REDISCOVERING THE LAW

Rediscovering the Law of Negligence offers a systematic exploration of the law of negligence. Its aim is to re-establish the notion that thinking about the law ought to and can proceed on the basis of principle. As such, it is opposed to the prevalent modern view that the various aspects of the law are and must be based on individual policy decisions and that the task of the judge or commentator is to shape the law in terms of the relevant policies as she sees them. The book, then, is an attempt to re-establish the law of negligence as a body of law rather than as a branch of politics.

The book argues that the law of negligence is best understood in terms of a relatively small set of principles enunciated in a small number of leading cases. It further argues that these principles are themselves best seen in terms of an aspect of morality called corrective justice which, when applied to the most important aspects of the law of negligence reveals that the law—even as it now exists—possesses a far greater degree of conceptual unity than is commonly thought. Using this method the author is able to examine familiar aspects of the law of negligence such as the standard of care; the duty of care; remoteness; misfeasance; economic loss; negligent misrepresentation; the liability of public bodies; wrongful conception; nervous shock; the defences of contributory negligence, voluntary assumption of risk and illegality; causation; and issues concerning proof, to show that when the principles are applied and the idea of corrective justice is properly understood then the law appears both systematic and conceptually satisfactory. The upshot is a rediscovery of the law of negligence.

Rediscovering the Law of Negligence

Allan Beever

·H A R T·
PUBLISHING

OXFORD AND PORTLAND, OREGON
2009

Published in North America (US and Canada) by
Hart Publishing
c/o International Specialized Book Services
920 NE 58th Avenue, Suite 300
Portland, OR 97213-3786
USA
Tel: +1 503 287 3093 or toll-free: (1) 800 944 6190
Fax: +1 503 280 8832
E-mail: orders@isbs.com
Website: www.isbs.com

Hart Publishing, Worcester Place, Oxford, OX1 2JW
Telephone: +44 (0)1865 517530 Fax: +44 (0)1865 510710
E-mail: mail@hartpub.co.uk
Website: http://www.hartpub.co.uk

British Library Cataloguing in Publication Data
Data Available

ISBN-13: 978-1-84113-686-8 (hardback)
ISBN-10: 1-84113-686-7 (hardback)
ISBN: 978-1-84113-975-3 (paperback)

Typeset by Hope Services Ltd, Abingdon
Printed and bound in Great Britain by
CPI Antony Rowe, Chippenham, Wiltshire

For Charles Rickett

The particular form of bad conscience which betrays itself in the vainglorious eloquence of . . . superficial philosophy may be remarked on here; for, in the first place, it is precisely where it is at its *most spiritless* that it has most to say about *spirit*, where its talk is driest and most lifeless that it is freest with the words 'life' and 'enliven', and where it shows the utmost selfishness of empty arrogance that it most often refers to the 'people'. But the distinctive mark which it carries on its brow is its hatred of law. That right and ethics, and the actual world of right and the ethical, are grasped by means of *thoughts* and give themselves the form of rationality—namely universality and determinacy—by means of thoughts is what constitutes *the law*; and it is this which is justifiably regarded as the main enemy of that feeling which reserves the right to do as it pleases, but that conscience which identifies right with subjective conviction. The form of right as *duty* and a *law* is felt by it to be a *dead, cold letter* and a *shackle*; for it does not recognize itself in the law, and thereby recognize its own freedom in it, because the law is the reason of the thing and reason does not allow feeling to warm itself in the glow of its own particularity. The *law* is therefore . . . the chief shibboleth by which the false brethren and friends of the so-called 'people' give themselves away.

GWF Hegel, *Elements of the Philosophy of Right*, Preface

Acknowledgements

First thanks must go to Ernest Weinrib, to whom I owe the largest intellectual debt. A great deal of the content of this book can be traced directly back to his lectures that I was fortunate enough to attend as an MSL student at the Faculty of Law at the University of Toronto in 1999–2000. Those lectures shattered my dogmatic and largely complacent picture of the law and forced me to think more deeply about the law's underlying structure. I hope that in this book I have been true to the spirit of intellectual enquiry that those lectures, and Professor Weinrib's work in general, so powerfully exemplify.

I am also most grateful to all of my colleagues with whom I have discussed this material and with whom I have agreed or disagreed on these or related matters, in person or in print. I am most grateful for the amount that I have learnt from you all. In that regard, I would like to mention in particular Peter Benson, Peter Birks, Vaughan Black, Russell Brown, Neil Campbell, Peter Cane, David Cheifetz, David Dyzenhaus, James Edelman, James Gordley, Ross Grantham, Michael Jones, Lewis Klar, David McLauchlan, Geoff McLay, Janet Mclean, John Murphy, Paul Myburgh, Jason Neyers, Ken Oliphant, Charles Rickett, Arthur Ripstein, Andrew Robertson, Elsabe Schoeman, John Smillie, Lionel Smith, Stephen Smith, Jane Stapleton, Robert Stevens, Stephen Todd, Stephen Waddams and Richard Wright. Forgive my trespasses.

I would also like to thank all of the students I taught at the University of Auckland Faculty of Law, whose probing and criticising has done a great deal to improve the arguments herein. I am also very grateful for the very able research assistance of Xiaojiang Ren, whose assistance was generously sponsored by Chapman Tripp Barristers and Solicitors, New Zealand.

Further, I would like to offer my heartfelt thanks to the Alexander von Humboldt Foundation, if not for forcing me to learn German, then for making possible my 20 month research stay in Germany, during part of which I worked on this book. In that regard, I would also like to thank my host institute, the Max-Planck-Institut für ausländisches und internationales Privatrecht, Hamburg, and my academic host, Reinhard Zimmermann, for his hospitality. Thanks also to all of Professor Zimmermann's *Mitarbeiter*.

I would also like to thank Cathryn Wilson for her continued, unflagging and selfless support of my research, and to Beth Beever for encouraging me and supporting me so that I could begin it.

Finally, I would like to thank most especially Charles Rickett for his contribution to my life as a mentor, an example, a critic and a friend. For encouraging me to persist through difficult times and for giving me hope. In other words, for being that most rare and misunderstood creature: a colleague. This book is dedicated to you.

Contents

Table of Cases

Australia

Canada

New Zealand

United Kingdom

United States of America

Table of Legislation

United Kingdom

1

Introduction

I. THE DISINTEGRATION OF THE MODERN LAW

A. Very Brief History

I BEGIN WITH A story about the law of negligence. The story is not new and it is not intended that the reader will learn much from it. Indeed, the vast majority of modern negligence lawyers already accept it, though it does not have a happy ending.[1]

The law of negligence is a relatively recent invention, being at the beginning of the nineteenth century, in the words of PH Winfield, little more than 'a bundle of frayed ends'.[2] Moreover, although the law developed throughout the nineteenth century, it nevertheless remained highly 'fragmentary'.[3] Hence, in 1932 Lord Atkin accurately described the law as containing:

> an elaborate classification of duties as they exist in respect of property, whether real or personal, with further divisions as to ownership, occupation or control, and distinctions based on the particular relations of the one side or the other, whether manufacturer, salesman or landlord, customer, tenant, stranger, and so on. In this way it can be ascertained at any time whether the law recognizes a duty, but only where the case can be referred to some particular species which has been examined and classified.[4]

However, towards the end of the nineteenth century, the law began to coalesce around general conceptions of the duty of care. Most significant in this regard were the judgments of Brett MR in *Heaven v Pender*[5] and Lord Escher in *Le Lievre v Gould*.[6] Support for a general test for the duty of care was also forthcoming from important academic commentators such as Winfield,[7]

---

[1] The story is largely taken from DJ Ibbetson, *A Historical Introduction to the Law of Obligations* (Oxford University Press, Oxford, 1999).

[2] PH Winfield, 'The History of Negligence' (1926) 42 *LQR* 184, 185. See also Ibbetson, above n1, 167: '[i]t would be premature to see a "Tort of Negligence" in existence at the end of the eighteenth century'.

[3] *Ibid*, 178–81.

[4] *M'Alister (or Donoghue) (Pauper) v Stevenson* [1932] AC 562 (HL Sc), 579–80.

[5] (1882–1883) LR 11 QBD 503 (CA).

[6] [1893] 1 QB 491 (CA).

[7] PH Winfield, 'The History of Negligence' (1926) 42 *LQR* 184.

Frederick Pollock,[8] and John Salmond.[9] The breakthrough came with Lord Atkin's judgment in *Donoghue v Stevenson*, which introduced the 'neighbour principle', a general conception of the duty of care based on the notion of reasonable foreseeability.

However, the impact of the neighbour principle in practice tended to be rhetorical rather than direct.[10] In reality, judges and commentators continued to regard the law of negligence as consisting of a series of separate duties of care that applied only to particular situations. Importantly, despite the neighbour principle, liability was not countenanced for injury to trespassers or for loss suffered consequent to negligent misstatements.[11] Of course, none of this is to say that the neighbour principle had no impact. But the influence of Lord Atkin's judgment tended to be abstract rather than concrete. Instead of being applied directly, the neighbour principle led in time to an increasing generalism in the law, which slowly moved away from the idea of individual duties of care.

Because of this generalism, the middle years of the twentieth century witnessed an expansion in liability as individual and specific duties of care were generalised and so expanded into new territories. The most important case in this regard was *Hedley Byrne & Co Ltd v Heller & Partners Ltd*,[12] which for the first time allowed recovery for pure economic loss. Eventually, the generalist approach won out in Lord Reid's judgment in *Home Office v Dorset Yacht Co Ltd*[13] and most significantly in Lord Wilberforce's judgment in *Anns v London Borough of Merton*.[14]

However, it was soon realised that the generalist approach suffered from a crucial flaw: it was unable sensibly to contain liability. In particular, judges and commentators came to realise that the generalist approach would produce indeterminate liability for economic loss, a conclusion that would be unacceptable in practice. Hence, the generalist approach has been abandoned to a degree. The law has now retreated to a position which sometimes invokes the generalist approach (particularly in cases of personal injury), but sometimes adopts an individual duties of care methodology (particularly in cases of economic loss).[15] For instance, it is said that, despite *Hedley Byrne*, liability for economic loss will usually exist only if the defendant made a negligent misstatement and then only in certain specific circumstances. For these reasons, the focus of modern negligence lawyers largely surrounds elucidating the circumstances in which the generalist approach should and should not apply and the appropriate scope of the individual duties such as the one for negligent misstatement.

---

[8] F Pollock, *The Law of Torts* (13th edn, Stevens, London, 1929) 21.

[9] J Salmond, *Torts* (7th edn, Sweet & Maxwell, London, 1929) 63–70.

[10] Ibbetson, above n1, 191.

[11] *Ibid.*

[12] [1964] AC 465 (HL).

[13] [1970] AC 1004, 1026–7 (HL).

[14] [1978] AC 728, 751 (HL).

[15] For an explicit espousal of this view, see eg NJ McBride and R Bagshaw, *Tort Law*, 2nd edn (Pearson Education Ltd, Harlow, 2005) chs 4–8.

B. Implications of the Development of the Modern Law: The Role of Policy

The most noticeable effect of the rejection of the generalist approach has been the growing reliance on 'policy' arguments by courts and commentators. The terms 'policy' and its contrary 'principle' are difficult to define and more will need to be said about them later, but the following picture will suffice for the moment. 'Principle' refers to the rules and doctrines of the law itself. The idea that accepted offers made with consideration are binding as contracts is a paradigm example of a principle from the law of contract. 'Policy', on the other hand, can be defined only negatively. 'Policy' is everything apart from principle. For example, policy has been held to include issues of distributive justice, social morality, economic efficiency, public opinion and so on. But it is impossible to define the content of these terms exactly, because people disagree on what constitute the rules and doctrines of the law. Accordingly, there is no 'theory neutral' way of defining the content of principle and of policy. And, for reasons discussed below, the distinction between them is crumbling. For some modern commentators, the distinction is incoherent.

Returning to the picture of the law developed above, imagine that a court is faced with a claimant who maintains that she was injured as a consequence of the violation of a duty of care owed to her by the defendant. Imagine also that the defendant disputes the existence of the alleged duty of care and that there is no clear authority binding on the court. Assume further that, if the generalist approach were to be adopted, the claimant would win, but the defendant argues that an individual duties approach should be utilised and the claimant's action should be held to lie outside the relevant duties. Where is the court to look for the answer to this dilemma?

The answer cannot be to the law or its principles. If the court looks to the generalist approach, then it begs the question against the defendant. If it looks to the individual duties approach, then it ignores the argument of the claimant. And there is, of course, no 'meta-generalist' approach that provides principles to allow the court to choose between the generalist and individual duties approaches. So where is the court to turn? The answer is to policy. In other words, in settling controversial issues, the court must look outside the existing legal rules and doctrines to something else, and the general term we use for this something else is 'policy'.

Over the years, this something else has grown from a small suburb outlying the town of legal principle into a metropolis that now dwarfs and encroaches upon the town. Thus, in a rightly famous paper published in 1998, Jane Stapleton identified 50 policy concerns utilised by courts to determine the duty of care stage of the negligence enquiry.[16] This already long list was not intended

---

[16] J Stapleton, 'Duty of Care Factors: A Selection from the Judicial Menus' in P Cane and J Stapleton (eds), *The Law of Obligations: Essays in Celebration of John Fleming* (Clarendon Press, Oxford, 1998).

to be exhaustive but rather indicative of the kinds of concerns raised in courts, and there have been many more policy concerns utilised by courts since.

These policy concerns are highly controversial in two ways. First, their cogency is controversial. So, in the paper mentioned above, Stapleton did not merely list 50 concerns, she also recommended 29 of these for future courts' consideration, while arguing against the application of 21. Others, naturally, disagree with Stapleton's lists and argue that some of the 29 concerns on the in list should not be there, that some of the 21 on the out list should be on the in list, or that other concerns that Stapleton did not discuss should be on the in list. In fact, the potential lists seem endless. Hence, according to Stephen Todd, '[t]he question of responsibility for negligence may be argued in an almost unlimited range of circumstances, and *all kinds of considerations* may be taken into account in deciding how it ought to be resolved'.[17]

The policy concerns are also controversial in terms of their content. For instance, on Stapleton's list of concerns recommended for courts' attention is the notion that duties of care should not be recognised when they 'would discourage socially beneficial forms of hospitality'.[18] Obviously, what counts as a socially beneficial form of hospitality is a matter for considerable debate and about which there is much disagreement.[19] But, according to Stapleton, it must be appropriate for judges to engage in that debate and in many similar debates when deciding the duty of care stage of the negligence enquiry.

Consider also the following examples from Stapleton's in list said to constitute good reasons against imposing a duty of care.

(1)   That the proper vindication of the law's concern with the liberty of the individual justifies a refusal to recognise any duty of affirmative action towards a stranger. . . .

(3)   The plaintiff himself had adequate means of avoiding the risk eventuating and causing loss.

(4)   The imposition of a duty might produce a specified unattractive socio-economic impact such as the disproportionate distortion of the budgets and/or activities of public bodies to the detriment of a specified public interest. . . .

(7)   Recognition of a duty here might bring the law into disrepute or otherwise injure its dignity.

(8)   Imposition of a duty might threaten the control of public order, the conduct of military operations or national security. . . .

(19)   Recognition of a duty might overall have deleterious effects on those in the position of the plaintiff. . . .

(22)   Avoidance of breach of such a duty would be particularly onerous on disadvantaged groups.[20]

[17] S Todd, 'Negligence: Breach of Duty' in S Todd (ed), *The Law of Torts in New Zealand,* 3rd edn (Brookers, Wellington, 2001) 151 (emphasis added).
[18] Stapleton, above n16, 95.
[19] See eg *Childs v Desormeaux* [2006] SCC 18.
[20] Stapleton, above n16, 93–5.

None of these could be said to provide *determinants* of the duty of care; rather they are invitations to engage in wide ranging debates on issues about which there is nothing even approaching a general consensus.

As a result of this development, major disagreements as to the shape and direction of the law have become commonplace. Hence, to take just one example, some argue that recovery for economic loss should be significantly expanded,[21] while others argue that it should be dramatically contracted.[22] The point is not that people disagree over these matters when we turn to law reform, or even that such disagreements exist per se, neither of which would be surprising or inappropriate, but rather that these disagreements are found within the *mainstream* analysis of the law of negligence. Moreover, even when a consensus does exist, it is often merely on outcome rather than over appropriate reasoning. For instance, in *White v Jones*,[23] one of the most famous recent cases, a majority of the House of Lords agreed that the claimants should be able to recover from the defendant, but their Lordships gave quite different reasons for that conclusion. And, although the academic community has greeted the case with widespread acceptance, there appears to be no consensus on why the case was rightly decided (apart from the banal claim that it was 'fair'). The above has also led to the existence of curious arguments that appear to lead nowhere. For instance, despite the consensus that general liability for economic loss would be intolerable, Basil Markesinis and Hannes Unberath note that in French, Belgian and Dutch law 'tort compensation for pure economic loss is, quite simply, a non-problem'.[24] If it is true that recovery for pure economic loss exists in these jurisdictions,[25] then on what basis can it be assumed that it must not be permitted by the common law? Often, gut instinct seems to be the determining factor.

In summary, the law is awash with conflicting policy arguments that can be utilised to support any conceivable position. This is not to say that all positions are *equally* supported by the policy arguments, of course. But the point is that there is no longer any consensus on the type of arguments that are relevant and irrelevant. Any argument is prima facie relevant.

We have become so familiar with this situation that it is unlikely to raise any eyebrows, but is it not possible still to recapture some of the surprise that would have been felt by our juridical ancestors were we able to explain to them the current state of the law? Imagine how, say, Lord Atkin would have reacted to the idea that the modern law of negligence functioned in this manner. In fact, it is

[21] See eg C Witting, 'Justifying Liability to Third Parties for Negligent Misstatements' (2000) 20 *OJLS* 615.
[22] See eg A Tettenborn, 'Property Damage and Economic Loss: Should Claims by Property Owners Themselves be Limited?' (2005) 34 *Common Law World Review* 128.
[23] [1995] 2 AC 207 (HL). This case is examined in detail in ch 7.
[24] BS Markesinis and H Unberath, *The German Law of Torts: A Comparative Treatise,* 4th edn (Hart Publishing, Oxford, 2002) 53.
[25] The truth is somewhat more complicated. Though there is no absolute bar against the recovery of economic loss in these jurisdictions, various methods are employed to determining liability that prevent indeterminate liability.

not necessary to conduct this thought experiment. One need only consult those colleagues who research in other areas of the law of obligations or who are civil lawyers. Consider our common law colleagues. It is a striking difference between negligence lawyers on the one hand and contract or unjust enrichment lawyers on the other that only the first compile long lists of allegedly relevant policies.[26] Few contract lawyers in particular would even entertain accepting an understanding of contract law that mirrors the modern negligence lawyer's understanding of negligence.[27] Surely, I cannot be the only negligence lawyer who has noticed amongst his contract law colleagues a certain amused condescension. I would only add that, at least when directed to the law and not *ad hominem*, the condescension is largely deserved. After all, even amongst negligence lawyers themselves, it is widely recognised that the law of negligence is in a bad state.[28] To some, the law seems so ad hoc, so indeterminate, that it should be abolished.[29]

Moreover, as the discussion of Stapleton's paper above revealed, the reliance on policy has led to an increasing politicisation of the law. Consider, for instance, Stapleton's recent address to the High Court of Australia. 'I see every reason to hope that our tort law, the law of wrongs, as nourished by our present and future High Courts will attract renewed public confidence because of the supporting role it will play in righting the most grievous wrongs in Australia's history.'[30] Notice the automatic inference from the claim that an issue is important for society as a whole to the conclusion that it is an appropriate matter for the courts to consider in tort cases. Certainly, there are very significant wrongs in Australia's past that require righting, but why does it follow that *the High Court of Australia*, or other *courts*, should seek to remedy even some of those wrongs *in tort law*? The answer, I suppose, is that if the courts in tort cases are engaged in the kind of political debates witnessed earlier, then why not in other debates as well, such as the one concerning the past treatment of people in Australia? But how can we accept the existence of an unelected and unaccountable judiciary making such decisions?

---

[26] Compare R Grantham and C Rickett, *Enrichment and Restitution in New Zealand* (Hart Publishing, Oxford, 2000) 44–5: 'if the rationale for the imposition of a restitutionary obligation was simply that that was serving other substantive ends, the law of restitution could not be rationalized as a coherent subject. Its content would be at most a policy-oriented jumble. The law of restitution certainly could not stand alongside the law of consent as a meaningful part of the private law of obligations. And it is unlikely that it could stand *even* with the law of wrongs' (emphasis added).

[27] This is not to say that policy reasoning plays no part in the law of contract. Rather, the point is that the *ubiquitous* and *direct* appeal to policy is unique to tort.

[28] For a recent statement, see DJ Ibbetson, 'How the Romans did for Us: Ancient Roots of the Tort of Negligence' (2003) 26 *University of New South Wales Law Journal* 475, 475.

[29] See eg PS Atiyah, 'Personal Injuries in the Twenty-First Century: Thinking the Unthinkable' in P Birks (ed), *Wrongs and Remedies in the Twenty-First Century* (Clarendon Press, Oxford, 1996); J Smillie, 'Certainty and Civil Obligation' (2000) 9 *Otago Law Review* 633, 651; J Smillie, 'Let's Abolish Negligence: Commentary on a Paper by J G Fogarty QC', 1996 New Zealand Law Conference Papers (New Zealand Law Society,Dunedin 1996).

[30] J Stapleton, 'The Golden Thread at the Heart of Tort Law: Protection of the Vulnerable' (2003) 24 *Australian Bar Review* 135, 149.

Returning to the specific issue discussed by Stapleton, while many agree that the wrongs of the past should be remedied, we do not all agree on what those wrongs were or on how they should be remedied. And some deny that there were wrongs or, if there were, that they should now be remedied. In fact, this is close to the position taken by the current Australian Prime Minister. Nor do we necessarily agree on what constitutes 'a proper vindication of the law's concern with the liberty of the individual', 'a specified unattractive socio-economic impact', bringing 'the law into disrepute', an appropriate concern with 'public order, the conduct of military operations or national security', or about the implications of *any* of the policy factors Stapleton mentions. The point here is not that there may or may not be correct answers to these questions. Nor is it that complete uniformity cannot be expected on these matters. Rather, the point is that, as the answers to the relevant questions are not transparent and as there is a *wide* variation on how the questions are answered by individuals, these questions are deeply political, and hence the answers to them will be highly politically controversial.[31] Hence, the injunction to a judge to consider, say, the proper vindication of the law's concern with the liberty of the individual is an injunction to the judge to apply her beliefs about the proper vindication of the law's concern with the liberty of the individual, and those beliefs are almost certain to vary widely between judges and between judges and members of society as a whole. Accordingly, this vision of law contains an invitation to judges to enforce their personal and politically controversial conceptions of the good.[32] The problem with this view of the courts' role—and I assert this here without argument as I cannot see that one is needed—is that this is just not law. If judges are constrained only by their beliefs as to these and similar issues, then we have the rule of judges, not the rule of law.

It is apparent that the politicisation of the law and its consequences are coming to be recognised by the non-legal fraternity. Recently, writing in response to the civil liability legislation that has swept Australia in the wake of its apparent insurance crisis, Peter Underwood J has drawn attention to the way in which Australian legislatures have begun to respond in an ad hoc and unprincipled manner to individual tort judgments.[33] Underwood J rightly laments this development.

> [I]t appears there is no need to refer anything to a review panel. Indeed, it appears that there is no need even to study this development in the common law. It is sufficient if there is a perception that a common law development might cause a financial problem or some other problem for there to be legislative action to remove that development and deny others in the situation of the respondents a remedy that the law has decided is their entitlement.

---

[31] In fact, it is at least arguable that the *questions* Stapleton poses are ideologically loaded.

[32] Some have attempted to respond by suggesting that the judge's role is to enforce the public's conception of the good—as if there were such as thing. I have explored this argument in A Beever, 'Particularism and Prejudice in the Law of Tort' (2003) 11 *Tort Law Review* 146, 153–5.

[33] P Underwood, 'Is Ms Donoghue's Snail in Mortal Peril?' (2004) 12 *Torts Law Journal* 39, 59–60.

This is a very dangerous development, not only for Ms Donoghue's snail, but also for all other aspects of the common law. It will become uncertain. No one will know whether a particular aspect of the common law will or will not fall under the legislative knife; a knife wielded in accordance with the political beliefs of the party that happens to be in power from time to time. Historically, legislative incursions into the common law have been restrained and largely remedial. Recently, all that has changed. Legislation is enacted instantaneously and as an immediate response to perceived, but untested, economic factors. More likely than not the legislation will vary from jurisdiction to jurisdiction so that the common law of the country will be fragmented. In effect, there is every danger of the judicial development being subject to the unnecessary superior and instantaneous editing of the legislature.[34]

This is a very perceptive criticism. However, if (as Underwood J does not contend) the law of negligence is about the promotion of lists of policies such as the ones examined above, then one could hardly blame the legislature for questioning the policies of the courts and substituting their own. There is no reason democratically elected legislatures should accept the different policy preferences of non-elected judges. In fact, one might regard the Australian legislatures as asserting the will of the people in the face of the non-representative and elitist preferences of the legal community—which is, no doubt, how the legislators see it. Of course, one may disagree with the policy choices of the legislatures, but if the law of negligence were based on the kinds of contentions examined earlier, then there could be no doubting the political legitimacy (and not merely the legal validity) of the interference of the legislatures per se. I, for one, would demand that the legislatures seize control of the law of negligence, replace the common law with statute, and supplant judges with democratically accountable officials.

C. Implications of the Development of the Modern Law: The Role of Principle

The reliance on policy has become so ubiquitous that modern lawyers no longer understand what a principled account of the law would be like. Hence, in her address to the High Court of Australia, Stapleton also maintained that it is 'simply not feasible' for courts to ignore policy concerns such as the ones listed above.[35] According to this view, the very idea of a successful account of the law of negligence that does not rely on the routine appeal to policy is *incomprehensible*. Why?

One can discover the answer by looking at one of Stapleton's leading forerunners, John Fleming. Consider, for instance, Fleming's discussion of the development of the duty of care since *Donoghue v Stevenson*.

---

[34] P Underwood, 'Is Ms Donoghue's Snail in Mortal Peril?' (2004) 12 *Torts Law Journal* 39, 60 (citation omitted).

[35] Stapleton, above n30, 136.

Lord Atkin's proximity has cast a baleful shadow over judicial ruminations on duty. . . . it became a convenient screen for not disclosing any specific reasons behind a decision for or against a finding of duty. The judicial tendency to take refuge in seemingly bland, neutral concepts, like foreseeability and proximity, under the pretence that they represent 'principle' has its roots in the embarrassment with which the British conservative tradition has generally treated the role of policy in judicial decision making. . . . The [more recent] inclusion [in judgments] of 'what is just (fair) and reasonable' is a discreet acknowledgement at long last of what in academic and popular discourse is more forthrightly referred to as policy.[36]

The most important feature of this passage is what it is missing from it. While I argue in Chapters 5, 7 and 8 that Fleming is right to condemn much judicial use of these terms, Fleming ignores the possibility that foreseeability and proximity are not bland but are meaningful terms that do, or at least can, play a justificatory role in deciding cases. Moreover, it is possible to detect in this passage, as well as in Fleming's other writing, a hostility toward the notion of principle altogether (hence his use of scare quotation marks).[37] We can explain the reason for this as follows. If a court is or is not to impose liability on a defendant, then the court should have reasons for its decision. Those reasons should be elucidated in the court's judgment. And, Fleming crucially assumes, those reasons cannot be ones of legal principle, but must refer to issues such as extra-legal ideas of morality and justice, administrative convenience, economic efficiency and so on.[38] In other words, only policy is justificatory; principle is at best a screen to hide behind.

For that reason, in John Fleming's great work, *The Law of Torts*,[39] the law of negligence is interpreted as a pragmatic response to social circumstances in a way that minimises the role of legal principle. In fact, it is perhaps not going too far to say that *The Law of Torts* is so significant a book precisely because it does away with principle and attempts to explain everything about the law in terms of policies, often unenunciated by the judges who decided the relevant cases.

Stapleton goes a step further by arguing that no meaningful distinction can be made between principle and policy, and that the contrary view is odd.[40] The reason for this is that, according to Stapleton, 'principle' and 'policy' are just labels for reasons and the issue is, or should be, whether a reason is good or bad, and not whether it is arbitrarily labelled as principle or as policy. Hence, the insistence that the law be principled as opposed to policy driven is, for Stapleton, merely an attempt to act on some reasons (arbitrarily labelled principle) rather than on others (arbitrarily labelled policy) without elucidating one's reasons for doing so. And because the labels are arbitrarily applied, this is merely a covert

---

[36] J Fleming, *The Law of Torts,* 9th edn (LBC Information Services, Sydney, 1998) 153.

[37] Consider in particular Fleming's treatment of remoteness (*ibid*, 232–3) with the one developed in ch 4.

[38] *Ibid*, 154.

[39] *Ibid*.

[40] J Stapleton, 'The Golden Thread at the Heart of Tort Law: Protection of the Vulnerable' (2003) 24 *Australian Bar Review* 135, 135–7.

and dishonest attempt to do something without explaining why one is doing it. Hence, Stapleton responds to the critics of policy that 'we must "let daylight in on magic" '.[41] For both Fleming and Stapleton, then, the insistence on principle over policy is simply the refusal to explain. It is a form of obscurantism.

The approach advocated by Fleming and Stapleton is sometimes described as a 'realistic' approach to the law—'realistic' in the sense that it follows central teachings of the school known as 'legal realism' believed by its adherents to be realistic. Though different versions of 'realism' are available, most modern negligence lawyers accept the view that the fundamental question when deciding important matters of liability is the interests of society at large, and that appeal to 'principle' that ignores such interests can only be self-defeating. In that sense, books like The Law of Torts are attempts to explain away legal principle in terms of what are perceived to be the law's underlying objectives.

Philosophers call a theory that attempts to explain away a phenomenon an 'error theory'. A good example of an error theory is John Stuart Mill's account of the esteem given to virtue. According to Mill, originally virtue was valued only for the happiness that it produced. However, people became habituated over time to placing value on virtue, and so came to value virtue for its own sake. This is similar to the process by which people have come to value money. Initially money was valued only for what it could buy, but over time people gained the habit of valuing it for itself.[42] Mill provides an error theory of the esteem given to virtue, because he explains that esteem, not by elucidating virtue's intrinsic value, but by explaining the belief in that intrinsic value by reference to something else that, according to Mill, really is intrinsically valuable. Hence, on this view, the belief in the intrinsic value of virtue is at best a kind of shorthand or mistaken description for what truly is valuable, ie happiness.

This closely mirrors mainstream accounts of the law of negligence, where commentators tend to regard the purported principles of the law as shorthand descriptions for consolidations of policies not contained in those principles. Witness, for example, the almost ubiquitous description of the duty of care as a 'control device': a method for cutting back on liability in order, for reasons of economic and social policy, to prevent liability from being overly extensive.[43] This is despite the fact that the leading formulations of the duty of care are presented in precisely the opposite light. They appear to be focused, not on excluding instances of liability, but on determining what is to be included based on a conception of appropriate care. Mainstream accounts of the law of negligence, then, are error theories with respect to the principles of negligence law.

---

[41] J Stapleton, 'The Golden Thread at the Heart of Tort Law: Protection of the Vulnerable' (2003) 24 *Australian Bar Review* 135, 138.

[42] JS Mill, *Utilitarianism* (Hackett, Indianapolis, Ind, 1979) 35–7.

[43] J Fleming, 'Remoteness and Duty: The Control Devices in Liability for Negligence' [1953] *Canadian Bar Review* 471. For discussion of this general idea, see NJ McBride, 'Duties of Care—Do they Really Exist?' (2004) 24 *OJLS* 417.

This should give us pause. Given that the judges who created the law of neg-ligence attempted to justify their decisions, admittedly sometimes by policy, but often by reference to general conceptions of principle that they believed were both instantiated in law and morally justified, it is at least surprising that it should have become almost universal to adopt an error theory about those prin-ciples. Moreover, it is worrying as well as surprising that attempts to show otherwise have almost disappeared. A browse through today's law reviews will reveal the broad range of current analysis of the law. It is now accepted practice to explore and analyse the law from a plethora of viewpoints. This is valuable. But the one perspective seldom to be found in the law reviews is the law's own— taking seriously the law's principles.

The reply is that judges' commitment to principles of law is and always has been insincere. In fact, so it is said, judging has always been about sometimes overt but often covert policy-making.[44] This conspiracy theory may turn out to be true; but it is an unattractive view that we should be reluctant to accept with-out examining all the alternatives.

D. Less 'Realistic' Views

I have been concentrating on the views of Fleming and Stapleton because, for reasons examined below, these authors take the modern understanding of the law to its logical conclusion. Their work is most significant, then, not only because of its inherent quality, but also because it most clearly and powerfully captures and elucidates the modern conception of law. For that reason, it receives much attention in this and in following chapters.

But not all commentators would accept that Fleming's or Stapleton's charac-terisation of the law of negligence is appropriate. Some would prefer a more conservative approach. In particular, it may be argued that the ubiquitous ref-erence to policy has a tendency to undermine legal certainty by producing large and rapid changes in the positive law. But it is important to understand the nature of that criticism.

Stapleton accepts that valid disagreements may arise over the appropriate rate of legal change, but, for her, this disagreement is itself over best policy.[45] In other words, if the law should change slowly, that is because of the negative social impact created by dramatic changes. Hence, those who object to Stapleton on the ground that her approach would lead to too much change, and that that would be a bad thing for society, in fact agree with her approach. The disagreement here, if there really is one, is a disagreement over the weight of the relevant policies. For instance, a commentator may think that legal certainty is more important than

---

[44] The foremost statement of this view in this area is *Lamb v Camden London BC* [1981] 1 QB 625, 636–7 (CA) (Lord Denning MR).
[45] Stapleton, above n40, 139.

Stapleton does. But this does not call into question the primacy of policy itself. Simply, at least as stated, legal certainty is itself a policy, and so the insistence on legal certainty cannot lead away from the policy-driven model.

Consider, for instance, the claim that it is permissible for judges to consult policy in their decision making, but they should exercise care or restraint in doing so. What do these terms 'care' and 'restraint' mean? Why should judges be careful or exercise restraint? There are two kinds of responses to these questions. First, one could maintain that judges should be careful and restrained *just because*. Clearly, that is a form of obscurantism that fails to explain why judges should be careful and restrained. On the other hand, one could argue that judges should be careful and restrained for some reasons. But those reasons will themselves be reasons of policy. Accordingly, this position is Stapleton's position in disguise.

Consider also Heydon J's recent extrajudicial attack on judicial activism.[46] First, his Honour defines judicial activism as 'using judicial power for a purpose other than that for which it was granted, namely doing justice according to law in the particular case'.[47] He then defines doing justice according to law as following precedent or adapting precedent through analogy.[48] This approach is intended to avoid large changes in the law and to preserve the rule of law.

But this method alone is doomed to failure. I discuss this issue in more detail in Chapter 5 when I explore the so-called 'incremental approach' to the duty of care, but it is enough for the moment to say that there is one major flaw in Heydon J's position as it stands. When one incrementally extends or contracts legal principle, when one adapts precedent by analogy, why does one do so? This is Heydon J's answer:

> When new cases arose, existing principles could be extended to deal with them, or limited if their application to the new cases was unsatisfactory. As business or technical conditions changed, the law could be moulded to meet them. As inconveniences came to light, they could be overcome by modifications. The changes could be effected by analogical reasoning, or incremental growth in existing rules, or a rational extension of existing rules to new instances not foreseen when the existing rule was first developed. Particular rules might be modified by the detection of more general principles underlying them or a more rigorous reformulation of some traditional concept.[49]

What do the terms 'unsatisfactory', 'inconveniences', 'rational', 'detection of more general principles' and 'rigorous reformulation' mean in this context? To Stapleton and others, the answer is clear. They are covert references to policy.[50] To them, Heydon J will appear to give no reason to think otherwise.

---

[46] JD Heydon, 'Judicial Activism and the Death of the Rule of Law' (2003) 23 *Australian Bar Review* 110. Stapleton's address to the High Court of Australia was intended as, in part, a response to this article.

[47] *Ibid*, 113.

[48] *Ibid*, 114–15.

[49] *Ibid*, 6.

[50] See especially J Stapleton, 'The Golden Thread at the Heart of Tort Law: Protection of the Vulnerable' (2003) 24 *Australian Bar Review* 135, 138.

Consider also Stapleton's claim that:

> such pro-incrementalism, pro-legalism critics of 'the conscious making of new law by radical judicial destruction of the old' have a problem in explaining why it is that the most admired tort judgments are those characterised by realism and creativity such as that in *Donoghue v Stevenson* by Lord Atkin.[51]

If *Donoghue v Stevenson* was good, then Stapleton appears right to claim that it was good because it was good policy.

Hence, Stapleton seizes on Heydon J's subsequent judgment in *Cattanach v Melchior*.[52]

> Justice Heydon based his reasoning in large part on a consideration of matters that would seem better described in moral, social or scientific terms such as: basic legal assumptions about human life in families; the psychology of litigants, parents and children; a parent's moral duties even though these are not enforceable by the law; and the 'disquieting possibilities' in relation to other much more ambitious claims of a type not before the court that might create 'an odious spectacle'. In my opinion, therefore, we should ditch both the 'principle' and 'policy' terminology, and simply describe these concerns *neutrally* as 'legal concerns' while openly acknowledging that 'the law takes on new values and sheds old ones as society changes'.[53]

If all this is right, then the debate between Stapleton and Heydon J comes down to three issues. First, Stapleton insists—surely rightly—that courts clearly elucidate the reasons for their decisions. It must be wrong to maintain, as Heydon J's argument appears to imply, that courts should disguise their reasons by adopting methods of analogous reasoning. Secondly, Stapleton and Heydon J disagree over the impact of dramatic changes to the law. For reasons of policy, Heydon J thinks that these changes are disastrous, while Stapleton is less convinced. It is unclear who is right here, but the evidence seems to be with Stapleton. *Some* large changes, such as *Donoghue v Stevenson*, seem to have been valuable. Thirdly, Heydon J maintains that it is illegitimate for judges to make policy decisions of the kind under discussion, that being the appropriate role for elected politicians.[54] Stapleton responds that there is no reasonable alternative. If judges admit that they have the authority to alter the positive law, then their decisions to change or, just as importantly, not to change the law must be based on reasons of policy. Therefore, we must rethink the traditional understanding of the separation of powers.[55]

But there is another option neglected by Stapleton: The common law should be abolished in this area and replaced by a statutory code. To respond to this suggestion, it is not enough to point to the purported practice of the courts. It is

---

[51] *Ibid* (reference omitted).

[52] [2003] HCA 38, (2003) 215 CLR 1.

[53] Stapleton, above n50, 138 (references omitted).

[54] JD Heydon, 'Judicial Activism and the Death of the Rule of Law' (2003) 23 *Australian Bar Review* 110, 14–22.

[55] Stapleton, above n50, 135.

necessary to justify the alleged political power of judges. Considering that we are not dealing with issues of 'fundamental rights' such as those found in Bills of Rights or Charters, a contentious issue in itself, it is hard to see how a justification could proceed. We appear to be on the horns of a dilemma. In order to perform what almost all regard as their role, it seems necessary for judges to appeal (overtly or covertly) to policy; but in doing so they appear to step outside the scope of their legitimate function. They are, on this view, unelected, unaccountable officials enforcing their personal political preferences on a sometimes unwilling public, apparently inconsistently with the notion of democracy.

Nevertheless, if there is nothing more to be said for Heydon J's position, then Stapleton appears to have the better of the argument. But there is much more to be said. This can be brought out by examining some hypothetical examples.

Consider *Donoghue v Stevenson* again. As all know, this case involved a woman who was allegedly injured when she drank from a bottle of ginger beer that contained the decomposing remains of a snail that was in the bottle because of the defendant's negligence. We have seen that, according to Stapleton, this case revolutionised the law and did so in a 'realistic' and 'creative' fashion, in other words through the implementation of policy.[56] But imagine that, in addition to the argument given, Lord Atkin found in favour of the claimant because snails perform a vital ecological role, and hence their species should be protected against the negligence of those such as ginger beer manufacturers. Or imagine that it was not *Donoghue v Stevenson* that reached the House of Lords, but the previous 'mouse case', *Mullen v A G Barr & Co Ltd*,[57] a decision of the Inner House that was followed by the Inner House when it heard *Donoghue v Stevenson*.[58] In that case, a claimant was said to have been injured by drinking a bottle of ginger beer with a mouse in it. Imagine that in our hypothetical *Mullen* case before the House of Lords Lord Atkin had argued, in addition to the reasons he gave in *Donoghue v Stevenson*, that the defendant should be liable because his negligence amounted to cruelty to animals.

The question is: are these relevant reasons for finding in favour of the claimant? Note what the question is not. It is not: are these reasons *sufficient* for finding for the claimant? They are clearly not sufficient, but the issue is whether they strengthen the claimant's case in conjunction with the other reasons given by Lord Atkin in *Donoghue v Stevenson*. Nor is the question: are these reasons at all morally persuasive? For instance, it may be possible to argue that there are enough snails in Scotland for it to make no difference to Scots ecology that a few end up in bottles of ginger beer or the like. But it is not reasonable to argue that mice drowning in bottles of ginger beer is of no moral concern. One might think

---

[56] Stapleton, above n50, 138 (reference omitted). As noted above, Stapleton maintains that the distinction between principle and policy is at best rhetorical, but I continue to use these terms for convenience for the moment. They are defined more precisely below.

[57] 1929 SLT 341 (IH).

[58] 1930 SN 138 (IH).

that the concern is of little moment, but the pain of animals is not an *irrelevant* moral concern. The question is whether these arguments are relevant to deciding liability in negligence.

Imagine also a case involving a traffic accident in which a judge refuses recovery, inter alia, on the ground that a decision for the defendant would discourage people from driving cars and hence would be beneficial because it would reduce traffic congestion, pollution, and make the country cleaner and greener. These claims appear to be inappropriate considerations for a court in a traffic accident case, despite the fact that they are morally pertinent issues. Indeed, they are ones that legislatures should take into account when considering legislation in this area. Again, the question is not whether the judge's decision would be right, but whether these are the kinds of issues that judges should be taking into account.

The general point is this. We agree that there are concerns that courts should not take into account even though the concerns are morally relevant. If the concerns listed above are not convincing, others could be found. These concerns should not be taken into account because they are *irrelevant,* and not merely because they are outweighed or excluded by other concerns in a sense that I now elucidate.[59]

Concern x is outweighed by concern y if y is stronger than x. For instance, if I believe that I will make my wife happy by visiting my in-laws but I also believe that I will be very much happier if I stay at home, and hence believe that I should stay at home, then I believe that my greater happiness outweighs my wife's lesser happiness. On the other hand, concern x excludes concern y if x gives reason not to act on y. If I believe that I should visit my in-laws because I have promised my wife that I will, then I believe that my promise excludes my happiness as a reason for not going. I should not act on my happiness, because I have promised to go. My happiness is not merely outweighed by my promise; my promise gives me reason to disregard my happiness as a reason. My claim is that concerns such as animal cruelty in the hypothetical mouse case are not merely outweighed or excluded. First, those who support the outcome in *Donoghue v Stevenson* cannot argue that the concern is outweighed, because it argues in favour of their preferred result. In any case, the point is that it seems wrong even to consider the force of this concern. It is irrelevant, not merely weak. But nor it is right to regard the concern as excluded, or at least it is not right to regard the concern as excluded by other reasons of policy. This is because one knows immediately that the concern is an inappropriate concern to be taken into account in court even before one examines the policy arguments. It does not have to be excluded; it never gets into the picture in the first place. It is, as it were, excluded by the nature of the forum and not by other arguments of policy.[60]

---

[59] For general discussion of these issues see J Raz, *Practical Reason and Norms,* 2nd edn (Oxford University Press, Oxford, 1999) 35f.

[60] Of course, one could dispute these claims and argue that there are no concerns that are irrelevant in this way and that it is legitimate for courts to consider all morally relevant issues. Perhaps we will be forced to this position, but I doubt that many will be comfortable with it. If any are, then,

That means that the model of law promoted by Fleming and Stapleton must be wrong. Because they collapse the distinction between principle and policy and, which is the same, between law and politics, they cannot accept that there exists any argument that is irrelevant to judicial decision making in the sense described above.

Again, to make things clear, it is of course open to claim that some concerns should not be taken into account because they are excluded or should not be acted upon because they are outweighed. But if one holds, as I think we do all hold, that some arguments are irrelevant in law though they are morally valid and politically relevant, then the law is not about policy as defined but about something else, something narrower.[61]

We tend not to notice this point because lawyers usually argue *from* a conservative perspective in the following sense. The traditional view was that courts do not make law but only declare what the law had always been, and so do not, or do not rightly, appeal to policy.This position has not completely faded away. Hence, one of the goals of the revisionist academic is to show that appeals to policy are legitimate. The heat, then, is in the argument between those who argue that policy is, and those who argue that it is not, legitimate. Because of this, most of those on the revisionist side of the fence have not realised the logical consequences of their position. If it is legitimate for courts to take policy into account, where policy means any relevant moral concern, then it is legitimate for courts to take into account any morally relevant concern. But I doubt that anyone really thinks this. Accordingly, no one accepts the logical consequences of the position taken by most modern academics.

Note again that it is no reply to argue that one can accept the revisionist view but maintain that there are good reasons of policy that some other policies should be outweighed or excluded. Some policies are irrelevant, but the revisionist view cannot account for that. For this reason, it is impossible to agree with the general position that policy has a legitimate role to play in the law of negligence, but hold that Fleming's and Stapleton's specific approaches to the law are too wide. One could not, for instance, accept that the law is based on policy but argue that the 29 concerns that Stapleton lists are inappropriate and that courts' consideration should be restricted to a lesser and less open-ended list of concerns. If policy is relevant, then it is relevant. It cannot be relevant only when it is narrow or some such thing. Nor it is helpful to label some concerns 'legal' and others 'non-legal'.[62] There must be reasons why certain concerns are

---

apart from the political argument mentioned above, I have no response except astonishment. This book has nothing to say to those, hopefully non-existent, people who are happy to hold so extreme a view about the role of judges. But if things had come so far that such views were welcome, then nothing I or anyone else could do would be sufficient to rescue the common law. It would be time for it to be replaced.

[61] This is not to say that there will be no overlap between the concerns of politics and those of law, of course.

[62] J Stapleton, 'The Golden Thread at the Heart of Tort Law: Protection of the Vulnerable' (2003) 24 *Australian Bar Review* 135, 137.

legal and others not. An open policy-based account is not in a position to provide those reasons. If it is right for courts to take into account the impact of a decision on the community as a whole, then *all* impacts are relevant.

A good illustration of this point concerns the relevance of insurance as an issue in deciding the existence of a duty of care, an issue that we return to in Chapter 5. Some maintain that insurance is clearly a relevant concern.[63] The question now is whether one is entitled to appeal to insurance in some cases while ignoring, say, cruelty to animals or traffic congestion in others. The answer to this question depends on why insurance is said to be relevant. If the reason is that insurance relates to the maximisation of economic efficiency, then the question becomes: why is economic efficiency important? If the answer to that question is because economic efficiency is socially beneficial, then rationality demands that, if insurance is relevant to deciding the duty of care, then all concerns of social benefit are also relevant. Moreover, in the absence of reasons to the contrary, all concerns of social benefit must also be relevant to the other stages of the negligence enquiry.

The reply 'but that would clearly be going too far' is no reply at all. I agree that it is going too far, but one must accept the logic of one's own position. The point can be put simply. If it is right to appeal to moral consideration x in determining liability in case y, then all x-type considerations are relevant in all y-type cases.

This conclusion echoes the famous words of Burrough J in *Richardson v Mellish*.

> I, for one, protest . . . against arguing too strongly upon public policy;—it is a very unruly horse, and once you get astride it you never know where it will carry you. It may lead you from the sound law. It is never argued at all but when other points fail.[64]

If policy is relevant, then it is relevant. It cannot be relevant only when it feels right to the judge or commentator. It has led us from the sound law. It is always argued these days because all other points have failed. This is the disintegration of the modern law.

E. Defining Policy Narrowly

In order to avoid these conclusions, it is necessary to define the permissible scope of legal reasoning more narrowly. Naturally, one cannot do so arbitrarily—by allowing insurance but not traffic congestion *just because*, for example. Instead, one must elucidate a coherent sphere of reasoning appropriate for legal decision making. One seemingly attractive way of doing so is to argue that only distributive justice, perhaps in conjunction with corrective justice, has a role to play in

---

[63] See eg *Canadian National Railway Co v Norsk Pacific Steamship Co Ltd* [1992] 1 SCR 1021, 1119.

[64] (1824) 2 Bing 229, 130 ER 294, 303.

determining the law.[65] The hope is that distributive justice is sufficiently narrow that it avoids the consequences of an appeal to policy writ large.

To demonstrate the plausibility of this project, one would need to show why distributive justice, rather than policy writ large, was appropriate for judicial decision making—unless, of course 'distributive justice' in this context is merely a synonym for policy writ large (as I suspect it often is), in which case we need not bother with the theory further.[66] Moreover, one would have to develop a theory of the appropriate sphere of distributive justice for the law of negligence. It is important to recall that in his famous book, *A Theory of Justice*, John Rawls considers distributive justice in respect of one aspect of society only, what Rawls calls the 'basic structure' of society.[67] But the law of negligence is concerned, not with the basic structure, but with many relationships: between manufacturers and consumers,[68] railway operators and passengers,[69] sports clubs and users of footpaths,[70] fathers and sons,[71] and so on. Many issues in addition to those considered by Rawls would need to be taken into account if the law of negligence were concerned with distributive justice with respect to these relationships. Though no such theory has been developed, it seems safe to say that distributive justice in this context would be almost as unruly a horse as policy. Moreover, appealing to distributive justice will do nothing to rescue the law from politicisation, as questions of distributive justice lie at the heart of politics.

I conclude that Fleming and Stapleton are right in that, if a purely principled account of the law of negligence is not forthcoming, and if the appeal to policy is acceptable and indeed required, then the law of negligence cannot be other than deeply political. The law is and always will be a battlefield upon which various political views fight for supremacy. Until it is abolished, the law will continue to see the kind of wide ranging debates and experience no greater consensus than exists at present.

We are faced with a choice: believe in principle or in policy—or more accurately, believe in principle rather than in policy or deny that there is any meaningful distinction between the two. But the first seems impossible. We must, it appears, adopt an error theory with respect to the law of the past and hold it odd to believe that there is any such thing as legal principle.[72] But when put starkly like that, it is, I think, the strangest view of all. Is it not possible to

---

[65] See eg P Cane, 'Distributive Justice and Tort Law' [2001] *New Zealand Law Review* 401; R Mullender, 'Corrective Justice, Distributive Justice, and the Law of Negligence' (2001) 17 *Professional Negligence* 35; SR Perry, 'On the Relationship Between Corrective and Distributive Justice: Fourth Series' in J Horder (ed), *Oxford Essays in Jurisprudence* (Oxford University Press, Oxford, 2000). I examine this view in more detail in ch 2.

[66] A Beever, 'Particularism and Prejudice in the Law of Tort' (2003) 11 *Tort Law Review* 146.

[67] J Rawls, *A Theory of Justice: Revised Edition* (Belknap, Cambridge, Mass, 1999) 3.

[68] Eg *M'Alister (or Donoghue) (Pauper) v Stevenson* [1932] AC 562 (HL Sc).

[69] Eg *Palsgraf v Long Island Railroad Co* 162 NE 99 (NY CA 1928).

[70] Eg *Bolton v Stone* [1951] AC 850 (HL).

[71] *Talbert v Talbert* 199 NYS 2d 212 (NY SC 1960).

[72] Compare J Stapleton, 'The Golden Thread at the Heart of Tort Law: Protection of the Vulnerable' (2003) 24 *Australian Bar Review* 135, 135.

find an alternative? Could it not be that our legal ancestors, whom we accuse of dishonesty in their presentation of the law,[73] knew something that we do not? Could it be that their 'dishonesty' is really our ignorance? The answer to all of these questions is yes.

II. AN ALTERNATIVE

We must find a tame horse, an understanding of the law that is capable of providing an alternative to the modern mess. In light of the argument above, the alternative must do two things. First, it must define the sphere of reasoning appropriate to the law of negligence so that legal decision making can proceed in a perspicuous fashion. It must not permit appeal to all morally relevant concerns, but only to a subset thereof so that it permits judicial decision making to occur in a rational and orderly fashion. Moreover, that sphere of reasoning cannot be arbitrarily chosen but must be morally appropriate for the kind of decisions that have to be made in the law of negligence. Secondly, the alternative must define the sphere of legal reasoning in such a way that it allows judges to make decisions without those decisions being the judicial usurpation of democratic authority. These two themes run throughout the rest of this book: our understanding of the law must provide perspicuous grounds for judicial decision making, and those grounds must be apolitical.[74]

My task is to provide an account of the law of negligence that satisfies these two criteria. I begin with a new story.

A. History Revisited

The account of the historical development of the law of negligence related above ignores something of great importance. By focusing on the duty of care—a topic that receives inordinate attention from modern lawyers, as we shall see—the account is blind to a crucial part of the law's intellectual history. In particular, it underestimates the impact of Lord Atkin's judgment in *Donoghue v Stevenson*. It is certainly true that that judgment led to an expansion in liability through an expansion in the duty of care, but there is a tendency to underplay the wider impact of the judgment on the law of negligence as a whole. Most importantly, in *Donoghue v Stevenson* Lord Atkin argued for a general conception of the law of negligence, a conception that was exemplified by, but not restricted to, the neighbour principle as it applied to the duty of care. In particular, the judgment had a significant impact on future formulations of the standard of care and remoteness of damage. The most important cases in this

---

[73] See eg J Fleming, *The Law of Torts*, 9th edn (LBC Information Services, Sydney, 1998) 153.
[74] The precise meaning of 'apolitical' is discussed in ch 2.

regard are well known: *Bolton v Stone*[75] and *The Wagon Mound (No 2)*[76] with
respect to the standard of care, and *The Wagon Mound (No 1)*[77] with regard to
remoteness. However, despite the fact that these cases are familiar, they are not
generally studied alongside Lord Atkin's judgment in *Donoghue v Stevenson*, as
they must be if they are to be understood fully.

These cases, along with others to be introduced in subsequent chapters, present not merely a historical stage in the law of negligence, but a *theoretical*
understanding of that law founded on the neighbour principle. This understanding flowed from an attempt to define the boundaries of negligence in a
coherent fashion so that the law would both function successfully in practice
and, just as importantly, be normatively appealing. Unfortunately, academic
commentators largely ignored the understanding of the law developed by the
courts, mostly because of the reluctance of the common lawyer to think about
case law in general theoretical terms. The clearest example of this was the tendency, already mentioned above, to treat *Donoghue v Stevenson* itself as a case
that applied merely to products liability and that did not directly threaten the
individual duties of care approach.[78] Further, for most jurists, cases such as *The
Wagon Mound (No 1)* were understood to implement only a new rule regarding
remoteness of damage. It was not generally noticed that the case was also
another building block in the structure of a developing coherent legal schema.
The Wagon Mound (No 1) did not merely harmonise the law of remoteness
with the neighbour principle (a point that was noticed), but it was also an
important step along the route to a complete and unified account of the law of
negligence, an account that had all its essentials in place with the decision in *The
Wagon Mound (No 2)*.

But, as I have said, this was not generally noticed. In consequence, when Lord
Wilberforce set out his approach to the duty of care in *Anns*, it was widely
regarded as a development of the long line of thought that began with *Heaven v
Pender* and ran though *Donoghue v Stevenson* rather than, as it really was due
to its incorporation of policy and its consequent abandonment of the approach
introduced by Lord Atkin, a rejection of that line of thought. In that sense, the
Anns test was a victory of ignorance from which we have not yet recovered and
which we are in fact cementing.[79] Moreover, when the *Anns* test came to be
rejected or modified, this was seen as a rejection of the approach heralded in
Donoghue v Stevenson itself. But this is not correct. In fact, that approach has

[75] [1951] AC 850 (HL).
[76] *Overseas Tankship (UK) Ltd v Morts Dock & Engineering Co Ltd (The Wagon Mound, No 2)* [1961] AC 611 (PC).
[77] *Overseas Tankship (UK) Ltd v Morts Dock & Engineering Co Ltd (The Wagon Mound, No 1)* [1961] AC 388 (PC).
[78] See eg the discussion in RFV Heuston, 'Donoghue v. Stevenson in Retrospect' (1957) 20 *MLR* 1.
[79] I do not mean to claim that Lord Wilberforce was ignorant of the approach that I am describing. It may well be that we have misunderstood his intentions and that he did not intend the *Anns*
test as we understand it at all. In particular, it may be that Lord Wilberforce would have allowed a
much smaller role for policy than modern courts and commentators are happy with.

seldom been taken seriously by academics, and it is now almost universally ignored by academics and courts alike, even as an aspect of legal history.

This book examines that approach which, for reasons discussed below, I call the 'principled approach'. It has much to teach us about the law of negligence and offers us a way out of the malaise that is the modern law.

B. Strategy and Methodology

I now elucidate the strategy and methodology used in this book. I begin by clarifying the nature of the account of the law provided here. I explain that I present an interpretive legal theory rather than a descriptive or prescriptive account. I then explore the methodology of interpretive legal theory in relation to Rawls' notion of reflective equilibrium. Following this, I examine in more detail the way in which the methodology is applied to the law of negligence. I end by elucidating the scope of the enquiry conducted here.

(i) General Strategy

(a) *Interpretive Legal Theory* It will be evident that this book does not present a purely descriptive or historical account of the law. But nor is the account prescriptive. This book does not depict how the law ought to be according to some account of political morality or what have you. Instead, the goal is to present an interpretive theory of the law of negligence.[80] An interpretive theory is, as Stephen Smith puts it, an attempt to reveal 'an *intelligible order* in the law, so far as such an order exists'.[81] It is an attempt to help us to make sense of the law and to see it in a coherent and meaningful light.

Smith argues that interpretive theories should be evaluated along four axes: fit, transparency, coherence and morality.[82] For Smith, a theory fits the case law if it generates outcomes that match the case law, and a theory satisfies transparency if it coheres with the general reasoning adopted by courts. Moreover, a theory satisfies the morality criterion to the extent that it reveals 'how the law *might be thought to be* justified even if it is not justified'.[83] The idea is to explain how judges and others could have regarded the law as justified, even if, at the end of the day, the law is not justified. The reason this is important is that judges and commentators have apparently considered the law to have been justified and to have developed it in that light. Hence, while they may have been

---

[80] For a general account of interpretive legal theory see SA Smith, *Contract Theory* (Clarendon Press, Oxford, 2004) ch 1. For a defence of this view against common misconceptions, see A Beever and C Rickett, 'Interpretive Legal Theory and the Academic Lawyer' (2005) 68 *MLR* 320. As that article makes clear, opponents of interpretive legal theorists often mistake interpretive legal theory for descriptive or prescriptive accounts.

[81] Smith, above n80, 5.

[82] *Ibid*, 7–32.

[83] *Ibid*, 18.

mistaken, part of revealing the law's intelligibility lies in showing how the judges and others could have possessed the views that they did.

Smith also distinguishes between two understandings of coherence. According to the first (weak) notion, a theory satisfies coherence to the extent that it shows the law to be non-contradictory. According to the second (strong) notion, a theory achieves coherence only if it shows that the law can be understood as a unified system, perhaps under a single principle. It is particularly important to notice what both of these notions rule out. They exclude what I call 'limited rationality'. Imagine a position according to which the duty of care in negligence is based on principle x (or set of principles x) and the standard of care on principle y (or set of principles y). If x is inconsistent with y, then the position asserts that the law is incoherent on both of Smith's notions.[84] I refer to this as *limited* rationality, because the position is not *entirely* irrational. It analyses the separate parts of the negligence enquiry—the duty of care and the standard of care—rationally, but does so in a way that renders the entire enquiry inconsistent. Hence, the rationality is limited to particular spheres. The overall approach is, therefore, irrational.

Unfortunately, the common law suffers a great deal from limited rationality. It is, perhaps, its fundamental problem. A classic example is the willingness of some courts to take insurance into account in setting the duty of care in cases involving economic loss, but not in those dealing with personal injury without explaining why insurance is relevant in the former but not the latter case.[85] Another example is the common appeal to deterrence as a policy said to justify a particular instance of tort liability, when there are a great many examples of unwanted behaviour that tort law does precisely nothing to deter and when most would feel, including those raising the deterrence argument, that it would be inappropriate for tort law to deter that behaviour. For instance, tort law does nothing to deter unsocial activities that do not result in specific harm to individuals and grossly under-deters certain kinds of behaviour because it imposes liability only if harm to an individual results. Unless one is happy with the notion of tort liability without a claimant, or at least without a claimant who is the victim of the tort, then appeals to deterrence are examples of limited rationality.[86] Many other examples could be found, particularly in this context, as we see below, from judgments and commentary related to the issue of economic loss where it is routine to appeal to policies inconsistent with the general law.

---

[84] Notice that x must be *inconsistent* with y for this consequence to follow. If x and y are different but consistent, then this is compatible with at least one of Smith's notions.

[85] See, for instance, the decisions of the Supreme Court of Canada in *Canadian National Railway Co v Norsk Pacific Steamship Co Ltd* [1992] 1 SCR 1021 (economic loss) and *Dobson v Dobson* [1999] 2 SCR 753 (personal injury).

[86] J Coleman, *The Practice of Principle* (Oxford University Press, Oxford, 2001) 3–63; M Stone, 'The Significance of Doing and Suffering' in GJ Postema (ed), *Philosophy and the Law of Torts* (Cambridge University Press, Cambridge, 2001); EJ Weinrib, *The Idea of Private Law* (Harvard University Press, Cambridge, Mass, 1995) 39–42; A Beever, 'The Law's Function and the Judicial Function' (2003) 20 *New Zealand Universities Law Review* 299, 301–2; A Beever, 'Particularism and Prejudice in the Law of Tort' (2003) 11 *Tort Law Review* 146, 149–51.

The criticism, then, is not that many judges and commentators are irrational. Quite to the contrary, in dealing with specific issues, lawyers usually produce highly rational and sophisticated accounts. But because the reasons and justifications they posit to explain that specific area conflict with the reasons and justifications said to apply elsewhere, the rationality fails. One is therefore forced to the conclusion that, despite the apparent rationality, the positions adopted are, in fact, irrational.

Let us return to Smith's two understandings of coherence. Smith argues that the search for strong coherence should be abandoned. He maintains, for instance, that in relation to contract:

> there is no reason to suppose that the basis for invalidating restrictive covenants is the same as the basis for invalidating prostitution contracts—or that either of these rules can be explained on the same basis that orders of specific performance are explained. I conclude, then, that a requirement of perfect unity seems not only unattainable in practice, but also inappropriate in theory.[87]

However, the conclusion does not follow from the argument. It remains possible that these three features of the law of contract have the same fundamental explanation. For instance, the reason behind all three could be (and this is intended only as a suggestion) respect for autonomy. Of course, that respect would play out differently in each case. One might argue that specific performance is called for in some cases because it is a general requirement of autonomy that one be responsible for one's agreements, and in some instances the only way adequately to hold someone responsible for her agreements is to require her to perform her promises. On the other hand, one may claim that respect for autonomy does not always lead to the conclusion that one be responsible for one's agreements. In particular, agreements that, if enforced, would undermine autonomy should not be enforced—hence the reason for invalidating restrictive covenants.[88] One could also argue that prostitution contracts are invalid because, given its nature, prostitution undermines the autonomy of women. The issue is not whether this argument succeeds. The point is that it does not follow from the fact that each of these rules can be justified at one level only in terms of different considerations—the autonomy of prostitutes is irrelevant to the issue of specific performance, for example—that no more abstract principle underlies the whole of the law in this regard.

Imagine again the position which holds that the duty of care is based on principle x while the standard of care is based on principle y, but assume now that x and y are not inconsistent. Smith argues that this position is incompatible with strong coherence, and that we can therefore see that strong coherence is unrealistic and inappropriate. But it is wrong to think that strong coherence is necessarily incompatible with this position. This is because principles x and y could

---

[87] SA Smith, *Contract Theory* (Clarendon Press, Oxford, 2004) 12–13.

[88] Compare JS Mill, 'On Liberty' in JS Mill, *Three Essays* (Oxford University Press, Oxford, 1975) 125–6 (ch V, para 11).

themselves be justified in the light of principle z. In such a case, it would be principle z that would be seen to bring unity to the law. Principles x and y would be different because principle z would have different consequences when applied to different circumstances, here the duty of care and the standard of care.

Furthermore, this discussion enables us to see the significant advantages of strong over weak coherence. Take the following two positions. According to the first position, the duty of care is justified by principle x, the standard of care by principle y, where x and y are not inconsistent but no further principle can be given. According to the second position, the duty of care is justified by principle x, the standard of care by principle y and principle z explains why principle x applies to the duty of care and principle y to the standard of care. It must be clear from this that the second position presents a deeper understanding of the law of negligence than the first. This is because only it can explain why the approaches to the duty of care and the standard of care are different, only it can explain why the duty of care functions as it does while the standard of care functions as it does. This point holds universally. Hence, the desire for unity is identical to the desire to explain.

Recall the specific example discussed by Smith. Let us say that we are offered the following explanations. First, courts do not enforce agreements in restraint of trade because such agreements are economically inefficient. Secondly, courts do not enforce prostitution contracts because such are immoral. Given these explanations, we are entitled to ask why the law is interested in economic efficiency in one case and in morality in the other. We cannot claim fully to understand these aspects of the law of contract without an answer to this question. And a proper answer to the question will provide an account of why economic efficiency is relevant in the first case while morality is pertinent in the second, and will therefore show that economic efficiency and morality are not isolated concerns applied in an ad hoc manner but will reveal how those issues relate normatively to the law of contract. In other words, the answer will produce greater unity.

This is not to say that the desire for unity will always be satisfied. It is certain to be the case that points will be reached where no more explanation is forthcoming, where explanation 'bottoms out', and where certain 'brute facts' need to be accepted. And it may be the case that justifications for legal phenomena such as negligence liability immediately reach those points. But the discovery of unity is clearly desirable and, if we want to explain the law as best we can, it is something that we must search for, even if we do not find it. Importantly, it must not be assumed that it does not exist.

Smith is right, then, to deny that strong coherence is a *requirement* of interpretive legal theory. But he is wrong to deny that it is *desirable* and maintain that the search for it should be abandoned. Because unity leads to greater coherence, and hence to a theory possessing greater explanatory power, other things being equal, a theory that provides a unified explanation of the law in the sense elucidated is preferable to one that does not. Unity may not be mandatory, but it is attractive.

There is no priority between the four categories outlined by Smith. Fit is no more or less important than coherence or morality (transparency is a special case and is explored further below). One theory is better than another, then, to the extent that it satisfies all of these categories, but there is no formula for judging the success of a theory. That, like everything of its kind, requires judgement with the appropriate criteria in mind.

(b) Reflective Equilibrium   John Rawls argues that the appropriate procedure for ethical enquiry is one of reflective equilibrium. According to this view, in relation to justice:

> In describing our sense of justice an allowance must be made for the likelihood that considered judgments are no doubt subject to certain irregularities and distortions. . . . When a person is presented with an intuitively appealing account of his sense of justice . . . he may well revise his judgments to conform to its principles even though the theory does not fit his existing judgments exactly. He is especially likely to do this if he can find an explanation for the deviations which undermines his confidence in his original judgments and if the conception presented yields a judgment which he finds he can now accept. From the standpoint of moral theory, the best account of a person's sense of justice is not the one which fits his judgments prior to his examining any conception of justice, but rather the one which matches his judgments in reflective equilibrium. . . . [T]his state is one reached after a person has weighed various proposed conceptions and he has either revised his judgments to accord with one of them or held fast to his initial convictions . . .[89]

I describe this theory in relation to ethics in general.[90]

Human beings possess moral intuitions. These are our pre-reflective attitudes towards morality, our immediate moral likes and dislikes. We can utilise these intuitions to produce general accounts of morality; ie general principles or theories. For instance, if one has the intuition that it is good to make others happy, then one could generalise this and say that all actions are good if they maximise happiness.[91] However, this theory may conflict with other intuitions one has. For instance, one may also possess the intuition that persons have rights that must not be violated whatever the outcome in terms of happiness. Rawls argues that this clash between theory and intuition provides us with a choice.[92] Rawls means that when we have an intuition that clashes with our theory, we can do one of three things: we can revise our theory so that it accommodates our intuition; we can reject our intuition; or we can partially revise the theory and

---

[89] J Rawls, *A Theory of Justice: Revised Edition* (Belknap, Cambridge, Mass, 1999) 42–3. See also J Rawls, 'Outline of a Decision Procedure for Ethics' in S Freeman (ed), *John Rawls: Collected Papers* (Harvard University Press, Cambridge, Mass, 1999); J Rawls, 'The Independence of Moral Theory' in *ibid*.

[90] The distinction between 'ethics' and 'justice' as I use the terms is discussed in ch 2.

[91] A highly influential moral theory is based on precisely that intuition: utilitarianism. See eg J Bentham, *The Principles of Morals and Legislation* (Prometheus Books, Amherst, NY, 1988); JS Mill, *Utilitarianism* (Hackett, Indianapolis, Ind, 1979).

[92] J Rawls, *A Theory of Justice: Revised Edition* (Belknap, Cambridge, Mass, 1999) 18.

partially reject our intuition.[93] Rawls insists that all three possibilities are open to us. In that sense we are faced with a choice. But 'choice' is not the best term as it suggests that we are entirely free to adopt one of the three strategies as if our decision could just as well be made by rolling a die. But that is not correct. Though we must decide which of the three strategies to adopt, that decision is not arbitrary but involves judgement. I explore judgement briefly in Chapter 2, but suffice it to say for the moment that, while reasonable people sometimes disagree in their judgements, this does not imply that judgement is arbitrary or that judgements do not have truth values. In other words, though judgement is far from a mechanical process, and though it is to a large extent inscrutable, judgements can be right or wrong.[94]

For our purposes, the crucial element in the process of reflective equilibrium is the possibility of rejecting our intuitions because they conflict with our theory. According to Rawls, this is likely to happen when our theory enables us to see that our intuitions are suspect. For instance, many nineteenth century citizens of the United States came to see that slavery was wrong, in part because slavery was inconsistent with the notion of human equality thought to lie behind such documents as the US Constitution.[95] Though US citizens could have rejected that principle or defined it in a way that did not cover human beings of African descent (as they often did, in fact), the intuitive force of the principle eventually overcame the intuitive reluctance of many to recognise the immorality of slavery.[96] Accordingly, theory has a crucial role to play in reflective equilibrium. It forces us critically to examine our intuitions and provides us with a perspective from which to do so. It also produces the aspiration to make all our intuitions consistent with each other and with general principle. As Rawls envisages the process of reflective equilibrium, as time passes people will alter their general principles in the light of their intuitions, and their intuitions in the light of their general principles, in order to produce greater equilibrium between intuition and theory. This is a continuous process and there is no reason to believe that people will ever achieve perfect equilibrium. Nevertheless, if we are to make progress in our understanding of ethics, we must engage in this process.

---

[93] Rawls neglects the last possibility, but it is entailed by his view.

[94] If this were not true, then knowledge would be impossible. For discussion of the nature of judgment see I Kant, *Critique of the Power of Judgment* (trans P Guyer and E Matthews, Cambridge University Press, Cambridge, 2000).

[95] Note that the constitution did not actually contain an equality clause until the 14th amendment was passed after the civil war.

[96] Note that this judgment has a truth value. Those who judged that slavery was wrong because it conflicted with equality were right. Those who judged otherwise were wrong. Note also that this process is far from unusual and is not confined to morality. The vast majority of philosophical and many other disputes involve similar clashes in intuition. For instance, most believe that one cannot be harmed by something unless one either knows about that something or that something physically impacts on one ('what you don't know can't hurt you'). But we also hope that others are not talking about us behind our backs, and not just because we might find out about it or because it might impact on us in the future. One of these intuitions must go. For discussion see T Nagel, 'Death' (1970) 4 *Nous* 73.

Hence, reflective equilibrium steers a course between foundationalism and intuitionism. Foundationalists begin with a theory and insist that intuitions are justified only if they match that theory.[97] There are two main problems with this approach. First, the subjection of intuition to theory leaves it unclear why the theory should be accepted in the first place. Is the theory meant to be attractive because it is intuitively appealing or for some other unknown reason? Secondly, the position appears to be dogmatic. What resources do we have for checking whether the theory is correct or whether we correctly understand it? Intuitionism, on the other hand, is beset by the problem that it promotes prejudice to the level of moral truth. It is widely recognised that we should not accept that a moral claim is true simply because it sits well with our prejudices.[98] Reflective equilibrium avoids the pitfalls of both foundationalism and intuitionism by allowing theory to be derived from intuition and by allowing theory to check and examine intuition. The result ought to be a developing and constantly improving understanding of ethics.[99]

The process described by Rawls is almost identical to the one I employ here, but there is one important difference. Although the distinction between intuition and theory remains important, the chief focus of this book is on the relationship between *case law* and theory. That is because this is an exercise in interpretive legal theory and not in prescriptive theory. Hence, the appropriate starting point is not intuitions concerning what is right, but the case law. The method employed is to derive a theoretical understanding of the law from the case law that can then be used to re-examine the case law. Hence, my method is not to stipulate first principles and then apply them to the law. Rather, it is to engage in a process of reflective equilibrium considering the case law. In that sense, the theory advanced here is a *legal theory* rather than a *legal philosophy*.[100]

Before I discuss how I apply reflective equilibrium to the law in more detail, it will be helpful to discuss the relationship between Rawls' concept of reflective equilibrium and Smith's account of interpretive legal theory. According to reflective equilibrium, one must begin with one's intuitions. With respect to the law, this refers to the case law. At this level, ie before conducting any reflective equilibrium, there is of course a perfect fit between one's account and the case

---

[97] This view is informatively examined and rejected in JJC Smart, 'An Outline of a System of Utilitarian Ethics' in JJC Smart and B Williams (eds), *Utilitarianism: For and Against* (Cambridge University Press, Cambridge, 1973).

[98] I have explored these issues in more detail in A Beever, 'Particularism and Prejudice in the Law of Tort' (2003) 11 *Tort Law Review* 146.

[99] This does not imply that all changes will be improvements. Certain intuitions could arise that, as it were, infect theories. Racist intuitions are likely to be a case in point. Moreover, some improvements may be able to come about only if theories move for a while further away from the truth. These possibilities need not detain us further.

[100] Compare J Rawls, 'The Independence of Moral Theory' in S Freeman (ed), *John Rawls: Collected Papers* (Harvard University Press, Cambridge, Mass, 1999) 286; EJ Weinrib, 'Correlativity, Personality, and the Emerging Consensus on Corrective Justice' (2001) 2 *Theoretical Inquiries in Law* 107, 111–12, 153.

law—one's account simply is the case law. But that is only where the enquiry begins. In order to satisfy the criteria of transparency, coherence and morality, one must attempt to explain the case law in an intelligible fashion. When one does so, one is almost certain to encounter problems of fit—there will be cases that do not fit with one's account. When this happens, one can attempt to revise one's theory so that it fits the difficult cases. But that is not necessarily appropriate. Fit is not the only value at play here. One may be able to make the cases fit only at great sacrifice of transparency, coherence and/or morality. It may be more attractive, then, to decide that some of the cases are to be rejected. That has a cost in terms of fit, but the pay off in terms of transparency, coherence and morality may be worthwhile.

(c) Transparency, Policy, Judicial Decision Making, and Reflective Equilibrium
As indicated above, there is no relationship of priority between the categories of fit, transparency, coherence and morality. However, transparency requires special treatment when applied to the modern law of negligence. This is because, as we have seen, modern cases contain reasoning that cannot be reconciled into a general theory. Hence, no theory could ever hope to provide a high degree of transparency. But that does not mean that transparency is irrelevant. As we discover in the following chapters, a general account of the law is forthcoming from the case law, although not from the modern case law. The theory presented here is transparent with respect to that case law.

   Moreover it is important to remember that judges have the unenviable task of having to make a decision with comparatively (compared to academics) little time to reflect on the case. Sometimes, judges have to make decisions when they are not sure which outcome is right. Though it is difficult to obtain any evidence, I suspect that at the highest appellate levels that happens only infrequently. Much more common is that judges have a strong feeling for what the result ought to be but do not know how best to argue for that conclusion.[101] In such circumstances, it is not surprising that judges reach for policy arguments, as a policy argument can be found to favour any conclusion. It *may* even be appropriate, or at least justifiable, for judges at lower levels sometimes to do this, even if the argument of this book is entirely correct. But it is inconsistent with the role of the academic to accept at face value policy arguments that cannot be combined into a general account of the law. It is the job of the academic to find more general, theoretically satisfactory explanations for the cases. This is important in order to find the appropriate legal justification for a decision or, as the case may be, to reveal why the decision was wrongly decided.

(ii) Applying the Methodology to the Law of Negligence

(a) The Principled Approach   The theory that I advance is based primarily on the approach to the law of negligence set out in five great cases: *Donoghue v*

---

[101] That is surely a common experience for academics as well.

Stevenson, Palsgraf v Long Island Railroad Co,[102] *Bolton v Stone, The Wagon Mound (No 2)* and *The Wagon Mound (No 1)*. With respect to those cases, it is not necessary to engage in a process of reflective equilibrium, because the judges have already done that for us. Accordingly, our task is merely to observe the way in which the judges developed their understandings of the case law and principle in order to produce a general account of the law.

What we discover is a theory of the law of negligence that appears capable of explaining that law in a conceptually satisfactory fashion. I call that theory the 'principled approach' and maintain that it is based on a form of justice known in legal circles as 'corrective justice'. Hence, although I present a 'corrective justice theory of the law of negligence', this does not mean that I focus on corrective justice *rather than* on the case law, or that I argue that the positive law should be replaced with a system based on corrective justice. At this point at least, I am rediscovering the law, not recreating it. Though, for reasons of convenience explored at the beginning of Chapter 2, it is necessary to explore corrective justice *before* examining its application to the principled approach developed in the cases noted above, this does not mean that corrective justice is a 'first principle' from which I derive that approach. Rather, I maintain that the leading cases mentioned above *instantiate* corrective justice. I use the word 'instantiate' advisedly. My claim is not that the cases apply corrective justice in the sense that the judges who decided the cases had a general theory of corrective justice in mind that they utilised to generate principles and outcomes (though I do not rule that out either). But nor is my claim merely that the cases are consistent with corrective justice. My claim is that the cases contain reasons that are reasons of corrective justice. They are reasons of corrective justice because corrective justice demands the application of those reasons to the case and because other forms of morality do not demand the application of those reasons but may, in fact, demand the application of conflicting reasons. Hence, as the leading cases that I discuss proceed on the basis of those reasons demanded by corrective justice, those cases are not merely compatible with corrective justice, they are *instances* of corrective justice. In that sense, this part of the book is an essay in normative archaeology.

The principled approach to the law of negligence presents us with a model for comprehending that law that is, at least prima facie, far superior to the modern understanding. In particular, the modern understanding's necessary reliance on policy is removed. In fact, viewing the law of negligence in terms of the principled approach is designed to eliminate both the need for appeal to policy considerations and the permissibility of that appeal. It removes the need to appeal to policy by providing an account of the scope of liability that refers only to corrective justice. It renders the appeal to policy impermissible because it reveals both that policy concerns are *irrelevant* to the conception of justice that informs the law of negligence and that policy concerns are *inconsistent* with that

---

[102]   162 NE 99 (NY CA 1928).

conception of justice. Hence, if successful, the principled approach provides a perspicuous and apolitical account of legal reasoning.[103]

In the light of the principled approach and of corrective justice, we will see that the law of negligence possesses a conceptually coherent, indeed conceptually *unified*, structure. By this I mean that the various stages of the negligence enquiry—the standard of care, the duty of care, remoteness, factual causation and defences—are seen as parts of a conceptually integrated whole and not, as they are usually understood, a series of conceptually separate questions brought together under the rubric 'the law of negligence' for reasons of public policy. The principled approach shows that the negligence enquiry can be reduced almost entirely to a single question: Did the defendant create an unreasonable risk of the claimant's injury?

(b) The Modern Law   I then apply the principled approach to the modern law. Here the fit is not perfect. Generally speaking, with regard to transparency the reasoning of modern judges does not instantiate corrective justice or the principled approach. Nevertheless, I argue that the principled approach is the best theory of the modern law. I now explore what this claim means.

To begin with, it will help if we imagine all case law falling into four general categories that I label: central cases, standard cases, controversial cases and divisive cases. Central cases are ones of utmost importance to the law. *Donoghue v Stevenson* is an obvious example of such a case. These cases form the backbone of the negligence curriculum for tort students and are found in all casebooks. Standard cases are the general run of the mill cases that broadly exemplify the principles found in the central cases. Because they contain little that is new or exciting, they seldom find their way into casebooks. Controversial cases are (as I define them) those that are, at least on their face, consistent with other existing case law but nevertheless remain controversial because they appear to jar with the general law in some way. According to the dissent in *White v Jones*, that was such a case as the finding of the majority was inconsistent with general features of the law of contract.[104] Finally, divisive cases are ones that are inconsistent with other cases. Prominent examples of divisive cases are the divergent judgments of Commonwealth courts regarding economic loss caused in the construction of a building.[105] Casebooks often contain both divisive and controversial cases, because those cases present interesting debates for students and academics alike. However, it is crucial not to overestimate their importance to the law as a whole.

---

[103] The apolitical nature of this reasoning is examined in ch 2.

[104] [1995] 2 AC 207, 251 (HL) (Lord Keith). At this point, it is not important whether this claim was correct.

[105] *Anns v London Borough of Merton* [1978] AC 728 (HL); *Murphy v Brentwood District Council* [1991] 1 AC 398 (HL); *Bryan v Maloney* (1995) 182 CLR 609 (HCA); *Winnipeg Condominium Corp No 36 v Bird Construction Co* [1995] 1 SCR 85; *Invercargill City Council v Hamlin* [1994] 3 NZLR 513 (CA); *Invercargill City Council v Hamlin* [1996] AC 624 (PC).

As indicated above, the general aim of this book is to develop a picture of the law that captures the case law. Naturally, an ideal theoretical explanation of the case law would be one that fits every decided case that has not been superseded. But no such theory will be forthcoming, as there will always be some cases that fall outside a general theory. It is tempting, then, to hold that the best theory is the one that fits with the most cases. But this is wrong. Not all cases are created equal. It is more important that the theory fit the central cases than the standard cases, the standard cases than the controversial cases, and the controversial cases than the divisive cases.

The theory that I develop in the following completely satisfies fit and transparency with respect to the central cases. That is, the theory is consistent with both the outcome of and the reasoning utilised in those cases. The theory also satisfies fit and transparency with regard to most of the standard cases. However, the theory cannot satisfy transparency with respect to a few of the standard cases. With respect to these cases, my aim is to show that the principled approach would have allowed the court to reach the same result, but with far more elegant and unified reasoning,[106] with reasoning that was consistent with that used in other cases, and without the need to appeal to controversial and conflicting policies. In short, the argument is that, though the court did not realise it, there was a *legal* rather than a policy-based route to the same answer. Hence, in regard to these cases, the principled approach is the best theory because it provides the most elegant and appropriate method of reaching the conclusions preferred by the court.

Moreover, the principled approach is incompatible with a number of divisive cases, in terms both of fit and transparency. But it would obviously be wrong to treat these cases as simple counterexamples to the principled approach, because other case law exists that is, as it were, a counterexample to those counterexamples. Rather, the goal here must be to determine which of the inconsistent cases were rightly decided and why. I argue that the cases consistent with the principled approach were rightly decided because they adopt reasons that are more elegant, consistent with the law in general, and appropriate to judicial decision making than the alternatives. If successful, this will also show that the principled approach is the best theory of the modern law, as it tells us which of the divisive cases were rightly decided and why they were rightly decided.

Finally, the principled approach is inconsistent with a few controversial cases that fall into two general groups: cases that deal with the thin skull rule (which are, I believe, widely regarded as unsatisfactory[107]) and cases that concern economic loss caused to intended but not actual will beneficiaries (the so-called

---

[106] This is not an aesthetic concern, despite the claims of S Hedley, 'The Empire Strikes Back? A Restatement of the Law of Unjust Enrichment' (2004) 28 *Melbourne University Law Review* 759, 774. The elegance of an argument relates to the simplicity and unity of the underlying general theory and is widely recognised in the natural and social sciences to be a desirable property of theories.

[107] In fact, the description of one of them was greeted with hilarity at a conference I recently attended.

'disappointed beneficiary cases'). Hence, it is only in these very narrow areas that the modern law in outcome is actually inconsistent with the principled approach. Moreover, with respect to the disappointed beneficiary cases, I suggest other avenues for satisfying one's intuitions. Hence, if the rest of the argument is successful, the existence of a handful of cases inconsistent with a theory that captures the rest of the law could hardly be said to defeat that theory. Quite the contrary. Though the theory may conflict with a few cases that at first glance appear to be rightly decided, we must always recognise the possibility that our intuitions are mistaken. The theory advanced here may help us to see why those intuitions are mistaken and why those cases were in fact wrongly decided. We must recognise that it is always possible that our reason will drive us to conclusions with which we are not immediately happy—the same was true for many racists in the southern United States.

It is curious that many common lawyers are as attached as they are to the case law, especially given that it is widely recognised that the modern law is in a state approaching chaos. According to David Ibbetson, for instance, '[t]hat the tort of negligence is in a mess goes almost without saying'.[108] Why are we so enchanted by this mess? Stapleton, for instance, rejects Peter Benson's theory of the irrecoverability economic loss in negligence[109] on the ground that it fails to fit *one* case, and a case that is inconsistent with all the leading authorities from other Commonwealth jurisdictions.[110] If we are to tidy up this mess, some of it will have to be thrown out.

Although it does not fit everything, the theory advanced here both is highly unified and captures the vast majority of the case law; so much so in fact that—though the theory will of course require improvement—it would be surprising if the theory were on the wrong track. Instead, it must represent a leap forward in our understanding of the law. Or, rather, a very welcome leap backwards.

I have distinguished between central, standard, controversial, and divisive cases. How does one know which cases belong to which category? The answer, *the only answer that is available*, is to conduct a reflective equilibrium. In other words, one can tell which cases are central only by examining both one's intuitions and one's theory. Some are inclined to see a sleight of hand in this, claiming that certain cases are marginalised, not because they really are unimportant,

---

[108] DJ Ibbetson, 'How the Romans did for Us: Ancient Roots of the Tort of Negligence' (2003) 26 *University of New South Wales Law Journal* 475, 475.

[109] P Benson, 'The Basis for Excluding Liability for Economic Loss in Tort Law' in D Owen (ed), *Philosophical Foundations of Tort Law* (Oxford University Press, Oxford, 1995).

[110] J Stapleton, 'Comparative Economic Loss: Lessons from Case-Law-Focused "Middle Theory"' (2002) 50 *University of California of Los Angeles Law Review* 531, 573. The one case is *Winnipeg Condominium Corp No 36 v Bird Construction Co* [1995] 1 SCR 85. It is inconsistent with *Murphy v Brentwood District Council* [1991] 1 AC 398 (HL); *Bryan v Maloney* (1995) 182 CLR 609 (HCA); *Invercargill City Council v Hamlin* [1994] 3 NZLR 513 (CA); and *Invercargill City Council v Hamlin* [1996] AC 624 (PC). These cases are explored in ch 7. Stapleton also notes that Benson acknowledges that his account *may be* inconsistent with *Biakanja v Irving* 320 P 2d 16 (Calif SC 1958) and *White v Jones* [1995] 2 AC 207 (HL).

but merely because they do not fit one's preferred theory.[111] There is no doubt that this danger exists, but there are two replies to the challenge.

First, cases are rightly categorised on the basis of both theory *and intuition*. Theory is informed by intuition and intuition is informed by theory. So, for example, in effect I claim in Chapter 7 that *White v Jones* is best regarded as a controversial case. I believe this is correct both because the outcome and reasoning in that case clash with the principled approach and because it seems to me that *White v Jones* is intuitively wrong. Of course, my intuition is in part influenced by my theory, but it would be a mistake to see this as question begging. This can be brought out by considering the alternative—the second reply. If one holds that *White v Jones* is, say, a central case without justifying that result partly in terms of theory, then on what is one basing one's claim? Sheer gut feeling?[112] But that cannot be appropriate in this context. We cannot see whether *White v Jones* is a central case without having some idea about what the law of negligence is and how *White v Jones* fits into it. In other words, we cannot see whether the case is central without a theory that tells us what 'central' means in this context. Accordingly, if one wished to prove that *White v Jones* were in fact a central case, the only way to do so would be to develop a rival theory to the one that I present here that does a better job of explaining the law and that reveals *White v Jones* to be central.

At this point, it is important to note that, although lawyers do not usually describe their methodology as I have, the strategy that I adopt here is by no means unique. Nor is it limited to normative enquiries. The attempt to understand apparently diverse phenomena in terms of general accounts or theories is the way in which every academic discipline progresses, with the sole, thankfully partial, exception of the common law. Hence, the strategy employed here is an attempt to produce a conception of the law of negligence of a kind that matches our understanding of every other aspect of our world. There is no reason why investigations into the law of negligence, especially academic investigations, should be different in kind from those undertaken by moral philosophers, physicists,[113] chemists, psychologists, historians and the like into their subject matter. In fact, one might expect that investigation into law would have much

---

[111] SM Waddams, *Dimensions of Private Law: Categories and Concepts in Anglo-American Legal Reasoning* (Cambridge University Press, Cambridge, 2003) 21–2, 222.

[112] Remember that we are talking of the case being central to the law. The issue is not whether the case was important to the business community, was controversial at the time it was decided, was welcome or unwelcome to the profession, or other similar concerns.

[113] I England, *The Philosophy of Tort Law* (Dartmouth, Aldershot, 1993) ch 5 points out that modern physicists sometimes present 'complementary' rather than unitary explanations of phenomena and concludes from this that unitary accounts are not required in law either. But England's argument relies on a false analogy between law and physics. See A Levin, 'Quantum Physics in Private Law' (2001) 14 *Canadian Journal of Law and Jurisprudence* 249. In any case, physicists have adopted non-unitary accounts because they have been forced to do so, not because they thought that non-unitary accounts were per se preferable to unitary ones. Hence, modern physics does nothing to question the *desirability* of unitary accounts of phenomena.

in common with moral philosophy in particular.[114] Still less should enquiry into the law of negligence differ to the extent it does from the investigations of the laws of unjust enrichment and contract, which often are presented as general, theoretical accounts.

(c) An Internal, not External, Analysis   This book is concerned entirely with legal doctrine. It is an attempt to show that the law of negligence can be explained and justified from an appropriate legal perspective. There are many other perspectives from which the law may informatively be analysed and evaluated, and this book is in no way intended to close off those avenues of understanding. But those perspectives are not the central one for a lawyer.[115] Hence, while it must be valuable to consider the impact of the law of negligence on economic efficiency, for example, I show that the inner normativity of the law is exclusively corrective justice and does not involve economic efficiency. Therefore, economic efficiency does not belong to the law's self-understanding.

In order to appreciate this point, it is important to perceive an often over-looked distinction between the value of something and the way that that some-thing works. Unfortunately, we tend to use the word 'function' to refer to both of these concepts, and we therefore tend to equivocate over the concepts. An example is found in Peter Cane's rejection of the idea that the private law is solely a system of corrective justice:

> Why is it inconsistent with the ideas of private law and of corrective justice to say that private law serves the function of co-ordinating human behaviour, or of resolving cer-tain sorts of disputes between individuals, or of maintaining social order, or of giving effect to ideas of personal responsibility, or . . . of setting standards for behaviour and of punishing and deterring certain types of conduct? . . .

---

[114] It is sometimes said that a crucial difference exists between law and philosophy that explains the difference in methodology between the two disciplines. This difference is said to be that, unlike philosophers, lawyers must reach decisions that have immediate real world impact. But this not true. Certainly, judges make such decisions, but academic lawyers do not. Their position is closely parallel to the philosophers'.

One apparent difference between scientific investigation and legal investigation as I have described it is that scientists are not free to reject some phenomena as I have suggested that we must reject some case law as wrongly decided. This difference recognises the fact that judges can some-times get things wrong while the laws of nature cannot. Moreover, there is more similarity here than first appears. Scientists are not prepared to abandon their theories as soon as they encounter any experimental data that are inconsistent with their theories. For one thing, the theory may give good reason to believe that the experimental data are flawed because of human error.

[115] M Oakeshott, 'The Concept of a Philosophical Jurisprudence: Part I' [1938] *Politica* 203, M Oakeshott, 'The Concept of a Philosophical Jurisprudence: Part II' [1938] *Politica* 345. Compare the criticism of EJ Weinrib, *The Idea of Private Law* (Harvard University Press, Cambridge, Mass, 1995) in P Cane, 'Tort Law as Regulation' (2002) 31 *Common Law World Review* 305, 310–11. Cane censures Weinrib for considering only legal doctrine and ignoring the wider impact of private law. But it is no objection to a theory of law that it does not consider every perspective possible on law but only the uniquely legal perspective. That is, surely, the central (though by no means only) task of the legal academy.

In fact, private law can be seen as serving a number of different and sometimes conflicting goals which are reflected in incoherence and inconsistencies in the institution itself.[116]

This passage begins by examining the law's function in the sense of there being a value to the law. Cane is right to point out that the law has many functions in that sense. However, Cane ends by speaking of the law's *goals*. A goal is not merely something valuable that is achieved but is something *at which one aims*. But Cane does not show that private law aims at the goals he perceives it to have. In short, establishing that the law is valuable because of *x* does not show that practising lawyers should seek to achieve *x* in law. The value of *x* does not necessarily reveal how *x* works.[117] Despite the fact that the law of negligence has many functions in the sense that it is valuable (and disvaluable) from many perspectives, the workings of the law may be able to be explained and justified by corrective justice alone.

Moreover, the analysis in this book is internal in another sense: it is internal to the law of negligence in particular. Hence, this is an essay on the common law of negligence, though it includes discussion of statutes long thought to be relevant to the law of negligence itself. What it is emphatically not is an exploration of the effect of legislation such as the various 'Bills of Rights', 'Charters', etc that are now in force. This is not because these issues are unimportant, or because I insist that such can have no effect on the law of tort. On the contrary. It is only because that is not the chosen focus of this discussion.[118]

It is also important to clarify my position on the issue of vicarious liability. Although vicarious liability is not part of the law of negligence, it often applies to negligence actions, and many of the cases explored in this book involve vicarious liability. There are two main ways of dealing with this issue. First, one could argue that vicarious liability is consistent with corrective justice.[119] Secondly, one could maintain that vicarious liability is anomalous, and hence need not be incorporated into a general account of the law of negligence. To say that vicarious liability is anomalous is not necessarily to assert that vicarious liability is unjustifiable, but rather to say that vicarious liability cannot be justified in terms of the ordinary justifications of tort law. Hence, it is possible to produce a convincing theoretical account of the law of negligence that does not and cannot explain vicarious liability.

It is not necessary to take a stand on which is the preferable position. It suffices for the purposes of this book to note that vicarious liability is external

---

[116] P Cane, 'Corrective Justice and Correlativity in Private Law' (1996) 16 *OJLS* 471, 484 (citation omitted).

[117] For further discussion see A Beever, 'The Law's Function and the Judicial Function' (2003) 20 *New Zealand Universities Law Review* 299, 299–307.

[118] For that discussion, see eg D Friedmann and D Barak-Erez (eds), *Human Rights in Private Law* (Hart Publishing, Oxford, 2001).

[119] Eg *Ira S Bushey & Sons Inc v United States of America* 398 F 2d 167 (US 2d Cir 1968) 171; 1266;1266 EJ Weinrib, *The Idea of Private Law* (Harvard University Press, Cambridge, Mass, 1995) 185–7.

to the law of negligence. This is because vicarious liability allows the claimant to sue one person for the tort of another. Hence, vicarious liability is parasitic on the law of tort. To take the standard case in the law of negligence, the claimant can sue an employer only if the claimant would have been able to establish the elements of negligence (duty, breach, proximate and factual causation) against the employer's employee. Therefore, my argument is that, whether or not corrective justice is sufficient to explain why the claimant can sue the employer who was not negligent, corrective justice explains why the employee is potentially liable, and thus is necessary to explain why the employer is liable.

That point is crucial for the following reason. If the law of negligence determines liability in accordance with the relationship between the parties as I contend, then, in cases involving vicarious liability, the employer's liability is determined (i) by the relationship between the employee and the claimant and (ii) by the relationship between the employer and the employee. The first part of this equation (i) relates to the law of negligence; the second part (ii) to vicarious liability. Hence, because this is a book about the law of negligence and not about vicarious liability, I ignore the second part of the equation (ii). Therefore, I generally disregard the fact that the defendant in these cases is not the person who committed the wrong, and I speak of the parties as if they were the claimant and the employee. This is appropriate because, as I have shown, vicarious liability is parasitic on the law of tort.

Despite appearances, there is no similar problem with wrongful death actions. At common law, such actions were not available.[120] In many jurisdictions, this has been altered by statute. Hence, in these cases the claimant's ability to recover is parasitic on the ability of the deceased to recover were he alive, and hence the relevant relationship is not between the claimant and the defendant but between the deceased and the defendant. This is appropriate because it is mandated by statute.

(iii) Format of the Book

The strategy employed in this book presents a problem of presentation. This is because the book attempts to do two things at once: to provide a theoretical account of the law and to show that a theoretical account of the law can be derived from the law's leading cases. If the task were to do only the former, then it would be best to begin with general and abstract features of the theory and then apply that systematically to the various areas of the law in descending order of abstraction. But if the task were to do only the latter, then it would be best to begin with the leading cases and work up towards the theory from there. And

---

[120] *Baker v Bolton* (1808) 1 Camp 493; *Admiralty Commissioners v SS Amerika* [1917] AC 38 (HL).

there is another problem. In order to convince the reader unfamiliar with the theory and unused to thinking of the case law in its light that the law of negligence can rightly be understood in terms of the theory, it is not possible to begin with that theory itself. Rather, it is necessary to convince the reader, piece by piece, that the law is capable of being so understood.

The solution I have adopted is as follows. First, I outline in Chapter 2 the general theory upon which the book is based. This is necessary in order to provide a point of reference for the discussion that follows. After that, I have organised the chapters of this book so that they correspond roughly to the order of a normal casebook on the law of negligence. I hope that the order of the materials will reflect the reader's own first investigations of the law. It is my aim to convince the reader to see the cases in a new light as we travel though our enquiry and, as it were, to relearn the law in the same order as she first learnt it. In doing so, not only may her understanding of the law in general change, but also her interpretation of the individual cases themselves. In all areas, but perhaps most in this, one's appreciation of the cases is influenced by one's general picture of the law. Accordingly, one of the tasks is to request the reader, at least temporarily, to abandon her policy focused reading of the cases and entertain instead a more principled analysis.

In the above, I maintained that the law of negligence can be understood as a single question: Did the defendant create an unreasonable risk of the claimant's injury? For analytic purposes, both courts and commentators break this question down into smaller questions, of which three are the most important. The first question is: did the defendant create an unreasonable risk? This corresponds to the standard of care stage of the negligence enquiry and is explored in Chapter 3. My argument is that the standard of care is designed to do justice between the claimant and the defendant. Hence, I show that both the objective standard and the manner in which it is sometimes adjusted reflect corrective justice. I also argue that the approach to determining reasonable care in the Commonwealth is based on corrective justice, despite claims that it reflects utilitarian concerns. The second and third questions are: 'was the claimant placed at an unreasonable risk?' and 'was there an unreasonable risk of the claimant's injury?'. These questions correspond to the duty of care and remoteness stages of the negligence enquiry respectively. I examine them together in Chapter 4. My argument is that the duty and remoteness enquires are both designed to determine whether the defendant was at fault for creating the risk of the injury that actually occurred. Hence, the question is whether the appropriate normative connection can be established between the defendant's negligence and the claimant's injury. I discuss these issues in a single chapter because they involve concerns so intimately related that they cannot adequately be explored separately.

In Chapter 5, I compare the principled approach with the modern approaches to the duty of care: the *Anns* test and the incremental approach. I maintain that the modern approaches are significantly inferior to the principled approach.

In fact, I argue that the modern approaches cannot rightly be regarded as competitors with the principled approach as they are conceptually empty. By this, I mean that the modern approaches have no inherent content and thus are incapable of directing judicial decision making.

I then begin to explore the central problems said to defeat the principled approach. In Chapter 6, I start by clarifying the fundamental structure of the principled approach in the light of previous chapters. Then, in Chapters 7 and 8, I explore two important problems said to haunt the law of negligence. The first is the issue of economic loss. After examining the largely unsuccessful attempts of the modern approaches to deal with the issue, I show that the principled approach faces no problem in relation to economic loss. This is because the principled approach imposes liability only if the defendant violated a right in the claimant, but, in the cases said to pose problems of economic loss, the claimant possessed no relevant right. The second, and closely related, issue is recovery for loss caused by negligent misrepresentation. Again, I examine the deficiencies of the modern approaches in this area. I then show that the cause of action known as 'negligent misrepresentation' is not a form of negligence liability. Instead, it belongs primarily to the law of consents and is irrelevant to our understanding of the law of negligence proper. Finally, I examine the issue of nonfeasance and the liability of public authorities in Chapter 9.

I turn to the defences in Chapter 10. I examine contributory negligence, voluntary assumption of risk and illegality. My argument is that these defences are mandated by corrective justice. Contributory negligence is designed to preserve equality in the relationship between the parties by applying standards of care equally to both parties. Voluntary assumption of risk reflects the fact that the defendant cannot have violated the claimant's rights if the claimant willed the defendant's actions. Finally, I argue that the defence of illegality can be understood only by examining the nature of the legal system as a whole. While this means that this defence cannot be understood solely in terms of the application of corrective justice to the law of negligence, that conclusion is not in tension with the thesis of this book. That is because the defence of illegality is mandated by the application of corrective justice, not to the law of negligence alone, but to the common law as a whole.

In Chapter 11, I explore the subjects of wrongful birth, wrongful conception and nervous shock. With respect to the first, I reveal why corrective justice demonstrates that there can be no recovery. With regard to the second, I show why corrective justice reaches a similar conclusion to that adopted by the House of Lords in *Rees v Darlington Memorial Hospital NHS Trust*[121] and also explore the exceptions that corrective justice would allow to that result. I then turn to nervous shock, though that discussion is only brief and important issues remain unresolved. This is because recovery for nervous shock is problematic, as the common law contains at best an obscure and partially incoherent account

---

[121] [2003] UKHL 52, [2004] 1 AC 309.

of the right to psychological integrity. Accordingly, this problem will be solved only by elucidating an adequate account of that right. But, for reasons examined in Chapter 11, that enquiry lies beyond the scope of this book.

In Chapter 12, I examine factual causation. First, I insist that factual causation in law means factual causation *simpliciter*. In particular, I reject the notion that there is a special legal conception of causation. However, I accept that deciding liability raises issues that *appear* to require the adoption of a peculiarly legal understanding of causation. But I maintain that those issues can be resolved by seeing them in the light of corrective justice. Hence, I argue that these issues are not ones of factual causation, but are normative concerns relevant to corrective justice.

Finally, in Chapter 13, I explore issues of uncertainty that arise in the law of negligence. In particular, I discuss *res ipsa loquitur*, factual uncertainty and loss of a chance. I maintain that *res ipsa loquitur* and loss of a chance are conceptually confused and that they should be eliminated from our understanding of the law. With respect to factual uncertainty, I again argue that the important issues in this area are best resolved by the application of corrective justice.

III. CONCLUDING REMARKS

In ending this introduction, it is important to spell out what this book is not. It is not a comprehensive analysis of the law of negligence and the commentary that surrounds it. No book of this size or kind could possibly be one. It therefore does not examine each area of the law in complete detail. Nor does it examine all areas of the law, though the most important ones are covered. In summary, it is not a textbook on the law of negligence. What it is is an attempt to demonstrate that the general strategy it employs, which I call the principled approach, provides an analytic framework for understanding the law of negligence that possesses far greater explanatory power than the current dominant models. And it attempts to show that that model applies throughout at least the most important areas of the law. Of course, not all will agree with how I have applied the approach to particular cases. Not all will read the cases as I do. Some will think that the principled approach has other consequences. And there will be issues not covered that, at first sight, appear to conflict with the principled approach and, naturally, new cases will arise that will throw up issues not considered here. Perhaps this too will be explained by the principled approach as described here, or perhaps it will cause that approach to be revised. While the latter would certainly constitute an objection to the claims made in this book, it is consistent with its general thesis. In that sense, this book is best regarded as a contribution to the beginnings of a research project than as a statement about the end of one. The project is to re-establish general principle in our understanding of the law of negligence. First and foremost, the aim of this book is to give reason to believe that that project is feasible.

On a personal level, then, my chief goal is not so much to establish the particular claims made herein, but rather to show that the law of negligence can genuinely be law and that it deserves to take its place in the legal pantheon alongside areas of the law such as contract and the modern law of unjust enrichment. In fact, in my view, as I hope to give some reason to accept, the law of negligence correctly understood is the greatest achievement in the history of the common law. If only we allowed ourselves to see it.

2

Corrective Justice, Negligence and Tort Law

THIS CHAPTER EXAMINES the nature of corrective justice. It does so first by distinguishing corrective justice from other forms of morality, then by elucidating corrective justice itself. I then examine the role that corrective justice plays in defining the distinction between principle and policy adopted here and the apolitical nature of corrective justice. In end by exploring two possible objections that may be raised to the thesis of this book. The first is that any account of the law of negligence based on corrective justice must be incomplete, because it cannot explain the nature of the rights upon which corrective justice is said to operate. The second is that the corrective justice model of the law of negligence is inconsistent with other areas of the law of tort.

As discussed in the previous chapter, I am here interested in corrective justice because it provides the theoretical background necessary to comprehend the principled approach. I do not proceed by imposing corrective justice on the case law. On the face of it, then, it would be better to leave discussion of corrective justice until later. If I claim to find corrective justice in the case law, then why not wait until I have found it before I exhibit it? The answer is that corrective justice may be difficult to find if we do not know what we are looking for. Outlining a general conception of corrective justice now will facilitate our investigations in further chapters.

Because the aim in this chapter is to introduce corrective justice, the following has the air of theory. But it is important to remember that I am not presenting a theory of corrective justice. For my purposes, the appropriate account of corrective justice is the one that emerges through reflective equilibrium on the case law. Hence, my goal in this chapter is to present corrective justice only in outline. For that reason, though commentators have disagreed over how corrective justice is best understood, this debate is at best of only incidental relevance here.[1] Nor it is necessary to explore criticisms of corrective justice

---

[1] See eg J Coleman, *The Practice of Principle* (Oxford University Press, Oxford, 2001); RA Epstein, 'A Theory of Strict Liability' (1973) 2 *The Journal of Legal Studies* 151; EJ Weinrib, *The Idea of Private Law* (Harvard University Press, Cambridge, Mass, 1995); EJ Weinrib, 'Corrective Justice in a Nutshell' (2002) 52 *University of Toronto Law Journal* 349. In any case, the amount of disagreement is generally overstated. See EJ Weinrib, 'Correlativity, Personality, and the Emerging Consensus on Corrective Justice' (2001) 2 *Theoretical Inquiries in Law* 107, 109.

theory such as the one presented by Benjamin Zipursky, who prefers the notion of civil recourse.[2] The differences between Zipursky's view and the one he criticises, while important from the perspective of corrective justice theory, are not important here. I am not pursuing theories of corrective justice and their competitors, but providing a theory of the law of negligence.

I. SPHERES OF MORALITY

Accounts of morality seek to answer a number of different questions. Some attempt to elucidate a conception of the good person. Others focus on right action. Still others concentrate on social justice or the obligations states owe to other states. Accordingly, spheres of moral enquiry can be distinguished in terms of the nature of the questions they seek to answer.

Consider the following questions: how should I behave in order to be a good person? How must I treat and be treated by others? How should we organise our society so that it is just? How should our nation behave with regard to other nations? Each of these is a moral question, but each focuses on a different area of morality. For instance, the first question concerns the individual; the last question concerns the state.

Although it is possible to distinguish between many potential spheres of morality, for our purposes it is helpful to discriminate between the following four.

1. Personal;
2. Interpersonal;
3. Societal;
4. International.

Personal morality asks how an individual should behave in order to be a good person. Interpersonal morality considers interactions between one individual and another. The focus here is on how persons should conduct themselves vis-à-vis one another as two individuals rather than as isolated individuals or as members of a collective. The third sphere is societal. The concern here is how to govern society and how to regulate the behaviour of individuals for the common good. The final sphere is the international. This sphere considers the impact of our actions on everyone, whether they belong to our political community or not, or the impact of our state on other states.

Not all moral theories place much significance on such distinctions. According to classical utilitarianism, for instance, all questions of morality are settled by reference to the principle of utility: Act so as to maximise the greatest happiness for the greatest number. Hence, the questions 'how should I behave

---

[2] BC Zipursky, 'Civil Recourse, Not Corrective Justice' (2003) 91 *Georgetown Law Journal* 695.

in order to be good?', 'how should I behave in order to avoid wronging that person?' and 'how should our society be governed?' reduce to the question, 'how can I maximise pleasure for everyone?' This feature of utilitarianism is thought by its supporters to be one of the theory's greatest strengths, and by its opponents to be one of the theory's greatest weaknesses. Nevertheless, there are many, including some modern utilitarians, who would reject this reduction. On their view, truths about one level of morality are not necessarily applicable, or at least not directly applicable, to other levels.

The enquiry that goes by the name 'philosophical ethics' usually focuses on the first sphere of morality: personal morality. Hence, introductory university courses called 'Ethics' or 'Moral Philosophy' teach utilitarianism, Kantianism, virtue ethics and other theories, as attempts to provide answers to the questions: 'which actions should an agent perform?' and 'what makes a person morally good?' In accordance with this tendency, I refer to this sphere of morality as 'ethics'.[3]

In other university courses, perhaps also taken at introductory level, students learn about distributive justice. This belongs to the third sphere of morality. The problem of distributive justice is how best to allocate a society's benefits and burdens amongst its members. Also belonging to this sphere is retributive justice, which is concerned with the appropriate response to those who breach the rules a society imposes for the benefit of its citizens.[4]

Distributive justice is also relevant to international morality,[5] although it is not always studied in that context. There, distributive justice is used to explore issues such as the proper behaviour of states with respect to each other and the appropriate conduct of international institutions such as the United Nations.

But there is another area of morality usually ignored by philosophers.[6] This is the second sphere: interpersonal morality. This area concerns the justice pertinent to transactions between individuals and deals with the legitimate expectations of one person with respect to the actions of another, where the two persons are regarded *as individuals* rather than as members of a wider community. In other words, interpersonal morality views transactions between two

---

[3] This distinction is also designed to mirror a similar distinction make by Kant: I Kant, 'The Metaphysics of Morals' in M Gregor (ed), *Practical Philosophy* (Cambridge University Press, Cambridge, 1996) 512 [6:379].

[4] This benefit is usually cashed out in terms rights, deterrence or rehabilitation. However, some argue that that retributive justice is linked to interpersonal morality and corrective justice. See eg P Cane, 'Retribution, Proportionality, and Moral Luck in Tort Law' in P Cane and J Stapleton (eds), *The Law of Obligations: Essays in Celebration of John Fleming* (Oxford University Press, Oxford, 1998).

[5] See eg J Rawls, *The Law of Peoples* (Harvard University Press, Cambridge, Mass, 1999).

[6] This may appear ironic, as it was discovered by Aristotle: Aristotle, *Nicomachean Ethics* (trans T Irwin, Hackett, Indianapolis, Ind, 1999) 72–6 [1131b25–1134a16]. However, as we will see, the most appropriate place to teach this sphere of morality is not in modern philosophy departments but in law schools.

individuals through a narrow lens that focuses on those two individuals alone rather than through a wide lens that sees the individuals in terms of their relationships with the collective.

Each of the four spheres of morality outlined above is distinct from the others and different, although similar, considerations are appropriate in each sphere.[7] Accordingly, it is important to keep the spheres separate in our analyses of law and morality. In particular, it is important not to draw conclusions about one sphere of morality based on arguments not pertinent to that sphere. To illustrate, I now provide an example of this error.

As we see in Chapter 3, the law of negligence sometimes imposes liability on defendants who are not ethically to blame for the claimant's injury. For instance, a defendant may be held liable although she was unable to avoid causing the claimant's injury. From the ethical perspective, this seems to be the imposition of liability on the innocent. It is tempting to conclude that the law of negligence is either immoral or amoral. But it is not clear that either conclusion is warranted. If the law of negligence does not belong to the ethical sphere of morality, but rather to that of interpersonal morality or distributive justice, then the defendant's lack of ethical blameworthiness may be irrelevant.

In legal circles, it has become common to refer to that part of interpersonal morality with which we are primarily concerned here as 'corrective justice'. I do so in this book.

---

[7] Even on the assumption that these spheres of morality are distinct in an important sense, this raises the question whether hybrids between the spheres are possible. There is a sense in which hybrids are possible and a sense in which they are not. It is possible for a system to incorporate concerns that relate to more than one sphere of morality. The legal system as a whole is one example of such a system. But a system can be coherent only if it calls for individual issues to be settled by the application of only one sphere of morality. Hence, a system that calls on an agent to apply, say, distributive and corrective justice to the same issue cannot be coherent. This is because these areas of justice call on the agent to make two separate judgements that cannot be combined into a single judgement. One consequence is that if the judgements do not agree—if the issue is an injustice in distributive justice but is correctively just, say—then the agent is both called on to remedy the situation and to maintain the status quo. This is not coherent. Note that this is distinct from the claim that the spheres of morality must not overlap in the sense that, outside a system, an issue can be of relevance to one sphere only. This is not the case. For instance, outcomes of the law of negligence are relevant at least to corrective and distributive justice. For instance, a poor, negligent defendant being required to pay a wealthy claimant may be just from the perspective of corrective justice but unjust in the eyes of distributive justice. There is nothing incoherent about that. But it would be incoherent to combine corrective and distributive justice in a system such as the law of negligence and ask a judge to do both corrective and distributive justice in such a case. For discussion, see EJ Weinrib, 'Deterrence and Corrective Justice' (2002) 50 *University of California of Los Angeles Law Review* 621; A Beever, 'Particularism and Prejudice in the Law of Tort' (2003) 11 *Tort Law Review* 146, 149–53; A Beever, 'Aristotle on Justice, Equity, and Law' (2004) 10 *Legal Theory* 33, 33–5, 44–50.

II. THE FORM OF CORRECTIVE JUSTICE[8]

An interpersonal injustice occurs when one person wrongs another or, which is the same, when one person interferes with the rights of another.[9] In determining wrongdoing, then, the focus is on the personal interaction between the wrongdoer and the wrong-sufferer. The focus is not on the consequences of the wrongdoer's action for society as a whole. The injustice committed by the wrongdoer is an instance of personal wrongdoing and the injustice suffered by the wrong-sufferer is an instance of personal wrong suffering. Therefore, a wrong-sufferer has a claim in corrective justice only if the wrongdoer violated *her* right, and she can claim from the wrongdoer only if her right was violated by *that particular wrongdoer*. 'What the [wrong-sufferer] must show is "a wrong" to herself, *i.e.*, a violation of her own right, and not merely a wrong to some one else, nor conduct "wrongful" because unsocial, but not "a wrong" to any one.'[10]

As the name suggests, when one of the rights of the wrong-sufferer is violated, corrective justice sees this as an injustice and aims to correct the injustice. In other words, the goal of corrective justice is to undo the wrongdoer's wrong as far as it is possible to do. As the wrong was personal, the remedy is also personal: the wrong consists in the wrongdoer interfering with the wrong-sufferer's right, the remedy in requiring the wrongdoer to undo that wrong, typically by compensating the wrong-sufferer. Accordingly, the reason for insisting that the wrongdoer pay compensation is the same reason as the one for requiring that the compensation be given to the wrong-sufferer. Corrective justice takes from the wrongdoer in order to give to the wrong-sufferer and gives to the wrong-sufferer in order to take from the wrongdoer.

Compare this with Peter Birks' notion that '[t]here would be nothing incoherent in a system making the policy choice . . . by using multiple measures of damages or even by visiting beatings and other humiliations upon the defend-

---

[8] The following discussion owes so much to EJ Weinrib, 'Corrective Justice in a Nutshell' (2002) 52 *University of Toronto Law Journal* 349, a very useful summary of corrective justice, that I do not cite this piece further.

[9] Here, rights are defined simply as the correlatives of wrongs. Note that this account of wrongdoing incorporates both tort and breach of contract. Note also that this does not mean that an injustice in corrective justice occurs only when a wrong is committed. Corrective justice may also be relevant to the law of unjust enrichment. See EJ Weinrib, 'Restitutionary Damages as Corrective Justice' (2000) 1 *Theoretical Inquiries in Law* 1; R Grantham and C Rickett, *Enrichment and Restitution in New Zealand* (Hart Publishing, Oxford, 2000) 45; L Smith, 'Restitution: The Heart of Corrective Justice' (2001) 79 *Texas Law Review* 2115.

[10] *Palsgraf v Long Island Railroad Co* 162 NE 99 (NY CA 1928) 343–4 (Cardozo CJ).

[11] P Birks, 'The Concept of a Civil Wrong' in D Owen (ed), *Philosophical Foundations of Tort Law* (Oxford University Press, Oxford, 1995) 36. Birks' attitude to tort law is very revealing. Outside tort, Birks has done a great deal to reveal the conceptual bases of liability, obviating the need to rely on policy by emphasising the structure of the common law of obligations as a whole. In tort, however, Birks himself reverts to a policy-based approach, perhaps indicating a belief that tort law has no inherent structure.

ant at the insistence of the claimant'.[11] Birks is right that this would not be incoherent in itself, but it is inconsistent with corrective justice.[12] If a wrongdoer wrongly causes loss to a wrong-sufferer worth £100, then correcting this wrong requires the wrongdoer to pay the wrong-sufferer £100, no less and no more.[13] To require the wrongdoer to pay the wrong-sufferer more than £100 would require the wrongdoer to do more than correct his wrong to the wrong-sufferer. Hence, it is impossible to find any reasons *in corrective justice* why the wrong-doer should pay more than £100. Moreover, barring contributory negligence or other defences,[14] there can be no reasons in corrective justice to make the wrongdoer pay less than £100. The appropriate quantum of damages is deter-mined by the injury wrongfully caused. Hence, on the corrective justice model, while the enquiries into liability and into damages are separate, they are con-ceptually linked.

In corrective justice, then, the focus is on the *relationship between the parties* rather than on the parties as solitary individuals or as members of a wider com-munity.[15] We are interested in the wrongdoer only because he wronged the wrong-sufferer, and we are interested in the wrong-sufferer only because he was wronged by the wrongdoer. Hence, the reasons for holding the wrongdoer liable are the same reasons for finding that liability is owed to the wrong-sufferer. In corrective justice, the relationship between the parties forms a conceptual unity. This is intended only as a sketch of corrective justice, but that is all that we require for the moment. Given the strategy adopted here, the flesh that we need to put on these bones will come from reflection on the case law and not from more theory.

III.   CORRECTIVE JUSTICE, THE PRINCIPLED APPROACH AND THE ROLE OF JUDGEMENT

It is clear from the above that corrective justice so expressed is highly abstract. Though it is not empty, it is not sufficiently concrete for everyday courtroom analysis. For instance, imagine a case in which the issue is whether the defendant fell below the standard of care. The injunction 'do justice between the parties'

---

[12] As Birks is happy to accept: *ibid*, 36–7. Birks calls the argument here a 'common distraction' and maintains that tort law need not be consistent with corrective justice. Perhaps in some sense it *need* not, but this book argues that it *is*.

[13] Strictly, it requires the defendant to give the claimant something worth £100 to the claimant. This need not be done via a monetary award, but that is usually the most convenient method for both parties. Moreover, corrective justice does not permit punitive responses. See A Beever, 'The Structure of Aggravated and Exemplary Damages' (2003) 23 *OJLS* 87, 105–10; EJ Weinrib, 'Punishment and Disgorgement as Contract Remedies' (2003) 78 *Chicago-Kent Law Review* 55.

[14] These are examined in ch 10.

[15] Hence, while corrective justice is not societal, it remains social. It does not treat persons as iso-lated 'atomistic' individuals.

is too abstract to provide the kind of guidance that judges need for their decision making. But it does not follow from this that corrective justice lacks the content required in order to produce appropriate guidance.[16]

Judges need concrete principles that are tailored to specific issues to aid them in their decision making. They require more precise principles regarding the standard of care, the duty of care, remoteness and so on. But there is every possibility that reflection on corrective justice will provide such principles. That is, though the injunction 'do justice between the parties' is too abstract to enable judges to make decisions about the standard of care, for example, we may be able to produce a more concrete principle that, if followed, would do justice between the parties in terms of setting the standard of care. That principle would be a principle of corrective justice. It would be corrective justice applied to a particular area of concern.

The following picture emerges. Corrective justice provides the most abstract explanation of the law of negligence. But, for practical reasons, the principle of corrective justice is not applied directly to the facts when deciding cases. Instead, the law adopts various 'mid-level' principles, such as the neighbour principle, that are used to determine the various stages of the negligence enquiry. These mid-level principles constitute the principled approach. They are designed to achieve corrective justice when applied to the particular areas of the negligence enquiry to which they pertain.[17]

We do not have to assume that there is only one set of these 'mid level' principles appropriate to corrective justice, or even that there is only one set of principles that best exemplifies corrective justice. It may be the case that a number of different principles embody corrective justice or, more likely, that numbers of different collections or sets of principles reflect corrective justice more or less equally. Therefore, although I claim that the common law of negligence reflects corrective justice, this does not mean, for example, that the German or French laws of delict do not or do so less well. It may be the case that the common, German and French law all achieve corrective justice roughly as efficiently though the adoption of packages of principles that together achieve that end.

Importantly, then, it does not follow from the theory presented here that the relationship between corrective justice and the principles of the law is mechanical. The latter cannot be deduced logically from the former. For instance, in Chapter 3, we explore a disagreement between the House of Lords in *Bolton v Stone*[18] and the Privy Council in *The Wagon Mound (No 2)*[19] with respect to the determination of the standard of care. I suggest that this argument is best under-

---

[16] Against: P Cane, 'Distributive Justice and Tort Law' [2001] *New Zealand Law Review* 401, 415.

[17] Compare T Aquinas, *Summa theologica* (trans English Dominicans, Benziger Bros, New York, 1947) 1, 2, 94–5.

[18] [1951] AC 850 (HL).

[19] *Overseas Tankship (UK) Ltd v Morts Dock & Engineering Co Ltd (The Wagon Mound, No 2)* [1961] AC 611 (PC).

stood as a debate about the optimal method of realising corrective justice in terms of setting the standard of care. This matter requires considerable judgement and cannot be settled merely by deduction.

Nor do I argue that that the mid level principles of the principled approach apply mechanically to fact patterns. For instance, I argue in the next chapter that a defendant is rightly found to have been negligent if he created a 'substantial' risk in the sense defined in that chapter. But while there are guidelines for deciding what a 'substantial' risk is, there is no formula. Such determinations require judgement; calculation alone is insufficient.

Given that corrective justice does not call for mechanical judicial decision making, it does not follow from the fact that a disagreement exists that the disagreement exists over something other than corrective justice. In particular, it does not follow, as Peter Cane contends, that because it is appropriate to debate the proper standard of care to be applied in individual cases the standard of care must be set in accordance with distributive justice or policy.[20] This would follow only if corrective justice outlawed such debates, but it does not. As Ernest Weinrib has said, 'When construing a transaction in accordance with corrective justice, the adjudicator does not choose one scheme of correction over another [a distributive task] but rather specifies the meaning of corrective justice with respect to the transaction in question'.[21] In our example, the debate is over what corrective justice demands in setting the standard of care. In general, the issue is how best to achieve corrective justice in particular contexts, not how to do something else.

Another result of this discussion is that it does not follow from the view presented here that the law should be forever unchanging. Though our general understanding of corrective justice is likely to remain very stable—it has, after all, changed little since Aristotle—our understanding of its best application is sure to vary with time. Those who argue that the law reflects contemporary thinking are surely right in this respect—though again it does not follow from this that the law reflects modern conceptions of distributive justice or policy as many seem to assume.[22]

At this point, it is useful to deal with an objection sometimes raised in this context. According to this view, if a principle is incapable on its own of specifying (ie without judgement) an outcome, then the principle captures only some of the normative concerns relevant to the application of that principle. Hence, if principles of corrective justice and the principled approach are not able to determine specific outcomes, then those principles must provide incomplete accounts of the norms relevant to the law of negligence.[23]

[20] Cane, above n15, 415.
[21] EJ Weinrib, *The Idea of Private Law* (Harvard University Press, Cambridge, Mass, 1995) 212.
[22] The issue of legal change and its relationship to corrective justice is examined in ch 14.
[23] A version of this argument is employed in P Cane, 'Corrective Justice and Correlativity in Private Law' (1996) 16 *OJLS* 471, 478–80 and in SM Waddams, *Dimensions of Private Law: Categories and Concepts in Anglo-American Legal Reasoning* (Cambridge University Press, Cambridge, 2003) 2.

This argument is fallacious as it denies the very possibility of judgement. Judgement is required because there is an essential logical gap between principles and actions. For instance, the principle 'promises should not be broken' is not an algorithm that, in conjunction with data, can churn out specific rules for action. Principles are not like computer programs. Hence, in utilising a principle, an agent must always make a judgement as to how the principle applies in the particular case. For instance, if I say to a student that I will do my best to help her in her future career but she then turns to bank robbing, in deciding what my promise requires I have to decide, inter alia, whether helping her rob banks lies within the scope of my promise. In doing so, I must make a judgement, but that does not mean that I have to appeal to principles other than the one that promises should not be broken. Similarly, the concept of a drinking glass does not specify which objects in the world are drinking glasses; judgement is required. But that does not mean that one must appeal to a concept other than the concept of drinking glass in order to make the judgement about whether something is a drinking glass. The fact that a principle cannot itself *specify* a result does not entail that one can apply the principle only if one adds another normative concern to it. Nor does it follow from the fact that corrective justice cannot itself *specify* results of cases that there are normative concerns other than corrective justice relevant when cases are decided.

Simply, there is always a gap between principles and decisions, but that does not mean that the gap must be filled by other principles or policies. In fact, it would be futile to attempt to fill the gap in this way, because there would always be a gap between those other principles and policies and the decision. That is the very reason why judgements must be made. It is a feature of the distinction between our minds and the external world. These points were powerfully expressed by Kant:

> General logic contains no precepts at all for the power of judgment, and moreover cannot contain them. For since it abstracts from all content of cognition, nothing remains to it but the business of analytically dividing the mere form of cognition into concepts, judgments, and inferences, and thereby achieving formal rules for all use of the understanding. Now if it wanted to show generally how one ought to subsume under these rules, i.e., distinguish whether something stands under them or not, this could not happen except once again through a rule. But just because this is a rule, it would demand another instruction for the power of judgment, and so it becomes clear that although the understanding is certainly capable of being instructed and equipped through rules, the power of judgment is a special talent that cannot be taught but only practiced.[24]

Note also that, as this gap cannot be filled by other principles, it is no failure on the part of judges when their judgments contain these gaps. Throughout this

---

[24] I Kant, *Critique of Pure Reason* (trans P Guyer and A Wood, Cambridge University Press, Cambridge, 1998) 268–9 [A133/B172–73].

book, I argue that judges must enunciate their reasoning in making decisions. This means that they must elucidate all the normative concerns upon which their decisions are based and show how those concerns apply to the facts of the case. But it is important to recognise that, in doing so, they will be required to make judgements that leave gaps in the sense discussed above. This is unobjectionable, as long as the principles and the facts to which the judge applies the principles are explained.

This is another area in which judgement is required. As I have indicated, there will always be a gap between principles and facts, and hence the judge will always have to make a certain 'leap' from the principles to her decision. It is a matter of judgement as to how wide this gap can permissibly be. As the gap widens, at some point we will have to say that the gap is so wide that the purported principle upon which the judge claimed to act cannot genuinely be said to justify the outcome of the case. A clear example of this is the bland suggestion that a certain outcome is warranted because it is fair. Fairness in the round is too abstract a principle, and its content too uncertain, to be said to ground judicial decision making. In Chapter 5, I claim that the same holds for modern uses of the term 'proximity'. But the problem with these purported principles is not that they call for judgement or that their application can be controversial, but rather because they lack the content required sufficiently to direct decision making. The principle of fairness in the round is not objectionable because deciding what is fair requires judgement or because people can disagree about what is fair. Rather, the principle is inappropriate because it is so wide open that it does not sufficiently direct judicial decision making and is so controversial that no consensus on its application could be expected. The degree of precision and consensus required is, of course, itself a matter for judgement.

IV. CORRECTIVE JUSTICE AND THE DEFINITION OF PRINCIPLE AND POLICY

In this book, I make much use of the distinction between policy and principle. The distinction is problematic, hard to define, and often inconsistently used. For instance, WVH Rogers insists that policy is identical to reason and good sense,[25] but then endorses Lord Lowry's claim in *Spring v Guardian Assurance*[26] that policy should be appealed to only in those rare cases in which the threat to the public interest is clear.[27] Reason and good sense are relevant only in rare cases? Surely, 'policy' was used equivocally. Moreover, the terms have become evaluatively loaded. Sometimes a decision or position is described as 'principled' simply if it is liked. Hence, to say that a decision is 'unprincipled' is merely

[25] WVH Rogers, *Winfield and Jolowicz on Tort,* 16th edn (Sweet & Maxwell, London, 2002) 129.
[26] [1995] 2 AC 296, 326 (HL).
[27] Rogers, above n25, 130.

to say that one disagrees with it. On the other hand, as we have seen, it has also become *de rigueur* to dismiss as unrealistic any view that fails to give policy a leading role in negligence. Accordingly, although principle and policy are said to be different and in tension, it is claimed that it is good to be principled and good to accord a high importance to policy. It is not clear that this account is coherent.

Because of our treatment of the terms 'policy' and 'principle', when I describe a certain position in the following chapters as principled and recommend it as such, this cannot but have the appearance of rhetoric. Perhaps, then, it would be better to eschew use of these terms altogether. However, I do not do so, as I believe that the position I recommend is recognisably principled in a non-value laden sense.

On the other hand, some of the arguments I utilise may appear to be based on policy. Again, this is because of the slipperiness of the terms. On some views, it is true by definition that any argument purporting to *justify* some conclusion must be an argument of policy. However, this understanding of the term eradicates the point of having a distinction between principle and policy. It will turn out that even legal principles are policies. Similarly, some use 'principle' as a synonym for precedent and 'policy' to mean everything else. But that usage is not adopted here. At least since *Donoghue v Stevenson*, principles in the law of negligence are found in precedents, but the precedents are merely examples or instances of principles that exist independently of any individual case.[28] Principle, then, is more abstract than precedent and, as we shall see, it is normative in a way that precedent cannot be.

In Chapter 1, I said that 'principle' refers to the doctrines of the law and 'policy' to everything else. I also acknowledged that this definition does not reveal the content of the terms, because people disagree over the substance of the doctrines of the law. But this book presents a theory of those doctrines. Accordingly, *for my purposes*, principle is what I say that law is, as revealed in reflective equilibrium on the case law, while policy is everything else. Hence, when I refer to something as 'principle', that must not be understood to argue in favour of that thing. Nor, when I refer to something as 'policy', am I to be regarded as thereby arguing against that thing. Such arguments would beg the question. I do not assume that principle is good and policy is bad; I argue for that conclusion. But to begin with, the terms are merely convenient labels for types of arguments: ones that fit with my theory ('principle', 'the principled approach') and ones that do not ('policy', 'the policy-driven approach').[29]

---

[28] *M'Alister (or Donoghue) (Pauper) v Stevenson* [1932] AC 562, 580 (HL Sc) (Lord Atkin).
[29] R Mullender, 'Corrective Justice, Distributive Justice, and the Law of Negligence' (2001) 17 *Professional Negligence* 35, 37–8, also holds that principle in the law of negligence is to be identified with corrective justice.

V. THE APOLITICAL NATURE OF CORRECTIVE JUSTICE

All too often, corrective justice is interpreted as a version of distributive justice. One example of this is the nonfeasance rule discussed in Chapters 6 and 9. As we see, nonfeasance cannot result in liability, because in committing an act of nonfeasance the nonfeasor does not interfere with the claimant's rights. Hence, a person who fails to rescue another from injury cannot be liable, because the person who required rescuing had no right as against the potential rescuer to be rescued. Accordingly, the issue is decided entirely between the parties. In some sense, the nonfeasor may be a wrongdoer, but because she did not interfere with the rights of the claimant, she did not wrong the claimant in interpersonal morality. No wider implication can be drawn from this concerning the law's attitude towards the desirability of helping others. In particular, this is not libertarianism or some other political viewpoint.[30] It is not a view about distributive justice at all. It is, as Arthur Ripstein has pointed out, perfectly compatible with other legal condemnation of the nonfeasor, such as criminal liability.[31]

Unlike the account of the law of negligence examined in Chapter 1, the position developed here is in an important sense apolitical. It is necessary to distinguish the sense in which the approach is apolitical from the sense in which it is not.

Assume that the law of negligence instantiates corrective justice. One can then ask: should we govern the sphere of human life covered by the law of negligence in terms of corrective justice? This is a political question. It is to be resolved by consulting a potentially limitless range of concerns, importantly including both corrective and distributive justice. This book takes no stand on the answer to this question. Hence, the arguments presented in the following chapters are not intended to demonstrate, and do not demonstrate, that *statutes* should not be passed that alter the law from the model presented here. Therefore, no necessary objection whatsoever is expressed to statutes such as the Injury Prevention, Rehabilitation, and Compensation Act 2001 (NZ) (this is New Zealand's latest accident compensation Act that prevents tort recovery for personal injury) or to other Acts such as those that provide workers' compensation. Of course, the merit of these statues is open to debate but, while the argument presented here is relevant to that debate, that debate must take into account many concerns not pertinent here.

In Chapter 1, I argued that the law of negligence should not be based on politically sensitive policy considerations. That argument also was largely political. However, it should not be regarded as politically controversial in the way that

---

[30] Against: J Stapleton, 'Duty of Care Factors: A Selection from the Judicial Menus' in P Cane and J Stapleton (eds), *The Law of Obligations: Essays in Celebration of John Fleming* (Clarendon Press, Oxford, 1998) 73–4.

[31] A Ripstein, 'Three Duties to Rescue: Moral, Civil, and Criminal' (2000) 19 *Law and Philosophy* 751.

the policy concerns are. For instance, the notion that a duty of care should be denied if it would produce a specified unattractive socio-economic impact calls for judges to make decisions on matters about which there is widespread disagreement. Conversely, all, in the absence of good reason to think otherwise, can accept the idea that unelected judges should not enforce their personal political preferences. That view has widespread agreement, though lawyers sometimes, at least implicitly, reject it.

Two other questions one can ask are: given that the law instantiates corrective justice, how is the law best understood and how does it apply in particular cases? These are not political questions. They are questions about how best to realise corrective justice in particular cases. In the next chapter, we examine an example of this disagreement in *Bolton v Stone* and *The Wagon Mound (No 2)*. The disagreement is real, but it is not political.[32]

Moreover, even if corrective justice is more political than I claim, it is infinitely less political than the approach explored in Chapter 1, which calls for judges to answer a list of highly politically controversial questions. It is also clearly less political than an approach that would base the law of negligence on distributive justice. Questions over how to distribute the benefits and burdens of society are political to the core. Hence, one can argue that corrective justice is an entirely or a relatively apolitical conception of justice, and for that reason, among others, is appropriate for judicial decision making.[33] Either is sufficient for our purposes.

The above should also be sufficient to eliminate the charge sometimes made against those who reject the policy based approach to the law of negligence: that they must be covertly pursuing a conservative or right-wing political agenda.[34] We saw in Chapter 1 why it is believed that the attempt must be covert: appeal to principle is believed to be the refusal to explain. The attempt is also believed to be right-wing because it is tied to libertarianism. But that is wrong. It is consistent with any mainstream political philosophy.

Moreover, thinkers who regard themselves as progressive have good reason to reject the policy-driven account of the law. The idea that social justice is

---

[32] See also A Beever, 'Aristotle on Justice, Equity, and Law' (2004) 10 *Legal Theory* 33, 45–7; EJ Weinrib, *The Idea of Private Law* (Harvard University Press, Cambridge, Mass, 1995) 210–14.

[33] This does not mean that judges should never be permitted to deal with concerns of distributive justice. They may do so when required to by statute. But the legislator would be wise to elucidate her conception of distributive justice rather than make the unsound assumption that the judge will share it. Compare Beever, above n32, 44–5.

[34] See eg F Carrigan, 'A Blast from the Past: The Resurgence of Legal Formalism' (2003) 27 *Melbourne University Law Review* 163; J Stapleton, 'The Golden Thread at the Heart of Tort Law: Protection of the Vulnerable' (2003) 24 *Australian Bar Review* 135. Compare R Unger, 'The Critical Legal Studies Movement' (1983) 96 *Harvard Law Review* 561; R Unger, *What Should Legal Analysis Become?* (Verso, New York, 1996). Unger rejects arguments of the kind advanced in this book, but also argues that more respect should be given to the decisions of legislatures and less to the preferences of judges. I agree with the latter claims and insist that they are consistent with the argument presented here.

promoted when political power is given into the hands of a small socio-economic elite is not credible. Though the democratic nature of our societies is sometimes said to argue in favour of the courtroom relevance of policy,[35] this argument is one of the great ironies of the modern common law. The claim that we in democratic societies must be able to change the law so that it can respond to our concerns is familiar. But to whom does 'we' in that claim refer? It refers to lawyers. The claim actually means that *lawyers* in democratic societies must be able to change the law so that it can respond to *their* concerns (including *their* conception of the *appropriate* concerns of others). This is anything but supported by democracy. A democracy is a state in which the people as a whole decide, usually though elected representatives. It is not one in which a small section of the socio-economic elite are appointed to unaccountable positions of political power where they enforce their personal conceptions of the good, advised by a slightly larger section of the socio-economic elite; although it is understandable that members of those elites may tend not to see this point as clearly as they might. Nor is a democracy a state in which those elites condescend to tell 'ordinary people' what their interests are—even if those elites are conscientious and well motivated, as I am sure they almost always are. In a democracy we, meaning all citizens, must be able to change the law so that it can respond to our concerns *though statute*, but that is not what excites the modern negligence lawyer. It is untenable to argue that only conservatives would oppose the judicial aristocracy supported by those who argue that judges should settle negligence cases by examining concerns of policy. Furthermore, with the very notable exception of law and economics scholars, those who recommend policy do so without advocating any general principles by which to determine policy. Hence, 'policy' in practice reflects little more than someone's intuitions and prejudices in particular circumstances. The idea that the judicial enforcement of such could be consistent with democracy is incredible. In reality, the fact that we live in democratic societies demonstrates that the modern picture of the law of negligence is even more deeply problematic than the first chapter of this book gave us reason to believe.

This may be less clear than it has been at other times in history because it is probably generally true that courts in recent times have been more 'progressively' minded than legislatures. But this has not always been so, and there is no reason to expect that it will be so in the future. No doubt, when the change comes, those 'progressives' who now argue in favour of policy will decamp and begin to fight for principle while (political) conservatives will do the opposite. But this is a dance that one should sit out.

Further, it is sometimes argued that the law adopts policies in order to help vulnerable persons and, hence, that only a conservative would oppose this. However, though the appeal to policy has often been aimed at helping the

---

[35] See eg Lord Steyn, 'Perspectives of Corrective and Distributive Justice in Tort Law' (2002) 37 *Irish Jurist* 1.

vulnerable, it has damaged the position of those very people. Because appeal to policy leads to uncertainty, which makes prompt resolution of disputes impracticable, the cost of justice has increased. In consequence, by attempting to make the law more flexible in order to protect the vulnerable, courts have created a situation in which the vulnerable cannot afford access to justice.[36] If they could afford it, then they would find a more sympathetic law, but, while that may allow lawyers to sleep easier, it is cold comfort to the intended beneficiaries of that flexibility. Academics and judges, perhaps, are less likely to notice this than practising lawyers, as parties that cannot afford access to justice do not appear in courtrooms or law reports to prick our consciences. In any case, when the law is uncertain it is not surprising that the biggest beneficiaries are 'the strong', particularly those with the resources to outlast their opponents.[37] It has been said that it is no longer infrequent in New Zealand criminal trials for an accused who knows himself innocent to plead guilty, because the impact of the sentence on his life will be less than the impact of having to defend the charge, even if successfully.[38] If that is true of criminal law, the situation can only be worse in tort. However well motivated those responsible for this state of affairs were, this is a most significant injustice.

Finally, the certainty principle can provide is important from the perspective of justice as it enables people to know their legal rights and obligations. It also means that law is public in the sense of being accessible to all citizens, rather than residing in the at least partly unexpressed intuitions of judges. And, most fundamentally, there is no reason to believe that justice is anything like as ad hoc as the modern law of negligence. Why have we simply assumed the implausible view that justice is unprincipled? In fact, in political philosophy, it is the progressive who insists on principle and the conservative who rejects it. Policy and justice do not go hand in hand, and principle is not justice's antithesis. On the face of it, justice calls for more principle, not less.[39] It is time to see whether the law of negligence can be so understood.

VI. TWO POTENTIAL OBJECTIONS

I now deal with two potential objections to the thesis advanced here: that the thesis must be incomplete and that it is inconsistent with other areas of the law of tort.

---

[36] Legal aid is only a partial answer, particularly in private law.

[37] It is the inexplicable blindness to this point that, as much as anything else, mars Lord Denning's jurisprudence.

[38] B Robertson, 'The Court System Through the Eyes of the Citizenry' [2002] *New Zealand Law Journal* 267, 267.

[39] I have explored these issues in more detail in A Beever, 'The Law's Function and the Judicial Function' (2003) 20 *New Zealand Universities Law Review* 299; A Beever, 'Particularism and Prejudice in the Law of Tort' (2003) 11 *Tort Law Review* 146. It is also worth noting that this attitude of the common lawyer conflicts with one of the most fundamental assumptions of the civilian lawyer: that the search for general principle is a search for justice.

A. The Incompleteness Objection and the Rights of Corrective Justice

(i) The Incompleteness of Corrective Justice

In this section, I examine a perceived difficulty with corrective justice theory that flows from its apparent inability to provide an account of rights. I suggest that it is possible to meet the problems thought to follow from this difficulty.

If we accept the view that a tort involves the violation of a right in the claimant by the defendant, then three questions arise:

1. With respect to which things do we have rights?
2. Against what sort of behaviour do those rights protect us?
3. How should the law respond when a right has been violated?

According to the dominant modern understanding, corrective justice is relevant only to question 3. That is, if one takes corrective justice to be simply about correcting injustices, as the name suggests, then corrective justice can begin only when we have decided that an injustice has been committed. On this view, then, corrective justice is solely about how to respond to violations of the claimants' rights and cannot inform us about the nature of those rights.

But this is not how corrective justice is understood in the tradition of legal thought to which it belongs. According to that line of thought, 'corrective justice' refers to an area of interpersonal morality that both defines rights persons possess against each other as individuals and elucidates how one should respond to violations of those rights. In order to see this point, it is useful briefly to examine Aristotle's discovery of the distinction between distributive and corrective justice in his *Ethics*.[40]

For Aristotle, distributive justice deals with the overall spread of 'honour or money or such other assets as are divisible among members of the community'.[41] This form of justice is achieved when goods are divided in such a way that they are held in appropriate amounts by the right people. This means that those who are equal, according to the appropriate account of equality relevant for distributive justice, have the same while those who are unequal have differing shares.[42] Corrective justice, on the other hand, deals with the justice of 'transactions' between individuals.[43] Typically, it is called into play when one person wrongly inflicts harm on another. In such circumstances, a judge, in accordance with corrective justice, 'tries to restore this unjust situation to equality, since it is unequal. For [not only when one steals from another but] also when one is

---

[40] Aristotle, *Nicomachean Ethics* (trans T Irwin, Hackett, Indianapolis, Ind, 1999) 71–4 [1131a–1132b]. I have dealt with this issue in much more detail in A Beever, 'Justice and Punishment in Tort: A Comparative Theoretical Analysis' in R Grantham and C Rickett (eds), *Justifying Remedies in Private Law* (Cambridge University Press, Cambridge, forthcoming, 2007).

[41] Aristotle, above n40, 71 [1130b–1131a].

[42] *Ibid*, 71 [1131a].

[43] *Ibid*, 72–4 [1131b–1132b].

wounded and the other wounds him, or one kills and the other is killed, the action and the suffering are unequally divided [with profit for the offender and loss for the victim]; and the judge tries to restore the [profit and] loss to a position of equality, by subtraction from [the offender's] profit'.[44]

This is Aristotle's paradigm example of corrective justice, but it would be hasty to conclude that the example exhausts corrective justice. Moreover, though the second form of justice is usually called (in English) 'corrective justice', one cannot assume that it is concerned merely with correcting injustices. In particular, it is important to remember that the name for this form of justice may be misleading. Of course, Aristotle did not call this form of justice 'corrective justice' but referred to it by the term 'συνάλλαγμα'; and even if 'corrective' were a perfect translation for 'συνάλλαγμα', it would be wrong to assume that Aristotle's *use* of 'συνάλλαγμα' was identical to the standard meaning of 'corrective'.

In fact, in discussing corrective justice, Aristotle frequently uses key terms in a non-standard fashion. For instance, his use of the terms 'profit' and 'loss' in the passage quoted above extends the meaning of those terms beyond the normal. According to Aristotle, for example, a person who batters another makes a 'profit', though that person may have made no factual gain. Aristotle recognises that his use of this term is non-standard, saying that it 'is not the proper word',[45] but he uses it nevertheless. Similarly, a person whose land is trespassed on but who suffers no factual damage is described by Aristotle as suffering a 'loss'. Furthermore, as we have seen, Aristotle defines corrective justice as dealing with 'transactions',[46] but gives as examples cases in which one person steals from another or batters another. Again, this is a non-standard use of the term 'transaction'. Why, then, did Aristotle use these terms?

To answer this question, one must remember that, in this area and in others, Aristotle's philosophy was revolutionary. Frequently, he introduced concepts, and indeed whole areas of thought, that did not exist before. In doing so, Aristotle was faced with a choice. To refer to a new concept, he could either invent a neologism for it or extend the meaning of an existing term to cover it. Though is it possible to do only the former, it is at best an uncomfortable strategy, and so, often, Aristotle adopted the latter tactic—just as many do today.[47] Hence, while Aristotle's use of 'profit', 'loss' and 'transaction' was non-standard, these terms would have been the closest in meaning to Aristotle's intention that he could find. Consequently, Aristotle' intention in using 'συνάλλαγμα' may not correspond to the exact use of the term in contemporary Greek. In using that term, he may have been intending to identify a concept that

---

[44] *Ibid*, 73 [1132a] (the additions are the translator's).

[45] *Ibid*.

[46] *Ibid*, 72–4 [1131b–1132b].

[47] The tort lawyer is likely to be most familiar with this phenomenon: 'negligence' that does not require carelessness; 'battery' that can be a mere touching, 'assault' that requires no touching at all, 'conversion' that leaves property unchanged, annoying persons who are not 'nuisances', and so on.

did not before exist. Therefore, we cannot assume that 'corrective' justice, for Aristotle, is merely about correcting injustices, even were 'corrective' a perfect translation for 'συνάλλαγμα'.

None of this would be important if there were no evidence that Aristotle actually thought that corrective justice was informative about the justice of transactions. But that evidence exists. Though Aristotle spends most of his time discussing corrective justice in the light of practices with which his contemporary audience would have been familiar—ie the operations of the Greek courts—his discussion ends with this crucial passage:

> [H]aving more than one's own share is called making a profit, and having less than what one had at the beginning is called suffering a loss, in buying and selling, for instance, and in other transactions permitted by law. . . . And when people get neither more nor less, but precisely what belongs to them, they say they have their own share and make neither a loss nor a profit. Hence the just is intermediate between a certain kind of loss and profit, since it is having the equal amount both before and after [the transaction].[48]

According to this passage, in a transaction such as buying and selling, persons can end up with more or less than that which rightly belongs to them. There is no suggestion that this can result only as a consequence of a breach of the terms of the transaction. In fact, the transaction Aristotle explores is one of sale, and he claims that after the sale has taken place persons can have more, less, or as much as justice allows. This appears to be a reference to what became known as the *laesio enormis*, the idea that there is a fair price independent of the agreed price that can be enforced by courts, an idea that survives in the modern civil law but less so, if at all, in the common law.[49] In fact, Reinhard Zimmermann traces the ideas that gave rise to the *laesio enormis* in the *ius commune* precisely to the passage quoted above.[50]

The idea, then, is that corrective justice determines, inter alia, how much persons should receive in transactions, an amount which will sometimes not equate with what it is for which the parties actually contracted. Now, it does not matter whether corrective justice has exactly *this* consequence; the crucial point is rather that this takes us well outside the view that corrective justice is informative only about correcting injustices. Aristotle holds that corrective justice tells us how transactions ought to proceed—'[t]he just in transactions . . . though it is a sort of equality (and the unjust a sort of inequality), accords with numerical proportion, not with the [geometrical] proportion of the other species'[51]—and not merely how transactions that have not proceeded as they should have done should be remedied. Accordingly, for Aristotle, corrective

---

[48] Aristotle, above n40, 74 [1132b] (the addition is the translator's).

[49] For discussion see R Zimmermann, *The Law of Obligations: Roman Foundations of the Civilian Tradition* (Oxford University Press, Oxford, 1996) 259–70.

[50] R Zimmermann, *Roman Law, Contemporary Law, European Law: The Civilian Tradition Today* (Oxford University Press, Oxford, 2001) 266.

[51] Aristotle, above n40, 73 [1132a].

justice is not merely about correcting injustices, but also about defining justice and injustice in transactions between individuals.

The point is even clearer in Aquinas, who, following the old Latin translation of Aristotle's *Ethics*, distinguished between commutative justice (*commutativa justitia*) and distributive justice rather than between corrective justice and distributive justice. However, it would be wrong to think that Aquinas' commutative justice is different from Aristotle's corrective justice. Aquinas took himself to be referring to the same thing as Aristotle:[52]

> [J]ustice is directed to the private individual, who is compared to the community as a part to the whole. Now a twofold order may be considered in relation to a part. In the first place there is the order of one part to another, to which corresponds the order of one private individual to another. This order is directed by commutative justice, which is concerned about the mutual dealings between two persons. In the second place there is the order of the whole towards the parts, to which corresponds the order of that which belongs to the community in relation to each single person. This order is directed by distributive justice, which distributes common goods proportionately.[53]

Corrective justice is concerned with 'the order' that regulates the interaction of one individual with another. It determines what is just and unjust within that sphere and how to respond to injustices when they occur.[54] Hence, for Aquinas, one acts in accordance with corrective justice when one performs a just contract; one does not merely not bring corrective justice into play by not violating a contract. Corrective justice is relevant to the performance of a contract, not merely to its breach.[55] This is also why Aquinas discusses corrective justice and restitution separately. Restitution is that aspect of corrective justice which deals with correcting injustices, but corrective justice is also involved with defining the kinds of injustices that call for restitution.[56] Accordingly, corrective justice refers to that area of morality that determines how individuals should behave with respect to each other as individuals.[57]

---

[52] T Aquinas, *Summa theologica* (trans English Dominicans, Benziger Bros, New York, 1947) SS Q61. See also H Grotius, *The Law of War and Peace* (trans FW Kelsey, Clarendon Press, Oxford, 1925) 36–8 [I i 8]; S Pufendorf, *Of the Law of Nature and Nations* (trans HC and WA Oldfather, Clarendon Press, Oxford, 1934) 119–21, 123–4 [I vii 8–10, 12]. See also T Hobbes, *Leviathan* (Oxford University Press, Oxford, 1996) 99–100 [XV 14]. According to Finnis, however, Aquinas' allegiance to Aristotle is disingenuous. J Finnis, *Natural Law and Natural Rights* (Clarendon Press, Oxford, 1980) 179. There is insufficient evidence to determine this, but the matter is in part decided by the correct interpretation of Aristotle's views. Moreover, against Finnis' assertion, Aquinas was likely to have interpreted Aristotle in the manner given here, particularly as it fits his own view of the *laesio enormis*: T Aquinas, *Summa theologica* (trans English Dominicans, Benziger Bros, New York, 1947) SS Q77 A1.

[53] *Ibid*, SS Q61 A1.

[54] Similarly, distributive justice deals with 'the order' that regulates people as members of a society generally. For Aquinas, the claim that corrective justice is restricted to correcting injustices would be as unintuitive as the claim that distributive justice can tell us only about just distributions given certain accounts of equality but has no role in explaining what sort of equality really is relevant to distributive justice.

[55] Aquinas, above n53, SS Q61 A2.

[56] See also *ibid*, SS QQ64–66.

[57] See also Pufendorf, above n52, [I vii 10].

In other words, corrective justice is a theory of interpersonal morality. It provides answers to all of questions 1–3 explored above.

This understanding of corrective justice is not shared by most common law academics. A good example of the view adopted there is found in the decision of the High Court of Australia in *Harriton v Stevens*.[58] In that case, the claimant, who had been injured by the defendant, argued that corrective justice indicated that he should be able to recover. Crennan J responded that:

> there remains a problem in Aristotle's analysis, relevant to this submission. In emphasising 'corrective justice', even as added to by his consideration of 'distributive justice', Aristotle left unexplored the dependence of 'correction' on the prior establishment of principles. As Finnis puts it, '"[c]orrection" and "restitution" are notions parasitic on some prior determination of what is to count as a crime, a tort, a binding agreement, etc'. . . .
>
> [Therefore] a need for 'corrective justice' alone could never be determinative of a novel claim in negligence.[59]

This statement seriously misdescribes the tradition of Aristotelian corrective justice theory. In that tradition, corrective justice is not merely about correcting injustices but is also concerned with defining justice in transactions between individuals.[60]

'Corrective justice', then, is a *proper name* for the area of morality that deals with interactions between individuals. It is not a description thereof, and has no semantic content.

Why, then, call it 'corrective justice' when this seems to imply that it is concerned only with correcting independently defined injustices? Why not find a better name? The first answer is that 'corrective justice' is the term adopted by most of the scholars who work in this area. Moreover, the term is adopted by those scholars because they see themselves as belonging to the Aristotelian tradition, and Aristotle used the term συνάλλαγμα to describe this kind of justice, which is usually translated as corrective justice.[61]

The leading alternative comes from the old Latin translation of Aristotle's ethics, which rendered συνάλλαγμα as *commutativo*, and was picked up by Aquinas who spoke of *commutativa justitia*, or commutative justice. However, this term has its own problems. The Oxford English Dictionary defines 'commutative' as '[p]ertaining to exchange or mutual dealings'. This definition fits contract well, but not the law of tort where the parties are likely to be strangers

---

[58] [2006] HCA 15.

[59] *Ibid*, paras [274]–[275] (citations omitted) citing J Finnis, *Natural Law and Natural Rights* (Clarendon Press, Oxford, 1980) 178–9.

[60] This also indicates that the claimant was wrong to hold that corrective justice indicated necessarily that recovery should follow. Corrective justice has that implication only if it indicates that the defendant violated one of the claimant's rights. See ch 11 for further discussion.

[61] Terence Irwin translates the terms as 'rectificatory', but this presents the same difficulties as 'corrective': Aristotle, *Nicomachean Ethics,* 2nd edn (trans T Irwin, Hackett Publishing Co Ltd, Indianapolis, Ind, 1999) 72.

and not involved in either exchange or dealings. The term is also archaic and not used in general legal discourse.[62]

Perhaps 'interpersonal justice' would be the best term, but I have chosen to stick with 'corrective justice' for the reasons elucidated above and because, in any case, this book is concerned primarily with the corrective or restorative element of corrective justice, however that term is best defined. That is, this book is concerned with questions 2 and 3 above, and not, or only incidentally, with question 1. In the following, we explore what behaviour our rights protect us against and how the law should respond when one of our rights has been violated. The book presents no theory of the rights that we have.

Moreover, it is worth noting that a similar difficulty faces the use of the term 'distributive justice'. At first glance, distributive justice is concerned solely with distributing. Accordingly, it tells us about fair patterns of distribution, but must presuppose an account of what it is that should be distributed and to whom it should be distributed. On this understanding, these questions must be extrinsic to distributive justice, as no amount of reflection on just distributions will reveal what should be distributed and to whom. But, of course, distributive justice theorists have presented accounts of these issues. For this reason, we have come to regard these issues as intrinsic to distributive justice. There is no reason that 'corrective justice' cannot be similarly used. Just as distributive justice is not solely concerned with how to distribute but also looks beyond to what should be distributed and to whom, corrective justice is involved with more than merely correcting but looks beyond to what should be corrected and why it should be.[63]

I conclude that corrective justice is not incomplete in the way often supposed.

The importance of these points cannot be overstated. No one who holds the view that corrective justice is concerned only with correcting independently defined injustices will be able to understand the argument of this book. Corrective justice is a form of morality that deals with interactions between individuals. It tells us how to correct matters when those interactions go wrong, but it also tells us what it means for those interactions to go wrong.

(ii) The Incompleteness of the Principled Approach

As indicated above, this book presents no theory of the rights upon which the law of negligence operates. This means that this book presents an incomplete account of the law of negligence. In addition to answering questions 2 and 3, a complete theory of the law of negligence would need to present a theoretical justification of the rights that persons have, the negligent violation of which calls

---

[62] The major exception is Finnis, above n59.

[63] And, clearly, we must not assume that theorists who have been labelled 'corrective justice theorists' cannot explain the rights base of negligence law just because of the label they have been given. In Weinrib's case, we must not forget ch 4 of *The Idea of Private Law* (Harvard University Press, Cambridge, Mass, 1995). Nor should we assume that Kantian right is too abstract to ground legal rules. At the very least, we must examine that theory to see whether that is so.

for restoration. I call this 'the rights base of negligence law'. We examine this rights base in some detail in later chapters, but we can say immediately that these rights include most importantly rights to the person, such as the right to bodily integrity, and property rights. Accordingly, a complete account of the law of negligence would need to provide a theoretical explanation and justification of these rights.

I hope that it is clear that this cannot be provided here. This book is a theoretical examination of the law of negligence as it operates in terms of the categories of enquiry with which we are familiar: the standard of care, the duty of care, remoteness, defences and causation. Without becoming entirely unwieldy—and impossibly long—it cannot also become a philosophical investigation of personal and property rights. Accordingly, I must be forgiven for not providing such. In any case, the demand for completeness is inappropriate when made with regard to individual pieces of research, as no research is ever complete in this sense.

Instead of providing a theory of the rights base of negligence law, I accept largely uncritically those rights as they exist in the positive law and leave to another time the justification of those rights. I say that I accept extant rights '*largely* uncritically' because, as we see in Chapter 7, the sum of extant rights is to a degree incoherent. This is because, in a few cases, courts have implicitly recognised rights that conflict with other areas of the law in ways that cannot sensibly be isolated. In other words, in these areas the law is inconsistent with itself. I argue that, for that reason, we must regard some of these cases as wrongly decided. But this is a special form of argument. The claim is not that we should reject these cases because they adopt a false view of rights—a claim that would require theoretical justification that I do not provide—but because they adopt a view of rights inconsistent with general features of the common law.

This strategy must be legitimate, but it creates a specific problem in this context that must be dealt with before the investigation of the law of negligence can begin. Some have argued that the rights base of negligence cannot be justified by corrective justice, but must instead be justified by distributive justice or by policy.[64] If that is so, then it appears that the thesis of this book is undermined. If the law's rights base is grounded in distributive justice or policy, then it cannot be right to maintain that corrective justice provides the best analysis of the law of negligence.

As indicated above, I cannot deal with this problem by developing a theory of the rights base of negligence law. Instead, I respond in two stages. First, I argue that it is not implausible to hold that the rights base of the law of negligence is grounded in corrective justice. I then argue that it is unattractive to hold that the rights base of negligence law is founded on distributive justice. Though this argument is incomplete in that it does not elucidate the ground of the rights

---

[64] See, eg, P Cane, 'Distributive Justice and Tort Law' [2001] *New Zealand Law Review* 401.

base, it is sufficient to show that the view that the rights base of the law of negligence is consistent with corrective justice is plausible, and hence is sufficient to clear the way for the main enquiry—ie the examination of the law in the light of corrective justice.

To summarise, if the argument below is successful, then the thesis developed in the rest of this book cannot be rejected on the ground that the rights base of the law of negligence *is* grounded on distributive justice or policy. This is because it will have been shown that the rights base *could be* grounded in corrective justice. In other words, it would show that the objection was guilty of begging the question. Moreover, while rights are logically prior to wrongs and hence the rights base of negligence law is conceptually prior to the remainder of that law, it does not follow that investigations into the law of negligence must begin with its rights base. One can start at the top and work down, but one can just as profitably start at the bottom and work up. Hence, if the book succeeds in showing that distributive justice has no role to play in the area of the law that it examines, it will have done much to show, in addition to the arguments above, that the rights base of negligence law is not founded on distributive justice. It will not have definitively proved such, of course, but will have given reason to think that corrective justice also explains the rights base.

(iii) The Rights Base of the Law of Negligence and Corrective Justice

Recall the argument above: the rights base of negligence law cannot be founded on corrective justice; hence, the rights base of negligence law must be founded on distributive justice. Obviously, this argument fails if the rights base can be founded on corrective justice.

According to Weinrib, the rights base of private law is grounded on Kantian right.[65] This is a conception of 'personality'—a conception of the person appropriate to the normative sphere in which the private law operates. Accordingly,

---

[65] EJ Weinrib, *The Idea of Private Law* (Harvard University Press, Cambridge, Mass, 1995) ch 4. According to Weinrib, however, Kantian right is distinct from corrective justice. For Weinrib, corrective justice 'presupposes the existence of entitlements' provided by Kantian right. Hence, Kantian right is understood as separate from corrective justice: EJ Weinrib, *The Idea of Private Law* (Harvard University Press, Cambridge, Mass, 1995) 80. However, this difference is merely terminological. For Weinrib, interpersonal morality consists of corrective justice and Kantian right. For me, 'interpersonal morality' and 'corrective justice' are synonyms. Nothing substantive turns on this difference. It is also important to note the mistake Cane makes in attributing the following position to Weinrib: P Cane, 'Distributive Justice and Tort Law' [2001] *New Zealand Law Review* 401, 409. Cane argues that because Weinrib recognises only two forms of justice (distributive and corrective) and because Weinrib holds that corrective justice *presupposes* a set of entitlements, implying that these entitlements cannot belong to corrective justice, Weinrib must hold that these entitlements belong to distributive justice. That argument fails because, on Weinrib's view, corrective justice does not exhaust interpersonal morality. Rather, for Weinrib, Kantian right is part of interpersonal morality, though it is not part of justice. This view is appropriate if one takes justice to be about, at its most general, *giving* to persons what they deserve and not about the nature of desert itself. I have preferred a wider definition of justice and would reply to a similar claim to Cane's by maintaining that the relevant entitlements do indeed belong to corrective justice.

it belongs to corrective justice as defined here. It is not my job to examine this view in any detail. My task is only to show that it, or something like it, is plausible enough to defeat the claim that the rights of tort law cannot belong to corrective justice.

Distributive justice is concerned with the distribution of benefits and burdens between persons in a society. Theorists of distributive justice debate the appropriate pattern of distribution. But there are two further, or rather prior, questions: What is a person in this context and what in the relevant sense are benefits and burdens? As well as discussing fair patterns of distribution, distributive justice theorists provide answers to these two questions. John Rawls, for instance, argues that relevant benefits are things that he calls 'primary goods', things such as 'rights, liberties, and opportunities, and income and wealth'.[66] He argues that these are the primary goods because they 'are things which it is supposed a rational man wants whatever else he wants'.[67] Hence, the selection of the primary goods is based on a conception of the person, and because distributive justice is concerned with the fair distribution of primary goods *for the reason that those things are needed and wanted*, the conception of the person adopted by Rawls is one that takes into account persons' needs and wants.

Notice that the conception of the person adopted by Rawls is not derived from an account of fair distribution. Though that conception is *sensitive to* the notion of fair distribution in that it is designed to reflect aspects of persons that are relevant to such distribution (ie needs and wants), it is not *based on* a view of fair distribution. Simply, no amount of reflection on theories about just patterns of distribution will reveal what should be distributed and to whom.

It is quite plausible that interpersonal morality has the same structure. Perhaps the rights upon which corrective justice operates are based on a conception of the person designed to reflect the norms that are appropriate to interpersonal morality. Weinrib presents Kantian right in precisely that light. Because corrective justice abstracts from particularities such as the moral goodness of the parties, their wealth and so on, a highly abstract account of the person is appropriate that does not refer to needs and wants.[68] This also appears to have been Aristotle's view.[69] We need not decide whether this is the correct account, just that an account of this kind is plausible, and it is eminently so.

Consider, for instance, the law of battery. It is trite law that an unwanted touching of another is illegal as a battery. Why is this? Weinrib would say that this is because, in line with Kantian right, the law has adopted a conception of the person as a free and rational agent, and that this implies that people have an entitlement to be free from interference with their bodies by other people. As one might say, because people are free and rational, they are not to be used as the means to others' ends. On the other hand, one who held that the rights base of negligence

---

[66] J Rawls, *A Theory of Justice: Revised Edition* (Belknap, Cambridge, Mass, 1999) 79.
[67] *Ibid.*
[68] Weinrib, above n65, 80–3.
[69] Aristotle, *Nicomachean Ethics* (trans T Irwin, Hackett, Indianapolis, Ind, 1999) 71 [1132a–1–6].

was grounded on distributive justice would say that the law has recognised that people possess a right to bodily integrity because the law has decided that it is a fair distribution of risk for the risks of unwanted touching to be borne by the person touching rather than by the person being touched.[70] Even on its face, this is much less plausible than Weinrib's position. But it is also important to be clear about the claim. It must not be allowed to piggy-back on Weinrib's. The position cannot be that distributing the risk to the person touching is fair because that would be the only way to respect the person being touched as free and rational. That is just Weinrib's position in disguise. One must say that the scheme is fair because it distributes benefits and burdens fairly throughout society as a whole.[71] Perhaps this will turn out to be right, but it is not very intuitive.

Moreover it does not seem to be the case that the courts have based the idea of a right to bodily integrity on distributive justice. Moreover, it would have been rather odd if they, or if anyone else, had. Our bodily integrity is not something that we deserve because of the fair distribution of risks throughout society. It is something that we can demand because we are free and rational.[72] Similarly, Rawls does not argue that we are entitled to 'freedom of the person' (which incorporates bodily integrity) because a state that respects freedom of the person distributes fairly. Rather, he argues that freedom of the person is a requirement of distributive justice because people are free and rational. Respecting freedom of the person is not a way of distributing justly. Rather, Rawls' point is that freedom of the person is *not something that should be distributed*, because people are free and rational and hence their bodies are not to be used for others' ends. Hence, freedom of the person is not founded on fair distribution, but it is relevant to distributive justice because a state that tried to distribute freedom of the person would be unjust. Freedom of the person is based on an abstract conception of the person or, as Kant and Weinrib put it, on personality.[73]

My point has not been to defend Weinrib per se. Rather, there are two points. First, the approach which holds that the rights base of the law of negligence is founded on Kantian right is plausible. Accordingly, it cannot be argued against the thesis of this book that the rights base of the law of negligence must be founded in distributive justice or policy unless this position is undermined.[74]

---

[70] See eg P Cane, 'Distributive Justice and Tort Law' [2001] *New Zealand Law Review* 401, 415.

[71] In fact, crucially, Cane resiles from this position, as we see below.

[72] At least this is so for the Kantian. It *may not* be true for some forms of consequentialism. But if the rejection of positions such as Weinrib's turns on the *assumption* of a consequentialist perspective, as I think it often does, then it would be sufficient to show that it is open for me to proceed with my enquiries by pointing to the compendious non-consequentialist literature that exists.

[73] J Rawls, *A Theory of Justice: Revised Edition* (Belknap, Cambridge, Mass, 1999) 53.

[74] For that position in detail, in a legal context, see eg EJ Weinrib, *The Idea of Private Law* (Harvard University Press, Cambridge, Mass, 1995) ch 4; P Benson, 'The Unity of Contract Law' in P Benson (ed), *The Theory of Contract Law: New Essays* (Cambridge University Press, Cambridge, 2001); A Ripstein, 'Authority and Coercion' (2004) 32 *Philosophy and Public Affairs* 2; SB Byrd and J Hruschka, 'Duty to Recognize Private Property Ownership: Kant's Theory of Property in his *Doctrine of Right*' (2006) 56 *University of Toronto Law Journal* 217; SB Byrd and J Hruschka, 'Kant on 'Why Must I Keep my Promise?' (2006) 81 *Chicago-Kent Law Review* 47.

Secondly, more generally, it does not matter for this study whether Kantian right forms the rights base of the law or whether Weinrib's understanding of Kantian right is correct. The point is simply that it is plausible to hold that the rights upon which tort law operates are ones of corrective justice. Perhaps Weinrib shows where those rights belong or perhaps there are better theories. I take no stand on that issue here.

(iv)   The Rights Base of the Law of Negligence and Distributive Justice

On the face of it, it is tempting to hold that the rights base of negligence is grounded on distributive justice, while responses to violations of those rights *ordinarily* proceed in accordance with corrective justice. However, when the outcome suggested by corrective justice would violate distributive justice, an exception should be created that preserves distributive justice.[75]

On the face of it, this both accurately reflects the operation of the modern law and makes good sense. It reflects the operation of the modern law, because courts do sometimes utilise concerns such as 'public policy' to negative prima facie rights in the claimant. It also appears to make sense because, if the rights base of negligence is founded on distributive justice, as many assume, then it appears that distributive justice should also play a role in determining responses to violations of those rights that are, *per* hypothesis, based on distributive justice.

In fact, however, the position is incoherent. Consider the following injunction: Do corrective justice unless that would be distributively unjust, in which case do distributive justice. That is simply a long winded way of saying: 'do distributive justice'.[76] Though a person following the injunction may sometimes apply the same reasoning as someone doing corrective justice would apply, if she applies this reasoning only because doing so is not not distributively just (and the double negative is instructive), then she is merely using the reasoning of 'corrective justice' as a heuristic for achieving distributive justice. Corrective justice has no real role to play on this model. The hypothetical possibility that corrective justice and distributive justice may sometimes, often, or even always lead to the same results makes no difference to this argument.

Alternatively, one might claim that corrective justice should be followed unless the distributive injustice would be *significant*, or some similar epithet. But why should the courts follow corrective justice when there would be a distributive injustice, though it would not be 'significant'? The answer to this question must refer to distributive justice or to corrective justice. If it refers to

---

[75] This is, in effect, the position advanced by R Mullender, 'Corrective Justice, Distributive Justice, and the Law of Negligence' (2001) 17 *Professional Negligence* 35, though he does not present it in that light. This is because Mullender appears to interpret corrective justice as an individual focused form of distributive justice.

[76] See also P Cane, 'Distributive Justice and Tort Law' [2001] *New Zealand Law Review* 401, 416; SR Perry, 'Tort Law' in D Patterson (ed), *A Companion to Philosophy of Law and Legal Theory* (Blackwell, Cambridge, Mass, 1996) 71–2.

distributive justice, then it is incoherent as it is claiming that there are good reasons of distributive justice not to be distributively just. Conversely, the claim that distributive justice should not always be followed because that would lead to inefficiency is, if it is coherent, the claim that it is not really distributively just to do what distributive justice *appears to but does not really* require. We have nothing more than distributive justice here. The second reply, that distributive justice should sometimes not be done because that would not be correctively just, raises the question: then why ever do what is distributively just when that conflicts with corrective justice?

The general problem here is that corrective and distributive justice are two forms of justice. The former focuses on the relationship between two individuals; the latter on the place of people in society generally. They are, then, incommensurable. It is, therefore, impossible in a case of conflict between corrective and distributive justice to, as it were, weigh the corrective justice against the distributive injustice.[77] Hence, if the law does in fact respond to rights violations by importing both corrective and distributive justice, then the law is incoherent. And so the modern law often is, as we see in Chapter 5. Hence, though the position examined here may accurately describe the operation of the modern law, it is not an attractive picture. It therefore gives us reason for revising our understanding of the law if we are able to do so.

On the other hand, Cane attempts to keep the perceived distributive and corrective elements of the law of negligence separate. According to Cane, the rights base of negligence law is grounded on distributive justice, but responses to violations of rights proceed solely in accordance with corrective justice.[78] On the face of it, this is coherent because it means that courts do not have to attempt to weigh incommensurables in one enquiry. Rather, courts elucidate rights by considering distributive justice and then respond to rights violations by doing corrective justice.

However, this does raise the question: if rights are based on distributive justice, then why should distributive justice not play a role in deciding how violations of those rights are handled by the courts? It is not possible to reply that, at least ideally, the rights would be so defined that in responding to violations of those rights in accordance with corrective justice courts will always produce outcomes that are distributively just. This reply destroys the theory it is meant to protect. On this view, the rights are tailored to achieve distributive justice when the violations of them are corrected. 'Corrective justice', therefore, is only the heuristic means of achieving distributive justice.

Hence, though Cane avoids arguing that courts must conduct an enquiry into incommensurables, his position remains problematic because it posits the

---

[77] It may be possible to respond that distributive justice and corrective justice can be 'weighed' in an entirely intuitive manner; however, as such must be entirely private, judges doing so would violate the principle that they should justify their decisions. See generally A Beever, 'Particularism and Prejudice in the Law of Tort' (2003) 11 *Tort Law Review* 146.

[78] Cane, above n76, 412.

existence of two normative enquiries—one concerning rights into distributive justice and the other concerning responses into corrective justice—without explaining why the enquiry should be divided in this manner, apart from his observation that the modern law seems to him to work this way. But that could show only how problematic the modern law is. Moreover, what reasons could be given for dividing the enquiry in this way? If the reasons are ones of distributive justice, then the theory collapses into distributive justice, if of corrective justice, then the theory collapses into corrective justice. And that is what happens in fact.

Cane anticipates some of the points made here and in response maintains:

> It does not follow from [the notion that the rights base of tort law is founded on distributive justice] that in tort law, distributive justice is logically prior to corrective justice. On the contrary, corrective justice provides the structure of tort law within which distributive justice operates. As a result, tort law might be judged, all things considered, to be a distributively unfair way of dealing with harm even if it was judged distributively just *as between doers and sufferers of harm*. This contrast could be captured by distinguishing between distributive justice in a global sense and principles of distributive justice that are 'local' to tort law.[79]

Note that in the last two sentences of this passage Cane uses 'distributive justice' in two different senses. First, there is distributive justice per se, and then there is distributive justice as between doers and sufferers of harm. According to Cane, only the latter is relevant to tort law. But Cane is using 'distributive justice' in a non-standard fashion. As indicated above, distributive justice is taken by almost all commentators to refer to the justice of distributing benefits and burdens throughout society. It belongs to societal morality as defined above. But Cane's 'distributive justice as between doers and sufferers of harm' does not. It belongs rather to interpersonal morality. In fact, then, Cane is not talking about distributive justice as the term is generally meant. He agrees with corrective justice theorists that distributive justice in its normal sense is irrelevant to tort law.[80] His argument, then, should be seen as consistent with and as *strengthening* the position adopted here.[81] 'Distributive justice' as between doers and sufferers of harm is a form of corrective justice.

---

[79] Cane, above n76, 413.

[80] Why, then, did Cane use the term 'distributive justice' in this fashion? The answer is that he believes that any justice that calls for distribution is, by definition, distributive justice. (See A Beever, 'Perspectives of Responsibility in Law and Morality' (2003) 27 *Melbourne University Law Review* 905, 914–15.) It is certainly true that the term could have been used in that manner, but it is not the standard use. Moreover, if Cane's use were right, then it would follow that responding to violations of rights would also be distributive justice as it would involving distributing assets from defendants to claimants or refusing to do so.

[81] See also SR Perry, 'On the Relationship Between Corrective and Distributive Justice: Fourth Series' in J Horder (ed), *Oxford Essays in Jurisprudence* (Oxford University Press, Oxford, 2000).

(v) Conclusion

Accordingly, it is not implausible to hold that the rights base of the law of negligence is grounded in corrective justice and not in distributive justice. This means that it is plausible to hold that property rights and rights to the person, such as bodily integrity, are founded on a conception of interpersonal morality—on a view of how persons should treat each other as individuals.

Though this position is unlikely to be familiar to the modern mind, it was the standard view for many centuries. As David Ibbetson has pointed out, the writings of the natural lawyers had an important impact on the development of the law of negligence as a whole,[82] and those theorists argued that the private law is based on corrective (commutative) rather than distributive justice.[83] And as Samuel Fleischacker has reminded us with respect to property rights:

> according to the tradition that had drawn this distinction [between corrective and distributive justice], distributive justice had little or nothing to do with property arrangements. Not a single jurisprudential thinker before [Adam] Smith—not Aristotle, not Aquinas, not Grotius, not Pufendorf, not Hutcheson, not William Blackstone or David Hume—put the justification of property rights under the heading of distributive justice. Claims to property, like violations of property, were matters for commutative justice; no one was given a right to claim property by distributive justice.[84]

Accordingly, even if these thinkers were wrong to hold that property rights can be justified by corrective justice, that view must have been extremely influential in the formation of our property law.

One area in which this can be seen is—ironically given the arguments of those who hold that the rights base of negligence law must lie in distributive justice—in our intuitive understanding of the operation of distributive justice. According to most modern theories of distributive justice, this form of justice calls for a redistribution in wealth from the rich to the poor.[85] This is generally understood to involve taking some of the property of the wealthy and transferring it to the poor. But if the notion of property was itself based on distributive justice, then it would appear to make no sense to think this way. If person *A* does not deserve property *x* as a matter of distributive justice, and property is based on distributive justice, then it appears natural to conclude, not that property in *x* must be taken away from *A*, but that *A* does not have property in *x*. But we do not think this way. This indicates that, even when we are thinking in terms of distributive justice, we think of property as conceptually prior to that form of justice. This

[82] DJ Ibbetson, *A Historical Introduction to the Law of Obligations* (Oxford University Press, Oxford, 1999) 166–7.

[83] A Beever, 'Justice and Punishment in Tort: A Comparative Theoretical Analysis' in R Grantham and C Rickett, *Justifying Remedies in Private Law* (Cambridge, Cambridge University Press, 2007).

[84] S Fleischacker, *A Short History of Distributive Justice* (Harvard University Press, Cambridge, Mass, 2004) 27.

[85] The leading example is J Rawls, (Belknap, Cambridge, Mass, 1999).

does not mean that property trumps distributive justice, as if property disallows distributive justice from redistributing.[86] Rather, the point is that the very notion of distributive justice calling for *re*distribution of property presupposes a non-distributive account of the basis of property rights.

Pursuing this line of though further, we can discover how this non-distributive account is likely to appear. Consider the way in which our societies typically redistribute resources from the wealthy to the poor, viz income tax. In non-legal terms, we say that in charging us income tax, the state takes some of *our* money to pay for public goods, and that it does so, at least arguably, in terms of distributive justice. This claim is particularly interesting in the light of the fact that, at least usually, the money is taken from us *before we receive it*. Why, then, do we regard it as *our* money? And why do we regard it as our money even if we believe that distributive justice requires that we be deprived of it? The answer must be because we do not believe that it is distributive justice that makes the money ours. Rather, we believe that the money is ours because that is what our employers agreed to pay us in return for our labour. In other words, we believe that the money is ours because of the relationship that we have with our employer, and this is a matter of corrective justice as defined here. The money is ours because there is a form of justice that operates as between ourselves and our employers that indicates that we should get the money, but we are rightly deprived of some of that money, because of justice within the community as a whole. Intuitively, then, we regard property as based on corrective, not distributive, justice. This becomes difficult to understand only when one internalises the misguided assumptions of most modern legal theories.

None of this has been intended as a knockdown argument against the notion that the rights base of the law of negligence is based on distributive justice. But it has been sufficient to show that it is far from implausible to hold that the rights base lies in corrective rather than in distributive justice.

B. The Inconsistency Objection: Corrective Justice and the General Law of Tort

The following chapters develop an account of the law of negligence based on corrective justice. At various points, it may appear that the claims made generate inconsistencies between the law of negligence and other areas of the law of tort. For instance, in Chapter 3, I argue that corrective justice calls for the adoption of an objective standard of fault in judging the defendant's behaviour. This may appear to be inconsistent with the existence of different standards in the law, such as strict liability in the torts of trespass.

I have two replies. The first is that this book argues that the law of negligence can be understood in a unified and consistent manner in accordance with cor-

---

[86] In effect, this is the argument of R Nozick, *Anarchy, State, and Utopia* (Blackwell, Oxford, 1975).

rective justice. I am not *here* arguing that the whole of the law of tort is based on corrective justice. Because of this, it is not clear what it would reveal to show that, say, the law of trespass is inconsistent with this model. Proving that the law of trespass is not based on corrective justice does not prove that the law of negligence is not so based.

The object of this book is to show that the law of negligence can be understood in a principled way without appeal to policy. The goal is not to show that policy plays no role in the law in general. In Chapter 1, I claimed that it would be better if policy played no role in law. In following chapters, I maintain that the law of negligence can be understood in such a way that policy plays no role. My conclusion is that we should understand the law of negligence in that way. None of this can be defeated by pointing to the purported role that policy analysis is said to play outside the law of negligence.

On the other hand, I should perhaps confess that it is my belief that at least almost all of the law of tort, and the private law more generally, is based on corrective justice. That view is not advanced in this book, but nor is it undermined. Corrective justice calls for different approaches to different circumstances. As we see in Chapter 3, the standard of care is rightly adjusted in certain situations. It also remains possible that corrective justice would call for strict liability in certain instances. It cannot be taken for granted, then, that the existence of strict liability is inconsistent with corrective justice or provides any objection to the thesis advanced here.

Of course, one could show that the law of tort as a whole is based on corrective justice only by examining that law in detail. Again, like an exploration of the rights base of the law of negligence, an investigation of the law of tort in its entirety cannot be conducted here. This is a work on the law of negligence. It cannot also become a work on the whole of the law of tort. For the moment, we must be content with the *possibility* that corrective justice explains that law.

However, there are two occasions on which the relationship between corrective justice and the wider law of tort requires special treatment. These surround an apparent inconsistency between the argument concerning the standard of care in Chapter 3 and the existence of strict liability, and between the discussion of economic loss in Chapter 7 and the economic torts. These are dealt with in those chapters.

3

The Standard of Care

T HE STANDARD OF care in negligence law is crucial, not merely as a determinant of liability, but because it is of primary importance in elucidating the concept of negligence. If a defendant performs an action that falls below the standard of care, then he is said to be negligent. Conversely, if the defendant does not fall below the standard of care, then he cannot be found negligent. Moreover, while the duty of care tells us to whom one owes care, and remoteness tell us in respect of which injuries one owes care, the standard of care tells us what having care means.

It may seem peculiar to discuss the standard of care before the duty of care. After all, this means that 'breach of duty' is explored before 'duty' itself. But that is not inappropriate. A defendant acts negligently if he creates an unreasonable risk of injury to someone, but that someone need not be the claimant. Accordingly, it is possible for a defendant to be negligent but not owe a duty of care to the claimant. This was most famously the case in *Palsgraf v Long Island Railroad Co.*[1] In terms of the negligence enquiry, then, it is possible for the claimant to be able to prove that the defendant was in 'breach of duty', although she cannot show that the defendant owed her a duty of care. In other words, 'breach of duty' is shorthand for breach of the *standard of care*, not for breach of the *duty of care*. The standard of care, then, is not parasitic on duty, and it is not irrational to discuss it first.[2] Moreover, as we will see, it is impossible to understand the duty of care without prior examination of the standard of care.

This chapter is divided into five parts. The first examines when it is appropriate to apply the standard of care. The answer is that the standard of care is applied only to defendants who have manifested their will in action. I argue that this is so because corrective justice is a form of moral responsibility, and moral responsibility can be predicated only of actors in respect of their actions. The second part of the chapter explores the objective standard and the way in which it is sometimes adjusted. It rejects policy-based justifications of the objective standard and insists instead that the standard is designed to do justice between the parties. Moreover, it maintains that the standard is sometimes adjusted in order to preserve equality between the parties by reflecting relevant features of

---

[1] 162 NE 99 (NY CA 1928).

[2] J Fleming, *The Law of Torts,* 9th edn (LBC Information Services, Sydney, 1998) 117–18; T Weir, *Tort Law* (Oxford University Press, Oxford, 2002) 55. Compare WVH Rogers, *Winfield and Jolowicz on Tort,* 16th edn (Sweet & Maxwell, London, 2002) 103.

the relationship between the parties. The third part of the chapter examines the issue of reasonable care and unreasonable risk. I explore both the 'utilitarian' and corrective justice approaches to this question and conclude that the corrective justice model best captures the law of the Commonwealth, in particular the leading English cases. I also consider some problematic cases. Accordingly, the first three sections of this chapter establish that the standard of care stage of the negligence enquiry is best understood an instantiation of corrective justice.

In the fourth part of the chapter, I examine in outline the relationship between fault, strict liability and corrective justice. I show why it is that corrective justice calls for fault based liability in negligence while imposing strict liability for torts such as trespass to the person, to land and to goods. Finally, the fifth part of the chapter examines the impact of recent legislation on the way that courts should determine the standard of care.

I. THE DISTINCTION BETWEEN ACTION AND MERE BEHAVIOUR

The law of negligence imposes liability only on those who have manifested their will in action. It does not impose liability on those who merely behave. Of course, this is not unique to the law of negligence. The principle also holds for torts such as trespass. A trespasser is not someone who is pushed onto someone else's land, for instance.

The rule that the defendant cannot be liable unless the claimant can trace her injury to a wrongful action of the defendant's does not entail that the defendant must have *chosen* to act in an illegal fashion. Action is not coextensive with choice. If I wander onto your land in a daydream, my wandering onto your land is an action, although it is not chosen.

What is the difference between choosing and acting? This is a controversial philosophical issue and I can only gesture at the solution to it here. Actions are behaviours over which the agent has the requisite degree of control. This is sometimes captured by saying that a behaviour is an action if the behaviour was under the command of the agent's will. The precise meaning of this is the subject of much philosophical debate, but whatever it means we can conclude that an action can be attributed to the free will of the agent.

Choice is something more than this. For an action to be chosen, it must be the specific product of the agent's deliberation. Specific deliberation, then, is a necessary condition for choice but not for action. If I decide to feed myself because I am hungry, then my walking to the refrigerator, opening the door, cutting the chocolate cake, etc, are choices. But, if I do not specifically decide to open the refrigerator door with my right rather than my left hand, then I do not choose to do so. However, as I could have chosen to open the door with either hand, not to have opened it at all, etc, my opening the door with my right hand was under the control of my will, and hence remains an action. Similarly, blinking is a behaviour under the command of my free will—I can blink immediately or cease for a time—hence the behaviour is an action, although it is seldom chosen. But why are actions singled out as peculiarly capable of giving rise to liability? The answer in corrective justice is that legal liability is a form of moral responsibility and moral responsibility can coherently be predicated only of actors in respect of their actions.

We owe to Immanuel Kant the most eloquent elucidation of the notion that attributing moral responsibility to an object is meaningful only if that object possesses free will.[3] When our ancestors sat in judgment on stones and trees, they evidenced what today seems a curious inability to distinguish moral from merely causal responsibility.[4] Of course, the tree that fell and crushed the claimant's leg was causally responsible for the claimant's injury, but it was not and could not have been morally responsible for doing so, because the tree lacked free will. It is not a thing to which the concept of moral responsibility can apply.[5] Hence, Kant insists that the concept of fault is that of an unintentional (or better, not necessarily intentional) transgression of a duty that can be *imputed* to the agent.[6] But, if mere behaviour is not action, then it cannot be imputed to a person any more than the falling of a tree can be imputed to the tree.

For these reasons, failing to act does not function as a defence to liability; rather, liability can be aimed only at actions—ie only actions are candidates for liability. Attempting to establish liability against a defendant for mere behaviour is the equivalent of attempting to establish liability against a tree.

In *Buckley and The Toronto Transportation Commission v Smith Transport Ltd*,[7] the first claimant was injured and the streetcar (tram) that he was operating was damaged when the tractor and trailer 'driven' by the defendant's employee at high speed slammed into his vehicle. The defendant's employee, Taylor, was 'driving' too fast for the conditions and had failed to give way. However, Taylor was suffering from syphilis of the brain and was under the remarkable delusion that the tractor was not being driven by him but was being operated by remote control from head office. He died from the disease one month after the accident.

The Ontario Court of Appeal ruled that the defendant could not be liable in negligence, because Taylor 'suddenly and without warning, had become

---

[3] Eg I Kant, *Critique of Pure Reason* (trans P Guyer and A Wood, Cambridge University Press, Cambridge, 1998) 533–4 [A 534/B 562]; I Kant, 'Critique of Practical Reason' in M Gregor (ed), *Practical Philosophy* (Cambridge University Press, Cambridge, 1996) 139–42 [5:3–8].

[4] However, they may not have been as irrational as we think them. See A Watson, *Legal History and a Common Law for Europe* (Institutet för Rättshistorisk Forskning, Stockholm, 2001) 142–9.

[5] Some torts are actionable even though the defendant did not commit a wrongful act. These torts, such as nuisance, are not based on any wrong*doing* by the defendant. This does not mean that they are not forms of moral responsibility or that they are not based on corrective justice. Rather, the link between these torts and moral responsibility and corrective justice is more indirect. See EJ Weinrib, *The Idea of Private Law* (Harvard University Press, Cambridge, Mass, 1995) 187–203.

[6] I Kant, 'The Metaphysics of Morals' in M Gregor (ed), *Practical Philosophy* (Cambridge University Press, Cambridge, 1996) 378 [6:224].

[7] [1946] OR 798 (Ont CA). See also *Slattery v Haley* [1923] 3 DLR 156 (Ont SC App Div).

insane'.[8] His insanity made Taylor incapable of carrying out the duty that lay on him, hence, in the eyes of the law, Taylor was an automaton and his behaviour was incapable of giving rise to liability.

Roach JA maintained that liability in negligence could follow only if Taylor had been capable of understanding that he had a duty to take care and had been able to carry out that duty.[9] This is a very close approximation of the truth, but it must be remembered that the real question is whether the defendant acted. Usually, the defendant will not have acted unless Roach JA's conditions are met, but that will not always be the case. For instance, if the defendant is both compelled to behave in a manner that infringes the claimant's rights *and* chooses to do so, then, though he is unable to carry out his duty, his behaviour is an action and can ground liability. For example, if the defendant is pushed onto the claimant's land but also intends to enter that land, then the defendant commits a trespass.[10] This is because the entry onto the claimant's land was an action of the defendant's even though the defendant was compelled. In *Buckley*, on the other hand, the driving of the tractor was not an act of Taylor's.

We have no test for deciding whether something is an action or a mere behaviour; at least that is so if what we mean by 'test' is a formula that one can mechanically apply to pick out instances of action from those of mere behaviour. The line between action and mere behaviour will often be a grey one, but that is a feature of the law generally, indeed of life generally, and the desire to avoid it will necessarily go unfulfilled.

In the above, I suggested that liability in negligence could arise only in respect of a defendant's actions because liability is based on moral responsibility and because moral responsibility can be predicated only of actors in respect of their actions. This leads to a potential problem. While the notion that liability is based on moral responsibility indicates that mere behaviour cannot generate liability, it also seems to indicate that many actions should not be candidates for liability. A powerful reason for thinking that this is so is that some actions are performed without the agent having an alternative.

Moral philosophers commonly insist that moral responsibility can rightly be attributed only to people who could have acted otherwise. 'Ought implies can', it is said. But it is surprisingly difficult to understand this concept.[11] What do we mean by 'can' in 'ought implies can'? Imagine the following examples:

---

[8] *Buckley and The Toronto Transportation Commission v Smith Transport Ltd* [1946] OR 798, 800 (Ont CA).

[9] *Ibid*, 806.

[10] For clarity, the case I have in mind is one in which there are two causes of the entrance to the claimant's land that overdetermine that result. In other words, the defendant would have entered the claimant's land even if either the third party did not push or the defendant did not have the relevant intention. Also, the claim is that action is a necessary, not a sufficient, condition for liability. Hence, it does not follow from that fact that the defendant was on the claimant's property as the result of an action that the defendant must be liable. If the defendant was under duress, etc, then he may not be liable. This is not because the defendant did not act, but because he acted under duress; a fact which absolves the defendant. Ie, unlike an absence of action, duress functions as a defence.

[11] T Honoré, *Responsibility and Fault* (Hart Publishing, Oxford, 1999) ch 7.

1. While *A* was driving, the steering column on *A*'s car breaks through no fault of *A*'s. As a result, *A*'s car goes into a skid and collides with the claimant.
2. While driving, *B* slams on the brakes when he notices a vehicle, failing to give way, emerging from a side road. *B* does all that he can reasonably do to prevent injury to those in the vicinity, but must swerve to avoid the vehicle. As a result, *B*'s car goes into a skid and collides with the claimant.
3. While driving, due to a weakness in *C*'s peripheral vision, *C* collides with another vehicle. As a result, *C*'s car goes into a skid and collides with the claimant.
4. While driving, *D* rummages around on the back seat for his favourite compact disk and fails to pay attention to the road. As a result, *D*'s car goes into a skid and collides with the claimant.

If 'can' means 'physically possible', then the drivers are responsible for the claimants' injuries in all of the cases above. In case 1, for instance, it was physically possible for *A* to have driven more slowly, to have bought a different car, to have stayed at home that day, etc. But few would say that *A* was morally responsible for the claimant's injury in case 1. The same holds for *B* in case 2. Whatever we mean by 'ought implies can', we do not mean that the attribution of responsibility relies only on physical possibility. By 'can' we do not mean 'physically can'.

Perhaps we mean by the 'can' in 'ought implies can' that the action is something that *can be expected of* the agent. So, *B* is not to be held responsible for the claimant's injury in case 2, because we cannot expect *B* to have prevented that injury. But this opens its own can of worms. What is meant by 'can be expected of'? There are at least two possible interpretations of this phrase. The first and more familiar—at least to those who are not private lawyers—is subjective. Here, we determine whether we could have expected better of the agent by consulting the agent's knowledge, intelligence, reflexes, etc. In case 2, we are likely to say that *B* was not responsible because it would have been unreasonable in the circumstances to expect *B* to behave in any other manner. Likewise, in case 3 we will say that *C* was not responsible, because, given *C*'s impairment, one could not expect *C* to have done otherwise. Conversely, in case 4 we will say that *D* was responsible, because one could expect *D* to realise that he should have kept his eyes on the road.

But this is not the only interpretation of 'can be expected of' available. We may decide whether more could have been expected of the agent by reference to a standard set independently of the agent's particular abilities. A prerequisite for taking my advanced course in tort law is a passing grade in the basic first-year tort course. Hence, I may say to a student in my first year class who intends to take the advanced class that, given his pre-enrolment in *Advanced Tort*, it is expected of him that he will pass the basic course. I may say this to him with no expectation that he will pass the basic course. So, I may expect (subjective) that the student will fail while imposing the expectation (non-subjective) on him that he will pass. When he does fail, I may say that he failed to live up to a standard expected of him and of all my students.[12]

When dealing with such a non-subjective standard, the dictum 'ought implies can' must be understood to mean, not that it must have been possible for the agent to do such and such in this particular case, but that it is generally possible for agents of a kind similar to this agent to do things of such and such a kind. At first glance, it may appear unfair to impose such expectations on individuals when it is unrealistic to expect those individuals to live up to that standard. But, as I argue below, it is unfair only in an irrelevant sense.

II. THE OBJECTIVE STANDARD

The defendant in *Vaughan v Menlove*[13] built his rick of hay next to the claimant's barn. The rick caught fire, which spread to and destroyed the barn and other property of the claimant's. At trial, Patterson J instructed the jury that they were to find the defendant negligent if in building the rick the defendant had failed 'to proceed with such reasonable caution as a prudent man would have exercised under such circumstances'.[14] Apparently, in nineteenth century England it was common knowledge that ricks of hay are prone to catch fire. Accordingly, the jury found the defendant liable. On appeal, the defendant accepted that a reasonable man would have known of the risk of fire and would have built the rick elsewhere. However, the defendant maintained that he could not have been expected to be aware of the risk due to his remarkable stupidity. The Court of Common Pleas ruled that this reply was irrelevant.[15]

According to Tindal CJ, the question was not what could have been expected of the defendant but what could have been expected of 'a man of ordinary prudence'.[16] Speaking generally, then, the standard of care is not determined with regard to the peculiarities of the defendant, but rather by reference to a creation of the law: the ordinary reasonable person. This raises two questions: who is the ordinary reasonable person, and why is the law interested in him rather than in the actual defendant? I begin with the latter question.

---

[12] The position enunciated here bears some similarity to that enunciated in *ibid*. However, there are important differences. Honoré maintains that there is a particular and a general sense of 'can' that is used with reference to the agent. I do not disagree, but I am arguing that there is a sense of 'can', at least as used in the phrase 'ought implies can', that refers beyond the agent.

[13] (1837) 3 Hodges 51, 132 ER 490.

[14] *Ibid*, 492.

[15] G Fletcher, 'The Fault of not Knowing' (2002) 3 *Theoretical Inquiries in Law* 265, 277 argues that there was no evidence that the defendant could not have avoided the risk to the claimant's barn. This is to maintain that the defendant's evidence was unreliable, as it surely was. However, the Court did not argue in this manner. It held that the defendant would have lost even if he really were too stupid to have avoided the fire. Fletcher, then, can explain the outcome of the case, but not the reasoning upon which it was based.

[16] *Vaughan v Menlove* (1837) 3 Hodges 51, 132 ER 490, 493.

A. Justifying the Objective Standard

On its face, it seems that the objective standard is adopted for convenience rather than from a concern for justice. This is because, at first glance, a subjective standard that holds a defendant negligent only if he were personally culpable seems preferable from the standpoint of justice. Conversely, the objective standard seems based on policy concerns—most likely convenience of proof. It is possible to read Tindal CJ's claim that if a subjective standard were applied then 'liability for negligence should be co-extensive with the judgment of each individual, which would be as variable as the length of the foot of each individual' in this manner.[17] If a subjective standard were adopted, then it would be too difficult to prove that the defendant was negligent.[18]

However, the objective standard is not based on this policy. In fact, the objective standard is not merely consistent with corrective justice; corrective justice demands the adoption of an objective standard.

First, it is important to recognise that the objective standard is not always harsh on defendants. If the defendant is an ordinary reasonable person in the relevant respect, then he will be asked to do no more than he is able to do. Moreover, if the defendant has abilities superior to those of the ordinary reasonable person, then the objective standard will ordinarily impose a standard of care on the defendant that is easier to meet than a subjective standard would be. Hence, in such circumstances the objective standard will impose fewer obligations on the defendant than does ethics.[19] From the perspective of ethics, this may appear soft on the defendant and harsh on the claimant. The objective test is not claimant friendly, then. Rather, at least in the usual cases, it is a 'one size fits all' standard that sometimes benefits claimants, but sometimes benefits defendants over a subjective standard. The question, then, is why the law adopts this approach when it seems clear that one size does not fit all.[20]

I answer this question by considering an approach recently enunciated by the English Court of Appeal in *Mansfield v Weetabix Ltd*.[21] This approach departs from a long line of authority partly examined below.[22] In *Mansfield*, the defendant's employee, Tarleton, driving in a manner that fell below the reasonable person standard, caused extensive physical damage to the claimant's shop. The defendant argued that the ordinary reasonable driver standard—ie the ordinary objective standard relevant in such cases—should not be applied. This was because Tarleton's consciousness was impaired because he was suffering from

[17] *Ibid.*
[18] See eg S Todd, 'Negligence: Breach of Duty' in S Todd (ed), *The Law of Torts in New Zealand*, 3rd edn (Brookers, Wellington, 2001) 383.
[19] Recall that the ethical standard is identified with the subjective. See ch 2.
[20] This is not to say that the standard is never adjusted. That issue is explored below.
[21] [1998] 1 WLR 1263 (CA).
[22] See eg *R v Isitt* [1978] RTR 211 (CA); *Rabey v R* [1980] 2 SCR 513; *Roberts v Ramsbottom* [1980] 1 WLR 823 (QBD); *R v Hennessey* [1989] 1 WLR 287 (CA); *A-G's Reference (No 2 of 1992)* [1993] 3 WLR 982 (CA).

a malignant insulinoma that produced hypoglycaemia. Tarleton was not aware, and it was not reasonable to expect him to have been aware, that he was suffering from hypoglycaemia at the time of the accident. A unanimous Court of Appeal accepted the defendant's argument. Leggatt LJ said:

> There is no reason in principle why a driver should not escape liability where the disabling event is not sudden, but gradual, provided that the driver is unaware of it. A person with Mr Tarleton's very rare condition commonly does not appreciate that his ability is impaired, and he was no exception. Although by the time of trial Mr Tarleton was dead, and there was no direct evidence of his actual state of awareness, the judge held that he 'would not have continued to drive if he had appreciated and was conscious that his ability was impaired.' Of course, if he had known that it was, he would have been negligent in continuing to drive despite his knowledge of his disability. So also if he ought to have known that he was subject to a condition that rendered him unfit to drive . . .
>
>   In my judgment, the standard of care that Mr Tarleton was obliged to show in these circumstances was that which is to be expected of a reasonably competent driver unaware that he is or may be suffering from a condition that impairs his ability to drive. To apply an objective standard in a way that did not take account of Mr Tarleton's condition would be to impose strict liability. But that is not the law.[23]

The Court did not discuss *Vaughan v Menlove*, but it is clear that the decisions are inconsistent. If it is unfair to hold a driver to a standard that he cannot meet, then it is also unfair to hold a stacker of hay to a standard that he cannot meet. Moreover, being stupid is no more morally culpable than having hypoglycaemia. In fact, stupidity may be less culpable: a party with hypoglycaemia can ordinarily make plans accordingly, whereas it is in the nature of stupidity that the stupid person cannot adequately plan to avoid the consequences of his stupidity. Nevertheless, it cannot be denied that the decision of the Court of Appeal in *Mansfield* has significant intuitive attraction. If Tarleton was not to blame for having hypoglycaemia or for failing to notice that it was affecting his driving, then it seems harsh to impose liability. Perhaps, then, we should follow *Mansfield* and reject *Vaughan v Menlove*?

However, there is something missing from the deliberations of the Court of Appeal in *Mansfield*: *the claimant*. While it may be harsh to say that Tarleton was driving negligently when he was not personally to blame for doing so, the actual outcome of the case was harsh on the claimant, who was at least as innocent as Tarleton and now must suffer an uncompensated loss.

Of course, the innocence of the claimant per se is neither here nor there. The law of negligence compensates the claimant only if she was the victim of another's wrongdoing. But this does show that appealing to the innocence of one or other of the parties does nothing to settle the issue of liability. If the personal innocence of the claimant was irrelevant, then, as a matter of justice, so must Tarleton's have been.

---

[23] *Mansfield v Weetabix Ltd* [1998] 1 WLR 1263, 1268 (CA).

If the claimant in *Mansfield* had been injured by a driver without hypo-glycaemia or a similar condition, then the claimant would have been able to recover.[24] Accordingly, *Mansfield* held that the duties of the defendant were determined in part by Tarleton's capacities: the case imposed a *subjective* stand-ard. Consider again Leggatt LJ's language, this time with my emphases:

> There is no reason in principle why a driver should not escape liability where the dis-abling event is not sudden, but gradual, provided that *the driver* is unaware of it. A person with Mr Tarleton's very rare condition commonly does not appreciate that *his ability* is impaired, and *he* was no exception. Although by the time of trial Mr Tarleton was dead, and there was no direct evidence of his actual state of awareness, the judge held that *he* 'would not have continued to drive if *he* had appreciated and was conscious that *his* ability was impaired.' Of course, if *he* had known that it was, *he* would have been negligent in continuing to drive despite *his* knowledge of *his* dis-ability. So also if *he* ought to have known that *he* was subject to a condition that ren-dered him unfit to drive . . .[25]

The argument was that Tarleton was not to blame, and so the defendant could not be liable. The question asked by the Court of Appeal was ethical rather than one of corrective justice.

Accordingly, in *Mansfield* the standard of care was determined by consider-ing only the defendant's side of the equation. In effect, then, the idiosyncrasies of the defendant determined the scope of the claimant's rights. This is a one-sided approach to determining negligence and is incompatible with the formal equality of the parties imbedded in the law. It privileges the defendant by hold-ing that his peculiarities determine the relationship between the parties. Of course, it is unfortunate that Tarleton suffered from hypoglycaemia, but that does not justify transferring the consequences of that misfortune to the claimant.[26]

To achieve justice, therefore, the law of negligence requires a standard for judging the behaviour of the defendant that treats the claimant and the defen-dant as equals; a standard that mediates between the interests of the parties.[27] This is the objective standard. This approach sets the rights and duties of the parties, not by reference to the defendant alone (as does the subjective stand-ard), nor by reference to the claimant alone (as does strict liability),[28] but by

[24] Moreover, as is explored below, the claimant would have been able to recover even if a young child had been driving.

[25] *Mansfield v Weetabix Ltd* [1998] 1 WLR 1263, 1267–8 (CA).

[26] OW Holmes, *The Common Law* (Dover Publications, New York, 1881) 108.

[27] Also required is a standard that judges *the claimant* in order to mediate between the interests of the parties. See *Rogers v Elliott* 15 NE 768 (Mass SJC 1888). For general discussion, see EJ Weinrib, 'Towards a Moral Theory of Negligence Law' (1983) 2 *Law and Philosophy* 37, 51; EJ Weinrib, *The Idea of Private Law* (Harvard University Press, Cambridge, Mass, 1995) 180–3.

[28] Strict liability is discussed by EJ Weinrib in *ibid*, ch 7. The general strategy is to show either that purported instances of strict liability are in fact fault based or that they are justified because, in the relevant and restricted context, the position of the claimant is paramount. This issue is explored in the final section of this ch.

reference to a hypothetical person who embodies a standard universalisable across the community as a whole. Its purpose is to set an *impersonal* benchmark for judging action so that the parties are treated as equals. This is the right way to understand Tindal CJ's claim in *Vaughan v Menlove* that a subjective standard should not be applied, as it would mean that 'liability for negligence should be co-extensive with the judgment of each individual, which would be as variable as the length of the foot of each individual'.[29] A subjective standard cannot do justice between the parties as it focuses entirely on the defendant.

There are two important consequences of the above. First, negligence is not a state of mind. We are interested in whether the defendant acted in accordance with a standard of care set to mediate between the interests of the parties. Accordingly, we are uninterested in what went on inside the defendant's head. Negligence, then, is not carelessness or the failure to give due consideration. It is not a mens rea standard. Nor is it concerned with whether the defendant tried hard enough or made sufficient effort to avoid injury.[30] It is simply the failure to live up to the standard of the ordinary reasonable person. Secondly, as a consequence of the above, a finding of negligence does not necessarily imply that the defendant acted unethically or is deserving of punishment.[31]

An excellent illustration of these points is found in *Roberts v Ramsbottom*.[32] The claimant suffered personal injury and property damage when the defendant driver collided with her vehicle. The defendant insisted that he was driving poorly because he had suffered a stroke that impaired his consciousness. This stroke rendered him unfit to drive and unable fully to appreciate that he was not

---

[29] (1837) 3 Hodges 51, 132 ER 490, 493. See also S Todd, 'Negligence: Breach of Duty' in S Todd (ed), *The Law of Torts in New Zealand*, 3rd edn (Brookers, Wellington, 2001) 383.

[30] Against: T Weir, *Tort Law* (Oxford University Press, Oxford, 2002) 56–7. J Gardner, 'The Purity and Priority of Private Law' (1996) 46 University of Toronto Law Journal 459, 485 claims that 'negligence liability . . . is liability which imposes a duty to pay attention, and a duty to pay attention is none other than a duty to engage in a certain kind of mental activity, that is, a positive duty [to care for others]'. But this argument is fallacious. The duty is to act as a reasonable person would. Gardner comments that this '*imposes* a duty to pay attention' (emphasis added), and that may be right, but it does not follow from this that the duty to act as a reasonable person would *is* the duty to pay attention (or even that the latter is a subset of the former). That *x* imposes *y* does not show that *x* is *y* (or that *y* is part of *x*). Though the standard of care might, in practice, require persons to pay attention (such as when they are driving), it is not a duty to pay attention. Furthermore, to the extent that one must pay attention, the obligation is to avoid injuring the legal rights of others. It seems wrong to characterise this as care for others, because, inter alia, it is compatible with complete distain for the interests of others—eg, one acts legally even if one's reasons for avoiding injuring others were entirely self-regarding and one, in fact, hated all others. Finally, the law imposes liability on those who have paid as much attention as they could have done, so long as they fell below the standard of the ordinary reasonable person.

[31] This must call into question accounts that explain the law in terms of retribution. See eg P Birks, *Harassment and Hubris: The Right to an Equality of Respect* (University College Dublin Faculty of Law, Dublin, 1996); P Cane, 'Retribution, Proportionality, and Moral Luck in Tort Law' in P Cane and J Stapleton (eds), *The Law of Obligations: Essays in Celebration of John Fleming* (Oxford University Press, Oxford, 1998); JM Kelly, 'The Inner Nature of the Tort Action' (1967) 2 *Irish Jurist (NS)* 279.

[32] [1980] 1 WLR 823 (QBD).

fit to drive. Consistently with *Vaughan v Menlove*, Neill J ruled that these factors were irrelevant and held the defendant liable, remarking that:

> if [the driver] retained some control, albeit imperfect control, and his driving, judged objectively, was below the required standard, he remains liable. His position is the same as a driver who is old or infirm. In my judgment unless the facts establish what the law recognises as automatism the driver cannot avoid liability on the basis that owing to some malfunction of the brain his consciousness was impaired.[33]

Neill J stressed that 'the defendant was in no way morally [ie ethically] to blame, but that is irrelevant to the question of legal liability in this case'.[34]

This approach was criticised in *Mansfield* on the ground that it imposed strict liability on the defendant.[35] Moreover, Leggatt LJ pointed out that Neill J implied that the defendant could escape liability only if he could prove that he was not driving, but, Leggatt LJ argued, that issue was irrelevant.[36]

But *Roberts v Ramsbottom* did not impose strict liability. Certainly, Neill J said that the defendant could not avoid liability by showing that he was doing his best,[37] but that is to reject only a subjective standard. Liability is strict if it is imposed without reference to standards such as that of the ordinary reasonable person; if liability lies solely in *causa* rather than also in *culpa*. But there was no sign of that in Neill J's judgment. Neill J imposed liability because the defendant's driving fell below the standard of care to be expected of an ordinary reasonable person, and that is fault-based, not strict, liability. Simply, the Court in *Mansfield* forgot that there is a standard intermediate between the subjective and strict liability and that legal fault does not imply ethical wrongdoing.

On the other hand, the Court of Appeal in *Mansfield* correctly interpreted Neill J as holding that it was relevant to ask whether the defendant was driving. But the Court of Appeal was wrong to dismiss this concern. If in this context the defendant was not driving, then he was behaving as an automaton, lacked volition, and hence was not acting. Therefore, if the defendant was not driving he could not be liable. Alternatively, if he was driving, then he was acting volitionally and should have been held to the objective standard. Neill J's analysis of the objective standard in *Roberts v Ramsbottom* was exemplary.

Despite the claims made in *Mansfield*, the objective standard is morally justified from the normative perspective relevant to interactions between two parties, one as the doer and the other as the sufferer of an alleged injustice. This is almost, but not quite, to say that the objective standard is demanded by corrective justice. That issue is explored below. Suffice it to say for the moment that, when a moral judgement is called for that must determine which of two parties must bear a loss, it would be wrong for the judgement to be determined

---

[33] *Ibid*, 832.

[34] *Ibid*, 833.

[35] *Mansfield v Weetabix Ltd* [1998] 1 WLR 1263, 1268 (CA).

[36] *Ibid*, 1266.

[37] This was rejected for two reasons: Neill J did not believe it was true and, if true, that it would be relevant: *Roberts v Ramsbottom* [1980] 1 WLR 823, 832–3 (QBD).

by a one-sided focus on either party. Instead, the judgement must look to do jus-tice between the parties, and in the law of negligence it does so by adopting a standard that mediates between their interests. Because the parties were strangers in *Mansfield*, the objective standard would mediate between their interests by (i) ignoring the idiosyncrasies of the driver, (ii) refusing to find the defendant liable merely because the claimant was injured and (iii) by applying an impersonal standard that generates liability only if the driver's driving fell below the standard of that of an ordinary reasonable person.

This discussion also reveals why the law refuses to take into account the defendant's disabilities, although that refusal seems unjust on its face. In discussing *Vaughan v Menlove*, it was pointed out that the objective standard benefits defendants who enjoy natural talents over those who do not. This may be an injustice from the perspective of distributive justice as the distribution of natural talents is undeserved.[38] If so, then that injustice must be ameliorated by means other than the law of negligence. However, the claim here is not that the objective standard is distributively just. It is only that the standard is just from the normative perspective relevant to an interaction between two parties.[39]

B. Who is the Ordinary Reasonable Person?

In order to mediate between the interests of the parties, the law adopts an objective, impersonal standard: the ordinary reasonable person. But who is the ordinary reasonable person? First, is the ordinary reasonable person an ordinary person who is reasonable or a reasonable person who is ordinary? (This is a serious question!) The answer must be the latter. The point of the objective standard is to mediate between the interests of the parties by setting an imper-sonal standard by which to judge the defendant's actions. This aim cannot be achieved if the standard is determined by reference to ordinary, ie actual, per-sons. As Tony Weir has said, 'the normal and the normative are not necessarily congruent'.[40] A standard determined entirely by reference to the manner in which people usually act would be set, not fairly as between the parties, but by reference to third parties. Hence, that standard would inappropriately incor-porate elements external to the relationship between the parties and hence external to corrective justice. To be true to its nature, then, the objective stand-ard must be normative, not sociological.

---

[38] J Rawls, *A Theory of Justice: Revised Edition* (Belknap, Cambridge, Mass, 1999) 444–7.

[39] M Moran, *Rethinking the Reasonable Person: An Egalitarian Reconstruction of the Objective Standard* (Oxford University Press, Oxford, 2003) argues that the reasonable person standard should be replaced by an egalitarian objective standard. In Moran's view, inherent biases are bound to arise if we speak of reasonable *persons*. Also, Moran argues that the reasonable person standard as it has been applied in practice has not been genuinely objective, and hence has not done justice as between the parties. See especially *ibid*, at 52–4. If these important claims are true, then we should change our practice and our terminology, but the justification for the standard is untouched.

[40] T Weir, *Tort Law* (Oxford University Press, Oxford, 2002) 60.

Take the following case. Paul injures Peter in a traffic accident. Paul was driving too fast for the conditions, but plausibly argues that ordinary persons regularly drive too fast for the conditions. We must not say that, as Paul was driving as an ordinary person would, Paul did not fall below the standard of care. To do so would be to judge Paul's behaviour by that of third parties rather than by a standard that mediates between Paul and Peter. In effect, Paul's argument is that he was not negligent, because he was only doing something that many people do, which is drive carelessly. But, from the perspective of corrective justice, that argument is irrelevant.[41]

Accordingly, in *Bolitho v City and Hackney HA*, the House of Lords made it clear that the negligence of medical practitioners is not to be determined solely by reference to conventional medical practice, and that it is therefore proper for courts to reach judgments about appropriate medical practice:

> the court has to be satisfied that the exponents of the body of opinion relied on can demonstrate that such opinion has a logical basis. In particular, in cases involving, as they so often do, the weighing of risks against benefits, the judge before accepting a body of opinion as being responsible, reasonable or respectable, will need to be satisfied that, in forming their views, the experts have directed their minds to the question of comparative risks and benefits and have reached a defensible conclusion on the matter.[42]

The standard of care to be expected of medical practitioners is not determined by how medical practitioners usually behave, but is designed to do justice between the parties.

Similarly, in *Edward Wong Finance Co Ltd v Johnson Stokes & Master*,[43] the Privy Council ruled that an action done in accordance with an almost universal commercial practice was negligent, as the risks involved were clear. The issue was not what the ordinary person *would* have done, but what she *should* have done. This is the point of referring to the legal construct as an ordinary *reasonable* person. We are not referring to any actual person or statistical average, but are making a judgement about what ordinary persons *should* do.

Hence, the ordinary reasonable person is primarily a reasonable person or, in other words, the ordinary reasonable person is not a person but a value judgement about how persons should behave.[44]

Why, then, do we speak of *ordinary* reasonable persons? 'Ordinary' serves as a reminder that we are not to set the standard by considering how people ought to behave were they saints or heroes with 'the courage of Achilles, the wisdom

---

[41] This kind of case is also explored below in connection with *McHale v Watson* (1966) 115 CLR 199 (HCA).

[42] [1988] AC 232, 241–2 (HL). This judgment purports to deal with issues of causation not relevant here, but the quoted passage is nevertheless relevant to the standard of care. J Fleming, *The Law of Torts*, 9th edn (LBC Information Services, Sydney, 1998) 121 claims that the decision in *Bolam v Friern Hospital Management Committee* [1957] 1 WLR 582 (QBD) means that English courts have no jurisdiction to examine the reasonableness of medical practices, but he appears to admit that this is wrong at 121 n34.

[43] [1984] AC 296 (PC).

[44] In the next section, I argue that the value judgement is one of corrective justice.

of Ulysses or the strength of Hercules',[45] but by contemplating how they ought to behave given the kind of beings that they are. Again, this is a reflection of the fact that the standard is designed to do justice between the parties. To set a standard appropriate for a saint would be to set the standard above that required one to mediate between the interests of the parties.

C. The Objective Standard and Corrective Justice

In the above, I argued that the law adopts an objective standard in order to mediate between the interests of the parties. I contrasted this with a subjective standard that judges the defendant's behaviour entirely in terms of her abilities and strict liability that judges the defendant solely in terms of whether she injured the claimant. In the context in which negligence actions arise (examined below), the subjective standard and strict liability are both inconsistent with corrective justice because they focus on one party in isolation rather than mediate between the interests of the parties. But this does not mean that the objective standard is consistent with corrective justice. In fact, on the face of it, the objective standard also violates corrective justice. I explore this issue now.

Corrective justice demands that the law mediate between the interests of the parties. However, the objective standard appears to *ignore* the actual parties to the case and instead impose a *societal* standard. Consider *Mansfield* again. In that case, an objective test would attempt to do justice by mediating between an imaginary ordinary reasonable driver and an imaginary ordinary reasonable shop owner.[46] But why not do justice by mediating between the disabled driver and the actual shop owner? Why not impose a standard that requires the parties to take each other as they find each other?[47]

The answer is that the objective standard does require the parties to take each other as they find each other. In *Mansfield*, the driver and the shop owner were strangers. The driver, then, was someone who knew nothing of the shop owner's peculiarities. Similarly, the shop owner was someone who knew nothing of the driver's idiosyncrasies. Hence, the parties' idiosyncrasies were normatively irrelevant to the interaction that occurred between them. To require a claimant to adjust to the peculiarities of a defendant when the claimant does not know about those peculiarities would remove the claimant's rights in the name of the defendant's idiosyncrasies. Conversely, to insist that a defendant take into account the peculiarities of a claimant when the defendant does not know about those peculiarities would impose obligations on the defendant in the name of the

---

[45] RE Megarry, *Miscellany-at-Law: A Diversion for Lawyers and Others* (Stevens & Sons Ltd, London, 1955) 260.

[46] As indicated above, while the idiosyncrasies of the claimant are usually not relevant in these cases, the objective standard nevertheless ignores the idiosyncrasies of both parties. See n 27 above.

[47] I am grateful to Paul Myburgh for discussion of these issues.

claimant's idiosyncrasies.[48] To take these peculiarities into account would be to attempt to fuse two ethical judgements rather than to make one judgement in corrective justice. Accordingly, the objective standard does, in fact, reflect corrective justice.

I have argued that the ordinary objective standard must be applied when the defendant does not know about the claimant's peculiarities. I have not argued that the ordinary standard should not apply whenever the defendant does have this knowledge. Rather, as I examine now, the standard should be adjusted when, and only when, the idiosyncrasies of one or both of the parties affect the normative character of the interaction that occurred between them. Knowledge is relevant here, but it is not sufficient to determine when the standard should be adjusted.

D. Adjusting the Objective Standard

The defendant in *McHale v Watson*,[49] a boy of 12 years, threw a piece of sharpened metal at a wooden post. The metal ricocheted off the post and struck the claimant, a girl of similar age, in the eye. It was argued for the defendant that the standard to be expected of the defendant was not that of an ordinary reasonable person but that of an ordinary boy aged 12. A majority of the High Court of Australia accepted this argument, found that the defendant had not fallen below the standard to be expected of a normal 12-year-old boy, and hence ruled that the defendant was not negligent.

Assuming that the principle applied in *McHale v Watson* was correct, the conclusion seems to be that the law is prepared to allow exceptions to the ordinary objective test, at least in respect of children. The questions are whether this is so and, if it is so, why the law permits this.

The decision of the High Court is particularly interesting because the majority accepted that the idiosyncrasies of the defendant must not remove rights from the claimant. However, the majority maintained that they were not relying on an idiosyncrasy in taking into account the defendant's age. As McTiernan ACJ said, 'I do not think that I am required to disregard altogether the fact that the defendant Barry Watson was at the time only twelve years old. In remembering that I am not considering "the idiosyncrasies of the particular person". Childhood is not an idiosyncrasy'.[50] Similarly, Kitto J remarked:

a defendant does not escape liability by proving that he is abnormal in some respect which reduces his capacity for foresight or prudence. . . . The principle is of course applicable to a child. The standard of care being objective, it is no answer for him, any more than it is for an adult, to say that the harm he caused was due to his being

[48] Compare *Rogers v Elliott* 15 NE 768 (Mass SJC 1888).
[49] (1966) 115 CLR 199 (HCA). See also *Mullin v Richards* [1998] 1 WLR 1304 (CA).
[50] (1966) 115 CLR 199, 203 (HCA).

abnormally slow-witted, quick-tempered, absent-minded or inexperienced. But it does not follow that he cannot rely in his defence upon a limitation upon the capacity for foresight or prudence, not as being personal to himself, but as being characteristic of humanity at his stage of development and in that sense normal. By doing so he appeals to a standard of ordinariness, to an objective and not a subjective standard.[51]

The suggestion is that, because childhood is not an idiosyncrasy, taking the age of the defendant into account is consistent with the objective approach of the law.

While this argument is on the right track, it is not itself sufficient to justify the Court's approach. First, the approach is inconsistent with the manner in which the common law judges the behaviour of other classes of person such as the elderly. Although the elderly often pose risks to others additional to those posed by the ordinary reasonable person, as a general rule the standard of care is not adjusted downwards for the aged. Older drivers often suffer from poor eyesight, for example, but this is not taken to lower the standard to be expected of such drivers. This is a particularly telling point, since old age is no more an idiosyncrasy than childhood.[52]

Not all elderly persons suffer from poor eyesight or other disabling conditions, of course. But this is beside the point. The argument under examination is that a lower standard should be applied to children because children *usually* lack certain capacities. Hence, if the reasoning is to carry through, the same should be true of the elderly. Moreover, there are exceptional children whose appreciation of risk far exceeds that normal for their age. Accordingly, the fact that the standard is not lowered for the elderly indicates that, although childhood is a normal aspect of human development, that cannot be the *reason* why the standard of care is lowered for children.

Furthermore, although in one sense childhood is not an idiosyncracy, it is not clear that this is the relevant sense. Certainly, childhood is something we all go through. But what is the significance of that fact for the determination of liability in negligence? We all go through periods of depression and almost everyone gets drunk at least once, but these facts usually do not feature in setting the standard of care for depressed or drunk defendants. Moreover, the fact that children make up a significant proportion of the population is not to the point. Many people are short sighted and stupidity is far from uncommon, yet these are not usually taken into account in setting the standard of care. Perhaps it is simply that we have a soft spot for children?

A further difficulty with the High Court's reasoning is that the standard of care is not always lowered when the defendant is a child of 'tender years'. When the child defendant is engaged in an 'adult activity', she is judged according to the ordinary adult standard. In *McErlean v Sarel*,[53] the parties, who were

---

[51] (1966) 115 CLR 199, 203 (HCA), 213.

[52] Not everyone reaches old age, but this does not make old age an idiosyncrasy. One is unlikely to remark: 'She is nearly 90. How idiosyncratic!'

[53] (1987) 42 DLR (4th) 577 (Ont CA).

unknown to each other, were riding trail bikes when the defendant collided with the claimant causing personal injury. The defendant was 13 years old. However, a unanimous Ontario Court of Appeal maintained that:

> Where a child engages in what may be classified as an 'adult activity', he or she will not be accorded special treatment, and no allowance will be made for his or her immaturity. In those circumstances, the minor will be held to the same standard of care as an adult engaged in the same activity.[54]

Here, then, the standard is not adjusted. Why not?

Alan Linden (quoted in *McErlean v Sarel*[55]) argues that a child who engages in an adult activity is held to the adult standard for reasons of policy. In his view:

> Special rules for children make sense, especially when they are plaintiffs; however, when a young person is engaged in an adult activity which is normally insured, the policy of protecting the child from ruinous liability loses its force. When the rights of adulthood are granted, the responsibilities of maturity should also accompany them. The legitimate expectations of the community are different when a youth is operating a motor vehicle than when he is playing ball. As one American court suggested, juvenile conduct may be expected from children at play, but 'one cannot know whether the operator of an approaching automobile . . . is a minor or adult, and usually cannot protect himself against youthful imprudence even if warned'.[56]

Though Linden cites the American Court[57] in support of his claims, in fact Linden and the American Court give diverging rationales for their conclusions. Linden argues that the standard of care should not be lowered when the child is engaged in an adult activity by reference to social policies relevant to distributive justice: insurance and the legitimate expectations of the community. Conversely, the American Court is focused entirely on the relationship between the parties, on corrective justice. Moreover, Linden's policy argument is confused. Although it is true that a child who engages in an adult activity engages in an activity that is *usually* insured, the child herself will usually be *uninsured*, particularly in cases that do not involve motor vehicles. Hence, the insurance argument cannot function in the way that Linden uses it. Also irrelevant is Linden's observation that, '[w]hen the rights of adulthood are granted, the responsibilities of maturity should also accompany them', as the rights of adulthood have *not* been granted to the child defendant in the relevant cases.

Turning now to the position of the American Court, the argument is that the standard of care should not be affected by the fact that the defendant is a child in such cases, because claimants would not be able to adjust their behaviour in light of the age, lack of experience, etc, of the defendant. To take the defendant's age into account in such a case would fail to do justice between the parties. It

---

[54]   *Ibid*, 592–3.

[55]   *Ibid*, 593.

[56]   AM Linden, *Canadian Tort Law*, 7th edn (Butterworths, Markham, 2001) 145 (citation omitted).

[57]   *Dellwo v Pearson* 107 NW 2d 859, 863 (Minn 1961).

would privilege the position of the defendant. Why should the claimant bear the risks associated with the defendant's youth?

Corrective justice shows that both the rule (that children are to be held to a special standard) and the apparent exception to that rule (that the ordinary adult standard applies when the child is engaged in an adult activity) are part of the same approach. The standard of care is adjusted when applying the ordinary reasonable person standard would be unfair as between the parties. If we focus on the relationship between the parties, the position is that the ordinary standard applies unless one party's peculiarities affect that relationship. This is why the situation of children playing together (*McHale v Watson*) is relevantly different from one in which a child is driving a motor vehicle and collides with a child stranger (*McErlean v Sarel*). When children are playing together, the fact that they are children affects the normative character of their interaction. In such circumstances, the claimant cannot but expect the defendant to behave as a child. It would privilege the position of the claimant to insist on the application of the ordinary adult standard to the child defendant when it was clear to the claimant that the defendant was a child and the claimant engaged with the defendant as such. It would allow the claimant to say to the defendant, as it were, 'though I know we're just kids, you must behave like a grown up'. On the other hand, the fact that the driver of an out of control motor vehicle is a child cannot impact on the relationship between that driver and the stranger with whom she collides.

One important consequence of this discussion is that it is not appropriate to decide whether the adult standard should be imposed on children by asking whether the child was engaged in an adult activity. The issue is not the quality of the defendant's behaviour per se,[58] but the impact of the nature of that behaviour on the *relationship between the parties*.

This is a fortunate conclusion, as the truth is that we have no idea how to distinguish adult from non-adult activities except in the most obvious cases. For instance, is drinking coffee an adult activity? If a child defendant spills coffee over a claimant in a café, which standard is to apply? Is playing 'Cowboys and Indians' with a real bow and arrow an adult activity?[59] Does it matter if the bow and arrow were purchased from a toyshop? In fact, it is not beyond dispute that the defendant in *McErlean v Sarel* was engaged in an adult activity: Is it an adult activity to ride a trail bike? Note that the problem here is not that these cases are difficult—that would be no necessary objection. Rather, the problem is that it is both impossible and artificial to settle them by asking whether the defendant was engaged in an adult activity.

Moreover, what should happen if a child defendant attaches a string to a real bow in the course of a game and shoots a passer-by through the eye with an arrow? Despite its similarly with *McHale v Watson*, in this case it is unjust to

---

[58] Such would make the test subjective.
[59] Compare *Walmsley v Humerick* [1954] 2 DLR 232 (BCSC).

lower the standard of care in favour of the defendant. This is because, unlike in *McHale v Watson* itself, the passer-by and the defendant were strangers, and hence the passer-by could not be expected to take the defendant's age into account and modify his behaviour accordingly. Conversely, imagining the same fact situation with the exception only that the claimant was not a passer-by but was involved in the game, then it would be just to lower the standard.[60] This is because the claimant knew that the defendant was a child and was playing with him as such.

Moreover, not only is the 'adult activity' standard vague, it may also produce inappropriate results. Imagine that an adult claimant lets a child defendant drive his car on a private road and becomes injured because of the child's driving. On the face of it, it would be inappropriate to judge the child by the standard of an ordinary reasonable driver, given the interaction between the claimant and the defendant. I explain this by saying that the defendant's youth and inexperience were relevant to the relationship between the parties. The contemporary approach could achieve the same result by insisting that the defendant was not engaged in an 'adult activity'.[61] But that denudes the 'adult activity' standard of meaning, as it appears plain that driving a car is an adult activity.

The contemporary approach to setting the standard of care for children is partially misconceived. The law as currently understood is that (i) the ordinary reasonable person standard normally applies, (ii) unless the defendant is a child, in which case the standard of care will be lowered, (iii) unless the defendant is engaged in an adult activity. On the view advanced here, (i) the standard of care is that of the ordinary reasonable person, (ii) unless there is something in the relationship between the parties that indicates that the standard should be raised or lowered. As we see immediately below, this is not a special rule for children. The common law's current approach and the view argued for here will usually produce the same result. However, the current approach will do so only by distorting either the concept of an 'adult activity' or another area of the law. Hence, my view is more economical and has greater explanatory power than the alternative.[62]

This explanation of when and why the objective standard is altered is by no means peculiar to cases that involve child defendants. It was supported by Salmon LJ in *Nettleship v Weston* with respect to adult drivers:

---

[60] This is not necessarily to say that the defendant should escape liability. It is just to say that the standard should be lowered.

[61] The alternative is to appeal to the *volenti* defence. However, for reasons explored in ch 10, the defence need not apply in this kind of case. Hence, taking this approach to the standard of care will tend to result in distortion of the *volenti* defence.

[62] I have sometimes encountered the view amongst lawyers that if an idea makes no practical difference, then the idea is unimportant. There are two replies. First, reaching a better understanding of a subject is likely to lead to the elimination of confusion and error. Secondly, and most importantly, the fundamental issue is whether a particular position is *true*, not whether it is useful. Hence, a theory should *never* be rejected simply on the ground that its implementation would make no practical difference. Compare I Kant, *Critique of the Power of Judgment* (trans P Guyer and E Matthews, Cambridge University Press, Cambridge, 2000) 236 [5:363]: 'the question of limited minds: for what is this knowledge useful?'

As a rule, the driver's personal idiosyncrasy is not a relevant circumstance. In the absence of a special relationship what is reasonable care and skill is measured by the standard of competence usually achieved by the ordinary driver. In my judgment, however, there may be special facts creating a special relationship which displaces this standard or even negatives any duty, although the onus would certainly be upon the driver to establish such facts.[63]

Moreover, in *Bolam v Friern Hospital Management Committee*, McNair J said that:

where you get a situation which involves the use of some special skill or competence, then the test whether there has been negligence or not is not the test of the man on the top of a Clapham omnibus, because he has not got this special skill. The test is the standard of the ordinary skilled man exercising *and professing* to have that special skill.[64]

Here, then, the peculiarities of the defendant serve to raise the standard of care. Again, this is not because of the defendant's peculiarities alone, but because those peculiarities are relevant to the relationship between the parties. It is because the expert professes his expertise to the claimant, or because the defendant's expertise is in some other way relevant to the relationship between the parties, that that expertise is relevant in setting the standard of care.[65] Conversely, although surgeons are said to possess steady hands, the care they are expected to take towards strangers while carrying cups of coffee in cafés is that of an ordinary reasonable person.

This discussion is also relevant when considering the idiosyncrasies of the claimant. The claimant in *Paris v Stepney Borough Council*[66] entered the employ of the defendants in 1942. Unknown to the defendants, the claimant was blind in his left eye. In 1946, the defendants conducted a medical examination of the claimant and discovered his disability. In 1947, the claimant was injured when he struck a U-bolt with a hammer, dislodging a shard of metal that entered his right eye causing complete blindness. The claimant argued that the defendants were negligent in failing to provide him with safety glasses.

Importantly, the claimant's argument was not that all employees should have been provided with safety glasses. Rather it was that, given that the claimant was already blind in one eye, the defendants should have taken into account the seriousness of the injury if the other eye was damaged. Accordingly, while it was not negligent to fail to provide glasses to other employees, the seriousness of the potential injury to the claimant meant that the defendant was obliged to take special precautions in relation to the claimant.[67] The House of Lords agreed, apparently implying that the idiosyncrasies of the claimant can impose obligations on the defendant.

---

[63] [1971] 2 QB 691, 703 (CA).

[64] [1957] 1 WLR 582, 586 (QBD) (emphasis added).

[65] This does not mean that the defendant must communicate directly with the claimant as to his expertise.

[66] [1951] AC 367 (HL).

[67] As discussed below, the seriousness of the potential injury to the claimant is relevant in determining the standard of care.

Again, however, it is possible to explain this result in terms of corrective justice. The peculiarity of the claimant was rightly held to have been relevant in determining the standard of care owed by the defendant, as the claimant's idiosyncrasy affected the relationship between the parties. The defendants employed the claimant knowing that he was partially blind, and hence knowing of the increased risk posed to the claimant, without providing the claimant with safety glasses. Of course, the standard should have been raised only if the claimant's blindness did affect the relationship between the parties. Accordingly, the claimant's partial blindness would not have been relevant if the claimant's injury had occurred prior to his medical examination in 1946.[68]

It is important to note that the standard of care is rightly adjusted only if the peculiarities of one of the parties affected the *relationship* between the parties. So, for instance, one cannot insist that one's driving be judged by a lower standard than that of the ordinary reasonable driver simply because one attached a 'learner plate' to one's car. Similarly, though the claimant in *Vaughan v Menlove* knew of the defendant's stupidity, as the parties were not engaged in an activity together, the defendant's stupidity was not relevant to the relationship between the parties. To lower the standard of care in these cases would *unilaterally* remove rights from the claimants in the name of the defendants' idiosyncrasies. On the other hand, if the parties were in a relationship with respect to the activity that led to the claimant's injury, then the standard should be adjusted. Imagine, for instance, that our hypothetical claimant knew about the learner plate and agreed to enter a 'drag race' with the defendant in the light of that knowledge, or that the claimant and defendant in *Vaughan v Menlove* were engaged in collective farming on their properties.

In *McHale v Watson*, McTiernan ACJ described the categories to be applied to children as follows:

(a) Children who are so young as to be manifestly incapable of exercising any of the qualities necessary to the perception of risk. This group would comprise babies and children of very tender years and instead of formulating a standard of care for them it suffices to say that they are incapable of negligence.

(b) Infants who, although they have not yet attained majority, are capable as adults of foreseeing the probable consequences of their actions. In view of the capabilities of this class the standard of care required of them is the same as that required of adults.

(c) Children who come between the extremes indicated in the above categories and whose capacities are infinitely various. The standard of care required of these children is that which it is reasonable to expect of children of like age, intelligence and experience.[69]

---

[68] *Bourhill v Young* [1943] AC 92, 109–10 (HL) (Lord Wright); WVH Rogers, *Winfield and Jolowicz on Tort* (16th edn, Sweet & Maxwell, London, 2002) 200. It may have been possible to argue that the defendants were negligent in not discovering that the claimant was blind in one eye before the examination. This is a different argument, however. The thin skull cases are examined in ch 4.

[69] *McHale v Watson* (1966) 115 CLR 199, 207 (HCA). This is derived from *Restatement of the Law of Torts* (American Law Institute Publishers, St Paul, Minn, 1934) para 283.

McTiernan ACJ rightly made clear that the standard applied in categories (b) and (c) is objective, although it is an adjusted objective standard in (c). McTiernan ACJ also correctly identified that the objective standard is not applied in (a). But this does not mean that (a) involves the application of a subjective standard. Rather, if the defendant fell into category (a) then his behaviour was not an action and he is not a candidate for tort liability. Defendants who fell under (a) lacked volition and were not agents, hence *no standard applies*. This approach is in accordance with that explored in the first section of this chapter.

If the defendant acted, if he is a responsible agent, then the standard applied in the law of negligence judges his behaviour objectively. The court is not interested in the particular child but in the ordinary reasonable child of the relevant age. Similarly, the court is not interested in the defendant doctor but in the ordinary reasonable doctor; not in the defendant driver, but in the ordinary reasonable driver. Only in cases in which the claimant and the defendant are very familiar with each other will this mean that the parties are treated on what appears to be an 'individual basis', and, even then, the parties' idiosyncrasies are relevant only because they determine in part justice between the parties. The law of negligence will never rightly seek to do justice only to the defendant by adopting a subjective standard.

In *McErlean v Sarel*, the Ontario Court of Appeal said that the standard of care applied to children when not engaged in an adult activity '[i] is essentially a subjective test which recognises that the capacities of children are infinitely various and accordingly [ii] treats them on an individual basis and, [iii] out of a public interest in their welfare and protection, [iv] in a more lenient manner than adults'.[70] But we have seen enough to conclude that all four claims are incorrect. First, alterations to the normal objective standard are designed to effect justice between the parties in particular cases. Therefore, the standard remains objective. For that reason, secondly, the defendant is not treated on an individual basis. We are interested in what can be expected of the particular child defendant only when it is relevant to the relationship between the parties. Thirdly, adjusting the ordinary reasonable person standard is designed to do justice between the parties and does not aim to further public policy. Fourthly, the standard is also adjusted for adults, and is adjusted for the same reason as it is adjusted for children.

In light of this discussion of corrective justice and the standard of care, we can see that the correct principle was applied in *McHale v Watson*. But the principle was not applied correctly. There were two related errors. First, Kitto J asked himself: 'did the respondent, in throwing the spike as he did though aware of the proximity of the appellant, do anything which a reasonable boy of his age would not have done in the circumstances . . .?'.[71] Kitto J's answer what that the

---

[70] (1987) 42 DLR (4th) 577 (Ont CA). See also J Fleming, *The Law of Torts,* 9th edn (LBC Information Services, Sydney, 1998) 125–6.

[71] *McHale v Watson* (1966) 115 CLR 199, 215 (HCA).

defendant did not. But Kitto J's characterisation of the question is ambiguous. Was Kitto J imagining a judicially constructed boy of 12 who acts appropriately for a child of that age, or was his Honour imagining the average Australian boy of 12 in the 1960s? The wider judgment makes clear that Kitto J in fact imagined the second. But that is the wrong approach. Unless the defendant's idiosyncratic propensity was relevant to the relationship between the parties, and there is no reason to believe that it was, the question was not whether an ordinary boy of 12 *would* have thrown the piece of metal against the post, but whether an ordinary boy of 12 *would have known that he should not* have thrown the piece of metal against the post. It may well be that the ordinary boy of 12 frequently does what he knows he should not do, but he nevertheless engages in wrongdoing when he does so. Determining the standard of care involves a judgement about whether the defendant had placed the claimant at an unreasonable level of risk. This cannot be answered simply by enquiring into what most persons, or what most persons of a particular kind, do in certain situations.

Accordingly, if it can be expected that an ordinary child of 12 would know that he should not throw sharpened objects at wooden posts in the presence of others, then it is negligent for a boy of 12 to do so. And one can expect children of 12 to know that they should not throw sharpened objects when others are around. Hence, it must be clear that *McHale v Watson* was wrongly decided. As Menzies J pointed out, the result reached by the majority was inconsistent with their own formulation of the correct approach.[72]

The second error is that there is more than a hint of sexism in the judgments of the majority. For instance, Kitto J said:

> It is, I think, a matter for judicial notice that the ordinary boy of twelve suffers from a feeling that a piece of wood and a sharp instrument have a special affinity. To expect a boy of that age to consider before throwing the spike . . . would be, I think, to expect a degree of sense and circumspection which nature ordinarily withholds till life has become less rosy. . . .
>
> [C]hildren, like everyone else, must accept as they go about in society the risks from which ordinary care on the part of others will not suffice to save them. One such risk is that boys of twelve may behave as boys of twelve; and that, sometimes, is a risk indeed.[73]

One wonders what the Court's position would have been if the girl had thrown the dart and hit the boy in the eye.[74]

But, despite drawing criticism, none of this is a problem for corrective justice. Corrective justice does not predict that judges will be free of bias and will

---

[72] *Ibid*, 226.

[73] *Ibid*, 215–16.

[74] However, if there are relevant differences between the behaviour of boys and girls (and men and women), and if these differences are relevant to the relationship between the parties, then the courts are to take them into account. I doubt that this is often, if at all, relevant. Of course, those differences must be real and not merely perceived by judges. In particular, judges should not take judicial notice of such differences. If they exist, expert witnesses should be called to testify to that effect.

always decide matters according to a right-minded application of the correct principles. In this case, corrective justice illuminates the Court's error.

In conclusion: corrective justice provides a unified and compelling explanation for the operation of the objective standard to determine negligence. Instead of seeing the common law's position as the adoption of a standard for reasons of policy coupled with a list of exceptions each motivated by its own policy concerns—a veritable hodgepodge—in the light of corrective justice the apparent exceptions to the objective standard are revealed as entirely principled reflections of the desire of the law to do justice between the parties. The exceptions are not policy-based. They are not even rightly understood as exceptions. No less than the ordinary objective test itself, the 'exceptions' are attempts to treat the parties as equals. The objective standard is an instantiation of corrective justice.

III. REASONABLE CARE

A. The Leading Cases

We have seen that the law imposes an objective test to determine the standard of care. The question we must now ask is: how is the standard determined in particular cases? In this area more than any other, our understanding of the law lives in the shadow of the United States. In one of the most famous negligence cases, *United States v Carroll Towing*,[75] Learned Hand J set out his famous test for determining negligence. His Honour argued that a defendant is negligent if he creates a risk where the probability of the risk occurring (P) multiplied by the seriousness of the risk if it materialises (L) is greater than the burden of eliminating the risk (B). Hence, we have the 'Hand formula': the defendant is negligent if $B<PL$.[76] On this view, then, the aim of the law of negligence is to find the lowest cost avoider.

This formula has had a significant impact on Commonwealth commentators' understandings of the standard of care. For instance, John Fleming claims:

> The gravity of the risk created by the defendant must be weighed against the utility of his conduct. The question is whether 'the game is worth the candle'. If all vehicles travelled at only 10 kilometres an hour there would be fewer accidents, but life would be intolerably slowed down: the additional safety would be procured at too high a price in terms of general convenience. By the same token it is sometimes permissible to take

---

[75] 159 F 2d 169 (US 2nd Cir 1947).

[76] Whether this is actually followed in the US is another matter. For commentary see R W Wright, 'Negligence in the Courts: Introduction and Commentary' (2002) 77 *Chicago-Kent Law Review* 425; R W Wright, 'Justice and Reasonable Care in Negligence Law' (2002) 47 *American Journal of Jurisprudence* 143; R W Wright, 'Hand, Posner, and the Myth of the "Hand Formula"' (2003) 4 *Theoretical Inquiries in Law* 145. Wright argues that this formula is not generally followed in the US and was not usually followed by Learned Hand J himself. Moreover, Wright maintains that the Hand formula was not applied even in *Carroll Towing*.

a 'calculated risk', as a doctor might in undertaking a risky operation or in prescrib-
ing a radical drug to alleviate a condition so serious that it is worth running the risk of
harmful side effects. . . .

The conduct claimed to be negligent may have value to the actor or to someone else;
it may be impelled by selfishness or altruism. In either case, the law will assess its value
against the risk of harm.[77]

Later Fleming also argues:

The negligence concept . . . has a decidedly utilitarian flavour. Indeed, it has been
forcibly argued that the negligence matrix reflects norms of economic efficiency, tending to maximise wealth and minimise costs, by encouraging cost-justified accident
prevention while discouraging excessive investment in safety. If the loss caused by a
given activity to the actor and his victim is greater than its benefit, the activity should
be (and is) discouraged by being labelled negligent and requiring the actor to compensate the victim; if the balance is the other way, the actor may go ahead scot-free.[78]

However, Commonwealth commentators' acceptance of the Hand formula is
ambivalent. In the very next paragraph after the one quoted immediately above,
Fleming insists:

But negligence cannot be reduced to a purely economic equation. True, economic factors are given weight, especially regarding the value of the defendant's activity and the
cost of eliminating the risk. But in general, judicial opinions do not make much of the
cost factor, and for good reasons. For one thing, our legal tradition in torts has strong
roots in an individualistic morality with its focus primarily on interpersonal equity
rather than broader social policy. . . . Secondly, the calculus of negligence includes
some important non-economic values, like health and life, freedom and privacy,
which defy comparison with competing economic values. Negligence is not just a matter of calculating the point at which the cost of injury to victims (that is the damages
payable) exceeds that of providing safety precautions. In particular, avoiding harm is
commonly considered more important than promoting increased public welfare. In
short, the reasonable man is by no means a caricature cold blooded, calculating
Economic Man. Lastly, courts remain sceptical of their ability, let alone that of juries,
to pursue economic analyses; especially as precise data are rarely available, particularly in personal injury cases, to quantify the relevant factors.[79]

Fleming seems to commit himself to the view that the Hand formula does and
does not capture the law of the Commonwealth.

It is particularly interesting that Commonwealth commentators generally
describe the standard of care with only passing reference to what was actually
said in the leading Commonwealth cases on the point. When we return to these,
the source of Fleming's ambivalence becomes clear: in the leading cases
efficiency is not an ingredient in setting the standard of care.

---

[77] J Fleming, *The Law of Torts*, 9th edn (LBC Information Services, Sydney, 1998) 129.
[78] *Ibid*, 131.
[79] *Ibid*, 131–2. For similar statements see S Todd, 'Negligence: Breach of Duty' in S Todd (ed),
The Law of Torts in New Zealand, 3rd edn (Brookers, Wellington, 2001) 395–6.

In *Bolton v Stone*,[80] members of the defendant cricket club were playing against a visiting team when one of the visitors drove the ball out of the ground, over a seven foot high fence, and onto an adjacent, little used, road. The ball struck and injured the claimant. It was estimated that a ball was driven out of the ground on average once every five years. In deciding for the defendants, Lord Reid said:

> In my judgment the test to be applied here is whether the risk of damage to a person on the road was so small that a reasonable man in the position of the appellants, considering the matter from the point of view of safety, would have thought it right to refrain from taking steps to prevent the danger.
>
> In considering that matter I think that it would be right to take into account not only how remote is the chance that a person might be struck, but also how serious the consequences are likely to be if a person is struck, but I do not think that it would be right to take into account the difficulty of remedial measures. If cricket cannot be played on a ground without creating a substantial risk, then it should not be played there at all.[81]

Lord Reid divided risks into two kinds: substantial and extremely small. His Lordship claimed that in determining the size of a particular risk one is to take into account both the likelihood of the risk materialising and the seriousness of the likely injury if the risk materialises. But Lord Reid stated explicitly that the burden of eliminating the risk was irrelevant. Hence, we could express Lord Reid's view as: Risk = PL. However, there is no formula for determining whether a risk is substantial or extremely small, and the burden of eliminating the risk is held to be irrelevant in determining the standard of care. Therefore, *Bolton v Stone* contains no economic test of negligence whatsoever. In fact, it explicitly rejected 'utilitarian considerations'.[82]

Lord Reid reconsidered his position in *The Wagon Mound (No 2)* and adopted a more complicated standpoint.[83] Again, risk was divided into two kinds. But here the distinction was between real risks and fantastic or far fetched (FOFF) risks. Real risks were in turn divided into two subcategories: substantial risks and small risks. On Lord Reid's reconsidered view, a defendant is negligent if he creates a substantial risk, but he is not negligent if he creates a FOFF risk. However, if the defendant creates a small risk then he is liable unless 'he had some valid reason for doing so'.[84] One such reason is the expense of eliminating the risk.[85] Hence, the position can be represented according to Table 3.1.

---

[80] [1951] AC 850 (HL).

[81] *Ibid*, 867.

[82] According to EJ Weinrib, *The Idea of Private Law* (Harvard University Press, Cambridge, Mass, 1995) 151 n 12, utility can be a relevant consideration when the defendant is a public authority. This is because the defendant has a duty to promote the public interest, as a private defendant does not. However, see the discussion of *Watt v Hertfordshire County Council* [1954] 1 WLR 835 (CA) below.

[83] *Overseas Tankship (UK) Ltd v Morts Dock & Engineering Co Ltd (The Wagon Mound, No 2)* [1961] AC 611 (PC).

[84] *Ibid*, 666.

[85] *Ibid*.

Table 3.1: Risk and Negligence

1. Real Risks	1a. Substantial Risks	Defendant is negligent
	1b. Small Risks	Defendant is negligent unless he had good reason not to have eliminated the risk
2. FOFF Risks		Defendant is not negligent.

Though reference is made to the burden of eliminating the risk in *The Wagon Mound (No 2)*, this does not mean that the case imposed an economic test. First, the burden of eliminating the risk is relevant only when the risk is small. For substantial or FOFF risks, economic considerations are entirely irrelevant. Moreover, Lord Reid did not suggest that an economic test should apply to small risks. In order to see this point, it will help to examine Lord Reid's reinterpretation of *Bolton v Stone*.

In *The Wagon Mound (No 2)*, Lord Reid recognised that the risk created by the cricket club in *Bolton v Stone* was not FOFF. It was extremely small, but nevertheless not fantastic or far fetched. Hence, in the language of *The Wagon Mound (No 2)*, the risk was real. However, because the chance of injury was 'infinitesimal',[86] it was classed as a small rather than a substantial risk. Hence, the defendants could escape liability if they had good reason for failing to avoid the risk. In *The Wagon Mound (No 2)*, Lord Reid seems to have been of the view that the defendants in *Bolton v Stone* could have avoided creating the risk to the claimant only at considerable expense. Accordingly, the defendants had good reason for not eliminating the risk and were rightly found not to have been negligent. But it is also clear that Lord Reid believed that the burden on the defendant had to be high to justify this conclusion. Crucially, although the risk to the claimant was small because of the 'infinitesimal' probability of an injury occurring, the burden needed to be high—ie *much larger than infinitesimal*—for the defendant to escape liability. It was not sufficient that the burden was merely higher than PL. Therefore, even with respect to the creation of small risks, negligence may be found even if B≥PL.

In light of the above, there are two reasons why *The Wagon Mound (No 2)* cannot be said to contain an economic test. First, the assessment of risk, and of the burden when appropriate, is casuistic rather than formulaic.[87] It relies on judgement rather than measurement. Secondly, the case does not suggest a search for the lowest cost avoider. If the defendant creates a substantial risk, then he is negligent despite the fact that the claimant may have been the lowest

---

[86] *Ibid.*

[87] EJ Weinrib, *The Idea of Private Law* (Harvard University Press, Cambridge, Mass, 1995) 151. Some have argued that the assessment is purely intuitive and relies on the personal beliefs of the judge. See eg WVH Rogers, *Winfield and Jolowicz on Tort,* 16th edn (Sweet & Maxwell, London, 2002) 190; S Todd, 'Negligence: Breach of Duty' in S Todd (ed), *The Law of Torts in New Zealand,* 3rd edn (Brookers, Wellington, 2001) 384. This view is mistaken. It is discussed in detail with respect to remoteness of damage in ch 4.

cost avoider. Similarly, if the defendant creates only a FOFF risk, then the defendant cannot be liable even if he is the lowest cost avoider. Finally, if the defendant creates a small risk, then he will be liable unless the burden of eliminating the risk is high—not merely higher than the risk. This will often result in a finding of negligence when the claimant is the lowest cost avoider.

Consequently, neither *Bolton v Stone* nor *The Wagon Mound (No 2)* contains economic tests for determining negligence. Neither is concerned with efficiency. The ubiquitous claim that the 'gravity of the risk created by the defendant must be weighed against the utility of his conduct'[88] is, as Richard Wright has argued, an 'academic myth'[89] inconsistent with the leading cases.

Note, however, that this does not mean that all concerns thought to be ones of distributive justice are irrelevant. Consider, again, an example suggested by Fleming. 'If all vehicles travelled at only 10 kilometres an hour there would be fewer accidents, but life would be intolerably slowed down: the additional safety would be procured at too high a price in terms of general convenience'.[90] The conclusion that Fleming wants—that what we regard as safe driving is not negligent—can be reached without appeal to the 'general convenience'. On the view presented here, while it is negligent to create substantial risks while driving, the creation of less significant risks should not be regarded as negligent, because of the burden that they would impose on the defendant. Hence, Fleming's desired conclusion is justified by corrective rather than distributive justice. As indicated earlier, the general problem is that corrective justice has been ignored by most English speaking theorists for centuries, so that most arguments based on corrective justice appear to the commentator to be grounded in distributive justice. But this bad habit must be unlearnt.[91]

At this point, it is useful to clarify the nature of the risk in question. The court is interested in the *foreseeable* risk to the claimant, not in the actual risk.[92] The risk is to be gauged with reasonable foresight, not hindsight. Hence, when one is assessing the risk as substantial, small or FOFF, the question is not how large the risk was in fact, but how large it would have appeared to a reasonable person. This is unsurprising, given that we are asking whether the defendant has been negligent. It cannot be negligent to create a FOFF risk, even if the actual—although unknown and not reasonably knowable—chance of that risk materialising was very high.

---

[88] J Fleming, *The Law of Torts,* 9th edn (LBC Information Services, Sydney, 1998) 129.

[89] R W Wright, 'Hand, Posner, and the Myth of the "Hand Formula"' (2003) 4 *Theoretical Inquiries in Law* 145, 273. Note that Wright primarily discusses case law in the US, the ostensible home of the Hand Formula.

[90] Fleming, above n88, 129.

[91] See A Beever, 'Justice and Punishment in Tort: A Comparative Theoretical Analysis' in R Grantham and C Rickett (eds), *Justifying Remedies in Private Law* (Cambridge University Press, Cambridge, forthcoming 2007).

[92] As HM Hurd and MS Moore, 'Negligence in the Air' (2002) 3 *Theoretical Inquiries in Law* 333 point out, if the claimant was injured then the actual risk was always a certainty, while if the claimant was not injured it was certain not to happen. Hence (despite Hurd and Moore's claims to the contrary), the actual risk cannot be relevant.

The decision in *Bolton v Stone*, even as reinterpreted in *The Wagon Mound (No 2)*, has generated a large amount of criticism. Chief among the allegations are the following three claims: the decision (i) is contrary to principle, (ii) neglects the position of the claimant and (iii) was inappropriately motivated by a desire to protect England's national, and their Lordships' favourite, sport. For instance, in *Wyong Shire Council v Shirt*,[93] Murphy J said that the standard of care is correctly set in terms of foreseeability alone and remarked:

> In other areas, different considerations have prevailed. An extreme instance is the decision in *Bolton v Stone* . . . that suggests that if the chances of harm are very slight, the event is not foreseeable. Policy considerations concerning English cricket seem to have been paramount in that case which, in my opinion, is not a guideline for negligence law in Australia.[94]

First, however, it is quite clear that Lord Reid did *not* say that 'if the chances of harm are very slight, the event is not foreseeable'. Rather, his Lordship ruled that if the chances of harm were slight then the defendant was not negligent, even though the event was foreseeable.

Secondly, the claim that their Lordships were concerned to protect cricket is a remarkably uncharitable accusation in this case.[95] Is it really negligent to passers-by to play cricket on a ground when on average a ball is driven out of the ground once every five years onto a little used road? As Lord Reid said, 'the chance of [an accident] happening in the foreseeable future was infinitesimal. A mathematician given the data could have worked out that it was only likely to happen once in so many thousand years.'[96] Surely, judicial and academic rhetoric aside, no one believes that the creation of such a risk is negligent in the circumstances. Who would say to the defendants, 'you should stop playing cricket. Don't you realise that there is a million to one chance that you might hit a passer-by with the ball?'

Moreover, if the cricket club was negligent in allowing cricket to be played on its ground, then the players must also have been negligent. When playing cricket, one cannot but be aware of the possibility of injury to bystanders, however small. Hence, if negligence equals the creation of a merely foreseeable risk, then playing cricket almost anywhere is negligent. But few would regard that as accurate.

This reasoning applies outside the playing of cricket. Football players know that the ball may escape from the field of play and that a bystander may trip on

---

[93] *Wyong Shire Council v Shirt* (1980) 146 CLR 40 (HCA). See also T Weir, *Tort Law* (Oxford University Press, Oxford, 2002) 61 who claims that the case was designed to preserve 'British [*sic*] manhood'.

[94] *Wyong Shire Council v Shirt* (1980) 146 CLR 40, 49–50 (HCA). See also D Lloyd, 'Note' (1951) 14 MLR 499.

[95] *Miller v Jackson* [1977] QB 966 (CA) is a different story, but there it would be impossible to miss Lord Denning's fondness for the game or the impact of that fondness on the outcome of the case.

[96] *Overseas Tankship (UK) Ltd v Morts Dock & Engineering Co Ltd (The Wagon Mound, No 2)* [1961] AC 611, 666 (PC).

it and sprain an ankle. But it does not follow that football players are negligent to play football.[97] When one chooses to drive one's car, one knows that no matter how careful one tries to be, another may be injured. Again, it does not follow that any accident caused by driving is caused by negligence. Moreover, this discussion must also be relevant to the defence of contributory negligence. When one walks down the road, one knows of the possibility of being injured by passing vehicles, falling objects, or other users of the footpath. But this does not mean that when one suffers a foreseeable injury caused by another's negligence, one must have been contributorily negligent.

The argument here is *not* that liability would be overly extensive were we to adopt Murphy J's understanding of negligence (that would be an argument of policy). Rather, the point is that, *contra* Murphy J, it is not plausible to contend that these examples involve negligence. Therefore, negligence cannot be the creation of a merely foreseeable risk.

In *Bolton v Stone*, the House of Lords said that negligence was the creation of a substantial risk. In *The Wagon Mound (No 2)*, the Privy Council said that it was the creation of a real risk—ie not a FOFF risk—unless the risk was small, in which case the defendant was innocent if he had good reason not to eliminate the risk. Far from being the unprincipled attempt to protect cricket clubs, the decisions are remarkably successful elucidations of the nature of negligence and reasonable care.

Although the defendants in *Bolton v Stone* succeeded in the House of Lords, they had already paid damages to the claimant after the claimant had won in the Court of Appeal. Moreover, the defendants made no attempt to recover this money. Harold Luntz and David Hambly ask, 'What does this show about the relationship of the law of negligence and the general public sentiment as to when compensation should be paid?'[98] Reading between the lines, the suggestion seems to be that the decision of the House of Lords in *Bolton v Stone* was contrary to public sentiment and must, therefore, be motivated by policies such as the perceived desirability of cricket.

If this is Luntz and Hambly's intention, then their claim is unfounded. We can agree that it was morally *desirable* for the cricket club to compensate the claimant for her injuries. But that point is irrelevant. The question is whether it was morally *obligatory* for the defendants to do so. If one thinks—as I suspect critics of *Bolton v Stone* do think—that it would have been right to require the cricket club, *but not the player who struck the ball*, to compensate the claimant, then this can have nothing to do with negligence. It was no less foreseeable to the player than to the club that someone would be injured.

The feeling that the club should pay may arise from one of two sources. First, it may be based in distributive justice. The idea is that a wealthy defendant has

---

[97] Compare *Hilder v Associated Portland Cement Manufacturers Ltd* [1961] 1 WLR 1434 (QBD) where the defendant created a real risk of injury in a similar case.

[98] H Luntz and D Hambly, *Torts: Cases and Commentary*, 4th edn (Butterworths, Sydney, 1995) 196–7.

caused injury to a less wealthy claimant and so the defendant should compensate the claimant. But this has nothing to do with whether the defendants placed the claimant at an unreasonable risk. To say that the defendants were negligent simply in order to achieve distributive justice in this manner would be pretence. The second possible source of the intuition that the defendant should compensate the claimant is the notion that the defendant created the risk, and hence should be responsible for the consequences that flow from the risk. Certainly, it is said, the balance of justice lies with the claimant who did nothing to create the risk. But this argument fails for two closely related reasons.

First, the argument cannot distinguish the defendant cricket club from the players. If the cricket club can be sued because it created a risk that materialised, then so can the player who struck the ball, the bowler and anyone who contributed to the game being played. This also means that the cricket club would be able to claim contribution from such persons if sued by the claimant. Secondly, the idea that the claimant did nothing to create the risk is false. She created the risk to herself by walking past the cricket ground. Moreover, that risk was foreseeable. Hence, on the approach under examination, the balance of justice does not lie with the claimant.

It may be possible to refine the argument somewhat by maintaining that the balance of justice lies with the claimant because the injury, rather than the risk, was caused by the defendant.[99] But the same reply can be made: the claimant caused her injury by walking down the lane.[100] In any case, the argument cannot be used here, as it is an argument for strict liability. In negligence, liability requires both *causa* and *culpa*.

In consequence, the opposition to *Bolton v Stone* is not well reasoned. The position seems to be that the defendants should compensate the claimant because they can afford to, or because they caused the claimant's injury. Neither notion has any place in the law of negligence.

B. The Standard of Care and Corrective Justice

The Hand Formula is clearly inconsistent with corrective justice.[101] It does not attempt to do justice between the parties, but defines negligence as acting against society's interests. Hence, if a person's activity has high social value, the Hand Formula permits, and in the economic sense encourages, the creation of risk to others. If one is conducting a very risky activity that is also highly socially

---

[99] See eg RA Epstein, 'A Theory of Strict Liability' (1973) 2 *The Journal of Legal Studies* 151.
[100] A Ripstein, *Equality, Responsibility, and the Law* (Cambridge University Press, Cambridge, 1999) 32–42.
[101] EJ Weinrib, *The Idea of Private Law* (Harvard University Press, Cambridge, Mass, 1995) 148. Compare SR Perry, 'Responsibility for Outcomes, Risk, and the Law of Torts' in GJ Postema (ed), *Philosophy and the Law of Torts* (Cambridge University Press, Cambridge, 2001).

beneficial, then the Hand Formula will justify imposing that risk on other individuals. This would involve injustice from the perspective of corrective justice.

From that perspective, the fundamental problem with the Hand Formula is that it holds the rights of the claimant hostage to the interests of society. The objection to this is not that this is necessarily bad for the claimant. The Hand Formula protects some claimants more and some less than do the principles in *Bolton v Stone* and *The Wagon Mound (No 2)*. Moreover, all may be better off in terms of welfare in the long run under a system that imposed the Hand Formula than under the principles in *Bolton v Stone* and *The Wagon Mound (No 2)*.[102] Rather, the objection is that the Hand Formula treats the entitlements of the claimant, and hence also the freedom of action of the defendant, as a product of social convenience. The Hand Formula, then, is an example of treating the parties as a means to an end: the parties are viewed as methods by means of which communal interests can be achieved. This *may* be justified in terms of distributive justice,[103] but it is fundamentally incompatible with corrective justice.

On the other hand, the English approach, as exemplified by *Bolton v Stone* and *The Wagon Mound (No 2)*, is consistent with corrective justice. There, the issue is whether the defendant created an unreasonable level of risk to the claimant. What counts as reasonable is determined by examining the relationship between the parties, without recourse to the interests of those outside that relationship: this is less clear in *The Wagon Mound (No 2)* than it is in *Bolton v Stone* due to the relevance in the former of the burden of eliminating the risk when the risk is small. Perhaps, in its reference to the burden, *The Wagon Mound (No 2)* is in part a concession to the Hand Formula and a departure from corrective justice?

However, *The Wagon Mound (No 2)* can be interpreted in two ways, depending on how small risks are distinguished from substantial risks. Commonwealth commentators tend to read the case as opening up a wide new categorisation of risk—small risks—that would have counted as substantial risks under *Bolton v Stone*. On this view, *The Wagon Mound (No 2)* allows defendants to escape liability for creating such risks if they can show that the burden of eliminating the risk was high. Hence, *The Wagon Mound (No 2)* seems more defendant friendly than *Bolton v Stone*. The fact that the risk created by the defendant in *Bolton v Stone*—there categorised as 'extremely small'—is described in *The Wagon Mound (No 2)* as 'small' lends *some* support to this. However, in *The Wagon Mound (No 2)* itself, Lord Reid suggested that the risk created by the defendant in *Bolton v Stone* was 'infinitesimal'.[104]

---

[102] L Kaplow and S Shavell, 'Fairness Verses Welfare' (2001) 114 *Harvard Law Review* 961.

[103] Compare J Rawls, *A Theory of Justice: Revised Edition* (Belknap, Cambridge, Mass, 1999) 19–24.

[104] *Overseas Tankship (UK) Ltd v Morts Dock & Engineering Co Ltd (The Wagon Mound, No 2)* [1961] AC 611, 666 (PC).

Many risks that are extremely small, and hence could not give rise to negligence under *Bolton v Stone*, are not FOFF. Accordingly, such risks count as small risks under *The Wagon Mound (No 2)* and hence may attract liability. Therefore, although it benefits defendants that courts consider the burden of eliminating the risk when the risk is small, this is offset by the fact that the creation of extremely small though not FOFF risks may, if not accompanied by a good excuse, generate liability. Overall, then, *The Wagon Mound (No 2)* is neither more nor less defendant friendly than *Bolton v Stone*.

Moreover, in light of the judgment in *The Wagon Mound (No 2)*, it can be seen that *Bolton v Stone* suffered from two related flaws. The first was that it regarded the creation of an extremely small but foreseeable risk as reasonable even when that risk could easily have been eliminated. This fails to show sufficient concern for the position of the claimant, and therefore fails to achieve corrective justice. (Here *Bolton v Stone* seems too defendant friendly.) Secondly, *Bolton v Stone* held that a person who creates a small risk is negligent, even if it would have been extremely difficult to eliminate that risk. But this fails to show sufficient concern for the defendant's interests. (Here *Bolton v Stone* seems too claimant friendly.) Hence, the overall problem with *Bolton v Stone* is not that it is too defendant or too claimant friendly, but that it is not sufficiently subtle in achieving justice between the parties.

The Wagon Mound (No 2) better instantiates corrective justice than *Bolton v Stone* because it more accurately reflects the moral dimensions of the relationship between the parties. Both cases agree that the creation of a substantial risk cannot be justified, while the creation of a FOFF risk needs no excuse. But only *The Wagon Mound (No 2)* holds correctly that a defendant who creates an extremely small but foreseeable and easily eliminated risk of injury to a claimant wrongs the claimant if that risk materialises. The chance of a child drowning in a fenced swimming pool with the gate left open for only a few hours is extremely small. Nevertheless, given the low burden of preventing this risk—closing the gate, installing spring hinges, etc—the homeowner wrongs the child if she drowns in his pool.[105] Conversely, provided the category of small risks is appropriately (narrowly) defined, it is not wrong to expose another to a small risk when the burden of eliminating that risk is high. It is not negligent to play cricket on a well-designed ground, although that will expose others to small risks.

The approach of the Privy Council in *The Wagon Mound (No 2)* is more in accord with corrective justice than that in *Bolton v Stone*. Consequently, in the remainder of the book I take the notion of an unreasonable risk to be defined in terms of *The Wagon Mound (No 2)*. That is, for the purpose of this book, an *unreasonable risk* is either a substantial risk or a small risk created without good

---

[105] In this case, the case could not be brought by the child but would be taken by others because of the wrong to the child. For reasons explored in more detail in ch 1, wrongful death actions must be seen as parasitic on the wrong the defendant committed against the deceased. This is because there is no violation of the claimant's rights in these cases.

reason. Further, I refer to risks that are not unreasonable as FOFF risks. Although this is not strictly accurate, as some risks are neither FOFF nor unreasonable (ie those that are small when the burden of eliminating them was high), calling all these risks FOFF avoids the awkwardness of having to refer to risks that materialised in injury to a claimant as reasonable.

C. Summary

It is not negligent to create a FOFF risk. A claimant cannot reasonably expect a defendant to protect him from risks that the defendant could not, as a reasonable person, foresee. Conversely, it is negligent to create substantial risks. A defendant cannot reasonably expect a claimant to accept the imposition of such risks. Finally, the creation of a small risk is negligent unless there was good reason for creating that risk. This is in order to balance the interests of the parties. Determining the standard of care is casuistic, not formulaic. It requires judgement about the degree of risk created by the defendant. The aim is to take into account equally the interests of both parties. Moreover, the judgement is neither consequentialist nor anti-consequentialist. Although the predominant concern is for the right of the claimant to be free of injury that results from real risks, the court takes into account consequences to the parties in balancing their interests.[106]

D. Problematic Cases

I do not claim that the outcomes of all cases, or the reasoning used in all cases, is consistent with corrective justice. However, there are fewer cases incompatible with corrective justice than one might expect. For instance, in *Morris v West Hartlepool Steam Navigation Co*, the claimant suffered personal injury when he fell through an uncovered and unfenced deck hatch. The claimant argued that the defendants were negligent in failing to cover or fence the hatch, as it would have been easy to do so. Lord Reid said:

> it is the duty of an employer, in considering whether some precaution should be taken against a foreseeable risk, to weigh on the one hand the magnitude of the risk, the likelihood of an accident happening and the possible seriousness of the consequences if an accident does happen, and on the other hand the difficulty and expense and any other disadvantage of taking the precaution.
>
> Here the . . . consequences of any accident were almost certain to be serious. On the other hand, there was very little difficulty, no expense and no other disadvantage in taking an effective precaution. Once it is established that danger was foreseeable and,

---

[106] Incidentally, this does not conflict with the notion that tort law is broadly Kantian. See eg A Wood, *Kant's Ethical Thought* (Cambridge University Press, Cambridge, 1999) 306–9.

therefore, that the matter should have been considered before the accident, it appears to me that a reasonable man weighing these matters would have said that the precaution clearly ought to be taken.[107]

It would be too quick to conclude that Lord Reid said that in every case the 'gravity of the risk created by the defendant must be weighed against the utility of his conduct'.[108] First, the burden is relevant only when the risk is not FOFF. Secondly, and crucially, Lord Reid said that an employer has a duty to consider the relevant costs. His Lordship did not say that an employer is innocent if the cost of the precautions exceeds the cost of the accident, if B<PL. That claim would be quite different, and much more radical, than the one made by Lord Reid, and any tendency to 'read it in' to Lord Reid's judgment should give us pause. In *Morris*, the claimant was exposed to a small risk where the burden of eliminating the risk was low.[109] Accordingly, the House of Lords accepted that the defendant was negligent. This decision is quite consistent with the later judgment of the Privy Council in *The Wagon Mound (No 2)*. There is no conflict with corrective justice here.

Another example is *Wyong Shire Council v Shirt*. After a very considered and accurate discussion of *The Wagon Mound (No 2)*, Mason J concluded:

> In deciding whether there has been a breach of the duty of care the tribunal of fact must first ask itself whether a reasonable man in the defendant's position would have foreseen that his conduct involved a risk of injury to the plaintiff or to a class of persons including the plaintiff. If the answer be in the affirmative, it is then for the tribunal of fact to determine what a reasonable man would do by way of response to the risk. The perception of the reasonable man's response calls for a consideration of the magnitude of the risk and the degree of the probability of its occurrence, along with the expense, difficulty and inconvenience of taking alleviating action and any other conflicting responsibilities which the defendant may have. It is only when these matters are balanced out that the tribunal of fact can confidently assert what is the standard of response to be ascribed to the reasonable man placed in the defendant's position.[110]

Stephen Todd comments, '[s]o on the one hand the reasonable person takes account of the probability of harm and its potential gravity and on the other the social value of the activity in question and the burden of precautionary measures. The judge needs to balance these factors'.[111] But, in light of the above, this reading of Mason J's judgment begs the question in favour of the utilitarian approach. Mason J said that a reasonable man would consider 'the expense, difficulty and inconvenience of taking alleviating action', but his Honour did not

[107] [1956] AC 552 (HL) 574–5
[108] J Fleming, *The Law of Torts*, 9th edn (LBC Information Services, Sydney, 1998) 129.
[109] *Morris v West Hartlepool Steam Navigation Co*, above n107.
[110] *Wyong Shire Council v Shirt* (1980) 146 CLR 40, 47–8 (HCA).
[111] S Todd, 'Negligence: Breach of Duty' in S Todd (ed), *The Law of Torts in New Zealand*, 3rd edn (Brookers, Wellington, 2001) 396. Todd goes on to argue that the balancing is impressionistic only.

say that this should be balanced against the risk to the claimant in some utilitarian fashion. Again, the crucial claim is being 'read into' the judgment. As a
general rule, commentators are too quick to reach conclusions on such matters.
Particularly in its wider context, Mason J's judgment is quite consistent with
The Wagon Mound (No 2).

A more difficult case is the decision of the English Court of Appeal in *Watt v
Hertfordshire County Council*.[112] Although this case was decided before *The
Wagon Mound (No 2)* and so could, for our purposes, be ignored, it is nevertheless instructive to consider it. The London Transport Executive lent a jack
for moving heavy objects to a fire station for which the defendant was responsible. As the jack was rarely used, the fire station possessed only one vehicle
designed to transport it and that vehicle was elsewhere when the station received
an emergency call concerning a woman who had been trapped under a heavy
vehicle. The scene of the emergency was 200 or 300 yards from the fire station.
The station's commanding officer ordered that the jack be placed on another
truck and taken to the scene along with a number of firemen. While on route,
the driver of the truck had to brake forcefully. The jack moved inside the truck
and injured the claimant fireman. The Court of Appeal unanimously ruled that
the claimant could not recover, as he was not the victim of negligence.

The reasoning of Singleton and Morris LJJ is consistent with both *Bolton v
Stone* and *The Wagon Mound (No 2)*. Their Lordships argued that the risk was
small and the burden high. This seems plausible, given the need to rescue the
third party and the fact that the rescue was to take place only 200 or 300 yards
from the fire station.[113]

The judgment of Denning LJ is a rather different story:

> It is well settled that in measuring due care one must balance the risk against the mea-
> sures necessary to eliminate the risk. To that proposition there ought to be added this.
> One must balance the risk against the end to be achieved. If this accident had occurred
> in a commercial enterprise without any emergency, there could be no doubt that the
> servant would succeed. But the commercial end to make profit is very different from
> the human end to save life or limb. The saving of life or limb justifies taking consider-
> able risk, and I am glad to say there have never been wanting in this country men of
> courage ready to take those risks, notably in the fire service.[114]

As usual, in this passage Denning LJ latches onto a deeply held intuition in justifying his position. The fact that the defendant exposed the claimant to the risk
of injury in order to rescue a third party should make a difference, it seems.

Denning LJ's argument was that the defendant could not be liable in negligence because the truck was used to rescue a third party. But that is inadequate.

---

[112] [1954] 1 WLR 835 (CA).

[113] I say that it *seems* plausible because, for reasons discussed below, it is actually false. The point
here, however, is that the reasoning of their Lordships was consistent with corrective justice, even if
they adopted false premises.

[114] *Watt v Hertfordshire County Council* [1954] 1 WLR 835, 838 (CA). See also J Fleming, *The
Law of Torts*, 9th edn (LBC Information Services, Sydney, 1998) 129.

The fact that the commanding officer had a good motive does not justify the creation of unreasonable risks to others. This is particularly clear in relation to this case. As the scene of the accident was only 200 or 300 yards from the fire station, there appears to have been no need for the claimant to have travelled in the truck, and hence there was no need to expose him to the risk.[115] It was necessary to transport the jack on the truck, but the claimant could have been ordered to *run* the 200 or 300 yards to the scene of the accident. Surely, therefore, there was negligence in this case.

This reply to Denning LJ is available only because the scene of the emergency was so close to the fire station. The claimant could not have been expected to run to the scene of an accident five miles away. But transporting the jack in the truck for five miles would likely have exposed the claimant to a *significant* risk of injury, and hence also would have been negligent.

Moreover, the reasoning in the case—and our intuitive reactions to it—is confused because we are dealing with firemen who have consented to take on employment that exposes them to certain risks. Hence, the defendant's liability may rightly be negatived by the claimant's consent to undergo certain risks.[116] This is why it makes a difference, as Denning LJ recognised, that the claimant was a fireman (although it does not make the difference Denning LJ thought it made). There is a world of difference between imposing a risk on a party who knows of it and chooses to accept it and imposing the risk on a bystander. Moreover, there are features of the relationship between the defendant and claimant in this case that affect their relationship, due to the nature of the claimant's employment. This alters the standard of care without any appeal to policy. Denning LJ's premature leap to policy obscures all of this.

Imagine, then, that the risk created was not to a fireman but to a member of the public and that the risk was significant. Imagine that *A* is driving an injured person, *B*, to hospital at excessive speed. *A* is doing so in the reasonable belief that *B* requires immediate treatment to save his life. *A* collides with and seriously injures *C*, a pedestrian. One is likely to feel much less comfortable with the assertion that *A* was not negligent as 'one must balance the risk against the end to be achieved'. One may or may not think that *A* acted unethically, but one cannot be comfortable with the assertion that *C* should bear this uncompensated loss because *A* had good reasons for what he did. Why should *C* pay for *B's* rescue?

---

[115] However, Singleton LJ said at 369 that the claimant held the jack while it was being transported. Perhaps, then, it was necessary for the claimant to ride in the vehicle in order to hold the jack in place because there was no other reasonable way of transporting it. It is impossible to discern this for certain from the judgment. It seems, however, that the claimant held the jack, not to prevent damage to the vehicle or to the jack (which in any case would not be sufficient to show that the defendant was not negligent), but to prevent injury to himself. See also *ibid*, 210–11. Note also that I am assuming that the claimant was ordered to travel in the truck. If that was not so, then either the claimant did not know of the risk and should have been warned by his employer or had consented to run the risk and was thus *volens*. See ch 10.

[116] See ch 10.

Denning LJ himself argued that the creation of such risk would be negligent:

> I quite agree that fire engines, ambulances and doctors' cars should not shoot past the traffic lights when they show a red light. That is because the risk is too great to warrant the incurring of the danger. It is always a question of balancing the risk against the end.[117]

But this reasoning must be mistaken. The taking of very significant risks may be justified if the question is one of balancing the risk against the end. Imagine an ambulance driver with a patient or patients who must be rushed to hospital. The ambulance driver may reason rightly that shooting past red traffic lights is justified in terms of balancing the risk against the end, as the end is the saving of a life or lives. Recall that the point is not that A did something unethical. Rather, the question is whether C must bear the consequences of *A's* driving.[118] In such circumstances, Denning LJ insisted that running the red light is negligent, but it can be justified in utilitarian terms. Hence, even Denning LJ balks at his own official conception of negligence.

Note also that emergency vehicles raise special issues according to the ordinary principles of law. Driving in a particular manner may be negligent for an ordinary driver, although it may not be when a specially trained driver is using a specially painted vehicle that is equipped with flashing lights and a siren. The point of the training, the paint, the lights and the siren is, of course, to reduce the risk involved. Hence, what may count as the imposition of a substantial risk by one driver may not when another is driving an emergency vehicle using flashing lights and a siren. Once it is recognised that the threshold for the creation of a substantial risk is higher for those driving emergency vehicles than for others, much of the intuitive appeal of the claim that a driver of an emergency vehicle should not be held liable for the creation of substantial risks evaporates.

Moreover, if one believes that drivers of emergency vehicles require more protection from the law of negligence than do ordinary drivers, then it is misleading to regard the treatment of emergency vehicles as an example of ordinary principle, as did Denning LJ. In both law and ordinary perception, the treatment of emergency vehicles is *exceptional*, reflected in the fact that they enjoy special statutory exceptions to general rules. Frankly, if we think that drivers of emergency vehicles should be able to expose persons to substantial risks without incurring liability, that should be entrenched in statute.[119]

Despite initial appearances, then, the standard of care owed by and to members of the emergency services is better understood in terms of corrective justice than in terms of utilitarian calculation.[120] Tort law in this area may or may not advance social policy, but its standards are not ones of social policy.

---

[117] *Watt v Hertfordshire County Council* [1954] 1 WLR 835 (QBD) 838

[118] Again, this indicates the irrelevance of ethics for the law of negligence.

[119] See eg s 4A(7) Motor Traffic Act 1909 (NSW); s 37 Transport Act 1949 (NZ).

[120] Recall, however, that corrective justice does not ignore consequences. It is not in that sense anti-consequentialist.

E. Conclusion

It is commonly believed that the standard of care consists of a mishmash of rules that apply to particular cases, each motivated by a unique set of policies. It is widely accepted that the basis for all this is utilitarian, although Commonwealth commentators do not consistently hold this view. On the contrary, I have suggested that seeing the standard of care in terms of corrective justice allows one to comprehend it as a unified field of enquiry. Hence, the explanatory power of corrective justice exceeds by orders of magnitude other attempts to capture the setting of the standard of care.

IV. STRICT LIABILITY AND CORRECTIVE JUSTICE

In *Vaughan v Menlove*, the defendant built a rick of hay next to the claimant's barn. The rick caught fire and the fire spread to the barn. The claimant's allegation—which was accepted, as we saw above—was that the defendant should not have built the rick of hay where he did, given the danger to the claimant's barn. Note, then, that the claimant's allegation related to the defendant's use of his own property on his own land. Consider also a standard traffic accident case involving the collision of two vehicles. Here, both parties are using their property in a public space when one causes injury to the other. In the above, I have claimed that in these circumstances, which we may call 'the circumstances of negligence', an objective standard is appropriate because it gives equal weight to the interests of the parties in determining whether the defendant wrongfully injured the claimant.[121]

But the situation is different where the allegation is not that the defendant was inappropriately using his own property or some publicly available property, but where the complaint is that the defendant was using the claimant's property. Here, fairness between the parties dictates that the defendant acted rightly only if his use of the claimant's property was with the claimant's consent.[122]

This explains why the torts of trespass require intention but neither fault nor damage. I can be liable for converting your vehicle only if I intend to do something with it that indicates that I have asserted possession of the vehicle, because without that intention I cannot be said to be using your property. And if I am using your property without your consent, then I wrong you even if I am not at fault for using your property (for instance, I have good reason to believe that I have the authority to use it[123]) and I do not damage it. Your property is yours and I must use it only with your consent.

---

[121] For a more in-depth, theoretical analysis, see EJ Weinrib, *The Idea of Private Law* (Harvard University Press, Cambridge, Mass, 1995) 179–83.

[122] This consent can sometimes be implied. There are also, of course, defences available, such as necessity.

[123] See, eg, *Wilson v New Brighton Panelbeaters Ltd* [1989] 1 NZLR 74 (CA).

The same argument applies even more obviously to the torts of trespass to the person. Fairness between persons indicates that one person is entitled to use the body of another only with that other's consent. To adopt an objective standard here would imply that we are allowed to use others' bodies as long as we are careful in doing so. This is not fair as between the parties.[124]

Although it would take a full scale investigation of the torts of trespass and other instances of strict liability to bring these points out fully, we have seen enough to know that it is likely that corrective justice can provide a theoretically satisfactory account of both fault based and strict liability. Again, then, the explanatory power of the corrective justice understanding of the law exceeds the alternatives by a considerable margin.

V. RECENT LEGISLATION

In many jurisdictions, the common law has been amended though statutory intervention. For instance, according to section 1 of the Compensation Act 2006 (UK):

> A court considering a claim in negligence . . . may, in determining whether the defendant should have taken particular steps to meet a standard of care (whether by taking precautions against a risk or otherwise), have regard to whether a requirement to take those steps might—
>
> (a) prevent a desirable activity from being undertaken at all, to a particular extent or in a particular way, or
> (b) discourage persons from undertaking functions in connection with a desirable activity.

According to the explanatory notes that accompanied the relevant Bill,[125] this section was not designed to alter the status quo but 'reflects the existing law and approach of the courts'.

Key to interpreting this section is defining what 'desirable' means in this context. It is important to see that it can be given an interpretation based either on corrective or distributive justice. Interpreting the section in line with corrective justice produces the following picture. In determining whether the defendant was negligent, the court may take into account the impact of liability on the defendant in terms of the activities that the defendant needs to carry out in order to lead a worthwhile life. In other words, 'desirable' is to be cashed out by examining the defendant's life, and the desirability of certain factors from that perspective is a matter to be taken into account in determining the standard of care.

---

[124] Incidentally, both this and the argument concerning the standard of care above indicate that fairness between the parties is not merely a matter of formal equality—ie treating the parties in the same way. Instead, the parties must be treated in accordance with a conception of what persons are appropriate to corrective justice. In Weinrib's view, this is Kantian right: EJ Weinrib, *The Idea of Private Law* (Harvard University Press, Cambridge, Mass, 1995) ch 4.
[125] Compensation Bill (2005–11 HL–155).

That interpretation of the section is entirely in line with the approach to the standard of care advanced here, and it is, indeed, in line with the leading decisions of the courts. Its function is to remind the courts (if any reminder is needed) that, even though it was the defendant who injured the claimant, the defendant's interests are not to be disregarded. In fact, justice can be done only if the defendant's interests are given equal weight to the claimant's. In particular, the section reminds the court that the defendant is not to be treated merely as a deep pocket, a loss spreader or a compensator, but must be approached as the moral equal of the claimant.

There is certainly a perception that this reminder is necessary. Consider the following scenario: A paediatrician makes an error of medical judgement that results in permanent injury to an infant. Whether or not it is accurate, there is a perception that courts will tend to find that the paediatrician has been negligent, even if her mistake was in fact reasonable, out of sympathy with the child (coupled, perhaps, with the knowledge that the defendant is likely to be insured). If that is so, then the section serves to remind the court that they must not ignore the defendant's interests in this, or like, manner.

The alternative interpretation of 'desirable' in the section above is based on distributive justice. According to this view, in deciding whether the defendant was negligent, the court may take into account the social burdens of imposing liability on the society as a whole. Hence, on this view, 'desirable' is to be cashed out in terms of the interests of the community. Though, as we have seen, this is the view held by the majority of modern academics, it is not the one found in the leading Commonwealth cases.

Moreover, this interpretation of the section leads to morally unacceptable results—*even in terms of distributive justice*. It would mean that a defendant who violated corrective justice with respect to a claimant could escape liability because of the benefit of the defendant's activity to third parties. But it is entirely unclear why, as a matter of justice, the claimant should in effect pay for that benefit. If the benefit is to the public, then the public should pay for it. Given that, as this example assumes, the injury to the claimant is one of the costs of the defendant's activities, then if the activity should continue because it is in the public interest the public should pay for that injury. At least in terms of the law of tort,[126] the best way of ensuring this result is to hold the defendant liable because he is much more likely to be able to pass those costs on to the public who benefit.

Furthermore, in implying that the court 'may' take into account distributive justice in setting the standard of care, this interpretation of the section would render judicial decision making hopelessly intuitionistic. This can be brought out by imagining a case in which corrective justice calls for liability but distributive justice would lead to the converse result. If the judge finds for the claimant, on what basis is she to justify her failure to use distributive justice to

---

[126] Alternative compensation schemes have different ways of achieving this result, of course.

trump corrective justice? No appeal to justice can do so, so she is forced to rely on her gut instincts. Similarly, if she finds for the defendant, on what basis is she to justify the trumping of corrective justice by distributive justice? She cannot, but must rely only on her raw intuition. This is an inappropriate method of judicial decision making.

Accordingly, not only is the distributive justice interpretation of section 1 of the Compensation Act inconsistent with the law as it stands, it is morally objectionable and inconsistent with the nature of judicial decision making. Thankfully, it is not the only interpretation available.

Unfortunately, the same cannot be said for those Acts passed in the wake of Australia's recent insurance crisis. For instance, section 9 of the Civil Liability Act 2003 (QLD) reads:

(1) A person does not breach a duty to take precautions against a risk of harm unless—

(a) the risk was foreseeable (that is, it is a risk of which the person knew or ought reasonably to have known); and
(b) the risk was not insignificant; and
(c) in the circumstances, a reasonable person in the position of the person would have taken the precautions.

(2) In deciding whether a reasonable person would have taken precautions against a risk of harm, the court is to consider the following (among other relevant things)—

(a) the probability that the harm would occur if care were not taken;
(b) the likely seriousness of the harm;
(c) the burden of taking precautions to avoid the risk of harm;
(d) the social utility of the activity that creates the risk of harm.[127]

Everything in this section is in accordance with the argument presented here except the last clause. It is objectionable for the reasons outlined above. Of course, however, Queensland courts are bound by it, but it would be better if it were repealed. Ironically, this section and the statute that contains it were a response to a crisis in the Australian insurance industry that was believed to have resulted from the judicial expansion of liability,[128] an expansion that, as the first chapter of this book has indicated and we see in the following, was produced in part by a departure from corrective justice. The appropriate solution would have been to refocus on corrective justice rather than to attempt to use the problem as the solution.

---

[127] See also s5B Civil Liability Act 2002 (NSW); s5B Civil Liability Act 2002 (WA).
[128] For a thoughtful discussion of these circumstances see P Cane, 'Reforming Tort Law in Australia: A Personal Perspective' (2003) 27 *Melbourne University Law Review* 649.

4

Duty and Remoteness

T HIS CHAPTER EXPLORES the nature of the duty of care and remoteness stages of the negligence enquiry. The discussion is designed to contrast two approaches. First, the 'policy model' that adopts general principles but qualifies those principles with a list of exceptions that are so important that the principles appear to have no practical relevance. That approach is also explored in more detail in Chapter 5. Secondly, the 'principled approach' that treats the stages of the negligence enquiry as forming a unified investigation. This investigation is an enquiry into whether the unreasonable risk created by the defendant (standard of care) was an unreasonable risk of injury to the claimant (the duty of care) and an unreasonable risk of the injury that the claimant suffered (remoteness). I also apply the principled approach to the issues of the duty of care owed to rescuers, the duty of care owed to non-existent claimants, novus actus interveniens and the thin skull rule.

I. THE DUTY OF CARE

A. The Nature of the Duty of Care

(i) Winterbottom v Wright[1]

The development of the duty of care in the law of negligence features a recurring counterpoint. It is in this area that we see the common law's greatest advances and its most ignominious defeats. We begin with one of those defeats: *Winterbottom v Wright*.

The defendant contracted with the Postmaster General to supply and maintain a mail coach. The Postmaster General contracted with Atkinson to operate the coach. Atkinson contracted with the claimant to drive the coach. The defendant had not maintained the coach properly, in breach of his contractual obligations with the Postmaster General. As a result an accident occurred in which the claimant suffered personal injury. The claimant brought a cause of action against the defendant.

---

[1] (1842) 10 M & W 109, 152 ER 402.

The claimant failed. Lord Abinger CJ said:

> I am clearly of opinion that the defendant is entitled to our judgment. We ought not to permit a doubt to rest upon this subject, for our doing so might be the means of letting in upon us an infinity of actions. . . . Here the action is brought simply because the defendant was a contractor with a third person; and it is contended that thereupon he became liable to every body who might use the carriage. . . . There is no privity of contract between these parties; and if the plaintiff can sue, every passenger, or even any person passing along the road, who was injured by the upsetting of the coach, might bring a similar action. Unless we confine the operation of such contracts as this to the parties who entered into them, the most absurd and outrageous consequences, to which I can see no limit, would ensue.[2]

Alderson B remarked:

> I am of the same opinion. . . . If we were to hold that the plaintiff could sue in such a case, there is no point at which such actions would stop. The only safe rule is to confine the right to recover to those who enter into the contract: if we go one step beyond that, there is no reason why we should not go fifty.[3]

Clearly, something had gone wrong here.[4] To the modern common lawyer, the something is likely to appear obvious: the Court was surreptitiously implementing a policy the judges held to be important at the time. The decision now seems a legal monstrosity because the policies that motivated the Court in *Winterbottom v Wright* no longer motivate us. As John Fleming put it:

> In the decision whether to recognise a duty in a given situation, many factors interplay: the hand of history, our ideas of morals and justice, the convenience of administering the rule and our social ideas as to where the loss should fall. Hence, the incidence and extent of duties are liable to adjustment in the light of evolving community attitudes. 'The categories of negligence are never closed.' In 1842, Lord Abinger foresaw that 'the most absurd and outrageous consequences, to which I can see no limit, would ensue', if it should ever be held that a party to a contract was under a duty to anyone but the promisee. This standpoint, based on the fear of impeding industrial development, has long since given way to a policy of making negligent manufacturers, repairers and others shoulder the accident losses of ultimate consumers. Here, the advent of

[2] (1842) 10 M & W 109, 152 ER 402, 404–5.

[3] *Ibid*, 405.

[4] Some have attempted to explain away the difficulty by suggesting that the claimant's sole claim was in contract. See eg *M'Alister (or Donoghue) (Pauper) v Stevenson* [1932] AC 562, 588–9, 610 (HL Sc). However, this seems more an ex post facto rationalisation of the case than an explanation of it. It is remarkably uncharitable to the claimant's case to see him as claiming recovery for the defendant's breach of contract with the Postmaster General. Moreover, this interpretation is inconsistent with the claims made in the case. See eg: '[t]he plaintiff in this case could not have brought an action on the contract; if he could have done so, what would have been his situation, supposing the Postmaster-General had released the defendant? that would, at all events, have defeated his claim altogether. By permitting this action, we should be working this injustice, that after the defendant had done everything to the satisfaction of his employer, and after all matters between them had been adjusted, and all accounts settled on the footing of their contract, we should subject them to be ripped open by this action of tort being brought against him': *Winterbottom v Wright* (1842) 10 M & W 109, 152 ER 402, 405 (Lord Abinger CB). These claims are incoherent on the assumption that the plaintiff's cause of action is in contract rather than negligence.

insurance and a more realistic appreciation of the methods available for the distribution of losses has led to an enormous widening of the field of duty.[5]

However, despite the wide acceptance of this view, there are two significant problems with Fleming's analysis. First, it conflicts with other decisions of the same Court.[6] Fleming claims that the judges in *Winterbottom v Wright* restricted liability in order to protect industrial development. However, within four months of the decision in *Winterbottom v Wright*, the same Court, with an almost identical bench, decided *Davies v Mann*.[7] That case instituted the so-called 'rule of last opportunity' or 'last clear chance rule' relevant to the defence of contributory negligence. This rule limited the availability of the defence of contributory negligence and, hence, *Davies v Mann* expanded the scope of liability. Moreover, Fleming attempts to explain the approach to contributory negligence that was applied *before Davies v Mann* in terms of protecting industrial development.[8] But, given *Davies v Mann*, the desire to protect industry seems to have lasted only 153 days after *Winterbottom v Wright*. Although they say that a week is a long time in politics, this nevertheless casts significant doubt on Fleming's argument.

Of course, it is possible to invent policy reasons to explain why the Court may have been prepared to expand liability in *Davies v Mann* but limit it in *Winterbottom v Wright*. Perhaps there is some economic reason why an expansive defence of contributory negligence would have damaged English industry. But we have no reason to attribute any such view to the judges in *Davies v Mann* or, indeed, to attribute to the judges in *Winterbottom v Wright* the views described by Fleming. In respect of that case, Ernest Weinrib asks, '[w]as this factor [the protection of industry] mentioned by . . . Lord Abinger? What evidence would be required to substantiate Fleming's statement?'[9] Weinrib's questions make it clear that—and this must be put bluntly—Fleming is making up the facts. It is taken for granted that the Court in *Winterbottom v Wright* was motivated by unexpressed policy and that that policy was the protection of industry. Although such has become the received wisdom, it is an invented wisdom. Certainly, it is not beyond belief that judges were concerned with the strength of the industrial revolution—even as late as 1845—but there is no evidence that it actually affected the judgment in *Winterbottom v Wright*.

Fleming's failure to substantiate his claim is particularly disappointing, as the judges' arguments are in themselves more than sufficient to explain (as opposed to justify) their decisions. Indeed, the concerns that explicitly motivated the judges remain familiar today and motivated Fleming himself.[10]

---

[5] J Fleming, *The Law of Torts,* 9th edn (LBC Information Services, Sydney, 1998) 154.

[6] EJ Weinrib, *Tort Law: Cases and Materials* (Emond Montgomery Publications Ltd, Toronto, 1997) 253.

[7] (1842) 10 M & W 546, 152 ER 588.

[8] Fleming, above n5, 304.

[9] Weinrib, above n6, 111.

[10] Fleming, above n5, 193–207.

There are two reasons why the claimant's case was denied in *Winterbottom v Wright*. The first was the belief that the law of tort has no room to operate when the claimant's injury was caused by an event covered by contract. Hence, the Court was concerned with the relationship between tort and contract. The second was the fear of indeterminate liability.[11] The irony is that both of these concerns are still very much with us today. Accordingly, although we may disagree with the emphasis the judges in *Winterbottom v Wright* gave to these concerns, it is not difficult to understand why they came to their conclusions. There is no need to look beyond the judgment for the 'real basis of the decision' in economic policy.

The second problem is that, assuming that the policy of protecting industry was valid in 1842, Fleming's analysis holds that *Winterbottom v Wright* was rightly decided; although perhaps a similar case should be decided differently today. But that is not correct. The reasoning in *Winterbottom v Wright* was flawed. It was flawed in 1842 and it would have been flawed at any time.

The argument in *Winterbottom v Wright* was mistaken for the following reason. The Court ruled that the presence of a contract between the defendant and the Postmaster General could not ground a cause of action in the claimant. This amounts to the notion that the contract could not create a right in the claimant. This was because the claimant was not in privity. Hence, the Court concluded, the claimant had no basis for his cause of action. But that conclusion does not follow. The correct conclusion is that, as the claimant was not in privity, the contract was *irrelevant* to the claimant's rights and obligations. The privity argument, then, neither aids nor hinders the claimant's case. Accordingly, the Court could not rightly escape examination of the relationship between the claimant and the defendant through the lens of tort law.[12] Hence, the only plausible reason given for denying liability in tort was the fear of indeterminate liability. But this argument is also spurious. In fact, it is always spurious, and it is the task of much of the rest of this book to show why.

(ii) Donoghue v Stevenson[13]

The claimant was given a bottle of ginger beer, bought by her friend from a café. The defendant was the manufacturer of the ginger beer. The ginger beer was said to have contained the decomposing remains of a snail, the drinking of which caused the claimant personal injury (gastroenteritis). As Lord Buckmaster pointed out, the case was on all fours with *Winterbottom v*

---

[11] This is a policy argument, but it does not necessarily indicate a concern with protecting industrial development. The meaning of the term 'indeterminate liability' is discussed in detail in ch 7.

[12] Two points are to be noted here. First, the issue is not one of concurrent liability. Because the claimant had no contract with the defendant, there is no issue of concurrent liability. Secondly, the issue is not the independence of *tort* law (as opposed to the law of negligence) from contract. No court would have held that a contract between *A* and *B* not to trespass against *C* would undermine *C's* ability to sue *A* for a trespass.

[13] *M'Alister (or Donoghue) (Pauper) v Stevenson* [1932] AC 562 (HL Sc).

Wright.[14] In fact, perhaps Donoghue's case was intuitively even weaker than the claimant's in *Winterbottom v Wright*, given that Donoghue had no contract with her friend. Nevertheless, the House of Lords ruled that the defendant owed Donoghue a duty of care.

Of course, the case is celebrated by Commonwealth lawyers as the most significant decision in the history of the law of tort, if not in the history of the whole of the common law.[15] There are three reasons why it is such an important case.

The least important reason, at least for our purposes, is that *Donoghue v Stevenson* introduced 'products liability'. No doubt that was an important development in terms of the economic structure of British society. But, from the perspective of legal principle, the point is trivial.

Of much more importance was Lord Atkin's proposal of a general, principled approach to determining the existence of a duty of care. In Lord Atkin's view, a defendant owed a duty of care to all those placed at a reasonably foreseeable risk of injury by the defendant's actions. As Lord Atkin famously said:

> You must take reasonable care to avoid acts or omissions which you can reasonably foresee would be likely to injure your neighbour. Who, then, in law is my neighbour? The answer seems to be—persons who are so closely and directly affected by my act that I ought reasonably to have them in contemplation as being so affected when I am directing my mind to the acts or omissions which are called in question.[16]

Why? Lord Atkin claimed that this was 'no doubt based upon a general public sentiment of moral wrongdoing for which the offender must pay'.[17] But what does 'public sentiment' mean here? In order to answer this question, it is necessary to be clear about the subject matter of the enquiry into the duty of care.

The role of the duty enquiry is to determine to whom the defendant was under an obligation to observe the standard of care. In less formal (and less accurate) terms, the question is: of whom must the defendant exercise care? Before *Donoghue v Stevenson*, the answer to this question was muddled:

> The Courts are concerned with the particular relations which come before them in actual litigation, and it is sufficient to say whether the duty exists in those circumstances. The result is that the Courts have been engaged upon an elaborate classification of duties as they exist in respect of property, whether real or personal, with further divisions as to ownership, occupation or control, and distinctions based on the particular relations of the one side or the other, whether manufacturer, salesman or landlord, customer, tenant, stranger, and so on.[18]

The picture painted by Lord Atkin is of a law of negligence that imposed a duty of care in an arbitrary fashion. *Winterbottom v Wright* is an excellent example of this. To quote Alderson B again:

---

[14] *Ibid*, 568.
[15] However, see *MacPherson v Buick Motor Co* 111 NE 1050 (NY CA 1916).
[16] *M'Alister (or Donoghue) (Pauper) v Stevenson* [1932] AC 562, 580 (HL Sc).
[17] *Ibid*.
[18] *Ibid*, 579.

> If we were to hold that the plaintiff could sue in such a case, there is no point at which such actions would stop. The only safe rule is to confine the right to recover to those who enter into the contract: if we go one step beyond that, there is no reason why we should not go fifty.[19]

The argument was that liability must end somewhere and so it may as well end here. There is no reason why liability should end at this particular point, but then there is no reason why it should end at any particular point. Here is as good as anywhere. Given the existence of the contract between the defendant and the Postmaster General, this is, perhaps, a convenient place at which to set the limits of liability.

Lord Atkin's judgment in *Donoghue v Stevenson* could not be more opposed to this approach. His Lordship's answer to the question, 'to whom was the defendant under an obligation to observe the standard of care?', is a general one, designed to avoid arbitrariness. A duty of care is owed to all those placed at a reasonably foreseeable risk of injury by one's actions.

Although Lord Atkin's derivation of this principle was based on the parable of the Good Samaritan, and hence is in that sense a Christian doctrine, clearly its appeal does not depend on an acceptance of Christianity. Moreover, Lord Atkin was at pains to point out that the law's conception of duty is not coextensive with that of Christian ethics, even in the case of the Good Samaritan from which the neighbour principle derives. First, the law insists on an objective approach to mediate between the interests of the parties. Secondly, the law defines the scope of an actionable injury in terms of the parties' rights.[20] Nevertheless, the notion that duty is based on foreseeability is itself quite in accord with public sentiment.[21] If one (Christian or not) is after a general answer to the duty enquiry in negligence, it is hard to see how the approach could be different.

We can understand Lord Atkin's reasoning as follows. We are dealing with the law of negligence. What is negligence? It is the creation of an unreasonable risk.[22] Hence, if the defendant created an unreasonable risk, then he is said to have been negligent. However, the unreasonable risk must be a risk *to someone*. Therefore, the defendant has been negligent to someone only if he has created

---

[19] (1842) 10 M & W 109, 152 ER 402, 405.

[20] Compare Lord Atkin, 'Law as an Educational Subject' [1932] *Journal of the Society of Public Teachers of Law* 27, 30: '[i]t is quite true that law and morality do not cover identical fields. No doubt morality extends beyond the more limited range in which you can lay down definite prohibitions of law'. See also JC Smith and P Burns, 'Donoghue v. Stevenson—The Not So Golden Anniversary' (1983) 46 *MLR* 147, 147–8. See further ch 7. In this way, the doctrine is perhaps strictly closer to Confucianism than to Christianity, whose golden rule is not 'do unto others as you would have them do unto you', but 'do not do unto others as you would not have them do unto you'.

[21] Hence, the suggestion in H Luntz and D Hambly, *Torts: Cases and Commentary,* 4th edn (Butterworths, Sydney, 1995) 196–7, that the fact that the defendants did not attempt to recover the damages in *Bolton v Stone* [1951] AC 850 (HL) shows that Lord Atkin was wrong in this regard, is not to the point.

[22] Recall that 'unreasonable risk' was defined in ch 3.

an unreasonable risk of injury to that person.[23] If the defendant created an unreasonable risk to someone other than the claimant, then the defendant was not negligent to the claimant. The duty of care, then, is not a Christian 'import' into the common law. Rather, it is connected to the very concept of negligence itself as it operates in corrective justice, that is, as between two parties.

The third reason *Donoghue v Stevenson* is an important case is that Lord Atkin insisted on a general conception of negligence:

> [T]he duty which is common to all the cases where liability is established must logically be based upon some element common to the cases where it is found to exist. . . . At present I content myself with pointing out that in English law there must be, and is, some general conception of relations giving rise to a duty of care, of which the particular cases found in the books are but instances.[24]

It is important to understand this argument. Lord Atkin did not claim that, as a matter of policy, a general conception of negligence should be adopted because it would be efficient, easy to apply, predictable or whatever. On the contrary, he insisted that it is in the nature of law itself that it adopts a general conception of negligence. Law is general principle. A system of arbitrary rules could not be a legal system in its proper sense. This provides an interesting and enlightening comparison with the situation that existed before *Donoghue v Stevenson*.

Recall that, prior to *Donoghue v Stevenson*, duties of care were imposed on defendants in a more or less arbitrary fashion. Limits to liability were determined for convenience, rather than to reflect any understanding of the nature of the law of negligence itself. This demonstrates that the understanding of the duty of care prior to *Donoghue v Stevenson* was in principle *un*limited. Of course, in practice liability was limited; but it was so arbitrarily, by unprincipled limitations placed on the duty of care for convenience. In modern terms, we would say that the duty of care was wide open in principle though it was restricted in particular instances for reasons of policy.[25]

---

[23] Of course, this does not mean that the defendant must have been able to foresee injury to the *particular* claimant. It is sufficient that the claimant is within the class of persons placed at reasonably foreseeable risk by the defendant. This does not mean that the duty of care is owed to the class of persons. Instead, the duty of care is owed individually to each member of the class of persons that the defendant placed at foreseeable risk.

[24] *M'Alister (or Donoghue) (Pauper) v Stevenson* [1932] AC 562, 580 (HL Sc).

[25] There are at least two ways of understanding the law as it existed prior to *Donoghue v Stevenson,* above n24. From the perspective of the legal historian, the situation is likely to appear as follows. Before *Donoghue v Stevenson*, the law witnessed a gradual expansion in the scope of negligence liability. This expansion produced *Donoghue v Stevenson* and continued for a long time after that case. The picture, then, is of a narrowly defined duty of care expanding. See eg S Todd, 'Negligence: The Duty of Care' in S Todd (ed), *The Law of Torts in New Zealand,* 3rd edn (Brookers, Wellington, 2001) 143–7; T Weir, *Tort Law* (Oxford University Press, Oxford, 2002) 3. The legal historian sees the law this way, because her interest typically is in the practice of the law. That is, the legal historian is typically concerned with changes in the scope of liability. This is not the perspective with which I am interested. It is a perfectly valid perspective, but not the most illuminating for our purposes. The perspective relevant here is that of a legal theorist. My question is not how the law functioned in practice, or even how lawyers of the time understood the law, but how the law of the period is best understood from the standpoint of theory. This perspective

Clearly, this was anathema to Lord Atkin. The law cannot work this way: 'in English law there must be, and is, some general conception of relations giving rise to a duty of care, of which the particular cases found in the books are but instances'.[26] It would be inconsistent with the nature of legal principle to hold that those principles, rightly understood, are incapable of determining the sphere of liability so that liability would be, without the addition of policy, unlimited. Hence, it is no defence of the law prior to *Donoghue v Stevenson* to point out that liability was restricted by policy in practice. The task of legal principle must be to discover the conceptual boundaries of liability.

In Lord Atkin's view, then, the point of legal principle is to determine the frontiers of liability, to elucidate the boundaries of legal responsibility. The task of legal principle is to tell us what the law is and, importantly, why it is that way. Accordingly, if legal principles generate indeterminate liability, then they must be the wrong principles. Not wrong, or not merely wrong, as a matter of policy, but wrong as a matter of principle. The fact that a suggested set of principles generates indeterminate liability constitutes a *reductio ad absurdum* of that suggested set. Lord Atkin's aim in *Donoghue v Stevenson*, then, is to develop a coherent general understanding of his subject matter. As discussed in Chapter 1, this is the task faced by scholars of all disciplines.

On the other hand, even scholars sympathetic to a more principled law than exists at present have questioned Lord Atkin's assertions. For instance, Nicholas McBride and Roderick Bagshaw claim that:

> There seems to be no justification for Lord Atkin's statement that '. . . in English law there must be, and is, some general conception of relations giving rise to a duty of care, of which, the particular cases found in the books are but instances'. The better view, we would submit, is that there are many *different* kinds of situations and relationships in which one person will owe another a duty of care; to think that all these different situations and relationships have something in common which accounts for why they give rise to a duty of care is folly and it can only lead to confusion.[27]

However, while Lord Atkin's quest may never be fully achieved, embarking on it is not folly.

First, Lord Atkin did not argue that all cases in which a duty of care exists 'have something in common' if this is taken to mean that they must all possess some non-legal, factual property in common. Perhaps that would be folly. But what Lord Atkin claimed was that there must be 'some general conception of relations giving rise to a duty of care', and that is a quite different thing. This can be brought out by examining McBride and Bagshaw's positive position.

Imagine that, in situation 1, a defendant is held to owe a claimant a duty of care for reasons *x*. In situation 2, however, a defendant is held not to owe a duty

generates a view of the law prior to *Donoghue v Stevenson* that is, while consistent with that of the legal historian, in interesting contrast to that view.

[26] *M'Alister (or Donoghue) (Pauper) v Stevenson* [1932] AC 562, 580 (HL Sc).
[27] NJ McBride and R Bagshaw, *Tort Law*, 2nd edn (Pearson Education Ltd, Harlow, 2005) 67 n5.

of care to a claimant for reasons *y*. Further imagine that adopting reasons *x* in situation 2 would have produced the opposite result, ie that a duty of care would have been owed. Here we have circumstances as described by McBride and Bagshaw. We have two different situations or relationships; one set of considerations is applied to the first and a different set of considerations is applied to the second.

It must be clear that leaving things as described is unacceptable however, at least for the academic. This can be revealed by asking a simple question: *why* are reasons *x* applied to situation 1 and reasons *y* to situation 2? An answer to this question will either replace *x* and *y* or combine with *x* and *y* to show why it is that a duty of care exists in situation 1 but not in situation 2. But that means that the answer will produce a 'general conception of relations giving rise to a duty of care' in situations 1 and 2. That is what Lord Atkin was after. On the other hand, refusing to answer this question would involve succumbing to limited rationality as defined in Chapter 1.

The task of legal principle is to tell us what the law is and why it is that way. In the absence of a 'general conception of relations giving rise to a duty of care', it cannot achieve that task. Accordingly, the search for such a conception is imperative, despite the possibility that one will never be found.

Thus, *Winterbottom v Wright* and *Donoghue v Stevenson* present two models for understanding the development of law. For convenience and for reasons that must now be obvious, I call the model instantiated in *Winterbottom v Wright* the 'policy model' and that enunciated by Lord Atkin the 'principled approach'. I now explore these models further by examining their implementation in a case. Case law could not be more helpful here. The clash between the two models is almost perfectly illustrated by the decision of the New York Court of Appeal in *Palsgraf v Long Island Railroad Co.*[28]

(iii) Palsgraf [29]

The defendant's employees pushed a man onto a moving train, dislodging a package the man was carrying. The defendant's employees did not know, and could not reasonably have known, that the package contained fireworks. These exploded, causing scales far down the platform to fall onto the claimant,[30] resulting in personal injury. All accepted that it was negligent to push a man onto a moving train. All accepted that the claimant was not placed at a reasonably foreseeable risk of injury.

The policy model of law was brilliantly illustrated by Andrews J's dissent. His Honour first asked what it is that makes an act wrongful. His answer was

---

[28] 162 NE 99 (NY CA 1928).

[29] For discussion of *Palsgraf*, see also EJ Weinrib, *The Idea of Private Law* (Harvard University Press, Cambridge, Mass, 1995) 159–64.

[30] At least it was said that the claimant was far down the platform. Compare RA Posner, *Cardozo: a Study in Reputation* (Chicago University Press, Chicago, Ill, 1990) 33–48.

that an action is wrongful if it creates a risk of injury to someone. But Andrews J concluded that the rightfulness or wrongfulness of an act is a property that attaches to the act itself and has nothing to do with the relationship between the parties:

> Should we drive down Broadway at a reckless speed, we are negligent whether we strike an approaching car or miss it by an inch. The act itself is wrongful. It is a wrong not only to those who happen to be within the radius of danger but to all who might have been there—a wrong to the public at large. Such is the language of the street.[31]

Hence, given that the defendant's employees created an unreasonable risk to the man boarding the train, their acts were wrongful.

Moreover, Andrews J maintained that the aim of the law is to protect society at large, rather than to protect particular persons. 'Due care is a duty imposed on each one of us to protect society from unnecessary danger, not to protect A, B or C alone.'[32] Therefore, when the defendant's employees created an unreasonable risk to the man boarding the train, they wronged everyone. Accordingly, prima facie, anyone injured as a result of the defendant's employees' conduct had a cause of action:

> The proposition is this. Every one owes to the world at large the duty of refraining from those acts that may unreasonably threaten the safety of others. Such an act occurs. Not only is he wronged to whom harm might reasonably be expected to result, but he also who is in fact injured, even if he be outside what would generally be thought the danger zone.[33]

Therefore, the claimant was owed a duty of care by the defendant.

So far, Andrews J's judgment seems perfectly principled. However, the rub is not far away. After setting up his approach to the duty of care, Andrews J tells us that the 'right to recover damages rests on additional considerations'.[34] These additional considerations are those of remoteness of damage (proximate or legal causation). At this point, Andrews J's views are more than a little different from those discussed above. Instead of basing remoteness on the concept of wrongdoing, Andrews J argues that it is purely a matter of policy:

> A cause, but not the proximate cause. What we do mean by the word 'proximate' is, that because of convenience, of public policy, of a rough sense of justice, the law arbitrarily declines to trace a series of events beyond a certain point. This is not logic. It is practical politics. . . . We may regret that the line was drawn just where it was, but drawn somewhere it had to be.[35]

After laying out a seemingly principled approach to the duty of care (and after criticising Cardozo CJ on the ground that his approach was less principled),

---

[31] *Palsgraf v Long Island Railroad Co* 162 NE 99, 102 (NY CA 1928).
[32] *Ibid*.
[33] *Ibid*, 103.
[34] *Ibid*.
[35] *Ibid*, 103–4.

Andrews J adopted an entirely arbitrary—his word—approach to remoteness in order to restrict liability. 'It is all a question of expediency' we are told.[36]

There could not be a clearer illustration of the policy model. The principles for determining liability are wide open, allowing liability a scope even Andrews J regarded as unacceptable. Hence there is a need to restrict liability in terms of arbitrarily chosen policies. Liability must end somewhere; here is as good as anywhere.

Moreover, on Andrews J's version of the policy model, the duty of care is redundant. If the duty is owed to everyone, then it must be owed to any claimant. Accordingly, after the standard of care is determined (which is at least officially decided according to the Hand Formula in the United States[37]) as the duty of care stage is the only stage even apparently principled, all the work is done by policy. There appears to be no point in having a duty of care stage of the enquiry, and no point in having principle.

While other versions of the policy model do not necessarily divide principle and policy between duty and remoteness as Andrews J did, the emphasis on policy over principle is common to all such views. The model is genuinely policy-*driven*. As we see in Chapter 5, although each version of the policy model has its own set of ostensible principles, in fact these principles mean little or nothing. All the work is done by policy.

Cardozo CJ's judgment contrasts starkly with Andrews J's. Not only did Cardozo CJ reach a different conclusion on the facts of the case, he did so by adopting a radically different method of reasoning. In what vies with Lord Atkin's judgment in *Donoghue v Stevenson* for the greatest single judgment in the history of the law of negligence, Cardozo CJ laid out the principled model's approach to the duty of care.

First, Cardozo CJ pointed out that, while the defendant's employees may have been negligent to the man boarding the train, they were not negligent to the claimant:

> The conduct of the defendant's guard, if a wrong in its relation to the holder of the package, was not a wrong in its relation to the plaintiff, standing far away. Relatively to her it was not negligence at all. Nothing in the situation gave notice that the falling package had in it the potency of peril to persons thus removed.[38]

A defendant falls below the standard of care if he creates a risk that a reasonable person would not create. In English law, the question is whether the defendant created an unreasonable risk as defined in Chapter 3. An unreasonable risk of what? An unreasonable risk of injury to another. The risk, then, is relational:

---

[36] *Ibid*, 104. The policy is arbitrary, not because it is chosen for no good reason, but because the choice of any particular policy is not related to wrongdoing or negligence. Hence, it is arbitrary from the perspective of the enquiry into negligence.

[37] But see R W Wright, 'Hand, Posner, and the Myth of the "Hand Formula"' (2003) 4 *Theoretical Inquiries in Law* 145.

[38] *Palsgraf v Long Island Railroad Co* 162 NE 99, 99 (NY CA 1928).

'risk imports relation'.[39] In *Palsgraf*, the defendant's employees were negligent because they placed the owner of the package at risk of suffering personal injury and property damage. But they were not negligent in creating a risk of scales falling on the claimant. The defendant's employees did create such a risk, but, as that risk was not reasonably foreseeable, they did not act unreasonably in creating that risk. In the language of the English law, the risk to the claimant was FOFF.

Accordingly, as Cardozo CJ argued, the claimant in *Palsgraf* was not placed at an unreasonable risk. The defendant's employees were not negligent to the claimant. Hence, the claimant was not wronged by the defendant's employees. If the claimant was not wronged, then she could not have had a cause of action. To have held otherwise would have been to allow the claimant to sue for the wrong done to another, to have allowed her to sue for the wrong done to the owner of the package.[40] But '[t]he plaintiff sues in her own right for a wrong personal to her, and not as the vicarious beneficiary of a breach of duty to another':[41]

> Negligence, like risk, is thus a term of relation. Negligence in the abstract, apart from things related, is surely not a tort, if indeed it is understandable at all . . . Negligence is not a tort unless it results in the commission of a wrong, and the commission of a wrong imports the violation of a right, in this case, we are told, the right to be protected against interference with one's bodily security. But bodily security is protected, not against all forms of interference or aggression, but only against some. One who seeks redress at law does not make out a cause of action by showing without more that there has been damage to his person. If the harm was not willful, he must show that the act as to him had possibilities of danger so many and apparent as to entitle him to be protected against the doing of it though the harm was unintended. Affront to personality is still the keynote of the wrong. . . . The victim does not sue derivatively, or by right of subrogation, to vindicate an interest invaded in the person of another. Thus to view his cause of action is to ignore the fundamental difference between tort and crime . . . He sues for breach of a duty owing to himself.[42]

According to Cardozo CJ, then, as the claimant was not placed at a reasonably foreseeable risk by the defendant's employees' acts, she was not owed a duty of care. Therefore, she had no cause of action.

Cardozo CJ's judgment is a wonderful example of the principled approach. This can be seen very clearly in Cardozo CJ's treatment of the relationship between the standard of care and the duty of care. For Cardozo CJ, these two parts of the negligence enquiry are parts of a single question, which is: 'was the defendant negligent to the claimant?' This question can be divided into two

---

[39] *Palsgraf v Long Island Railroad Co* 162 NE 99, 99 (NY CA 1928), 100.

[40] This assumes that a wrong was done to the owner of the package, but even this is unclear. It was at least arguable that the defendant's employees were acting reasonably to prevent injury to that person: *ibid*, 99.

[41] *Ibid*, 100.

[42] *Ibid*, 101.

parts.[43] The first part is to ask: was the defendant negligent? This is answered by asking whether the defendant created an unreasonable risk of injury to someone. We refer to this as the standard of care stage of the negligence enquiry. The second part of the question is to ask: was the claimant someone towards whom the defendant should have been careful? Here we ask whether the defendant placed the claimant at a reasonably foreseeable risk. We refer to this as the duty of care stage of the negligence enquiry. But, as Cardozo CJ pointed out, instead of dividing the enquiry in this manner, we could also ask whether the defendant created an unreasonable risk of injury to the claimant, conducting both stages of the enquiry at once.[44] 'The risk reasonably to be perceived defines the duty to be obeyed.'[45]

In consequence, on Cardozo CJ's model, the standard of care and the duty of care fit into a coherent picture of negligence.[46] Moreover, there is no need to limit the ambit of liability in terms of policy. Rather, Cardozo CJ's principles elucidate acceptable and coherent conceptual limits of liability.

The difference between the judgments is further revealed by considering their application to the facts of the case and to some hypothetical versions of it.

In *Palsgraf* itself, Cardozo CJ argued that the claimant could not recover, because she was not placed at a reasonably foreseeable risk of injury and so was not owed a duty of care. For Andrews J, on the other hand, the claimant was owed a duty of care, because the wrong committed by the defendant's employees was a wrong to the whole world—including the claimant, of course. However, remoteness remained to be considered and was to be decided in accordance with policy.[47] Evidently, Andrews J thought that it was expedient for the claimant to recover in *Palsgraf* itself, but we have no idea why. Moreover, as Andrews J insisted, there must be some point at which liability ends. Imagine that the explosion injured another person who was standing even further away from the train than the claimant. At some point, Andrews J would conclude that that person was standing too far away for it to be expedient to allow that person to recover.[48] Now imagine that this person sues the defendant, but fails because her injury is held to be too remote. She wants to know why Andrews J ruled that Mrs Palsgraf could recover but she cannot. Recall Andrews J's answer:

> [B]ecause of convenience, of public policy, of a rough sense of justice, the law arbitrarily declines to trace a series of events beyond a certain point. This is not logic. It is practical politics. . . . We may regret that the line was drawn just where it was, but drawn somewhere it had to be.[49]

---

[43] It eventually needs to be divided into three parts, as is discussed later in this ch.

[44] *Palsgraf v Long Island Railroad Co* 162 NE 99, 101 (NY CA 1928).

[45] *Ibid*, 100.

[46] Compare AJE Jaffey, *The Duty of Care* (Dartmouth, Aldershot, 1992) 6–8 who generates his disaffection with the principled approach to the duty of care by *assuming* that each stage of the negligence enquiry must involve distinct considerations and not be part of a unified enquiry.

[47] *Palsgraf v Long Island Railroad Co* 162 NE 99, 103–5 (NY CA 1928).

[48] See eg the discussion of the negligent driver: *ibid*, 104.

[49] *Ibid*, 103–4.

How impressive would this sound to our hypothetical victim? She does regret that the line was drawn here and she does not find it at all convenient. Moreover, it is positively irrational to expect her to be satisfied when she is told she cannot recover because the law '*arbitrarily* declines to trace a series of events beyond a certain point'. In this light, no matter how useful it may be to lawyers, Andrews J's argument is contemptuous of the claimant. She is given *no reason whatsoever* to accept the judgment. Likewise, in *Palsgraf* itself, Andrews J's view was contemptuous of the defendant.

Andrews J's judgment is seriously deficient. Because it holds that the duty of care is owed to the whole world and therefore to *all* potential claimants, it adopts a principle that is effectively meaningless and insists that cases be decided in terms of unstated policies. The judgment, therefore, is completely empty. The common response is to insist that judicial policy making be explicit.[50] But this follows only if the sole alternative to covert policy making is overt policy making. But this, as the judgments of Cardozo CJ and Lord Atkin reveal, is an assumption that should not be made.

Cardozo CJ in *Palsgraf* and Lord Atkin in *Donoghue v Stevenson* set out to discover the conceptual boundaries of the law of negligence. Those judges were not prepared to resign decision making to the case-by-case application of policy. Theirs is an approach with much to recommend it. For those interested in *understanding* the law, the task must be to uncover the conceptual limits of liability. Now, it may be that a completely principled account of law will prove elusive, and it may not be the case that the law of negligence is based on corrective justice, but the search for the rational foundation of liability is imperative.

B. The Duty of Care and Corrective Justice

Lord Atkin in *Donoghue v Stevenson* and Cardozo CJ in *Palsgraf* provided brilliant illustrations, not only of the principled approach to legal adjudication, but of the application of corrective justice. For both judges, the duty of care is set in terms of the relationship between the parties. Lord Atkin rejected the view that a duty of care could be negatived by concerns external to the relationship between the parties. Cardozo CJ rejected the view that a duty of care could be created by concerns external to the relationship between the parties. Moreover, both decisions fit neatly with the understanding of the standard of care discussed in the previous chapter.

It is in this light that one is to understand Cardozo CJ's criticism that Andrews J's judgment failed to respect the distinction between tort and crime.[51] Recall Andrews J's claim that his view—that the defendant wrongs everyone when he creates an unreasonable risk to someone—is 'the language of the

---

[50] See eg *Hunter v Canary Wharf* [1997] AC 655 (HL) (Lord Cooke).
[51] *Palsgraf v Long Island Railroad Co* 162 NE 99, 101 (NY CA 1928).

street'.[52] Andrews J was undoubtedly correct in this, at least as a general rule. But the issue is whether the type of wrong committed against everyone is the type of wrong addressed by tort law. A person who drives down Broadway at reckless speed wrongs *both* only those he foreseeably injures and everyone, because there are two types of wrongs involved. The wrong to those foreseeably injured is an injustice in the eyes of corrective justice and is remedied in tort. The wrong to everyone is not an injustice from the perspective of corrective justice. Nevertheless, it is a wrong and it is legally actionable. It is a crime. The wrong done by the defendant to particular persons is relevant to the private law and is actionable in tort. The wrong done to society at large is relevant to public law and is actionable in criminal law.[53]

On the corrective justice model, the role of the standard of care is to determine the appropriateness of the defendant's behaviour by adopting a standard that mediates between the interests of the parties. The judgment, then, is about the parties taken as a unit. The duty of care is also concerned to link the parties by tracing the defendant's negligence to the claimant. Accordingly, both the duty and the standard of care operate as between the parties.

II. REMOTENESS OF DAMAGE

A. The Nature of Remoteness[54]

(i) Polemis[55]

Our discussion of remoteness closely mirrors the exploration of the duty of care above. We begin with a case that is in many ways the parallel of *Winterbottom v Wright* and of the judgment of Andrew's J in *Palsgraf: In re Polemis and Furness*.

An employee of the defendants negligently knocked a plank into the hold of a ship, causing a spark that ignited the large quantity of petrol vapour in the hold, causing a fire that destroyed the ship. It was accepted that the destruction of the ship was not a reasonably foreseeable consequence of the defendants' employee's negligence. The issue for the English Court of Appeal was whether this fact demonstrated that the damage was remote.

The Court ruled that proximate causation should not be decided in terms of reasonable foreseeability. This was despite the fact that, inter alia, foreseeability

---

[52] *Ibid*, 102.

[53] Note that the above makes no commitment to the view that criminal law protects societal *rather than* individual interests. The criminal law may well protect the interests of individuals, but it does so by adopting social, not merely interpersonal, norms. Hence, it remains the case than when one violates the criminal law, one commits a social wrong, regardless of the nature of the interest the criminal law protects.

[54] Remoteness is sometimes referred to as 'proximate causation' or 'legal causation'.

[55] *In re Polemis and Furness* [1921] 3 KB 560 (CA).

was relevant in determining the standard of care. Instead, the Court ruled that the claimant could recover if his injury was a *direct* result of the defendant's negligence.

But what does it mean for a result to be direct? How is the distinction drawn between direct and indirect causation? Scrutton LJ's answer was that the defendant's action was an indirect cause of the claimant's injury if the injury was 'due to the operation of independent causes having no connection with the negligent act, except that they could not avoid its results'.[56] What does this mean? Evidently, Scrutton LJ himself did not know. For instance:

> Perhaps the House of Lords will some day explain why, if a cheque is negligently filled up, it is a direct effect of the negligence that some one finding the cheque should commit forgery . . . while if some one negligently leaves a libellous letter about, it is not a direct effect of the negligence that the finder should show the letter to the person libelled . . .[57]

Hence, although Scrutton LJ appealed to directness in order to explain the basis of his decision in *Polemis*, his Lordship admitted that he had no idea what 'directness' really meant, but hoped that the House of Lords would one day enlighten him.

However, Scrutton LJ argued that the instant case was relatively clear cut.[58] But Scrutton LJ's optimism was certainly unfounded. If we do not know how to draw the distinction between direct and indirect causation, then there are no simple cases. This is not a slippery slope argument. The claim is not that, because we cannot draw a fine line between direct and indirect causation, the distinction is useless. Rather, the point is that without a definition of even paradigm instances of direct and indirect causation, we cannot understand the distinction at all. Although we cannot locate the precise moment at which an acorn turns into an oak tree, we know what acorns and oak trees are. But we do not know what direct or indirect causation is. The approach, then, 'leads to nowhere but the never ending and insoluble problems of causation.'[59]

The decision in *Polemis* bears a striking resemblance to that of Andrews J in *Palsgraf*.[60] First, neither the English Court of Appeal nor Andrews J had any interest in developing a coherent approach to adjudication. Instead, the standard of care, the duty of care and remoteness are seen as unconnected, conceptually separate, elements of the cause of action. Secondly, Andrews J and the English Court of Appeal shared similar views as to the content of remoteness. The latter adopted a distinction it could not comprehend. The former claimed that remoteness is all about expediency. In both judgments, then, policy is called

---

[56] *In re Polemis and Furness* [1921] 3 KB 560 (CA), 577.
[57] *Ibid.*
[58] *Ibid.*
[59] *Overseas Tankship (UK) Ltd v Morts Dock & Engineering Co Ltd (The Wagon Mound, No 1)* [1961] AC 388, 423 (PC) (Viscount Simonds).
[60] Andrews J drew attention to this point: *Palsgraf v Long Island Railroad Co* 162 NE 99, 103 (NY CA 1928).

on to do the work in deciding actual cases. Although the judgments appeal to putative principles, the principles have no content and so cannot guide deliberation. As Andrews J was honest enough to admit, '[i]t is all a question of expediency'.[61]

The approach to remoteness enunciated in *Polemis* could not survive *Donoghue v Stevenson*. After the latter case, the search was on for a more principled approach that cohered with the standard and duty of care. That was definitively to come with the decision of the Privy Council in *The Wagon Mound (No 1)*.[62]

(ii) The Wagon Mound (No 1)

Employees of the defendants negligently allowed a large quantity of bunkering oil to spill into the bay. This oil fouled the claimant's slipways and also caught fire, causing severe damage to the claimant's wharf. The trial judge found that only the fouling of the claimant's slipways was reasonably foreseeable. The damage by fire was not reasonably foreseeable because, apparently, it was not foreseeable that bunkering oil floating on water was flammable.

Viscount Simonds set out a new approach to remoteness:

> It is a principle of civil liability . . . that a man must be considered to be responsible for the probable consequences of his act. To demand more of him is too harsh a rule, to demand less is to ignore that civilised order requires the observance of a minimum standard of behaviour. This concept, applied to the slowly developing law of negligence has led to a great variety of expressions which can, as it appears to their Lordships, be harmonised with little difficulty with the single exception of the so-called rule in Polemis. For, if it is asked why a man should be responsible for the natural or necessary or probable consequences of his act (or any other similar description of them), the answer is that it is not because they are natural or necessary or probable, but because, since they have this quality, it is judged, by the standard of the reasonable man, that he ought to have foreseen them.[63]

Moreover, Viscount Simonds claimed that this approach was required so that the enquiry into remoteness would cohere with that into the standard and duty of care:

> [I]f some limitation must be imposed on the consequences for which the negligent actor is to be held responsible . . . why should that test (reasonable foreseeability) be rejected which, *since he is judged by what the reasonable man ought to foresee*, corresponds with the common conscience of mankind . . .[64]

---

[61] *Ibid*, 104.
[62] *Overseas Tankship (UK) Ltd v Morts Dock & Engineering Co Ltd (The Wagon Mound, No 1)* [1961] AC 388 (PC).
[63] *Ibid*, 422–3.
[64] *Ibid*, 423 (emphasis added).

> [T]he essential factor in determining liability is whether the damage is of such a kind as the reasonable man should have foreseen. This accords with the general view thus stated by Lord Atkin in *M'Alister (or Donoghue) v. Stevenson* . . .[65]

In this light, it can be seen that the rule in *Polemis* is both over- and under-inclusive:

> [I]f it would be wrong that a man should be held liable for damage unpredictable by a reasonable man because it was 'direct' or 'natural', equally it would be wrong that he should escape liability, however 'indirect' the damage, if he foresaw or could reasonably foresee the intervening events which led to its being done . . . Thus foreseeability becomes the effective test.[66]

Polemis is a case in which the rule is over-inclusive. An example in which it is under-inclusive is a doctor who gives a patient a drug that she knows is likely to cause cancer, though only *indirectly* through a long, slow process.[67] Surely, the patient is entitled to recover.

B. Remoteness and Corrective Justice

The view of remoteness expounded by the Privy Council in *The Wagon Mound (No 1)* accords with corrective justice. In order to be guilty of an injustice in the eyes of corrective justice, the defendant must create an unreasonable risk as defined above that materialises in injury to the claimant. If the unreasonable risk created by the defendant is to a person other than the claimant, then the defendant's negligence did not wrong the claimant, despite the fact that the claimant was injured. We say that the defendant did not owe the claimant a duty of care. Similarly, if the injury suffered by the claimant was not a foreseeable consequence of the defendant's negligence, then the claimant was also not wronged, though he was injured. We say that the claimant's injury was too remote.

In *Polemis*, the unreasonable risk created by the defendant's employees was that cargo in the hold would be damaged. The employees also created a risk of the destruction of the claimant's vessel by fire, but that risk was FOFF. Hence, the claimant could not establish the appropriate connection between the defendant's employee's negligence and his injury and therefore should have failed. The defendant's employees created the risk of the destruction of the vessel by fire, but they were not negligent in creating that risk. Hence, on the corrective justice

---

[65] *Overseas Tankship (UK) Ltd v Morts Dock & Engineering Co Ltd (The Wagon Mound, No 1)* [1961] AC 388 (PC), 426. Compare WS Seavey, 'Mr. Justice Cardozo and the Law of Torts' (1939) 39 *Columbia Law Review* 20, 34: '[p]rima facie at least, the reasons for creating liability should limit it'. See also M Stauch, 'Risk and Remoteness of Damage in Negligence' (2001) 64 *MLR* 191, 194–5.

[66] *Overseas Tankship (UK) Ltd v Morts Dock & Engineering Co Ltd (The Wagon Mound, No 1)* [1961] AC 388, 426 (PC).

[67] I am assuming that this is indirect, though that is of course questionable, as 'indirect' has no fixed meaning.

model, the claimant was not injured, in the relevant sense, as a consequence of the defendant's wrongdoing.

The five great cases we have explored so far—*Bolton v Stone*, *The Wagon Mound (No 2)*, *Donoghue v Stevenson*, *Palsgraf* and *The Wagon Mound (No 1)*—develop the following picture:

1. The defendant was negligent if he created an unreasonable risk of injury to another.
2. The defendant owed a duty of care to the claimant if it was reasonably foreseeable that the claimant would be injured by the defendant's action.
3. The defendant's negligence was a proximate cause of the claimant's injury if the injury was a reasonably foreseeable consequence of the defendant's action.

These combine into a unified enquiry.

4. The defendant wronged the claimant if he created an unreasonable risk to the claimant of the injury that the claimant suffered.

This accords perfectly with corrective justice.

If the defendant fell below the standard of care (ie was negligent to someone) but did not owe a duty of care to the claimant (ie was not negligent to the claimant), then the claimant cannot recover because the defendant did not wrong the claimant. Similarly, if the defendant fell below the standard of care (ie was negligent to someone), and did owe a duty of care to the claimant (ie was negligent to the claimant), but the claimant's injury was remote (ie the defendant was not negligent in creating a risk of the claimant's injury), then again the claimant cannot recover because, at least in relation to that injury, the defendant did not wrong the claimant.[68] Neither of these is a policy based limitation on liability. Instead, they reflect the nature of the kind of wrongdoing relevant to tort law. They are not control mechanisms. They are part of the concept of negligence as it operates in corrective justice.

C. Remoteness, the Injury and the Accident

(i) *The General Approach*

In *Hughes v Lord Advocate*,[69] employees of the defendant were working down a manhole. The presence of the site was indicated by red paraffin warning lamps. Without securing the site properly, the defendant's employees left to take

---

[68] The claimant may have suffered other injuries that were not remote for which she can recover. This is what happened in *Overseas Tankship (UK) Ltd v Morts Dock & Engineering Co Ltd (The Wagon Mound, No 2)* [1961] AC 611 (PC).

[69] [1963] AC 837 (HL Sc).

tea. While the workmen were away, the claimant and his 10-year-old uncle arrived on the scene and set about meddling with the gear on the site:

> They took with them into the shelter the ladder, a length of rope and a tin can . . . and also one of the red warning lamps, which they swung at the end of the rope. They placed the ladder in position in order to explore the manhole. . . . According to the appellant's own account, he had stumbled over the lamp and knocked it into the hole, when a violent explosion occurred and he himself fell in. A passer-by named Bruce, who was 100 yards or so along the street at the time, described the explosion as having made a roar of sound like a 'woof' and said that a flame shot up some 30 feet into the air. When the lamp was recovered from the manhole, its tank was half out and its wick-holder was completely out of the lamp. The explanation of the accident which was accepted was that when the lamp fell down the hole and was broken, some paraffin escaped, and enough was vaporised to create an explosive mixture which was detonated by the naked light of the lamp.[70]

Lord Reid argued that the defendant's employees were negligent, as they created an unreasonable risk of injury to passing children, who would be inclined to play with the lamps.[71] Hence, the behaviour of the defendant's employees fell below the standard of care. Moreover, as the defendant's employees created an unreasonable risk to persons of a class that included the claimant—viz children—the claimant was owed a duty of care. The remaining issue was whether the damage suffered by the claimant was proximate.

Lord Reid argued that:

> the injuries suffered by the appellant, though perhaps different in degree, did not differ in kind from injuries which might have resulted from an accident of a foreseeable nature. . . . The cause of this accident was a known source of danger, the lamp, but it behaved in an unpredictable way.
>
> The explanation of the accident which has been accepted, and which I would not seek to question, is that, when the lamp fell down the manhole and was broken, some paraffin escaped, and enough was vaporised to create an explosive mixture which was detonated by the naked light of the lamp. The experts agree that no one would have expected that to happen: it was so unlikely as to be unforeseeable.[72]
>
> This accident was caused by a known source of danger, but caused in a way which could not have been foreseen, and in my judgment that affords no defence.[73]

This case stands as authority for the rule that the defendant's negligence was a proximate cause of the claimant's injury if the *kind* of damage the claimant suffered was reasonably foreseeable. Proximate causation requires that neither the extent nor the precise circumstances of the claimant's injury be foreseeable.[74] According to Lord Reid, as the claimant's injury in *Hughes* was of a kind that

[70] [1963] AC 837 (HL Sc), 839–40.
[71] The issue of novus actus interveniens is discussed below and contributory negligence is explored in ch 10.
[72] *Hughes v Lord Advocate* [1963] AC 837, 845–6 (HL Sc).
[73] *Ibid*, 847.
[74] *Ibid*, 855–6 (Lord Guest).

was foreseeable, though the extent of the injury was not foreseeable, the claimant was entitled to recover. However, this case must be understood in the light of a later decision of the English Court of Appeal.

In *Doughty v Turner Manufacturing Co Ltd*,[75] one of the defendant's employees negligently knocked an asbestos and cement cover into a cauldron containing a sodium cyanide solution at 800 degrees Celsius. This caused a small splash that injured no one. However, after one or two minutes, an explosion occurred that expelled some of the solution from the cauldron, burning the claimant. Tests later discovered that the materials from which the covers were made undergo a chemical reaction at high temperature that produces water. This water would turn to steam and, coming into contact with a liquid at high temperature, would cause an explosion, such as the one that injured the claimant in *Doughty*. At the time of the accident, however, that was unforeseeable.

The claimant appealed to Lord Reid's assertion in *Hughes v Lord Advocate* that 'a defender is liable, although the damage may be a good deal greater in extent than was foreseeable. He can only escape liability if the damage can be regarded as differing in kind from what was foreseeable.'[76] In *Doughty*, it was foreseeable that the defendant's employee's negligence would cause the claimant to be burnt. This was because it was foreseeable that knocking the cover into the vat could cause a splash that would expel liquid that would cause burns. Hence, the claimant maintained, according to the principle enunciated by Lord Reid, his injury was not remote.

The Court of Appeal disagreed. Diplock LJ said:

> The former risk [of a splash] was well-known (that was foreseeable) at the time of the accident; but it did not happen. It was the second risk [of the explosion] which happened and caused the plaintiff damage by burning. The crucial finding by the learned judge . . . was that this was not a risk of which the defendants at the time of the accident knew, or ought to have known. This finding, which was justified by the evidence and has not been assailed in this appeal, would appear to lead logically to the conclusion that in causing, or failing to prevent, the immersion of the cover in the liquid, the defendants, by their servants, were in breach of no duty of care owed to the plaintiff, for this was not an act or omission which they could reasonably foresee was likely to cause him damage.[77]

Accordingly, *Doughty* shows that 'injury' must be defined by reference both to the type of accident that occurred and to the type of damage that the claimant suffered. Both must be foreseeable if the claimant is to recover. Hence, the claimant in *Doughty* failed, because the defendant's employee did not create an unreasonable risk of the injury (specifically the accident) that the claimant suffered. The claimant was injured as a result of the realisation of a FOFF risk.[78]

---

[75] [1964] 1 QB 518 (CA).

[76] *Hughes v Lord Advocate* [1963] AC 837, 845 (HL Sc).

[77] *Doughty v Turner Manufacturing Co Ltd* [1964] 1 QB 518, 530 (CA).

[78] Compare M Stauch, 'Risk and Remoteness of Damage in Negligence' (2001) 64 *MLR* 191, 198–9.

On its face, justice may appear to lie with the claimant in *Doughty* (especially if we ignore the issue of vicarious liability). While the claimant was entirely innocent, the defendant owed the claimant a duty of care, the defendant's employee acted negligently (ie fell below the standard of care), the claimant was injured, and the claimant suffered damage of a kind that could have been foreseen. But that sense of justice is not corrective justice and is not relevant in the law of negligence. The defendant's employee was not negligent in creating the risk of an explosion, and hence was not negligent in creating the risk of the injury that the claimant in fact suffered. Therefore, no matter how unethical the defendant's employee's behaviour was, and no matter how distributively unjust the result, the claimant suffered no injustice in corrective justice and had no cause of action.[79] In effect, to have found for the defendant would have been to apply the rule in *Polemis*: to allow the claimant to recover for the realisation of a FOFF risk as long as it was 'direct'. Diplock LJ said as much when he remarked that, if the claimant's submissions were correct:

> the mere fact of an explosion consequent on the immersion of some substance in the liquid would render the defendants liable, however meticulous the care they had taken to see that the substance was chemically inert at 800 degree C, for the fact of the explosion would show that the substance 'could' cause one.
> This is to impose on the defendants a 'strict liability' . . .[80]

The decision in *Doughty* is not grounded on any policy-based attempt to limit liability. The ultimate principle is that the defendant wronged the claimant only if he created an unreasonable risk of the injury suffered by the claimant. The coherence of the three doctrines explored above—the standard of care, the duty of care and remoteness—is explicitly referred to by Diplock LJ in the course of his judgment:

> There is no room today for mystique in the law of negligence. It is the application of common morality and common sense to the activities of the common man. He must take reasonable care to avoid acts or omissions which he can reasonably foresee would be likely to injure his neighbours; but he need do no more than this. If the act which he does is not one which he could, if he thought about it, reasonably foresee would injure his neighbour it matters not whether he does it intentionally or inadvertently. The learned judge's finding, uncontested on appeal, that in the state of knowledge as it was at the time of the accident the defendants could not reasonably have foreseen that the immersion of the asbestos cement cover in the liquid would be likely to injure anyone, must lead to the conclusion that they would have been under no liability to the plaintiff if they had intentionally immersed the cover in the liquid. The fact that it was done inadvertently cannot create any liability, for the immersion of the cover was not an act which they were under any duty to take any care to avoid.[81]

---

[79] For other compelling reasons to reject the argument under review see EJ Weinrib, *The Idea of Private Law* (Harvard University Press, Cambridge, Mass, 1995) 163.
[80] *Doughty v Turner Manufacturing Co Ltd* [1964] 1 QB 518, 531 (CA).
[81] *Ibid*, 531–2.

The fact that Diplock LJ felt no need to distinguish between the duty of care and proximate causation helps to bring out the point that these elements of the negligence enquiry are meant to form parts of a unified whole.

This discussion of *Doughty* raises difficulties with regard to the decision of the House of Lords in *Hughes v Lord Advocate*, in which, it seems, the accident was unforeseeable and yet the claimant recovered. However, before we are able to examine that issue in detail, it is necessary to consider some other important matters that arise in connection with remoteness.

(ii) The Chain of Events

Consider the decision of the Supreme Court of Canada in *Bradford v Kanellos*.[82] The defendant was the owner of a restaurant whose employees had failed adequately to clean a grill. As a result, fat built up around the edge of the grill and caught fire. The fire was immediately put out by an automatic extinguisher. The operation of the fire extinguisher caused no injury to the claimant. However, the fire extinguisher made a hissing or popping noise that was heard by one of the restaurant's patrons who shouted that gas was escaping and that there was going to be an explosion. This outburst caused a stampede as diners fought for the door. The claimant was injured in the crush.

The majority of the Court ruled that the claimant's injury was too remote from the negligence of the defendant's employees. Martland J said:

> The judgment at trial found the respondents to be liable because there had been negligence in failing to clean the grill efficiently, which resulted in the flash fire. But it was to guard against the consequences of a flash fire that the grill was equipped with a fire extinguisher system. . . .
>
> This system, when activated, following the flash fire, fulfilled its function and put out the fire. This was accomplished by the application of carbon dioxide on the fire. In so doing, there was a hissing noise and it was on hearing this that one of the customers exclaimed that gas was escaping and that there was danger of an explosion, following which the panic occurred, the appellant wife was injured. . . .
>
> Was that consequence fairly to be regarded as within the risk created by the respondent's negligence in permitting an undue quantity of grease to accumulate on the grill? The Court of Appeal has found that it was not and I agree with that finding.[83]

The defendant's employees created only a FOFF risk that the claimant would be injured in a stampede. Hence, the claimant could not recover.

However, in dissent, Spence J maintained:

> I am of the opinion that any reasonable person knew that a greasy grill might well take fire and that in such event a CO2 fire extinguisher is put into action either automatically or manually and that such fire extinguisher makes a hissing and popping sound and he could not fail to anticipate that a panic might well result. The panic did result

---

[82] [1974] SCR 409.
[83] *Ibid*, 412–13. Novus actus interveniens is discussed below.

and on the evidence the whole affair from beginning to end was almost instantaneous.[84]

Spence J did not ask whether the claimant's injury was reasonably foreseeable
from the perspective of the defendant's negligence. Instead, his Honour arbitrarily divided the causal sequence into a number of steps and asked whether
each step was foreseeable from the perspective of the preceding step. Given that
the grill was not cleaned, it was reasonably foreseeable that there would be a
fire; given that there was a fire, it was reasonably foreseeable that the extinguisher would come on; given that the extinguisher came on, it was reasonably
foreseeable that it would make a hiss or a pop; given that it made a hiss or a pop,
it was reasonably foreseeable that someone would mistake it for gas escaping;
given that someone mistook it for gas escaping, it was reasonably foreseeable
that he would shout to warn other patrons; given the shout, it was reasonably
foreseeable that there would be a stampede; given the stampede, it was reasonably foreseeable that the claimant would be crushed. As long as one divides the
sequence in the 'right' way, nothing will turn out to be unforeseeable on this
model.

According to corrective justice, the issue is whether the appropriate normative connection exists between the defendant's negligence and the claimant's
injury. We are interested in whether the defendant was negligent because he created an unreasonable risk of the claimant's injury. In this case, it is helpful to
express the question in the following manner. Would it have been sensible to
have said to the defendant's employees, 'Don't forget to clean the grill, because
if you don't someone might get crushed in a stampede'? Although there is room
for disagreement, the natural answer appears to me to be 'No'. The claimant's
injury was too remote.

Incidentally, I believe that there is much to be gained by addressing the facts
in this manner, putting aside the convoluted and sometimes distracting legal
language. Consider *Palsgraf*: 'don't push people onto trains. People standing on
the other side of the platform may be injured by scales falling over on them.' Or
Polemis: 'don't knock planks of wood into the hold of the ship. The ship may be
destroyed by fire.' Compare *Winterbottom v Wright*: 'don't fail to maintain the
coach. The driver may be injured.'

The above demonstrates that in deciding whether the claimant's injury is or
is not remote, we are interested neither in the precise circumstances of the accident nor in the foreseeability of each step in the causal chain from the perspective
of the one before. The question is whether the defendant, as a reasonable
person, should have prevented the claimant's injury from occurring.

---

[84] [1974] SCR 409, 414. The notion that the negligence was proximate because the injury followed almost instantaneously appears to rely on the notion of directness.

(iii) The Extent of the Claimant's Injury

Reflection on *Doughty* shows that it cannot strictly be correct to say that the claimant's injury needs to be of a foreseeable kind *though not of a foreseeable extent*. This is because, if the *damage* suffered by the claimant is of an unforeseeable extent, then the *accident* must have been of an unforeseeable kind. Moreover, it is sometimes said that if the damage to the claimant was much greater in extent than was foreseeable, then the difference in the extent of damage amounts to a difference in the kind of damage. For instance, if I prick you with a pin, it is foreseeable that this will cause a minute bleed, but not that it will cause you to bleed to death. Hence, if you do bleed to death, your death is too remote to ground a cause of action in negligence. This conclusion is correct, but the example shows that the distinction between the extent and the kind of injury is unhelpful. We have said that recovery is not available, because your injury is so much larger than was foreseeable that this amounts to an injury of an unforeseeable kind. This means that the extent of your damage *is* relevant, *contra* Lord Reid in *Hughes v Lord Advocate*.

However, this constitutes no objection to the result in *Hughes v Lord Advocate*, which did not in fact involve recovery for an injury of unforeseeable extent. Lord Reid said:

> If the lamp fell and broke it was not at all unlikely that the boy would be burned and the burns might well be serious. No doubt it was not to be expected that the injuries would be as serious as those which the appellant in fact sustained. But a defender is liable, although the damage may be a good deal greater in extent than was foreseeable. He can only escape liability if the damage can be regarded as differing in kind from what was foreseeable.[85]

However, the fact that it was 'not to be *expected* that the injuries be as serious' as they were does not mean that those injuries were of an *unforeseeable* extent. Lord Reid, following the decision of the trial judge, maintained that it was foreseeable that the lamp would be broken and the paraffin would escape, and that the claimant would be burnt as a result. Surely, then, despite the trial judge's conclusion, it *was* foreseeable that the claimant would be very seriously burnt. In fact, I submit that it could not be said to be unforeseeable that someone would be killed by being burnt by paraffin escaping from a lamp. Hence, given a proper interpretation of the facts, the principle as stated by Lord Reid was unnecessary to decide *Hughes v Lord Advocate* in favour of the claimant. Certainly, the claimant's injuries were not to be expected in the sense that they were not likely, but that does not mean that they were unforeseeable in the sense that the defendant did not create an unreasonable risk of those injuries.

---

[85] *Hughes v Lord Advocate* [1963] AC 837, 845 (HL Sc).

(iv) Remoteness and Judgement

In deciding whether the claimant's injury is or is not remote, the Court is called on to make a twofold judgement. The second part of the judgement, explored above, concerns whether the claimant's injury was foreseeable from the perspective of the defendant's negligence. The first part of the judgement involves adopting an appropriate description of the defendant's negligence and the claimant's injury. Importantly, these are two parts of one judgement; they are not two separate judgements. One cannot decide whether the claimant's injury was foreseeable from the perspective of the defendant's negligence without deciding how to describe that injury and that negligence, and the fact that one is trying to decide whether the claimant's injury was foreseeable from the perspective of the defendant's negligence must guide the way one describes the injury and the negligence.

Consider *Hughes v Lord Advocate* once again. There are an infinite number of ways in which to describe that case. On some descriptions, the claimant's injury will clearly not be foreseeable. For instance, was it foreseeable that a boy would arrive with his 10-year-old uncle, play with the lamps by tying them to some rope, swing the lamps around, trip over a lamp, knock the lamp into the manhole, causing an explosion that in turn caused the claimant to fall into the manhole, causing serious burns, while being watched by a man named Bruce? No. Conversely, the claimant's injury will clearly be foreseeable according to some descriptions. For example, was it foreseeable that the claimant would suffer personal injury? Yes. Accordingly, it is the task of the court to choose the most appropriate description of the events from the infinite number of possibilities available.

There is no rule for this. Judgement is required. The appropriate description will depend on the nature of the circumstances and should be designed to reflect the relationship between the parties. The ultimate question is whether the claimant's injuries were within those risks by reason of which the defendant's conduct was characterised as negligent.[86]

---

[86] EJ Weinrib, *The Idea of Private Law* (Harvard University Press, Cambridge, Mass, 1995) 222–7. See also I Kant, *Critique of Pure Reason* (trans P Guyer and A Wood, Cambridge University Press, Cambridge, 1998) 268–9 [A132–34/B171–73]: '[g]eneral logic contains no precepts at all for the power of judgment, and moreover cannot contain them. For *since it abstracts from all content of cognition*, nothing remains to it but the business of analytically dividing the mere form of cognition into concepts, judgments, and inferences, and thereby achieving formal rules for all use of the understanding. Now if it wanted to show generally how one ought to subsume under these rules, i.e., distinguish whether something stands under them or not, this could not happen except once again through a rule. But just because this is a rule, it would demand another instruction for the power of judgment, and so it becomes clear that although the understanding is certainly capable of being instructed and equipped through rules, the power of judgment is a special talent that cannot be taught but only practiced . . . . A physician therefore, a judge, or a statesman, can have many fine pathological, juridical, or political rules in his head, of which he can even be a thorough teacher, and yet can easily stumble in their application, either because he is lacking in natural power of judgment (though not in understanding), and to be sure understands the universal *in abstracto* but cannot distinguish whether a case *in concreto* belongs under it, or also because he has not received adequate training for this judgment through examples and actual business.

Hence, in *Hughes v Lord Advocate*, the defendant's employees were negligent inter alia because they created an unreasonable risk that children would be lured into the tent to play with the lamps and would get burnt. That is what happened. Hence, the claimant's injury was not too remote. Conversely, in *Doughty*, the defendant's employee was negligent in creating an unreasonable risk that the claimant (and others) would be splashed. But that is not what happened. Accordingly, the claimant's injury was too remote. In *Hughes v Lord Advocate*, the claimant's injury was the kind of thing from which he should have been protected by the defendant's employees. In *Doughty* it was not. The question, then, is whether the claimant's injury (accident and damage) lay within the scope of the defendant's negligence.

It is important to stress once again that this is not a formulaic approach. I am not pretending that these results can be reached from formulae. I am making judgements, not applying mechanical rules.[87] But the judgements are not esoteric. We constantly make similar judgements in our ordinary lives. To put this into less formal language again, the question in *Hughes v Lord Advocate* and *Doughty* was whether it would have been sensible to have said to the defendant's employees, 'you should have realised that you shouldn't have done that; look what happened'. That clearly would not be sensible in *Doughty*, although, to me at least, it would make sense in *Hughes v Lord Advocate*.

Importantly, these judgements are what Kant called 'determining judgments' rather than 'reflecting judgments'. Judgement is determining when the universal is given and the agent must determine whether a particular falls under the universal. Conversely, judgement is reflecting when a particular is given and a universal must be found to accommodate it.[88] Both kinds of judgement are ubiquitous in thought, but perhaps the paradigm examples of reflecting judgements come from natural science, where they occur inter alia in the discovery of natural laws. Einstein's discovery of the effect of gravity on light is a good example. The particular is the observation that a star remains visible even when it lies wholly behind another object such as a planet. The reflecting judgement occurs when that phenomenon is explained by the postulation of the natural law that gravity bends light; hence the star can be seen because the light it produces is bent by the gravity of the planet that would otherwise obscure it. Of course, there are many other examples. Again, examples of determining judgements abound. I have the concept of a drinking glass, and when I look around me I make judgements on whether particular objects fall into this class. There are two important conclusions. First, the kind of judgement that judges are called upon to make is ubiquitous rather than unusual. Secondly, the judgement is not

---

[87] Applying rules also requires judgement. See SA Kripke, *Wittgenstein on Rules and Private Language: An Elementary Exposition* (Blackwell, Oxford, 1982); I Kant, *Critique of Pure Reason* (trans P Guyer and A Wood, Cambridge University Press, Cambridge, 1998) 268–9 [A132–34/B171–73]; I Kant, *Critique of the Power of Judgment* (trans P Guyer and E Matthews, Cambridge University Press, Cambridge, 2000).

[88] Kant, above n 87, 66–8 [5:179–81].

unconstrained, or even creative, in the way that reflecting judgements sometimes are. The task is simply to determine whether the facts of the case fall under
the principles of the law.

Although it is impossible to eliminate entirely the judge's subjectivity from
these judgements (just as it is impossible to eliminate entirely differences of
opinion on which objects count as drinking glasses), the aim of the common law
is to minimise subjectivity as much as possible. Although it is said that findings
of fact have no precedential value in the sense that they are not binding,[89] this
does not mean that judges should ignore previous findings of fact. The role of
the judge is not to determine whether *she* feels that the claimant's injuries are or
are not remote, but whether *the law* does. The law's view of the matter is to be
found by examining previous judgments in similar cases in the law reports.[90]

In consequence of the above, the idea that the claimant's injury must be of a
foreseeable kind though not of a foreseeable extent, is better elucidated as follows. The defendant must have created an unreasonable risk of the accident and
the damage the claimant suffered. In determining this, it is necessary to describe
the accident and the damage appropriately, not in too particular a fashion
(privileging the defendant) or in too general a fashion (privileging the claimant).
The task, as always, is to do justice between the parties. This involves judgement, but it is a judgement directed at the relationship between the parties and
constrained by legal principles and case law. It is a determining judgement, not
a policy-based free-for-all.[91]

(v) Hughes v Lord Advocate *Again*

Finally, it is necessary to address a further problem in reconciling *Doughty* with
Hughes v Lord Advocate. In the latter case, the defendant argued with some
force that the accident was unforeseeable. Lord Reid appears to have been persuaded:

> The explanation of the accident which has been accepted, and which I would not seek
> to question, is that, when the lamp fell down the manhole and was broken, some
> paraffin escaped, and enough was vaporised to create an explosive mixture which was
> detonated by the naked light of the lamp. *The experts agree that no one would have
> expected that to happen: it was so unlikely as to be unforeseeable. . . .*
>
> This accident was caused by a known source of danger, *but caused in a way which
> could not have been foreseen,* and in my judgment that affords no defence.[92]

If Lord Reid is rightly interpreted as saying that the type of accident need not
be reasonably foreseeable, then I submit that his Lordship was mistaken. As

---

[89] *Qualcast (Wolverhampton) Ltd v Haynes* [1959] AC 743 (HL).
[90] The law adopts essentially the same approach to determining damages for non-pecuniary loss,
as we see in ch 11.
[91] EJ Weinrib, *The Idea of Private Law* (Harvard University Press, Cambridge, Mass, 1995)
165–7.
[92] *Hughes v Lord Advocate* [1963] AC 837, 845, 847 (HL Sc) (emphasis added).

Doughty makes clear, if the accident was unforeseeable then it cannot have been the manifestation of an unreasonable risk created by the defendant. Hence, the accident was not something for which the defendant was responsible in corrective justice.

However, this does not mean that *Hughes v Lord Advocate* was wrongly decided. Lord Guest correctly maintained that the precise circumstances of the accident need not be foreseeable. To insist that the precise circumstances be foreseeable is to contend that the appropriate interpretation of the accident is always particular rather than general. But that would bias the enquiry in favour of the defendant. The issue in *Hughes v Lord Advocate*, then, was whether the unforeseeability of the actual sequence of events was relevant to an appropriate interpretation of the accident. Although it is certainly arguable that the claimant's injury in *Hughes v Lord Advocate* was remote—in that sense *Hughes v Lord Advocate* is a borderline case[93]—in my judgement the claimant's injury was sufficiently proximate to the defendant's negligence. This is because, given the relationship between the parties and the nature of the defendant's employee's negligence, and given that the interpretation of the accident is designed to affect corrective justice, the fact that there was an explosion was not relevant to an appropriate interpretation of the accident.

III. THE ROLE OF REASONABLE FORESEEABILITY IN DUTY AND REMOTENESS

It is sometimes said that the requirement of foreseeability is empty or misleading. This is because, at some level, everything is foreseeable. This is a serious challenge to any view according to which the standard of care, the duty of care and remoteness are unconnected. That is, if the duty of care and remoteness are independent of the standard of care, then the former stages appeal to an undefined and potentially limitless conception of foreseeability. This fuels the view that judicial appeals to 'reasonable foreseeability' are, in fact, empty and serve only to obscure the real reasons for courts' decisions.[94] But this problem arises only because the duty of care and remoteness are understood independently of the standard of care, and, as we have seen, it is a mistake to separate the stages of the negligence enquiry in this fashion.

What do we mean when we speak of 'reasonable foreseeability'? In particular, why do we refer to *reasonable* foreseeability? One possible answer is that 'reasonable foreseeability' is more restrictive than 'foreseeability' in the sense that there are fewer events that are reasonably foreseeable than are foreseeable, and hence the introduction of reasonableness into the formula is intended to

---

[93] The lower courts had found in favour of the defendant on the plausible ground that the accident was unforeseeable.

[94] See eg J Fleming, *The Law of Torts,* 9th edn (LBC Information Services, Sydney, 1998) 153.

restrict the scope of liability. But why do we wish to restrict liability in that fashion? The modern common lawyer is likely to answer that the restriction is desired for reasons of policy,[95] but the above has revealed a quite different answer.

According to Lord Atkin:

> You must take reasonable care to avoid acts or omissions which you can reasonably foresee would be likely to injure your neighbour. Who, then, in law is my neighbour? The answer seems to be—persons who are so closely and directly affected by my act that I ought reasonably to have them in contemplation as being so affected when I am directing my mind to the acts or omissions which are called in question.[96]

Hence, one owes a duty of care to those whose interests one *ought* to have considered. What is the content of this ought? In particular, how can we tell if someone has violated this obligation? The most natural answer in this context is that someone violated this obligation if he was negligent. And we know that someone is negligent if he violated the standard of care. Accordingly, one violates a duty of care owed to another if one falls below the standard of care with respect to that person, in other words, if one creates an unreasonable risk of injury to that person in the sense of 'unreasonable' defined in Chapter 3. Hence, asking whether the defendant put the claimant at a reasonably foreseeable risk is shorthand for asking whether the defendant created an unreasonable risk of injury to the claimant.

The connection between the standard of care and remoteness is even clearer in the judgment of Viscount Simonds in *The Wagon Mound (No 1)*:

> if it is asked why a man should be responsible for the natural or necessary or probable consequences of his act (or any other similar description of them), the answer is that it is not because they are natural or necessary or probable, but because, since they have this quality, it is judged, by the standard of the reasonable man, that he ought to have foreseen them.[97]

A man ought to have foreseen certain consequences if he created a real risk of them, but not if he created a FOFF risk of those consequences. Hence, the claimant's injury is not remote if the defendant created an unreasonable risk of it. Therefore, asking whether the claimant's injury was reasonably foreseeable is shorthand for asking whether the defendant created an unreasonable risk of that injury. As Lord Hoffmann has said, 'the law limits liability to those consequences which are attributable to that which made the act wrongful'.[98]

The judicial appeal to 'reasonable foreseeability', then, does not involve the obscuring of the real reasons for the court's decision. Completely the reverse,

---

[95] See eg ibid; H Luntz and D Hambly, *Torts: Cases and Commentary*, 4th edn (Butterworths, Sydney, 1995) 118.

[96] *M'Alister (or Donoghue) (Pauper) v Stevenson* [1932] AC 562, 580 (HL Sc).

[97] *Overseas Tankship (UK) Ltd v Morts Dock & Engineering Co Ltd (The Wagon Mound, No 1)* [1961] AC 388, 423 (PC).

[98] *South Australia Asset Management Co v York Montague Ltd* [1997] AC 191, 213 (HL).

the appeal *presents* those reasons. And when correctly using this term, courts do not refer to a general and undefined notion, but to precisely the concept required to link the defendant's wrongdoing (standard of care) to the claimant's (duty of care) injury (remoteness).

IV. ILLUSTRATIONS OF DUTY AND REMOTENESS

A. Liability to Rescuers

In *Wagner v International Railway Co*, Cardozo CJ said:

> Danger invites rescue. The cry of distress is the summons to relief. The law does not ignore these reactions of the mind in tracing conduct to its consequences. It recognizes them as normal. It places their effects within the range of the natural and probable. The wrong that imperils life is a wrong to the imperiled victim; it is a wrong also to his rescuer. The state that leaves an opening in a bridge is liable to the child that falls into the stream, but liable also to the parent who plunges to its aid . . . The railroad company whose train approaches without signal is a wrongdoer toward the traveler surprised between the rails, but a wrongdoer also to the bystander who drags him from the path . . . The risk of rescue, if only it be not wanton, is born of the occasion. The emergency begets the man. The wrongdoer may not have foreseen the coming of a deliverer. He is accountable as if he had.[99]

This statement can be read in one of two ways.

First, Cardozo CJ could have intended that, although the actions of a rescuer need not be reasonably foreseeable, the law will treat them *as if* they were. On this reading, then, the treatment of rescuers is an exception to the principles enunciated above, an exception that is likely to have been motivated to encourage rescues.[100] This reading is apparently supported by the claim that the wrongdoer need not have foreseen the rescue.

However, the notion that the defendant need not have foreseen the rescue is merely a consequence of the objective standard. The test is whether a reasonable person would have foreseen the risk, not whether the defendant actually foresaw it. In that light, it is more natural to read Cardozo CJ as arguing that a duty of care is owed to a rescuer because, and to the extent to which, the rescue was foreseeable to an ordinary reasonable person.

On this view, then, rescuers are treated in the same way as all other claimants. The claimant and the claimant's injury must be within the ambit of the risk created by the defendant. This will often be the case, as rescues are frequently

---

[99] 133 NE 437, 437–8 (NY CA 1921).

[100] See eg J Fleming, *The Law of Torts*, 9th edn (LBC Information Services, Sydney, 1998) 186; S Todd, 'Negligence: The Duty of Care' in S Todd (ed), *The Law of Torts in New Zealand*, 3rd edn (Brookers, Wellington, 2001) 167. Fleming also attempts to justify liability to rescuers by appeal to ethics: Fleming, above, 188.

reasonably foreseeable: 'The cry of distress is the summons to relief.' However, if the attempted rescue is wanton, then it constitutes a novus actus interveniens.[101]

For example, in *Haynes v Harwood*,[102] the defendant's employee negligently left unattended the defendants' two-horse van. The horses became scared and bolted. The claimant, a police officer who was sitting in a nearby police station, saw the horses galloping along the road and saw that others were placed at risk. He ran out of the station and seized one of the horses. Although he prevented others being harmed, the claimant was injured when one of the horses fell on him.

One of the questions for the Court was whether the claimant was owed a duty of care. Greer LJ said:

> What is meant by negligence? Negligence in the air will not do; negligence, in order to give a cause of action, must be the neglect of some duty owed to the person who makes the claim. In this case, if the duty was owed to, among others, the plaintiff—if he is one of a class affected by the want of care or the negligence of the defendants, that is negligence of which the plaintiff can avail himself as a cause of action. What is the negligence complained of here? Mr. Hilbery rightly described it as a failure to use reasonable care for the safety of those who were lawfully using the highway in which this van with the two horses attached was left unattended. I personally have no doubt that a policeman—or indeed any one, and still more a policeman, using the highway for the purpose of stopping a runaway horse and thereby preventing serious accidents and possibly preventing loss of life, is within the category of those lawfully using the highway.[103]

For Greer LJ, the issue was simply whether the claimant was of a class of persons reasonably foreseeably placed at risk by the defendants' employee's negligence. The defendants' employee was negligent because he created an unreasonable risk that lawful users of the road would be injured. The claimant was a lawful user of the road. Hence, a duty of care was owed to the claimant. The fact that the claimant was conducting a rescue had no impact on the principles of the law whatsoever. The claimant would not have used the roadway were he not attempting the rescue, but the rescue was reasonably foreseeable and that is what counted.

No policy is required in order to reach this result. The law has no soft spot for rescuers. The result in *Haynes v Harwood* is a simple application of the principle enunciated in *Donoghue v Stevenson*. 'Assuming the rescuer not to have acted unreasonably . . . he must normally belong to the class of persons who

---

[101] This is explored below. See also JW Neyers, '*Donoghue* v. *Stevenson* and the Rescue Doctrine: A Public Justification of Recovery in Situations Involving the Negligent Supply of Dangerous Structures' (1999) 49 *University of Toronto Law Journal* 475, 496–503.

[102] [1935] 1 KB 146 (CA).

[103] *Ibid*, 152–3.

ought to be within the contemplation of the wrongdoer as closely and directly affected by the latter's act'.[104]

Similarly, in *Urbanski v Patel*,[105] the defendant surgeon negligently removed a patient's only kidney during a tubal ligation. The claimant, who was the patient's father, offered one of his kidneys for transplant. However, the transplant was unsuccessful and the claimant sued the defendant for the loss of his kidney. The Manitoba Court of Queen's Bench found the defendant liable. Wilson J said:

> In testifying before me, Dr. Thomson spoke of 123 kidney transplants in Winnipeg alone; both he and Dr. Fenton spoke of the many thousands performed in the United States and Europe. If not routine . . . certainly I think it can fairly be said, in light of today's medicine, kidney transplant is an accepted remedy in renal failure. Certainly defendant here can hardly be heard to deny its 'foreseeability', in the dictionary sense of that word. . . . In other terms, the transplant, surely, must be viewed as an expected result, something to be anticipated, as a consequence of the loss of normal kidney function.[106]

As, given the circumstances, the claimant's actions were readily foreseeable, the defendant clearly owed the claimant a duty of care. Despite the apparent complications raised by the facts, as a matter of law the case was easily decided.[107]

The same approach applies when the defendant is the person being rescued. In *Harrison v British Railways Board*,[108] the defendant fell from a train due to his own negligence. The claimant, a guard on the train, was injured attempting the defendant's rescue. The defendant argued that the claimant could recover only if the defendant was under a duty to rescue him. The House of Lords rejected that argument. The issue was only whether the claimant's rescue —here of the defendant—was reasonably foreseeable. It was, so the defendant owed the claimant a duty of care.

In *Talbert v Talbert*,[109] the defendant attempted suicide by locking himself in a garage with a car engine running. The claimant, the defendant's son, was injured when he broke a window attempting to rescue his father. Again, the claimant successfully recovered. The defendant must have owed the claimant a duty of care, as the rescue was perfectly foreseeable.[110]

---

[104] *Ward v T E Hopkins* [1959] 3 All ER 225, 242 (CA) (Willmer LJ). See also JW Neyers, 'Donoghue v. Stevenson and the Rescue Doctrine: A Public Justification of Recovery in Situations Involving the Negligent Supply of Dangerous Structures' (1999) 49 *University of Toronto Law Journal* 475, 496–509.

[105] (1978) 84 DLR (3d) 650 (Man QB).

[106] *Ibid*, 671.

[107] Note, then, that the claimant would have been able to recover even if the transplant had been successful.

[108] [1981] 3 All ER 679 (QBD).

[109] 199 NYS 2d 212 (NY SC 1960).

[110] Note that *Talbert v Talbert* does not show that one owes a duty not to kill oneself. Rather, it shows only that one must not kill oneself in a way that exposes others to unreasonable risks.

As far as the duty of care goes, this is all that needs to be said. However, we must revisit the issue of rescuers when we examine the defence of *volenti non fit injuria*.

B. Not-yet-existent Claimants

In *Renslow v Mennonite Hospital*,[111] the defendants gave the claimant's mother a blood transfusion of an inappropriate blood type more than eight years before the claimant was conceived. The transfusion caused a sensitisation of the claimant's mother's blood, which resulted in injury to the claimant both *in utero* and post-natally. The defendants argued that, as the claimant did not exist at the time of the negligent transfusion, no duty of care could have been owed to the claimant.

The Illinois Court of Appeal refused to accept this argument, and rightly so. The issue was whether the claimant belonged to a class of persons put at reasonably foreseeable risk by the defendants' negligence. In this case, the claimant clearly belonged to that class:

> The complaint alleges that the defendants transfused the wrong type of blood into a teenage girl who several years later became the plaintiff infant's mother and that such conduct on the part of the defendants caused damage to the unborn infant which resulted in permanent physical injuries to the infant. We emphasise that the defendants are a doctor and a hospital. There has been no showing that the defendants could not reasonably have foreseen that the teenage girl would later . . . bear a child and that the child would be injured as the result of the improper blood transfusion.[112]

To doctors at least, one of the clearly foreseeable results of giving a woman an incorrect blood transfusion is that the foetuses she carries in the future may be damaged, leading to the birth of injured children. The claimant fell into this class, so the defendants owed the claimant a duty of care. Again, despite the complexity of the facts, this is a perfectly simple case.

This reasoning does not apply only to human claimants. In *Welbridge Holdings Ltd v Greater Winnipeg*,[113] the defendant municipality enacted a byelaw rezoning an area of land in order to permit the building of high-rise apartments. Sixteen months after the passage of the byelaw, the claimant company was incorporated in order to take advantage of the business opportunity presented by the byelaw. However, third parties successfully contested the byelaw, causing loss to the company. While the Manitoba Court of Appeal accepted that the defendant had been negligent, the Court ruled that the municipality did not owe the claimant a duty of care, as the claimant did not exist at the time of the negligent act.[114] The Court of Appeal said that the 'neighbour'

---

[111]   351 NE 2d 870 (Ill CA 1976).
[112]   *Ibid*, 874.
[113]   [1971] SCR 957.
[114]   *Welbridge Holdings Ltd v Greater Winnipeg* [1971] 12 DLR (3d) 124 (Man CA).

principle enunciated in *Donoghue v Stevenson* did not extend to an entity not yet in existence. However, in the Supreme Court of Canada, Laskin J disagreed and held that the duty of care could be owed to the claimant company.[115] Again, this flows from *Donoghue v Stevenson*. It was reasonably foreseeable that a company would be incorporated to take advantage of the byelaw. Hence, the claimant was owed a duty of care.

C. Novus Actus Interveniens

The issue of novus actus interveniens is perhaps the most difficult and complicated area of the law of negligence. The developing case law on this issue has moved further and further away from a principled approach and has descended into chaos. I begin by exploring this descent. I then propose an alternative, principled approach to novus actus interveniens that is based on corrective justice and on the discussion of duty and remoteness earlier in this chapter.

(i) Case Law

In *Home Office v Dorset Yacht Co Ltd*,[116] the claimant alleged that the defendant's employees failed appropriately to supervise a group of borstal boys. As a result, the boys attempted an escape. Given that they were on an island, the boys chose the only realistic means of escape available: they stole a yacht. This yacht collided with and damaged a yacht belonging to the claimant.

The issue for the House of Lords concerned the appropriate impact of the actions of third parties on the relationship between the claimant and the defendant. In *Dorset Yacht*, the question was whether the wrongdoing of the borstal boys meant that the defendant could not be liable. Over Viscount Dilhorne's dissent, the House of Lords ruled that the claimant was owed a duty of care, the claimant's injury was not too remote, and therefore the defendant was liable. Lord Reid asked:

> What, then, is the dividing line? Is it foreseeability or is it such a degree of probability as warrants the conclusion that the intervening human conduct was the natural and probable result of what preceded it? There is a world of difference between the two. If I buy a ticket in a lottery or enter a football pool it is foreseeable that I may win a very large prize—some competitor must win it. But, whatever hopes gamblers may entertain, no one could say that winning such a prize is a natural and probable result of entering such a competition.
>
> In *Haynes v Harwood*, Greer LJ said . . .
>
> > 'If what is relied upon as novus actus interveniens is the very kind of thing which is likely to happen if the want of care which is alleged takes place, the principle

---

[115] *Welbridge Holdings Ltd v Greater Winnipeg* [1971] SCR 957, 966.
[116] [1970] AC 1004 (HL).

embodied in the maxim is no defence. The whole question is whether or not, to use the words of the leading case, *Hadley v. Baxendale*, the accident can be said to be "the natural and probable result" of the breach of duty.'[117]

In fact, as we see below, Lord Reid misread Greer LJ's judgment in *Haynes v Harwood*. Nevertheless, Lord Reid's claim was that, when the wrongdoing of a third party intervenes between the defendant's negligence and the claimant's injury, the defendant can be liable only if the claimant's injury was a *natural and probable* consequence of the defendant's negligence. In other words, the claimant could recover only if the defendant's negligence made her injury *likely*.[118]

However, as Lord Denning MR noticed in *Lamb v Camden London BC*,[119] Lord Reid's position is inconsistent with the principles enunciated in *The Wagon Mound (No 1)*. In that case, liability was said to rely on reasonable foreseeability, not likelihood. Moreover, it is widely believed that Lord Reid's view extends liability too widely.[120]

Alternatively, Lord Diplock concluded:

I should therefore hold that any duty of a borstal officer to use reasonable care to prevent a borstal trainee from escaping from his custody was owed only to persons whom he could reasonably foresee had property situate in the vicinity of the place of detention of the detainee which the detainee was likely to steal or to appropriate and damage in the course of eluding immediate pursuit and recapture. Whether or not any person fell within this category would depend on the facts of the particular case including the previous criminal and escaping record of the individual trainee concerned and the nature of the place from which he escaped.[121]

Not only is this open to the same objections raised in connection with Lord Reid's view above, Lord Diplock's position is entirely unprincipled. Why is liability limited only to those who are in the vicinity of the escape? This appears to be an ad hoc response to the particular facts of *Dorset Yacht*. Lord Diplock called for an arbitrary restriction to avoid what he regarded as overly extensive liability. Lord Diplock's position is a partial return to *Polemis*: the claimant can recover from the defendant only if her injury was a 'direct' consequence of the defendant's negligence. But we are in no better position here than we were in *Polemis* itself.

Moreover, Lord Diplock justified the defendant's potential liability as follows:

In the present appeal the place from which the trainees escaped was an island from which the only means of escape would presumably be a boat accessible from the shore

---

[117] [1970] AC 1004 (HL), 1028. Quotation from *Haynes v Harwood* [1935] 1 KB 146, 156 (CA).
[118] It is important not to put too much emphasis on this word. It is a term of convenience that is useful in order to distinguish Lord Reid's position from those discussed below.
[119] [1981] 1 QB 625, 633–5 (CA). For reasons discussed below, Lord Denning's criticism was more than a little disingenuous.
[120] See the discussion that follows.
[121] *Home Office v Dorset Yacht Co Ltd* [1970] AC 1004, 1070–1 (HL).

of the island. There is thus material . . . for holding that the respondents, as the owners of a boat moored off the island, fell within the category of persons to whom a duty
of care to prevent the escape of the trainees was owed by the officers responsible for
their custody.

   If therefore . . . it was reasonably foreseeable by the officers that if these particular
trainees did escape they would be likely to appropriate a boat moored in the vicinity
of Brownsea Island for the purpose of eluding immediate pursuit and to cause damage
to it, the borstal officers would be in breach of a duty of care owed to the respondents
and the respondents would, in my view, have a cause of action against the Home
Office as vicariously liable for the 'negligence' of the borstal officers.[122]

Accordingly, the reason the defendant was potentially liable was that the
claimant's injury was a reasonably foreseeable consequence of the defendant's
employee's negligence. But if that was so, then the limitations Lord Diplock
placed on liability shatter the coherence of the enquiry. If liability arises *because
of* the reasonable foreseeability of the claimant's injury, then it should arise
whenever the claimant's injury is reasonably foreseeable. We cannot have *The
Wagon Mound (No 1)* and *Polemis* together if the law is to make sense.

   The differences between Lord Reid's and Lord Diplock's judgments in *Dorset
Yacht* were fundamental and important. As if that were not bad enough, the law
fell into a state of absolute chaos from which it has not recovered with the decision of the English Court of Appeal in *Lamb v Camden London BC*.[123]

   The claimant left her house in the care of a tenant. The defendant council
conducted road works outside the house. The defendant's employees broke a
water main, causing water to flood the house. As a result, the tenant moved out
and the claimant removed her furniture from the house. Later, because the
house was unoccupied and unfurnished, squatters moved in and caused considerable damage. The claimant wanted to recover that loss from the defendant
council, but the defendant argued that the behaviour of the squatters constituted
a novus actus interveniens.

   A unanimous Court of Appeal ruled against the claimant. But their Lordships
could not agree about why. Oliver LJ claimed that the loss was not reasonably
foreseeable,[124] but Lord Denning[125] and Watkins LJ[126] rejected that view.
Moreover, although their Lordships could not agree on the correct approach to
novus actus interveniens, they all disagreed (explicitly) with Lord Reid and
(implicitly) with Lord Diplock.

   Oliver LJ maintained that a claimant could recover only if her injury was a
very likely consequence of the defendant's negligence. However, Oliver LJ did
not define 'very likely' but left the standard to be considered on a case-by-case
basis:

---

[122] *Ibid*, 1071.
[123] This was a case decided in nuisance, however, the relevant principles are the same in negligence.
[124] *Lamb v Camden London BC* [1981] 1 QB 625, 643–4 (CA).
[125] *Ibid*, 632–3.
[126] *Ibid*, 639–40.

There may, for instance, be circumstances in which the court would require a degree of likelihood amounting almost to inevitability before it fixes a defendant with responsibility for the act of a third party over whom he has and can have no control. . . . [T]hat does not arise here, and the problem can be left for a case in which it directly arises.[127]

Which circumstances? Why does that not arise here? Oliver LJ did not say.

The approach enunciated by Oliver LJ collapsed into complete incoherence in Lord Mackay's judgment in *Smith v Littlewoods Organisation Ltd*:

The more unpredictable the conduct [of the intervener] in question, the less easy to affirm that any particular result from it is probable and in many circumstances the only way in which a judge could properly be persuaded to come to the conclusion that the result was not only possible but reasonably foreseeable as probable would be to convince him that, in the circumstances, it was highly likely.[128]

What does 'reasonably foreseeable as probable' mean? Whatever the answer to that question, how could showing that an event was reasonably foreseeable as probable possibly require showing that the event was highly likely?

The failure to state a principled basis for dealing with novus actus interveniens is also clear in Watkins LJ's judgment in *Lamb*. Ironically, after insisting that courts show respect for the principle enunciated in *The Wagon Mound (No 1)*, Watkins LJ's said:

A robust and sensible approach to this very important area of the study of remoteness will more often than not produce, I think, an *instinctive feeling* that the event or act being weighed in the balance is too remote to sound in damages for the plaintiff. I do not pretend that in all cases the answer will come easily to the inquirer. But that the question must be asked and answered in all these cases I have no doubt.

To return to the present case, I have the instinctive feeling that the squatters' damage is too remote. I could not possibly come to any other conclusion, although on the primary facts I, too, would regard that damage or something like it as reasonably foreseeable in these times.[129]

The unsuccessful claimant cannot have been very impressed by this argument. Instinctive feelings do not make a robust and principled approach to the law.

Moreover, though his Lordship said that:

the very features of an event or act for which damages are claimed themselves suggest that the event or act is not upon any practical view of it remotely in any way connected with the original act of negligence. These features will include such matters as the nature of the event or act, the time it occurred, the place where it occurred, the identity of the perpetrator and his intentions and responsibility, if any, for taking measures to avoid the occurrence and matters of public policy.[130]

---

[127] *Lamb v Camden London BC* [1981] 1 QB 644.
[128] [1987] 1 AC 241, 261 (HL).
[129] *Lamb v Camden London BC* [1981] 1 QB 625, 647 (CA) (emphasis added).
[130] *Ibid*.

His Lordship also maintained that the claimant's injury was reasonably fore-seeable.[131] On the face of it, these claims are inconsistent and are not made less so by reference to instinctive feelings.

Note, that the criticism of Watkins LJ's position is not that it calls for judge-ment. On the contrary, Watkins LJ was surely right that, at the end of the day, the judge will have to make a judgement on whether the claimant's injury was remote or not. Rather, the criticism is that Watkins LJ called for judgement without the guidance of principle. The judgement should be based on one or more principles that serve to guide and constrain it. The process should not be left wide open, providing no guidance, as does Watkins LJ's reference to instinc-tive feelings.

But all this was overshadowed by Lord Denning's incendiary judgment. His Lordship argued that principle had no role to play in the law, because principle was merely a smokescreen for judicial policy making. Under the heading 'The Truth', his Lordship explained himself as follows:

> The truth is that all these three, duty, remoteness and causation, are all devices by which the courts limit the range of liability for negligence or nuisance. As I said recently in *Compania Financiera Soleada SA v Hamoor Tanker Corpn Inc, The Borag* . . .' . . . it is not every consequence of a wrongful act which is the subject of compen-sation. The law has to draw a line somewhere.'
> Sometimes it is done by limiting the range of the persons to whom duty is owed. Sometimes it is done by saying that there is a break in the chain of causation. At other times it is done by saying that the consequence is too remote to be a head of damage. All these devices are useful in their way. But ultimately it is a question of policy for the judges to decide. I venture to repeat what I said in *Dutton v Bognor Regis Urban District Council* . . .
>
>> It seems to me that it is a question of policy which we, as judges, have to decide. The time has come when, in cases of new import, we should decide them according to the reason of the thing. In previous times, when faced with a new problem, the judges have not openly asked themselves the question: what is the best policy for the law to adopt? But the question has always been there in the background. It has been concealed behind such questions as: Was the defendant under any duty to the plain-tiff? Was the relationship between them sufficiently proximate? Was the injury direct or indirect? Was it foreseeable or not? Was it too remote? And so forth. Nowadays we direct ourselves to considerations of policy.[132]

Even ignoring Lord Denning's repeated appeal to himself as an authority, this argument is extraordinary. According to Lord Denning, the judges of the past—and, we might add, those of the present who prefer to base their decisions on legal principles—were dishonest. They pretended to base their decisions on the principles they enunciated in the cases, but this was really the intentional concealing of the true basis of their decisions, viz their personal political

[131] *Ibid.*
[132] *Ibid*, 636–7.

preferences, which they chose to hide from public scrutiny. Though this view is quite popular in contemporary circles, it is a conspiracy theory of the first order. And, like most conspiracy theories, it is backed up by almost no evidence. Why is it so hard to believe that the judges of the past honestly presented their reasons in their judgements, even if we happen to disagree with them?

Moreover, if Lord Denning were right—if the law of negligence simply were nothing more than the case-by-case application of judges' sense of what was best for the community—then the law of negligence surely ought to be abolished. We cannot justify a system in which judges—a small section of the socio-economic elite, usually trained only in law, unelected, protected from public criticism, removable from office only in extreme circumstances, and appointed until a late retirement date—make decisions about what is good for the rest of the community in this manner.[133] Unless one believes in a kind of aristocracy *and* would select judges as one's chosen aristocrats, Lord Denning's argument not only attacks his opponents, but destroys the position he intends to defend. In that sense, Lord Denning's judgment is the judicial equivalent of a suicide bombing.

In any event, what were the policies that Lord Denning considered decisive in *Lamb*?

> I ask myself: whose job was it to do something to keep out the squatters? And, if they got in, to evict them? To my mind the answer is clear. It was the job of the owner of the house, Mrs Lamb, through her agents. That is how everyone in the case regarded it. It has never been suggested in the pleadings or elsewhere that it was the job of the council.[134]

This argument relies on an equivocation in the meaning of 'keep out'. Taking the argument to mean that it was the job only of the claimant physically to prevent the squatters from entering the property, then Lord Denning's claims are correct. But on that interpretation the argument does nothing to show that the claimant should have failed. This is because the claimant was suing the defendant, not for failing physically to prevent the squatters from entering the property, but for wrongfully creating the opportunity for the squatters to enter the property. On this interpretation, therefore, the argument is entirely irrelevant. However, the argument appears to be relevant because the question 'whose job was it to do something to keep out the squatters?' appears to ask a wider question than 'whose job was it physically to prevent the squatters to enter the property?', viz 'whose job was it to make sure that the squatters did not enter the property?' In other words, the argument appears to be relevant because it seems to incorporate the question: 'whose job was it to prevent the squatters having the opportunity to enter the property?' But that is the question that the case had

---

[133] I explore these points in more detail in A Beever, 'The Law's Function and the Judicial Function' (2003) 20 *New Zealand Universities Law Review* 299.
[134] *Lamb v Camden London BC* [1981] 1 QB 625, 637 (CA).

to decide and Lord Denning simply *assumed* that the answer refers only to the claimant. On this interpretation, it is certainly not true that its not being the defendant's job was 'how everyone in the case regarded it', as it was the claimant's contention that that was precisely the defendant's job. What we require is a *reason* why this job was the claimant's and not the defendant's, but Lord Denning does not provide one.

The second string to Lord Denning's bow was insurance:

> On broader grounds of policy, I would add this: the criminal acts here, malicious damage and theft, are usually covered by insurance. By this means the risk of loss is spread throughout the community. It does not fall too heavily on one pair of shoulders alone. The insurers take the premium to cover just this sort of risk and should not be allowed, by subrogation, to pass it on to others.[135]

The claimant in *Lamb* may not have had insurance, but Lord Denning concluded that she should have had insurance and so, if she did not, 'that [was] her misfortune'.[136]

Again, this argument is circular. The reason Lord Denning concluded that the claimant should have been insured was that he believed that it was the claimant's responsibility to protect herself from the damage caused by the squatters. If his Lordship had believed that it was the defendant's responsibility, then he would have argued that the defendant should have been insured (as the defendant surely was). Hence, the insurance argument has as its premise the notion that the claimant was responsible, and so cannot argue for the truth of that premise. The truth or falsity of that premise is precisely the issue in the case. In effect, then, Lord Denning's view collapses into Watkins LJ's. While he intends to provide an argument for his conclusions, in fact his Lordship's conclusions are based on his instinctive feelings.

Finally, Viscount Dilhorne suggested a further possibility in *Dorset Yacht*: the defendant cannot be liable at all. In a passage that could almost be a paraphrase of Alderson B's judgment in *Winterbottom v Wright*, Viscount Dilhorne argued that the only way to prevent indeterminate liability was arbitrarily to cut it off.[137] Moreover, both harking back to Lord Buckmaster in *Donoghue v Stevenson*[138] and anticipating the incremental approach, Viscount Dilhorne maintained that the existence of a duty of care should be decided almost exclusively by reference to precedent. 'We are concerned not with what the law should be but with what it is. The absence of authority shows that no such duty

---

[135] *Ibid*, 637–8.

[136] *Ibid*, 638.

[137] *Home Office v Dorset Yacht Co Ltd* [1970] AC 1004, 1043 (HL).

[138] *M'Alister (or Donoghue) (Pauper) v Stevenson* [1932] AC 562, 566–78 (HL Sc). See especially ibid, 567: '[t]he law applicable is the common law, and, though its principles are capable of application to meet new conditions not contemplated when the law was laid down, these principles cannot be changed nor can additions be made to them because any particular meritorious case seems outside their ambit'.

now exists. If there should be one, that is, in my view, a matter for the legislature and not for the courts.'[139]

We are offered a choice between unprincipled discretion, arbitrary restrictions to the principled approach, or abandonment of that approach in favour of a pre-*Donoghue v Stevenson* style 'elaborate classification of duties' that would prevent liability in cases such as *Dorset Yacht* and *Lamb*.[140]

It is immediately apparent that the latter is untenable. If *D* cannot be liable to *C* when a necessary condition for *C*'s injury was the wrongful intervention of a third party, then no liability would be possible in a case such as *Dorset Yacht*—not even the borstal boys could be sued (even if they had sufficient funds). This is because the injury to the claimant occurred only because of the actions of both the borstal boys and the Home Office employees. The boys and the employees were both necessary conditions for the claimant's injury.

Perhaps, however, it might be suggested that only the borstal boys should be liable, because only they were *really* to blame. What does 'really' mean here though? If this is not a purely intuitive judgement, then it must be possible to explicate the claim in terms of the principles of the law of negligence. But it is not. According to those principles, both the boys and the employees were really to blame (which is not to say that they were equally to blame).

(ii) An Alternative

Is there a better way to decide these cases? I argue now that there is. However, the view advanced here cannot answer all of the concerns raised in the cases explored above. But this is because, so I argue, those concerns are misplaced.

In *Haynes v Harwood*, Greer LJ said:

> If what is relied upon as novus actus interveniens is the very kind of thing which is likely to happen if the want of care which is alleged takes place, the principle embodied in the maxim is no defence. The whole question is whether or not, to use the words of the leading case, *Hadley v. Baxendale*, the accident can be said to be 'the natural and probable result' of the breach of duty. If it is the very thing which ought to be anticipated by a man leaving his horses, or one of the things likely to arise as a consequence of his wrongful act, it is no defence; it is only a step in the way of proving that the damage is the result of the wrongful act.[141]

---

[139] *Home Office v Dorset Yacht Co Ltd* [1970] AC 1004, 1045 (HL). See also T Weir, 'The Staggering March of Negligence' in P Cane and J Stapleton (eds), *The Law of Obligations: Essays in Celebration of John Fleming* (Clarendon Press, Oxford, 1998) 99.

[140] *M'Alister (or Donoghue) (Pauper) v Stevenson* [1932] AC 562, 579 (HL Sc)(Lord Atkin).

[141] *Haynes v Harwood* [1935] 1 KB 146, 156 (CA). Not surprisingly, this brilliant judgment was produced soon after *Donoghue v Stevenson*. Nor is it surprising that, as the law departs further and further from *Donoghue v Stevenson*, this issue becomes more and more clouded in confusion. However, it is possible to interpret parts of both Lord Reid's judgment in *Dorset Yacht* and Watkins LJ's judgment in *Lamb* as coinciding with Greer LJ's position in *Haynes v Harwood*. See also EJ Weinrib, *The Idea of Private Law* (Harvard University Press, Cambridge, Mass, 1995) 219–22.

As discussed above, in *Dorset Yacht* Lord Reid interpreted this as a departure from the principle of reasonable foreseeability. But that is not the most natural way to read Greer LJ's judgment.

In *Haynes v Harwood*, the defendant's employee negligently left a two-horse van unattended in the street. The horses were scared when a boy, 'obviously with a mischievous propensity',[142] threw a stone at them. The horses bolted, causing injury to a police officer. Greer LJ said:

> In considering this case one must take into account the nature of the street in which the two horses were left. A little way to the left of Quiney's Yard, on the opposite side of the road, are certain tenement dwellings, and just opposite Quiney's Yard there are dwelling-houses. Coming along on the same side as were the horses and van, one finds a church, a school entrance, and a number of houses which, having regard to the locality, are probably occupied by working-class people with families. We are told that altogether there are three schools in this neighbourhood, and that between 4 and 5 o'clock in the afternoon there are always many children about. It was in this kind of place the defendants' driver chose to leave his vehicle.[143]
>
> There can be no doubt in this case that the damage was the result of the wrongful act in the sense of being one of the natural and probable consequences of the wrongful act. It is not necessary to show that this particular accident and this particular damage were probable; it is sufficient if the accident is of a class that might well be anticipated as one of the reasonable and probable results of the wrongful act.[144]

One of the reasons the defendant's employee was negligent was that he created an unreasonable risk that children would come along and scare the horses, causing them to bolt and do injury to users of the road. This meant that, although the injury to the claimant required the wrongful intervention of a third party, the defendant must remain liable.

On Greer LJ's view, then, to be liable not only must the defendant have created an unreasonable risk of the claimant's injury; the defendant must also have created an unreasonable risk of the third party intervention.[145] This is no new policy-based rule designed to cut back on liability, but is merely the application of the approach to remoteness explored in *Doughty*. If the defendant did not create an unreasonable risk of the third party's intervention, then the *type of accident* would not have been reasonably foreseeable and the claimant would have been injured as a result of the materialisation of a risk created by the defendant that was FOFF.

In my view, that is all that there is to be said about novus actus interveniens. Hence, the search for policy to limit liability is unmotivated. The appropriate limits to liability are found within the ordinary principles of the law as enunciated in

---

[142] *Haynes v Harwood* [1935] 1 KB 146, 151 (CA).
[143] *Ibid*.
[144] *Ibid*, 156. See also M Stauch, 'Risk and Remoteness of Damage in Negligence' (2001) 64 *MLR* 191, 211–14.
[145] This is the 'step in the way of proving that the damage is the result of the wrongful act': *Haynes v Harwood* [1935] 1 KB 146, 156 (CA).

the leading cases explored above. In the following, I apply this reasoning to *Dorset Yacht* and to *Lamb* as well as to a hypothetical example explored by Oliver LJ in the latter case.

In *Dorset Yacht*, the defendant's employees created an unreasonable risk that the borstal boys would steal a yacht and cause damage to the claimant's property. Hence, the House of Lords were right to say that a duty of care could be owed in such circumstances and that the claimant's injury was not too remote. Note that this means that, in finding such a defendant liable (ignoring vicarious liability), the defendant is being found responsible for its own wrong. Although the negligence committed by the defendant would not have materialised in injury to the claimant without the additional wrong of the third parties (the borstal boys), this cannot show that the defendant did not wrong the claimant. The defendant created an unreasonable risk of the very injury suffered by the claimant.[146]

This can usefully be contrasted with *Wright v Lodge*.[147] The first defendant's car broke down and she negligently failed to push it to the side of the road. The second defendant, driving at grossly excessive speed, crashed into the back of the first defendant's car, injuring the claimant passenger.[148] The English Court of Appeal ruled that, while the second defendant's negligence was a proximate cause of the claimant's injury, the first defendant's negligence was too remote. This was because the first defendant was not negligent for creating the risk that the claimant would be injured by a third party driving at grossly excessive speed. The second defendant's action, then, was a novus actus interveniens. Note that the reason the second defendant's action was a novus actus interveniens was *not* because it was illegal, but because the first defendant did not create an unreasonable risk of it.

The situation in *Lamb* is somewhat more complicated. Part of the problem with this case lies in the difficultly of assessing the magnitude of the risk created by the defendant's nuisance that squatters would occupy the claimant's house. One imagines that the risk was small, though certainly not FOFF in the England of the day.[149] But, when the defendant's employees caused the water main to burst, increasing the risk of squatters, it was incumbent on the defendant to eliminate only that risk—ie the increased risk that squatters would move in. The defendant did not have to eliminate any FOFF risks or the risk of squatters moving in altogether. How could the defendant eliminate that risk?

As Lord Denning rightly argued, few options were open to the defendant:

> The council were not in occupation of the house. They had no right to enter it. All they had done was to break the water main outside and cause the subsidence. After they

---

[146] Compare T Weir, 'The Staggering March of Negligence' in P Cane and J Stapleton (eds), *The Law of Obligations: Essays in Celebration of John Fleming* (Clarendon Press, Oxford, 1998) 99.

[147] [1993] 4 All ER 299 (CA).

[148] The issue arose because the second defendant was attempting to recover contribution from the first. The claimant was not attempting to recover from the first defendant.

[149] Conversely, it probably would not have been reasonably foreseeable in New Zealand.

had left the site, it was Mrs Lamb herself who paved the way for the squatters by moving out all her furniture and leaving the house unoccupied and unfurnished.[150]

In fact, the defendant's first duty was to pay damages to the claimant to repair the harm caused by the water. If the defendant did so and the claimant chose not to spend this money on repairs, then any adverse outcomes would have been the claimant's responsibility.[151]

Of course, however, the defendant was entitled to dispute its liability to the claimant for the initial water damage, and so was entitled to withhold compensation until the matter had been settled by a court of law. But if the defendant did so, the defendant would have had to compensate the claimant for any continuing loss, subject to the claimant's 'duty' to mitigate. In *Lamb*, if the defendant had chosen to dispute its liability to the claimant for the water damage, and the claimant had acted reasonably in not conducting repairs pending the outcome of the trial, and as a result squatters occupied the house, then the defendant should have been liable for the loss caused by the squatters. But that is not what happened in *Lamb*. As Lord Denning pointed out, the claimant did not act reasonably to prevent squatters. Rather, she 'paved the way for the squatters by moving out all her furniture and leaving the house unoccupied and unfurnished'.[152] This, then, was a novus actus interveniens, and hence the defendant was responsible only for the water damage.[153]

As above, it helps to express the idea in less formal language. Would it have been sensible to have said to the defendant's employees, 'Be careful with that pick. The owner might choose to move all her furniture out and then squatters might move into that house.'[154] In my view, it would not.

Finally, I turn to the hypothetical situation explored by Oliver LJ in *Lamb:*

> Suppose that as a result of the carelessness of a prison officer a prisoner escapes and commits a crime of the same type as that for which he is in custody a fortnight later and 400 miles away from the place at which he escaped. . . . [I]s the Home Office to be liable without limit until the prisoner is apprehended? Does it make any difference if he is, at the date of his escape, on remand or due for parole?[155]

Watkins LJ insisted that finding liability in such circumstances 'would plainly be a ludicrous conclusion'.[156]

---

[150] *Lamb v Camden London BC* [1981] 1 QB 625, 637 (CA).

[151] Compare *ibid*, 637–8.

[152] *Ibid*, 637.

[153] This could also be expressed by saying that the claimant failed to mitigate.

[154] This treats the case as if it were in negligence rather than nuisance, but the point remains. This discussion also reveals that part of the problem with *Lamb* was that their Lordships committed the same error as diagnosed in regard to *Bradford v Kanellos* above. That is, their Lordships argued that, if the water main was broken, then it was reasonably foreseeable that the house would be damaged. Given the damage, it was reasonably foreseeable that the tenant would move out. Given that the tenant moved out, it was reasonably foreseeable that squatters would move in. Given that squatters moved in, it was reasonably foreseeable that they would cause damage.

[155] *Lamb v Camden London BC* [1981] 1 QB 625, 643 (CA).

[156] *Lamb v Camden London BC* [1981] 1 QB 646.

Imagine that a prisoner with a record of violent crime escapes due to a defendant prison officer's negligence. Imagine also that the prisoner violently assaults someone 400 miles from the prison. Why is it plainly ludicrous to hold that the defendant should be liable? One reason prison officers should be careful to prevent the escape of violent offenders is that such offenders are likely to commit violent offences. 'If what is relied upon as novus actus interveniens is the very kind of thing which is likely to happen if the want of care which is alleged takes place, the principle embodied in the maxim is no defence.'[157] While the judges in *Lamb* would regard this conclusion as absurd, there is nothing remotely absurd about it.

Oliver LJ placed much emphasis on the idea that the claimant's injury was physically distant from the occurrence of the defendant's negligence. But why is this significant? Oliver LJ called for a return to the law before *Donoghue v Stevenson*. As Lord Atkin noted,[158] in *Le Lievre v Gould* Lord Esher said that *Heaven v Pender*:[159]

> established that, under certain circumstances, one man may owe a duty to another, even though there is no contract between them. If one man is near to another, or is near to the property of another, a duty lies upon him not to do that which may cause a personal injury to that other, or may injure his property.[160]

Ironically, in *Donoghue v Stevenson* itself, the claimant was injured in a place close to the defendant's bottling premises. Hence, *Donoghue v Stevenson* could have been decided according to Lord Esher's statement of the law and did not require the legal revolution that it represents. One suspects that Lord Atkin was aware of this. But, even if so, his Lordship's reluctance to accept the law as expressed in *Le Lievre v Gould* is understandable. The defendant's liability in *Donoghue v Stevenson* should not have turned on such accidents as the physical proximity of the defendant's bottling plant. For this reason, Lord Atkin instead interpreted 'nearness' to refer to mental rather than physical proximity. What is of normative significance is not physical proximity but reasonable foreseeability. Hence, the location of the claimant's injury mattered not one iota in *Donoghue v Stevenson* and nor should it in Oliver LJ's hypothetical case. If one should not allow prisoners to escape because they may commit crimes 400 miles away, then one should be liable if one's negligence contributes to the escape and a crime is committed 400 miles away.

This does not mean that physical distance is always irrelevant. If the defendant did not create an unreasonable risk of injury to anyone over a certain distance away, then duties of care were not owed to such persons. This is not because of their physical distance *simpliciter*, but because their physical distance

---

[157] *Haynes v Harwood* [1935] 1 KB 146, 156 (CA).
[158] *M'Alister (or Donoghue) (Pauper) v Stevenson* [1932] AC 562, 580–1 (HL Sc).
[159] (1882–1883) LR 11 QBD 503 (CA).
[160] [1893] 1 QB 491, 497 (CA).

from the defendant's negligence meant that injury to them was not reasonably foreseeable. However, as escaped prisoners are liable to travel far—in fact, one of the reasons they should not be permitted to escape is that they are apt to travel far—this point is not relevant to our hypothetical case.

But while physical distance is irrelevant per se, is distance in time also irrelevant? What if the escaped prisoner commits a crime two years after escaping? What about three years? What about 10 years?[161] The answer to these questions depends on the risk created by the defendant. If the defendant created a substantial risk that the prisoner would escape and be at large for 10 years, then the defendant should be liable. If the defendant created a small risk of the escaped prisoner being at large for 10 years and the burden of eliminating that risk was not high, then again the defendant should be liable. I take it, however, that that will rarely be the case. The risk of an escaped prisoner being at large for a long period, while not FOFF, is small and the burden of eliminating such risks is likely to be high. However, this changes if recapture rates are low. But if recapture rates are low, all the more reason why prison officers should be careful to ensure that prisoners do not escape.

Moreover, it follows from the above that if the escaped prisoner commits an offence while at large of which the defendant did not create an unreasonable risk, then the claimant's injury will be remote. For instance, in *State of New South Wales v Godfrey & Godfrey*,[162] an escaped prisoner, apparently thought to pose little risk to the public,[163] committed an armed robbery, threatening the first claimant with a shotgun. The first claimant, who was 23 weeks pregnant, suffered nervous shock and as a result her child, the second claimant, was born prematurely with disabilities. The appropriate question, then, was whether the actions of the prison authorities created a substantial risk, or a small risk where the burden of eliminating that risk was not high, that the first claimant would suffer nervous shock in an armed robbery and that the second claimant would be born premature and disabled. Though the facts are not available, it is most likely that the risk of these injuries was small and the burden of eliminating them was high. Accordingly, as the New South Wales Court of Appeal decided for different reasons, the State of New South Wales should not have been liable.

Finally, what should happen if the prisoner is on remand or parole? First, the defendant cannot be negligent for failing to do something he was under a legal obligation not to do. Hence, if the defendant is not entitled to keep the offender in custody, the defendant cannot be negligent for failing to keep the offender in custody. Secondly, the defendant can be negligent only if the offender posed an unreasonable risk to the public, but if the offender posed such a risk, then he

---

[161] One response is to point to limitation statutes. However, I do not rely on these here, because they limit liability beyond the principled approach. This is why these limitations must be statutory.

[162] [2004] NSWCA 113, [2004] Aust Tort Reports 81-741.

[163] At least this is how I interpret the fact that the prisoner escaped from a 'minimum security section of Bathurst Gaol': *ibid*, [1].

should not have been released. Subject to the third point below, it would appropriate to find liability in such circumstances. Thirdly, if the defendant has
statutory authority to release the offender even though the release poses an
unreasonable risk to the public in the sense relevant in negligence, then the
defendant's potential liability is extinguished by statute. Similarly, if the defendant enjoys other immunity from liability, then he cannot be sued. Hence, in normal circumstances at least, judges cannot be sued for giving bail to dangerous
criminals.[164]

Of course, as the above also demonstrates, if we as a community do not like
the implications of a principled approach to these cases, we are entitled to
amend the common law through legislation. But whether we should do so is not
the issue here. We are concerned with the proper understanding of the common
law in respect of novus actus interveniens. This understanding may or may not
cohere with the best social policies, but that is irrelevant. However, at the very
least, a correct application of the principles enunciated in *The Wagon Mound
(No 1)* and *Doughty* to situations of novus actus interveniens is far from
ludicrous.

D. The Exception: The Thin Skull Rule

I have argued above that seemingly difficult problems can be solved relatively
easily by taking seriously the principled approach as revealed in a number of
leading cases. But there is one notable exception: the thin skull rule. As courts
have interpreted this rule, it is inconsistent with the principles of the law and
generates inappropriate results.

In *Smith v Leech Brain & Co Ltd*,[165] the claimant's husband was employed in
an iron works, inter alia to galvanise articles by lowering them by crane into a
tank. Due to the defendant's negligence in not providing better safety equipment, the claimant's husband had to shelter behind a piece of corrugated iron in
order to avoid being burnt by substances escaping from the tank. During one
operation, a piece of molten metal struck the claimant's husband, causing a relatively minor burn. However, the site of the burn later ulcerated and grew. It
was discovered that the claimant's husband had cancer, of which he later died.
The claimant sued for the wrongful death of her husband.

Lord Parker CJ maintained that the principle enunciated by the Privy Council
in *The Wagon Mound (No 1)* did not apply to this or to relevantly similar
cases.[166] His Lordship also insisted that, in this case:

---

[164] Nonfeasance is also an issue here. See ch 6 and EJ Weinrib, *The Idea of Private Law* (Harvard
University Press, Cambridge, Mass, 1995) 152–4 n16.

[165] [1962] 2 QB 405 (QBD). In the following, I ignore the fact that this was a wrongful death
claim. Wrongful death actions are discussed briefly in ch 1.

[166] *Ibid*, 415.

The test is not whether these defendants could reasonably have foreseen that a burn would cause cancer and that Mr. Smith would die. The question is whether these defendants could reasonably foresee the type of injury which he suffered, namely, the burn. What, in the particular case, is the amount of damage which he suffers as a result of that burn, depends on the characteristics and constitution of the victim.[167]

On this view, when dealing with personal injury, if the initial injury suffered by the claimant was reasonably foreseeable, then all consequences of that injury are proximate, whether reasonably foreseeable or not. This is a departure from *The Wagon Mound (No 1)*, as it entails that a defendant can be liable for the materialisation of FOFF risks. As Viscount Simonds said in *The Wagon Mound (No 1)*:

> Their Lordships have already observed that to hold B liable for consequences, however unforeseeable, of a careless act, if, but only if, he is at the same time liable for some other damage, however trivial, appears to be neither logical nor just. This becomes more clear if it is supposed that similar unforeseeable damage is suffered by A and C, but other foreseeable damage, for which B is liable, by A only. A system of law which would hold B liable to A but not to C for the similar damage suffered by each of them could not easily be defended.[168]

But this is just what the thin skull rule requires. In *Leech Brain*, the risk of cancer was FOFF; nevertheless the defendant was found liable for creating it.

Not only is the thin skull rule inconsistent with the law's approach to remoteness, but there are at least three other crucial problems with it. These can be brought out by considering three questions. First, must the unforeseeable consequences of the reasonably foreseeable initial injury also constitute personal injury? Secondly, must the consequences of the reasonably foreseeable initial injury occur to the victim of that injury in order for the claimant to recover? Thirdly, why does the thin skull rule apply only to personal injury? I explore these questions in the context of real and hypothetical cases below.[169]

In *Cotic v Grey*,[170] the defendant negligently caused serious head injuries to the claimant's husband in a driving accident. Before the accident, the claimant's husband had suffered from neuroses and was prone to depression. The head injuries sustained in the accident aggravated this condition. Sixteen months after the accident, the claimant's husband committed suicide. The Ontario Court of Appeal found the defendant liable for his death. This is inconsistent with the approach to proximity illustrated in *The Wagon Mound (No 1)* and *Doughty*. The defendant created only a FOFF risk that the claimant's husband would commit suicide.[171]

[167] Ibid.
[168] *Overseas Tankship (UK) Ltd v Morts Dock & Engineering Co Ltd (The Wagon Mound, No 1)* [1961] AC 388, 425 (PC).
[169] These questions cannot be answered by insisting that the claimant's ultimate injury must be a *direct* consequence of the initial injury. For the reasons explored earlier in this ch in relation to *In Re Polemis*, that answer is empty.
[170] (1981) 124 DLR (3d) 641 (Ont CA).
[171] Moreover, the injury to the actual claimant was not a personal injury.

In *Kavanagh v Akhtar*,[172] the defendant's employees negligently dropped a box of perfume onto the claimant's shoulder causing injury. Because of her injury, the claimant could no longer care for her long hair and decided to cut it short. This angered the claimant's husband, a strict Muslim, so much that he separated from his wife. In consequence, the claimant suffered psychiatric injury. The New South Wales Court of Appeal applied the thin skull rule and held that the claimant's psychiatric injury was not too remote from the defendant's negligence.

If the claimant's husband had also suffered psychiatric injury because of the separation, should he also have been able to recover? If the claimant's husband had battered the claimant, should the claimant have been able to recover for that injury from the defendant? If the claimant chose to sue her husband for that injury, should the husband have been able to claim contribution from the defendant? Should the defendant have been liable if the claimant's psychiatric injury caused her to damage her property?

Finally, in *McColl v Dionisatos*,[173] Young CJ applied the thin skull rule to a case involving property damage and no personal injury.

The problem is this. If the thin skull rule should be applied in *Leech Brain*, why should it not also be applied in *Cotic v Grey*, *Kavanagh v Akhtar* and *McColl v Dionisatos*? If the thin skull rule applies to allow recovery for unforeseeable personal injuries, then why must the unforeseeable injury be personal injury, why does the injury have to be to the person who suffered the reasonably foreseeable initial injury, and why does the rule apply only to personal injury? Moreover, if the rule allows recovery for unforeseeable injuries, why does the claimant have a cause of action only if she can prove that her initial injury was reasonably foreseeable? And why does that initial injury have to be a personal injury?

Another way of putting these questions is to ask: how is the thin skull rule consistent with *The Wagon Mound (No 1)* and *Doughty*? The answer is that it is not consistent. Given *The Wagon Mound (No 1)* and *Doughty*, then, the questions raised above cannot be answered adequately.

It is sometimes said that the thin skull rule reflects the general principle that the tortfeasor must take the victim as he finds him.[174] But it is misleading to describe this as a general principle that applies in this context. The principle applies appropriately to the law of damages. The idea is that, if the defendant wrongfully caused the claimant's loss, then the claimant should be able to recover that loss even if a different claimant would not have suffered that loss. If, for instance, I negligently destroy a car that belongs to a family of 10 with only one car, then I will ordinarily have to pay more compensation to that

---

[172] (1988) 45 NSWLR 588 (CA).

[173] [2002] NSWSC 276, [2002] Aust Tort Rep 81-652 causation. Hence, despite Young CJ's claims to the contrary, the case raised no issue of remoteness whatsoever and the thin skull rule should not have been applied.

[174] See eg *Smith v Leech Brain & Co Ltd* [1962] 2 QB 405, 415 (QBD).

family than I would to a family of four with two cars. This is because the loss of the car to the family of 10 is likely to be a bigger loss than the loss of a car to the family of four. It is not open to me to argue that I should be excused from paying for some of this loss, because it was I who wrongly caused it.

But these issues are not relevant to the thin skull rule. There, we are not concerned with the extent of the defendant's liability for wrongfully caused loss, but with whether the defendant caused any loss wrongfully. That is, the issue is liability not damages. Unfortunately, here and elsewhere, the analytical distinction between the enquiry into liability and that into damages has been collapsed in recent times. Much of the material from Chapter 7 on can be understood as, in part, an attempt to re-establish that distinction.

In the example above, I am liable for the family's loss, even though I may not have foreseen how large it would have been, because I wrongfully caused it. But in determining what is wrongful, in the law of negligence at any rate, it is necessary to take into account what I, or a reasonable person in my position, could have foreseen. Hence, if I could not have foreseen that my action could have caused the injury that the claimant suffered, then I cannot have been negligent in respect of that injury. Accordingly, I did not wrongfully cause that injury. I must take my victim as I find him, but my behaviour is to be judged by standards fair as between us. The rule in relation to damages for wrongdoing must not be allowed to pervert the different, though closely related, enquiry into wrongdoing itself.

Furthermore, in *Stephenson v Waite Tileman Ltd*,[175] the defendant had negligently failed to maintain a wire cable. The cable was rusted and had begun to de-strand itself so that small sprags of wire split off from the cable. This was said to have been negligent, because it posed a real risk that someone would be scratched or cut by the sprags.[176] As it happened, the claimant steeplejack was scratched on the hand when the cable broke away from its sheave. The claimant argued that an unknown virus had entered through his broken skin, resulting in severe disability, including inability to concentrate, loss of balance and recurring headaches.

Richmond J argued that the thin skull rule should apply and consequently found for the claimant. His Honour referred to the influential argument of Glanville Williams:

> [W]here the plaintiff has suffered bodily injury, it is difficult to maintain the cold logical analysis of the situation [as called for in *The Wagon Mound (No 1)*]. Human bodies are too fragile, and life too precarious, to permit a defendant nicely to calculate how much injury he may inflict without causing more serious injury.[177]

---

[175] [1973] 1 NZLR 152 (CA).
[176] *Ibid*, 153–4.
[177] G Williams, 'The Risk Principle' (1961) 77 *LQR* 179, 196. See also J Fleming, *The Law of Torts*, 9th edn (LBC Information Services, Sydney, 1998) 235.

First, however, this argument cannot justify the rule that the claimant's initial injury must be reasonably foreseeable. Secondly, there are many things besides human bodies that are 'too fragile . . . to permit a defendant nicely to calculate how much injury he may inflict without causing more serious injury', but injury to these things does not attract the thin skull rule. Thirdly, the relevance of calculation is opaque. The issue is the *reasonable foreseeability* of the risk, not the calculability of its precise likelihood or seriousness.

In fact, *contra* Williams, the difficulty of predicting the outcome of an initial injury means that *more, not fewer*, ultimate injuries are reasonably foreseeable. Hence, the fact that it is difficult to calculate how much personal injury an event will inflict shows that a great many personal injuries are reasonably foreseeable. Conversely, if it were easy to predict personal injuries, then far fewer personal injuries would be reasonably foreseeable. Accordingly, the fact that it is difficult to predict personal injuries shows that there is *less* need for the thin skull rule than there would be were such injuries easy to forecast. Therefore, Williams' argument tends to the opposite conclusion from the one he reached: the principle of reasonable foreseeability is quite adequate to deal with personal injury.

Finally, the ultimate difficulty with the thin skull rule is that it is inconsistent with the negligence enquiry to which it is meant to apply. It calls for a regime of strict liability to operate within the bounds of the law of negligence. According to the rule, the defendant can be liable only if he causes a reasonably foreseeable injury, but he can also be liable for unforeseeable injuries. If the law is to make sense in this area, we will have to choose. Moreover, in consequence of the above, the thin skull rule is inconsistent with the concerns that underlie the standard of care, as examined in Chapter 3. As we discovered, the law adopts an objective standard to judge the behaviour of the defendant. This means that the defendant is to be judged according to the standard of the ordinary reasonable person unless the parties possess idiosyncrasies that affect their relationship. This was contrasted with a subjective standard, that privileges the defendant, and strict liability, which biases the enquiry in favour of the claimant. But, as it is a restricted form of strict liability, the thin skull rule permits the claimant to assert his idiosyncrasies, thereby biasing the enquiry in his favour. This must not be permitted if the law is to be fair as between the parties.

V. CONCLUSION

The thin skull rule aside, the principled approach to duty and remoteness develops a coherent enquiry that focuses on the connection between the defendant's negligence and the claimant's injury. The enquiry is neither policy-based nor arbitrary. It is an ideal embodiment of corrective justice. Moreover, we have again seen that corrective justice is a powerful model for elucidating the duty of care and remoteness stages of the negligence enquiry. As we will see in the next chapter, the policy-driven approaches do significantly worse.

5

Modern Approaches to the Duty of Care

T HE DEVELOPMENT OF the approach to negligence explored in Chapters 3 and 4 was one of the greatest achievements in the history of the common law. It is one of the common law's greatest tragedies that it has been abandoned and forgotten. At the beginning of the twenty-first century, we have not only lost faith in the notion that a coherent account of the law of negligence will be forthcoming, we have also forgotten that it was attempted with remarkable success over a period beginning as recently as 80 years ago. In consequence, the modern view of law is profoundly different from Lord Atkin's or Cardozo CJ's. Their project is misunderstood and rejected as naïve and unrealistic, or even dismissed as a distortion and a distraction.[1]

As we shall see, their approach is far more resilient than ours, and is quite capable of dealing with the problems of the modern world. Moreover, the approaches developed in various common law jurisdictions since the 1970s are at best pale shadows of the principled approach. Frankly, negligence law as it exists today is lamentable. It is particularly so because it has arisen by abandoning an understanding of law infinitely superior to it.

Why has this happened? Although there are many reasons, the most important is found in the story of the modern law with which this book began. As we saw in Chapter 1, according to that view the generalist approach to the law of negligence, elucidated so powerfully in cases such as *Donoghue v Stevenson*[2] and *The Wagon Mound (No 1)*,[3] never completely gained the upper hand because it called for liability in circumstances where that appeared inappropriate. For our purposes, there are three major areas in which it is said to occur: with respect to liability for economic loss, for omissions and for the causation of mental injury. According to standard readings of the law, liability in these areas constrained only by the principled approach would be unacceptable, and so it is necessary to appeal to policy in order to keep liability within sensible limits.[4]

---

[1] J Fleming, *The Law of Torts*, 9th edn (LBC Information Services, Sydney, 1998) 193–4; JC Smith and P Burns, '*Donoghue v. Stevenson*—The Not So Golden Anniversary' (1983) 46 *MLR* 147.

[2] *M'Alister (or Donoghue) (Pauper) v Stevenson* [1932] AC 562 (HL Sc).

[3] *Overseas Tankship (UK) Ltd v Morts Dock & Engineering Co Ltd (The Wagon Mound, No 1)* [1961] AC 388 (PC).

[4] See eg GC Christie, 'The Uneasy Place of Principle in Tort Law' in D Owen (ed), *Philosophical Foundations of Tort Law* (Oxford University Press, Oxford, 1995); Fleming, above n4, 154–5,

In Chapters 7 and 8, I show that this story is a fiction. The principled approach does not generate inappropriate liability. Before demonstrating that, however, I compare the approach to the duty of care explored in the last chapter with more modern methods. I argue that the modern approaches are seriously flawed as they either lack content altogether or lack the kind of content necessary for them to play their justificatory role. Accordingly, the modern approaches are incapable of providing the law of negligence with a secure foundation.

Conducting this argument before examining the issue of liability for economic loss, omissions and mental injury that largely motivates the modern approaches may appear hollow and unfair. But even if the principled approach were defective, it would not follow that the modern alternatives were desirable. In this chapter, I demonstrate that, whatever the truth about the principled approach, the modern approaches are seriously inadequate. Hence, even if they were the lesser of two evils, they would be nevertheless very great evils indeed.

The modern law contains two general approaches for determining the existence of a duty of care: the *Anns* approach and the incremental approach. Both grew out of the decision of the House of Lords in *Anns v London Borough of Merton*.[5] I explore each in turn before briefly examining a potential new approach that focuses on the vulnerability of the claimant.

I. THE *ANNS* APPROACH

A. The Development of the *Anns* Approach

In *Home Office v Dorset Yacht Co Ltd*, Lord Reid said:

> In later years there has been a steady trend towards regarding the law of negligence as depending on principle so that, when a new point emerges, one should ask not whether it is covered by authority but whether recognised principles apply to it. *Donoghue v Stevenson* may be regarded as a milestone, and the well-known passage in Lord Atkin's speech should I think be regarded as a statement of principle. It is not to be treated as if it were a statutory definition. It will require qualification in new circumstances. But I think that the time has come when we can and should say that it ought to apply unless there is some justification or valid explanation for its exclusion.[6]

In *Anns*, Lord Wilberforce paraphrased Lord Reid as follows:

> Through the trilogy of cases in this House, *Donoghue v Stevenson*, *Hedley Byrne & Co Ltd v Heller v Partners Ltd* and *Home Office v Dorset Yacht Co Ltd*, the position

---

193; Smith and Burns, above n1, 152–5. S Todd, 'Negligence: The Duty of Care' in S Todd (ed), *The Law of Torts in New Zealand*, 3rd edn (Brookers, Wellington, 2001) 252; T Weir, *Tort Law* (Oxford University Press, Oxford, 2002) 45.

[5] [1978] AC 728 (HL).
[6] [1970] AC 1004, 1026–7 (HL).

has now been reached that in order to establish that a duty of care arises in a particular situation, it is not necessary to bring the facts of that situation within those of previous situations in which a duty of care has been held to exist. Rather the question has to be approached in two stages. First one has to ask whether, as between the alleged wrongdoer and the person who has suffered damage there is a sufficient relationship of proximity or neighbourhood such that, in the reasonable contemplation of the former, carelessness on his part may be likely to cause damage to the latter, in which case a prima facie duty of care arises. Secondly, if the first question is answered affirmatively, it is necessary to consider whether there are any considerations which ought to negative, or to reduce or limit the scope of the duty or the class of person to whom it is owed or the damages to which a breach of it may give rise . . .[7]

This is referred to as the '*Anns* test' or the 'two-stage test'. The first stage involves an enquiry into proximity and the second into policy. On Lord Wilberforce's version of the test, policy functions only to negative prima facie duties of care. This formulation of the test was also adopted in Canada in *Kamloops (City) v Nielsen*.[8] As expressed by Cory J in *Dobson v Dobson*:

before imposing a duty of care, the court must be satisfied: (1) that there is a sufficiently close relationship between the parties to give rise to the duty of care; and (2) that there are no public policy considerations which ought to negative or limit the scope of the duty, the class of persons to whom it is owed, or the damages to which a breach of it may give rise.[9]

Again, policy plays only a negative role. It may negative a duty of care but it cannot create one.

Things are more complicated in New Zealand however. In the leading case in that jurisdiction, *South Pacific Manufacturing Co Ltd v New Zealand Security Consultants & Investigations Ltd*,[10] three different approaches to the duty of care were expressed.

First, Casey J held that:

in deciding whether a duty of care lies, foreseeability of loss is only a factor among others going to make up the necessary relationship of proximity between the plaintiff and the defendant, of such a nature that it is fair just and reasonable that the latter should be held responsible for loss occasioned by his carelessness. If such a relationship of proximity is found, policy considerations may—probably in rare cases only—still negative the existence of a duty.[11]

Hence, Casey J would have allowed policy only a small ambit: the role of policy is purely negative and arises in rare cases only.

---

[7] *Anns v London Borough of Merton* [1978] AC 728, 751–2 (HL).
[8] [1984] 2 SCR 2.
[9] [1999] 2 SCR 753, 766.
[10] [1992] 2 NZLR 282 (CA). This case adopts an intermediate position between the *Anns* test and the incremental approach. However, it is generally understood in New Zealand to be a version of the *Anns* test, hence it is interpreted here in that light. As we shall see, nothing important hangs on this categorisation.
[11] *Ibid*, 312. Casey J also supported the 'incremental approach' explored below.

Compare this with Richardson J's position:

> The ultimate question is whether in the light of all the circumstances of the case it is just and reasonable that a duty of care of broad scope is incumbent on the defendant . . . It is an intensely pragmatic question requiring most careful analysis. It has fallen for consideration in numerous cases in this Court over recent years and, drawing on *Anns v Merton London Borough Council*, we have found it helpful to focus on two broad fields of inquiry. The first is the degree of proximity or relationship between the alleged wrongdoer and the person who has suffered damage. . . . The second is whether there are other policy considerations which tend to negative or restrict—or strengthen the existence of—a duty in that class of case.[12]

As duties of care do not come in degrees, and hence do not need strengthening, the only plausible way to read this claim is that policy can both negative prima facie duties and create duties when no prima facie duty exists.

Finally, compare the judgment of Cooke P, who said:

> A broad two-stage approach or any other approach is only a framework, a more or less methodical way of tackling a problem. How it is formulated should not matter in the end. Ultimately the exercise can only be a balancing one and the important object is that all relevant factors be weighed. There is no escape from the truth that, whatever formula be used, the outcome in a grey area case has to be determined by judicial judgment. Formulae can help to organise thinking but they cannot provide answers.[13]

In other words, determining the existence of a duty of care is all about policy and has nothing to do with principle.[14]

Accordingly, it is somewhat misleading to speak of there being one approach based on *Anns*. Supporters of Lord Wilberforce's account in *Anns* itself may have no time for Richardson J's or Cooke P's reformulation of the approach in *South Pacific*. Nevertheless, as we see below, Cooke P's judgment most accurately depicts the operation of the *Anns* approach in practice, however that approach is officially formulated.

B. Criticism of the *Anns* Approach

The two-stage test is meaningful only if it is possible to elucidate each stage of the test. But that is impossible. Beginning with the second stage of the *Anns* test, while one can say that policy may negative a prima facie duty of care, and perhaps create a duty of care where no prima facie duty exists, this means nothing concrete unless 'policy' has some determinate content. But it has no such

---

[12] [1992] 2 NZLR 305. The text replaced by the second ellipsis is crucial and is explored below.
[13] *Ibid*, 294.
[14] See further A Beever, 'The Law's Function and the Judicial Function' (2003) 20 *New Zealand Universities Law Review* 299, 318.

content. In fact, policy is entirely open-ended.[15] As outlined in Chapter 1, Jane Stapleton identifies 50 policy concerns that have been raised by the courts.[16] It is unlikely that she caught them all, and others must have appeared since the publication of her article. Accordingly, it has been argued that 'any attempt to provide an exhaustive list of every factor which might conceivably weigh in the scale is to pursue a will-o'-the-wisp'.[17] But this means that the second stage of the *Anns* test is empty. It is a *tabula rasa* that judges are called on to fill in however they see fit in individual cases.

Stapleton attempts to mitigate this difficulty with the *Anns* test by distinguishing lists of convincing and unconvincing policies from the 'melange'[18] of considerations relied on by the courts. Nevertheless, she has 29 considerations on her convincing list, and there is no reason to think that these are, or that Stapleton thinks that they are, the only 29 available. Moreover, not all will agree with the lists Stapleton provides. For instance, Stapleton insists that the argument advanced by Lord Bridge in *Murphy v Brentwood District Council*[19]— that the claimant cannot recover economic loss suffered as the result of purchasing a poorly constructed building, as such would be to give the claimant the benefit of a contract to which he was not a party—belongs on the unconvincing list.[20] As we see in Chapter 7, I disagree. Moreover, Stapleton lists as convincing the idea that a duty of care should be denied if finding a duty would encourage abortion or discourage rescues.[21] My own view is that such concerns are irrelevant.

The point is not that my attitude to these policies must be correct while Stapleton's must be mistaken, but rather that the *Anns* test provides absolutely no direction as to how these disputes should be settled. This is a necessary cost of the appeal to policy: the *Anns* test invites and requires judges to make

---

[15] For the sake of clarity, the claim is not that 'policy', or anything else, need be *fully* determinate in the sense that it could be applied by a computer or such. Rather, the claim is that the second stage of the test has content only if it directs judges to consider a perspicuous set of considerations. However, the second stage of the test is a licence for judges to consider *anything* they believe important. Hence, the content of the second stage is entirely indeterminate and is, therefore, empty. See also EJ Weinrib, *The Idea of Private Law* (Harvard University Press, Cambridge, Mass, 1995) 23, 25, 222–7.

[16] J Stapleton, 'Duty of Care Factors: A Selection from the Judicial Menus' in P Cane and J Stapleton (eds), *The Law of Obligations: Essays in Celebration of John Fleming* (Clarendon Press, Oxford, 1998) 92–5. It should be noted that Stapleton is no friend of the *Anns* test or the incremental approach, referring to both as 'vacuous': J Stapleton, 'The Golden Thread at the Heart of Tort Law: Protection of the Vulnerable' (2003) 24 *Australian Bar Review* 135, 137. However, her approach to policy fits with the second stage of the *Anns* test and so is examined here.

[17] S Todd, 'Negligence: The Duty of Care' in S Todd (ed), *The Law of Torts in New Zealand*, 3rd edn (Brookers, Wellington, 2001) 151–2.

[18] EJ Weinrib, 'Does Tort Law Have a Future?' (2000) 34 *Valparaiso University Law Review* 561, 566.

[19] [1991] 1 AC 398, 480–1 (HL).

[20] J Stapleton, 'Duty of Care Factors: A Selection from the Judicial Menus' in P Cane and J Stapleton (eds), *The Law of Obligations: Essays in Celebration of John Fleming* (Clarendon Press, Oxford, 1998) 93.

[21] *Ibid.*

open-ended political decisions.[22] Accordingly, many will disagree with Stapleton's list of convincing factors because they do not share her political views. For instance, Stapleton maintains that duties of care should be denied if they would 'be particularly onerous on disadvantaged groups'.[23] Libertarians would disagree. Moreover, many of the policies enunciated by Stapleton depend on political views for their content. For example, Stapleton claims that duties of care should be denied if the duty would encourage exploitation of others in breach of good faith principles, there are 'explicit and sound reason(s) the area is one more appropriate to Parliamentary action', the duty would conflict with the appropriate ambit of free speech and so on.[24] But there will be wide disagreement as to what these ideas mean in practice. Accordingly, not only is the second stage of the *Anns* test a *tabula rasa*, it is an invitation for judges and commentators to pursue their personal visions of the good society. In other words, the second stage of the *Anns* test is an invitation to judges to abandon the rule of law in favour of the rule of judges.

One reply is that most judges constrain their appeal to policy so as to prevent the law degenerating into ad hoc politicking in which only a handful have the vote. But the criticism of the *Anns* test is unaffected by the truth of this reply. According to the test, the desire to prevent this degeneration could be only yet one more policy to consider. The test itself allows judges to appeal to anything. If a judge's personal commitment to the rule of law prevents her from taking advantage of that opportunity, then she is to be congratulated, but the test is not.

A related problem with the *Anns* test is that, in applying the second stage of the test, courts involve themselves with concerns that lie beyond their institutional competence. For instance, Stapleton includes on her convincing list the policy of denying a duty of care if the alternative would 'produce a *specified* unattractive socio-economic impact'.[25] But judges are not in a position to make these decisions, both because they lack the necessary information and because they usually lack the training to deal in an informed matter with the information if they had it.[26]

---

[22] Note that the claim is not that the *Anns* test forces judges to make decisions that are *relevant* to politics. Arguably, all decisions are so relevant. Rather, the point is that the test forces judges to consider political arguments in making decisions. Hence, the decisions are themselves political, and not merely relevant to politics. Of course, some insist that all judicial decision making is political in both senses. I reject this claim and this book is intended as a partial refutation of such views.

[23] Stapleton, above n20, 95.

[24] *Ibid*, 94.

[25] *Ibid*, 93.

[26] P Benson, 'The Idea of a Public Basis of Justification for Contract' (1995) 33 *Osgoode Hall Law Journal* 273, 313; JW Neyers, '*Donoghue v. Stevenson* and the Rescue Doctrine: A Public Justification of Recovery in Situations Involving the Negligent Supply of Dangerous Structures' (1999) 49 *University of Toronto Law Journal* 475, 481–2; EJ Weinrib, 'Does Tort Law Have a Future?' (2000) 34 *Valparaiso University Law Review* 561, 566; A Beever, 'The Law's Function and the Judicial Function, (2003) 20 *New Zealand Universities Law Review* 299, 307–9.

It is sometimes held that the public would support this kind of approach. For instance, Lord Steyn has recently claimed that 'today the ever more knowledgeable public would be astonished if they thought that judges did not regard the attainment of practical justice as their main task'.[27] This certainly does not reflect my experience of the attitudes of non-lawyers, but in any case, if it were true that the general populations of the societies in which we live—rather than merely lawyers in those societies—were content to allow judges to make policy decisions of this kind, then that would be curious indeed. Why would we be prepared to spend considerable effort and taxpayers' money setting up ministries containing expert policy analysts in order to ensure that ministers get the best advice possible, and yet be prepared to allow judges with little or no social policy training, advised by lawyers with little or no social policy training, to make social policy choices in the absence of the data necessary to make those choices informed ones? Judges may be entitled to rely on reports prepared by ministries, etc. But there are three problems with this strategy. First, policy advice is often conflicting and judges are generally not in a position to decide on the merits of such advice. Secondly, the accurate interpretation and application of policy advice often calls for expertise in the subject matter of the advice. Thirdly, if it is argued that judges may rely on ministry reports because those reports were prepared by persons with significantly greater expertise than the judges themselves in a subject matter relevant to judging, then we should replace those currently on the bench with the experts who write the reports. According to the view under examination, judges are novices in the task they must perform as judges and so must be advised by the experts. But it would be desirable to have the experts actually making the decisions, at least in final appellate courts. (On the view advanced in this book, on the other hand, it is right for judges to be making judicial decisions, because the judges are the experts as judicial decisions are legal and not political.)

Moreover, I expect that the general populations of our societies would *not* be happy with the picture of the law developed by the *Anns* test. In fact, I would expect them to be outraged by it and, indeed, all to whom I have explained this view have been outraged by it. It is worth remembering that lawyering is not exactly the world's most respected profession, and the idea that judges know best is likely to be much less appealing to the layman than to the lawyer.

A further objection to the second stage of the *Anns* test is that it calls for a balancing of incommensurables.[28] As a general rule (subject to the argument of the following chapters), if the claimant's injury was a reasonably foreseeable

[27] Lord Steyn, 'Perspectives of Corrective and Distributive Justice in Tort Law' (2002) 37 *Irish Jurist* 1, 3.
[28] Weinrib, above n26, 567. R Mullender, 'Corrective Justice, Distributive Justice, and the Law of Negligence' (2001) 17 *Professional Negligence* 35, 41–3 argues that this incommensurability can be overcome by reference to the notion of 'qualified deontology'. But Mullender does not explain how qualified deontology achieves this. Moreover, Mullender appears to interpret corrective justice as an individual focussed form of distributive justice and so does not confront the real incommensurability.

consequence of the defendant's negligence, then corrective justice dictates that the claimant may recover. However, on the *Anns* test, this can be negatived if policy concerns are sufficiently weighty. Conversely, if the claimant's injury was not a reasonably foreseeable consequence of the defendant's negligence, corrective justice dictates that the claimant cannot recover. However, on New Zealand's version of the *Anns* test, the claimant may nevertheless recover if policy is believed to be sufficiently important. 'Sufficiently weighty' or 'sufficiently important' must mean sufficient to outweigh corrective justice. But how is one to compare the weight of corrective justice with that of policy?

Concerns such as corrective justice cannot appropriately be treated as mere preferences to be balanced along with others in a utilitarian fashion, inter alia, because, to the extent to which they can be regarded as preferences at all, they are preferences not to be subject to utilitarian calculation. For instance, the 'preference' for rights is, inter alia, a 'preference' that some things not be balanced against others in utilitarian terms.[29] Hence, the attempt to balance all such considerations at the second stage of the *Anns* test is farcical. As such, the second stage of the *Anns* test:

> requires judges to balance categorically different considerations, in order to determine whether in a given case the policy considerations are more important than the justice considerations that they can displace. How is this balancing of incommensurables to be done? In effect, the two-stage test puts into circulation two different normative currencies between which no rate of exchange exists.[30]

Moreover, conflicting policies themselves often involve incommensurable concerns: economic efficiency and social justice perhaps.

As a result, despite the insistence of those who support a policy-driven approach to the law of negligence that courts should present good reasons for their decisions, the policy-driven model removes the ability of courts to do just that. In the following chapters, we explore some prominent examples of this in regard to economic loss and negligent misstatement, and we have also seen this in relation to Lord Denning's judgment in *Lamb v Camden London BC*[31] in Chapter 4. Accordingly, for the moment it will suffice to present one example that lies outside these areas.

In *McFarlane v Tayside Area Health Board*[32]— a case discussed in more detail in Chapter 11—the claimants were falsely and negligently told by the defendant that they were no longer able to have children. But, when the claimants ceased using birth control, the female claimant fell pregnant. The claimants kept the child and endeavoured to recover the costs of raising the child.

---

[29] See eg R Dworkin, *Taking Rights Seriously* (Harvard University Press, Cambridge, Mass, 1977) pxi.

[30] EJ Weinrib, 'Does Tort Law Have a Future?' (2000) 34 *Valparaiso University Law Review* 561, 567.

[31] [1981] 1 QB 625 (CA).

[32] [2000] 2 AC 59 (HL Sc). Compare *Cattanach v Melchior* [2003] HCA 38, (2003) 215 CLR 1.

The House of Lords ruled that the claimants were not able to recover these damages. According to Lord Steyn:

> It is possible to view the case simply from the perspective of corrective justice. It requires somebody who has harmed another without justification to indemnify the other. On this approach the parents' claim for the cost of bringing up [the child] must succeed. But one may also approach the case from the vantage point of distributive justice. It requires a focus on the just distribution of burdens and losses among members of a society. If the matter is approached in this way, it may become relevant to ask of the commuters on the Underground the following question: should the parents of an unwanted but healthy child be able to sue the doctor or hospital for compensation equivalent to the cost of bringing up the child for the years of his or her minority, ie until about 18 years? My Lords, I have not consulted my fellow travellers on the London Underground but I am firmly of the view that an overwhelming number of ordinary men and women would answer the question with an emphatic No.[33]

For the moment, let us assume that corrective justice argues in favour and distributive justice against recovery.[34] In finding for the defendant on this issue, Lord Steyn came to the conclusion that the considerations of distributive justice were more important than those of corrective justice, but how did he reach that conclusion? We have no idea. Lord Steyn's reason for choosing distributive over corrective justice is absent from his judgment.

But the fault here is not that that reason should have been revealed—by some additional discussion of policy or whatever. Because corrective and distributive justice are incommensurable, it is impossible to give reasons for choosing one over the other. Consequently, all decisions in a system that deals with both forms of justice in this manner must be unprincipled. In *McFarlane*, Lord Steyn apparently chose distributive justice over corrective justice, but he did nothing to justify that choice, which was made by his Lordship in a private and entirely intuitive manner. We must 'let daylight in on magic',[35] but it cannot be done in this manner.

As we saw in Chapter 1, those who support the judicial appeal to policy justify their position by arguing that such appeal is the only way that judges can make clear the bases for their decisions. But we have now seen that this is not true. Not only can appeal to principle provide proper explanations—as we saw in Chapters 3 and 4—the appeal to policy in fact requires judges to make decisions of a kind that cannot be made in a public and open manner but must be made in an intuitive and private one. Supporters of the policy based approach

[33] *McFarlane v Tayside Area Health Board* [2000] 2 AC 59, 82 (HL Sc). See also *Rees v Darlington Memorial Hospital NHS Trust* [2003] UKHL 52, [2004] 1 AC 309, [4]; Lord Steyn, 'Perspectives of Corrective and Distributive Justice in Tort Law' (2002) 37 *Irish Jurist* 1, 1–7.
[34] In fact, as revealed in ch 11, the former is more complex. The latter is also questionable, as I have shown in A Beever, 'Particularism and Prejudice in the Law of Tort' (2003) 11 *Tort Law Review* 146, 151–3.
[35] J Stapleton, 'The Golden Thread at the Heart of Tort Law: Protection of the Vulnerable' (2003) 24 *Australian Bar Review* 135, 138.

are right to insist that judges present their reasons in their judgments, but the appeal to policy cannot satisfy that demand.

The specific problem under examination is particularly acute because, as indicated in Chapter 2, corrective justice and policy belong to different moral spheres. While corrective justice focuses on the relationship between the parties, policy is generally concerned with distributive justice, with overall social well-being.[36] In practice, therefore, the policies applied by courts ignore either one or both parties. For instance, in his discussion of the policies governing the duty of care, entirely in line with modern sentiments, Stephen Todd lists as relevant the following concerns: (i) encouraging reasonable care and deterring wrongdoing, (ii) preventing indeterminate liability, (iii) protecting important interests in the claimant, and (iv) maintaining existing bases of liability.[37] The first two concerns ignore the claimant, the third ignores the defendant and the fourth appears to ignore both parties.

These points are crucial, because they show that the law of negligence under the *Anns* test is incapable of doing justice between the parties in respect of the dispute that brought the parties to court. Instead, in applying the *Anns* test, the court treats the dispute as an occasion on which to engage in social policy debate, often ignoring one or both parties. But it cannot be appropriate to treat the specific concerns of the parties, as articulated in the litigation though the principles of the law, as instrumental in this manner. If we are to have judges making social policy, then we should at least spare the litigants the expense and indignity of having it made with the pretence of dealing with their dispute.

For instance, imagine a case in which a claimant was injured by the defendant's negligence. However, the court rules that the claimant cannot recover, because to do so would unfairly disadvantage vulnerable groups, though that was not an issue between the claimant and the defendant because the defendant was not a member of one of those groups. (Similar cases are explored at the end of this section and in the final section of this chapter.) This treatment of the claimant is contemptuous and cannot be justified, even if the court were to reach the appropriate result. If courts are to institute such rules, they should not wait until unfortunate claimants present them with the opportunity to do so.

Similarly, imagine a case in which, prima facie, justice lies with the claimant, but finding for the claimant would produce, though not in this particular case, indeterminate liability. The harshness of indeterminate liability may on one level justify excusing the defendant, but this does not extinguish the justice of the claimant's case. The claimant is still able to say that she was wrongfully injured by the defendant. But we deny recovery because it would create a situation that would be bad for society or, the greatest of all insults, for the defendant. In other words, the appeal to such one-sided policy concerns 'amounts to

---

[36] In fact, as 'policy' has no determinate meaning, it could refer to all spheres of morality or indeed to anything at all.

[37] S Todd, 'Negligence: The Duty of Care' in S Todd (ed), *The Law of Torts in New Zealand*, 3rd edn (Brookers, Wellington, 2001) 151–63.

the judicial confiscation of what is rightly due to the plaintiff in order to subsidise policy objectives unilaterally favourable to the defendant and those similarly situated'.[38] The claimant is treated merely as a means to others' ends.

Finally, as a consequence of the points above, the *Anns* test has caused the collapse of the structure of the law of negligence. In effect, this means that neither stage of the test is comprehensible, as I now explain.

In the previous chapter, we saw that the role of reasonable foreseeability is to link the defendant's wrongdoing to the claimant's injury: the defendant can be liable only if he created an unreasonable risk of the claimant's injury. But this is not how the first stage of the *Anns* test functions, despite its use of language derived from *Donoghue v Stevenson*. Because the issue of reasonable foreseeability is not tied to the creation of an unreasonable risk, reasonable foreseeability is interpreted to mean mere comprehensibility—thus an injury is 'reasonably foreseeable' if its occurrence was not incomprehensible. Accordingly, almost any situation will pass the first stage of the *Anns* test.

This creates the illusion—an illusion from which the modern law of negligence greatly suffers—that almost any damage is recoverable unless policy dictates otherwise, whether or not the damage is to something over which the claimant has a legal right. In other words, the *Anns* test applies a variation of the prima facie tort doctrine: the negligent defendant is liable for all injuries unless he can find a policy to excuse himself.[39]

Sensitive to this criticism, in *South Pacific* Richardson J insisted that the first stage of the enquiry 'is not of course a simple question of foreseeability as between the parties. It involves consideration of the degree of analogy with cases in which duties are already established and . . . reflects an assessment of the competing moral claims.'[40] This involves an appeal to the incremental approach explored below. But it also makes clear that, in order to prevent all conceivable injuries getting past the first stage of the test, Richardson J maintained that policy concerns are relevant at that stage also.

A similar attempt was made by McLachlin J in *Canadian National Railway Co v Norsk Pacific Steamship Co Ltd*. 'In determining whether liability should be extended to a new situation, courts will have regard to the factors traditionally relevant to proximity such as the relationship between the parties, physical propinquity, assumed or imposed obligations and close causal connection.'[41]

---

[38] EJ Weinrib, 'Does Tort Law Have a Future?' (2000) 34 *Valparaiso University Law Review* 561, 566.

[39] JC Smith and P Burns, '*Donoghue v. Stevenson*—The Not So Golden Anniversary' (1983) 46 *MLR* 147 refers to this as the prima facie duty doctrine. See also J Smillie, 'Formalism, Fairness and Efficiency: Civil Adjudication in New Zealand' [1996] *New Zealand Law Review* 254. In A Beever, 'Justice and Punishment in Tort: A Comparative Theoretical Analysis' in R Grantham and C Rickett (eds), *Justifying Remedies in Private Law* (forthcoming, Cambridge University Press, Cambridge, 2007), I refer to this as the 'common law conception of tort'.

[40] *South Pacific Manufacturing Co Ltd v New Zealand Security Consultants & Investigations Ltd* [1992] 2 NZLR 282, 306 (CA).

[41] [1992] 1 SCR 1021, 1153. See also *Sutherland Shire Council v Heyman* (1985) 157 CLR 424, 497–8 (HCA) (Deane J).

These are traditionally relevant factors, but the factors relate to two different and conflicting traditions. Focus on the relationship between the parties is part of the principled approach, as exemplified by *Donoghue v Stevenson* and Cardozo CJ's judgment in *Palsgraf*. Conversely, physical propinquity and close causal connection are relevant to the policy-based approach seen in cases such as *Winterbottom v Wright*,[42] Andrews J's judgment in *Palsgraf* and *In Re Polemis and Furness*.[43] Assumed or imposed obligations are explored in Chapter 8 of this book.

Moreover, it is opaque how this enquiry is to be conducted. Does proximity exist if the injury to the claimant was unforeseeable but occurred in physical proximity to the defendant's negligence and there was a short causal chain? It is impossible to balance these concerns in anything but an obscurantist fashion. Further, physical proximity, the length of the causal chain and other similar factors are unrelated to the normative connection between the defendant's wrongdoing and the claimant's injury. As Viscount Simonds pointed out in *The Wagon Mound (No 1)*, the claimant's injury may be perfectly foreseeable even though there is a long causal chain between it and the defendant's negligence. But if the defendant created an unreasonable risk of that injury, then it cannot be justified to find for the defendant, no matter how long the causal chain.[44] Finally, McLachlin J's list was not intended to be exhaustive. The number of concerns relevant to proximity is potentially infinite. If that is so, then the first stage of the *Anns* test, the enquiry into proximity, is also a *tabula rasa* and is incapable of directing judicial decision making. Again, then, the policy based approach has led to less daylight rather than more.

In fact, as the context of *Norsk* makes clear, the factors other than the relationship between the parties are introduced in order to prevent indeterminate liability.[45] In other words, they are motivated by policy. Policy also motivated Richardson J's formulation of the *Anns* test, as explored above. Therefore, the first stage of the *Anns* test involves policy and is no more principled or predictable than the second. In consequence, the first stage of the *Anns* test has been swallowed by the second. As Todd, aptly puts it, 'It is apparent . . . that resolution of the stage one issue may involve a wide-ranging inquiry into matters of policy and principle, raising the question as to the function of stage two'.[46] Because proximity has come to mean anything and nothing, the duty of care is in fact determined by policy, as Cooke P clearly perceived in *South Pacific*.[47]

---

[42] (1842) 10 M & W 109, 152 ER 402.

[43] [1921] 3 KB 560 (CA).

[44] *Overseas Tankship (UK) Ltd v Morts Dock & Engineering Co Ltd (The Wagon Mound, No 1)* [1961] AC 388, 426 (PC).

[45] *Canadian National Railway Co v Norsk Pacific Steamship Co Ltd* [1992] 1 SCR 1021, 1153.

[46] S Todd, 'Negligence: The Duty of Care' in S Todd (ed), *The Law of Torts in New Zealand*, 3rd edn (Brookers, Wellington, 2001) 148.

[47] See also J Stapleton, 'The Golden Thread at the Heart of Tort Law: Protection of the Vulnerable' (2003) 24 *Australian Bar Review* 135, 137.

The dominance of policy does not end with the duty of care. Not only has the second stage of the *Anns* test swallowed the first, it has the entire law of negligence in its mouth.[48] For instance, in *South Pacific*, Cooke P maintained that the likelihood that the defendant's action would result in harm was a factor to be taken into account in determining a duty of care.[49] But that is properly an issue for the *standard* of care, not for the duty of care. Similarly, in *Takaro Properties Ltd v Rowling*, the Privy Council argued that courts should be slow to impose duties of care on ministers carefully to construe statutes, as such might lead ministers to waste too much time and money obtaining legal advice.[50] And in *Hill v Chief Constable of West Yorkshire Police*, the House of Lords ruled that the police could not owe a duty of care to the public in relation to their investigation of a crime, as such would tend to make the police overly defensive in conducting their investigations.[51] If they are compelling at all, these issues also rightly relate to the standard of care rather than to the duty of care. The issue is whether the defendant acted unreasonably; not, assuming *arguendo* that the defendant did act unreasonably, whether the defendant acted unreasonably *to the claimant*.

Duty has also begun to swallow remoteness. For instance, the modern law holds that some kinds of injury are irrecoverable, because they involve loss of a particular kind—most importantly economic loss or mental injury. If this approach were correct, then the damage would be irrecoverable because of the *type of injury* to the claimant, because the injury was too remote.[52] But this is not how the issue is actually treated under the *Anns* test. Instead, it is treated as relevant to the duty of care. As a result, remoteness has been relegated to an issue of little concern. For instance, the authors of *The Law of Torts in New Zealand* deal with the standard and duty of care in four separate chapters—chapters 4 to 7—which constitute 276 pages. Conversely, remoteness is discussed in a chapter together with factual causation—chapter 20—and merits only 16 pages. Less dramatically, one of English law's leading textbooks, *Winfield and Jolowicz on Tort*, devotes 96 pages to the duty and standard of care and 24 to remoteness. Remoteness is again discussed after factual causation and is treated as a subset of causation.[53] Although the impact of the *Anns* test is

---

[48] Compare T Weir, *Tort Law* (Oxford University Press, Oxford, 2002) 30.

[49] *South Pacific Manufacturing Co Ltd v New Zealand Security Consultants & Investigations Ltd* [1992] 2 NZLR 282, 295 (CA).

[50] [1987] 2 NZLR 700, 710 (PC).

[51] [1989] 1 AC 53 (HL). This case was decided before the House of Lords finally rejected the *Anns* test in *Murphy v Brentwood District Council* [1991] 1 AC 398 (HL).

[52] *SCM v Whittall* [1971] 1 QB 337, 343–4 (CA) (Lord Denning MR); *Spartan Steel & Alloys Ltd v Martin & Co (Contractors) Ltd* [1973] QB 27, 36–7 (CA) (Lord Denning MR); JC Smith and P Burns, 'Donoghue v. Stevenson—The Not So Golden Anniversary' (1983) 46 MLR 147, 152.

[53] WVH Rogers, *Winfield and Jolowicz on Tort*, 16th edn (Sweet & Maxwell, London, 2002) 211–12. The association of remoteness with factual causation is one of the more unfortunate features of the modern law. Though we sometimes refer to the remoteness stage of the enquiry as 'proximate *causation*', remoteness has nothing to do with factual causation. We should not need to struggle to convince students, who believe themselves hopelessly confused, that they are in fact not at all confused, when they fail to understand how the actions of the defendant's employees in *Lamb*

less in England than in New Zealand, even in the former jurisdiction not only is remoteness seen as unconnected with the standard and duty of care, it is also believed to be comparatively trivial. This is a long way from the notion explored in the previous two chapters, that the standard of care, the duty of care and remoteness form a coherent and interdependent whole.

Furthermore, in *Fairchild v Glenhaven Funeral Services Ltd*, Lord Hoffmann argued that the defendant's negligence should be said to have been the factual cause of the claimant's injury, not if it actually was, but if it was fair, just and reasonable to say so.[54] In line with the discussion of the incremental approach below, this seems to indicate that factual causation is itself a policy matter that, under the *Anns* test, would be decided at the second stage of the test. Finally, in *Hall v Hebert* Cory J argued that the defence of illegality should be understood as a policy concern to negate a duty of care under the second stage of the *Anns* test.[55]

Is there anything not relevant to the duty of care? The answer must be 'No' because, according to the understanding under examination, the duty of care is simply a matter of policy, and so is the rest of the law.

In consequence, the law of negligence based on the *Anns* test looks remarkably similar to that propounded in *Winterbottom v Wright* and by Andrews J in *Palsgraf*. Recall that the Court in *Winterbottom v Wright* insisted that liability be restricted beyond principle in order to prevent indeterminate liability. That is the position of the modern law. This is why proximity, duty, remoteness, etc, are referred to as 'control mechanisms'. They are not seen as parts of a coherent enquiry, but rather as ways of cutting back on an incoherent enquiry. Recall also that in *Palsgraf* Andrews J held that, at the end of the day, liability was determined in accordance with 'not logic [but] . . . practical politics'.[56] 'It is all a question of expediency'.[57] But at least Andrews J could make sense of the different roles of the standard of care, the duty of care and remoteness—as we cannot. It is as if the great cases in the law of negligence were never decided and our understanding of the law of negligence has returned to the nineteenth century.

I now examine two stark signs of this decay. The first is Lord Templeman's judgment in *Hill v Chief Constable of West Yorkshire Police*. The claimant alleged that her daughter was killed by a serial murderer as a result of police incompetence in investigating the case. Lord Templeman insisted that '[t]he question for determination in this appeal is whether an action for damages is an appropriate vehicle for investigating the efficiency of a police force'.[58] He did

---

v Camden London BC [1981] 1 QB 625 (CA) did not cause the claimant's injury. They did cause the claimant's injury, but the claimant's injury was remote. Apart from the fact that 'proximate causation' contains the word 'causation', it is hard to imagine a more inappropriate place to discuss the concept than coupled with factual causation.

[54] [2002] UKHL 22, [2003] 1 AC 32, 72–3.
[55] [1993] 2 SCR 159, 201–5.
[56] *Palsgraf v Long Island Railroad Co* 162 NE 99, 103 (NY CA 1928).
[57] *Ibid*, 104.
[58] *Hill v Chief Constable of West Yorkshire Police* [1989] 1 AC 53, 64 (HL).

not believe that it was. In his Lordship's view, the claimant's action would have done 'more harm than good'.[59] Accordingly, Lord Templeman insisted that the claimant's case must fail.

The appropriate question was emphatically not the one identified by Lord Templeman. The right question was whether the claimant had been injured by a tort committed by the defendant. Specifically, the question was whether the defendant had failed to exercise due care in dealing with something over which the claimant's daughter had a legal right.[60] It is not my argument that a tort was committed in this case. Hence, I do not claim that the House of Lords committed an injustice in finding for the defendant. But I insist that Lord Templeman's handling of the case was nevertheless a most significant injustice to the claimant. As a matter of law, the claimant's case was that her daughter had been murdered because of the negligence of the police. That complaint was ignored. Lord Templeman settled the claimant's case by considering the role of the police force within society generally. In other words, he ignored the claimant's argument. In fact, Lord Templeman's focus was so far from the claimant that he was able to say,'[a]t the end of the day the court might or might not find that there had been negligence by one or more members of the police force. But that finding would not help anybody or punish anybody.'[61] The claim that the finding would not help anybody is obviously false. It would have helped the claimant.[62]

The second stark example of the collapse of the law of negligence is the existence in modern New Zealand law of instances of liability that the New Zealand Court of Appeal describes as *sui generis*.[63] Although this is less dramatic an example at a personal level than *Hill* above, in terms of legal structure, the approach of the New Zealand Court of Appeal is extraordinary. In describing an instance of liability as *sui generis*, the Court intends that the instance cannot be justified by general principle. That is to admit that the positive law is ad hoc and is therefore at least close to the overt admission that the positive law is unjustified. It is remarkable that the New Zealand courts have found themselves in this position.

---

[59] *Ibid*, 65.

[60] See the discussion of wrongful death actions in ch 1.

[61] *Hill v Chief Constable of West Yorkshire Police* [1989] 1 AC 53, 64 (HL).

[62] In this case, it would have helped the claimant, if only in the sense that it would have made her feel vindicated and also made her able to donate what would have been a considerable sum of money to charity.

[63] This was said of liability owed to potential beneficiaries of a will who fail to inherit because of the negligence of a solicitor in *Gartside v Sheffield, Young & Ellis* [1983] NZLR 37, 42 (CA) (Cooke J) and *Brownie Wills v Shrimpton* [1998] 2 NZLR 320, 325 (CA) (Blanchard J). In *A-G v Carter* [2003] 2 NZLR 160 (CA), a unanimous Court also described as *sui generis* liability for economic loss caused by negligent inspection and building of houses. That liability is a product of *Invercargill City Council v Hamlin* [1994] 3 NZLR 513 (CA) and *Invercargill City Council v Hamlin* [1996] AC 624 (PC).

II. THE INCREMENTAL APPROACH

The *Anns* approach was first rejected by the High Court of Australia in *Sutherland Shire Council v Heyman*.[64] Moreover, in *Caparo Industries v Dickman*[65] and *Murphy v Brentwood District Council*,[66] the House of Lords repudiated its own test. Finally, in *Cooper v Hobart*,[67] the Supreme Court of Canada followed suit.[68] This leaves New Zealand as the only jurisdiction to continue to apply the *Anns* test, although the New Zealand Court of Appeal has so modified the test that it bears only a passing resemblance to the judgment of Lord Wilberforce in *Anns* itself.

The rejection of *Anns* has seen the adoption of the so-called 'incremental approach'.[69] This approach has helped to reduce the level of chaos in the law of negligence outside New Zealand. However, the issue here is whether the incremental approach is preferable to the *Anns* test from the perspective of legal principle.

A. The Formulation of the Incremental Approach

The leading statement of the incremental approach is from Brennan J's judgment in *Sutherland Shire*:

> It is preferable, in my view, that the law should develop novel categories of negligence incrementally and by analogy with established categories, rather than by a massive extension of a prima facie duty of care restrained only by indefinable considerations which ought to negative, or to reduce or limit the scope of the duty or the class of person to whom it is owed. The proper role of the 'second stage' [of the *Anns* test], as I attempted to explain in *Jaensch v. Coffey*, embraces no more than 'those further elements [in addition to the neighbour principle] which are appropriate to the particular category of negligence and which confine the duty of care within narrower limits than those which would be defined by an unqualified application of the neighbour principle'.[70]

On this view, the incremental approach consists of three elements. First, the approach institutes incrementalism: the idea that the law should develop on a step-by-step basis. Secondly, the approach purports to limit or eliminate the role played by policy. Thirdly, the approach adds concerns to the neighbour principle in order to limit liability beyond the principled approach.

---

[64] (1985) 157 CLR 424 (HCA).

[65] [1990] 2 AC 605 (HL).

[66] [1991] 1 AC 398 (HL).

[67] (2002) 206 DLR (4th) 193 (SCC).

[68] Though not officially. See JW Neyers, 'Distilling Duty: The Supreme Court of Canada Amends *Anns*' (2002) 118 LQR 221.

[69] As indicated above, 'incrementalism' is also found in the judgment of Richardson J in *South Pacific*.

[70] *Sutherland Shire Council v Heyman* (1985) 157 CLR 424, 481 (HCA) (citations omitted, first addition mine, second in original).

My argument is that the incremental approach either collapses into the *Anns* test or undermines the ability of courts to justify their decisions. Hence, although the incremental approach may be preferable to the *Anns* test as a matter of legal practice, as a matter of principle the two approaches are equally moribund. The argument has two phases. In the first phase of the argument, I contend that the third element of the incremental approach either involves appeal to concerns that fail to justify the application of that approach or covertly relies on policy. If the former is correct, then the law of negligence is arbitrary and unjustified. If the latter is correct, then the first and second elements of the incremental approach are illusory and the incremental approach collapses into the *Anns* test. In the second phase of the argument, I maintain that the first element of the incremental approach, ie incrementalism, itself either is unjustified or involves appeal to policy, thus collapsing into the *Anns* test.

B. The Incremental Approach and the Neighbour Test

(i) Proximity and Reasonable Foreseeability

In *Sutherland Shire*, Gibbs CJ (arguing broadly in support of the *Anns* test) insisted that the notion of proximity applicable to the duty of care is not reducible to reasonable foreseeability. Rather, Gibbs CJ argued, the concept of proximity is a 'composite one'.[71] Gibbs CJ citied with approval Lord Keith's understanding of proximity in *Governors of the Peabody Donation Fund v Sir Lindsay Parkinson & Co Ltd*:

> The true question in each case is whether the particular defendant owed to the particular plaintiff a duty of care having the scope which is contended for, and whether he was in breach of that duty with consequent loss to the plaintiff. A relationship of proximity in Lord Atkin's sense must exist before any duty of care can arise, but the scope of the duty must depend on all the circumstances of the case.[72]

Gibbs CJ went on to say that '[i]n deciding whether the necessary relationship exists, and the scope of the duty which it creates, it is necessary for the court to examine closely all the circumstances that throw light on the nature of the relationship between the parties'.[73]

Two aspects of these arguments need to be explored. The first is the idea that proximity is to be distinguished from reasonable foreseeability, and the second is the claim that the duty of care is determined in accordance with 'the circumstances of the case'.

---

[71] *Ibid*, 441. See also *Murphy v Brentwood District Council* [1991] 1 AC 398, 489 (HL) (Lord Oliver).

[72] [1985] AC 210, 240 (HL). Cited *Sutherland Shire Council v Heyman* (1985) 157 CLR 424, 441 (HCA).

[73] *Sutherland Shire Council v Heyman* (1985) 157 CLR 424, 441 (HCA).

The first aspect of Gibbs CJ's judgment received support from Deane J, who claimed that 'Lord Atkin's notions of reasonable foreseeability and proximity were . . . distinct'.[74] This is plainly wrong. Though it is true that his Lordship argued that negligence in relation to words is exceptional,[75] as we see in Chapter 8, this is no exception to the principles enunciated in *Donoghue v Stevenson*. This is because those principles are not relevant in cases of negligent misrepresentation. Lord Atkin clearly did intend proximity, or the 'neighbour' test, to be based on reasonable foreseeability.

Furthermore, if proximity is not identified with reasonable foreseeability, then, as Robert Goff LJ pointed out in *Leigh and Sillivan Ltd v Aliakmon Shipping Co Ltd*,[76] 'proximity' is meaningless. This conclusion was resisted by Deane J in *Sutherland Shire*,[77] but it was accepted by a unanimous High Court of Australia in *Sullivan v Moody*:

> Notwithstanding the centrality of that concept [proximity], for more than a century, in this area of discourse, and despite some later decisions in this Court which emphasised that centrality, it gives little practical guidance in determining whether a duty of care exists in cases that are not analogous to cases in which a duty has been established. It expresses the nature of what is in issue, and in that respect gives focus to the inquiry, but as an explanation of a process of reasoning leading to a conclusion its utility is limited.[78]

This has been interpreted as a rejection of the role of proximity in the duty of care.[79]

Though *Sullivan v Moody* has met with strong criticism,[80] given the modern understanding of proximity, it is hard to see what other conclusion the High Court could have reached. If 'proximity' refers to a potentially limitless set of ideas unrelated to the ordinary meaning of 'proximity' (ie reasonable foreseeability), then it is better to abandon talk of proximity altogether.[81]

I turn now to the second feature of Gibbs CJ's judgment: that the existence of a duty of care is determined by reference to all the circumstances of the case. This view received support from Lord Jauncey in *Murphy v Brentwood District Council*, who said that '[a] relationship of proximity in the sense used by Lord

[74] *Ibid*, 495. See also *Gala v Preston* (1991) 172 CLR 243, 260 (HCA) (Brennan J).

[75] *M'Alister (or Donoghue) (Pauper) v Stevenson* [1932] AC 562, 582 (HL Sc).

[76] *Leigh and Sillivan Ltd v Aliakmon Shipping Co Ltd* [1985] QB 350, 395–6 (CA). See also *Caparo Industries v Dickman* [1990] 2 AC 605, 617–18 (HL) (Lord Bridge); *Gala v Preston* (1991) 172 CLR 243, 260–1 (HCA) (Brennan J).

[77] (1985) 157 CLR 424, 495–8 (HCA).

[78] *Sullivan v Moody* (2001) 207 CLR 562, 578–9 (HCA). See also WVH Rogers, *Winfield and Jolowicz on Tort*, 16th edn (Sweet & Maxwell, London, 2002) 116–17, 126.

[79] See eg C Witting, 'The Three-Stage Test Abandoned in Australia—or Not?' (2002) 118 *LQR* 214, 217.

[80] See eg *ibid*, 217–21.

[81] However, the High Court of Australia appears to have replaced proximity with the equally obscure concept of vulnerability. *Woolcock Street Investments Pty Ltd v CDG Pty Ltd* [2004] HCA 16, (2004) 216 CLR 515. This is explored below.

Atkin in *Donoghue* v. *Stevenson* . . . must exist before any duty of care can arise, but the scope of the duty must depend upon all the circumstances of the case'.[82]

These claims can be analysed in two ways. First, Gibbs CJ and Lord Jauncey were asserting only that it is necessary to examine the facts in order to assess whether the parties were in a relationship of proximity. That is correct, but it does not require abandoning the view that the duty of care is based on reasonable foreseeability. It entails only the perfectly sensible notion that one can determine whether the claimant was placed at a reasonably foreseeable risk by the defendant by looking at the facts of the case. Secondly, Gibbs CJ and Lord Jauncey were arguing that nothing more can be said about proximity than that it turns on the facts of the case. If this is a correct interpretation of Gibbs CJ's and Lord Jauncey's intentions, then their position must be rejected. The role of legal principle, and the role of the courts in elucidating legal principle, is to demonstrate *why* and *how* the circumstances of cases generate or fail to generate liability. It is not sufficient for a judge to examine the facts and then merely conclude that the defendant is or is not liable. Nor is it sufficient to enunciate putative principles that are incapable of elucidating the decision making procedure that produces judicial decisions. Such 'principles' are empty gestures.

If, as the High Court of Australia insisted in *Sutherland Shire*, proximity is not synonymous with reasonable foreseeability, then, if the Court is to utilise the concept of proximity, it is incumbent on it to elucidate that concept. In *Sutherland Shire*, Gibbs CJ attempted to avoid this by insisting that proximity is unanalysable. That approach is inadequate.

On the other hand, Mason and Dean JJ attempted to clarify proximity. Mason J argued that proximity was concerned with reliance:

> Reliance has always been an important element in establishing the existence of a duty of care. It has been suggested that liability in negligence is largely, if not exclusively, based on the plaintiff's reliance on the defendant's taking care in circumstances where the defendant is aware or ought to be aware of that reliance . . .[83]

There is a sense in which this claim is true. If driving negligently you injure me in a vehicle accident, there is a sense in which I was relying on you to drive carefully. But I was not relying on you specifically, nor did I have any right to rely on you in particular. In the same sense, then, the claimant in *Palsgraf* was relying on the defendant's employees not to push the owner of the package onto the train. But the sense of reliance used by Mason J is not the sense used in law. We do not say that the claimant in *Donoghue v Stevenson* suffered detrimental reliance on the belief that her bottle of ginger beer would not contain a decomposing snail. There would be no point. We say that the claimant was injured because her ginger beer contained a decomposing snail and she drank it. Hence, Mason J's attempt to explicate proximity failed.[84]

---

[82] [1991] 1 AC 398, 492 (HL).

[83] *Sutherland Shire Council v Heyman* (1985) 157 CLR 424, 461 (HCA).

[84] T Weir, *Tort Law* (Oxford University Press, Oxford, 2002) 36 says that reliance is a 'weasel word' in this context.

Deane J attempted to elucidate proximity by appeal to a number of concerns:

> The requirement of proximity . . . involves the notion of nearness or closeness and embraces physical proximity (in the sense of space and time) between the person or property of the plaintiff and the person or property of the defendant . . . and what may (perhaps loosely) be referred to as causal proximity in the sense of the closeness or directness of the causal connection or relationship between the particular act or course of conduct and the loss or injury sustained.[85]

This commits the same mistake analysed above in relation to McLachlin J's judgment in *Norsk*. Accordingly, because the High Court of Australia rejected the notion that proximity is synonymous with reasonable foreseeability, the Court was unable to provide an adequate account of proximity. Hence, the Court's treatment of the duty of care was inadequate.

In *Caparo*, the House of Lords provided an alternative approach to that taken by the High Court of Australia in *Sutherland Shire*, in the form of a three-stage test:[86]

1. Should the defendant have foreseen that the claimant was placed at risk of injury?
2. Was there a relationship of proximity between the parties?
3. Is it fair, just and reasonable to impose a duty of care on the defendant?

But the distinction between the steps in this argument is opaque. If 2 is different from 1, then 2 involves appeal to unstated concerns. This is no better than Gibbs CJ's position in *Sutherland Shire*. The same applies to the distinction between 3 and 1.

In *Governors*, Lord Keith said that 'in determining whether or not a duty of care of particular scope was incumbent upon a defendant it is material to take into consideration whether it is just and reasonable that it should be so'.[87] Of course, the law should be just and reasonable, but the role of courts such as the House of Lords is to elucidate what actually determines justice and reasonableness with respect to particular areas of law. As it stands, Lord Keith's assertion is empty. Nor does it help to add other equally vague and tautologous phrases, such as Lord Bridge's notion that a duty of care should be imposed if is fair, just and reasonable to do so.[88] Without analysis and elucidation, these are empty words. The role of legal principle is to tell us *why* certain outcomes are fair, just and reasonable.

It is also important to remember that, at least usually, the parties are in court because they both believe that their position is fair, just and reasonable. Accordingly, telling one of them that she must lose because her position is not

---

[85] *Sutherland Shire Council v Heyman* (1985) 157 CLR 424, 497–8 (HCA).

[86] *Caparo Industries v Dickman* [1990] 2 AC 605, 617–18 (HL) (Lord Bridge).

[87] [1985] AC 210, 241 (HL). See also *Sutherland Shire Council v Heyman* (1985) 157 CLR 424, 497–8 (HCA) (Deane J).

[88] See also *Caparo Industries v Dickman* [1990] 2 AC 605, 618 (HL); *A-G v Carter* [2003] 2 NZLR 160 (CA).

fair, just or reasonable is to tell her that she is wrong without telling her why. It is, then, contemptuous of that party. Why is she expected to accept the intuitive judgements of a few judges over her own? How could it be just to force her to do so?

On this interpretation of the incremental approach, the approach fails to provide reasons for imposing or refusing to impose a duty of care. The approach hides, rather than reveals, the basis of judicial decision making.

(ii) The Incremental Approach and Policy

On the other hand, John Fleming argues that 'fair', 'just' and 'reasonable' are code words for the judicial appeal to policy, that 'admits "instrumentalist" goals beyond the equities between *this* claimant and *this* defendant. . . . In short, it recognises the public law element in this area of private law.'[89] In other words, the dispute between the parties is treated as an occasion for an exercise in social engineering.[90] Perhaps one could also interpret Gibbs CJ's claim in *Sutherland Shire* that proximity cannot be analysed, and Mason and Dean JJ's suggestions for explicating proximity, as covert appeals to policy. If so, then the incremental approach is really just the *Anns* test in disguise and it is subject to the same criticisms raised in relation to that test in the first section of this chapter.

Recall the three-stage approach discussed above:

1. Should the defendant have foreseen that the claimant was placed at risk of injury?
2. Was there a relationship of proximity between the parties?
3. Is it fair, just and reasonable to impose a duty of care on the defendant?

In this light, 3 is code for policy. But then so is 2. Moreover, given that 1 is reduced to mere conceivability and hence receives an affirmative answer in all or almost all cases, the duty of care is determined entirely by policy. This is just the *Anns* test and its putative principles are entirely illusory.

The inability of the incremental approach to distinguish itself from the *Anns* test and the emptiness of the latter has occasionally been admitted. For instance, in *Caparo*, Lord Roskill said that:

> there is no simple formula or touchstone to which recourse can be had in order to provide in every case a ready answer to the questions whether, given certain facts, the law will or will not impose liability for negligence or in cases where such liability can be shown to exist, determine the extent of that liability. Phrases such as 'foreseeability,' 'proximity,' 'neighbourhood,' 'just and reasonable,' 'fairness,' 'voluntary acceptance of risk,' or 'voluntary assumption of responsibility' will be found used from time to time in the different cases. But, as your Lordships have said, such phrases are not precise definitions. At best they are but labels or phrases descriptive of the very different

---

[89] J Fleming, *The Law of Torts*, 9th edn (LBC Information Services, Sydney, 1998) 153–4.

[90] In passing, it is worth noting that the implication that the role of public law is to engage in social engineering strikes me as equally outrageous.

factual situations which can exist in particular cases and which must be carefully examined in each case before it can be pragmatically determined whether a duty of care exists and, if so, what is the scope and extent of that duty.[91]

This reliance on words that Lord Roskill admits have no determinate meaning is curious. If this picture is right, judges are simply making it up as they go along. 'It is all a question of expediency.'[92] The best we can hope for is 'an educated reflex to the facts'.[93] This is a form of extreme intuitionism.

If the incremental approach does collapse into the *Anns* test, then that would help to explain its hostility to the principled approach. For instance, in jurisdictions that adopt the incremental approach, it is widely regarded as axiomatic that no general principle governs the duty of care.[94] Parallel concerns led Lord Denning to dismiss the duty of care as a 'smokescreen' for policy in *Lamb v Camden London BC*.[95] Similarly, in *Sutherland Shire*, Deane J argued:

> Nor do I think that either the validity or the utility of common law concepts or principles is properly to be measured by reference to whether they can be accommodated in the strait-jacket of some formularised criterion of liability. To the contrary, it has been the flexibility of fundamental concepts and principles which has enabled the common law to reflect the influence of contemporary standards and demands and which has in no small part underlain its genius to provide a living element of the social compact of civilisation for different peoples through different ages and in different parts of the world.[96]

The desire to understand the law, to produce a coherent account of the scope and boundaries of liability, is described as the attempt to place the law in a straitjacket. Instead of principles that elucidate liability, flexibility—meaning wide judicial discretion or making it up as we go along—is preferred. This is to be expected from a policy-based approach to the law.

Furthermore, in assessing this argument, it is important to note that two general understandings of legal flexibility are available. According to the first view, a legal system is flexible if its decision makers are unconstrained by principles that guide their judgements in a perspicuous manner. It is this kind of flexibility

---

[91] *Caparo Industries v Dickman* [1990] 2 AC 605, 628 (HL). Compare *Lamb v Camden London BC* [1981] 1 QB 625, 636–7 (CA). See also *ibid*, 633 (Lord Oliver); *Stovin v Wise* [1996] AC 823, 932 (HL) (Lord Nicholls); J Stapleton, 'The Golden Thread at the Heart of Tort Law: Protection of the Vulnerable' (2003) 24 *Australian Bar Review* 135, 137.

[92] *Palsgraf v Long Island Railroad Co* 162 NE 99, 104 (NY CA 1928).

[93] *Smith v Littlewoods Organisation Ltd* [1987] 1 AC 241, 271 (HL) (Lord Goff).

[94] See eg *Governors of the Peabody Donation Fund v Sir Lindsay Parkinson & Co Ltd* [1985] AC 210, 239 (HL) (Lord Keith); *Leigh and Sillivan Ltd v Aliakmon Shipping Co Ltd* [1986] AC 785, 815 (HL) (Lord Brandon); *Sutherland Shire Council v Heyman* (1985) 157 CLR 424, 497 (HCA) (Deane J); *Caparo Industries v Dickman* [1990] 2 AC 605, 617 (Lord Keith), 628 (Lord Roskill), 635 (Lord Oliver).

[95] [1981] 1 QB 625, 636–7 (CA).

[96] *Sutherland Shire Council v Heyman* (1985) 157 CLR 424, 497 (HCA). Also detectable in this passage is the all too frequently asserted false dichotomy: the law must either be 'flexible' or be a system of mechanical formalism. In reality, there is a great deal of scope between these two notions.

for which Deane J argued in *Sutherland Shire* and the one most commonly appealed to by modern judges and commentators. According to the second view, however, a legal system is flexible if decision makers in that system have the power to correct wrong decisions in the light of better understandings. Examples of this include recognising that correct principles have been applied incorrectly in the past (as happened in *McHale v Watson*[97]) and that extant principles of the positive law do not reflect the appropriate normative concerns (as was recognised by the Courts in *Donoghue v Stevenson* and *Palsgraf*[98]). It is the authority of judges to do the second that is said to explain the common law's alleged advantage in terms of realising practical justice over the codified civilian systems.

This second notion of flexibility is compatible with, in fact demanded by, the principled approach. The first is not. But the first involves an obscurantist commitment to intuitionism and as such must be rejected as part of a methodology for judicial decision making.

Returning to the investigation of the incremental approach, Lord Keith in *Governors*[99] and the unanimous High Court of Australia in *Sullivan v Moody*[100] asserted that it had never been Lord Atkin's intention to provide a general account of negligence.[101] Again, this claim is plainly wrong. Although Lord Atkin did say that '[t]o seek a complete logical definition of the general principle is probably to go beyond the function of the judge',[102] this must be read in the light of the fact that he purported to elucidate the 'general conception of relations giving rise to a duty of care, of which the particular cases found in the books are but instances'.[103] Lord Atkin's judgment did not contain a 'complete logical definition' of the duty of care, and it must be understood in the light of other cases, but it clearly contained a general account of the duty of care. Moreover, even if Lord Atkin did not formulate a general account of the duty of care, it would not follow that one does not exist.

The automatic dismissal of the idea that a principled approach is possible must give us pause. Even if it were false, that certainly should not be regarded as axiomatic.

---

[97] (1966) 115 CLR 199 (HCA). See ch 3.
[98] See ch 4.
[99] [1985] AC 210, 239 (HL).
[100] (2001) 207 CLR 562, 577 (HCA).
[101] See also RFV Heuston, '*Donoghue* v. *Stevenson* in Retrospect' (1957) 20 *MLR* 1; JC Smith and P Burns, '*Donoghue* v. *Stevenson*—The Not So Golden Anniversary' (1983) 46 *MLR* 147, 147.
[102] *M'Alister (or Donoghue) (Pauper) v Stevenson* [1932] AC 562, 580 (HL Sc).
[103] *Ibid.*

C. Incrementalism and Justification

The errors above arise because of a fundamental flaw in the incremental approach. This is that the incrementalism in the approach either collapses into the *Anns* test or fails to justify legal outcomes.[104]

Consider the impact of insurance on tort liability. As a matter of principle, insurance is immaterial.[105] This is because it is not relevant to the relationship between the parties. If *D* injured *C* and a court finds for *D* because it does not want *I*, *D*'s insurer, to pay the damages award, then the court ignores the relationship it is meant to be analysing. Moreover, it is important to remember that, if *D* is found liable, *I* will have to pay only because *I agreed* to indemnify *D* for the financial consequences of his torts. Hence, finding *D* liable in no sense makes *I* 'vicariously liable' to *C*. *I* is merely called upon to perform his agreement with *D*, an obligation for which *D* contracted and paid. Hence, when a court denies or creates liability because of insurance, not only does this do violence to the coherence of tort law, it undermines freedom of contract. In the example above, the court would be saying to *I*, as it were, 'we don't think that you should have made that contract, so we will get you out of it'.[106]

---

[104] WVH Rogers, *Winfield and Jolowicz on Tort*, 16th edn (Sweet & Maxwell, London, 2002) 126–7. Rogers treats this as a reason for supporting the *Anns* approach. See also *Stovin v Wise* [1996] AC 823, 931–2 (Lord Nichols), 949 (Lord Hoffmann); *South Pacific Manufacturing Co Ltd v New Zealand Security Consultants & Investigations Ltd* [1992] 2 NZLR 282, 294 (CA) (Cooke P); S Todd, 'Negligence: The Duty of Care' in S Todd (ed), *The Law of Torts in New Zealand,* 3rd edn (Brookers, Wellington, 2001) 149; who argue that there is no real difference between the *Anns* test and the incremental approach.

[105] *Lister v Romford Ice and Cold Storage Co Ltd* [1957] AC 555, 798 (HL) (Viscount Simmonds); *Hunt v Severs* [1994] 2 AC 350, 363 (HL) (Lord Bridge), holding that accepting arguments based on insurance 'would represent a novel and radical departure in the law of a kind which only the legislature may properly effect'.

[106] Note that this does not entail the view that insurance has had no significant impact on the actual development of tort law. Sometimes appeal to insurance has produced important legal mistakes. Sometimes, it has allowed otherwise timorous judges to reach the conclusions they ought to have reached in terms of legal principle. For instance, it may be true that the judges in *Winterbottom v Wright*(1842) 10 M & W 109, 152 ER 402 would have decided that case differently had insurance been widespread in 1842. However, that would show that insurance has, as a matter of fact, led judges to do the right thing—ie enforce legal principle (according to which insurance is irrelevant). It could not show that the appeal to insurance is justified. Compare Kant's fascinating discussion of the role of Christianity in developing morality, though morality is entirely independent of religion: I Kant, *Critique of the Power of Judgment* (trans P Guyer and E Matthews, Cambridge University Press, Cambridge, 2000) 335 n2 [5:471]. A possible reply is that insurance must be relevant because of the very significant potential deleterious impact of tort law on the insurance market. The law of negligence is often blamed for Australia's recent insurance crisis for instance. However, what the insurance market needs is the certainty and sensible limits to liability provided by the principled approach. What it emphatically does not need is judges who know little about the workings of the insurance market making decisions based on what they intuit as being good for the market. If judges want to ensure a well functioning insurance market, they should ignore it. For discussion of the Australian situation, see P Underwood, 'Is Ms Donoghue's Snail in Mortal Peril?' (2004) 12 *Torts Law Journal* 39.

Finally, J Morgan, 'Tort, Insurance and Incoherence' (2004) 67 *MLR* 384, 393–4 (citations omitted) argues: '[a]ttempts have been made to argue that corrective justice does not require that the actor responsible for the injury actually pays [rather than his insurer], only that he is liable (and has

Imagine that a court appeals to insurance (or any other policy) in order to justify finding for a claimant. Now imagine that the same court is later faced with another claimant who also appeals to insurance. Assuming that the court wants to find for the defendant in the second case (so as to prevent indeterminate liability perhaps), can the court do so? There are two possible kinds of answers. (i) The court could point to a relevant difference between the first case and the second case that makes insurance relevant and liability appropriate in the former but not in the latter. (ii) The court could say that insurance is irrelevant and liability inappropriate in the second case, because to include it would produce an expansion in liability that was not incremental. But it is unclear how this argument is supposed to function. Again, this can be taken in two ways. (ii)(a) The court could say that expanding liability so far would be a bad thing for some reason. (ii)(b) The court could say that expanding liability so far would be a bad thing for no reason, or simply that liability should not be expanded because that would not be incremental.

The last of these options (ii)(b) fails to justify the result. To follow this view is to surrender entirely the notion that courts must justify their decisions. On the other hand, the other options, (i) and (ii)(a), collapse into the *Anns* test. On this view, incrementalism could only be a policy concern designed to prevent indeterminate liability and chaos.[107]

the responsibility for discharging that liability, whether from his personal funds or otherwise). With respect, such arguments do not ring true. While we have not quite reached the position which had emerged very early in some American states, whereby victims may always sue the liability insurer directly, the reality is that, whatever the name of the case in the law reports, it is the insurer which is the actual defendant. Indeed, insurers must pay out to the victim of a road accident in respect of which liability insurance is compulsory, even when they would be entitled to cancel the policy (ie against the insured driver). Furthermore, even when a tortfeasor-driver is uninsured, the victim has an action against the Motor Insurers' Bureau. As for vicarious liability, while the law has not formally developed to hold the master liable to the exclusion of the servant-tortfeasor, the reality is that employers do not seek to recover an indemnity for such damages from their workforce, and the courts have come close to holding such an indemnity irrecoverable. As Atiyah says, therefore, persons who are actually responsible for causing personal injury through their negligence would seem never to pay, and the actual working of tort is as a system of compensation. It needs to be justified as such.' In light of the argument above, the general point made by Morgan is irrelevant here. If the tortfeasor has arranged with someone else to pay for the consequences of his torts, then the fact that someone else will pay is neither here nor there. Nor is it significant that, in some jurisdictions, the legislature has determined, or the courts in response to legislation have determined, some outcomes that do not cohere with corrective justice. These points are completely irrelevant to corrective justice. Of course, *if* the corrective justice theorist also held that for some social reasons the actual defendant (not the insurer) should pay, then this would be a problem. But the corrective justice theorist is not in the business of doing social philosophy, which concerns are important, but not to the corrective justice interpretation of tort law. While the corrective justice model holds that tort law is a system of corrective justice, it does not (or not necessarily) also argue that it gets its political justification from the fact that corrective justice is something that our societies ought to enforce. That is an essentially separate political, rather than legal, matter and it confuses corrective justice for distributive justice to think that tort law must be interpreted in the light of it. The concerns that Morgan mentions are important, but they are not relevant here, as they are not features of the law of negligence or of corrective justice.

[107] It is no coincidence that this problem mirrors the difficulty that faces rule utilitarianism. See eg V Grassian, *Moral Reasoning: Ethical Theory and some Contemporary Moral Problems* (Prentice-Hall, Englewood Cliffs, NJ, 1981) ch 9.

This point can be brought out further by presenting the incremental approach as a three-stage test as is sometimes done, building incrementalism into the test. On this view, the test is as follows:

1. Is there a relationship of proximity between the parties?
2. Are there policy considerations that need to be taken into account?
3. Is the potential cause of action sufficiently analogous with established causes of action?

What is the content of 3? Is it a policy that could just as easily fall under 2? If so, then this is the *Anns* test in disguise. Is it not a policy? If not, then what could its justification possible be? It certainly cannot be corrective justice.

This problem with the incremental approach sometimes produces an almost schizophrenic approach in courts. For instance, in *Fairchild v Glenhaven Funeral Services Ltd*,[108] Lord Hoffmann went in great detail into the policies that he believed govern factual causation. This enabled his Lordship to reject the conclusion he felt the traditional but for test would have generated in *Fairchild* and substitute a new approach. However, one year later in *Channel Islands Knitwear Co Ltd v Hotchkiss*, on facts that apparently satisfied Lord Hoffmann's approach in *Fairchild*, Lord Hoffmann dismissed the claimant's case, saying 'it is an essential condition for obtaining the relatively generous compensation awarded by the law of negligence that, save in the most unusual case, the plaintiff should satisfy the court on a balance of probability that but for the defendant's negligent conduct she would not have suffered her injuries'.[109] How can it be right to dismiss this claimant without a broad discussion of policy when she satisfied Lord Hoffmann's criterion in *Fairchild*? The answer, I suppose, is that if you have an incremental approach you cannot write pages of policy in every decision. Indeed not, but that is hardly a justification.

One possible reply is to hold that the incremental approach is simply the traditional common law method, ie reasoning from precedent, and that such cannot be objectionable in the manner I have claimed. It should already be clear that this reply cannot succeed, but it may be useful briefly to demonstrate why.

Imagine a court which has in one or more cases departed from precedent because of policy. Imagine further that this court is now faced with a new case in which one of the parties argues that the court should depart from a different precedent because of policy concerns. Clearly, if incrementalism is to make any sense, it must at least sometimes be possible for the court to refuse such requests. But on what basis can the court do so? If the court gives a reason apart from the existence of the precedent itself, then it is not following the incremental approach or reasoning from precedent. For instance, a court that insisted on the observation of precedent because the alternative would be too big a change or would produce chaos would be attempting to justify its decision by appeal to

[108] [2002] UKHL 22, [2003] 1 AC 32.
[109] *Channel Islands Knitwear Co Ltd v Hotchkiss* [2003] PC 68, [39].

those policies. That is simply the *Anns* test in disguise. But nor can the court justify its decision to follow precedent simply because it is the precedent. If it is sometimes justified to depart from precedent because of policy, then there must be a reason why that is sometimes justified but sometimes not. A court can justify its decision only if it produces that reason. The mere appeal to precedent, of course, cannot provide such a reason.

Accordingly, the precedent-driven model of legal reasoning is available only in a system where judges have no authority to depart from established precedent, and it can even appear to be coherent only in a system that pretends to obey that rule. The *Practice Statement (Judicial Precedent)* of 1966 has definitively put an end to this.[110] Once it is acknowledged that judges can depart from precedent, they must give their reasons both for doing so when they do and for not doing so when they do not.

In fact, it is possible to state succinctly the fundamental difficulty with the incremental approach. It is that arguing in an incremental manner could be rational only if there were a principle or set of principles that lay under this approach.[111] For instance, if x is the law and a judge is asked to consider whether she should extend x to cover y, then her decision is rational, at least in law,[112] only if it is guided by some general considerations. The existence of those general considerations is precisely what the incremental approach attempts to do without.

D. Conclusion

At the beginning of this section, I argued that the incremental approach has been preferred because it has reduced the level of chaos created by the *Anns* test. Perhaps it is hard to see how the approach achieved this outcome given my arguments above. But this is because I have focused on the conceptual understanding of the law contained in the incremental approach. My conclusion has been that the incremental approach is no less chaotic than the *Anns* test *at the level of principle*. However, at the level of practice, the incremental approach has limited the damage done by the reliance on policy. It has done so in virtue of its insistence on incrementalism: the view that 'the law should develop novel categories of negligence incrementally and by analogy with established categories'.[113] Hence, the incremental approach limits the disturbing impact of policy

---

[110] [1966] 1 WLR 1234 (HL).

[111] The most important work in this regard is found in the writings of Immanuel Kant, particularly I Kant, *Critique of Pure Reason* (trans NK Smith, St Martin's Press, New York, 1965) and I Kant, *Critique of the Power of Judgment* (trans P Guyer and E Matthews, Cambridge University Press, Cambridge, 2000). The point is also made forcefully by N MacCormick, *Legal Reasoning and Legal Theory* (Clarendon Press, Oxford, 1978) 186.

[112] For the distinction between law and ethics, see A Beever, 'Particularism and Prejudice in the Law of Tort' (2003) 11 *Tort Law Review* 146.

[113] *Sutherland Shire Council v Heyman* (1985) 157 CLR 424, 481 (HCA) (Brennan J).

by insisting that—surely as a matter of policy—the law 'develop' slowly and only by analogy with previous cases.

While this approach aids adjudication, it cannot provide justification for the positive law. That a fact pattern does not fit with, or cannot closely be analogised to, previous cases cannot show that the claimant should fail as a matter of justice. Hence, at the level of principle, the incremental approach gives up on the justificatory function of legal principle. In this light, the reluctance of the New Zealand Court of Appeal to adopt the incremental approach seems laudable.

However, even from the perspective of principle, the incremental approach has been somewhat beneficial. This is because its incrementalism has limited the extent to which the law has departed from the principled approach. As a result (as I show in previous and following chapters), the principled approach is still able to explain most of the modern law. Hence, that approach is recoverable.

III. VULNERABILITY: A NEW APPROACH?

According to Stapleton, Commonwealth courts outside the United Kingdom have been developing a new approach that focuses on the vulnerability of the claimant.[114] According to this view, at least in cases involving economic loss, courts impose a duty of care on the defendant in cases in which the claimant was in a position of vulnerability. This approach appears to have received explicit support from recent decisions of the High Court of Australia.[115] But it cannot be regarded as an advance on the approaches elucidated above. First, in analysing the approach, Stapleton concentrates only on cases involving economic loss, and it is easy to see why. As a general matter, it is not credible to contend that the law of negligence is focussed on protecting the vulnerable as reflection on many cases in which the claimant loses demonstrates. The claimant in *Palsgraf* was undoubtedly vulnerable, but she was unable to recover. The same can be said for the claimants in *The Wagon Mound (No 1)*, *Doughty v Turner Manufacturing Co Ltd*[116] and a host of other cases. Simply, 'vulnerability' is far from providing an adequate account of the law of negligence.

If that is so, then the appeal to vulnerability in cases of economic loss is ad hoc at best. If vulnerable claimants can recover economic loss, then why cannot they recover for personal injuries or property damage? Any answer to this question will lead us away from vulnerability and back towards the *Anns* test. Hence, this approach is the reinvention of a broken wheel.

---

[114] J Stapleton, 'Comparative Economic Loss: Lessons from Case-Law-Focused "Middle Theory"' (2002) 50 *University of California of Los Angeles Law Review* 531. See also J Stapleton, 'The Golden Thread at the Heart of Tort Law: Protection of the Vulnerable' (2003) 24 *Australian Bar Review* 135.

[115] See *Perre v Apand Pty Ltd* (1999) 198 CLR 180 (HCA); *Woolcock Street Investments Pty Ltd v CDG Pty Ltd* [2004] HCA 16, (2004) 216 CLR 515.

[116] [1964] 1 QB 518 (CA).

In fact, vulnerability appears to be a particularly bad candidate for an explanation of even part of the law of negligence, because it is inconsistent with the important role played by reasonable foreseeability in that law. At least as a general matter, the less foreseeable the risk to the claimant the more vulnerable the position of that party. *Doughty* is a clear example of that. The claimant was extremely vulnerable precisely because it was not foreseeable that the cement cover would cause an explosion. If that had been foreseeable, then it would have been much less likely that the claimant would have been near the vat. Vulnerability, then, is not only incompatible with reasonable foreseeability; it is often directly opposed to it.

It might be tempting to reply that vulnerability counts in favour of liability only when the defendant should have realised that the claimant was vulnerable. But if that is worked out to its logical conclusion, it is just the principled approach in disguise. If the appeal to vulnerability were to herald even a covert return to the principled approach, then it might be welcomed, but I fear that it is more likely to lead the law in the opposite direction.

IV. THE MODERN APPROACHES AND THE PLACE OF TORT LAW WITHIN THE LAW OF OBLIGATIONS

A final important consequence of the modern approaches can be brought out by exploring Cooke J's judgment in *Gartside v Sheffield, Young & Ellis*.[117] *Gartside* was a disappointed beneficiary case. A third party instructed the defendant solicitor to draw up a will in the claimant's favour. The defendant negligently failed to do so and the third party died, depriving the claimant of the inheritance.

The claimant's case was presented on two fronts. First, he argued that he should have been able to recover as a third party beneficiary of the contract between the testator and the defendant. In support, the claimant appealed to section 4 of the Contracts (Privity) Act 1982 (NZ), which reads:

> Where a promise contained in a deed or contract confers, or purports to confer, a benefit on a person, designated by name, description, or reference to a class, who is not a party to the deed or contract . . . the promisor shall be under an obligation, enforceable at the suit of that person, to perform that promise . . .

Secondly, the claimant argued that he should have been able to recover in negligence.

Cooke J rejected the first argument:

> [O]n an ordinary and natural reading of the key s 4 of that Act, a prospective beneficiary under a proposed will could not invoke the Act. For the contract between the

---

[117] [1983] NZLR 37 (CA). The reasoning examined here was also adopted by Lord Goff in *White v Jones* [1995] 2 AC 207 (HL). That case and the wider issues are explored in detail in ch 7. For comment, see S Whittaker, 'Privity of Contract and the Tort of Negligence: Future Directions' (1996) 16 *OJLS* 191, 203.

testator and the solicitor would not itself contain a promise conferring or purporting to confer a benefit on the prospective beneficiary. Putting the point in another way, the solicitor has not promised to confer a benefit on him.[118]

That may well be correct, but I want to focus on the narrowness of Cooke J's interpretation of the Act.[119] The testator went to the defendant in order to benefit the claimant and the defendant was well aware of that. But, while one can loosely say that the transaction between the testator and the defendant was for the benefit of the claimant, one cannot say that *the contract* was for the claimant's benefit. This was because, strictly, the contract simply involved drawing up a will for the testator (in order to benefit the claimant). *The will*, not the contract, was for the claimant's benefit.

Compare this with Cooke J's treatment of the claimant's second argument:

> To deny an effective remedy in a plain case would seem to imply a refusal to acknowledge the solicitor's professional role in the community. In practice the public relies on solicitors (or statutory officers with similar functions) to prepare effective wills. It would be a failure of the legal system not to insist on some practical responsibility. After the client's death specific performance is out of the question as a remedy. The intended testamentary disposition can no longer be made. The client's estate must be distributed in accordance with the will (if any) that he has made or on intestacy, subject to claims under the family protection or testamentary promises legislation. . . . [T]o recognise that the solicitor owed a duty of reasonable care to the intended beneficiary would produce a just result. It offers a remedy that should be made available unless there is some technical objection. For the reasons already given I do not think that there is any technical objection.[120]

What happened to the rigorous legal analysis explored in relation to the claimant's first argument? Here, we are offered unrefined intuition. We are no longer closely analysing doctrines of law, but talking of 'plain cases', of conventions, of the public's expectations, of the fact that there appears to be no alternative remedy. In relation to the last issue, why is the solution to this problem not to alter the law of wills or the law of contract to provide an alternative remedy? Why is tort law seen as the appropriate place in which to create a solution to the problem presented by *Gartside*?

There are two points to note. First, as opposed to other areas of law, the law of negligence is seen to have no inherent content. Contract law cannot be altered as it contains doctrines that constrain judicial decision making, but tort law is

---

[118] *Gartside v Sheffield, Young & Ellis* [1983] NZLR 37, 42–3 (CA).

[119] Compare Cooke J's interpretation in *Donselaar v Donselaar* [1982] 1 NZLR 97 (CA) of s5(1) of the Accident Compensation Act 1972 (NZ)—which reads 'no proceedings for damages . . . shall be brought in any Court in New Zealand independently of this Act'—that 'no proceedings for damages' did not include exemplary damages. There, Cooke J was prepared to adopt a much more flexible approach to the interpretation of statues. This indicates that, not only does the common law of negligence attract more judicial flexibility than the common law of contract, but statutes that concern the law of negligence are also interpreted more flexibly than statutes that relate to the law of contract.

[120] *Gartside v Sheffield, Young & Ellis* [1983] NZLR 37, 43 (CA).

infinitely flexible and therefore—the second point—can respond to any perceived injustice that comes its way. Hence, whenever a problem arises, no matter what its real cause, tort law can fix it. Tort has become the Swiss Army knife of the common law.[121] But this is inconsistent with the notion that the law has a coherent conceptual structure. Moreover, as we will discuss further in Chapter 8, it has stunted the development of other parts of the law and our understanding of the private law as a whole.

V. COMPARING THE APPROACHES

I end this chapter by considering two similar cases, one from Canada under the *Anns* test and one from Australia under the incremental approach. The Canadian decision is particularly useful as it contains a dissent that accords with the principled approach (though it is officially based on *Kamloops*, the Canadian version of the *Anns* test). Hence, these cases enable us instructively to compare the approaches in practice. However, the point of discussing these cases is not to argue that the principled approach reaches a result with which all would agree. Some will prefer the result reached under the alternative approaches. Rather, the point of this discussion is that only the principled approach is able to resolve the disagreements that arise in the cases, and hence that we have good reason to adopt the principled approach even if the result it produces in this example does not align with our personal political preferences. As always, the result can be amended through statute if that is desired by the community as a whole.

The cases are *Lynch v Lynch*[122] and *Dobson v Dobson*.[123] In each case, the defendant damaged the foetus she was carrying while driving negligently. The claimants were the defendants' born alive children, each suffering from cerebral palsy. In *Dobson*, the Supreme Court of Canada used the *Anns* test to deny liability. In *Lynch*, the New South Wales Court of Appeal used the incremental approach to reach the opposite conclusion.

Before I begin, it is necessary to lay out some background legal principles applicable here. First, no duties of care are owed to foetuses. In order to gain legal personality and to be able to bring a cause of action, a child must be born alive. However, once born alive, the child can sue for injuries she suffers because of damage inflicted *in utero*.[124] Hence, prima facie, given that the defendant was negligent, the damage proximate and the claimant (the born alive child, not the

---

[121] I owe this phrase to Martin Klevstul. The law of unjust enrichment is also sometimes treated in this manner, particularly in Canada and New Zealand. See R Grantham and C Rickett, *Enrichment and Restitution in New Zealand* (Hart Publishing, Oxford, 2000) 9–12.

[122] (1991) 25 NSWLR 411 (CA).

[123] [1999] 2 SCR 753.

[124] *Watt v Rama* [1972] VR 353 (SC); *Burton v Islington Health Authority* [1993] QB 204 (CA); s 1 Congenital Disabilities (Civil Liability) Act 1976 (UK).

foetus) was within the class of persons put at risk by the defendant's negligence, the claimant had a good cause of action against the defendant.[125]

One important consequence of these background principles is that the discussion that follows says nothing whatsoever about the legality or morality of abortion. It is, I think, often felt that *Lynch* and *Dobson* are intimately linked with the issue of abortion, and in particular that opponents of the decision in *Dobson* must be anti-abortion in some sense. That is wrong. Because a foetus has no legal personality until it is born alive, successful abortions (ie ones that result in the death of the foetus) do not and cannot violate either the rights of the foetus, as the foetus has no rights, or the rights of the born alive child, as there is none. Hence, the issue of abortion is entirely irrelevant here.

I begin with *Dobson*. In concurring judgments, both Cory and McLachlin JJ appealed to a number of policies to negative the defendant's liability. Cory J argued that the unique relationship between a mother and the foetus she carries provides reasons for denying a duty of care.[126] As McLachlin J put it, '[p]regnancy is essentially related to womanhood. It is an inexorable and essential fact of human history [sic] that women and only women become pregnant. Women should not be penalised because it is their sex that bears children'.[127] Moreover, Cory J insisted that a finding of liability may have serious psychological repercussions on the defendant,[128] and maintained that liability would damage family harmony.[129] Perhaps more decisively, both Cory and McLachlin JJ argued that liability in such circumstances would interfere with women's privacy[130] and autonomy[131] rights.

With respect to privacy, Cory J said, '[I]f a mother were to be held liable for prenatal negligence, this could render the most mundane decision taken in the course of her daily life as a pregnant woman subject to the scrutiny of the courts'.[132] With regard to autonomy, Cory J maintained that:

> the consequences of imposing tort liability on a mother, for prenatally inflicted injuries causing damages to her born alive child, are far-reaching. It cannot be forgotten that the relationship between a mother-to-be and her foetus is such that everything the former does may affect the latter. To reiterate some of the most obvious examples—the ingestion of prohibited drugs, the consumption of alcohol, and the smoking of cigarettes—all could be found to breach a duty of care owed by a pregnant woman to her foetus [sic] or subsequently born child. Perhaps the decision to avoid eating fruits and vegetables could also be found to constitute tortious conduct. The same

---

[125] *Dobson v Dobson* [1999] 2 SCR 753, 805–6 (Major J).

[126] *Ibid*, 759, 769.

[127] *Ibid*, 800.

[128] *Ibid*, 781.

[129] *Ibid*.

[130] *Ibid*, 768, 771, 774 (Cory J) 800 (McLachlin J).

[131] *Ibid*, 768, 771–2, 779–81, 786–8 (Cory J) 799–801 (McLachlin J). Note that, unlike Cory J, McLachlin J based her arguments on the Canadian Charter of Rights and Freedoms, Part I of the Constitution Act, 1982, being Schedule B to the Canada Act 1982 (UK) 1982 c 11. I ignore this in the following.

[132] *Ibid*, 771 (Cory J).

conclusion might be reached with regard to unprotected sexual intercourse, rigorous exercise or no exercise. Every aspect of the life of a pregnant woman would be subjected to external scrutiny if liability for tortious conduct to her foetus were imposed.[133]

Furthermore, McLachlin J argued that imposing liability in this case would generate obligations on pregnant women additional to those placed on non-pregnant women and on men. This, according to McLachlin J, would conflict with the equality rights of pregnant women.[134]

These policy concerns were said to be sufficient to negative the prima facie duty of care. Accordingly, a majority of the Court concluded that the defendant did not owe the claimant a duty of care.

In *Lynch*, the New South Wales Court of Appeal came to the opposite conclusion. Whilst acknowledging the policy arguments that were to play so crucial a role in *Dobson*, Clarke JA argued that:

> the question with which this Court is concerned is a narrow one and does not, in my opinion, involve far reaching questions of policy. That question is whether a mother can be liable to her child, who was born with disabilities, in respect of injury caused to that child while a foetus by the mother's negligent driving of a motor vehicle.[135]

So, according to Clarke JA, the question was confined to injuries caused by motor vehicles and involved no wider issues. This was explicitly rejected by the Supreme Court of Canada in *Dobson*. Cory J insisted (somewhat ironically) that 'Courts, if they are going to create exceptions or distinctions, must do so in a more legally principled manner'.[136] Hence, his Honour maintained that the creation of special rules in relation to negligent driving was a matter for the legislature.

The difference between the majority of the Supreme Court of Canada and the New South Wales Court of Appeal can be seen to reflect the stylistic differences between the *Anns* test and the incremental approach. For the Canadian Court, the issues had to be ones of general policy. For the New South Wales Court, the issue was whether, on an incremental basis, liability should flow in this kind of case alone.

The Court in *Lynch* argued in favour of liability on the ground that the defendant was insured.[137] But again this was rejected by the Supreme Court of Canada. And it was rejected for good reason, as discussed above. Moreover, as Cory J noted with approval, in *Lister v Romford Ice and Cold Storage Co Ltd*, Viscount Simmonds said that '[a]s a general proposition it has not, I think, been

---

[133] *Ibid*, 792.
[134] *Ibid*, 800–1.
[135] *Lynch v Lynch* (1991) 25 NSWLR 411, 415 (CA).
[136] *Dobson v Dobson* [1999] 2 SCR 753, 793.
[137] *Lynch v Lynch* (1991) 25 NSWLR 411, 415–16 (CA). This was bolstered by the fact that liability insurance was mandatory under the Motor Vehicles (Third Party Insurance) Act 1942 (NSW).

questioned for nearly two hundred years that, in determining the rights inter se of A and B, the fact that one or other of them is insured is to be disregarded'.[138]

This indicates a serious problem with *Lynch* and with the approach applied in it. If insurance was relevant in *Lynch*, then it must be relevant outside that particular scenario. There is no reason to hold that insurance is relevant only when children are injured by their mothers as a result of damage suffered *in utero*. Moreover, if the policies enunciated in *Dobson* are compelling, then they apply equally to *Lynch*. To deny this on the grounds of incrementalism is to give up on the idea that legal outcomes must be justified. It is no answer that insurance was relevant in *Lynch* because the defendant's insurance was mandatory under the Motor Vehicles (Third Party Insurance) Act 1942 (NSW). On this view, insurance would always be relevant when it was mandatory: in all vehicle accident cases for example. But it is trite law that this is not the case. Furthermore, it cannot merely be stipulated that insurance is relevant only when it is mandatory. One must argue for that conclusion, but it is not obvious what that argument would be. Accordingly, the incremental approach fails to justify the outcome in *Lynch*.[139]

This failure of the incremental approach appears to point to the *Anns* test. If policies such as insurance are relevant, we must make sure that they are given weight in accordance with their strength in the particular case. Legal certainty is one such reason, but must be considered in terms of its relative strength vis-à-vis other relevant reasons. It will not do to make empty appeals to incrementalism. However, if we return to *Dobson*, we see that the *Anns* approach is also fundamentally flawed.

First, although the Court in *Dobson* rejected the insurance argument, its relevance was accepted in *Norsk*. That case involved economic loss, but it is hard to see any *reason* why insurance should be relevant only in economic loss cases, particularly given that liability in negligence produces a monetary award.[140]

Secondly, and more importantly, recall that the following reasons were given for negativing liability in *Dobson*: the unique relationship between a woman and the foetus she carries, family harmony, the psychological repercussions on the defendant, the privacy of pregnant women, the autonomy of pregnant women and equality between pregnant and non-pregnant women and between women and men. Of these concerns, only the first two pay any attention to the claimant.

For instance, in effect Cory J argued that the defendant's interest in her psychological wellbeing trumps the claimant's bodily integrity. He did not do so by

---

[138] [1957] AC 555 (HL); quoted *Dobson v Dobson* [1999] 2 SCR 753, 798.

[139] It is not possible to reply that insurance is relevant only in 'novel' cases. This is because a case can be novel only if there is a *reason* for it being so. This reason cannot be any old difference between the instant case and established cases, but must relate to wider issues of policy. Hence, this reasoning too collapses into the *Anns* test.

[140] See also EJ Weinrib, 'Does Tort Law Have a Future?' (2000) 34 *Valparaiso University Law Review* 561, 567.

comparing the strength of the claimant's interest in bodily integrity with the defendant's interest in psychological wellbeing. Rather, Cory J considered only the defendant's interests. Similarly, McLachlin J denied recovery because of equality concerns relevant to the relationship between the defendant and third parties,[141] again ignoring the claimant. Moreover, the appeal to family harmony, while paying some attention to the claimant, has the potential to sacrifice the claimant's interests to those of his wider family, many of whom are not parties to the action.[142] Finally, although the unique relationship between the woman and her foetus refers to both parties, it is hard to see how it amounts to a *reason* against liability. Furthermore, in McLachlin J's formulation, it involves a one-sided focus on the defendant. 'Pregnancy is essentially related to womanhood. It is an inexorable and essential fact of human history that women and only women become pregnant. Women should not be penalised because it is their sex that bears children.'[143] This does nothing to show that justice lies with the defendant *rather than with the claimant*. Imagine a variation on *Dobson* in which the claimant was a girl.

Hence, the arguments appealed to by the majority in *Dobson* were insufficient to justify their decision. The majority needed to, but did not, show that the policies relating to the defendant outweighed other policy matters concerning the claimant. It is understandable that the majority did not want to engage in that enquiry. This is because, for example, the claim that the autonomy of adult women is more important than the bodily integrity of their children is extremely politically controversial. It is also highly contentious to claim that family harmony is more important than the bodily integrity of children. Again, the point is not that the majority's assessment of these political issues was mistaken (though I believe it was), but that these are inappropriate questions for courts to be asking in these cases. If we agree with the position implicitly taken by the majority in *Dobson*, then we are entitled to attempt to enforce that view through statute, but these political matters are not for the courts to decide in tort cases.

The points of criticism made above were very forcefully put by Major J, dissenting in *Dobson*.

> The bare assertion of social policy concerns expressly and unilaterally centred on a pregnant woman's rights are not a sufficient answer to the question whether a

---

[141] I take it that it could not seriously be argued that healthy women are unfairly disadvantaged with respect to children with cerebral palsy.

[142] In *Dobson*, the claimant's interests were not sacrificed to those of his family. But this was not because the claimant's interests were not sacrificed. Rather, it was because the claimant's family, including the defendant, wanted the claimant to succeed, so that they would be able to gain access to the defendant's liability insurance in order to help with raising the disabled claimant. Hence, the interests of both the claimant and his family were sacrificed to those of other families. On the principled approach, these interests of the defendant are irrelevant, as the defendant had assigned her rights in the case to the insurance company in contract. However, this point does place the policy arguments in an interesting light. If policy is relevant, why ignore this issue?

[143] *Dobson v Dobson* [1999] 2 SCR 753, 800.

pregnant woman's rights should prevail over the equally recognized rights of her born alive child. It is no answer to the plaintiff in this case that unilateral concerns about a pregnant woman's competing rights are sufficient to 'negative' a negligent violation of his physical integrity. His rights, too, are at stake.[144]

In *Dobson*, then, we see 'the judicial confiscation of what is rightly due to the plaintiff in order to subsidise policy objectives unilaterally favourable to the defendant and those similarly situated'.[145]

Moreover, as Major J again pointed out, the policy concerns upon which the majority placed most emphasis were *irrelevant* in *Dobson*. This was because the defendant was not at liberty to drive negligently as she was already under a duty of care to other users of the highway. Hence, no issue of freedom or equality was at stake in *Dobson*.[146]

The majority rejected this argument because (so they claimed) it is impossible to formulate a standard of care for pregnant women that would allow liability in this case while protecting the autonomy and privacy rights of women in similar cases.[147] However, they gave no reason to prefer the autonomy of women to the bodily integrity of their children and, moreover, an adequate standard was suggested by Major J.[148] The accident that injured the claimant in *Dobson* also injured the driver of another vehicle. Accordingly, Major J argued:

> On the facts of this case, Ryan Dobson's prima facie right to sue in tort arises only on the same grounds and in the same way as that of the driver of the other car. In these circumstances, the appellant's freedom of action is not in issue, and the suggestion that her son's rights ought to be negatived so as to protect her freedom of action is misplaced.[149]

McLachlin J interpreted Major J as arguing that the defendant could be liable only if the claimant's injury resulted from the breach of a duty of care the defendant actually owed to a third party. But this, McLachlin J pointed out (with great irony given the above), 'violates the principle that the duty of care in tort must be founded on the relationship between the actual parties to the dispute before the court, and makes recovery conditional on the serendipitous coincidence that another person stood to be injured by the pregnant woman's act or omission'.[150] In other words, the duty to the claimant is parasitic on the duty to the third party, thus allowing the claimant to sue 'as the vicarious beneficiary of a breach of duty to another'.[151]

---

[144] *Ibid*, 813. See also *Lynch v Lynch* (1991) 25 NSWLR 411, 416 (CA) (Clarke JA).

[145] EJ Weinrib, 'Does Tort Law Have a Future?' (2000) 34 *Valparaiso University Law Review* 561, 566. See also LE Weinrib and EJ Weinrib, 'Constitutional Values and Private Law in Canada' in D Friedmann and D Barak-Erez (eds), *Human Rights in Private Law* (Hart, Oxford, 2001) 69.

[146] *Dobson v Dobson* [1999] 2 SCR 753, 809. Compare s2 Congenital Disabilities Act 1976 (UK).

[147] *Dobson*, above n146, 782–96 (Cory J), 801 (McLachlin J).

[148] *Ibid*, 810–12.

[149] *Ibid*, 810.

[150] *Ibid*, 801.

[151] *Palsgraf v Long Island Railroad Co* 162 NE 99, 100 (NY CA 1928).

However, as Major J made clear, the issue is not whether the defendant actually owed a duty of care to a third party, but whether the alleged duty of care was of a kind that *could have been* owed to a third party. Major J's stance was not that the default position is that no duty of care is owed to the claimant, but an exception is made when a duty of care is owed to a third party. Rather, Major J's view was that the default position is that a duty of care is owed to the claimant, but should be restricted—for reasons elucidated below—so that the defendant owes her future children no obligations additional to those owed to other persons. Hence, on Major J's view, the claimant should have been able to recover in *Dobson*, as his injury was caused in a motor vehicle accident and the alleged duty of care was of a kind that could be owed to other persons. Conversely, the defendant should not be liable for injuries caused by such activities as smoking, drinking alcohol, eating, exercising and so on—sometimes called 'lifestyle choices'—as duties of care in respect of those activities are not owed to other persons.[152]

Again, however, McLachlin J insisted that this 'violates the precept that a common law duty of care arises from the relationship of the parties before the court, not from the relationship between the defendant and a hypothetical claimant'.[153] This precept is not violated by Major J's position. In fact, Major J's restriction on the duty of care is justified by a consideration of the relationship between the parties.

As the majority identified, a fundamental question in *Dobson* and similar cases is: What level of care can a child reasonably expect his mother to have taken of him when he was *in utero*?[154] As discussed in Chapter 3, the law of negligence sets this level in accordance with a standard of care designed to mediate between the interests of the parties. The appropriate conclusion, then, is not that a woman enjoys an absolute immunity from liability in negligence in relation to injuries to her children suffered *in utero* (as the majority ruled). But nor is it that pregnant women must refrain from lifestyle choices that place their children-to-be at risk if such would significantly impact on the woman's autonomy (as the majority feared). Born alive children cannot reasonably expect their mothers to have been maximally efficient life-support machines. That would privilege the position of the child over his mother, failing to do justice between the parties.

What we need, then, is a standard that neither submerges the interests of the child to those of his mother or vice versa. One such standard (though perhaps not the only one[155]) is to hold the woman liable for injuries suffered *in utero* by

---

[152] S2 Congenital Disabilities Act 1976 (UK).

[153] *Dobson v Dobson* [1999] 2 SCR 753, 801.

[154] Note that the question is not: 'what level of care can a foetus expect from its mother to be?' At law, foetuses have no enforceable expectations.

[155] For discussion of the relationship between corrective justice, the principles of the law and their application, see the discussion of corrective justice, the principled approach and the role of judgement in ch 2.

204 Modern Approaches to the Duty of Care

her born alive children only if the woman's negligence was of a kind that could have injured a person other than the child. In other words, the woman is held to owe obligations to her born alive child only of a kind that she owes to others. This both recognises the born alive child as a person worthy of the law's protection and prevents the interests of the women being subverted to the interests of her children.[156]

In practice, then, whether or not one personally favours the outcome given by the principled approach, that approach is the only way to take seriously the interests of both parties who are actually in dispute. That approach, then, is vastly to be preferred to the modern approaches.

VI. CONCLUSION

At the beginning of this chapter, I indicated that the principled approach is rejected mainly because it cannot cope with concerns such as economic loss and liability for omissions. To demonstrate that this rejection is unfounded, I must show that the principled approach can deal with such issues. Accordingly, my attack on the law's modern approaches is only half completed. However, in this chapter I have shown that the modern law's alternatives to the principled approach are extremely unattractive. Though they purport to explain the law, they are systematically unable to do so. Conversely, I have shown in Chapters 3 and 4 that the principled approach is very attractive. Hence, we have reason to hope that my claims concerning the principled approach in relation to economic loss and liability for omissions can be made good.

---

[156] At this point, it may be useful to remind the reader that the need to 'balance the interests of the parties' does not imply that that balancing must be done in terms of distributive justice. The balancing may be done as between the parties and hence in accordance with corrective justice. Also, deciding these issues in accordance with corrective justice does not imply that the decisions will be entirely uncontroversial, just that the decisions are not political in the way that decisions about distributive justice are.

6

Misfeasance, Nonfeasance and the Rights Base of the Law of Negligence

ACCORDING TO FRANCIS Bohlen, '[t]here is no distinction more deeply rooted in the common law and more fundamental than that between misfeasance and nonfeasance'.[1] Despite that, outside certain narrow areas, the distinction is seldom discussed today. Many students, I suspect, leave law school without ever having heard of it. Nevertheless, Bohlen was right to claim that the distinction is of crucial importance. In particular, paying attention to the distinction is necessary if we are to understand the issues of economic loss, negligent misrepresentation and the liability of public bodies in the chapters that follow.

Although this chapter deals with the distinction between misfeasance and nonfeasance, the detailed examination of nonfeasance is postponed. That is because the issue is best explored after the discussions of economic loss and negligent misstatement. This chapter is concerned only to elucidate the distinction between misfeasance and nonfeasance and explore the relationship with the rights base of negligence law so that that discussion can begin.

I. THE TRADITIONAL UNDERSTANDING OF THE DISTINCTION BETWEEN MISFEASANCE AND NONFEASANCE

A. Acts and Omissions

The distinction between misfeasance and nonfeasance is often understood to be synonymous with that between acts and omissions.[2] This view has also recently found favour with Lord Hoffmann in *Gorringe v Calderdale MBC*. That case, explored further in Chapter 9, dealt with the responsibility of a borough council to ensure that the roads under its authority were safe. In discussing the history of such liability, Lord Hoffmann said:

> An individual who had suffered damage because of some positive act which the authority had done to make the highway more dangerous could sue for negligence

[1] FH Bohlen, 'The Moral Duty to Aid Others as a Basis of Tort Liability' (1908) 56 *University of Pennsylvania Law Review* 217, 219.
[2] See, eg, *ibid*.

. . . in the same way as he could sue anyone else. The highway authority had no exemption from ordinary liability in tort. But the [public law] duty to take active steps to keep the highway in repair was special to the highway authority and was not a private law duty owed to any individual. Thus it was said that highway authorities were liable in tort for misfeasance but not for non-feasance. Sometimes it was said that the highway authority was 'exempt' from liability for non-feasance, but it was not truly an exemption in the sense that the authority had a special defence against liability. The true position was that no one had ever been liable in private law for non-repair of a highway.[3]

Generalising from this case, it is said that usually one cannot be liable for an omission in the law of negligence and, although there are now some exceptions to this rule, the law remains very cautious in recognising such exceptions. This appears to count against the principled approach, as it is often foreseeable that injuries will result from omissions.[4]

However, defining the distinction between misfeasance and nonfeasance in terms of acts and omissions encounters a major problem: it is deeply inconsistent with the law of obligations as a whole. In fact, it has never been the case that omissions were immune from liability. Such liability has always been routine. For instance, if I contract to deliver my horse to you on Saturday, and instead of doing so I stay in bed, then I appear to be guilty of an omission but can be liable nevertheless. In contract, liability for omissions is commonplace. Moreover, though the principle of unjust enrichment is a recent discovery in the common law,[5] it has long been the case that one can recover, for instance, a mistaken payment even if the defendant had done nothing to procure it.[6] The likely reply is that the rule was only that omissions *in tort* were immune from liability, but there appears to be no good reason to separate the law of obligations in this manner—baring the desire to preserve the traditional understanding of the distinction between misfeasance and nonfeasance, that is—and, in any event, it has long been the case that omissions in tort were actionable. The tort of detinue dealt with the failure to return property to its rightful possessor. Nuisance requires no act on the part of the defendant.[7] Similarly, while it is not a trespass to be pushed onto another person's land, if one omits to leave then one commits a trespass. Other examples could be given. If we are looking for a deeply rooted and fundamental distinction in the common law, we have not found it. We must, then, replace the traditional understanding of the misfeasance/nonfeasance distinction with a view more consistent with the law, if one can be found.

---

[3] [2004] UKHL 15, [2004] 1 WLR 1057, 1063.

[4] See, eg, *ibid*, 1064 (WLR).

[5] *Lipkin Gorman (a firm) v Karpnale Ltd* [1991] 2 AC 458 (HL).

[6] See, eg, *Hewter v Bartholomew* (1598) Cro Eliz 614; *Aiken v Short* (1856) 1 H & N 210.

[7] '[I]t is not essential that there be an activity for there to be a nuisance': *Bank of New Zealand v Greenwood* [1984] 1 NZLR 525, 532 (HC). See also *Matheson v Northcote College* [1975] 2 NZLR 106 (SC), in which the defendant was found liable for the actions of schoolchildren on his property.

Of course, the apparent omissions described above can be redescribed as actions: the failure to return a chattel as the active keeping of it and the failure to leave the land as the active occupation of it, for example. But that just demonstrates how unhelpful the distinction between acts and omissions is. In *Fagan v Commissioner of Metropolitan Police*,[8] the defendant unintentionally drove his car onto a policeman's foot. When the defendant discovered what he had done, he refused to move. At least *arguendo*, all of the judges in that case accepted that the defendant could be guilty of a battery only if he had acted illegally; an omission would not suffice.[9] According to Bridge J, this meant that the defendant could not be liable:

> [A]fter the wheel of the appellant's car had accidentally come to rest on the constable's foot, what was it that the appellant did which constituted the act of assault? However the question is approached, the answer I feel obliged to give is: precisely nothing. The car rested on the foot by its own weight and, remained stationary by its own inertia. The appellant's fault was that he *omitted* to manipulate the controls to set it in motion again.[10]

However, James J and Lord Parker CJ, concurring, said that 'we see no difference in principle between the action of stepping on to a person's toe and maintaining that position and the action of driving a car on to a person's foot and sitting in the car whilst its position on the foot is *maintained*.[11] James J also claimed that '[t]he justices at quarter sessions . . . were satisfied . . . that the appellant "knowingly, provocatively and unnecessarily *allowed the wheel to remain* on the foot after the officer said 'Get off, you are on my foot'".[12] In other words, for James J, leaving the car on the victim's foot was an action, not an omission.

This argument is empty. It is true that the defendant in *Fagan* omitted to act and that he acted. As in *Fagan*, any omission can be described as an action. If I decide to stay in bed all day tomorrow not moving one muscle, that could equally well be described as the omission to perform any actions or the act of staying in bed. Or, to take an example used by Tony Honoré,[13] it is sometimes understood that beating one's child is an action, while starving it is an omission, but the latter need not be, and often is not, understood that way. Starving one's child is often regarded as an action—ie the act of depriving one's child of food.[14]

---

[8] [1969] 1 QB 439 (CA). This was a criminal case, but the differences between tort law and the criminal law do not concern us here.

[9] However, the prosecution argued that the defendant was under a duty to act, and hence violated that duty by omitting to do so. This was implicitly rejected by Bridge J, but James J expressed no conclusive opinion: *ibid*, 444.

[10] *Ibid*, 446 (emphasis added).

[11] *Ibid*, 444 (emphasis added).

[12] *Ibid*, 443 (emphasis added).

[13] T Honoré, 'Are Omissions Less Culpable?' in P Cane and J Stapleton (eds), *Essays for Patrick Atiyah* (Clarendon Press, Oxford, 1991) 33.

[14] We are likely to say of such parents, for instance, 'how could you *do that* to your child?'

A more recent example comes from the decision of the Supreme Court of Canada in *Childs v Desormeaux*.[15] At least as interpreted by the Court, this case involved the potential liability of a host of a social gathering to those injured by one of the host's guests who drove from the gathering in a state impaired by alcohol. One question was whether the host had committed nonfeasance or misfeasance. The Court concluded that, as the host did not supply his guest with alcohol, the host was guilty only of nonfeasance:

> [T]his is at best a case of nonfeasance. No duty to monitor guests' drinking or to prevent them from driving can be imposed having regard to the relevant cases and legal principles. A social host at a party where alcohol is served is not under a duty of care to members of the public who may be injured by a guest's actions, unless the host's conduct implicates him or her in the creation or exacerbation of the risk.[16]

Many would want to agree that this is an instance of nonfeasance, but this argument cannot support that conclusion. It is not plausible to argue that hosting a party creates no risk (or even only a very small risk anywhere that I have lived) that persons at that party will get drunk and drive in an impaired manner causing injuries to others. And when we recall that we are talking about the risk to the particular claimant injured in this case—ie the person using that stretch of road at that time of the night, etc—it is clear that the host was one of the persons who created the risk of injury to that person by holding the party.

One could attempt to support the Court's conclusion by arguing that, on the traditional understanding of the distinction between misfeasance and nonfeasance, given that the host did not serve alcohol, he did not *act* to create any risk and so could not be liable. But it is just as plausible to describe the case differently. The host acted by holding the party at which persons were invited to drink, and that action involved the creation of risk to third parties. If the traditional distinction between misfeasance and nonfeasance is correct, then it is completely unhelpful in this case and in all cases.

Take a different case. Imagine that I am driving down the road when I decide to close my eyes and drive with my feet on the dashboard. Not looking where I am going, I crash into your car. Is this misfeasance or nonfeasance? I might attempt to defend myself—as the defendant successfully did in *Childs*—by arguing that I simply failed to act. After all, I had my eyes closed and my feet on the dashboard. But, of course, this argument would not succeed. It would likely fail because a court would hold that I was acting by driving and that I was driving in an inappropriate manner. The problem is that this description is quite consistent with my own story. It is true both that I omitted to act by closing my eyes, etc, and that I acted by driving. Similarly, it was true in *Childs* that the defendant both omitted to act in not serving his guests and acted in holding the party. Hence, if we want to say that I was guilty of misfeasance and not nonfeasance and that the defendant in *Childs* committed nonfeasance and not misfeasance,

---

[15] [2006] SCC 18.
[16] *Ibid*, para [47].

then the distinction between misfeasance and nonfeasance cannot be that between acts and omissions.

The general point is this. Deciding not to act is itself an action. When I stay in bed all day I act, and the fact that my body does not move makes no difference to this conclusion. Similarly, I act when I decide to hold my breath *and* when I decide to start breathing again. All omissions are also actions. Hence, arguing over whether something is an action or an omission is like arguing over whether something is coloured or blue.

The distinction between misfeasance and nonfeasance is quite different. While one event can rightly be described both as an action and as an omission, no event can be both misfeasance and nonfeasance. The traditional understanding of the distinction must be flawed.[17] The logical structures of the relevant concepts are entirely different. They cannot, therefore, be the same. We must find another understanding of the distinction between misfeasance and nonfeasance if we can.

B. Justifications for the Act/Omission Distinction

One of the most stark and interesting features of the common law is that, outside certain special categories, it imposes no duty to rescue. So, to take and accentuate the standard example, if I am standing on a wharf when I see a child fall into the water and begin to drown, I have no duty to rescue that child. I am entitled to stand there and watch the child drown. Even if I could rescue the child simply by kicking into the water a lifebuoy that happens to be lying at my feet, I cannot be liable for failing to do so. What could possibly justify so extraordinary a rule?

Various suggestions have been made.[18] In *Stovin v Wise*, Lord Hoffmann summarised these into three categories: political, moral and economic.[19] Put shortly, the argument is that liability for failing to conduct a rescue would interfere with freedom (political), would arbitrarily single out individual defendants for liability who were no more to blame than anyone else for not conducting the rescue (moral), and would be economically inefficient (economic). Perhaps these arguments generally have weight, but they are hardly compelling when applied

---

[17] Note that this does not imply that enquiries such as the one conducted in Honoré, above n13, are without value. Honoré's aim is to justify the intuitive view that the culpability of those events we generally regard as actions is usually greater than that of those events we usually regard as omissions. No attack on that argument has been conducted here.

[18] For discussion, see, eg, L Bender, 'A Lawyer's Primer on Feminist Theory and Tort' (1988) 38 *Journal of Legal Education* 3, 33–8; RA Epstein, 'A Theory of Strict Liability' (1973) 2 *Journal of Legal Studies* 151, 197–201; A Ripstein, 'Three Duties to Rescue: Moral, Civil, and Criminal' (2000) 19 *Law and Philosophy* 751; EJ Weinrib, 'The Case for a Duty to Rescue' (1980) 90 *Yale Law Journal* 247; EJ Weinrib, 'Legal Formalism: On the Immanent Rationality of Law' (1988) 97 *Yale Law Journal* 949, 977–8.

[19] [1996] AC 823, 830–1 (HL).

to the case under discussion.[20] If these are the best arguments going, then one ought to be under a duty to rescue the child in the example above.

According to Jane Stapleton, the law at this point adopts a position of extreme libertarianism in its preference for freedom of action over the interests of the child.[21] This is in stark contradistinction to her claim that protection of the vulnerable lies at the heart of the law of tort,[22] and cuts against many of the policy concerns with which she recommends that courts engage in negligence cases.[23] And, in any case, it raises the question why the law should be libertarian at this point.

The non-existence of a duty to rescue is not easily explicable in terms of policy. If it is true that the law is concerned to promote the kinds of policies that we have discussed, then it appears inconceivable that it would not impose a duty to conduct easy rescues, at least in certain cases. The fact that continental systems do impose such duties in both civil law and, with the exceptions only of Finland and Sweden, in criminal law is further evidence that the common law is not responding to the kinds of concerns often thought to drive it.[24] In fact, the absence of a duty to rescue points away from the modern approaches altogether.

II. THE RIGHTS BASE OF THE LAW OF NEGLIGENCE

A. Primary Rights and Injuries

In his classic account of the role played by nonfeasance in the common law, Francis Bohlen writes:

> There is no distinction more deeply rooted in the common law and more fundamental than that between misfeasance and non-feasance, between active conduct working positive injury to others and passive inaction, a failure to take positive steps to benefit others, or to protect them from harm not created by any wrongful act of the defendant.[25]

---

[20] For an analysis of the moral argument see EJ Weinrib, 'The Case for a Duty to Rescue' (1980) 90 *Yale Law Journal* 247. For reasons of the kind discussed below, Weinrib now holds that a duty to rescue cannot be supported at common law. See, eg, EJ Weinrib, 'Legal Formalism: On the Immanent Rationality of Law' (1988) 97 *Yale Law Journal* 949, 977–8.

[21] J Stapleton, 'Duty of Care Factors: A Selection from the Judicial Menus' in P Cane and J Stapleton (eds), *The Law of Obligations: Essays in Celebration of John Fleming* (Clarendon Press, Oxford, 1998) 73–4.

[22] See J Stapleton, 'The Golden Thread at the Heart of Tort Law: Protection of the Vulnerable' (2003) 24 *Australian Bar Review* 135.

[23] For summary see Stapleton, above n21, 92–5.

[24] For a summary of the continental positions see JM Smits, *The Good Samaritan in European Private Law: On the Perils of Principles without a Programme and a Programme for the Future* (Kluwer, Deventer, 2000) 2–11.

[25] FH Bohlen, 'The Moral Duty to Aid Others as a Basis of Tort Liability' (1908) 56 *University of Pennsylvania Law Review* 217, 219.

Note that there are two potential definitions of the distinction between misfeasance and nonfeasance in this seminal passage. The first is between active and passive conduct, the second between conduct that causes injury and conduct that fails to benefit others or fails to prevent harm to others. I suggest that the later distinction is the more helpful. Misfeasance is the causing of injury and nonfeasance is the failure to benefit or, what is really an instance of a failure to benefit, the failure to prevent harm. We explore this notion further below, but for the moment our task is to elucidate the concept of an injury. What, in the eyes of the law, is an injury?

Generally, the position taken by modern common lawyers is that an injury is any factual deprivation suffered by the claimant, whether that be physical, financial, emotional or whatever. As we see in following chapters, this focus on factual injury has caused considerable damage to our understanding of the law, which adopts a quite different conception of injury.

The legal conception of injury can be seen in Lord Atkin's judgment in *Donoghue v Stevenson*.[26] Recall that Lord Atkin said that 'the lawyer's question, Who is my neighbour? receives a restricted reply'.[27] What is this restriction? Lord Atkin claimed that '[y]ou must take reasonable care to avoid acts or omissions which you can reasonably foresee would be likely to injure your neighbour'.[28] His Lordship then went on to ask, 'Who, then, in law is my neighbour?'[29] But there was another question, a question that was not important in *Donoghue v Stevenson* itself, but that is crucial here and in the chapters that follow: What is an injury? Although Lord Atkin did not elucidate the legal concept of an injury, his Lordship said enough for us to estimate what his answer might have been. Speaking generally about the law of tort, Lord Atkin remarked that 'acts or omissions which any moral code would censure cannot in a practical world be treated so as to give a right to every person injured by them to demand relief'.[30] The focus here is on rights to recover for injuries, but if we generalise this approach we will define injuries too in terms of rights. On this view, an injury or harm at law is the violation of a legal right. Hence, 'rules of law arise which limit the range of complainants and the extent of their remedy', in part because there can be no recovery unless the defendant violated a right in the claimant.[31] As Cardozo CJ said in *Palsgraf v Long Island Railroad Co*, '[n]egligence is not a tort unless it results in the commission of a wrong, and the commission of a wrong imports the violation of a right'.[32]

On this view, then, not all factual deprivations are injuries in the relevant, legal sense. Hence, if I compete with your business causing you financial loss,

---

[26] *M'Alister (or Donoghue) (Pauper) v Stevenson* [1932] AC 562 (HL Sc).
[27] *Ibid*, 580.
[28] *Ibid*.
[29] *Ibid*.
[30] *Ibid*.
[31] *Ibid*.
[32] 162 NE 99, 101 (NY CA 1928).

while I cause you a factual deprivation, I do not injure you in the eyes of the law. That is because in competing with you I interfere with no right that you hold. Similarly, I do not injure you when I insult you or when I steal your partner, though I do cause factual loss.

Injuries, then, are defined legally in terms of rights violations. Crucially, the rights in question are primary rights and not secondary rights. A primary right is a right recognised by the substantive law and includes the right to the performance of a contract, to property, to bodily integrity and to reputation.[33] It is the task of legal actions to protect and enforce these rights.[34] Secondary rights are those that arise when a primary right has been infringed; they are the law's response to invasions of primary rights. These are rights to compensation, disgorgement, etc. Naturally, it would make no sense to claim that one is injured in the eyes of the law only if someone has violated one's secondary rights, but that claim is not made here.

B. Primary Rights and the Structure of the Law of Obligations

Part of the problem with our understanding of the law of negligence, and part of the problem with our understanding of the private law as a whole, is that we tend to see that law as divided into five separate, though related, parts: property, contract, tort, unjust enrichment and equity.[35] The relationship between the first three is particularly important in this and in the subsequent five chapters of this book. First, though it is commonly perceived that parts of the law of tort are designed to protect property rights, tort law is also seen to be an independent area of the law. Hence, our picture of the law is something like the following:[36]

Area of Law	Responses to Contraventions of Law
Property ———————	Torts (eg trespass, conversion)
Contract ———————	(Breach of) Contract
Tort Law ——— ⌐ ———	Compensation
└ ———	Disgorgement

---

[33] BA Garner, *Black's Law Dictionary,* 7th edn (West Group, St Paul, Minn, 1999) 1323–4; DM Walker, *The Oxford Companion to Law* (Clarendon Press, Oxford, 1980) 1071.

[34] BA Garner, *A Dictionary of Modern Legal Usage* (Oxford University Press, Oxford, 1995) 451.

[35] For simplicity and to avoid entanglement in more controversy, I ignore unjust enrichment and equity for the most part in the following.

[36] This picture is not meant to be complete. It is meant only as an outline of the usual understanding of the conceptual layout of the law. Note also that it is perhaps the case that some property rights may be vindicated directly. In *Trustee of Jones v Jones* [1997] Ch 159 (CA), the English Court of Appeal may have recognised a common law version of the *vindicatio*. See R Grantham and C Rickett, *Enrichment and Restitution in New Zealand* (Hart Publishing, Oxford, 2000) 50 n27.

This picture is problematic for a number of reasons. The most important here is that these three areas of law deal with fundamentally different kinds of rights. For instance, property law recognises primary rights, but the enforcement of property rights falls to the law of tort.[37] Hence, property law deals only with primary rights. Contract law, however, deals with both primary and secondary rights. Introductory courses in contract law teach students how contractual rights and obligations come into existence (formation) and how the law deals with the violation of those rights (remedies). Tort law is a different beast again. This is because, at least on its face, tort law responds to violations of primary rights but does not recognise those rights. Hence, tort law appears able to recognise only secondary rights.

This is most clearly the case with respect to tort law's role in protecting property rights. For instance, a claimant can sue a defendant for converting a piece of property only if the claimant has legal possession of that property. Hence, in conversion, the claimant's primary right is a matter determined entirely by the law of property and about which tort law is silent.

But consider the torts of trespass to the person. The tort of battery protects the primary right of bodily integrity, but that right is not recognised by any explicit area of law. If one were asked to prove that a person possessed a property right to an item that he had purchased and that had been delivered, then one could point to cases in which judges say that title is transferred upon delivery following purchase. In other words, one could point to the explicit recognition of property rights in the law of property.[38] But if one were asked to prove that a person possessed a right to bodily integrity, one could point to no such case law. There is no explicit recognition of that right. But one can prove that the right to bodily integrity exists. One does so by pointing to cases in which claimants *recover* for violations of their bodily integrity and *inferring* from those cases that the right to bodily integrity exists. In the same way, we deduce the right to freedom of movement from the tort of false imprisonment and the right to reputation from the tort of defamation.

Accordingly, in order to develop a more coherent picture of the law, it is necessary to identify that tort law implicitly recognises primary rights. Most importantly, these are rights to the person.[39] Hence, while the law of property governs our primary rights over objects, the law of tort implicitly governs those rights that we possess simply by virtue of being persons. Moreover, as indicated above, tort law also protects both property rights and rights to the person. Therefore, it is also necessary to distinguish between the implicit primary-right-recognising and the explicit primary-right-protecting parts of the law of tort. I

---

[37] *Trustee of Jones v Jones* [1997] Ch 159 (CA) is the only possible exception, given that we are currently ignoring equity.

[38] Birksians may have qualms about this formulation, but see R Grantham and C Rickett, 'Property Rights as a Legally Significant Event',(2003) 62 CLJ 717. The existence of the right is also now given statutory backing. See eg ss 17–18 Sale of Goods Act 1979 (UK).

[39] These are not the only primary rights recognised by the law of tort. Other rights are analysed in ch 7.

do so by referring to the former as 'the law of persons'[40] and the latter as 'the law of wrongs'.[41] Hence, the following picture develops.[42]

Area of Law	Responses to Contraventions of Law
Property ——————	Torts (eg trespass, conversion)
Contract ——————	(Breach of) Contract
Tort Law ——————	Wrongs (eg battery, assault, defamation, false imprisonment)

   The question now is where the law of negligence belongs on this map. The answer is that it belongs in two places: the law of negligence protects primary rights that arise in the law of property and primary rights that arise in the law of persons.

Recognition of Primary Rights	Responses to Violations of Primary Rights— Secondary Rights
Property ——————	Wrongs (eg trespass, conversion, *negligence*)
Contract ——————	(Breach of) Contract
Law of Persons ————	Wrongs (eg battery, assault, defamation, false imprisonment, *negligence*)

The law of negligence is unique in this regard. Other torts are narrow and protect only one kind of primary right. Conversely, negligence is protean and protects many types of primary rights.

C. Standard Objections

This presentation of the law is likely to encounter the following familiar objection: The common law does not work this way. The civil law focuses on rights, the common law on remedies. The argument presented here is out of place.[43]

   At least in this context, this view is wrongheaded. Certainly, due to the historical idiosyncrasies of the common law, the causes of action are structured in

---

[40] This is not identical to the law of persons as it exists in French and Roman law. In my sense, the law of persons incorporates all those primary rights that persons possess simply in virtue of being persons. It may also include what could also be called the 'law of relationships', ie that area of the law that recognises special relationships such as those between parent and child. See also below n 58.

[41] 'Wrongs' is chosen so that it can accommodate equitable wrongs. These are touched on in ch 8.

[42] Note that this diagram is not intended to be complete. I continue to improve on it in chs 7 and 8.

[43] A leading statement of this view is SM Waddams, *Dimensions of Private Law: Categories and Concepts in Anglo-American Legal Reasoning* (Cambridge University Press, Cambridge, 2003). Compare N Jansen, 'Duties and Rights in Negligence: A Comparative and Historical Perspective on the European Law of Extracontractual Liability' (2004) 24 *OJLS* 443.

a way that focuses on remedies rather than rights. Hence, in our courts judges tend to focus likewise. But it does not follow that academics attempting to develop a systematic understanding of the law should ignore rights, which are the logical concomitants of wrongs and remedies.

A political scientist is not constrained to express her understanding of politics as if she were addressing the Speaker of the House at Question Time or an election rally. Academic lawyers, likewise, must be free to express themselves in the most appropriate fashion for their discipline. Naturally, academic lawyers must pay close attention to what courts have said and the manner in which they have said it, but they are not constrained to express themselves as the courts have done. If focusing on rights enables the academic better to explain the law than the courts with their focus on remedies are able to do, then she must adopt that methodology.

In doing so, the academic translates the language of the courts from remedies language into rights language. To the common lawyer, that language is likely to be unfamiliar. But it is important to remember that the translation from remedies to rights does not imply a rejection of the common law. Nor does it entail that the view of the courts is to be rejected, or even that courts should alter their practice. It is a translation not a replacement. Hence, it does not imply rejection any more than translation from one natural language to another does. Translating Shakespeare into German does not imply that he wrote badly in English. Moreover, there may be good reason why courts should continue to speak the language of remedies though academics should, at least at times, shift their focus to rights.[44]

The reason for translating remedies language into rights language in this context is that it enables us better to see and deal with the issues we must confront if we are adequately to resolve the problems of economic loss, liability for omissions, etc. In remedies language, we are likely to approach these problems by asking: did the claimant suffer actionable damage? The problem with this question is that it appears to allow any sort of answer. That is, it appears to be the case that, in arguing whether x is actionable damage, one can appeal to a potentially limitless range of concerns (ie policy). However, in translating the question into rights language, we identify the concerns appropriate to providing the necessary answer. In that language, the question is: did the defendant violate a primary right in the claimant? Here, it is apparent that the answer must refer to primary rights as they exist in the substantive law.

---

[44] Incidentally, this also shows that it would be wrong to conclude from the fact that the maps of the law that I present here are different from the ones suggested by, for instance, Peter Birks, that I reject Birks' understanding of the law. If Birks' maps and mine are *inconsistent*, then of course there is a disagreement. However, if they are merely *different* then that is not necessarily the case. There may be many valuable and consistent perspectives from which the law can be viewed. Some may be more useful when considering tort law, others when exploring unjust enrichment. For Birks' views, see especially P Birks, *Introduction to the Law of Restitution,* 2nd edn (Clarendon Press, Oxford, 1989); P Birks, *Unjust Enrichment* (Clarendon Press, Oxford, 2003).

It is also important to note that, although rights language may be unfamiliar, this translation does not involve the adoption of a radical, abstract-theoretical approach to lawyering—as if, say, the law of negligence were being replaced by abstract normative moral philosophy. The question we are asking—did the defendant violate a primary right in the claimant?—is answered by reference to the extant law, not to moral philosophy. As we see in Chapter 7, in many cases the question is answered by looking to the law of property and seeing whether the defendant violated a property right in the claimant. The approach, then, even though it is unfamiliar, is perfectly consistent with the traditional common law approach.

Furthermore, though the approach advanced here may be unfamiliar to common lawyers, it is not to lawyers from other traditions. For instance, in German law, section 823 of the Bundesgesetzbuch (BGB) reads, '[a] person who wilfully or negligently, unlawfully injures the life, body, health, freedom, property, or any other right of another is bound to compensate him for any damage arising therefrom'. Much can be learnt from analysis of the common law in a similar light. We should remember that the 'skill and ingenuity [of common lawyers] have laboriously brought them to ends they could have reached centuries earlier if they had shared in the mainstream of European legal development'.[45] In fact, as Nils Jansen has powerfully argued, the best understanding of all Western tort law may be provided by seeing it overall, and not just in this context, as a system of rights protection.[46]

It would be wrong to object to the approach advanced here on the ground that it involved a rejection of the common law. But it does conflict with the commonly held notion that the common law is a practical code rather than an abstract normative one,[47] and so is naturally focussed on actual harm rather than on interference with rights. Hence, Tony Weir explains why the person entitled to legal possession rather than the owner of an object can sue a bona fide purchaser in conversion by suggesting that 'the common law has always been more interested in the *physical* than the economic relationship between person and thing, and instead of asking who is eventually to have the benefit of the thing, it asks who is currently entitled to get his hands on it'.[48]

While it may well be that the law is more interested in physical than in economic relationships, is it true that physical relationships constitute the law's focus? In fact, Weir's example indicates not. In that example, the person in physical possession of the object is the bona fide purchaser, not the person in legal possession. As Weir rightly notes, the law is interested in 'who is currently *entitled* to get his hands on' the object. But that is another way of saying that the

[45] OF Robinson, TD Fergus and WM Gordon, *European Legal History,* 2nd edn (Butterworths, London, 1994) 152.

[46] N Jansen, 'Duties and Rights in Negligence: A Comparative and Historical Perspective on the European Law of Extracontractual Liability' (2004) 24 *OJLS* 443.

[47] See eg *Read v J Lyons & Co Ltd* [1947] AC 156, 173 (HL) (Lord Macmillan).

[48] T Weir, *Tort Law* (Oxford University Press, Oxford, 2002) 155 (emphasis added).

law is interested in the *right* to possession rather than in the physical fact of possession. Hence, the person with the right to possession and only that person can sue in conversion because conversion is designed to protect that right. Again, we see that, although the law gets by in practice without much reference to primary rights, the law cannot adequately be analysed without them.[49] The common law is not as practical as it would like to pretend, which is entirely unsurprising, given that entitlements are by their very nature normative, not physical, things.

III. THE DISTINCTION BETWEEN MISFEASANCE AND NONFEASANCE

In light of the above, we are now able to provide a conceptually satisfactory account of the distinction between misfeasance and nonfeasance consistent with the case law. Recall once more Bohlen's formulation of the distinction as 'between active conduct working positive injury to others and passive inaction, a failure to take positive steps to benefit others, or to protect them from harm not created by any wrongful act of the defendant'.[50] Misfeasance requires the causation of injury, which involves interference with a primary right in the claimant. Hence, misfeasance is an act or omission that violates a right in the claimant. Conversely, nonfeasance is an act or omission that does not violate a right in the claimant, though it may cause factual loss. Accordingly, the failure to perform a contract may be an omission and it may not cause loss, but it violates a right in the claimant and so is misfeasance and is actionable; while competing with the claimant's business is an action which causes loss, but it does not violate any right in the claimant, and so is nonfeasance and not actionable.[51] Unless indicated otherwise, the terms 'misfeasance' and 'nonfeasance' are used as defined here throughout the rest of this book.

This idea is nowhere better expressed than in *Fontainebleau Hotel Corp v Forty-Five Twenty-Five Inc*.[52] The claimant and defendant owned hotels on the Miami Beach strip. The defendant proposed to construct extensions to its hotel that would cast a shadow over the beachfront of the claimant's hotel during the height of the Florida tourist season. This would have resulted in considerable loss to the claimant, as its hotel would have been much less attractive to potential patrons. The claimant sought an injunction in nuisance to prevent the defendant carrying out the extensions.

---

[49] For the notion that the focus on rights is abstract rather than concrete and that this conflicts with the approach of the common law see SR Perry, 'The Moral Foundations of Tort Law' (1992) 77 *Iowa Law Review* 449, 478–88. For a reply, see EJ Weinrib, *The Idea of Private Law* (Harvard University Press, Cambridge, Mass, 1995) 126.

[50] FH Bohlen, 'The Moral Duty to Aid Others as a Basis of Tort Liability' (1908) 56 *University of Pennsylvania Law Review* 217, 219.

[51] See P Benson, 'The Basis for Excluding Liability for Economic Loss in Tort Law' in D Owen (ed), *Philosophical Foundations of Tort Law* (Oxford University Press, Oxford, 1995) 444–50; P Benson, 'Philosophy of Property Law' in J Coleman and S Shapiro (eds), *The Oxford Handbook of Jurisprudence and Philosophy of Law* (Oxford University Press, Oxford, 2002) 755 n 5.

[52] 114 So 2d 357 (Fla Dist CA 1959).

At trial, the claimant asserted the maxim *sic utere tuo ut alienum non laedas*. This maxim means: use your own property in such a way that you do not injure other people's. Clearly, the claimant pointed out, the defendant proposed to use his property in a way that would cause a factual injury to—ie decrease the value of—the claimant's property. Accordingly, the claimant's allegations were accepted at trial and an injunction was awarded to prevent the defendant building.

However, the Florida District Court of Appeal emphatically rejected that conclusion:

> This is indeed a novel application of the maxim *sic utere tuo ut alienum non laedas*. This maxim does not mean that one must never use his own property in such a way as to do any injury to his neighbor [despite what the maxim actually says]. . . . It means only that one must use his property so as not to injure the lawful *rights* of another.[53]

Consequently, the Court asked whether the defendant's proposed building would deprive the claimant of anything to which the claimant had a primary right. The right could not lie in the law of persons. It is no interference with someone's person to cast a shadow over her land. It appeared, then, that any right must lie in the law of property. But building on the defendant's land would not have damaged the property of the claimant. It would have made the claimant's land less valuable, but it would not have done so by damaging it. And, as there is no right that one's land possess any particular value, the only possible right was a right to sunlight. If the claimant could prove that it had a right to sunlight, then it could prove that the defendant's plans would interfere with its rights. However, according to the Court:

> No American decision has been cited, and independent research has revealed none, in which it has been held that—in the absence of some contractual or statutory obligation—a landowner has a legal right to the free flow of light and air across the adjoining land of his neighbor. Even at common law, the landowner had no legal right, in the absence of an easement or uninterrupted use and enjoyment for a period of 20 years, to unobstructed light and air from the adjoining land.[54]

Therefore, the claimant failed and the injunction was lifted. Although the defendant's proposed action would cause the claimant factual loss, that loss was of no legal significance, as it did not flow from a violation of the claimant's rights.

Despite the contemporary neglect of this issue, tort law, including the law of negligence, does not regard the causing of factual loss as even prima facie evidence of wrongdoing. To establish that the defendant committed a wrong, the claimant must show that the defendant damaged something over which she had a right. The law is not interested in loss per se, but only in losses that flow from a violation of the claimant's primary legal rights.

The consequence of this discussion for the law of negligence is easy to state, though it has profound implications: No matter how foreseeable the claimant's

---

[53] 114 So 2d 357 (Fla Dist CA 1959), 359 (emphasis in original).
[54] *Ibid.*

factual loss, the claimant cannot recover unless that loss was the result of the defendant's interference with a primary right that the claimant held against the defendant. As Cardozo CJ told us, '[n]egligence is not a tort unless it results in the commission of a wrong, and the commission of a wrong imports the violation of a right'.[55] The principled approach is not, then, committed to the view that all reasonably foreseeable losses are recoverable. It is committed only to the view that all reasonably foreseeable losses that flow from the violation of primary rights are recoverable.

Some are inclined to see these arguments as circular. For instance, Dean Prosser said of both Cardozo CJ and Andrews J in *Palsgraf* that '[b]oth of them beg the question shamelessly, stating dogmatic propositions without reason or explanation'.[56] We saw in Chapter 4 that this criticism is unfair of both judges, but what is to be made of the idea that the proposition 'the claimant can recover only if the defendant violated one of her rights' is tautologous? Prosser claimed that '[t]here is a duty if the court says that there is a duty',[57] and perhaps there is a right if the court says there is a right.

It is first important to remember that the rights in question are primary rights, not secondary rights. The argument that the claimant cannot recover because she had no *secondary* right is, of course, circular. To say that one has no secondary right is just to say that one cannot recover. But that argument is not being made here. The claim is that one can recover only if one's *primary* rights were violated. That argument is clearly not circular. Even if it were true that 'a primary right exists if the court says it exists', the argument would not be circular. If a court that utilised this argument failed to explain why the primary right did not exist, then the argument of the court would be incomplete, but that does not make it circular. Furthermore, for reasons we have seen, it is at least simplistic in the extreme to claim that 'a primary right exists if the court says it exists'.

The law is not merely a collection of rules. Those rules form a structure. It is, of course, a matter of debate just how consistent and well defined that structure is. But, at the very least, courts are not free to create rules that are logically inconsistent with other rules without undermining those other rules. The reason for this has nothing special to do with the law, but is demanded by the nature of rationality. The claim that an object is a cube cannot, even in law, sit alongside the claim that it is a sphere. Consequently, given that positive law exists and given that some of it is well settled by much case law, it is deeply misleading to say that 'a primary right exists if the court says it exists'. Our discussion of the issues contained in the next two chapters will be helped if we explore this issue in some detail here.

Imagine that a third party intended to transfer possession of a chattel from him to the claimant but, before he could do so, the chattel was stolen by the defendant. Imagine also that the claimant attempts to sue the defendant for

[55] 162 NE 99, 101 (NY CA 1928).
[56] WL Prosser, 'Palsgraf Revisited' (1953) 52 *Michigan Law Review* 1, 7.
[57] *Ibid*, 15.

converting the chattel. As we know, the claimant will fail because the claimant was not in possession of the chattel when it was stolen. But why does this fact prevent the claim in conversion? Why is this not question-begging, as Prosser's argument seems to imply?

The answer can be discovered by considering the consequences that would follow were the court to allow the claimant's argument to succeed. There are four possible consequences. First, the court could have left the tort of conversion unaltered, but implicitly created a new kind of possession according to which one can be in legal possession of an object merely because a possessor intended to transfer possession to one at a future date. Secondly, the court could have left current understandings of possession intact, but (i) created a new property right that relied simply on the fact that a possessor intended to transfer possession and (ii) extended the tort of conversion to protect this new right. Both of these first two strategies would cause considerable upheaval in the law of property and they are inconsistent with that law as it stands.

Thirdly, the court could have left the law of property as it is, but altered the tort of conversion so that it no longer responded only to interference with possession but also to other rights that lay elsewhere, such as in the law of persons, while creating such a right in the law of persons that relied on the intention of a possessor to transfer possession. In other words, the court could create a right in the law of persons such that the claimant possessed that right and such that that right was violated by the defendant, while extending the law of conversion so that it protected that right. This strategy is even less appropriate than the former two, because the right to an object cannot be a right that lies in the law of persons, but must lie in the law of property. It is the law of property that governs our rights to external objects. Hence, in effect this strategy does create new property rights, though it tries to hide that fact by pretending to locate the new rights in the law of persons. Accordingly, the strategy collapses into the first or second strategy.

Finally, in accepting the claimant's argument, the court could simply have created a remedy without a right, a secondary right without the violation of a primary right. But this strategy is incoherent. At least in private law, a wrong is the violation of a right. Hence, a remedy without the invasion of a right is a remedy without a wrong. But without a wrong, what is one remedying? Remedies without rights are incoherent.

Naturally, no court would find for the claimant in a case like this. This is because it is clear that the tort of conversion protects one particular right: the right to possession of a chattel. Hence, if the claimant was not in possession, it is clear that the claimant must fail. But things are much more complicated when we turn to negligence. The reason for this is that the law of negligence protects many rights, as we have seen above. Hence, when we ask whether a claimant can recover in negligence, it is easy to forget to ask whether the claimant had a primary right that was violated, as the right could be one of a large number of potential rights. We never forget to ask this question when dealing with the torts of trespass to land and chattels and the question is implicit in the torts of trespass to the person (who could imagine my successfully suing you in battery for your striking someone else, for instance?). The question is also implicit in the law of negligence—it is a proper *prerequisite* of the duty enquiry. But, because we tend to focus on remedies rather than rights, particularly in this area of the law when the rights are often not explicit, we forget to ask this question. When we remember to ask it, most of the problems said to haunt the law of negligence vanish.

Let us return to the duty to rescue and the drowning child. The reason that I am not obliged to rescue the drowning child is that I do not interfere with the child's rights by omitting to conduct the rescue. Hence, my failure to rescue the child is nonfeasance, not misfeasance, and cannot be actionable. Failing to rescue a child is not in the eyes of the law causing injury to the child; it is rather failing to benefit the child. But that demand is not actionable. That much is clear, but the more difficult question is why the child has no right to be rescued.

The short answer is that the unilateral actions of one person cannot impose obligations upon another. If I were obliged to rescue the child, then his choices—to play by the edge of the wharf, etc—create an obligation in me to act. This would violate the principle of corrective justice. Because the child did not fall into the water because of any wrongdoing of mine, there is no justification in corrective justice to hold that I now owe him an obligation to rescue him. That obligation is not required in order to correct anything that I have done to the child, and so imposing it on me would itself be an injustice in the eyes of corrective justice.

Of course, there is much more that needs to be said about this issue, but that must take place in the context of a complete discussion of the rights base of the law of negligence. For reasons discussed in Chapter 2, that is not the subject of this book. All that needs to be said here is that there is no duty to rescue because the failure to rescue violates no rights.

There are, of course, exceptions to the rule that there is no duty to rescue. But these are not exceptions to the rule that there is no liability for nonfeasance. When a duty to rescue exists, it exists because of a prior duty that comes into being for special reasons that do not apply generally. In other words, when a duty to rescue exists, it exists because the claimant has, as against a particular defendant or defendants, a special kind of primary right. There are two main areas in which these rights arise. First, children have these rights against their parents or guardians because of the nature of their relationship.[58] Hence, if one's own child is in danger then one may owe the child a duty to rescue him, not simply because the child is in danger, but because one has a pre-existing duty to attempt to rescue the child in situations of danger, a duty that arises because

---

[58] *Sutees v Kingston on Thames BC* [1992] *Personal Injuries and Quantum Reports* P 101. These duties exist only in very narrow circumstances. Hence, for instance, emergency services do not violate any duty if they fail to respond to emergency calls in a timely fashion: *Capital & Counties plc v Hampshire CC* [1997] QB 1004 (CA). However, the police do owe a duty to protect mentally disabled persons in their charge: *Kirkham v Chief Constable of Greater Manchester Police* [1990] 2 QB 283 (CA).

of the special relationship between oneself and one's child. Secondly, one may owe another a duty to rescue him because one consented to be placed under that obligation. When one violates this obligation, one is liable, not because one failed to rescue, but because one breached a promise that one had made. When one breaches a consensually formed obligation, such as contract, one fails to benefit someone, but one is not liable for failing to benefit someone, but rather for injuring someone in the eyes of the law by infringing their rights.

One may also have a duty to rescue someone if one is responsible for the danger that that person is in. For instance, if the child in our example fell into the water because of my negligence, then I have a duty to rescue the child. This duty exists because I violated the child's rights (to bodily integrity) by causing him to fall into the water, and so I am responsible for all reasonably foreseeable consequences of that negligence, including drowning if that was reasonably foreseeable. Again, I do not have a duty simply because the child is in danger, but because I am responsible for creating that danger. My obligation is merely to remove the harmful effects of my violation of the child's right to bodily integrity.[59]

It is apparent, then, that the common law consists of a system of negative rights. One owes no duty to benefit others or to save them from the harms caused by them or others, unless there is a pre-existing right that arises because of a relationship of dependency, such as that which exists between children and their parents, or because one consented to the existence of that right. Usually, then, there is no liability for what are generally regarded as omissions. This is not libertarianism. The position is perfectly consistent with the idea that persons who fail to conduct easy rescues should be criminally liable, for instance.[60] While failures to rescue do not violate any rights in potential claimants, it may be justifiable for societies to decide that such omissions are so antisocial, offensive or harmful in a sense not relevant to the law of tort that they should be penalised. The position is merely that, as failures to rescue violate no primary common law rights, they are not actionable at private law.[61]

IV. CONCLUSION

We have defined the distinction between misfeasance and non feasance in terms of invasions or non-invasions of primary rights, and we have seen that the principled approach is committed only to recovery for reasonably foreseeable consequences of invasions of primary rights. It is time now to turn this analysis to the problems which are believed to defeat the principled approach.

---

[59] This issue is explored further in ch 9.

[60] See A Ripstein, 'Three Duties to Rescue: Moral, Civil, and Criminal' (2000) 19 *Law and Philosophy* 751.

[61] Naturally, it is open to the legislature to alter this result if that should be judged desirable.

7

Economic Loss

I T IS TIME TO address the most pressing objection to the principled
approach: that it leads to indeterminate liability for economic loss. My task
is to demonstrate that this view is mistaken. Not only does the principled
approach have no problem with indeterminate liability for economic loss, it
would produce outcomes remarkably similar those of the modern law, particularly the modern English law. What is more, it manages to produce those results
without the interminable policy debates that infect the modern common law.

I begin by exploring the current approach to economic loss in the so-called
relational loss cases, before comparing this with the principled approach's
analysis of the same issues. Following that discussion, I do the same for
instances of pure economic loss.[1]

It is crucial to note that this chapter considers the issue of economic loss
separately from the kind of loss that occurs in negligent misstatement cases that
follow from *Hedley Byrne & Co Ltd v Heller & Partners Ltd*.[2] The issues relevant to those cases are explored in Chapter 8.

I. CONSEQUENTIAL AND RELATIONAL ECONOMIC LOSS

A. The Modern Approaches

The dispute in *Spartan Steel & Alloys Ltd v Martin & Co (Contractors) Ltd*[3]
arose when employees of the defendant contractors negligently damaged a
power cable that supplied electricity to the claimant's steel factory. When the
electricity was cut off, the claimant was engaged in converting a quantity of
metal into ingots in an arc furnace. In order to prevent serious damage to the

---

[1] The argument of this ch has greatly benefited from the excellent articles by P Benson, 'The Basis
for Excluding Liability for Economic Loss in Tort Law' in D Owen (ed), *Philosophical Foundations
of Tort Law* (Oxford University Press, Oxford, 1995) and JW Neyers, '*Donoghue* v. *Stevenson* and
the Rescue Doctrine: A Public Justification of Recovery in Situations Involving the Negligent Supply
of Dangerous Structures' (1999) 49 *University of Toronto Law Journal* 475. See also the important
R Brown, 'Still Crazy After All These Years: *Anns, Cooper v. Hobart* and Pure Economic Loss'
(2003) 36 *University of British Columbia Law Review* 159; R Brown, 'Justifying the Impossibility of
Recoverable Relational Economic Loss', (2004) 5 *OUCLJ* 155.
[2] [1964] AC 465 (HL).
[3] [1973] QB 27 (CA).

furnace, the claimant's employees were forced to melt the metal using oxygen and pour it from a tap out of the furnace. This caused physical damage to the metal or 'melt' worth £368. Moreover, the claimant estimated that it would have been able to sell the final product for a profit of £400 had it been able to complete the melt properly. Further, the factory was unable to operate for 14 hours and 20 minutes; a period long enough for the claimant's employees to have been able to process four more melts. Had they done so, it was calculated that the claimant would have made a profit on those melts of £1,767. The English Court of Appeal unanimously held that the claimant was entitled to recover £368 for the physical damage to and £400 for the loss of profit on the first melt. However, Lord Denning MR and Lawton LJ, Edmund Davies LJ dissenting, held that the loss of profit on the final four melts was not recoverable.

In the language of the modern common law, the loss of profit on the physically damaged melt was 'consequential loss'—ie loss consequent on physical damage to the claimant's property. Losses of this kind are recoverable. On the other hand, the loss of profit on the final four melts is labelled 'relational loss'—ie loss suffered 'in relation' to physical damage caused to the property of another, in this case physical damage to the electricity cable.[4] Generally at least, relational losses are irrecoverable.

In *Spartan Steel*, Edmund Davies LJ argued that the claimant should have been able to recover both the consequential and the relational loss. This was because, so his Lordship insisted, a principled approach does not and cannot distinguish between them:

> For my part, I cannot see why the £400 loss of profit here sustained should be recoverable and not the £1,767. It is common ground that both types of loss were equally foreseeable and equally direct consequences of the defendants' admitted negligence, and the only distinction drawn is that the former figure represents the profit lost as a result of the physical damage done to the material in the furnace at the time when power was cut off. But what has that purely fortuitous fact to do with legal principle? In my judgment, nothing . . .[5]

This passage expresses the view that the principled approach would allow recovery for economic loss restricted only by reasonable foreseeability. However, it is almost universally accepted that this would extend recovery too far. If the claimant could recover for its economic losses, then so could the claimant's customers who suffered loss, so could the customers of those customers and so on and on. The principled approach is nice in theory but intolerable in practice.

Lord Denning[6] and Lawton LJ[7] agreed with Edmund Davies LJ that the principled approach would generate recovery for relational loss. Lawton LJ said

---

[4] This terminology is by no means universal or consistent. However, it is convenient to define the terms in this manner here.

[5] *Spartan Steel & Alloys Ltd v Martin & Co (Contractors) Ltd* [1973] QB 27, 41 (CA).

[6] *Ibid*, 36.

[7] *Ibid*, 49.

that '[t]he differences . . . between what damage can be recovered in one type of case and what in another cannot be reconciled on any logical basis'.[8] But, logical or not, Lawton LJ insisted that the recovery of economic loss had to be restricted by policy to prevent absurd and unjust results. Strangely, however, Lawton LJ refused to enunciate the relevant policies. 'I agree with Lord Denning M.R. that such differences have arisen because of the policy of the law. Maybe there should be one policy for all cases; the enunciation of such a policy is not, in my judgment, a task for this court.'[9] This is a very curious position. If the distinction between recoverable and irrecoverable economic loss has no logical basis, then how can it be justified by policy? In any case, if a court is to deny the claimant recovery on policy grounds, it is surely incumbent on the court to say what those policies are. It is as if Lawton LJ said to the claimant, 'You cannot recover for some reasons, but I am not going to tell you what they are'.[10]

On the other hand, Lord Denning argued that relational loss is irrecoverable for five reasons. First, recovery for relational loss in this case would be in tension with the fact that the law does not permit recovery of relational loss in analogous cases.[11] Secondly, as the kind of loss is common, readily foreseeable and likely to be small, the claimant should have protected itself from those losses through insurance or some other means. Lord Denning described this self-protection as 'a healthy attitude which the law should encourage'.[12] Thirdly, 'if claims for economic loss were permitted for this particular hazard, there would be no end of claims'.[13] Fourthly, the loss should be spread as widely as possible and (though we are not told why) the claimant was best able to do so.[14] Finally, the claimant's case, being for economic loss rather than for physical damage to person or property, was not deserving.[15]

These arguments are inadequate. The second is inconsistent with the third. The fourth does not compare the position of the claimant with that of the defendant, and so does not show why the defendant should not be called on to spread the loss. The first begs the question: why should recovery for relational loss be denied in analogous cases? The second is usually understood as a reason for imposing rather than denying liability. We do not say in personal injury cases that if the injury was common and readily foreseeable the claimant should have been insured and cannot recover; quite the opposite, we say that because the injury was readily foreseeable the defendant should have protected the claimant from it. The fifth also begs all the relevant questions, despite its popularity. It is common to say that recovery for economic loss is less deserving than

---

[8] *Ibid.*

[9] *Ibid.*

[10] Judges on the Court of Appeal may choose to defer to policies enunciated by the House of Lords, but Lawton LJ did not do that either.

[11] *Spartan Steel & Alloys Ltd v Martin & Co (Contractors) Ltd* [1973] QB 27, 37–8 (CA).

[12] *Ibid*, 38.

[13] *Ibid*, 38–9.

[14] *Ibid*, 39.

[15] *Ibid.*

for physical injury,[16] but it is not common to explain why. On the face of it, certainly in terms of distributive justice or ethics, it is often false that recovery for economic loss is less deserving than that for property damage. Also problematic is the fact that the law routinely allows recovery for consequential economic loss.[17]

An interesting feature of both Lord Denning's and Lawton LJ's judgments is that their Lordships did not insist on a fixed approach to the recoverability of economic loss. Both judges saw recovery as a matter of policy to be decided on a case-by-case basis. However, in *Caltex Oil Pty Ltd v The Dredge 'Willemstad'*,[18] Stephen J rejected the case-by-case method and insisted on a more orderly approach to the recovery of economic loss.

While dredging, the defendant negligently broke an underwater pipeline belonging to a third party, Australian Oil Refining Pty Ltd (AOR). The pipeline carried petroleum products from a refinery to the claimant's oil terminal. Unable to use the pipeline, the claimant was forced to transport the petroleum by ship and road, incurring costs that the claimant attempted to recover from the defendant. As the claimant did not own the pipeline, the claim was for relational loss; ie loss suffered in relation to the physical damage to the pipeline owned by AOR.

In a celebrated judgment, Stephen J rejected the notion that the law should progress on a case-by-case basis, arguing that to 'apply generalised policy considerations directly, in each case, instead of formulating principles from policy and applying those principles, derived from policy, to the case in hand, is, in my view, to invite uncertainty and judicial diversity'.[19] Instead, Stephen J recommended a 'search for some more positive guidance as to the entitlement, if any, to recover in negligence for solely economic loss'.[20] In that light, it is ironic that Stephen J failed even to attempt that task in *Caltex Oil*, excusing himself with the claim:

> As the body of precedent accumulates some general area of demarcation between what is and is not a sufficient degree of proximity in any particular class of case of economic loss will no doubt emerge; but its emergence neither can be, nor should it be, other than as a reflection of the piecemeal conclusions arrived at in precedent cases. The present case contains a number of salient features which will no doubt ultimately be recognised as characteristic of one particular class of case among the generality of cases involving economic loss. . . . The existence of these features leaves no doubt in

[16] See eg *Spartan Steel & Alloys Ltd v Martin & Co (Contractors) Ltd* [1973] QB 27, 38–9 (CA); T Weir, *Tort Law* (Oxford University Press, Oxford, 2002) 47.

[17] C Witting, 'Distinguishing Between Property Damage and Pure Economic Loss in Negligence: A Personality Thesis' (2001) 21 *LS* 481 is one of the few to attempt to justify the distinction. See also A Tettenborn, 'Property Damage and Economic Loss: Should Claims by Property Owners Themselves be Limited?' (2005) 34 *Common Law World Review* 128, who argues that consequential economic loss should not be recoverable.

[18] (1976) 136 CLR 529 (HCA).

[19] *Ibid*, 567.

[20] *Ibid*.

my mind that there exists in this case sufficient proximity to entitle the plaintiff to recover its reasonably foreseeable economic loss.[21]

Again, we see that the distinction between the *Anns* test and the incremental approach is without a difference.

However, Stephen J pointed to five features of the case that suggested a decision in favour of the claimant:[22]

1. The defendant knew or should have known that the damage to the pipeline was 'inherently likely' to produce relational economic loss to the claimant.[23]
2. The defendant knew or should have known about the existence of the pipeline and the use to which the pipeline was put. Hence, the defendant knew or should have known about the risk of injury to the claimant.
3. The injury to the claimant resulted from a breach of a duty of care owed to AOR.
4. The nature of the loss to the claimant, ie its loss of use of the pipeline, demonstrated that there was a close degree of proximity between the claimant and the defendant.
5. The nature of the damages sought by the claimant, which reflect the loss of use of the pipeline rather than 'collateral commercial arrangements', indicates that there was a close degree of proximity between the claimant and the defendant.

These are not five different factors in favour of recovery. Factor 2 is merely an elucidation of factor 1. The defendant knew or should have known that damage to the pipeline would produce loss to the claimant only because the defendant knew or should have known that the pipeline existed and that the claimant used it to transport its products. Factor 4 is merely a repetition of factor 1. Factor 5 is either also a mere repetition of factor 1 or involves appeal to the notion of 'directness' examined and rejected above. Moreover, factor 3 cannot be treated as a 'salient factor' to limit the recovery of relational loss, because factor 3 holds of all relational loss cases. In fact, factor 3 is part of the definition of relational loss. In that light, the sole contribution of Stephen J's judgment to the issue of relational loss is the suggestion that the claimant can recover only if her injury was an 'inherently likely' consequence of the defendant's negligence. If we ignore 'inherent' for the moment, this implies that Stephen J's position is identical to the ordinary approach with the one exception that Stephen J insisted that the claimant be placed at a risk of *likely* injury rather than, as the ordinary approach maintains, at a reasonably foreseeable risk.[24] That would be insufficient to solve

[21] *Ibid*, 576.
[22] *Ibid*, 576–9.
[23] Stephen J called this loss 'consequential' loss. His Honour intended that the loss was a consequence of the defendant's damage to the property of the third party and was in that sense 'consequential' loss. However, the loss was relational loss as defined here.
[24] This is a repeat of Lord Reid's strategy in *Home Office v Dorset Yacht Co Ltd* [1970] AC 1004, 1028 (HL).

the issue of relational loss, because it is often the case that a great amount of relational loss is likely. Hence, Stephen J's position is helpful only if 'inherently likely' is sufficiently narrower than 'likely'. In fact, however, it means nothing to say that the likelihood of something is 'inherent'. It appears that 'inherently likely' is, like Gibbs CJ's use of 'proximity' in *Sutherland Shire Council v Heyman*,[25] no more than an appeal to raw intuition. Hence, the claimant's injury will be described as 'inherently likely' if and only if the court believes that the claimant should recover. For the reasons discussed in Chapter 5, this position is inadequate.

The High Court of Australia revisited this issue in *Perre v Apand Pty Ltd*[26] and more or less affirmed its decision in *Caltex Oil*. Hence, in *Perre*, the Court insisted that a claimant could recover only if she was a member of an ascertainable class of persons the defendant knew or should have known was put at risk.[27] The point of this test is to prevent liability getting out of hand. However, given that recovery based on reasonable foreseeability would be out of hand, this 'additional' requirement is no help as it is reasonable foreseeability in disguise: saying that the claimant must be a member of an ascertainable class the defendant knows or should know is at risk is another way of saying that the claimant must have been placed at reasonably foreseeable risk. *In practice*, then, the 'addition' does not mean what it says. In fact, it is a mechanism by which Australian courts restrict liability on an ad hoc, purely intuitive basis.[28] Despite Stephen J's high-minded search for principle, we are back with Lord Denning's case-by-case analysis in *Spartan Steel*.

Some see more promise in the approach of the Supreme Court of Canada in *Canadian National Railway Co v Norsk Pacific Steamship Co Ltd*.[29] The defendant negligently damaged a railway bridge owned by Public Works Canada (PWC). This meant that the claimant railway company was unable to use the bridge to carry freight and was forced to use routes that were more expensive. The claimant attempted to recover the ensuing costs from the defendant.

The main argument in *Norsk* focused on cost avoidance. Before we explore that argument in detail, however, it will be instructive to examine some of the subsidiary arguments.

McLachlin J, L'Heureux-Dubé and Cory JJ concurring, found for the claimant. Her Honour maintained that the parties were in a close relationship of proximity. As we saw in Chapter 5, 'proximity' for McLachlin J included, but was not restricted to, 'the relationship between the parties, physical propinquity, assumed or imposed obligations and close causal connection'.[30]

---

[25] (1985) 157 CLR 424, 441 (HCA). This issue was explored in ch 5.

[26] (1999) 198 CLR 180 (HCA).

[27] See eg *ibid*, 194–5 (Gleeson CJ).

[28] See eg S Todd, 'Negligence: Particular Categories of Duty' in S Todd (ed), *The Law of Torts in New Zealand*, 3rd edn (Brookers, Wellington, 2001) 260.

[29] [1992] 1 SCR 1021.

[30] *Ibid*, 1153.

Moreover, McLachlin J maintained that courts 'will insist on sufficient special factors to avoid the imposition of indeterminate and unreasonable liability. The result will be a principled, yet flexible, approach to tort liability for pure economic loss. It will allow recovery where recovery is justified, while excluding indeterminate and inappropriate liability'.[31] In other words, as in principle 'proximity' could mean anything, there is a relationship of proximity if the facts of the case give the judge the instinctive feeling that there is one. Evidently, McLachlin J had that instinctive feeling in *Norsk*.

McLachlin J supported that feeling by noting (i) that the defendant's negligence meant that the claimant could not enjoy the use of its property (ie could not enjoy driving its trains over PWC's bridge), (ii) that the claimant had provided advice and supplied materials for the construction of the bridge and (iii) the claimant was the predominant user of the bridge.[32] But the relevance of those issues is not at all clear. In particular, the notion that the claimant could not enjoy the use of its property is false. The claimant was able to transport freight, but had to use alternative means. It could enjoy driving its trains over other bridges. But even if (i) were true, its relevance would remain opaque.

Though the relevance of the second and third arguments is also not immediately obvious, those arguments are more interesting. This is because, as McLachlin J utilised them, they seem to suggest that the claimant had a *proprietary* interest in the bridge. However, the claimant had no such interest. As La Forest J noted, if the claimant and PWC were engaged in a 'common adventure' in relation to the bridge, then it may have been possible to find a proprietary right in the claimant to the bridge. But the claimant in *Norsk* and PWC were not engaged in a common adventure.[33] Moreover, if the claimant and PWC were engaged in a common adventure, and hence the claimant had a proprietary right in the bridge, then *Norsk* would not have been a case involving relational loss. Instead, the defendant would have violated the claimant's property rights. This would justify recovery, but, *contra* McLachlin J, it appears to have nothing to do with proximity.[34]

In dissent, La Forest J, Sopinka and Iaccobucci JJ concurring, maintained that the claimant could not recover. La Forest J's argument focused chiefly on cost avoidance; however his Honour also considered several subsidiary arguments that I examine now. First, La Forest J argued that the defendant did not owe a duty of care to the claimant, because the claimant could have protected itself from its loss through contract with PWC.[35] But the relationship between the claimant and PWC is irrelevant to the relationship between the claimant and

---

[31] *Ibid.*

[32] *Ibid*, 1161–2.

[33] *Ibid*, 1097–8. See also *Caltex Oil Pty Ltd v The Dredge 'Willemstad'* (1976) 136 CLR 529, 576 (HCA) (Stephen J).

[34] R Brown, 'Justifying the Impossibility of Recoverable Relational Economic Loss' (2004) 5 OUCLJ155, 159–65.

[35] *Canadian National Railway Co v Norsk Pacific Steamship Co Ltd* [1992] 1 SCR 1021, 1126. This is closely related to the cost avoidance argument. However, I discuss it here for convenience.

the defendant. Moreover, ignoring the cost avoidance argument for the moment, the absence of a duty of care does not follow from the fact that the claimant could have contracted with PWC. The issue is not what the claimant *could* have done, but what it *should* have done. The argument that the claimant should have contracted with PWC begs the question. One concludes that the claimant should have contracted with PWC only if one has already reached the conclusion that the defendant should not be liable. This is because, if the defendant were to be liable, then there would be no reason for the claimant to have contracted with PWC. Hence, to argue that the defendant did not owe the claimant a duty of care because the claimant should have protected itself is to beg the question that the case is supposed to answer.

Secondly, La Forest J argued that liability should not be imposed in relational loss cases, because it is impossible in those cases perfectly to quantify damage awards.[36] But this is usually impossible in cases of personal injury and property damage as well. In fact, prima facie, as both the loss and the remedy are in money, it ought to be easier to calculate the quantum of damages for relational economic loss than for personal injury or even property damage.

I turn now from the subsidiary arguments to cost avoidance. La Forest J argued that the defendant should escape liability as the claimant was the best cost avoider. First, the claimant was in at least as good a position as the defendant to estimate the potential risk of an accident. Secondly, the claimant was better able than the defendant to estimate the likely costs of an accident. Thirdly, the claimant was best able to protect itself from such losses, through contract with PWC, insurance, etc (this is a consequence of the first and second arguments). As a result, the claimant was in the best position to insure against the loss and should therefore have to bear it.[37]

McLachlin J replied that the defendant was the best cost avoider as the defendant was best able to estimate the probability of the accident occurring and the seriousness of the accident if it did occur.[38]

La Forest J was right. The claimant was best able to estimate the costs of an accident and best able to protect itself from the consequences of an accident. McLachlin J was also right. The defendant was best able to prevent the accident and was best able to estimate the risk of an accident occurring. What does this show? For one thing, it shows that McLachlin and La Forest JJ focused on different issues. La Forest J attempted to minimise the social cost of accidents when they occur, while McLachlin J attempted to minimise the number of accidents that occur. Crucially, the arguments in *Norsk* do nothing to settle which is the best approach. At least as utilised there, the cost avoidance argument leads nowhere, as it argues both in favour of and against liability.[39]

---

[36] *Canadian National Railway Co v Norsk Pacific Steamship Co Ltd* [1992] 1 SCR 1027.

[37] *Ibid*, 1063–8.

[38] *Ibid*, 1116–25.

[39] For further criticism of the reliance on cost avoidance, see J Stapleton, 'Torts, Insurance, and Ideology' (1995) 58 *MLR* 820.

So far, we have examined a 3–3 split in the Court. The result in *Norsk* was determined by the very different judgment of Stevenson J. His Honour argued that all reasonably foreseeable economic loss should be recoverable unless it would result in indeterminate liability. In *Norsk*, Stevenson J said, there was no issue of indeterminate liability, because the claimant was attempting to recover a fixed sum.[40] Hence, the claimant should succeed.

But there is never a danger of indeterminate liability *in any individual case*. The claimant is always suing for a particular loss. The issue is not whether finding for one claimant would result in indeterminate liability in the instant case—it never would—but whether indeterminate liability would result if the *reasoning* in the instant case were applied universally. If the claimant can recover in *Norsk*, then why cannot those who also suffer reasonably foreseeable loss, such as the claimant's clients who are likely to pay increased freight costs and other users of the bridge?

La Forest and McLachlin JJ reconsidered their positions in *Bow Valley Husky (Bermuda) Ltd v Saint John Shipbuilding Ltd*.[41] McLachlin J argued that:

> Despite [the] difference in approach [in *Norsk*], La Forest J. and I agreed on several important propositions: (1) relational economic loss is recoverable only in special circumstances where the appropriate conditions are met; (2) these circumstances can be defined by reference to categories, which will make the law generally predictable; (3) the categories are not closed. La Forest J. identified the categories of recovery of relational economic loss defined to date as: (1) cases where the claimant has a possessory or proprietary interest in the damaged property; (2) general average cases; and (3) cases where the relationship between the claimant and property owner constitutes a joint venture.[42]

As we see below, this paragraph exhibits a serious collapse in legal understanding. However, it will suffice for the moment to consider the structure of the duty of care according to this view.

First, in accordance with the *Anns* test, the judge must determine whether the parties were in a relationship of proximity. In doing so, the judge must consider any factors that appear to her to be relevant. Then the judge must consider policy. According to McLachlin J, in order to prevent indeterminate liability, the general policy is that economic loss is not recoverable.[43] However, for yet more reasons of policy, the previous policy is sometimes overlooked. Outside the three cases mentioned, the circumstances when such policies operate are left entirely open. Hence, the approach enunciated by McLachlin J is entirely empty. This situation is quite unsatisfactory.

In that light, it is worth revisiting Stephen J's claim in *Caltex Oil* that '[a]s the body of precedent accumulates some general area of demarcation between what is and is not a sufficient degree of proximity in any particular class of case of

---

[40] *Canadian National Railway Co v Norsk Pacific Steamship Co Ltd* [1992] 1 SCR 1021, 1183.
[41] [1997] 3 SCR 1210.
[42] *Ibid*, 1241–2.
[43] *Ibid*, 1249.

economic loss will *no doubt* emerge'.[44] That must be one of the most hopeful but least accurate predictions ever made. In *Tepko Pty Ltd v Water Board*, Fitzgerald J said:

> foreseeability of economic loss to another does not, of itself, establish a duty to take reasonable care to avoid causing loss, that there is, as yet, no general principle to determine whether or not such a duty exists, and that a general principle will not emerge until there is a sufficient body of cases decided on their particular facts. While that process evolves, individual cases will be decided by comparison with decided cases and by reference to material circumstances and policy considerations. The existence or absence of a relationship between the parties, the dependence of a party vulnerable to loss upon a party asserted to be under a duty of care, the number of vulnerable persons and the nature and extent of their possible claims, the control exercisable and responsibility assumed by a person asserted to be under a duty of care, the degree of foreseeability of reliance by a vulnerable party on the other party and the degree of foreseeability of loss by a vulnerable party, and of the magnitude of that loss, and, arguably, the degree of departure from standards of reasonableness are potentially material factors.[45]

Hence, Australian law has made no progress whatsoever in this area since 1976. The same is true of Canadian law. However, the law of England and Wales is another matter, as we see in the following.[46]

B. The Principled Approach

As noted above, in *Spartan Steel*, Edmund Davies LJ argued that the principled approach would allow recovery for consequential and relational economic loss. In fact, however, that is not the case. The view involves a very fundamental error that arises because of what David Stevens and Jason Neyers regard as the greatest weakness of the common law: its remedial mentality. With respect to the law of restitution, Stevens and Neyers examine four key errors in legal reasoning, and remark that:

> all of these related errors arise from the view that the controlling or master normativity in private law is to be found at the level of judicial remedies, when, in fact, remedies are driven entirely by rights and circumstances. Name the right, define it, and the rest is mere application in light of the circumstances. More juris, less prudence.[47]

[44] *Caltex Oil Pty Ltd v The Dredge 'Willemstad'* (1976) 136 CLR 529, 576 (HCA) (emphasis added).
[45] (1999) Aust Tort Rep 81-525 (NSWCA), [76]–[77].
[46] In this area, New Zealand law is something of a mixture of the Australian and Canadian approaches on the one hand and the English approach on the other. This is because of the influence of English law in New Zealand, due to the fact that the abolition of appeal to the Privy Council occurred only in 2004. However, it would be wrong to conclude that New Zealand law is preferable to Australian or Canadian. It is perhaps even more confused in this area, precisely because of the conflicting influences.
[47] D Stevens and JW Neyers, 'What's Wrong with Restitution?' (1999) 37 *Alberta Law Review* 221, 227. This is nicely contrasted with the claims of J Fleming, *The Law of Torts,* 9th edn (LBC Information Services, Sydney, 1998) 150 and T Weir, *Tort Law* (Oxford University Press, Oxford, 2002) 16, that the common law's lack of focus on rights has no substantive implications.

This perceptive criticism is no less pertinent in this area of tort law. The focus of analysis is invariably on the question 'should the claimant recover?', with various policies being offered for differing views. The prior question, 'does the claimant have a right that could ground recovery?', has gone largely unasked. The problem of economic loss will be solved if we balance the copious prudence (ie policy) that the topic of economic loss has engendered with a little juris (ie strict legal analysis). When we do so, we will see that we need not agree with David Ibbetson's lament that there is nothing in the law of negligence 'to restrain the urge to move from the proposition that a person has suffered loss from the negligence of another to the conception that the loss ought to be compensated'.[48] This formulation overlooks the distinction between factual losses that flow from the violation of a primary right and those that do not.

Before I turn to that issue in earnest, however, I explore the meaning of the term 'indeterminate liability' in more detail in order to clarify the problem with which we are dealing. I then examine the case from which all talk of indeterminate liability takes its cue, or at least believes it takes it cue: *Ultramares Corp v Touche*.[49]

(i) Indeterminate Liability

As we have seen, and entirely unsurprisingly, indeterminate liability is understood as a policy concern by the vast majority of modern negligence lawyers. The view is that liability must be kept within appropriate limits for reasons of social and economic convenience and the danger of this not occurring is referred to as the danger of indeterminate liability. Hence, it is often linked to the so-called 'floodgates' argument, according to which the courts must protect themselves against floods of litigation.

This problem, which certainly exists, is based on a deeper theoretical difficulty. At that level, the problem is that the principled approach appears unable to delimit the sphere of liability in a theoretically satisfactory manner. Hence, the issue is not merely that following the principled approach would lead to adverse social consequences, but that the principled approach appears to be inadequate even in terms of pure theory, because it is not able to achieve the primary goal of a theory of the relevant kind: to reveal the appropriate scope of liability. If the criticism is correct, then, the principled approach must be discarded in favour of an alternative understanding of the law.

In the following, I focus on the latter rather than the former problem. That is, the issue I explore is not how to avoid the alleged negative social consequences that would flow from indeterminate liability, but whether the principled approach is incapable of delimiting liability in a sensible fashion. Hence, as explored here, the problem of indeterminate liability is primarily theoretical

[48] DJ Ibbetson, 'How the Romans did for Us: Ancient Roots of the Tort of Negligence' (2003) 26 *University of New South Wales Law Journal* 475, 488.
[49] 174 NE 441 (NY CA 1931).

rather than practical. But, of course, if the principled approach is not beset by the theoretical problem, nor does it face the practical problem. That is, if I can show that the principled approach does, in fact, sensibly limit liability, then I will also have shown that the approach does not result in an opening of the floodgates of liability.

(ii) Ultramares

In *Norsk*, McLachlin J maintained:

> A fundamental proposition underlies the law of tort: that a person who by his or her fault causes damage to another may be held responsible. Where the fault is negligence, the duty extends to all those to whom the tortfeasor may foreseeably cause harm: *Donoghue* v. *Stevenson* . . . This is a proposition of great breadth. It was soon realised that it would be necessary to limit recovery for practical, policy reasons. As Cardozo J. put it in *Ultramares Corp.* v. *Touche* . . . limits were needed to prevent 'liability in an indeterminate amount for an indeterminate time to an indeterminate class'.[50]

This is an excellent illustration of the received wisdom outlined above: the principled approach results in indeterminate liability. Cardozo CJ is credited with recognising this and is held to have responded to the problem by asserting that, for reasons of policy, liability for economic loss ought to be restricted. If this view were correct, then it would damage the principled approach and the argument of this book, though perhaps only in an *ad hominem* fashion. As I demonstrated in Chapter 4, Cardozo CJ was one of the leading architects of the principled approach. Did he recognise its limits in *Ultramares* and abandon it?

He did not. Cardozo CJ's judgment in *Ultramares* is poorly understood. The claimant suffered loss in reliance on the defendant's negligently made statement. Famously, Cardozo CJ said:

> If liability for negligence exists, a thoughtless slip or blunder, the failure to detect a theft or forgery beneath the cover of deceptive entries, may expose accountants to a liability in an indeterminate amount for an indeterminate time to an indeterminate class. The hazards of a business conducted on these terms are so extreme as to enkindle doubt whether a flaw may not exist in the implication of a duty that exposes to these consequences.[51]

The standard, almost instinctive, reaction of the modern common lawyer is to interpret this passage as arguing that recovery must not be allowed because it would be bad for business. But that is not what Cardozo CJ actually said. He said that recovery would have results that would be 'so extreme as to enkindle doubt whether a flaw may not exist in the implication of a duty that exposes to these consequences'. Naturally, Cardozo CJ may have been aiming for rhetorical effect rather than accuracy here, but strictly interpreted he did not say that

---

[50] *Canadian National Railway Co v Norsk Pacific Steamship Co Ltd* [1992] 1 SCR 1021, 1137.
[51] *Ultramares Corp v Touche* 174 NE 441, 444 (NY CA 1931).

concerns for industry dictate that no recovery be available. Rather, Cardozo CJ's claim was that, were the claimant's contentions correct, extreme consequences would follow, and that that would be such a surprising result that we must doubt the accuracy of those contentions. The argument was not 'recovery would be inconsistent with policy *x* and so must be disallowed' but 'recovery would produce consequence *x* and *x* is so surprising that we should doubt whether recovery is legally warranted'. In fact, then, this is not really an argument against recovery at all, but is rather the observation that liability is likely to have been unjustified for reasons that Cardozo CJ had yet to examine.

Reading Cardozo CJ's judgment in this way also explains the pattern taken by the rest of the judgment. Cardozo CJ does not, as the standard interpretation would lead us to expect, conclude from the quotation above that for policy reasons no duty of care can be owed. On the contrary, at this point his argument *begins* rather than ends.

According to Cardozo CJ:

> The expression of an opinion is to be subject to a warranty implied by law. What, then, is the warranty, as yet unformulated, to be? Is it merely that the opinion is honestly conceived and that the preliminary inquiry has been honestly pursued, that a halt has not been made without a genuine belief that the search has been reasonably adequate to bring disclosure of the truth? Or does it go farther and involve the assumption of a liability for any blunder or inattention that could fairly be spoken of as negligence if the controversy were one between accountant and employer for breach of a contract to render services for pay?[52]

Note immediately Cardozo CJ's categorisation of the issue as broadly contractual. For that reason he then goes on to discuss privity of contract.[53] Cardozo CJ concluded that there was no authority binding on him that required him to recognise a relevant warrantee owed to the claimants in this case, and hence that the claimant was arguing, *not in accordance with established principle*, but for an *extension* to be made to the current law to allow recovery.[54] Crucially, he did not answer this question by referring to the costs of indeterminate liability on business. Rather, Cardozo CJ advanced two arguments. First, if recovery were allowed, then that would make recovery for negligent misstatement coterminous with that for fraud, but that was inconsistent with so long a line of authority, which insisted that the defendant must always be *sciens*, that only the legislature could produce that effect.[55] Secondly, Cardozo CJ noted that the duty to speak carefully would apply to many persons in many areas of life and that that would be intolerable.

Again, at this point the modern lawyer is likely to jump to the conclusion that Cardozo CJ's second argument was an appeal to the policy of indeterminate

---

[52] *Ibid*, 444–5.
[53] *Ibid*, 445–7.
[54] *Ibid*, 447.
[55] *Ibid*.

liability as we understand it. But it is important to pay close attention to what Cardozo CJ actually said. Consider, for instance, the following passage:

> Lawyers who certify their opinion as to the validity of municipal or corporate bonds, with knowledge that the opinion will be brought to the notice of the public, will become liable to the investors, if they have overlooked a statute or a decision, to the same extent as if the controversy were one between client and adviser. Title companies insuring titles to a tract of land, with knowledge that at an approaching auction the fact that they have insured will be stated to the bidders, will become liable to purchasers who may wish the benefit of a policy without payment of a premium. These illustrations may seem to be extreme, but they go little, if any, farther than we are invited to go now.[56]

It is clear that Cardozo CJ regarded this outcome as intolerable, but the question is why? Never in this passage, or in any other place in his judgment, does Cardozo CJ say that the claimants' contentions were unacceptable because they would produce consequences that were negative for business, etc. Rather, his argument seems to be merely an appeal to intuition: he regards these consequences as so clearly wrong that they count as almost self-evident counter-examples to the claimants' contentions.

The key point here is that there is no apparent appeal to policy in this judgment. But, of course, that does not mean that there is no covert appeal. Perhaps Cardozo CJ felt that his examples were self-evidently counterexamples because he had policy in mind that he did not reproduce in the law report. But, just as obviously, we are not compelled to this conclusion unless we are unable to find an alternative interpretation of Cardozo CJ's position. And an alternative interpretation is available that is consistent with the principled approach and with Cardozo CJ judgment in *Palsgraf v Long Island Railroad Co*,[57] as I now explain.

On its face, there are two possible readings of Cardozo CJ's discussion of indeterminate liability:

1. The claimant correctly enunciated the principles of the law but could not recover, because that would engender indeterminate liability, which is socially and economically undesirable.
2. Because the principles enunciated by the claimant would engender indeterminate liability, we can see that they could not be the correct principles of the law.

The first reading is not supported by any claim made by Cardozo CJ, it is inconsistent with his assertion that the claimant's contentions were not supported by the contemporary law, and the second reading is open.

Moreover, the second reading can be given two further interpretations:

2(a). Because the principles enunciated by the claimant would, if adopted, engender indeterminate liability, we should not, as a matter of policy, alter the extant principles to produce that result.

[56] *Ibid*, 448.
[57] 162 NE 99 (NY CA 1928).

2(b). Because the principles enunciated by the claimant would engender indeterminate liability, we can see that they cannot be the correct principles.

Again, in light of the above, Cardozo CJ intended 2(b) rather than 2(a). As we
saw in Chapter 4, the desire appropriately to delineate the scope of liability and
eliminate the need to impose arbitrary restrictions on recovery was at the centre
of his judgment in *Palsgraf*. On Cardozo CJ's view, then, it is analytic to the principled approach that it does not generate indeterminate liability. After all, as
Cardozo CJ's judgment in *Palsgraf* makes plain, the point of legal principle is to
determine the frontiers of liability, to tell us what the law is. Hence, if a proposed
principle generates indeterminate liability, then we know that it cannot be correct. The argument against the claimant in *Ultramares*, then, was not policy-
based at all. Rather, the argument was that, as the claimant's description of legal
principle would generate indeterminate liability, the claimant's description of
legal principle could not be correct. This is a *reductio ad absurdum*: the
claimant's argument cannot be correct, as his description of legal principle is
inconsistent with the nature of legal principle.[58] It is, therefore, the greatest irony
that Cardozo CJ is routinely cited as authority for the need to invent policies to
circumvent the principled approach in order to prevent indeterminate liability.

The question now is whether Cardozo CJ's vision can be realised. Can the
principled approach prevent indeterminate liability for economic loss?

(iii) Donoghue v Stevenson, *Nonfeasance and the Rights of Tort Law*

As outlined in Chapter 6, misfeasance is the invasion of a right. Conversely, an
action that violates no rights is nonfeasance. Hence, loss caused to another without violating that person's right is mere nonfeasance and is not actionable.

In *Donoghue v Stevenson*, the defendant's negligence violated the claimant's
bodily integrity, thus violating the primary rights of the claimant as contained in
the (implicit) law of persons. But, when a claimant sues for relational economic
loss, what right has been violated? Usually, the answer is: no right whatsoever.[59]
But that is nonfeasance. If the defendant did not violate a right in the claimant

---

[58] This is the standard way in which moral philosophers use examples to test general theories.
For instance, a Kantian might argue that the application of Classical Act Utilitarianism would generate injustice and so conclude that the theory is unacceptable. In doing so, she does not mean that
Classical Act Utilitarianism has to be supplemented by policy. She means that it cannot be the correct theory. See J Rachels, *The Elements of Moral Philosophy*, 3rd edn (McGraw-Hill, New York,
1999) 110–15. Law is not philosophy, but there is no reason a priori to insist that Cardozo CJ was
not engaging in a similar enquiry.

[59] The common law is sometimes compared to the German law in regard to economic loss. See
eg BS Markesinis and H Unberath, *The German Law of Torts: A Comparative Treatise*, 4th edn
(Hart Publishing, Oxford, 2002) 214–15. However, the situation in German law is crucially different. This is because the relevant section of the BGB, §823, reads '[a] person who wilfully or negligently, unlawfully injures the life, body, health, freedom, property, *or any other right* of another is
bound to compensate him for any damage arising therefrom' (emphasis added). Hence, German
courts are forced to consider whether a right to profits (patrimony) is 'any other right' in terms of
§823 BGB. There is no equivalent of this at common law. See D Jensen, 'Punitive Damages for
Breach of Fiduciary Obligation' (1996) 19 *University of Queensland Law Journal* 125, 444–6, 462–6.

then the defendant did not wrong the claimant. Hence, the claimant suffered no injustice in corrective justice and had no claim against the defendant.

Three points are crucial at this stage in the argument. First, the right in question is a primary right and not a secondary right. Of course, to argue that the claimant cannot recover because the claimant has no secondary right is circular. But that argument is not being made. Rather, the argument is that the claimant cannot gain a secondary right, because the defendant did not violate any primary right in the claimant. Secondly, asking whether the claimant possessed a relevant primary right held against the defendant is, in this context, not logically equivalent to asking whether the defendant owed the claimant a duty of care. The claimant was owed a duty of care only if she possessed a relevant right, but she can possess the right without being owed a duty of care. This point can be demonstrated by distinguishing between three kinds of case.

First, *A* reasonably foreseeably damages *B*'s car. Here, *B* has a right to the car and was owed a duty of care by *A*. Secondly, *C* unforeseeably damages *D*'s car. Here *D* had a right to the car, but was not owed a duty of care by *C*. Thirdly, *E* damages *G*'s car causing loss to *F*. Here, *F* has no right to the car and is therefore not owed a duty of care by *E* in relation to the car *whether or not E's damage of the car is reasonably foreseeable*. Hence, if *F* is to recover from *E*, *F* must show that she had some right in something that was injured by *E* other than the car. That may sometimes be possible, but in cases of economic loss it is generally not. In those cases, the defendant causes loss to the claimant, but it is impossible for the claimant to find a right to any of the things that were damaged. Hence, because there was no right, no duty of care could have been owed and the claimant must fail.

Finally, the argument is not that the claimants in the cases examined must fail because they do not possess any relevant *property* rights.[60] Rather, the argument is that they must fail because they possess no relevant primary rights at all. No special emphasis is placed on those rights being property rights.

In analysing the cases below, it is necessary to remind ourselves of two basic distinctions concerning the nature of rights and obligations.[61] These distinctions are not without controversy, but I use them as stipulated below. Though they can be defined slightly differently, these differences would not change the argument that follows in any substantial fashion.

The first distinction is that between rights *in personam* and rights *in rem*. A right *in personam* is a norm that exists as between persons with no essential reference to objects. Contractual rights are paradigm examples. On the other hand, rights *in rem* are rights to particular things, such as land or chattels. Common law property rights are the classic example.

---

[60] This interpretation appears to have resulted from a misreading of P Benson, 'The Basis for Excluding Liability for Economic Loss in Tort Law' in D Owen (ed) *Philosophical Foundations of Tort Law* (Oxford University Press, Oxford, 1995).

[61] In the following, I focus on rights and ignore obligations. This is merely for convenience. Obligations are, of course, the concomitants of rights.

The second distinction is that between paucital and multitial rights. Paucital rights are held against one person or a small set of persons. Multitial rights are held against everyone. Again, the paradigm example of a paucital right is a contractual right, while a common law property right is the classic example of a multitial right.

These distinctions are often used synonymously. That is, rights *in personam* are often regarded as paucital rights, while rights *in rem* are usually treated as multitial rights. But neither position is correct.[62] Some rights *in personam* are multitial. These are rights that belong to the law of persons. For instance, my bodily integrity is a right *in personam*, but it is held against the world.[63] Conversely, some equitable property rights are rights *in rem*—they are held in respect of specific pieces of property—though they are held only against a single person.

These distinctions are important because they help to direct our enquiry. That is, when we look at specific cases and ask whether the defendant violated a right in the claimant, knowing what kinds of rights there are helps us in our search.

C. The Principled Approach to Relational Loss

Recall *Spartan Steel*. The defendant damaged a power cable supplying electricity to the claimant's factory. The claimant suffered physical damage to a melt in progress (£368), loss of profit on that melt (£400) and loss of profit from not being able to process four further melts (£1,767). In this section, I analyse the claimant's rights in relation to the final four melts.

The claimant can recover only if the defendant violated one of its rights. What could this right have been? One response must be ruled out straight away. There is no right to be free of factual injury caused by negligence *simpliciter*. One can suffer many factual injuries that do not correspond to the violation of a right, and hence are irrecoverable. As we have seen, that is the essence of nonfeasance.

Let us begin with the claimant's paucital rights. Whether *in personam* or *in rem*, a paucital right could ground a cause of action against the defendant only if it were a right held by the claimant against the defendant. A paucital right held by a third party could not help the claimant as it would give the claimant no entitlement whatsoever. Moreover, a paucital right held by the claimant against a third party would not bind the defendant; hence, while the claimant may or

---

[62] In A Beever, 'A Rights-Based Approach to the Recovery of Economic Loss in Negligence' (2004) 4 *OUCLJ* 25, I conducted this analysis in terms of right *in personam* and rights *in rem* rather than paucital and multitial rights.

[63] JE Penner, *The Idea of Property in Law* (Clarendon Press, Oxford, 1997) 23 seems prepared to accept that rights to the person are rights *in rem*. However, this is difficult to accept as no *res* is present. In any case, this debate is not relevant to the argument presented here, because causing economic loss is clearly no violation of the victim's bodily integrity, freedom of movement, reputation, etc. This is particularly clear in cases in which the claimant is a company.

may not have had such rights, that issue is not relevant to the claimant's cause of action here. It is, therefore, irrelevant whether the claimant had a contractual right with the relevant electricity supply company to the supply of electricity. In the unlikely event that such a right existed, this right would bind the electricity company to supply electricity to the claimant. It would not bind the defendant. For the same reason, it was irrelevant whether third parties were contractually bound to purchase the products of the four melts. Any such rights in the claimant were held against the third parties, not the defendant.

Was there, then, a paucital right held by the claimant against the defendant that was violated? There was not. Recall that we are looking for a *primary* right: a right violated by the defendant's employees' negligence. Hence, the right must have existed before the defendant's employees' negligence and cannot have been a product of that negligence. Furthermore, the claimant's argument was not that the defendant *in particular* wronged the claimant, but that the defendant's employees had negligently caused reasonably foreseeable loss. That argument would apply to anyone in the defendant's position. (In other words, there was no 'special relationship' between the claimant and the defendant.) Therefore, the claimant's case cannot be based on any paucital right.

Can we find a multitial right in the claimant? If we can, then that right will have been held against the defendant and so could ground the claimant's cause of action. Was there a multitial right *in personam* violated by the defendant? Again, there was not. Causing someone economic loss could not plausibly be regarded as a violation of her bodily integrity, freedom of movement, reputation, etc. Interference with a person's patrimony is not an interference with their person.

Accordingly, to justify recovery we need to discover a multitial right *in rem* held by the claimant and violated by the defendant. At first glance, it appears that such a right did exist, as the claimant held property rights in the four melts in question. These were multitial rights *in rem* and so, of course, were held against the defendant. But it is important to recall what those melts were: they were lumps of metal. And the claimant's rights in those lumps were not infringed—the lumps of metal were not damaged or interfered with by the defendant's employees in any way. It was for that reason that the claimant's argument focussed, not on the melts themselves, but on the economic loss suffered by it being unable to process those melts. The claim was not 'you damaged my property' or 'you interfered with my property rights', but 'you caused me to lose profits'. Accordingly, it was incumbent on the claimant to find a right in relation to the profits that the defendant's employees violated.

What were these profits? Speaking loosely for the moment, they were sums of money held by the claimant's potential customers that those customers would have transferred to the claimant had the defendant's employees not negligently cut the cable and the melts been processed. Did the claimant have any right to those sums of money held against the defendants? It must already be apparent that the answer is no, but a complete analysis requires us to make some assumptions. These are required because the relevant facts were not revealed in *Spartan Steel* itself. The first assumption is unrealistic, but it is preferred for the moment because it establishes the point in issue in a clear and simple manner. A more realistic scenario is examined shortly. According to this assumption, had the melts not been interrupted, third parties would have purchased the product of the melts with banknotes in their possession at the time of the defendant's employees' negligence.

On this, unrealistic but possible, interpretation of the facts, the claimant could succeed only if he could show that he held rights to the relevant banknotes with which the defendant interfered. Moreover, for the reasons we have seen, these rights could not be paucital rights held against the potential customers or any other third parties, because such rights would not bind the defendant. Nor could they be paucital rights held against the defendant, because there is no warrant for asserting that such rights came into existence. Hence, the claimant had to show that it possessed multitial rights in the banknotes. As multitial rights to things are property rights *in rem*, this means that the claimant had to show that it possessed property rights to the banknotes. But whether that was so was a matter, not of the law of negligence, but of the law of property and, according to that law, no such rights existed. Therefore, the claimant had to fail.

Note that this does not imply that tort law responds only to breaches of rights *in rem*. The claim is only that the claimants needed to show that they had a right *in rem* in the banknotes with which the defendants had interfered *in this kind of case*, there being no other possible source of the claimant's primary right.

We now examine the more realistic assumption that the claimant's potential customers would have purchased the products of the melts by transferring a chose in action to the claimant. Unsurprisingly, nothing is altered on this interpretation. In order to recover on these facts, the claimant had to show that it had a right to the choses in action that it held against the defendant, with which the defendant interfered. But no such rights existed. First, there is no reason to believe that the claimant possessed *any* rights to the relevant choses in action. Secondly, if the claimant did possess such rights, they were almost certainly held only as against third parties. Thirdly, it is difficult to see how the defendant's employees could have interfered with the claimant's rights to the choses in action by damaging the cable, even on the most unlikely assumptions that the claimant possessed such rights and that they were held against the defendant.

Accordingly, the conclusion is that, in negligently damaging the third party's cable, the defendant's employees violated no right in the claimant in regard to the four melts under discussion. Accordingly, the claimant was rightly unable to recover in respect of them.

Note that the point here is not simply that the claimant possessed no primary right *in rem* upon which to establish his claim. The point is rather that the claimant possessed no relevant primary right whatsoever—paucital, multitial, *in personam* or *in rem*. Any paucital rights held by the claimant were held against third parties and the defendant did not interfere with any multitial rights held by the claimant. Hence, in relation to the final four melts in *Spartan Steel*, the defendant did not violate any of the claimant's rights. The claimant had no legal basis upon which to found his claim.

Despite the need to clear away the confusion created by the modern approaches, the general point can be put simply. Imagine three people: Peter, Paul and Mary. Peter owns a car. Mary, then, owes a duty of care to Peter in regard to the car. But she does not owe that duty of care to Paul. Why not? Because Paul has no primary right in the car—the car is Peter's.[64] Hence, if Mary negligently damages the car and Paul wants to sue her, Paul has to find some right that he holds against Mary that Mary violated. The right cannot be a right in the car because the law of property tells us that there is no such right. Imagine that Mary's negligence prevents Peter from giving Paul a lift and hence causes Paul loss. Paul still has no case against Mary, because the mere fact that Mary caused loss to Paul is insufficient to show that Mary violated one of Paul's primary rights. In damaging the car, Mary injures neither Paul's property nor his person, nor does she interfere with any other rights that Paul holds against Mary. The damage to Peter's car, then, was no wrong to Paul, no matter how much loss it may have caused him.

This argument was very clearly expressed by Lush J in *Seale v Perry*:

> A duty . . . cannot exist by itself. To the duty seen as imposed on the defendant, there must be a correlative right in the plaintiff: for either to exist, both must be capable of being identified.
>
> It is possible that this proposition is at the root of the reluctance of the common law, evident for a long time, to recognize purely economic loss as a form of damage recoverable in an action for negligence. If person or property were damaged, it was not difficult to identify the plaintiff's right as a right to have care taken not to cause that damage. If the plaintiff suffered an economic loss, such as the loss of the profits of a business, it was less easy to identify anything in the nature of a right to be protected by an action for negligence. . . .
>
> I venture to think that it is really the problem of identifying the right which the plaintiff is entitled to have protected which underlies the difficulties of allowing actions to be brought in cases were the plaintiff has suffered and suffered only economic loss.[65]

Unfortunately, this lucid expression of the principled approach to economic loss has been buried in the avalanche of policy that has fallen on the law in Australia and elsewhere.

On the principled approach, recovery is not denied because of policy concerns, or because the damage is held to be too remote.[66] Rather, there can be no

---

[64] In passing, note how odd it would be to hold that this position was guilty of question-begging. The reason Mary owes no duty of care to Paul is not because I assume that there is no right and hence no duty, but because the subject matter of the alleged duty—the car—does not belong to Paul.

[65] *Seale v Perry* [1982] VR 193, 200 (SC).

[66] Compare *SCM v Whittall* [1971] 1 QB 337, 343–4 (CA) (Lord Denning MR); *Spartan Steel & Alloys Ltd v Martin & Co (Contractors) Ltd* [1973] QB 27, 36–7 (CA) (Lord Denning MR); JC Smith and P Burns, 'Donoghue v. Stevenson—The Not So Golden Anniversary' (1983) 46 MLR 147, 152.

recovery because there was no wrong: in *Spartan Steel* the defendant's employees made the claimant worse off, but they did so by 'violating' a non-right. Hence, the appropriate conclusion is that the claimant possessed no relevant right and so the defendant could not have owed the claimant a duty of care.[67] Accordingly, the rule against the recovery of relational loss, as exemplified in *Spartan Steel*, is appropriately seen as a reflection of the rights of the parties in accordance with the principled approach.

In fact, the conclusion here is contained in Cardozo CJ's judgment in *Palsgraf v Long Island Railroad Co*. Recall Cardozo CJ's claim that:

> Negligence is not a tort unless it results in the commission of a wrong, and the commission of a wrong imports the violation of a right . . . The victim does not sue derivatively, or by right of subrogation, to vindicate an interest invaded in the person of another. Thus to view his cause of action is to ignore the fundamental difference between tort and crime . . . He sues for breach of a duty owing to himself.[68]

In relational loss cases, the claimant is attempting to recover for factual loss he suffered because of the violation of a third party's rights. To allow recovery would be to permit the claimant to 'vindicate an interest invaded in the person of another'. This view can be appropriate only on the understanding that the law regards wrongdoing as societal rather than as interpersonal, that is as a species of distributive injustice rather than corrective injustice. But, while this kind of wrongdoing is the focus of the criminal law, it is not of the law of tort.[69]

It is important to note that no objection has been stated to the recovery of economic loss per se. Accordingly, this chapter should not be read as arguing that recovery should never be available in cases that modern lawyers regard as economic loss cases. The modern view focuses on a kind of loss that it labels economic rather than physical and holds that recovery for the former should be restricted. The approach advanced here does not focus on the kind of loss at all, but rather on the underlying primary rights or their absence. On this view, the reason the claimant could not recover for the loss on the final four melts in *Spartan Steel* was not because that loss was economic, as the modern view has it, but because it was a loss of something in respect of which the claimant had no legally recognised interest. Recovery is denied, then, not for the reason that the loss fell into a class—economic rather than physical—that is excluded, but because the claimant had no right over that with which the defendant interfered.[70] The point turns not on the remedy but on the prior primary right.

[67] *Weller & Co v Foot and Mouth Disease Research Institute* [1966] 1 QB 569, 585–7 (QBD); *SCM v Whittall* [1971] 1 QB 337, 347 (Winn LJ), 354 (Buckley LJ).
[68] *Palsgraf v Long Island Railroad Co* 162 NE 99, 101 (NY CA 1928).
[69] See also A Beever, 'Justice and Punishment in Tort: A Comparative Theoretical Analysis' in R Grantham and C Rickett (eds), *Justifying Remedies in Private Law* (Cambridge University Press, Cambridge, forthcoming 2007).
[70] P Benson, 'The Basis for Excluding Liability for Economic Loss in Tort Law' in D Owen (ed), *Philosophical Foundations of Tort Law* (Oxford University Press, Oxford, 1995) 433–7.

While Spartan Steel produced the correct result in disallowing recovery for
relational loss, other cases have not. Two leading examples are *Caltex Oil* and
Norsk, discussed above. In these cases, the High Court of Australia and the
Supreme Court of Canada respectively ruled that the claimant could recover.
However, in neither case did the loss result from an interference with the
claimants' rights.

   The claimed loss in both cases was the increased expenditure the claimants
were forced to outlay in order to transport petroleum and to carry freight
respectively. At first glance, this seems different from *Spartan Steel*, in that this
expenditure directly came out of the claimants' pockets.[71] However, the relevant cost was a cost of the claimants doing business. The claimants had no right
to a particular level of cost of doing business. Or, to be more precise, the
claimants had no such right as against their defendants.

   In *Caltex Oil*, the claimants may have had some right, that they could no
longer exercise, to the use of the pipeline, and hence they may have had some
control over the cost of doing business in that regard. Were this right to exist, it
would have been generated by a contract between the claimants and the owners
of the pipeline.[72] Hence, the claimants' inability to utilise the pipeline may have
constituted a breach of the claimants' contractual rights. This possibility, however, was of no significance in *Caltex Oil*. Contracts create only paucital rights
and obligations *in personam*. Although there is impetus behind the view that
contracts may create rights in parties, not in privity,[73] it has never been held that
a contract creates obligations in third parties to the contract and the defendant
in *Caltex Oil* was a third party to the relevant contract (if there was one).[74] In
Caltex Oil, while the claimants may have had contracts with the owners of the
pipeline, this fact could not generate a right in the claimants as against the
defendants, since the defendants were not parties to the contracts.[75]

   These points were recognised by the Supreme Court of the United States in
1927 in *Robins Dry Dock & Repair Co v Flint*.[76] The defendant damaged the
propeller of a ship belonging to a third party. Because of the damage, the ship
was not delivered on time into the possession of the claimant, violating the

---

[71] Though this need not have been the case. Perhaps this extra expenditure resulted merely in
decreased revenue.

[72] This right did not exist in the Canadian case: *Canadian National Railway Co v Norsk Pacific
Steamship Co Ltd* [1992] 1 SCR 1021, 1126.

[73] Eg Contracts (Rights of Third Parties) Act 1999 (UK); Law Commission for England and
Wales, 'Contracts for the Benefit of Third Parties', 1996 242 ; R Flannigan, 'Privity—The End of an
Era (Error)' (1987) 103 *LQR* 564.

[74] *White v Jones* [1995] 2 AC 207, 251 (HL) 251 (Lord Keith). Agency is not a counterexample as
the principal is a party at law to a contract between his agent and another. In any event, the situations in *Caltex Oil* and *Norsk* are not analogous to agency. If the defendant knew about the
claimant's contractual relations with a third party and deliberately set out to cause a breach of those
obligations, then the defendant can be liable. None of the cases explored here fit this description,
however.

[75] P Benson, 'The Basis for Excluding Liability for Economic Loss in Tort Law' in D Owen (ed),
Philosophical Foundations of Tort Law (Oxford University Press, Oxford, 1995) 434–6.

[76] 275 US 303 (US SC 1927).

terms of the charterparty between the claimant and the third party. This caused the claimant loss that it attempted to recover from the defendant. This, then, was a standard relational loss case.

Holmes J, in just over three pages, demonstrated the invalidity of the claimant's case, instituting a precedent that stands today:

> The District Court allowed recovery on the ground that the respondents had a 'property right' in the vessel, although it is not argued that there was a demise, and the owners remained in possession. This notion also is repudiated by the Circuit Court of Appeals and rightly. The question is whether the respondents have an interest protected by the law against unintended injuries inflicted upon the vessel by third persons who know nothing of the charter. If they have, it must be worked out through their contract relations with the owners, not on the postulate that they have a right in rem against the ship.
>
> Of course the contract of the petitioner with the owners imposed no immediate obligation upon the petitioner to third persons as we already have said, and whether the petitioner performed it promptly or with negligent delay was the business of the owners and of nobody else. But as there was a tortious damage to a chattel it is sought to connect the claim of the respondents with that in some way. The damage was material to them only as it caused the delay in making the repairs, and that delay would be a wrong to no one except for the petitioner's contract with the owners. The injury to the propeller was no wrong to the respondents but only to those to whom it belonged. ... [N]o authority need be cited to show that, as a general rule, at least, a tort to the person or property of one man does not make the tortfeasor liable to another merely because the injured person was under a contract with that other unknown to the doer of the wrong.[77]

This is exactly in line with the argument here. The claimant had a right to the ship created by the charterparty. But that right was held only against the owners. Therefore, the claimant had no basis on which to sue the defendant for damaging the ship. To allow the claimant to do so would implicitly recognise rights *in rem* in the claimant to the ship, but those rights do not exist.

Similarly, in *Caltex Oil*, the existence of a contract between the claimants and the owners of the pipeline may have given the claimants a cause of action against the owners, AOR, but it could not have generated a cause of action against the defendant, who was a third party to the contract; only a multitial right could do that. And, as no relevant multitial rights *in personam* were violated by the defendant, the claimant needed to point to a multitial right *in rem*. But such rights belong to the law of property, and that area of the law tells us that there were no such rights.

This also demonstrates that it is not significant that the claimants may have had a chose in action exercisable in respect of the property of the third parties. This is because the relevant chose in action is property *in personam* not *in rem* and the relevant rights are paucital. Hence, such property produces only

[77] *Ibid*, 308–9.

paucital rights *in personam* between the claimants and the third parties; it does not generate obligations in the defendants.

In order to justify recovery against the defendants, the claimants needed to establish that they had a primary right that they held against the defendants and that the defendants interfered with this right. As there was no special relationship between the parties, the primary right could not have been paucital. Hence, given that the claimants succeeded, *Caltex Oil* and *Norsk* impliedly recognised multitial rights *in rem* in the claimants either to the pipeline and bridge or to the profits that the claimants insisted they lost. But no such rights are known to the law of property. These decisions, then, recognise a right *in rem* to a thing, and hence a 'property' right that, according to the law of property, does not exist.

It is impossible to reply to these points by claiming that tort law could recognise rights to the *use* of items such as bridges and pipelines, use rights are not independent of other areas of law in a way that would avoid the problems identified above. Where do use rights belong on our map?

Recognition of Primary Rights	Responses to Violations of Primary Rights—Secondary Rights
Property	Wrongs (eg trespass, conversion, *negligence*)
Contract	(Breach of) Contract
Law of Persons	Wrongs (eg battery, assault, defamation, false imprisonment, *negligence*)

For the reply to succeed, use rights would have to be independent of property and contract. But they are not. Rights to the use of an object are governed by consent[78] or by property. If the use right is a mere licence, then it generates only paucital rights *in personam* in the user and so cannot ground a claim in tort against a third party to the licence, such as the defendants in *Caltex Oil* and *Norsk*. Alternatively, the use right is multitial and *in rem*, in which case it is a possessory right governed by the law of property. But in the cases explored above, the law of property tells us that there are no such possessory rights. (Moreover, if there were, then the loss claimed would not be relational economic loss. Rather, it would be property damage or consequential loss. I turn to that topic now.)

D. The Principled Approach to Consequential Loss

As indicated above, the Court of Appeal in *Spartan Steel* held that the claimant could recover the loss of profit on the first melt. This *description* of the recovery

---

[78] The relationship between consent and contract is discussed in ch 8.

is inconsistent with the fact that the claimant had no right to that profit. However, the result, the award of £768 in damages, was appropriate. The explanation for this also lies in a consideration of the rights of the parties and the correct measure of damages.

The claimant had property in all five melts and no property in the profits. As the final four melts were not damaged, the defendant's employees did not interfere with any right in those melts. Conversely, the defendant's employees did interfere with the first melt, causing physical damage to it. Hence, in respect of that melt, the defendant's employees interfered with a right in the claimant and so the claimant was able to recover the cost of that interference.

In *Spartan Steel*, the negligent interference with the first melt made the claimant £768 worse off than the claimant would have been had the defendant's employees not interfered with the claimant's property right. At the relevant time, the claimant's factory was operating continuously. Presumably, this was because the claimant had orders or could otherwise sell all the stainless steel that they could produce. Therefore, the value to the claimant of the first melt was correctly calculated by reference to the market value of the finished product, not the market value of replacement raw materials. Despite appearances, that is what actually happened in *Spartan Steel*.

The claimant was awarded the loss of profit on, plus the physical damage to, the first melt. The loss of profit was calculated by subtracting the market value of the raw materials (RM) from the market value of the final product (FP).[79] The physical damage was arrived at by subtracting the market value of the melt after it had been poured off (PM) from the market value of the raw materials (RM). Hence, the calculation of the loss was (FP-RM)+(RM-PM). This equals FP-PM, ie the market value of the final product less the market value of the melt after pouring off. While this corresponds to the actual loss of profit suffered by the claimant, there is no need to describe this as recovery for loss of profit. The claimant merely recovered the cost to it of the interference with its rights *in rem*.

The claimant in *Spartan Steel* had a property right in the first melt that was infringed by the negligence of the defendant's employees. Hence, the claimant was able to recover the extent to which that interference made it worse off. This amounted to £768. It was neither legally correct nor necessary to describe part of this (£400) as recovery for loss of profit. The claimant was rightly awarded damages only on the basis of the value of the defendant's interference with its rights. In the language of another legal system, we would say that the economic loss suffered in relation to the final four melts was *damnum* but there was no *injuria*, while the economic loss suffered in relation to the first melt was *damnum* suffered as a result of *injuria*. Hence, though the reasoning in *Spartan Steel* was flawed, the result was correct.

---

[79] Note that this calculation is counterfactual. The 'loss of profit' is the amount the claimants would have made had the melt not been damaged. It is not the loss of profit that the claimants suffered in fact. The latter figure includes the physical damage.

This discussion reveals not only that the ability to recover consequential economic loss and the inability to recover relational economic loss accord with legal principle but also that the very distinction between consequential and relational loss turns on the fact that the former is suffered as a result of a violation of the claimant's primary rights, while the latter is not. Hence, though the law is not disposed to elucidate the claimant's rights, it nevertheless implicitly reflects them.

The above reveals that it is crucial to distinguish the *bases* of liability and damages from the methods by which the quantum of damages are calculated. To take a clear example, if one's house is destroyed by one's neighbour's nuisance, the calculation of damages is sure to include an assessment of the market value of the house prior to damage. But this does not show that one had a right that one's house have a specific value. There is no such right. Instead, one has a right to one's house, a right that entails a secondary right to recover for the value of wrongful damage to that house. This value is calculated with reference to the market.[80] Hence, it is important *not* to conclude from the fact that one can recover the loss of x that one has a right to x or that one can recover *for* the loss of x.

Imagine that a negligent defendant causes a claimant personal injury—to her leg let us say—so that the claimant cannot continue in her employment. The claimant is entitled to recover her lost future earnings (with the relevant discount). However, the claimant has a right to her future earnings due only to her employment contract with her employer. This contract generates no rights against the defendant. Therefore, the claimant has no right against the defendant to her future earnings. This seems to indicate either that the claimant can recover loss that resulted from no violation of the claimant's rights or that the claimant has a right to her future earnings held against the defendant. The first position is nonsensical, at least in this context. If the defendant did not violate a right in the claimant, then the claimant was not wronged and there was no tort at all. The second position misdescribes the claimant's rights. First, we do not have rights in our future earnings that we hold against the world. If that were true, then we would have to interpret employment contracts as *undermining*, rather than creating, rights to earnings in employees, because employment contracts would need to be seen as giving employers a right to deprive employees of those earnings by dismissing them. This is not sensible. Nor can we say that the right to future earnings is held only against the defendant. There is absolutely no reason to do so. People do not gain primary rights to earnings because of the negligence of others.

---

[80] This is to be distinguished from the claim that one has a secondary right to recover the value of damage to one's property, whatever that value is. Such a right does exist. However, the value of one's property may change without any infringement of one's property rights. The reason for this is that the value of property is a function of the market—of other persons' preferences—and one has no right to those preferences.

The solution to this problem is to note that the loss of future earnings is an element of the value to the claimant of her personal injury. In this case, it is part of the value to the claimant of her leg. So, this claimant can recover a sum calculated with reference to her future earnings, not because she had a right held against the defendant to those earnings or that her future earnings were in any legal sense an asset of the claimant's, but because the claimant had a right to her leg as against the defendant and she can recover for the cost of the interference with that right. Hence, though the claimant recovers her lost future earnings, she does not recover *for* the loss of those earnings. This is why the claimant can recover loss of future earnings even if she has no current employment contract and also why the terms of any current contract do not *determine* the amount of the award. The contract, if there is one, is of factual, not legal, significance; ie, it can be used to aid in the calculation of the value to the claimant of her personal injury, but it in no way forms the legal basis of the claimant's cause of action.

Applying this argument to *Spartan Steel*, we must not infer from the fact that the claimant recovered the loss of profit on the first melt that the claimant had a right to the profit on the first melt, or that the claimant correctly recovered *for* the loss of profit on the first melt. There were no such rights. The claimant merely recovered for the cost of the physical the interference with its property rights.

As discussed earlier in this section, in *Bow Valley Husky* McLachlin J claimed that, due to special considerations of policy, economic loss can be recovered if the claimant had a possessory or proprietary interest in the damaged property.[81] Hence, the position taken by modern Canadian law is the following:

1. The principles of the law of negligence allow for recovery of economic loss limited only by reasonable foreseeability.
2. However, for reasons of policy, the recovery of economic loss is restricted.
3. But, for yet more reasons of policy, that restriction is lifted when the economic loss is the result of damage to the claimant's property.

This neatly reveals why the modern approaches have great difficulty dealing with the issue of economic loss. Because the Court adopts the idea that the principles of the law of negligence permit recovery limited only by foreseeability, the Court must impose policy-based restrictions on recovery in order to prevent recovery for relational loss. But, once this policy-based restriction is in force, the Court must then restrict the restriction, for other reasons of policy, in order to permit recovery of consequential loss. However, as we have seen, none of this policy analysis is required. The principles of the law permit recovery only if the defendant created an unreasonable risk of the claimant's injury, where injury is defined as a violation of the claimant's primary rights. It follows logically from this position that consequential loss is recoverable and that relational loss is not.

[81] *Bow Valley Husky (Bermuda) Ltd v Saint John Shipbuilding Ltd* [1997] 3 SCR 1210, 1241–2.

Accordingly, the principled approach has nothing to fear from economic loss. The approach does not generate indeterminate liability. It is more than a little ironic that, with the exception of Australian law and the decision of the majority of the Supreme Court of Canada in *Norsk*,[82] the modern policy-driven approaches produce the same outcome as the principled approach, though they do so only through a host of convoluted and unpredictable policies. Far from constituting an objection to the principled approach, therefore, the issue of economic loss once again demonstrates the strength of that approach and its considerable superiority over its modern rivals.

II. PURE ECONOMIC LOSS

A. The Building Cases

(i) *The Principled Approach*

The argument made in the previous section was essentially the same as that of the House of Lords in *Murphy v Brentwood District Council*.[83] The claimant argued that the defendant's employee had been negligent in approving the design of a stabilising raft constructed under his house. Due to faults with the raft, the claimant's building suffered physical damage. The claimant was unable to afford the cost of repairs, and sold the building for £35,000 less than the amount for which he could have sold it had it been structurally sound. The claimant was not the first purchaser of the house.

In order to understand this case, it is necessary to see why the injury was economic loss rather than physical damage. Of course, the claimant's property suffered physical damage: cracks in the walls and so on. But this was not the wrongful infliction of physical damage on the claimants' property by the defendant. The reason for this is that the claimant bought his property with the faulty stabilising raft. Hence, when that raft caused cracks to appear in the walls, etc, that could not have been an interference with the claimant's property rights in the building. The claimant bought a house with a faulty raft: that was what he had a right to. Similarly, May Donoghue could not have sued Stevenson in tort for the damage to her ginger beer caused because a decomposing snail was in it. Because Donoghue acquired the ginger beer with the snail, it is impos-

---

[82] The outcome in *Bow Valley* is compatible with the principled approach. Despite some claims from New Zealand lawyers that economic loss is not a large issue in that jurisdiction, the New Zealand position, in terms of outcome, is very similar to that in England. See, for instance, *Taupo BC v Birnie* [1978] 2 NZLR 397 (CA), which is held to represent the limits of the recovery of economic loss in these cases. (S Todd, 'Negligence: Particular Categories of Duty' in S Todd (ed), *The Law of Torts in New Zealand,* 3rd edn (Brookers, Wellington, 2001) 253.) The loss in this case was consequential economic loss: the cost of the defendant's violation of the claimant's property rights caused by flooding the claimant's property.

[83] [1991] 1 AC 398 (HL).

sible to regard the continuing decomposition of the snail as an interference with Donoghue's property rights in the ginger beer. She had a right to the ginger beer with the snail.

In *Murphy*, the House of Lords ruled that the defendant did not owe the claimant a duty of care to prevent his economic loss. This was because the claimant held no rights as against the defendant in relation to that loss. The physical damage to the house was not a violation of the claimant's property rights. Nor did the claimant have a right as against the defendant that his house sell for any particular value. Accordingly, Lord Bridge argued that:

> A builder, in the absence of any contractual duty or of a special relationship of prox-
> imity introducing the *Hedley Byrne* principle of reliance, owes no duty of care in tort
> in respect of the quality of his work. . . . [T]o hold that the builder owed such a duty
> of care to any person acquiring an interest in the product of the builder's work would
> be to impose on him the obligations of an indefinitely transmissible warranty of
> quality.[84]

In other words, finding for the claimant would create a right in the claimant that does not exist. The most plausible candidate, or the least implausible, would be a contractual right that does not exist: a warranty of quality that the defendant may never have given to the first purchaser but that the first purchaser passed onto subsequent owners.[85] But, as the law of contract shows that this right does not exist, the defendant cannot have owed a duty of care to respect it. Hence, the defendant committed no wrong against the claimant.

This argument does not uniquely apply to defective buildings. The Supreme Court of the United States applied the argument to defective chattels, ruling that 'the injury suffered—the failure of the product to function properly—is the essence of a warranty action' and, hence, in the absence of a (real rather than invented) warranty, recovery is denied.[86]

The legal difference between *Donoghue v Stevenson* and *Murphy* is that between a case involving the violation of the claimant's right to bodily integrity and a case involving no violation of the claimant's rights whatsoever.[87] Shifting our focus from remedies to rights should expose this.

This discussion also reveals that there is no legally significant distinction to be made between relational and pure economic loss. As neither flows from the violation of a right in the claimant, neither is recoverable.

[84] *Ibid*, 480.
[85] See S Whittaker, 'Privity of Contract and the Tort of Negligence: Future Directions' (1996) 16 *OJLS* 191, 200–3.
[86] *East River Steamship Corp v Transamerica Delaval Inc* 476 US 858, 868 (US SC 1986) (Blackmun J).
[87] Compare WVH Rogers, *Winfield and Jolowicz on Tort*, 16th edn (Sweet & Maxwell, London, 2002) 110.

(ii) The Policy-driven Approaches

Despite the fact that *Murphy* was rightly decided, it has not found favour in the rest of the Commonwealth. This is not surprising. As we have seen, the problem with respect to economic loss is believed to be its tendency to result in indeterminate liability. However, in the building cases, recovery is limited to the damage to the specific building and a restricted amount of other damage. Hence, from this perspective, the situation is similar to recovery for physical damage to property.

Moreover, in *Bryan v Maloney*, Mason CJ and Deane and Gaudron JJ rejected the argument that finding the defendant liable would impose on him a transmissible warranty of quality. 'Their Lordships' view [in *Murphy*] seems to us . . . to have rested upon . . . a more rigid compartmentalisation of contract and tort than is acceptable under the law of this country'.[88] The argument seems to be that a finding of liability would not give the claimant a transmissible warranty of quality or any other contractual right. Instead, the claimant would be given only what she lost because of the defendant's negligence. It just so happens that these damages are equivalent to those that would have been awarded had the claimant successfully sued for the breach of a warranty of quality. But, while liability gives the claimant something that corresponds to a possible award in contract, it is actually an award in tort and not in contract. Hence, the award is objectionable only on a view that holds that awards in tort must never overlap with those in contract, but that is overly to compartmentalise the two areas of the law.

Mason CJ and Deane and Gaudron JJ interpret Lord Bridge as claiming that tortious liability cannot exist in cases such as *Murphy*, because the *remedy* in tort would overlap *remedies* in contract. Moreover, the judgment in *Murphy* is seen to depart from a principled approach on policy grounds in order to cut back on liability.[89] However, Lord Bridge's point did not concern the remedy but the claimant's primary right. In his Lordship's view, there was no primary right upon which to found the remedy. Hence, *Murphy* is perfectly in accord with the principled approach and is unassailable as a matter of common law.[90] This is obscured because of the focus of other courts and commentators on remedies rather than rights and on policy rather than principle.[91]

---

[88] *Bryan v Maloney* (1995) 182 CLR 609, 629 (HCA). See also *Winnipeg Condominium Corp No 36 v Bird Construction Co* [1995] 1 SCR 85, 103–4 (La Forest J); J Fleming, *The Law of Torts*, 9th edn (LBC Information Services, Sydney, 1998) 195; WVH Rogers, *Winfield and Jolowicz on Tort*, 16th edn (Sweet & Maxwell, London, 2002) 123–4.

[89] See also *Invercargill City Council v Hamlin* [1994] 3 NZLR 513, 546 (CA) (McKay J).

[90] I say as a matter of common law, because the above expresses no objection to the alteration of common law by statute.

[91] It has been suggested to me that Lord Bridge focussed, not on the rights of the claimant, but on the adverse non-legal consequences of imposing a duty of care on the defendant. However, Lord Bridge did not discuss any such consequences in the relevant sections of his judgment; in fact, his Lordship insisted that these concerns were a matter for the legislature. (His Lordship briefly referred to similar policy matters *only* in rejecting the idea that recovery could be given for, but restricted to,

In *Invercargill City Council v Hamlin*,[92] the New Zealand Court of Appeal substituted its own policies for the ones it wrongly believed the House of Lords implemented in *Murphy*.[93] Richardson J referred to the following concerns:[94]

1. New Zealand has a high proportion of owner-occupier housing.
2. In New Zealand, much housing construction is undertaken by small-scale building firms for individual purchasers.
3. There is and has been considerable Government support for private housing in New Zealand.[95]
4. New Zealand experienced a large housing boom in the 1950s and 1960s.
5. It is not common practice in New Zealand for those purchasing new houses to have those houses inspected by engineers or architects.

None of these points shows that the defendant ought to have been liable to the claimant. In particular, what could possibly be the significance of the fact that New Zealand underwent a housing boom in the 1950s and 1960s? Moreover, as Richardson J took himself to be showing why *Murphy* should not apply in New Zealand, the claims could have significance only if they showed that circumstances in New Zealand were different from those in the United Kingdom. But Richardson J conducted no comparative analysis whatsoever. Accordingly, Richardson J did *nothing* to show that 'the housing scene in New Zealand . . . is so very different from that in the United Kingdom'.[96] Consistent with the policy-driven approach in general, Richardson J's judgment in *Hamlin* was empty.

In fact, it is a sign of how bankrupt the modern approaches are that Richmond J's argument has been widely accepted in New Zealand. In *Hamlin*

---

damage posing an imminent danger to health and safety. Policy matters were, perhaps, relevant there, because the argument for the position rejected by Lord Bridge was itself based on policy.) Moreover, his Lordship recognised that alternative positions had been reached—without apparent adverse consequences—in other parts of the Commonwealth. Furthermore, I submit that, on reflection, it odd to interpret Lord Bridge's argument concerning transmissible warrantees of quality as an argument of policy. If it were such an argument, why would Lord Bridge choose to express it in that strange manner? Also, whatever Lord Bridge's actual intentions, why would we want to read the claim in this odd way? Of course, I expect that those who have been reading *Murphy* as based on policy for more than a decade and a half will not immediately find my interpretation of the case intuitive, but I note that those who interpret *Murphy* as being based on policy often express incomprehension at the judgments. See below n118. One ought to be at least uncomfortable with the idea that Lord Bridge clearly intended *x* and that *x* is incomprehensible.

[92] [1994] 3 NZLR 513 (CA).
[93] In *Invercargill City Council v Hamlin* [1996] AC 624 (PC), the Privy Council maintained that the New Zealand Court of Appeal was at liberty to do so and claimed that, despite the fact that the Privy Council was New Zealand's highest Court, the matter was rightly to be decided by the New Zealand Court of Appeal. Accordingly, I ignore the decision of the Privy Council in the following.
[94] *Invercargill City Council v Hamlin* [1994] 3 NZLR 513, 324–5 (CA). Richardson J listed six concerns, but the third and fifth are the same.
[95] This included the Building Act 1991 (NZ), discussed in *Hamlin,* above n94, 525–7. However, at 527, Richardson J admitted that this was not decisive, concluding merely that: 'there is nothing in the recent legislative history to justify reconsideration by this Court of its previous decisions in this field'.
[96] *Ibid*, 546.

itself it was referred to approvingly by Cooke P,[97] Casey[98] and MacKay JJ,[99] and it has been endorsed by Stephen Todd.[100] But even if one accepted that judicial decision making should proceed in terms of policy, one would hope that the policy discussions were more convincing than this.[101] In this case, and in many others, the so-called policy arguments really function as excuses for reaching a result believed just on almost entirely intuitive grounds. They therefore do nothing to 'let daylight in on magic', but are rather the magician's sleight of hand.

Cooke P and Casey J made better use of the five factors mentioned by Richardson J. Their Honours maintained that these factors, coupled with the Building Act 1991 (NZ) and other relevant issues, meant that the defendant had *assumed responsibility* to the claimant.[102] This view was endorsed by a majority of the High Court of Australia in *Bryan v Maloney*.[103]

The issue of assumption of responsibility and negligent misrepresentation is explored in detail in the next chapter. Suffice it to say for the moment that the argument succeeds only if it can be shown that the defendant voluntarily assumed responsibility to the claimant. In these cases, there was no direct communication between the claimant and the defendant, but that is not decisive (or so I shall argue). The issue is simply whether a builder or an inspector of a newly constructed building can reasonably be interpreted as assuming responsibility to subsequent purchasers of the building for the quality of the building. This is not a question of law but a question of fact.[104]

Of course, even putting the specific New Zealand context aside, builders generally do make some representations of quality with respect to their buildings. Simply referring to oneself as a respectable builder implies that one's buildings

---

[97] See *Hamlin*, above n 94, 519.

[98] *Ibid*, 530.

[99] *Ibid*, 546.

[100] S Todd, 'Negligence: Particular Categories of Duty' in S Todd (ed), *The Law of Torts in New Zealand,* 3rd edn (Brookers, Wellington, 2001) 299.

[101] S Todd, 'Policy Issues in Defective Property Cases' in JW Neyers, E Chamberlain and SGA Pitel (eds), *Emerging Issues in Tort Law* (Hart Publishing, Oxford, forthcoming 2007), has much improved on Richardson J's argument. Nevertheless, Todd does not demonstrate that the defendant violates a primary right in the claimant in these cases. In fact, like many others we have examined, Todd's argument assumes that the issue concerns the remedy rather than the primary right.

[102] *Invercargill City Council v Hamlin* [1994] 3 NZLR 513, 519 (Cooke P), 530 (Casey J).

[103] (1995) 182 CLR 609, 627 (HCA). See also *Woolcock Street Investments Pty Ltd v CDG Pty Ltd* [2004] HCA 16, (2004) 216 CLR 515. In the latter case, a majority of the High Court suggested that the claimant could recover only if he was 'vulnerable' in the sense of being unable to protect himself from the loss by other means. Hence, the Court found that a purchaser of commercial premises could not recover for their negligent construction because (so it was said) commercial purchasers are usually able to protect themselves through contract. In the sense in which that is true, however, it also applies to purchasers of dwellings. Moreover, as indicated earlier in this ch, this kind of argument is invalid, because the claimant should have to protect himself only if a duty of care was not owed.

[104] I am indebted to Russell Brown for discussion of these issues. The test for intention is objective, in line with the usual approach of contract law. Nevertheless, it will very seldom be appropriate to interpret builders or inspectors as providing a transmissible warrantee of quality to subsequent purchasers of a building on any test.

will be well constructed, for instance. But it is important to note that this argument applies not only to builders but to manufacturers of any object. In Europe, it is quite common for manufacturers to advertise themselves with a variation of the slogan: 'manufactures of fine *x* since 1624'. Clearly, this is a representation of quality as to the manufacturer's products. But this does not mean that the slogans are assumptions of responsibility for the quality of the products.

Imagine the following conversation between *A*, a watch manufacturer, and *B*, a potential customer. *B* asks if the watch is of good quality. *A* replies that it is and that it will last 25 years or more. In fact, *A* is so confident of the watch's quality, that he offers *B* a 10 year warranty free of charge. *B* responds, 'What do you mean? Why would I want a 10 year warranty when you have already guaranteed that the watch will last for 25 years?' We immediately recognise *B*'s response to be aberrant. Saying that the watch will last 25 years or more is not normally intended or understood as providing any sort of legally enforceable guarantee as to the watch's longevity. It is rather the expression of the *expectation* that the watch will last that long. If this were not the case, then it would be difficult to explain the role that warranties have. Ordinarily, we would have to understand them, counter-intuitively, as *restricting* the manufacturer's potential liability by undermining the force of other assumptions of responsibility made by the manufacturer as to the quality of his product. The fact that we do not understand them in this way reveals that we do not understand the kinds of representations ordinarily made in these contexts as assumptions of responsibility.

Moreover, returning to the building cases, Cooke P and Casey J's argument can succeed only if it is plausible to suggest that those in the position of the defendant in these cases—the builder of a house, the inspector of a building, etc—usually assumes responsibility, not merely to the first purchaser of the property, but to all subsequent purchasers. This is not plausible. In particular, given that the class of persons who could purchase the property is extremely wide and that persons may purchase the property for a variety of reasons, this constitutes strong evidence against the notion that the defendant assumed responsibility to all future owners of the property.[105] One assumes responsibility to an indeterminate class of persons only in extreme circumstances. As Lord Oliver said in *Murphy*, '[a]part from contract, the manufacturer of a chattel assumes no responsibility to a third party into whose hands it has come for the cost of putting it into a state in which it can safely continue to be used for the purpose for which it was intended'.[106] Prima facie, the case is the same with respect to defective buildings.

Accordingly, the conclusion that the defendant assumed responsibility either appears to be based on the view that the defendant *should have* assumed responsibility though he did not or is merely a veil for the raw intuition that the

---

[105] Compare *Caparo Industries v Dickman* [1990] 2 AC 605 (HL).

[106] *Murphy v Brentwood District Council* [1991] 1 AC 398, 481 (HL). See also *Bryan v Maloney* (1995) 182 CLR 609, 627 (HCA) (Mason CJ and Deane and Gaudron JJ).

defendant should be liable. The second possibility is inadequate on its face. The first possibility cannot justify liability on the ground that the defendant assumed responsibility, but must attempt to derive liability from general principles of the law of negligence. But, as we have seen, that cannot be done. Though Cook P's and Casey J's argument is the best one available, it fails because there is insufficient evidence to impute to the defendant the intention to assume responsibility to the claimant.

Note that the argument above is *not* that the defendant should escape liability because such would impose indeterminate liability. That claim would be false: as only owners of the property could sue; the liability would be determinate. The claim is that the argument for liability based on an assumption of responsibility relies on the notion that the defendant has actually assumed responsibility to an indeterminate class of persons. This is not impossible, but it would take very explicit language on the part of the defendant to justify that conclusion and that language is entirely absent in the relevant cases. I conclude, then, that an assumption of responsibility by the defendant cannot ground a right in the claimant.

(iii) The Risk to the Owner's Person and Property and Risk to Others

It remains to consider the apparent exceptions to the approach developed above adopted by the House of Lords in *Murphy*. These are that the claimant in some circumstances can recover for (i) personal injury and property damage caused by the building, (ii) 'unavoidable loss' such as the cost of removing possessions from a dangerous building and (iii) the cost of eliminating danger to the person and property of third parties.

In *Donoghue v Stevenson*, the claimant suffered injury when she drank a bottle of ginger beer gifted to her by her friend. When the claimant drank the ginger beer, it was her property. But the fact that the claimant owned the ginger beer did not prevent her claim against the defendant. Likewise, if Donoghue's friend had also drunk the ginger beer, then that person would have been able to recover from Stevenson. Similarly, '[i]f a builder erects a structure containing a latent defect which renders it dangerous to persons or property, he will be liable in tort for injury to persons or damage to property resulting from that dangerous defect'.[107]

This is entailed by the principled approach. In *Donoghue v Stevenson*, the claimant had a right to bodily integrity and the defendant interfered with that right by creating an unreasonable risk of personal injury to the claimant. The fact that a mechanism for that injury became the property of the claimant is irrelevant. If I pick up your gun and shoot you with it, your claim is not limited to conversion. The same reasoning would apply if Donoghue's friend had drunk the ginger beer. It also applies to injury to the claimant's other property. If the

---

[107] *Murphy v Brentwood District Council* [1991] 1 AC 398, 481 (HL) (Lord Bridge).

decomposition of the snail had produced a compound that dissolved Donoghue's false teeth, then she would have been able to recover for the damage to her teeth.[108] This is because the defendant would have created an unreasonable risk of injury to the claimant's property (teeth). Returning to *Murphy*, if the building caused damage to the claimant's person or *other* property, then the claimant should have been able to recover. This is because damage to the claimant's person or other property would be a violation of the claimant's bodily integrity or property rights.

But this conclusion follows only if the claimant was unaware of the defect in the building. 'If the defect becomes apparent before any injury or damage has been caused, the loss sustained by the building owner [to her other property] is purely economic [and therefore irrecoverable].'[109] This is because, if the claimant knew of the risk and chose to continue to expose herself to it, then either her decision means that she is *volens* or her actions constitute a *novus actus interveniens*. For reasons discussed in Chapter 10, if it was certain that the risk would materialise and the claimant could have moved out, then the claimant chose to be harmed and would be *volens*. This would happen only in the most unusual cases, however, and so is not examined further here. More likely is that the claimant would be aware of a risk of damage to her person or property and choose to take that risk. As revealed in Chapter 10, this does not make the claimant *volens*. But it does mean that her decision not to move out is a new intervening act. If the claimant knew about the risk and chose not to remove herself or her property from the danger, then the harm to her does not lie within the ambit of the risk created by the defendant's negligence.

Admittedly, this point is not easy to see in the building cases. As La Forest J plausibly argued in *Winnipeg Condominium Corp No 36 v Bird Construction Co*:

> The weakness of the argument is that it is based upon an unrealistic view of the choice faced by home owners in deciding whether to repair a dangerous defect in their home. In fact, a choice to 'discard' a home instead of repairing the dangerous defect is no choice at all: most home owners buy a home as a long term investment and few home owners, upon discovering a dangerous defect in the home, will choose to abandon or sell the building rather than to repair the defect.[110]

This point is quite correct, but it is not relevant. It could be relevant only if the claimant's property rights (or any other right held against the defendant) guaranteed her a building of a certain quality. But no such right exists in the relevant

---

[108] Assuming that such is a reasonably foreseeable consequence of the negligence.

[109] *Murphy v Brentwood District Council* [1991] 1 AC 398, 481 (HL) (Lord Bridge). See also *ibid*, 475 (Lord Keith). Strictly, the argument should have been that a claimant could not recover for an instance of damage if the risk of *that* damage was known to the claimant. Hence, if some damage occurs and the claimant then becomes aware of the risk, the claimant must take steps to remove the risk.

[110] [1995] 1 SCR 85, 199.

cases. The issue is not whether the claimant would ordinarily choose to repair the house rather than abandon it, but whether the claimant would act reasonably in knowing about the risk of injury to leave her property or her person in danger. An analogous case would be *Donoghue v Stevenson* but where Donoghue was warned that the ginger beer was likely to contain the snail and chose to drink it in the light of that knowledge. Here, that accident would not have been within the ambit of the unreasonable risk created by the defendant and hence, in line with the discussion of *Doughty v Turner Manufacturing Co Ltd* in Chapter 4,[111] the claimant's injury would have been remote.

While it is true that one cannot expect a homeowner to move out if she discovers a small risk of injury to herself or to her property, if she fails to protect herself from risks that she knows about, then that failure must be a novus actus interveniens. For instance, if the homeowner discovers a structural weakness in the roof affecting one bedroom, it may be unreasonable to expect her to vacate her house entirely, but it is reasonable to expect her to vacate the room. Failure to do so is a novus actus interveniens. On the other hand, if the entire house is in danger of collapse causing serious injury to the owner and her property, then it is reasonable to expect her to move out.[112]

Of course, as La Forest J pointed out, most people will believe that the result is harsh for the claimant from the perspective of distributive justice. But, from the perspective of corrective justice, if the claimant had no right that was violated then there was no wrong, no tort and no injustice. Accordingly, from this perspective the result is not harsh at all. Of course, if the members of our communities agree that the result is distributively unjust and that the distributive injustice is more important than the corrective justice in this context, then the situation could be amended by statute. But that is a quite different matter.[113]

An exception to the above arises if the claimant is genuinely unable to rescue herself from the danger. In such circumstances, the claimant can recover. But the claimant must be *unable* to eliminate the risk to herself. It is not sufficient that that elimination would produce hardship to the claimant, unless the claimant held a right as against the defendant that she not suffer that hardship (which is

---

[111] [1964] 1 QB 518 (CA).

[112] Note that this argument cannot apply to a third party suing in nuisance for damage suffered as the result of the collapse of the claimant's building.

[113] For discussion of the statutory context see S Whittaker, 'Privity of Contract and the Tort of Negligence: Future Directions' (1996) 16 *OJLS* 191, 200–3. The issues here are much more complex than policy-driven lawyers usually realise. For instance, allowing recovery would force up the price of new housing as builders, inspectors, etc would charge first purchasers for the 'insurance' they were forced to provide to subsequent purchasers. Hence, while recovery would protect current homeowners, it does so at the expense of those yet to enter the housing market. It should not be assumed that new entrants to the housing market would willingly pay for the 'insurance'. Rather, given that they have not in the past chosen to take out similar insurance, the evidence points the other way. In fact, then, recovery appears to support the 'rent seeking' of the middle class and middle aged (including judges, lawyers, etc) by sacrificing the interests of the poor and young. These matters require much deliberation, and deliberation of a kind that does not occur in common law courts.

almost certain not to be the case). If, for instance, the alternative to remaining in the building is death (because one is living in the north of Canada in the winter and no other shelter is available, for instance) or the destruction of one's property, then that too is an invasion of the claimant's rights for which the defendant is responsible. But these are extreme and unusual cases.

Note that it follows from the above that the claimant who needs to vacate her house in order to avoid injury to her person or to her other property is entitled to recover the cost of that move from the defendant. This is because the claimant has a right to bodily integrity and rights to that property, and so is entitled to rescue herself and her property from the danger imposed on it by the defendant.[114] Similarly, if the claimant's building poses a risk to others, then the claimant may remove that risk and claim the cost of doing so from the defendant. For instance:

> if a building stands so close to the boundary of the building owner's land that after discovery of the dangerous defect it remains a potential source of injury to persons or property on neighbouring land or on the highway, the building owner ought, in principle, to be entitled to recover in tort from the negligent builder the cost of obviating the danger, whether by repair or by demolition, so far as that cost is necessarily incurred in order to protect himself from potential liability to third parties.[115]

This is because the claimant is entitled to rescue third parties from injuries to their rights.[116]

The owner cannot recover more than the lowest amount required to remove the danger to third parties, even if that means recovery only of the cost of demolishing the building.[117] Also, if the owner chooses not to remove the danger and the defect develops, increasing the danger to third parties, then that constitutes a novus actus interveniens on the part of the owner, meaning that the third party can recover from the owner but not from the builder or inspector.[118]

---

[114] JW Neyers, '*Donoghue v. Stevenson* and the Rescue Doctrine: A Public Justification of Recovery in Situations Involving the Negligent Supply of Dangerous Structures' (1999) 49 *University of Toronto Law Journal* 475, 504. Compare P Benson, 'The Basis for Excluding Liability for Economic Loss in Tort Law' in D Owen (ed), *Philosophical Foundations of Tort Law* (Oxford University Press, Oxford, 1995) 437–44.

[115] *Murphy v Brentwood District Council* [1991] 1 AC 398, 481 (HL) (Lord Bridge).

[116] Neyers, above n114, 507.

[117] Note that the demolition of the building with the owner's consent does not amount to a violation of the owner's property rights in the building. See also EJ Weinrib, *The Idea of Private Law* (Harvard University Press, Cambridge, Mass, 1995) 176.

[118] It is interesting to observe that the modern approaches have great difficulty explaining the above. In fact, many commentators have found Lord Bridge's position in *Murphy* to be unintelligible. For discussion, see Neyers, above n114, 507 n 158. This highlights the inability of mainstream academic analysis in England to understand these decisions of the House of Lords.

B. The Disappointed Beneficiary Cases

I now examine the disappointed beneficiary cases. In an intriguing 3–2 decision, the House of Lords in *White v Jones* created an exception to the general rule that pure economic loss is irrecoverable.[119]

The claimants' father employed the defendant solicitor to alter his will. Had the solicitor done so, the claimants would have inherited £9,000 each on the death of their father. However, the solicitor failed to carry out this alteration. In consequence, when their father died, the claimants had no rights under the will. The claimants brought an action in negligence against the solicitor, claiming the £9,000 that they would have received had the solicitor not been negligent.

In order to justify recovery, the defendant must have interfered with a right in the claimants. What was the relevant right in *White v Jones*? In the view of the majority, the claimants possessed a right that the defendant take due care in altering the will, which the defendant had infringed. But what is the juridical basis of this right? Where does it belong on the map?

Lord Nolan's answer was that the right was produced by the claimants' reliance on the defendant:

> The appellants were acting in the role of family solicitors. As is commonly the case the contract was with the head of the family, but it would be astonishing if, as a result, they owed a duty of care to him alone, to the exclusion of the other members of the family. In the particular circumstances of the case, the degree of proximity to the plaintiffs could hardly have been closer. Carol White, the first plaintiff, had spoken to Mr Jones [the defendant] about the revised wishes of Mr Barratt [the testator] and the letter setting out those wishes was written for Mr Barratt by Mr Heath, the husband of the second plaintiff. It would be absurd to suggest that they placed no reliance upon the appellants to carry out the instructions given to them.[120]

This argument cannot establish liability even were it clear that the defendant had made a negligent misrepresentation to the claimants. In *White v Jones*, the claimants led no evidence that they relied to their detriment on any misstatement—that they would have sought the aid of another solicitor, for example.[121] Indeed, there was no evidence as to the content of any representation made to the claimants at all. In the absence of such evidence, all one can say is that the claimants' injury was caused by the defendant's negligence in not altering the will. There is insufficient evidence to conclude that it was caused by reliance on a negligent misrepresentation.

---

[119] [1995] 2 AC 207 (HL). See also *Whittingham v Crease & Co* (1978) 6 CCLT 1 (BCSC); *Hill v Van Erp* (1997) 142 ALR 687 (HCA); *Gartside v Sheffield, Young & Ellis* [1983] NZLR 37 (CA).

[120] *White v Jones* [1995] 2 AC 207, 294–5 (HL). Lord Nolan presented this as a response to certain objections raised, rather than an argument in its own right. Nevertheless, it is relevant to discuss it here.

[121] However, see *ibid*, 291–2 (Lord Mustill). Compare T Weir, *Tort Law* (Oxford University Press, Oxford, 2002) 36.

Though not central to his argument (which is examined below), Lord Browne-Wilkinson responded to this line of thought, saying that '[a]lthough in any particular case it may not be possible to demonstrate that the intended beneficiary relied upon the solicitor, society as a whole does rely on solicitors to carry out their will-making functions carefully'.[122] There are two ways of understanding this passage. The first is that society's general reliance is sufficient to establish on the balance of probabilities that these claimants actually relied. However, while society's general reliance could combine with other evidence to establish on the balance of probabilities proof of actual reliance, general reliance alone is insufficient to do so.

Alternatively, Lord Browne-Wilkinson could be read as arguing that, because society generally relies, the burden of having to prove detrimental reliance should be lifted from the claimants. Perhaps this is best put as an argument that society's general reliance justifies the adoption of a presumption of reliance in particular cases. But it is hard to see how this could be justified. The general rule is that the party making an assertion must prove it on the balance of probabilities. It is unclear how society's general reliance could justify a reversal of this.[123]

Moreover, *White v Jones* is held to enunciate a principle that extends beyond the particular facts of that case to all or almost all cases in which claimants have failed to benefit from an inheritance because of the negligence of a solicitor in altering a will.[124] In some of these cases, it will be clear that the claimants did not rely on any representation. In some cases, the claimants will not know that they stood to inherit until after the death of the testator. The argument for the claimants, therefore, must assert that a claimant need not prove that she relied to her detriment on the defendant's statement to establish a cause of action. The primary right, therefore, cannot have been generated by the claimants' detrimental reliance.

Lord Browne-Wilkinson denied the need to show reliance. Arguing by analogy from fiduciary obligation, his Lordship maintained that in deciding whether a duty of care exists, '[w]hat is important is not that A knows that B is consciously relying on A, but A knows that B's economic well being is dependent upon A's careful conduct of B's affairs'.[125] There is a crucial ambiguity in the final clause of that sentence.

Lord Browne-Wilkinson could be read as asserting one of the following two principles:

1. When *A* is involved in managing *B*'s affairs and knows that *B*'s wellbeing is dependent thereon, *A* owes *B* a duty of care.
2. When *A* is involved in managing *B*'s affairs and knows that *C*'s wellbeing is dependent thereon, *A* owes *C* a duty of care.

---

[122] *White v Jones* [1995] 2 AC 207, 276 (HL).

[123] These issues are explored further in ch 13.

[124] Moreover, it also extends beyond these cases. See *Gorham v British Telecommunications plc* [2000] 1 WLR 2129 (CA). Compare *Brownie Wills v Shrimpton* [1998] 2 NZLR 320 (CA).

[125] *White v Jones* [1995] 2 AC 207, 272 (HL).

The first principle is broadly correct, but is not applicable to *White v Jones*. There, the defendant was dealing with the claimants' father's affairs, not the claimants'. The second principle is applicable to *White v Jones* but is invalid. C does not acquire a right against A merely because A is managing the affairs of a third party. Nor does C have an innate right against A. That would mean that all those who have dealings with another would owe a duty to protect the interests of third parties they know might be affected. For instance, it would prevent two parties from contracting in the knowledge that the contract may damage the interests of a third party. But that is not the law. Such contracts are routine.

On the other hand, one may attempt to support Lord Browne-Wilkinson's position by appealing to the notion of vulnerability discussed in Chapter 5. On this view, 2 should be reformulated as follows:

2. When A is involved in managing B's affairs and knows that C's wellbeing is dependent thereon, and C is in a vulnerable position, then A owes C a duty of care.

However, even putting aside the objections to the reliance on vulnerability raised in Chapter 5, this argument will not do. First, it is not clear that the addition of vulnerability has added anything of substance to the formula. What is the difference between being dependant and being dependant and vulnerable? Secondly, the position remains flatly inconsistent with the case law. For instance, if I am an accountant for Peter and I manage Peter's accounts in a way that causes Peter's business empire to flourish but in the process drives Paul into poverty, I cannot be liable to Paul simply because Paul was vulnerable. The law does not require me to be altruistic in this manner; still less does it require me to be altruistic with Peter's money. The appeal to vulnerability in this context could only be an ad hoc attempt to justify the result in *White v Jones*.

A very different argument from the ones examined above was proposed by Lord Goff. His Lordship concluded that:

> the *Hedley Byrne* . . . principle cannot, in the absence of special circumstances, give rise on ordinary principles to an assumption of responsibility by the testator's solicitor towards an intended beneficiary. Even so, it seems to me that it is open to your Lordships' House . . . to fashion a remedy to fill a lacuna in the law and so prevent the injustice which would otherwise occur on the facts of cases such as the present. . . . In my opinion, therefore, your Lordships' House should in cases such as these extend to the intended beneficiary a remedy under the *Hedley Byrne* principle by holding that the assumption of responsibility by the solicitor towards his client should be held in law to extend to the intended beneficiary who (as the solicitor can reasonably foresee) may, as a result of the solicitor's negligence, be deprived of his intended legacy in circumstances in which neither the testator nor his estate will have a remedy against the solicitor.[126]

---

[126] *White v Jones* [1995] 2 AC 268.

Here, although Lord Goff argued that the claimants should recover under an extension of the law of negligent misrepresentation, it is clear that his Lordship regarded this as a unique case. In other words, in his Lordship's view, this case was to be treated as an exception to the general rules. It is in that sense *sui generis*.[127]

Lord Goff's main reason for finding liability in this case was captured in the following comment:

> [T]he real reason for concern in cases such as the present lies in the extraordinary fact that, if a duty owed by the testator's solicitor to the disappointed beneficiary is not recognized, the only person who may have a valid claim has suffered no loss, and the only person who has suffered a loss has no claim.[128]

This is not an *argument* to suggest that the claimants should recover; rather, it is the expression of the intuition, the instinctive feeling, that they should. Moreover, it is not clear that the only person (the testator) who had a valid claim suffered no loss, and while it may be the case that the only person (the intended beneficiary) who suffered loss had no claim, this is of no legal significance. I discuss the former point below, but the latter is explored here.

Lord Goff insisted that, absent liability, the claimants would have suffered incompensatable loss. This in itself is no argument for liability in negligence. If one is seriously injured by a non-negligent party, then one suffers loss, but one cannot recover for that loss in negligence. In that case, we do not say that the claimant must be able to recover or else the only person who suffered loss would have no valid claim. For a loss to be legally actionable, it must result from the violation of a primary right. But we have been unable to find a right in the claimants that was violated in *White v Jones*:

> [L]egal fault cannot exist in a vacuum; the person who complains of it must do so by virtue of a legal right. In the present instance it is tempting to say that the solicitor failed to do his job properly; that it was all his fault that the plaintiffs are less well off than they should have been; and that the law ought to do something about it. This temptation should in my opinion be resisted. The assertion of fault is either tautologous or inaccurate, and the analysis is safer without it.[129]

We now analyse the claimants' rights to the £18,000 itself. The testator's 'estate consisted principally of a house worth £27,000, about £1,000 in a building society, and insurances totalling some £1,000'.[130] Hence, before the claimants' father died, he possessed a right *in rem* to the house and choses in action *in personam* held against a building society and an insurance company or companies. When the testator died, those rights passed to the executors of the

[127] *Gartside v Sheffield, Young & Ellis* [1983] NZLR 37, 42 (CA) (Cooke J); *Brownie Wills v Shrimpton* [1998] 2 NZLR 320, 325 (CA) (Blanchard J).
[128] *White v Jones* [1995] 2 AC 207, 262 (HL). I accept *arguendo* that there is a loss here, rather than merely the failure to realise a benefit.
[129] *Ibid*, 277–8 (Lord Mustill).
[130] *Ibid*, 17 (Sir Donald Nicholls VC).

will, and those executors gained obligations to the will beneficiaries to distribute the estate in accordance with the terms of the will. It is unclear how this was done, but suppose that the executors sold the house and placed the proceeds in a new bank account, transferred the sum from the building society to that account, and cashed in the insurances and transferred those sums to the same account. When that occurred, the executors had a chose in action held against a bank and owed the will beneficiaries obligations to distribute the value of that chose in action, probably by transferring its value to accounts of the beneficiaries, thereby increasing the value of their choses in action. At no stage did the claimants, who were not the executors or the will beneficiaries, have any legal or equitable proprietary interest in the estate or in any subject matter relating to the £18,000.

Perhaps we can find a right *in personam* in the claimants that bound the defendant? For such a right to have existed, it would need to have been a right owed by the defendant. But, given the failure of the arguments above, the origin of this right is obscure. 'The intention to benefit the claimants . . . if it had received legal effect would have given them only a spes successionis of an ambulatory character.'[131]

There was no primary right in the claimants violated by the defendant in *White v Jones*. Again, this point was recognised by Lush J in *Seale v Perry*, another disappointed beneficiary case. 'In the present case, there is nothing in the position of the plaintiffs on which a right can be founded. They had no form of right at law, by contract or otherwise, to the benefaction.'[132] In effect, then, Lord Goff created a kind of recovery that relies on a primary duty without a primary right. This is all but admitted by the notion that the law is 'filling a lacuna' or is '*sui generis*'.[133] In the light of *White v Jones*, solicitors owe duties of care to those who stand to benefit from potential wills though a potential will generates no rights in its intended beneficiaries. This is incoherent.

It must be admitted, however, that there is a strong intuition that it would be erroneous for the law to ignore the apparent injustice in *White v Jones* and like cases. The intuition is likely to have one or more of three possible sources. First, the defendant behaved inappropriately and should not be able to escape responsibility. I accept this, but this is not sufficient to establish that the defendant is responsible *to the claimants in tort*. The intuition would lead to the establishment or strengthening of some kind of regulatory regime in relation to solicitors, but not to liability to the claimants in tort. It is important to recognise that the issue is not whether the defendant should be held responsible at all but whether he should be held responsible *in this fashion*.[134] If the claimants were not

---

[131] *White v Jones* [1995] 2 AC 251 (Lord Keith).

[132] [1982] VR 193, 200 (SC).

[133] Ironically, those who would support Lord Goff's conclusions by rejecting the argument of this ch would have difficulty explaining the lacuna *White v Jones* was said to fill. There is a lacuna because there is no primary right.

[134] *Ibid*, 278 (Lord Mustill).

wronged, they cannot rightly have a claim in tort against the defendant. This intuition, then, cannot be one of corrective justice and is irrelevant to the law of negligence. It should not be ignored, but it should be ignored here.

The second possible source of the intuition that the claimants should have recovered is that the claimants somehow deserved the money. Again, this is not an intuition of corrective justice and does not belong to the law of negligence. The intuition appears to be one of distributive justice. Perhaps this is the best light in which to understand Lord Goff's claim that:

> legacies can be of great importance to individual citizens, providing very often the only opportunity for a citizen to acquire a significant capital sum; or to inherit a house, so providing a secure roof over the heads of himself and his family; or to make special provision for his or her old age. In the course of the hearing before the Appellate Committee Mr. Matheson (who was instructed by the Solicitors Indemnity Fund to represent the appellant solicitors) placed before the Committee a schedule of claims of the character of that in the present case notified to the Solicitors' Indemnity Fund following the judgment of the Court of Appeal below. It is striking that, where the amount of the claim was known, it was, by today's standards, of a comparatively modest size. This perhaps indicates that it is where a testator instructs a small firm of solicitors that mistakes of this kind are most likely to occur, with the result that it tends to be people of modest means, who need the money so badly, who suffer.[135]

But, even as a matter of distributive justice, the outcome in *White v Jones* is highly questionable. It must be remembered that the defendant's negligence made the claimants no worse off than they would have been had their father not decided to alter his will.[136] In that sense, the claimants merely failed to realise a possible benefit. And, as a matter of distributive justice, at least as far as we know, the benefit to the claimants seems undeserved. This is most often so with inheritance. Usually, inheritance is a windfall to the inheritor that depends on the wealth and preference of the testator, not the desert of the beneficiary.[137] The rich give much to their rich children, the poor little to their poor children.

In this light, it is disappointing to observe the haste with which it has been assumed by judges and commentators that justice in cases such as *White v Jones* lies with the claimant. It is said that these are 'plain cases'[138] in which it is self-evident that the claimants should recover if only a legally 'intellectual sustainable means can be found'.[139] But this assertion is not related to corrective justice and is not self-evident even as a matter of distributive justice, which is in any case irrelevant.

[135] *Ibid*, 260.
[136] At least, that is so as far as we know. If in fact they had been made worse off, there may have been other avenues for rectifying this. For example, if the claimants had relied to their detriment on their father's assurance that they would inherit, it might have been possible for the claimants to recover from their father's estate.
[137] I thank Katie Sykes for reminding me of this point.
[138] *Gartside v Sheffield, Young & Ellis* [1983] NZLR 37, 43 (CA) (Cooke J); *White v Jones* [1995] 2 AC 207, 260 (HL) (Lord Goff).
[139] *White v Jones* [1995] 2 AC 207, 276 (HL) (Lord Mustill).

In fact, in both law and morality generally, the reason the wishes of the deceased are given force is the belief that those wishes deserve respect. This is why legislation was required in order to protect the interests of family members thought to be deserving on grounds not related to the testator's intentions or to the will itself.[140] This suggests that the intuition that the claimants should recover in cases such as *White v Jones* is best explained, not in terms of the desert of the intended beneficiaries, but by the intentions of the testator.[141] Surely, if we think that the claimants should recover in *White v Jones*, that is not because we think that they were deserving in themselves; we do not have enough information to make that judgment. Rather, we think that the claimants should inherit their father's money because their father wanted them to have it. If this is so, then it is most natural to interpret *White v Jones* as providing the claimants with a right to the £18,000 because of the intentions of their father with respect to his estate.[142] But the law of wills governs the legal effect of these intentions and the law of wills served to defeat the claimants' father's intentions by dictating that there was no such right—which, of course, is why the problem for the claimants arose in the first place. In *White v Jones*, therefore, the claimants were afforded a right of a kind that arises under the law of wills that, according to the law of wills, does not exist. This is liability for nonfeasance and is not consistent with the underlying structure of the law. Perhaps the law of wills should be changed, but again that is another matter.[143]

---

[140] See eg Inheritance (Provision for Family and Dependants) Act 1975 (UK). One problem with this view is the notion that the wishes of the deceased cannot have moral force because the deceased is deceased. However, see Aristotle, *Nicomachean Ethics* (trans T Irwin, Hackett, Indianapolis, Ind, 1999) 15, [1101a–b]; T Mulgan, 'The Place of the Dead in Liberal Political Philosophy' (1999) 7 *Journal of Political Philosophy* 52; T Nagel, 'Death' (1970) 4 *Nous* 73.

[141] *White v Jones* [1995] 2 AC 207, 260 (HL) (Lord Goff).

[142] Compare *ibid*, 251 (Lord Keith).

[143] However, in an important article, P Benson, 'Should *White v. Jones* Represent Canadian Law: A Return to First Principles' in J Neyers (ed), *Emerging Issues in Tort Law* (Hart Publishing, Oxford, forthcoming 2007) argues that the claimants should have been given standing to sue for the defendant's violation of the testator's contractual rights. According to Benson, as a matter of legal principle the testator is entitled to have his intentions, as expressed in the contract, realised. Because the testator's estate does not usually have an interest in enforcing those intentions (because it would result, for it, only in nominal damages) standing should be given to the persons whose interests normally align with those expressed in the contract between the testator and the defendant. Those are the intended beneficiaries and they should be able to enforce specific performance against the defendant. There is much to be said for this suggestion; however, it appears to suffer from the difficulty that the testator intended to benefit the claimants *through a will*, and that is now impossible. The difficulty becomes more apparent if the intention was to benefit the claimants by transferring something other than money, the family home for instance. Because of the law of wills, that intention cannot be realised by granting a claim in contract against the defendant. Also of high importance in this context is the suggestion in SM Waddams, 'Breach of Contract and Claims by Third Parties' in JW Neyers, E Chamberlain and SGA Pitel (eds), *Emerging Issues in Tort Law* (Hart Publishing, Oxford, forthcoming 2007), that the doctrine of subrogation should allow the claimants to sue the defendant for breach of contract.

III. ECONOMIC LOSS, PRIMARY RIGHTS AND THE GENERAL LAW

I have argued that claimants are unable to recover for relational or pure economic loss, because such losses do not result from the violation of any primary right in the claimant. Hence, the causing of such economic loss is mere nonfeasance. The reason I have insisted that no such rights are violated is that it is impossible to find one in the contemporary positive law: in particular in the law of property, the law of contract or the law of wills. In the relational loss cases, the claimant needs to show that the defendant interfered with a right of a kind that could belong only to the law of property when the law of property tells us that there was no such right. In the building cases, the claimant must appeal to a contractual right that according to the law of contract does not exist. In the disappointed beneficiary cases, the claimant must establish the violation of a right under the will that the law of wills demonstrates does not exist. To allow recovery in these cases is to introduce incoherence into the law as a whole by implicitly recognising property, contractual or testamentary rights 'in tort' while refusing to recognise them in property, contract or wills cases. In the case of disappointed beneficiaries, it is also inconsistent with statute.

However, I have not attempted to justify the contemporary positive law's picture of primary rights. This is because, as outlined in Chapter 2, this book largely accepts the rights base of the law of negligence. It is not my task here to defend the nature and arrangement of those rights. Hence, there are more issues to be solved than are solved here. Crucially, however, they are not issues of tort law. The relevant issues are why the law of property restricts property rights as it does, why contract law does not allow transmissible warranties of quality, and why the law of wills gives actual but not intended beneficiaries a right under the will. Though I doubt that it is difficult to explain the first two of these features, the issue is not explored further here.[144]

The situation may be different with respect to *White v Jones*. One of the reasons offered by Lord Goff for finding liability in that case was the need to protect 'the right of citizens to leave their assets to whom they please'.[145] This, however, can only indirectly justify the result in that case. Consider a variation on the facts. Imagine that *A* intended to alter her will so that the family home would pass to her daughter *B*. *A*'s solicitor negligently failed to alter *A*'s will. The extant will instructs that the family home is to go to *C*. *A* dies. Under the law as it stands, *C* gets title to the family home while *B* gets damages from the

---

[144] Moreover, it should not be assumed that the policies currently utilised to limit economic loss in the law of negligence would be apt in that context. In fact, it should not be assumed that the answer to these questions requires policy at all.

[145] *White v Jones* [1995] 2 AC 207, 260 (HL). This point may also justify the executors of the father's will recovering in contract. See AF Loke, 'Damages to Protect Performance Interest and the Reasonableness Requirement' [2001] *Singapore Journal of Legal Studies* 259. Very similar issues are explored in relation to *Bigg v Queensland Trusts* [1990] 2 Qd R 11 (SC) in C Rickett, 'Extending Equity's Reach through the Mutual Wills Doctrine?' (1991) 54 *MLR* 581.

negligent solicitor to the value of that property. This does not directly protect 'the right of citizens to leave their assets to whom they please'. This would require an alteration to the law of wills such that *B* would gain title to the family home.

White v Jones does protect 'the right of citizens to leave their assets to whom they please' indirectly, however. It does so by providing an incentive for solicitors to process alterations to wills in a timely manner. Perhaps this incentive should be preserved. But it cannot coherently be preserved by tort law, given the general law (in this case the law of wills and contract) as it stands. Moreover, such recovery does not cohere with the structure of the law of negligence. The injustice identified by Lord Goff was inflicted, not on the claimants, but on their father. The claimants, then, were not wronged. On this reasoning, the claimants in *White v Jones* sued as vicarious beneficiaries of a breach of duty owed to another.[146]

In *White v Jones*, it was thought that the easiest way to rectify the potential injustice was to allow recovery in tort. After all, tort law is the common law's Swiss Army knife. But this was not the correct way to rectify the injustice identified by Lord Goff, as the example above clearly reveals. Recall that Lord Goff claimed that, absent liability, 'the only person who may have a valid claim has suffered no loss'. But it is at least arguable that the claimants' father has in fact suffered loss, although that loss is not recognised in tort or contract. The loss here is the failure to have his intentions realised. The law of wills could be altered in order to provide a remedy for that loss, thus rendering *White v Jones* superfluous.[147]

There may be good reasons why the law of wills should not be changed. Whether or not that is so, the law of tort is not the appropriate place to deal with the type of injustice allegedly corrected in *White v Jones*. Moreover, and just as importantly, if the situation in *White v Jones* reveals that the law of wills ought to have been changed, then *White v Jones* has damaged not only the law of tort but also the law of wills. It has damaged the law of wills because, as the case was dealt with in terms of tort law, the court and many subsequent commentators have mislocated and misunderstood the wrong that occurred in that case. The wrong was failing to realise the testator's intentions, not failing to benefit the claimants per se. But it was necessary for the court to ignore the testator and concentrate instead on the claimants, because finding a wrong to the claimants was necessary to justify tort liability. As a result, the problem presented by *White v Jones* is poorly understood. Consequently, it is not widely recognised that *White v Jones* showed that there is a problem with the law of wills that

---

[146] Compare *Palsgraf v Long Island Railroad Co* 162 NE 99, 100 (NY CA 1928) (Cardozo CJ).

[147] See also *White v Jones* [1995] 2 AC 207, 278 (HL) (Lord Mustill). One possible alteration would be to allow those in the position of the claimants to prove the intentions of the testator (as they had to do in *White v Jones*) and have the will rectified in their favour. Compare Administration of Justice Act 1982, s 20. Note, that the fact that the father is dead does not necessarily mean that he cannot suffer loss. See above n140.

requires examination. The attempt to deal with this issue in tort has stunted our understanding of, and at least arguably also the development of, the law as a whole.

IV. ECONOMIC LOSS IN NEGLIGENCE AND THE ECONOMIC TORTS

At first glance, it may appear that the argument of this chapter is inconsistent with recovery in the so-called economic torts. A complete answer to this question can be provided only after a full discussion of the structure of the economic torts. In other words, I could answer this question only by subjecting the economic torts to the kind of analysis applied here to the law of negligence. This is not the appropriate place to conduct that enquiry. However, I have two shorter responses. The first is to deny that a problem for my theory would exist even if the economic torts were inconsistent with the argument presented here. The second is to maintain that some of the economic torts are clearly consistent with the argument of this chapter and that, at least without more analysis, we have no good reason for concluding that the others are not likewise consistent.

On its face, perhaps, at least some of the economic torts allow recovery for nonfeasance in that they appear to allow the claimant to recover damages for factual injuries that do not flow from the violation of any right in the claimant. But the notion that the claimant must base her case on a primary right is perhaps the most fundamental concept of the law of obligations.[148] There can be no obligation without a right. Hence, if the economic torts are inconsistent with the argument of this chapter because they posit wrongs where no rights exist, then the appropriate conclusion is that those areas of the law are problematic, not that my argument is flawed. It is irrational to argue against my view that recovery for economic loss in negligence should not be allowed as it would render the private law incoherent by positing a wrong where there was no right, by pointing out that the private law is incoherent elsewhere. The common lawyer's traditional attachment to the case law should not lead him to say things that do not make sense.

Of course, the economic torts may be inconsistent with my argument in another sense: they may be coherent but based on an understanding that conflicts with the one presented here. But there is no reason a priori to believe that that is the case, and the claim could be established only by conducting the appropriate analysis. That has not been done.

Moreover, some of the economic torts are obviously consistent with the argument here, and in fact lend support to it. Passing off is one example, which protects a property right: the claimant's goodwill. Naturally, there is much work to be done developing our understanding of goodwill and also in explaining

---

[148] See eg P Benson, 'The Idea of a Public Basis of Justification for Contract' (1995) 33 *Osgoode Hall Law Journal* 273, especially 315; P Birks, 'Definition and Division: A Meditation on *Institutes 3.13*' in P Birks (ed), *The Classification of Obligations* (Clarendon Press, Oxford, 1997) 23–4.

important features of the cause of action in passing off that distinguish it from the protection of other property rights—such as the need to prove damage which distinguishes passing off from trespass—but this constitutes no threat to the argument here.

The tort of loss of services is also explicable in terms of the argument here, though it is somewhat more problematic. If *D* injures *S* who is an employee of *M* and *M* suffers loss as a result of the injury to *S*, then an 'ancient remedy'[149] for that loss was available to *M*. This cause of action, while abolished in the United Kingdom,[150] remains available in limited circumstances in Australia,[151] Canada[152] and New Zealand.[153] The historical explanation for the availability of this cause of action is that a master traditionally was viewed as having a *proprietary interest* in the servant allowing the master to sue in trespass. The master could sue for loss of services, then, because he had a property right *in rem* in the servant that the defendant had infringed.[154] Given that it is no longer plausible or acceptable to regard employees as the property of their employers, recovery for loss of services should be abolished, as it has rightly been in the United Kingdom.[155] Again, far from constituting a counterexample to the argument of this chapter, the argument advances our understanding of the tort by revealing its historical basis and also why it is no longer viewed as appropriate.

A similar analysis is apposite for recovery in an action modelled on the priciple *per quod servitium amisit*. The traditional rule here was that a man could sue for the loss of his wife's love, affection and sexual favours, but a woman could not recover for the loss of her husband's. In line with the thesis advanced here, this asymmetry is to be explained by the fact that the wife was regarded as the property of her husband but not vice versa. Hence, the husband could sue for the violation of his property rights while the wife had no property rights and could therefore not sue. While some jurisdictions initially responded to the unacceptable sexism implied by the action by extending recovery to both spouses, the appropriate solution is to abolish the action altogether. Husbands and wives do not own each other. This solution has been achieved by legislation.[156] Again, this tort is no counterexample to the theory presented here, but is most clearly explicable in terms of that theory.

The torts of intimidation, conspiracy, unlawful interference with trade, and inducing breach of contract[157] are more difficult, but it is not obvious that the

---

[149] J Fleming, *The Law of Torts,* 9th edn (LBC Information Services, Sydney, 1998) 752.

[150] Administration of Justice Act 1982; *IRC v Hambrook* [1956] 2 QB 641 (CA).

[151] *Commonwealth Railways v Scott* (1959) 102 CLR 392 (HCA).

[152] *Genereux v Peterson* (1972) 34 DLR (3d) 614 (Ont CA).

[153] *A-G v Wilson* [1973] 2 NZLR 238 (CA).

[154] J Fleming, *The Law of Torts,* 9th edn (LBC Information Services, Sydney, 1998) 751–2.

[155] Alternatively, the interests hitherto protected by the cause of action could by protected by statute if this were desirable.

[156] For commentary, see J Fleming, *The Law of Torts,* 9th edn (LBC Information Services, Sydney, 1998) 719–20.

[157] See, however, P Benson, 'The Basis for Excluding Liability for Economic Loss in Tort Law' in D Owen (ed), *Philosophical Foundations of Tort Law* (Oxford University Press, Oxford, 1995) 455–7.

commission of these torts violates no primary rights in the claimant. That the contrary obtained with respect to the tort of conspiracy was clearly the view of Lord Brampton in *Quinn v Leathem*:[158]

> [T]he real and substantial cause of action is an unlawful conspiracy to molest the plaintiff, a trader in carrying on his business, and by so doing to invade his undoubted right, thus described by Alderson B. in delivering the judgment of the Exchequer Chamber in *Hilton v. Eckersley*[159]:
>
>> 'Primâ facie it is the privilege of a trader in a free country in all matters not contrary to law to regulate his own mode of carrying it on according to his own discretion and choice. If the law has in any matter regulated or restrained his mode of doing this, the law must be obeyed. But no power short of the general law ought to restrain his free discretion.'
>
> To this I would add the emphatic expression of the Lord Chancellor, Lord Halsbury, in the *Mogul Case*[160]: 'All are free to trade upon what terms they will'; and of Lord Bramwell, who in *Reg. v. Druitt*,[161] in a passage quoted by Lord Halsbury in the same case, said: 'The liberty of a man's mind and will to say how he should bestow himself and his means, his talents and his industry, was as much a subject of the law's protection as was that of his body.'

Of course, this account is problematic, particularly in its apparent confusion of claim rights and liberties. But it is nevertheless evidence that it would be premature to conclude from the fact that it is not apparent which, if any, primary right the law of conspiracy protects, that there is no such right.

No doubt, much more needs to be said about these torts before we are able to say with certainly what primary right or rights these torts protect. If we wish to develop our understanding of the economic torts, then, instead of rejecting the argument of this chapter, we should attempt to understand those torts in terms of the primary rights they protect. It is remarkable that this project has only barely begun.[162] But we can immediately say that it is at least premature to maintain that there are no such rights and, at this point, the assertion would simply beg the question against the thesis advanced here.

---

[158] [1901] AC 495, 525–6 (HL) (citations omitted).

[159] (1855) 6 E & B 74, 119 ER 781, 792.

[160] *Mogul Steamship Co Ltd v McGregor Gow & Co* [1892] AC 25 (HL).

[161] (1967) 10 Cox CC 592, 600.

[162] To my knowledge, the only attempt is P Benson, 'The Basis for Excluding Liability for Economic Loss in Tort Law' in D Owen (ed), *Philosophical Foundations of Tort Law* (Oxford University Press, Oxford, 1995) 455–7, and only inducing breach of contract is examined. Remarkably, T Weir, *Economic Torts* (Clarendon Press, Oxford, 1997) 29 discourages the analysis, though perhaps Weir's argument is merely that the economic torts should not be understood in terms of certain *kinds of* rights. See also AP Simester and W Chan, 'Inducing Breach of Contract: One Tort or Two?' [2004] *CLJ* 132 who attempt to justify the tort of inducing breach of contract in terms of distributive justice. However, the argument could be translated in terms of corrective justice, and indeed would be more forceful in that light, even in its own terms.

V. CONCLUSION

We began this chapter with the assertion that the principled approach is unacceptable because it cannot prevent indeterminate liability for economic loss. We now see that this view is unfounded. The principled approach has no difficulty with indeterminate liability. In fact, not surprisingly, due to its emancipation from policy, it is more constrained than the modern law. This conclusion is extremely ironic, given that the modern law's focus on policy is perhaps primarily motivated to restrict the recovery of economic loss beyond that believed allowed by the principled approach. But this is a confusion. Again, we see the enormous superiority of the principled over the modern approaches.[163]

---

[163] It is important to remember at this point that the issue is the ability of the approaches to settle disputes in accordance with a compelling conception of justice. Of course, we may disagree with the outcomes of the principled approach (because we do not think that corrective justice is appropriate in a particular context, for instance), and we are entitled to attempt to reform it *equally with all citizens* through our elected representatives and statute law.

8

Negligent Misrepresentation and Assumption of Responsibility

A S INDICATED IN Chapter 1, part of the story told of the law of negligence runs as follows. For reasons of policy, the law of negligence had always prevented recovery for relational and pure economic loss. Traditionally, the law adopted an absolute exclusionary rule. However, eventually it became clear that this absolute rule was unsustainable, and, in *Hedley Byrne & Co Ltd v Heller & Partners Ltd*,[1] the House of Lords announced that it would restrict the ambit of the exclusionary rule to permit some claims for pure economic loss.

On its face, this cuts against the argument of the last chapter. However, one must remember that no objection to the recovery of economic loss per se was stated in that chapter. My argument was that most economic losses are irrecoverable because they do not flow from a violation of a right in the claimant. Hence, recovery for loss caused by a negligent misrepresentation is unproblematic if it responds to the violation of a right in the claimant. The task is to identify that right.

In this chapter, I argue that the right protected by the so-called tort of negligent misrepresentation is based on the defendant's consent. It is a right given by the defendant to the claimant, rather than a right that the claimant possesses in virtue of being a person or of owning property. Hence, the right more closely resembles primary rights in contract law than bodily integrity or property rights. The conclusion is that the so-called tort of negligent misrepresentation does not rightly belong to the law of negligence and that it should be renamed better to reflect its true basis.

I begin by exploring the approach to negligent misrepresentation based on the general law of negligence: 'the negligence model'.[2] On its face, one would expect there to be three negligence models: one based on the principled approach, one on the *Anns* approach and one on the incremental approach. Tellingly, however, there is no principled negligence model. Moreover, mirroring the

---

[1] [1964] AC 465 (HL).

[2] In the following, I speak of the general or ordinary law of negligence. By 'ordinary law of negligence' I mean the law that applies outside negligent misrepresentation, to personal injury and property damage for instance. So that I do not beg the question against my opponents, for the sake of this argument I do not assume that the ordinary law is the principled approach.

discussion in Chapters 5 and 7, we will see that the *Anns* approach mires courts in concerns that they are not equipped to deal with and that the incremental approach either fails to provide justifications for decisions or collapses into the *Anns* test. I explore those issues before turning to the alternative understanding of negligent misrepresentation that I call 'the assumption of responsibility model'.

I. THE NEGLIGENCE MODEL

A. *Candler v Crane Christmas & Co*[3]

The claimant relied on a representation made by the defendants as to the financial viability of a mining company. In reliance on this representation, the claimant invested in the company. Within a year, the mining company had collapsed and the claimant had lost his investment. The representation had been negligently made and presented the company in an unrealistically favourable light.

Denning LJ's decision in *Candler* is one of the landmarks of twentieth century tort jurisprudence. Though written in dissent, it has had an enormous impact on the way we conceive the cause of action in negligent misrepresentation. In particular, three key elements of Denning LJ's judgment have echoed through subsequent jurisprudence.

First, Denning LJ characterised the claimant's potential cause of action as lying in negligence.[4] Accordingly, his Lordship saw the central issue as being whether the defendants owed the claimant a duty of care.[5] Further, Denning LJ held that it was significant that the defendants 'prepared and put before [the claimant] these accounts, knowing that [the claimant] was going to be guided by them in making an investment in the company'.[6] The reference to the defendants' knowledge indicates that the defendants' conduct fell below the appropriate standard of care. Moreover, Denning LJ argued that the cause of action protects foreseeable reliance. Hence, the defendants owed a duty 'to any third person to whom they themselves show the accounts, or to whom they know their employer is going to show the accounts, so as to induce him to invest money or take some other action on them'.[7]

Secondly, reinforcing the above, Denning LJ saw the claimant's cause of action as arising out of *Donoghue v Stevenson*.[8] If there is proximity between the parties, determined by Lord Atkin's neighbour test, then a duty of care

---

[3] [1951] 2 KB 164 (CA).
[4] *Ibid*, 176.
[5] *Ibid*.
[6] *Ibid*.
[7] *Ibid*, 180–1.
[8] *M'Alister (or Donoghue) (Pauper) v Stevenson* [1932] AC 562 (HL Sc).

arises.[9] Furthermore, Denning LJ argued in favour of liability by rejecting the suggestion that *Donoghue v Stevenson* does not apply to negligent misrepresentations.[10]

Thirdly, Denning LJ claimed that the scope of liability must be limited by special rules. These were that a duty of care is owed only by defendants with 'special knowledge and skill',[11] and that, in order to enjoy a duty of care, the claimant must rely on the statement in a manner consistent with the purpose for which it was made.[12] Moreover, though Denning LJ suggested that prima facie the defendant owed a duty to those who foreseeably relied on the statement, this was qualified:

> I do not think the duty can be extended . . . so as to include strangers of whom [the defendants] have heard nothing and to whom their employer without their knowledge may choose to show their accounts. Once the [claimants] have handed their accounts to [a third party] they are not, as a rule, responsible for what he does with them without their knowledge or consent.[13]

This departs from the principle of reasonable foreseeability, as it may readily be foreseeable that the statement will be shown to third parties who will rely on it without the defendant's knowledge or consent. Why should the defendant escape liability in such circumstances? Denning LJ's answer was that limiting liability in terms of foreseeability alone would produce indeterminate liability.[14] Hence, liability is restricted beyond principle for reasons of policy.

Importantly, indeterminate liability becomes an issue because the cause of action is characterised as a species of negligence liability. Were there such a thing, a principled negligence approach to negligent misrepresentation would allow recovery if the defendant created an unreasonable risk that materialised in the claimant's injury. This is almost universally believed to cast the net of liability too widely.[15] However, the need to construct special rules to avoid indeterminate liability did not lead Denning LJ to doubt that the cause of action for negligent misrepresentation was actually a species of negligence liability or that it was based on *Donoghue v Stevenson*. His Lordship regarded it merely as an instance of negligence liability where special rules should apply.[16]

In summary: in Denning LJ's view, the cause of action in negligent misrepresentation is a species of negligence liability based on *Donoghue v Stevenson* to which special rules apply for reasons of policy. Although Denning LJ was

[9] *Candler v Crane Christmas & Co* [1951] 2 KB 164, 179 (CA).
[10] *Ibid.*
[11] *Ibid*, 179–80.
[12] *Ibid*, 182–3.
[13] *Ibid*, 181.
[14] *Ibid*, 183–4.
[15] See eg J Fleming, *The Law of Torts,* 9th edn (LBC Information Services, Sydney, 1998) 189–90. However, see C Witting, 'Justifying Liability to Third Parties for Negligent Misstatements' (2000) 20 *OJLS* 615.
[16] Lord Denning, of course, did not think much of principle in any case. See *Lamb v Camden London BC* [1981] 1 QB 625, 636–7 (CA) and the discussion of this case in ch 4.

writing in dissent, the power of his judgment and the apparent justice of his conclusions seemed undeniable. As a result, many jurisdictions have followed Denning LJ's reasoning.

B. The *Anns* Test and Negligent Misrepresentation

Denning LJ's judgment in *Candler* has been closely followed in Canada. In *Hercules Managements v Ernst & Young*,[17] the defendant firm of accountants performed an audit of a third party company's financial statements for the company's AGM. The claimant shareholders of the company relied on this audit in choosing to invest in the company. It was alleged that the audit was conducted negligently and the claimants suffered detrimental reliance on the audit reports. However, the defendant did not prepare the reports to facilitate investment decisions of this kind.

Writing for a unanimous Supreme Court of Canada, La Forest J maintained that the cause of action for negligent misrepresentation belongs entirely within the law of negligence. In the Canada of the day, this meant that the *Anns* test was to be applied.[18] However, La Forest J also noted—in accordance with the argument in Chapter 5—that proximity under the *Anns* test is a 'vacuous' notion.[19] Hence, 'proximity' needed to be given a specific meaning that was appropriate in this context. La Forest J argued that, in negligent misrepresentation cases, proximity was closely aligned with reliance, and concluded that a relationship of proximity would exist if the claimant's reliance were reasonably foreseeable and reasonable.[20]

However, reliance is generally irrelevant in the law of negligence. Hence, the addition of reliance indicates that 'proximity' in this context has a different meaning from 'proximity' in the general law of negligence, a conclusion that undermines La Forest J's claim that his approach to negligent misrepresentation is part of the ordinary law of negligence.

It is possible to reply that the claimant's reliance is essential, because the defendant's negligence in making the statement could not have been the cause of the claimant's loss unless the claimant relied on the statement. This reply fails for two reasons. First, it is unrelated to the duty of care and confuses duty with factual causation. A defendant may be in a relationship of proximity with someone he does not injure. Secondly, the claimant's reliance is not necessary for factual causation. For instance, the claimant's loss may be caused through the reliance of a third party. Moreover, as that loss may be perfectly foreseeable, there is no reason to deny that the parties are in a relationship of proximity—no reason, that is, barring the desire to ensure that the defendant escape liability.

---

[17] [1997] 2 SCR 165.
[18] *Ibid*, 184–6.
[19] *Ibid*, 187.
[20] *Ibid*, 187–8.

Again, we are forced to the conclusion that the modern law uses 'proximity' as a term of art with an eye firmly fixed on the wanted result.

La Forest J also departed from the law's ordinary approach by insisting that the parties are in a relationship of proximity only if the claimant's reliance was reasonable. There is no equivalent to this in the ordinary law of negligence. There, if the claimant acts unreasonably she may be contributorily negligent— a partial defence not defeating the duty of care. Moreover, if her behaviour was so unreasonable that the defendant could not reasonably have foreseen it, then her injury may be remote. Again, though, that would not show that there was no relationship of proximity between the claimant and the defendant. Accordingly, despite La Forest J's claims, *Hercules* treated negligent misrepresentation as a special pocket of liability that does not fit into the ordinary law of negligence.[21]

In *Hercules* itself, La Forest J found that the claimant's reliance was both reasonably foreseeable and reasonable. Accordingly, his Honour concluded that the parties were in a relationship of proximity.[22] However, La Forest J felt that policy dictated that the claimant fail and so he applied the second stage of the *Anns* test to negative the duty of care.

La Forest J noted that imposing liability on the defendant would encourage auditors to take care in their work (this is the standard deterrence argument).[23] However, his Honour insisted that this concern was outweighed by the fact that imposing liability on auditors in such circumstances would cause premiums for auditors' liability insurance to rise, and that this would have two deleterious consequences. First, the cost of supplying accounting services would increase, thereby reducing the supply of accounting services as marginal companies would be driven to the wall. Secondly, the accounting firms would pass their increased costs onto their customers, thus increasing the cost of accounting services to the public.[24]

On the face of it, these arguments are in tension with each other. If the costs can be passed onto customers, why will firms be driven to the wall?[25] More importantly, La Forest J's arguments rely on the view that the quantum and cost of accounting services in the Canada of the day led to greater efficiency than would have occurred if liability had been imposed. But it is unclear how La Forest J came to that conclusion. In particular, it is not clear how La Forest J decided that the policies identified outweigh the deterrence argument. That is, it is not clear how to balance the quantum and cost of accounting services against the quality of those services. Moreover, one would have expected an economist to argue that the market determines the efficient quantum and cost of accounting services. Hence, whatever the shape of liability, the market for accounting

---

[21] Compare *ibid*, 186.
[22] *Ibid*, 200–2.
[23] *Ibid*, 194.
[24] *Ibid*, 194–5.
[25] I am grateful to Donna Wynd for raising this issue.

services will clear at the efficient point.[26] None of this is to say that La Forest J's view of the economic consequences of liability was necessarily mistaken. The problem is not that La Forest J was wrong, but that we have no idea whether he was right or wrong. Certainly, those reading the judgment in *Hercules* are not given sufficient information to make this decision. But that shows that La Forest J also lacked this information.[27] If such considerations are to play so decisive a role in the law, then we must radically reform legal procedure so that sensible conclusions on social and economic policy can be reached.[28]

Finally, even if we accept La Forest J's economic arguments, it is opaque how those concerns should be balanced against other non-economic factors such as corrective justice and fairness to the claimant. And that must remain unclear, as the correct balancing is entirely a product of one's political viewpoint, which judges do not adduce in their judgments and on which they should not base their judgments. Again, the appeal to policy is obscurantist.

These problems are amplified by the also unanimous judgment of the same Court in *Edgeworth Construction Ltd v M D Lea & Associates Ltd.*[29] The defendant engineers provided the Crown with specifications relating to the construction of a roadway. The claimant submitted to the Crown a successful tender to build the road. However, the claimant suffered loss in reliance on the specifications provided by the defendant. In *Edgeworth*, McLachlin J, La Forest J concurring, decided that the claimant should succeed.

Again, the claimant's reliance was said to be reasonable and reasonably foreseeable. Hence, as in *Hercules*, the real issue for the Court was one of policy. McLachlin J argued that the most pressing concern was that finding for the defendant would mean that tenderers would not be able to rely on specifications provided by engineers, and hence would have to conduct their own engineering work. Accordingly, the engineering job would have to be done twice, with much financial and opportunity cost.[30]

But it is unclear why a similar argument did not apply in *Hercules*. In fact, the argument seems stronger there. This is because *Hercules* indicates that investors must often conduct their own investigations into the financial viability of the

---

[26] This is essentially the point made in R Coase, 'The Problem of Social Cost' (1960) 1 *Journal of Law and Economics* 1.

[27] I am told that this was because counsel in the case, against the repeated prompting of La Forest J, were perverse enough to stick to the legal arguments and refused to be drawn into matters of policy.

[28] I have explored these issues in detail in A Beever, 'Particularism and Prejudice in the Law of Tort' (2003) 11 *Tort Law Review* 146, 161–5.

[29] [1993] 3 SCR 206.

[30] *Ibid*, 220–1. Again, this demonstrates that Cooke P was right to claim that there is no real difference between the various formulations of the *Anns* test. *South Pacific Manufacturing Co Ltd v New Zealand Security Consultants & Investigations Ltd* [1992] 2 NZLR 282, 294 (CA). Officially, in the Canada of the day, policy functioned only to negative a prima facie duty of care. Here, however, policy functions as a reason for not negativing a duty of care for other reasons of policy. There is no real difference between this and the notion that policy can create a duty of care, given that any conceivable injury can pass the first stage of the *Anns* test.

companies in which they invest, but they will frequently be unable to do this with any accuracy as they will not have access to the company's accounts. If investors cannot rely on audit reports, then how are they to ascertain the wisdom of their investments? While, with respect to each individual case, the economic waste may be smaller in investment cases than in engineering cases, the overall economic wastage is likely to be much higher in relation to investors than to construction firms.

Moreover, it is far from clear that imposing liability in *Edgeworth* would lead to efficiency. *Edgeworth* dictates that engineers are deemed to have guaranteed the accuracy of specifications they provide to third parties to all those they can reasonably foresee will rely on those specifications. Engineers will charge the third party for that guarantee and those costs will be passed on to others, probably including those in the position of the claimant in *Edgeworth*. It should not be assumed that this will be more efficient than allowing the parties to allocate their risks as they see fit. In fact, it appears that the result in *Edgeworth* will be efficient only if it simulates the arrangement for which the parties would have contracted were they rational agents and were transaction costs sufficiently low. But this means that, unless there is reason to think that the parties were not able to contract in their best interests, and we are given no reason to think that they were not, the efficient result is to leave tort law out of the picture. Moreover, given that future parties are able to contract in the light of the result in *Edgeworth*, that case cannot secure the policy concerns that motivated the Court.[31] Again, the point is not that the policy concerns raised in *Edgeworth* were necessarily mistaken, but that the judgment does not give enough information to decide this issue. Neither trials nor appeals are appropriate fora in which to conduct these kinds of enquiries. At least in law, the use of policy leads to obscurantism.

Furthermore, and crucially, on the approach of the Supreme Court of Canada, the only significant stage in the enquiry is the second stage of the *Anns* test: policy. Though the claimants in *Hercules* and *Edgeworth* were prima facie in the same legal position, the Court utilised policy to reach opposite results. Coupled with the inadequacy of the Court's policy arguments, this is a very significant problem.

The New Zealand Court of Appeal attempted to reduce the reliance on policy in *A-G v Carter*.[32] Writing for the Court, Tipping J accepted La Forest J's position in *Hercules* that a prima facie duty of care would exist only if the claimant's reliance was both reasonable and reasonably foreseeable.[33] However, Tipping J defined reasonable reliance more narrowly than did La Forest J. Tipping J insisted that, if a defendant makes a statement for one purpose, then any reliance on that statement for a different purpose is unreasonable. Moreover, his Honour

---

[31] R Coase, 'The Problem of Social Cost' (1960) 1 *Journal of Law and Economics* 1, 9–10.
[32] [2003] 2 NZLR 160 (CA).
[33] *Ibid*, 168.

asserted that it is not reasonable for a person to rely on a statement unless the statement was made for the benefit of that person.[34]

However, it is often reasonable to rely on statements in the relevant circumstances. In *Carter*, the claimant purchased a vessel, the *Nivanga*, from a third party. The claimant did so in the light of certificates issued by the Marine Division of the Ministry of Transport and Marine and Industrial Safety Inspection Services Ltd in accordance with section 206 of the Shipping and Seamen Act 1952 (NZ). The certificates indicated that the vessel was safe and seaworthy. The claimant alleged that he suffered loss in reliance on the negligently issued certificates. The Court found that the purpose of the Act, and hence the requirement in the Act to inspect vessels and issue certificates, is to ensure that waterborne vessels are safe and seaworthy. It is not to aid investment decisions. Hence, the Court argued that the claimant did not rely on the certificates in accordance with the purpose for which the certificates were made, and therefore the claimant's reliance on the certificates was unreasonable and the claimant could not recover. But the claimant's reliance was perfectly reasonable. In fact, it would have been irrational for the claimant not to have considered the certificates.

Similarly, if an auditor prepares a glowing report into a publicly listed company for purposes of the company's AGM, then it is reasonable for a member of the public to rely on that report (perhaps not in isolation) when deciding whether to invest in that company. In fact, it would be irrational not to do so. This is so whether or not the investor was a shareholder of the company at the time of the AGM, and hence whether or not the investor was a member of the class of persons for whom the report was prepared. To insist, as did the New Zealand Court of Appeal in *Carter*, that such reliance is unreasonable is to define 'unreasonableness' with reference to the desired outcome of the case: the claimant's reliance is said to be 'unreasonable', not because it was actually unreasonable, but because the court feels that the claimant should lose. Hence, the 'unreasonableness' of the claimant's reliance cannot *argue* against the imposition of liability and is therefore conceptually redundant. In other words, when 'unreasonable' is used in this manner, it is as vacuous as 'proximity'.

Some are inclined to reject this conclusion on the basis of the somewhat related remarks of La Forest J in *London Drugs Ltd v Kuehne & Nagel International Ltd.*[35] In that case, La Forest J distinguished 'mere reliance in fact and reasonable reliance on the employee's pocket-book'.[36] Hence, on this view, the question is not whether it was reasonable for the claimant to rely on the statement, but whether it was reasonable for the claimant to expect the defen-

[34] [2003] 2 NZLR 160 (CA), 169.

[35] [1992] 3 SCR 299. See eg *Williams v Natural Life Health Foods Ltd* [1998] 1 WLR 830, 836–7 (HL) (Lord Steyn); R Cooke, *Turning Points of the Common Law* (Sweet & Maxwell, London, 1997) 19–22.

[36] [1992] 3 SCR 299, 387. See also *Edgeworth Construction Ltd v M D Lea & Associates Ltd* [1993] 3 SCR 206, 210.

dant to compensate her for her, perhaps reasonable, detrimental reliance on the statement. Conceivably, then, it is possible to concede that the claimants' reliance may have been reasonable in fact, but insist that it would not be reasonable for the claimants to rely on the defendant's pocket book.

But this is an assertion rather than an argument. The suggestion is that, while it may have been reasonable for the claimant to have relied on the defendant's statement, it is not reasonable for the claimant to expect to be compensated by the defendant for that reliance. But we need to be shown *why* that expectation is unreasonable. Given the reasonableness and reasonable foreseeability of the claimant's reliance on the statement, the negligence model is incapable of answering this question.

In fact, then, although *Carter* promised to reduce the need for courts to rely on nebulous policy concerns in making decisions by more narrowly defining reasonable reliance, it adopts an understanding of reasonableness that is itself nebulous. The *Anns* test is inherently flawed. It is possible to hide its flaws only by shifting them from one stage of the test to the other.

I conclude, then, that the *Anns* approach is incapable adequately of capturing the so-called tort of negligent misrepresentation.

C. The Incremental Approach and Negligent Misrepresentation

The incremental approach does no better than the *Anns* test in elucidating liability for negligent misrepresentation. For instance, in *Caparo Industries v Dickman*,[37] the House of Lords ruled that a claimant was not entitled to rely on a statement for a purpose different from that for which the statement was made.[38] However, their Lordships were unable to elucidate any compelling reasons for that limitation. The claimant's case was rejected on the ground that it was not 'fair, just, and reasonable' to impose liability on the defendant.[39] Again, this is just an assertion. Prima facie, if negligent misrepresentation belongs to the law of negligence and the claimant's injury was reasonably foreseeable, then it would seem fair, just and reasonable to hold the defendant liable.[40] It seems clear, as John Fleming argues, that the Court's appeal to 'fair, just, and reasonable' is merely a smokescreen for the judges' sense of public policy.[41]

In *Esanda Finance Corp Ltd v Peat Marwick Hungerfords*,[42] the claimant, in reliance on an audit produced by the defendant, lent money to third party

[37] [1990] 2 AC 605 (HL).
[38] Eg *ibid*, 624 (Lord Bridge), 644–7 (Lord Oliver).
[39] *Ibid*, 618 (Lord Bridge).
[40] C Witting, 'Justifying Liability to Third Parties for Negligent Misstatements' (2000) 20 *OJLS* 615.
[41] J Fleming, *The Law of Torts,* 9th edn (LBC Information Services, Sydney, 1998) 153–4. Alternatively, their Lordships could be read as implicitly adopting the assumption of responsibility model as discussed below. However, as we will see, their Lordships explicitly rejected that model.
[42] (1997) 188 CLR 241 (HCA).

companies which failed and went into liquidation. In the High Court of Australia, Brennan, Dawson, Toohey and Gaudron JJ denied the claimant's case entirely on the basis of authority that was itself not justified.[43] While this makes sense on the incremental approach, it fails to justify the Court's position. On the other hand, McHugh J maintained that the claimant must not recover, as such would increase the cost of auditing services, decrease the supply of auditing services thus decreasing competition, lead to a reduction in the standard of the services and increase the likelihood and length of litigation. Moreover, McHugh J maintained that people in the position of the claimant are in a better position to absorb such losses than those in the position of the defendant and that people in the position of the claimant would have an indirect remedy against the liquidator of the failed company.[44] Appeal to these concerns is objectionable for the same reasons as discussed above: the Court is not in a position to make accurate judgments about these matters, and these are political decisions that are not within the Court's jurisdiction. Moreover, we again see that, to the extent that it attempts to provide justifications, the incremental approach collapses into the *Anns* test.

In conclusion, neither the *Anns* test nor the incremental approach to negligent misrepresentation justifies the position on negligent misrepresentation actually taken by Commonwealth courts. In consequence, both approaches end up relying almost exclusively on a politically controversial and poorly articulated set of policy concerns. As I now argue, these problems reflect a deeper difficulty: the negligence model of negligent misrepresentation is irreparably flawed at its base.

D. Rejection of the Negligence Model

In order to comprehend the cause of action known as negligent misrepresentation, it is necessary to identify the primary right or rights it protects. In order to do so, it will help first to elucidate what that primary right cannot be.

First, the right cannot be a right to rely on statements. There is no tort of innocent misrepresentation. Secondly, the right cannot be created by the claimant's decision to rely. That would allow the claimant unilaterally to impose an obligation on the defendant merely by choosing to rely.[45] Thirdly, the primary right cannot be some esoteric right not to be injured in reliance on negligently made statements. As we have seen many times, not all factual injuries are legally significant, even if caused by negligence. There is, for example, no cause of action for negligently induced breaches of contract. Moreover, as we

---

[43] (1997) 188 CLR 241–52 (Brennan J), 257–8 (Dawson J), 260–2 (Toohey and Gaudron JJ).

[44] *Ibid*, 272–89. See also ibid, 297–308 (Gummow J).

[45] B Feldthusen, *Economic Negligence,* 4th edn (Carswell, Scarborough, 2000) 45 criticises La Forest J's argument in *Hercules* for failing to attend to this point.

have seen in this chapter, Commonwealth courts do not allow recovery for merely reasonably foreseeable reliance on negligently made statements.

Fourthly, the right is usually not a property right or a right in the claimant's person. In order to see this point, it is necessary to distinguish two kinds of cases. In the first type of case, I negligently utter a statement that causes you to suffer personal injury or property damage. For instance, I tell you that a bridge is safe to drive over when I should know that it is not and the bridge collapses, injuring you and destroying your vehicle. In the second kind of case, I negligently utter a statement that causes you to suffer factual loss that is no violation of your person or property rights. For example, I negligently state that a certain company presents a good investment opportunity and you choose to invest in that company by transferring some of the value of a chose in action (bank account) in return for other choses in action (shares). Due to the weakness of the company, the value of the shares falls and you suffer factual loss. However, in making the statement, I did not interfere with your bank account, with your shares, or with any other property rights you possess. Simply, the shares are no longer worth what you paid for them, but this is no more an interference with your property rights in the shares than is a stock market crash.

The ordinary law of negligence applies to the first kind of case. The example given is similar to *Donoghue v Stevenson* itself. There, the claimant's injury arose because she chose to drink the ginger beer. Moreover, she assumed that the ginger beer would be safe because it was marketed as a beverage. She would not have been able to recover had she knowingly chosen to drink rat poison. But there is no temptation to describe *Donoghue v Stevenson* as a negligent misrepresentation case. Similarly, though your personal injury and property damage in the first example above are caused by your reliance on my representation, this should not be treated as a negligent misrepresentation case.[46]

Again, this indicates that 'negligent misrepresentation' is a misleading name for the cause of action. As we saw in previous sections of this chapter, not all injuries caused by negligently made representations are actionable and, as we have now discovered, not all actionable injuries caused by negligently made statements are actionable as negligent misrepresentations. The name of the cause of action is inappropriate. Moreover, as we also discovered with respect to economic loss, the law implicitly responds to differences in underlying primary rights. Because personal injury and property damage caused by negligent misrepresentations violate primary rights that the claimant possesses independently of the making of the representation, those injuries are remedied by the ordinary law of negligence, not by the law of negligent misrepresentation. Conversely, because purely economic losses caused by negligent misstatements violate no right that the claimant possesses independently of the making of the statement, the enquiry into the cause of action known as negligent misrepresentation

---

[46] Compare *Dutton v Bognor Regis Urban District Council* [1972] 1 QB 373, 410 (QBD) (Stamp LJ).

focuses on the circumstances of the making of the statement in order to determine whether the claimant gained a primary right. The distinction between the
ordinary law of negligence and the law of negligent misrepresentation is explicable only in terms of the primary rights protected by those areas of the law. All
this is obscured by the common law's focus on policy and remedies.

In the relevant cases, then, the primary right in the claimant violated by the
defendant must have been created by the defendant's making of the statement.
Unlike rights to the person and to property, therefore, the right to rely on a statement is derived from the defendant: it is a right somehow given to the claimant
by the defendant. Now, at common law, rights are given to another only if it is
reasonable to interpret, on an objective test, the giver as intending to furnish
those rights. There must be evidence of a donative intention. The law does not
presume a gift. Therefore, it is not sufficient merely that the defendant made the
statement. The defendant must both make the statement and provide a right to
the claimant to rely on the statement. In other words, there must be an assumption of responsibility.

This means that negligent misrepresentation does not in fact belong to the
ordinary law of negligence. Instead, it is a form of liability that responds to the
violation of assumed or consented to obligations. I call this 'the assumption of
responsibility model' of negligent misrepresentation and examine it now.

II. THE ASSUMPTION OF RESPONSIBILITY MODEL

A. The Judgments in *Hedley Byrne*

The defendant made representations containing disclaimers of responsibility to
the claimant in respect of the creditworthiness of a third party company. It was
alleged that the representations were made negligently and that the claimant
suffered loss as a result of its reliance on the representations.

Clearly, Denning LJ's decision in *Candler* had an enormous impact on the
judgments in *Hedley Byrne*. Lords Hodson and Pearce approvingly referred to
Denning LJ's reasoning.[47] Moreover, all the Lords characterised the claimant's
potential cause of action as lying in negligence,[48] and Lord Morris explicitly
applied the structure of negligence liability to the case.[49] Lords Devlin and
Pearce saw the cause of action for negligent misrepresentation as connected to
Donoghue v Stevenson,[50] and Lord Reid argued in favour of liability on the

---

[47] *Hedley Byrne & Co Ltd v Heller & Partners Ltd* [1964] AC 465, 509 (Lord Hodson), 538 (Lord
Pearce).
[48] *Ibid*, 481, 489 (Lord Reid), 498 (Lord Morris), 511 (Lord Hodson), 515–17, 528 (Lord Devlin),
536 (Lord Pearce).
[49] *Ibid*, 493. However, Lord Morris also argued that the claimant did not have to prove that the
defendant was negligent: *ibid*, 493.
[50] *Hedley Byrne & Co Ltd v Heller & Partners Ltd* [1964] AC 465, 524–5 (Lord Devlin), 536
(Lord Pearce).

ground that a relationship of proximity existed between the parties.[51] Lords
Reid and Morris referred to the defendant's knowledge of the claimant's future
reliance as a reason for imposing liability, indicating that the defendant had
fallen below the standard of care. Furthermore, Lord Morris maintained that
special rules must be applied limiting the duty of care to those with special
skills,[52] and Lord Pearce referred to the need to limit the duty of care to prevent
indeterminate liability.[53]

So far, then, the analysis in *Hedley Byrne* appears to mirror closely the dissenting judgment of Denning LJ in *Candler.* But there was another strand to
their Lordships' judgments. All the Law Lords argued that a duty of care arises
out of an assumption of responsibility by the defendant to the claimant.[54]
Hence, Lord Devlin maintained that the 'essence' of the cause of action was an
assumption of responsibility,[55] and Lord Reid explicitly denied that negligence
coupled with reasonable foreseeability was sufficient to ground a cause of
action.[56] This is in tension with Denning LJ's claim that prima facie a duty of
care is owed if the claimant's reliance was reasonably foreseeable. Moreover,
Lords Hodson and Devlin stressed the connection between contract and the
cause of action for negligent misrepresentation.[57] Lord Devlin maintained that
the relevant duty is 'a responsibility that is voluntarily accepted or undertaken',[58] and involves 'a relationship that is equivalent to contract',[59] and his
Lordship described the duty as arising 'where there is an assumption of responsibility in circumstances in which, but for the absence of consideration, there
would be a contract'.[60] On this view, the basis of liability is not negligence per
se but the defendant's consent.[61] Furthermore, Lords Reid and Pearce implied
that the cause of action was not based on *Donoghue v Stevenson.*[62] Finally, Lord

[51] *Ibid,* 482.
[52] *Ibid,* 502–3.
[53] *Ibid,* 533–4, 537.
[54] *Ibid* 487 (Lord Reid), 494 (Lord Morris), 505 (Lord Hodson), 528–32 (Lord Devlin), 533 (Lord
Pearce).
[55] *Ibid,* 531.
[56] *Ibid,* 483.
[57] *Ibid,* 508 (Lord Hodson) 532–3 (Lord Devlin).
[58] *Ibid,* 529.
[59] *Ibid,* 530.
[60] *Ibid,* 529. This view was restated by Lord Steyn in *Williams v Natural Life Health Foods Ltd*
[1998] 1 WLR 830, 836–8 (HL).
[61] R Grantham and C Rickett, 'Directors' "Tortious" Liability: Contract, Tort or Company
Law?' (1999) 62 *MLR* 133, 135–7; R Grantham and C Rickett, *Enrichment and Restitution in New
Zealand* (Hart Publishing, Oxford, 2000) 262–4. K Barker, 'Unreliable Assumptions in the Modern
Law of Negligence' (1993) 109 *LQR* 461, 465 argues that, as this suggestion is 'inconsistent with the
spirit of our existing law', Lord Devlin could not have intended it. I doubt this, but in any event we
are concerned not with the workings of Lord Devlin's mind but in the most reasonable way to interpret what Lord Devlin said. Given the references to voluntariness and contract, it is most reasonable
to interpret Lord Devlin as stating that the cause of action lies in the defendant's consent.
[62] *Hedley Byrne & Co Ltd v Heller & Partners Ltd* [1964] AC 465, 482 (Lord Reid), 539 (Lord
Pearce). This view is echoed by Lord Devlin: *ibid,* 515–16.

Devlin rejected the view that the duty of care should be restricted to those with special skills.[63]

According to this strand of their Lordships' judgments, liability for negligent misrepresentation is not imposed by the law as in the ordinary law of negligence, but is assumed as in contract. The basis of the defendant's potential liability is that he consented to something that placed him under an obligation that he did not then meet.[64]

I have not argued that the House of Lords in *Hedley Byrne* adopted the assumption of responsibility model rather than the negligence model. Rather, with the exception of Lord Devlin, their Lordships adopted both models.[65] To that extent, *Hedley Byrne* does not present a consistent exposition of the basis of liability. Nor have more recent cases settled this matter. For instance, in *Caparo Industries v Dickman*,[66] Lord Bridge presented the cause of action as being in negligence,[67] but also maintained that liability requires an assumption of responsibility.[68] This was despite his Lordship's criticism of the very notion of assumption of responsibility.[69] Similar remarks can be made of Lord Goff's judgment in *Henderson v Merrett Syndicates Ltd*[70] and of Lord Steyn's analysis in *Williams v Natural Life Health Foods Ltd*.[71] In that sense, though even proponents of the negligence model admit that the model is losing ground,[72] and though Lord Browne-Wilkinson clearly rejected the negligence model in *White v Jones*,[73] the issue cannot be said to have finally been settled by judicial pronouncements.

But one thing is immediately apparent: We cannot conclude from the fact that the House of Lords in *Hedley Byrne* agreed with Denning LJ in *Candler* that recovery may be available for detrimental reliance on negligently made mis-

---

[63] *Hedley Byrne & Co Ltd v Heller & Partners Ltd*, above n 62, 531.

[64] It may appear that there is a third alternative: that the defendant's responsibility arises from his *inducement* of the claimant's reliance. However, this notion is ambiguous. On the one hand, 'induce' could mean invite, which would reduce this approach to the assumption of responsibility model. On the other hand, 'induce' may mean bring about a state of affairs such that the claimant's reliance was reasonably foreseeable, which reduces to the negligence model.

[65] R Grantham and C Rickett, 'Directors' "Tortious" Liability: Contract, Tort or Company Law?' (1999) 62 *MLR* 133, 135–7.

[66] [1990] 2 AC 605 (HL).

[67] *Ibid*, 616.

[68] *Ibid*, 624.

[69] *Ibid*, 623 (Lord Bridge). See also *ibid*, 641 (Lord Oliver), 628–9 (Lord Roskill). Moreover, though Lord Oliver rejected the assumption of responsibility model, his Lordship was nevertheless unable to discuss the defendant's potential liability without reference to the concept. See *ibid*, 641.

[70] [1995] 2 AC 145, 178–81 (HL).

[71] [1998] 1 WLR 830, 836–8 (HL). See also the ambiguous comments in Lord Steyn, 'Perspectives of Corrective and Distributive Justice in Tort Law' (2002) 37 *Irish Jurist* 1, 6.

[72] Eg B Hepple, 'Negligence: The Search for Coherence' (1997) 50 *CLP* 69, 88. See also J Taylor, 'The Conceptual Basis of the Tort of Negligent Misstatement' (2003) 9 *New Zealand Business Law Quarterly* 177, 192; B Coote, 'Assumption of Responsibility and Pure Economic Loss in New Zealand' [2005] *New Zealand Law Review* 1.

[73] [1995] 2 AC 207 (HL). Compare *Merrett v Babb* [2001] EWCA Civ 214, [2001] QB 1174, 1192–4 (May LJ).

statements, that their Lordships agreed with Denning LJ as to the *basis* of such recovery. In fact, as I now argue, the actual decisions and the treatment of specific issues in *Hedley Byrne* and subsequent cases are better explained by the assumption of responsibility model than by the negligence model.

B. The Role of Assumption of Responsibility in Negligent Misrepresentation

This section argues that, although judgments in negligent misrepresentation cases often begin with a general statement of the negligence model, it is the assumption of responsibility model that is actually applied when courts turn to deciding the specific issues raised in such cases. Hence, though the negligence model appears to be the official basis of liability in negligent misrepresentation, this is illusory.

(i) Disclaimers

In *Hedley Byrne*, their Lordships were unanimous that the defendant's disclaimer negatived any possible liability. The issue for us is why the disclaimer had that effect. Outside negligent misrepresentation, a disclaimer on its own is of no relevance in negligence. For instance, I cannot avoid liability for driving negligently by attaching to my car a sign disclaiming responsibility.[74] Nor can I avoid an obligation to take care of my colleagues by warning them in advance that I am going to walk dangerously through the corridors of the faculty or gain a liberty to batter them by clearly disclaiming responsibility for their bodily integrity.[75] Were the law to give effect to such disclaimers, it would inappropriately allow one unilaterally to remove rights from others. In order for a disclaimer to be operative in tort, it must function to show that the claimant surrendered a right. In effect, this means that the claimant must have entered a contract excluding liability or, in the circumstances, the activity of the claimant in the face of the disclaimer must indicate that the claimant assumed or consented to the risk of the activity—in other words, the claimant must be *volens*.

Both of these approaches focus on the position of the claimant. In considering exclusion of liability, the court asks whether the claimant entered into a contract that contains a clause excluding liability. In considering the *volenti* defence, the court asks whether the claimant consented in the appropriate fashion. As we will see in Chapter 10, there are two general views about the nature of the *volenti* defence. In *Nettleship v Weston*, Lord Denning argued that the defence applies only if the claimant waived her right to sue.[76] Conversely, Salmon LJ maintained that the claimant need only know of the risk and choose

---

[74] *Harris v Wyre Forest District Council* [1988] QB 835, 853 (CA) (Kerr LJ).
[75] Hence, the issue is *not merely* one of reasonable notice.
[76] [1971] 2 QB 691, 701 (CA).

to go along with it.[77] At this point, it is not necessary to decide which, if any, of these views is correct. Rather, it is important to note that both Lord Denning and Salmon LJ focused on the claimant. On neither view will a defendant escape liability simply because he made a disclaimer.

For instance, in *Buckpitt v Oates*,[78] the claimant passenger was injured while riding in a vehicle negligently driven by the defendant. The defendant had placed in the vehicle a clearly visible notice stating that passengers rode in the car at their own risk. The claimant was aware of this notice. Given this, the claimant's decision to ride in the vehicle amounted to a voluntary assumption of risk. Accordingly, the reason the disclaimer was operative was not because it was made per se or merely that it was brought to the attention of the claimant, but that it was made, drawn to the claimant's attention, and the claimant chose to ride in the vehicle nevertheless. In the light of the circumstances, then, the claimant surrendered his right that the defendant take ordinary care and was therefore *volens*.[79]

None of their Lordships in *Hedley Byrne* treated the defendant's disclaimer in this manner.[80] Lord Devlin maintained that '[a] man cannot be said voluntarily to be undertaking a responsibility if at the very moment when he is said to be accepting it he declares that in fact he is not'.[81] The argument was not that the claimant had entered a contract excluding liability or was *volens*. Lord Devlin focused entirely on the defendant. His Lordship maintained that the disclaimer was operative simply because the defendant made it. In the language of contract, we would say that the defendant did not make the claimant an offer. In the language of negligent misrepresentation, we say that there was no assumption of responsibility.[82]

Similarly, Lord Hodson stated:

> I cannot exclude from consideration the actual terms in which the reference was given and I cannot see how the appellants can get over the difficulty which these words put in their way. They cannot say that the respondents are seeking, as it were, to contract out of their duty by the use of language which is insufficient for the purpose, if the

---

[77] [1971] 2 QB 691, 701 (CA), 704.

[78] *Buckpitt v Oates* [1968] 1 All ER 1145 (Devon Assizes).

[79] Either because the claimant waived his right to sue or knew of the risk and chose to go along with it. Things are more complicated when the claimant was not fully aware of the content of the disclaimer. See eg *Ashdown v Samuel Williams & Sons Ltd* [1957] 1 QB 409 (CA). However, these cases do not show that the mere fact that the disclaimer was made is decisive. This is demonstrated by the fact that the claimant's lack of awareness of the terms of the disclaimer is always an issue in these cases. It would not be were the disclaimer itself decisive.

[80] However, it could be argued that Lord Morris was ambivalent as to the role of disclaimer. *Hedley Byrne & Co Ltd v Heller & Partners Ltd* [1964] AC 465, 504 (HL). See also *Harris v Wyre Forest District Council* [1988] QB 835, 853 (CA) (Kerr LJ). Compare *Smith v Eric S Bush* [1990] 1 AC 831, 848 (HL) (Lord Templeman).

[81] *Hedley Byrne & Co Ltd v Heller & Partners Ltd* [1964] AC 465, 533 (HL).

[82] This reasoning was rejected in *Smith v Eric S Bush* [1990] 1 AC 831 (HL). This is unsurprising because the assumption of responsibility model is also rejected. This issue is explored further below.

truth of the matter is that the respondents never assumed a duty of care nor was such a duty imposed upon them.[83]

The argument is not that prima facie the defendant owed the claimant a duty of care but a defence arose because of the disclaimer. Rather, no defence was required, as the presence of the disclaimer meant that a duty of care never arose.[84] The defendant did not assume responsibility.

Lord Pearce considered the impact of disclaimers in negligence, but went on to say:

> [I]n any event [the representations including disclaimer] clearly prevent a special relationship from arising. They are part of the material from which one deduces whether a duty of care and a liability for negligence was assumed. If both parties say expressly . . . that there shall be no liability, I do not find it possible to say that a liability was assumed.[85]

The reference to both parties means that this could be read either way, but I submit that it is more natural to interpret the passage as denying liability on the ground that the defendant did not consent.

Lord Reid's view was somewhat more complicated. His Lordship said:

> The appellants founded on a number of cases in contract where very clear words were required to exclude the duty of care which would otherwise have flowed from the contract. To that argument there are, I think, two answers. In the case of a contract it is necessary to exclude liability for negligence, but in this case the question is whether an undertaking to assume a duty to take care can be inferred: and that is a very different matter. And, secondly, even in cases of contract general words may be sufficient if there was no other kind of liability to be excluded except liability for negligence: the general rule is that a party is not exempted from liability for negligence 'unless adequate words are used' . . . It being admitted that there was here a duty to give an honest reply, I do not see what further liability there could be to exclude except liability for negligence: there being no contract there was no question of warranty. I am therefore of opinion that it is clear that the respondents never undertook any duty to exercise care in giving their replies. The appellants cannot succeed unless there was such a duty.[86]

Certainly, some of the language used gives the impression that we are in the realm of tort rather than of contract, and hence that we are not dealing with *assumptions* of responsibility. However, that impression is misleading. Lord Reid focussed entirely on the defendant and did not argue that the claimant surrendered any right.

Moreover, it is important carefully to consider why Lord Reid argued that the rules governing the impact of disclaimers in contract were irrelevant. The claimant argued that the defendant's disclaimer was insufficient to negative

---

[83] *Hedley Byrne & Co Ltd v Heller & Partners Ltd* [1964] AC 465, 511 (HL).
[84] B Feldthusen, *Economic Negligence*, 4th edn (Carswell, Scarborough, 2000) 54.
[85] *Hedley Byrne & Co Ltd v Heller & Partners Ltd* [1964] AC 465, 540 (HL).
[86] *Ibid*, 492–3.

liability because it was not adequately clear. In support, the claimant pointed to the rules governing the impact of disclaimers on the interpretation of contracts. Lord Reid replied that those rules concern cases in which a contract has been formed that imposes a number of obligations, one of which is to take care, where the disclaimer is alleged to limit the obligations owed but not to deny the existence of a contract. The issue in *Hedley Byrne* was not that, but whether the defendant '*undertook* any duty to exercise care in giving their replies',[87] ie whether there was any assumption of responsibility at all. As Lord Devlin put it, '[t]he problem of reconciling words of exemption with the existence of a duty arises only when a party is claiming exemption from a responsibility which he has already undertaken or which he is contracting to undertake'.[88] In the language of contract, the question is not whether there was a contractual disclaimer, but whether there was an offer. Hence, the rules relating to the operation of disclaimers on parties bound by contract were irrelevant. In *Hedley Byrne* the issue was whether, in the face of the statement said to constitute the disclaimer, it was reasonable to say that the defendant had 'made an offer' to the claimant, and hence whether any 'contract' existed at all. Accordingly, though the approach of contract law in relation to disclaimers *in* contract was irrelevant, the approach of contract law with respect to interpreting whether statements constitute offers was pertinent and, therefore, we remain in the realm of assumed responsibilities.

On the other hand, commentators have argued that the role of disclaimers is consistent with the negligence model by suggesting that negligent misrepresentation protects only *reasonable* reliance and it would be unreasonable for the claimant to rely on the defendant's statement in the face of a disclaimer. For instance, Stephen Todd maintains that 'if advice is given subject to a stipulation disclaiming liability for it, the recipient is bound. He or she cannot accept the advice yet at the same time reject the stipulation.'[89] This conclusion is accurate, but how is it justified? On the negligence model, it is not clear why the claimant needs to *reject* anything. As her loss was a reasonably foreseeable consequence of the defendant's negligent misrepresentation, she does not have to reject the defendant's stipulation in order to recover. She can simply be indifferent to the stipulation, neither accepting nor rejecting it. The notion that the claimant must accept the stipulation is justified because the stipulation is a condition on which the advice was given. But this is another way of saying that the right to rely on the advice must be given by the defendant to the claimant and, in the presence of a stipulation limiting the defendant's responsibility, that right is circumscribed in accordance with that stipulation. None of this is explicable on the negligence model, but it fits perfectly with the assumption of responsibility model.

---

[87] *Ibid*, 493 (emphasis added).

[88] *Ibid*, 533.

[89] S Todd, 'Negligence: Particular Categories of Duty' in S Todd (ed), *The Law of Torts in New Zealand,* 3rd edn (Brookers, Wellington, 2001) 1067. See also J Blom, 'The Evolving Relationship Between Tort and Contract' (1985) 10 *Canadian Business Law Journal* 257, 293–4.

Moreover, reliance on advice given with a disclaimer is very often entirely reasonable. If the claimant has reason to believe that the defendant's statement is accurate, then she is not acting unreasonably when she relies on that statement. The claimant's reliance in *Hedley Byrne* was not unreasonable. It was not foolish or irrational. (And even if it were, that would constitute only contributory negligence—defined by statute as a partial defence.) In *Hedley Byrne*, it was not the claimant's reliance that was unreasonable, but the claimant's expectation that its reliance was at the defendant's risk. But why was that expectation unreasonable? As the defendant was negligent and the claimant's reliance was reasonably foreseeable, the negligence model has no answer to this question. The natural answer is that the claimant's expectation is unreasonable because the defendant did not assume responsibility.

Consequently, the impact of a disclaimer fits the assumption of responsibility rather than the negligence model of negligent misrepresentation. Disclaimer indicates that the defendant did not assume responsibility.

(ii) Casual Conversations

An issue of concern in both *Candler* and *Hedley Byrne* was whether the creation of liability for negligently made statements would entail potential liability for statements made in casual conversation.[90] Again, this concern is a creation of the negligence model. According to the ordinary principles of negligence, liability cannot depend on where the statement was made. Hence, on the view that negligent misrepresentation belongs to the ordinary law of negligence, it is believed necessary for policy reasons to invent special rules to limit the occasions upon which liability arises. But the assumption of responsibility model has no such problem. On this view, the issue is whether the defendant assumed responsibility for something by making the statement. It is normally unreasonable to interpret off-hand comments made in casual conversation as such. What this means is that the law of assumed responsibility contains and must contain an equivalent of the law of contract's demand that liability can exist only if there was an intent to create legal relations.[91]

However, the assumption of responsibility model posits no fixed rule in relation to statements made in casual conversation. It is possible for defendants to assume responsibility in any circumstances.[92] The relevance of the circumstances in which the statement is made is that the circumstances influence the appropriate interpretation of the statement. Utterances must be interpreted with

---

[90] *Candler v Crane Christmas & Co* [1951] 2 KB 164, 180 (Denning LJ), 194 (Asquith LJ); *Hedley Byrne & Co Ltd v Heller & Partners Ltd* [1964] AC 465, 496 (Lord Morris), 510 (Lord Hodson), 539 (Lord Pearce).

[91] Note that this does not imply that the defendant must have undertaken legal liability. If I promise to sell you my horse for £100, I undertake to sell you my horse for £100, which undertaking the courts will enforce. I do not undertake legal liability. The position is the same with respect to assumptions of responsibility.

[92] See eg *Hedley Byrne & Co Ltd v Heller & Partners Ltd* [1964] AC 465, 486 (HL) (Lord Reid).

an eye to the contexts in which they are made. But context alone does not determine the meaning of a statement, and context alone should not be decisive as to the legal effect of any statement. Again, the position argued for is identical to the interpretation of statements in contract law.[93]

Of course, it is possible for those who support the negligence model to invent yet more policies to reach the appropriate result. The position may be that (i) prima facie one is liable according to the ordinary principles of the law of negligence, but (ii) for policy reasons one will not be held liable for statements made in casual conversation, but (iii) for additional policy reasons rule (ii) will occasionally be abandoned. But if the point of introducing policy is to bend the negligence model so that it reaches the same conclusions as a principled application of the assumption of responsibility model, then we should simply adopt the assumption of responsibility model.

(iii) Special Skill

As examined above, the notion that only those with special skills should be liable for negligently made statements was supported by Denning LJ in *Candler* and by two of their Lordships in *Hedley Byrne*. It also received support from a majority of the Privy Council in *Mutual Life and Citizens' Assurance Co Ltd v Evatt*[94] and possible support from Lord Goff in *Henderson*[95] and in *Spring v Guardian Assurance*.[96] Again, the origin of this rule lies in the belief that liability would be overly extensive if imposed according to the ordinary principles of negligence. Therefore, for policy reasons, the duty of care is restricted to those with special skills.

However, as Lord Devlin pointed out in *Hedley Byrne*, this rule is inappropriate:

> If a defendant says to a plaintiff: 'Let me do this for you; do not waste your money in employing a professional, I will do it for nothing and you can rely on me,' I do not think he could escape liability simply because he belonged to no profession or calling, had no qualifications or special skill and did not hold himself out as having any. The relevance of these factors is to show the unlikelihood of a defendant in such circum-

---

[93] Similar comments are appropriate in relation to statements made to friends and acquaintances, against: K Barker, 'Unreliable Assumptions in the Modern Law of Negligence' (1993) 109 *LQR* 461, 466. Alternatively, one could argue that the assumption of responsibility model rules out liability for statements made in casual conversation, where 'casual' refers, not to the circumstances in which the conversation takes place, but to the intentions of the parties (objectively interpreted and hence with an eye on the context in which they are made) with respect to the conversation. This too fits the assumption of responsibility model.

[94] [1971] AC 793, 805 (HL). See however ibid, 812; B Feldthusen, *Economic Negligence,* 4th edn (Carswell, Scarborough, 2000) 72–7.

[95] *Henderson v Merrett Syndicates Ltd* [1995] 2 AC 145, 180 (HL).

[96] [1995] 2 AC 296, 318–19 (HL) Lord Goff's support was not conclusive. His Lordship insisted that those with special skills can be held liable. This does not logically entail the view that those without special skills cannot be liable.

stances assuming a legal responsibility, and *as such* they may often be decisive. But they are not theoretically conclusive and so cannot be the subject of definition.[97]

The defendant's expertise, or lack thereof, is a matter to be taken into account in interpreting the defendant's statement, but it cannot be decisive on its own in determining the legal effects of any statement. Again, this is on all fours with contract law, and hence with the concept of assumption of responsibility.

Once more, it is possible for those who support the negligence model to argue that (i) recovery is based on the ordinary principles of the law of negligence, but (ii) for reasons of policy the duty of care is restricted to those with special skills, but (iii) for yet more reasons of policy rule (ii) is sometimes overlooked. None of this is necessary or desirable.

(iv) The Purpose of the Representation and the Person for whose Benefit the Statement was Made

As discussed above, in *Caparo* the House of Lords ruled that, for them to have a cause of action, the claimants' reliance on the statement must be consistent with the purpose for which the statement was made. This result fits precisely with the assumption of responsibility model. In providing the statement for a particular purpose, the defendant assumed responsibility for uses of that statement that correspond to that purpose, but the defendant did not consent that the claimant might use the statement for other purposes. Hence, the result in *Caparo* was fair, just and reasonable, as their Lordships attested without explaining. This was because it would not be fair, just or reasonable to impose a consent-based obligation on a defendant who had not consented. Similarly, if the statement was not made to or for the claimant's benefit, then the defendant did not assume responsibility to the claimant and the claimant cannot recover.

Recall that in *Hercules*, the claimant suffered loss in reliance on an audit prepared by the defendant. However, the defendant did not prepare the report to be used in the way that the claimant used it. Moreover, in *Carter*, the New Zealand Court of Appeal said that a claimant could not recover for reliance on a negligently made statement unless the statement was made for the benefit of that person.[98] In both cases the claimants failed. Those results required no appeal to policy or to constructed meanings of 'unreasonableness'. In neither case did the defendants assume the relevant responsibility to the claimants. In the latter, there was no assumption of responsibility to the claimant at all. In the former, the claimant assumed responsibility only for losses suffered in reliance consistent with the purpose of the statement. If the defendant says, 'You can rely on these reports for your AGM', then he cannot be taken to have implied that the claimant can rely on the reports for other purposes as well. Similarly, no

---

[97] *Hedley Byrne & Co Ltd v Heller & Partners Ltd* [1964] AC 465, 531 (HL) (emphasis added).
[98] *A-G v Carter* [2003] 2 NZLR 160, 169 (CA). Compare *Hercules Managements v Ernst & Young* [1997] 2 SCR 165, 190–1.

appeal to policy is required to justify the results in *Caparo, Hercules, Carter* or *Esanda Finance*. The conclusions in those cases flow from an entirely principled approach to the law (though not a principled approach to the law of negligence, which is irrelevant in this context).

Moreover, the position taken by Tipping J in *A-G v Carter* is placed in doubt by Tipping J's own subsequent decision in *Frost and Sutcliffe v Tuiara*.[99] In the latter case, the claimant sold his family home to a third party on the under-standing that it would be sold back to the claimant by the third party six weeks later at a lower price. Before that could happen, the third party was placed in liquidation. The defendant had provided legal advice to the claimant and had also acted for the third party in the transaction. The defendant's advice to the claimant was clear:

> We note our advices to you as to our concern at advising family as regards to trans-actions of this type. This is especially the case when their own home is placed at risk. My initial advice to you would be 'don't'. . . . The effect of registration of the sale will mean that you have lost your home if anything goes wrong. . . . You will have a right against the security the Company grants but this would be likely to be of no value. . . . To summarise, our advice simply is it is better not to proceed with the transaction. . . . We note we have strongly recommended you consult an independent Solicitor in respect of the matter but you have declined to [do] so.[100]

Because of this, in the High Court Baragwanath J rejected Tuiara's claims for breach of contract and breach of fiduciary duty. Remarkably, however, Baragwanath J found the defendant liable in negligence.

This was rejected by Tipping J at the Court of Appeal:

> The contractual duty created by implied term, was to exercise such skill, care and dili-gence as was required in all the circumstances, including the scope of the retainer. In this case the contract of retainer could not sensibly be viewed as limiting the scope of liability to a greater extent in contract than in tort. The scope of the retainer was equally apt to influence what a competent practitioner should have done whether the obligation is analysed as contractual or tortious.
>
> There may be rare cases where, in a case like the present, it is possible to regard the tortious duty as wider than that in contract, but these must be very much the excep-tion rather than the rule. An express contractual limitation of the scope of the con-tractual duty in an artificial and improper way might result in the Court finding that the duty so excluded was nevertheless still owed in tort. The basis for that approach would be a policy one, preventing the professional person from improperly limiting the scope of their professional responsibilities by express contractual term. But there cannot be any suggestion of that in the present case. The three circumstances isolated by the Judge as relevant to the solicitors' duty in tort were clearly within the ambit of the duty in contract as well.[101]

---

[99] [2004] 1 NZLR 782 (CA).
[100] *Ibid*, 784–5.
[101] *Ibid*, 786–7.

In other words, as a matter of principle, the duties in the 'tort of negligent misrepresentation' and in contract are coextensive.

But it is not easy to explain this conclusion if '[i]n tort obligations are imposed, not assumed, as they are in contract'.[102] Rather, the fact that the duties have the same ambit indicates that they arise for the same reasons.

A more difficult case is the decision of the New Zealand Court of Appeal in *R M Turton & Co Ltd (in liq) v Kerslake and Partners*.[103] The defendant had contracted with a third party to supply specifications relating to the construction of a hospital. The claimant contracted with the third party to construct parts of the hospital. The claimant conducted its work in reliance on the specifications provided by the defendant to the third party. The specifications were inaccurate, causing the claimant to breach its contract with the third party, thus causing loss to the claimant. The claimant attempted to recover this loss from the defendant.

The contract between the defendant and the third party contained the following clauses:

4.2.1.3 The Consulting Engineer shall not be held to have given or implied any warranty as to the performance of the project which is the subject of his agreement with the Client.

4.2.1.5 The Consulting Engineer shall have no responsibility for or liability for costs, loss or damages of whatsoever nature arising from:

(a) any errors in or omissions from data, documents, plans, designs or specifications not prepared by the Consulting Engineer, his employees, or other personnel under his direct technical control;

(b) any act or omission or lack of performance or any negligent or fraudulent act or omission by the Client or any contractor or supplier to the Client or any employee or agent of the Client, contractor or supplier.

4.2.1.6 Notwithstanding any recommendation or lack of recommendation by the Consulting Engineer to the Client the Consulting Engineer shall not be held to have made any warranty, promise or representation as to the suitability, competence or performance of any contractor, subcontractor, supplier, professional adviser (other than the Consulting Engineer), or person engaged by the Client.[104]

Importantly, this did not mean that the defendant had disclaimed responsibility to the third party for the accuracy of the specifications.[105] However, the majority of the Court, Henry and Keith JJ, maintained:

---

[102] *A-G v Carter* [2003] 2 NZLR 160, 168 (CA).

[103] [2000] 3 NZLR 406 (CA). This discussion is also likely to be appropriate to *Edgeworth*. However, it is impossible to be certain, as the relevant facts of that case are not discussed in the reports.

[104] *Ibid*, 415.

[105] The importance of this point was overlooked in A Beever, 'All at Sea in the Law of Negligent Misrepresentation' (2003) 9 *New Zealand Business Law Quarterly* 101, 102.

The extent of any liability [to the third party] was governed by cls 4.2.2.1 to 4.2.2.8. It was limited to direct loss or damage and excluded 'any indirect or consequential loss of whatsoever nature'. There was also a time limit, a quantum limit, and an exclusion of the right to make any claim against an employee of the engineer. Also of significance, disputes were subject to an arbitration provision (cl 1.4.3). There is accordingly a careful allocation of risk as between the engineer, the architect and the area health board for negligence on the part of the engineer in fulfilling its obligations, including preparation of the specifications.[106]

Their Honours concluded that finding for the claimant would 'cut across and be inconsistent with the overall contractual structure which defines the relationships of the various parties to this work, and in the circumstances of this case it would not be fair, just or reasonable to impose the claimed duty of care'.[107]

This conclusion attracted the strong dissent of Thomas J who, adopting the negligence model, argued that the claimant owed the defendant a duty of care. Moreover, Thomas J argued that the existence of the contractual matrix could not negative a prima facie duty of care.[108] His Honour maintained that the majority failed to appreciate the impact of *Donoghue v Stevenson*. In effect, Thomas J argued that the majority in *Turton* reverted to the position in *Winterbottom v Wright*,[109] according to which a contract between the defendant and a third party that covered the subject matter of the alleged negligence would negative any liability in tort owed to the claimant. Clearly, however, this is the fallacy 'exploded by *Donoghue v Stevenson*'.[110] The terms of a contract between *A* and *B* cannot remove rights in *C*.

However, though the reasoning of the majority is not absolutely transparent, *Turton* was rightly decided. If *A* provides *B* with advice with no indication that he assumes responsibility to *C*, then it would be incredible to find *A* liable when *C* relies on that advice. On the negligence model, the defendant in *Turton* would have had to seek out all those who might reasonably and reasonably foreseeably rely on the specification and disclaim responsibility to them. But even that would not decide the matter. If *C* had a right to rely on the specifications absent the disclaimer, *A* could not remove that right unilaterally. Hence, *A* would remain bound if *C* refused to accept *A*'s disclaimer. But that is an absurd result.[111]

Similarly, in *Rolls-Royce New Zealand Ltd v Cater Holt Harvey Ltd*, a very similar case to *Turton*, the New Zealand Court of Appeal suggested that a

---

[106] *R M Turton & Co Ltd (in liq) v Kerslake and Partners* [2000] 3 NZLR 406, 415 (CA).

[107] *Ibid*, 417.

[108] *Ibid*, 440–1 (Thomas J); S Todd, 'Negligence: The Duty of Care' in S Todd (ed), *The Law of Torts in New Zealand,* 3rd edn (Brookers, Wellington, 2001) 232–6.

[109] (1842) 10 M & W 109, 152 ER 402.

[110] *Candler v Crane Christmas & Co* [1951] 2 KB 164, 179 (CA) (Denning LJ). See *R M Turton & Co Ltd (in liq) v Kerslake and Partners* [2000] 3 NZLR 406, 440–1 (CA) (Thomas J).

[111] The efficiency of the construction industry cannot justify imposing obligations on individual defendants. That would be to confiscate the liberties of the defendant in order to subsidise the industry.

claimant who suffered loss in reliance on advice given by the defendant to a third party could not recover from the defendant, because the claimant could have contracted, but did not contract, with the defendant in order to protect itself from that loss.[112] This is an unnecessarily circuitous way of saying that the defendant did not assume responsibility. There is no need to treat it as a policy matter that negatives liability.

Though the negligence model cannot reach the correct conclusion—as Thomas J's judgment in *Turton*, a flawless application of the negligence model, reveals—the assumption of responsibility model has no such difficulty. The fact that the defendant was so careful to define and restrict his obligations in his contract with the third party demonstrates that the contract contained no assumption of responsibility to the claimant. If you ask me to clean your house and I say that I will vacuum the floor, dust the shelves and clean the bathroom, but that I will not do the dishes, the washing or the ironing, then, even though I have not specifically mentioned it one way or the other, I have not agreed to clean the windows. Similarly, though the defendant in *Turton* did not specifically disclaim responsibility to the claimant for the accuracy of the specifications, the defendant elucidated his obligations in a way that meant no assumption of responsibility to the claimant for the accuracy of the specifications was plausibly made. Moreover, as there was no evidence outside the contract pointing to an assumption of responsibility, the conclusion must be that the defendant did not assume responsibility to the claimant and so was rightly found not to be liable.

Note that the disclamatory language in the contract between the defendant and the third party was not decisive on this view. It did not negative a prima facie duty of care as the contract did in *Winterbottom v Wright*. Rather, no duty arose, because the defendant did not assume responsibility to the claimant. The disclamatory language is only yet more evidence to that effect. This matter was perfectly captured by Lord Goff in *Henderson*:

> Let me take the analogy of the common case of an ordinary building contract, under which main contractors contract with the building owner for the construction of the relevant building, and the main contractor sub-contracts with sub-contractors or suppliers . . . for the performance of work or the supply of materials in accordance with standards and subject to terms established in the sub-contract. . . . But if the sub-contracted work or materials do not in the result conform to the required standard, it will not ordinarily be open to the building owner to sue the sub-contractor or supplier direct under the *Hedley Byrne* principle, claiming damages from him on the basis that he has been negligent in relation to the performance of his functions. For there is generally no assumption of responsibility by the sub-contractor or supplier direct to the building owner, the parties having so structured their relationship that it is inconsistent with any such assumption of responsibility.[113]

---

[112] [2005] 1 NZLR 324 (CA), [121]–[122].
[113] *Henderson v Merrett Syndicates Ltd* [1995] 2 AC 145, 195–6 (HL).

Therefore, the negligence model *as it has been applied in practice* produces the same results as the assumption of responsibility model, but it does so only by reference to a host of policy concerns that the assumption of responsibility model can do without. At the very least, this shows that the negligence model is redundant. Moreover, it unnecessarily complicates the enquiry and disguises the nature of the cause of action to base liability on a restrictively defined reasonable and reasonably foreseeable reliance or to distinguish 'mere reliance in fact and reasonable reliance on the employee's pocket-book' when the question is simply whether the defendant assumed responsibility to the claimant.

C. Perceived Difficulties with the Assumption of Responsibility Model

I have examined reasons for thinking that the assumption of responsibility model better explains the cause of action for negligent misrepresentation than does the negligence model. I now discuss perceived problems with the assumption of responsibility model.

(i) The Pigeonhole Argument

Two related difficulties with seeing negligent misrepresentation as based on assumption of responsibility are that the cause of action is called '*negligent* misrepresentation' and that it is widely regarded as part of the law of tort. The New Zealand Court of Appeal has said that '[c]oncerns have been expressed about the appropriateness of the concept of assumption of responsibility . . . The potential difficulty is with the word "assumption", which suggests a voluntary act. In tort obligations are imposed, not assumed, as they are in contract'.[114]

This assumes what is at issue. If one stipulates that liability for negligent misrepresentation is tortious and that all obligations in tort are imposed, then it must turn out that liability for negligent misrepresentation is not voluntarily assumed. But it cannot be taken for granted that the basis of liability for negligent misrepresentation is imposed rather than assumed. The fact that the cause of action is called '*negligent* misrepresentation' does not establish that its foundation lies in the ordinary law of negligence. As legal scholars, we must recognise the possibility that the cause of action has a misleading name and cannot take such trivial details as determinants of legal structure.

Though the argument is clearly inadequate, I suspect that it explains much of the intuitive reluctance to take seriously the assumption of responsibility model. It is natural to assume that a cause of action with negligence in its name is actually an ordinary form of negligence liability. Hence, to adopt the assumption of

---

[114] *A-G v Carter* [2003] 2 NZLR 160, 168 (CA). See also S Todd, 'Negligence: Particular Categories of Duty' in S Todd (ed), *The Law of Torts in New Zealand,* 3rd edn (Brookers, Wellington, 2001) 224–8.

responsibility model would require some reorganisation of our mental picture of the law. But this should not hold us back.

(ii) The Role of Proximity

As discussed above, Commonwealth courts continue to insist that a duty of care is owed only if the parties are in a relationship of proximity.[115] As proximity is an issue in negligence but not in contract, this supports the negligence model. However, as we saw above, courts are ambivalent as to the meaning of 'proximity' in this context. It is sometimes said that there must be a relationship of proximity or a *special relationship* between the parties, as if these statements were equivalent.[116] They are not. Donoghue and Stevenson were in a relationship of proximity, but they were not in a special relationship.[117] Hence, 'proximity' means one thing in negligent misrepresentation and another in the law of negligence proper. In fact, as the discussion above indicated, in negligent misrepresentation proximity equals a special relationship, which in turn equals an assumption of responsibility, which means consent.[118] Accordingly, 'proximity' exists between the parties only if the defendant assumed responsibility to the claimant. Given that, it would be better to abandon talk of proximity altogether and focus on the real issue: assumption of responsibility.

(iii) The Role of Reasonable Foreseeability

It is said that the defendant can be liable only if the claimant's reliance is reasonably foreseeable. Again, this may appear to suggest that negligent misrepresentation belongs more to tort than to contract. However, the assumption of responsibility model entails that the claimant's reliance must be reasonably foreseeable for liability to follow. If the reliance was not reasonably foreseeable, then responsibility for it cannot have been assumed; conversely, if responsibility for the reliance was assumed, then it must have been reasonably foreseeable. Hence, the reasonable foreseeability requirement is a logical consequence of the assumption of responsibility model, though an uninteresting one. Moreover, the issue of reasonably foreseeability is related to the claimant's ability to recover consequential loss, as in contract law.[119] Of course, reasonable foreseeability is not sufficient for liability on the assumption of responsibility model, but, as we have seen, that is accepted by all.

---

[115] See eg *Spring v Guardian Assurance* [1995] 2 AC 296 (HL), 325 (Lord Lowry), 342 (Lord Wolf).

[116] Eg *Caparo Industries v Dickman* [1990] 2 AC 605, 621 (Lord Bridge), 633 (Lord Oliver). For criticism see B Coote, 'The Effect of Hedley Byrne' (1966–1967) 2 *New Zealand Universities Law Review* 263, 266; B Feldthusen, *Economic Negligence*, 4th edn (Carswell, Scarborough, 2000) 41.

[117] *M'Alister (or Donoghue) (Pauper) v Stevenson* [1932] AC 562 (HL Sc).

[118] See eg *Merrett v Babb* [2001] EWCA Civ 214, [2001] QB 1174, 1201 (Aldous LJ).

[119] *Hadley v Baxendale* (1854) 9 Ex 341, 354 (Alderson B).

(iv) The Role of Reliance

It is sometimes said that a cause of action in negligent misrepresentation arises only if the claimant relies to her detriment on the defendant's statement.[120] It is true that the claimant normally must rely to her detriment, but detrimental reliance is not a necessary element of the cause of action.[121]

First, the issue of reliance is relevant, though not decisive, in determining whether the defendant voluntarily assumed responsibility to the claimant. If the evidence suggests that the defendant intended the claimant to rely, this tends to indicate an assumption of responsibility by the defendant rather than an off-the-cuff comment that should have no legal significance.

Secondly, if we ignore the disclaimer in *Hedley Byrne*, the defendant would have assumed a responsibility to protect the claimant from detrimental reliance. Accordingly, if the claimant did not suffer detrimental reliance, the claimant did not suffer a loss as a result of the defendant's failure to live up to his assumed responsibility. Hence, the claimant must rely to her detriment in order to recover from the defendant, but that is a matter relevant to factual causation rather than to general features of a duty of care.[122] Conversely, if a defendant assumes responsibility for something other than the claimant's detrimental reliance—such as a responsibility to perform a service—then detrimental reliance cannot be necessary to ground a cause of action any more than it is in contract.

The negligence model theorist could interpret liability for failing to perform a promised service as flowing from the claimant's detrimental reliance on the defendant's guarantee that she would perform the service, where the reliance equals not employing someone else to perform the service. But this also is unnecessary.[123] Simply put, the defendant is liable for not performing the service he promised to perform. There is no point in adopting more circuitous reasoning to reach the same result.

Imagine a version of Lord Devlin's hypothetical.[124] *A* is a self-employed bicycle courier. His bicycle gets a flat tire and *A* intends to have it mended at a bicycle shop. *B*, knowing of *A*'s business, tells *A*, 'Let me fix the tyre for you. Don't waste your money going to a shop. I will fix it for free.' However, *B* does not do so and *A*, not being able to use his bicycle for his business, suffers financial loss.

---

[120] *Merrett v Babb* [2001] EWCA Civ 214, [2001] QB 1174, 1192 (May LJ). But see *White v Jones* [1995] 2 AC 207 (HL) 270–3 (Lord Browne-Wilkinson). Compare *Henderson v Merrett Syndicates Ltd* [1995] 2 AC 145, 180 (HL) (Lord Goff).

[121] J Fleming, *The Law of Torts*, 9th edn (LBC Information Services, Sydney, 1998) 191.

[122] *Henderson v Merrett Syndicates Ltd* [1995] 2 AC 145, 180 (HL); *Williams v Natural Life Health Foods Ltd* [1998] 1 WLR 830, 836 (HL).

[123] '"[R]eliance" is a weasel word': T Weir, *Tort Law* (Oxford University Press, Oxford, 2002) 36.

[124] *Hedley Byrne & Co Ltd v Heller & Partners Ltd* [1964] AC 465, 531 (HL).

The negligence model theorist could interpret the liability in this case as flowing from *A*'s reliance on *B*'s promise to mend the tyre. Hence, the theorist may insist that reliance is required, not merely in order to cause *A*'s loss, but as part of the duty of care itself. But imagine now a variation on the case in which *A* paid *B* to mend the tyre. In that case, we do not insist that *B* can be liable only if *A* relied on *B* to his detriment. We say, simply, that *B* promised—ie contracted—to mend *A*'s tyre and failed to do so, rendering *B* liable for the foreseeable consequences of failing to live up to his promise. There is no reason we should not say the same in the original case. The analysis supplied by the negligence model is redundant. Putting the issue of causation aside, there is no practical difference between saying that *B* is liable because he failed to perform his promise and *B* is liable because he invited *A* to rely on his promise. In the (tenuous) sense in which reliance is required for recovery in negligent misstatement, it is also required for recovery in contract. Accordingly, the 'need' for reliance in negligent misstatement does not argue against the assumption of responsibility model.

(v) The Role of Negligence

With the exception of Lord Morris, their Lordships in *Hedley Byrne* were clearly of the view that negligence on the part of the defendant was a necessary condition for liability. Hence, it seems reasonable to conclude that the cause of action in negligent misrepresentation is based in negligence rather than on consent. After all, contractual liability is generally said to be strict.[125] Accordingly, if the basis of liability were consensual, one would expect the issue to be whether the defendant kept to his assumed responsibility, rather than whether he was negligent.

In fact, were it not for the disclaimer, the issue in *Hedley Byrne* would indeed have been whether the defendant had lived up to its assumed responsibility. Absent the disclaimer, the defendant would have 'accepted some responsibility for his answer being given carefully, or to have accepted a relationship with the inquirer which requires him to exercise such care as the circumstances require'.[126] In other words, absent the disclaimer there would have been a 'contract to be careful'.[127] Therefore, failure to be careful would have been necessary for breach of the 'contract'.[128]

Accordingly, the assumption of responsibility model has no difficulty explaining the essential role of negligence *in these cases*. The assumed obligation was to provide information with care. Given that the information was provided, the obligation was violated only if the defendant was not careful.

[125] GH Treitel, *The Law of Contract*, 11th edn (Sweet & Maxwell, London, 2003) 838–40.

[126] *Hedley Byrne & Co Ltd v Heller & Partners Ltd* [1964] AC 465, 486 (HL) (Lord Reid).

[127] *Ibid*, 492 (Lord Reid); citing *Robinson v National Bank of Scotland Ltd* [1916] SC(HL) 154, 157 (HL) (Lord Haldane).

[128] Compare *Hedley Byrne & Co Ltd v Heller & Partners Ltd* [1964] AC 465, 504 (Lord Morris), 539–40 (Lord Pearce).

Liability arises because of the defendant's carelessness, but the conceptual basis of the liability lies in the defendant's assumed responsibility not to be careless rather than in his negligence per se.

Again, this is identical to the situation in contract. If I make a contractual promise to be careful not to harm your business interests, I breach the contract if I am not careful. But, as a general rule, I owe no duty in negligence to look out for your business interests. Hence, though I am liable because of my negligence, the basis of the liability lies in my consent, not in my negligence. I am, as it were, strictly liable not to be negligent. Similarly, if I agree to build you a house, then (unless I disclaim) I owe a duty to you to build the house well, but that duty cannot lie in the law of negligence because there is no such duty there.[129] Accordingly, though I am liable because of my negligence, the basis of the liability lies in my agreement, not in my negligence. In *Hedley Byrne*, the defendant could not be liable absent negligence, but that does not show that its potential liability was in the law of negligence proper. Rather, it was a potential liability for breaching a 'contract to be careful' (an obligation that did not in fact exist, because the disclaimer showed that the defendant made no such 'contract').

This shows that negligence has no *essential* role in negligent misrepresentation. This is reflected in the fact that negligence is often irrelevant in cases of failure to perform a service. If the defendant does not perform the promised activity, then, according to the assumption of responsibility model, the defendant is liable even if not negligent. The liability is for failing to carry out the assumed obligation, not for negligence.

The negligence theorist may reply that there is negligence in these cases: given the representation, it was negligent for the defendant not to follow through on his representation. But it is not always negligent to fail to perform an assumed responsibility, just as it is not always negligent to breach a contract. Moreover, even were the claim plausible, this argument robs the negligence model of explanatory power. It asserts that it is negligent to fail to keep one's assumed obligations. This does nothing to show that the basis of liability for negligent misrepresentation lies outside an assumption of responsibility. Moreover, this argument would show that paradigm cases of liability for breach of contract are negligence based. Hence, the argument undermines the distinction between tort and contract and between imposed and assumed responsibilities, thus removing any point in having a *negligence theory* of negligent misrepresentation. The assumption of responsibility theorist is happy to concede that there is *some* concept of negligence upon which liability for negligent misrepresentation is based, but that is not the issue. The issue is whether the basis of liability for negligent misrepresentation lies in negligence in the sense in which 'negligence' is used in the law of negligence.[130]

---

[129] *Murphy v Brentwood District Council* [1991] 1 AC 398 (HL).

[130] This discussion points up the fact that, not only are the modern approaches damaging to the law of negligence, they undermine our understanding of the law in general, distorting that law so that it can appear to fit with our mistaken views of negligence.

(vi) Criticisms of the Notion of Assumption of Responsibility

In earlier chapters, we have seen that the principled approach to the law of negligence is rejected in part because of the largely unexamined belief that it cannot
cope with economic loss. Conversely, the assumption of responsibility model of
negligent misrepresentation is rejected for a number of explicit and specific reasons. Accordingly, in order to establish the assumption of responsibility model,
it is necessary to examine these objections.

The argument that the very notion of an assumption of responsibility is
flawed comes in two guises. First, some maintain that assumptions of responsibility do not exist outside (the twentieth century common law's paradigm of)
contract. Secondly, some allege that the phrase 'assumption of responsibility' as
used by the courts is unrelated to the defendant's intentions. I discuss each view
in turn.

Brian Coote argued that no one in his right mind assumes legal responsibility
without return.[131] Hence, assumptions of responsibility occur only for consideration and, therefore, assumption of responsibility has no role to play outside
contract. In my view, Coote was wrong to assume that only the insane enter into
legal obligations without return. Moreover, Coote ignored the fact that the
defendant may make the statement for return, though that return would not
count as consideration for the purposes of contract formation.[132] But, in any
event, the assumption of responsibility theorist holds that Coote focused on the
wrong issue. On the assumption of responsibility model, the issue is not whether
the defendant agreed to place herself under a legal obligation, and still less
whether the defendant agreed to be liable. The issue is whether the defendant
placed herself under a legal obligation by guaranteeing the accuracy of some
information, by consenting to do something, etc.[133] In that light, it can be seen
that people routinely assume responsibility. In fact, far from being an aberra-
tion, assumption of responsibility is a familiar and ordinary feature of our moral
discourse: 'But you said it was true.' 'But you said you would do it.' Finally, we
must remember that the doctrine of consideration is an idiosyncrasy of the common law. The claim that consensual agreements (assumptions of responsibility)
are made only for consideration ignores the reality of much of the world's legal
practice. Though, in the common law, we refuse to call such agreements

---

[131] B Coote, 'The Effect of Hedley Byrne' (1966–1967) 2 *New Zealand Universities Law Review*
263, 271. See also K Barker, 'Unreliable Assumptions in the Modern Law of Negligence' (1993) 109
LQR 461, 470–1. In B Coote, 'Assumption of Responsibility and Pure Economic Loss in New
Zealand' [2005] *New Zealand Law Review* 1, Coote retracted his former view and accepted the
general position advanced here. Nevertheless, Coote's original view is sufficiently interesting and
influential to deserve examination.

[132] W Bishop, 'Negligent Misrepresentation Through Economists' Eyes' (1980) 96 *LQR* 360,
374–5. Bishop points out that the defendant in *Hedley Byrne* made the statement for financial reasons.

[133] *White v Jones* [1995] 2 AC 207, 273–4 (HL) (Lord Browne-Wilkinson); B Coote, 'Assumption
of Responsibility and Pure Economic Loss in New Zealand' [2005] *New Zealand Law Review* 1,
20–1; B Feldthusen, *Economic Negligence,* 4th edn (Carswell, Scarborough, 2000) 50–1.

'contracts', this must not delude us into thinking that such agreements not do exist.

I now turn to the second objection: that courts find an assumption of responsibility when the defendant did not intend such. Kit Barker presents a number of arguments to this effect.[134] Barker's first argument is that courts have found defendants to have assumed responsibilities inconsistent with obligations the defendant owed to third parties. In Barker's view, this demonstrates that liability cannot be consensual, because '[o]ne must in the ordinary case presume that it is a defendant's intention to honour his prior obligations and that no promises are made to anyone else'.[135]

Though Barker does not argue in support of imposing liability in such circumstances, I accept that it should be imposed. In fact, *contra* Barker, the assumption of responsibility model shows why this is so.

First, Barker's argument rests on the mistaken view that one cannot act in an inconsistent fashion or intend inconsistent results. There is no problem believing that a person may have assumed conflicting responsibilities. It is, after all, a common enough experience in one's ethical life. Secondly, the standard for interpreting the defendant's actions and intentions in tort and in contract is objective.[136] Hence, the issue is not what the defendant actually intended but how the defendant's intentions reasonably appeared as between the parties.[137] Lord Slynn failed to appreciate this when he said in *Phelps v Hillingdon London Borough Council*:

> It is sometimes said that there has to be an assumption of responsibility by the person concerned. That phrase can be misleading in that it can suggest that the [defendant] must knowingly and deliberately accept responsibility. It is, however, clear that the test is an objective one . . . The phrase means simply that the law recognises that there is a duty of care. It is not so much that responsibility is assumed as that it is recognised or imposed by the law.[138]

Certainly, the standard is objective, but this does not show that responsibility is imposed rather than assumed, any more than it does in contract.[139]

---

[134] K Barker, 'Unreliable Assumptions in the Modern Law of Negligence' (1993) 109 *LQR* 461, 466–7. Barker discusses representations made in informal circumstances and disclaimers, which have been examined above. See also P Cane, *Tort Law and Economic Interests*, 2nd edn (Clarendon Press, Oxford, 1996) 775–86; B Hepple, 'Negligence: The Search for Coherence' (1997) 50 *Current Legal Problems* 69, 86–90. I do not explore Hepple's criticisms in detail in here, because they depend on the notion that contractual obligation should be imposed to protect reliance. I do not regard this as necessary or desirable.

[135] K Barker, 'Unreliable Assumptions in the Modern Law of Negligence' (1993) 109 *LQR* 461, 466.

[136] *Henderson v Merrett Syndicates Ltd* [1995] 2 AC 145, 180 (HL).

[137] For reasons for preferring this formulation, see JP Vorster, 'A Comment on the Meaning of Objectivity in Contract' (1987) 103 *LQR* 274, 283–4.

[138] *Phelps v Hillingdon London Borough Council* [2001] 2 AC 619, 654 (HL).

[139] The fact that contract law adopts an objective standard has inclined some to conclude that contractual obligations are also imposed. However, this debate is irrelevant here, as the dispute between the negligence and assumption of responsibility models is premised on the existence of a division between tort and contract; a division which may as well be captured by speaking of assumed and imposed obligations, however those terms are correctly analysed.

Returning to the example discussed by Barker, if the claimant knew nothing of the defendant's other obligations, then those obligations are irrelevant in determining whether the defendant assumed responsibility to the claimant. Moreover, even if the claimant was aware of those obligations, the obligations are relevant only in providing a context in which the meaning of the defendant's utterances should be interpreted. That is, the objective meaning of the defendant's statement may be affected by knowledge of the other obligations. But the existence of the other obligations is not decisive. One can form inconsistent contracts and also assume inconsistent responsibilities.

Barker's second argument is that courts may find that a defendant has assumed responsibility though she has structured her obligations in a way that indicates that she did not intend to assume that responsibility. Barker advances *Junior Books Ltd v Veitchi Co Ltd*[140] in support of this claim, although he notes that it is not clear that the liability in that case actually lay in negligent misrepresentation.[141] Nevertheless, the claim is acceptable in principle. For instance, if A contracts with B who contracts with C, and A's contract with B is structured to exclude any liability on the part of A, though C is not aware of that, and A makes representations to C that indicate an assumption of responsibility, then it is appropriate to interpret A as having assumed responsibility to C. On the other hand, if C is aware of the structure of A's contractual obligations to B, then that is a matter to be taken into account in determining the meaning, on the objective test, of A's utterances to C.[142] The second argument fails for the same reasons as the first.

Barker's third argument is that one can be liable in negligent misrepresentation to a claimant with whom one has had no direct contact.[143] Again, though he cites only the questionable *Smith v Eric S Bush*[144] in support, such liability is explicable as a matter of principle. If A makes an utterance to B indicating that he assumes responsibility for something to C, in the knowledge that B will pass that information on to C, then it is reasonable to conclude that A has assumed responsibility to C. Similarly, one can make offers and acceptances through third party intermediaries in the law of contract.

Merrett v Babb is an instructive case in this context.[145] In order to purchase a property, the claimant and her mother applied to a building society for a mortgage. The building society instructed a firm of surveyors and valuers to value the

---

[140] *Junior Books Ltd v Veitchi Co Ltd* [1983] 1 AC 520 (HL).

[141] K Barker, 'Unreliable Assumptions in the Modern Law of Negligence' (1993) 109 *LQR* 461, 466 n 19. See also *Muirhead v Industrial Tank Specialities Ltd* [1986] 2 QB 223, 517 (CA) (Robert Goff LJ).

[142] Compare *R M Turton & Co Ltd (in liq) v Kerslake and Partners* [2000] 3 NZLR 406 (CA).

[143] K Barker, 'Unreliable Assumptions in the Modern Law of Negligence' (1993) 109 *LQR* 461, 467.

[144] [1990] 1 AC 831 (HL). The case is questionable because it explicitly rejects the assumption of responsibility model, but that rejection must now be reconsidered. Moreover, some argue that the claimants could and should have succeeded on other grounds. Eg B Feldthusen, *Economic Negligence*, 4th edn (Carswell, Scarborough, 2000) 56. This case is explored below.

[145] [2001] EWCA Civ 214, [2001] QB 1174.

property. The defendant employee of the firm conducted the investigation. The defendant knew the reason for the valuation and the names of the claimant and her mother were included in the instructions issued to the firm. The valuation produced by the defendant was passed from the defendant to the firm, from the firm to the building society and from the building society to the claimant and her mother. However, the name of the defendant and of the defendant's company was not included on the valuation when it was passed from the building society to the claimant and her mother. The valuation was conducted negligently, over-valuing the property, and the claimant suffered loss as a result.

Aldous LJ adopted the assumption of responsibility model but ruled that, as there was no direct communication between the parties, the defendant had not assumed responsibility and thus did not owe a duty of care.[146] Conversely, May LJ adopted the negligence model and held that an 'assumption of responsibility' should be imposed on the defendant.[147] Finally, Wilson J, though agreeing with May LJ's reasoning, also maintained that an assumption of responsibility had been made in the case.[148]

Though this case sits somewhere near the borderline (hence the split court), in my view the correct analysis requires a mixture of Wilson J's judgment with Aldous LJ's dissent. An assumption of responsibility is required, and there was one in *Merrett v Babb* despite the fact that there was no direct communication between the parties.[149] In order to see this, I begin by examining May LJ's reasons for concluding that no assumption of responsibility had been made:

> [I]n the circumstances of this case and particularly since Mr Babb was an employee of the firm instructed by the building society, there was no assumption of responsibility by Mr Babb personally. He knew that the valuation report which he prepared would be relied on by Miss Merrett and her mother. But his duty was to the firm by which he was employed. The purchasers should be taken to have relied on the firm, not on him personally. It was the firm that assumed responsibility to them.[150]

---

[146] [2001] EWCA Civ 214, [2001] QB 1201–3.

[147] *Ibid*, 1192–5.

[148] *Ibid*, 1198.

[149] This argument cannot apply to *White v Jones* [1995] 2 AC 207 (HL). In *Merrett v Babb*, though only the third party had direct dealings with the defendant, the third party asked the defendant to perform an action, in part, on behalf of the claimant. That is, part of the reason that the third party asked the defendant to value the property was so that the claimant could make a reasonable investment decision. The defendant knew that and agreed to perform that action. In *White v Jones*, on the other hand, the third party (the testator) did not even in part approach the defendant on the claimant's behalf. The third party merely asked the defendant to draw up a new will so that the third party's estate would benefit the people he wanted to benefit (who happened to be the claimants). However, if there were something in the dealings between the third party and the defendant—such as an assurance from the defendant to the third party that the claimants would be looked after where that assurance would be passed onto the claimants—then the defendant could have been liable for breach of an assumed responsibility. There is insufficient information to reach that conclusion in *White v Jones*.

[150] *Merrett v Babb* [2001] EWCA Civ 214, [2001] QB 1174, 1181.

First, it is not clear why the fact that the defendant had a duty to his employers shows that he did not assume responsibility to the claimant. I suppose that the idea is that the defendant conducted the valuation only because his employers instructed him to do so, and hence it is not reasonable to interpret his actions as an assumption of responsibility to the claimant. Normally that would be sufficient to justify the conclusion that no assumption of responsibility was made. But this case is different. As Wilson J pointed out:

> Mr Babb is a professional person and, by writing his name and professional qualifications at the end of the report, expressly represented, to those with access to that part of it, that it was the product of his professional expertise. Indeed, under section 13(1)(c) of the Building Societies Act 1986 the society had to seek to ensure that the officer assessing the application for an advance 'will have furnished to him a written report on the value of the land . . . made by a person who is competent to value, and is not disqualified under this section from making a report on, the land in question'.
>
> To this end, the society's printed report form required signature, name, qualifications and date to be appended to the following certificate: 'I certify that I am not disqualified under section 13 of the Building Societies Act 1986 from making this report.'
>
> This certificate was signed by Mr Babb . . . and the qualifications recited were those of Mr Babb . . . [I]t is clear to me that Mr Babb's assertion was that it was he . . . who had the necessary competence to value; he . . . who was not disqualified for any of the reasons set out in section 13(2) of the Act; and he . . . who was accordingly 'making this report'.[151]

In other words, because of the peculiar nature of the defendant's employment, it is not appropriate to view him merely as having acted for his employers. Instead, he was also acting to a degree independently, and hence it is not necessarily inappropriate to view his valuation of the house as also an assumption of responsibility to the claimant.[152]

Secondly, the fact (assuming that it is one) that the firm assumed responsibility to the claimant does nothing to show that the defendant did not also. Hence, the only reason we have for denying that the defendant assumed responsibly to the claimant was that the defendant's name was not on the document that was transferred from the building society to the claimant. But this seems to count against an assumption of responsibility only if we allow ourselves to be confused by the law of contract currently understood. The fact that the claimant did not know who the defendant was gives no reason to conclude that the defendant did not assume responsibility to the claimant. The issue is the defendant's state of mind (interpreted in accordance with the objective test), not the claimant's. As May LJ said, 'The instruction form stated that the building society was considering an application for a mortgage on the property from Miss Merrett and her

---

[151] *Ibid*, 1198.

[152] In that light, with respect to its second defendant, *Williams v Natural Life Health Foods Ltd* [1998] 1 WLR 830 (HL) is an entirely different case. See *ibid*, 837–8 where Lord Steyn makes it clear that the second defendant was not independent in this sense.

mother'.[153] Accordingly, the purpose of the valuation was plain to the defendant and he acted independently in producing it. The fact that the claimant did not know who he was does nothing to show that he did not assume responsibility to the claimant. To adopt for a moment the language of contact, the fact that the claimant did not know who the defendant was presents a problem for one who wants to claim that the claimant 'accepted', but no problem for the notion that the defendant made an 'offer'. Of course, for an 'offer' to have legal effect it must be communicated to the claimant; but it was. As May LJ noted, the claimant 'knew that it was a report prepared for [the] Building Society by an independent valuer, but [the claimant] did not know who the valuer was'.[154] Note also that May LJ accepted that the firm assumed responsibility to the claimant. But the claimant knew no more about the firm than she did about the defendant. If the firm assumed responsibility to the claimant, prima facie, so did the defendant.[155]

Apparently against this, in *Williams v Natural Life Health Foods Ltd* Lord Steyn said:

> The touchstone of liability is not the [subjective or actual] state of mind of the defendant. An objective test means that the primary focus must be on things said or done by the defendant or on his behalf in dealings with the plaintiff. Obviously, the impact of what a defendant says or does must be judged in the light of the relevant contextual scene. Subject to this qualification the primary focus must be on exchanges (in which term I include statements and conduct) which cross the line between the defendant and the plaintiff.[156]

The only problem with this passage is Lord Steyn's use of the word 'exchanges', which seems to imply that an assumption of responsibility can be made only if there were, direct or indirect, communications from the defendant to the claimant *and* from the claimant to the defendant. But only the former is required for the defendant to make an assumption of responsibility to the claimant. Lord Steyn was certainly right that there must be a communication 'which cross[es] the line between the defendant and the plaintiff', but that does not require an exchange in the strict (and probably unintended) sense of the term.

Barker's fourth argument is that assumptions of responsibility have sometimes been found when there was no evidence that one had been made. Barker cites three cases in support of this claim, two of which are the concurrently decided: *Smith v Eric S Bush* and *Harris v Wyre Forest District Council*.[157] The claimants borrowed money from third parties in order to purchase property.

---

[153] *Merrett v Babb* [2001] EWCA Civ 214, [2001] QB 1174, 1181. Note also that this means that the assumption of responsibility was not made to an indeterminate class of persons but to specific people, the claimant and her mother. This, then, does not conflict with the argument against imposing an assumption of responsibility on builders for the quality of their products to subsequent purchasers in ch 7.

[154] *Ibid.*

[155] Recall that all reference to the defendant and his employers was omitted from the forms given to the claimant.

[156] *Williams v Natural Life Health Foods Ltd* [1998] 1 WLR 830, 835 (HL).

[157] [1990] 1 AC 831 (HL).

The third parties arranged for the defendants to conduct valuations of the properties. The defendants knew the purpose of the valuations and so knew that the claimants would rely on the valuations. The valuations were conducted negligently and the claimants suffered loss as a result. The defendants disclaimed any responsibility to the claimants. Nevertheless, the defendants were found liable.

A majority of their Lordships ruled that, while the disclaimers would have negatived liability at common law, the defendant was precluded from appealing to them, and thus the disclaimers were of no effect because, in the circumstances, they were unreasonable under section 11(3) of the Unfair Contract Terms Act 1977.[158] Though their Lordships founded this conclusion on the negligence model, it is at least equally consistent with the assumption of responsibility model. Again, we are not interested in whether the defendant subjectively intended to assume responsibility, but in whether he did so on an objective test. In line with the discussion of *Merrett v Babb* above, absent the disclaimers the defendants assumed responsibility to the claimants. Given that, the disclaimers were the only evidence suggesting that the defendants did not assume responsibility. But the defendants were precluded from relying on the disclaimers by the Unfair Contract Terms Act. Hence, it was reasonable to conclude that the defendants assumed responsibility to the claimants. This is evidenced by the fact that, if the claimants had paid the defendants for the valuation, they would have been able to sue for breach of contract. As Bruce Feldthusen has argued, '[t]he fate of the voluntary assumption of responsibility approach in other contexts should be determined in comparison to other options. The speeches in *Smith* offer nothing useful in that regard'.[159] Actually, the fact that their Lordships believed that the Unfair *Contract* Terms Act was relevant tends to indicate support for the assumption of responsibility rather than the negligence model.

The third case mentioned by Barker, *Ministry of Housing and Local Development v Sharp*,[160] is also unproblematic. The claimant registered a planning charge on a piece of property with the defendants for £1,828 11s 5d. A third party company asked the defendants to conduct an official search to determine, inter alia, whether any planning charges were registered on the property. The search was conducted negligently and the third party company was informed that no charge existed. In light of that information, the company purchased the property. As the charge could not be recovered from the company, the claimant alleged that it had lost the benefit of its charge due to the defendants' negligence. The Court of Appeal accepted that argument and allowed the claimant to recover £1,828 11s 5d from the defendant. The defendants had made no assumption of responsibility to the claimant. However, the defendants were under a statutory duty carefully to search the register and that statutory duty was designed to protect, inter alia, people in the position of the claimant.[161]

---

[158] I do not claim that this finding was correct. Nor does my argument rely on its being correct.
[159] B Feldthusen, *Economic Negligence,* 4th edn (Carswell, Scarborough, 2000) 56.
[160] [1970] 2 QB 223 (CA).
[161] *Ibid*, 265 (Lord Denning MR).

Hence, liability can be supported on two possible heads: either the defendants were liable for breach of a statutory duty or for breaching an assumption of responsibility that they were statutorily obliged to make. On the latter view, the assumption of responsibility is fictional, but not fictional in the sense that it has been invented to support the assumption of responsibility model. Rather, it is a fictional creation of statute, much like the legal personality of companies. There is no objection to the assumption of responsibility model here.

Barker's criticisms of the assumption of responsibility model are not compelling.

D. Conclusion

The so-called tort of negligent misrepresentation is based on an assumption of responsibility by the defendant to the claimant. Moreover, as we have seen, although negligence is usually required in order to support a cause of action, that is not always the case. Accordingly, there is no law of negligent misrepresentation if we mean a law whose basis of liability lies in negligently made statements. This should be recognised openly. We should say that the law of negligent misrepresentation does not exist and find a better name for the cause of action. The liability is for the breach of an assumed obligation.

Accordingly, liability for 'negligent misrepresentation' is in no way inconsistent with the argument in Chapter 7. Moreover, it is a perfectly principled head of liability that needs no help from policy in order to set sensible limits to recovery.

Moreover, a correct understanding of 'negligent misrepresentation' again reveals the weakness of the modern approaches. Given the very important differences between assumption of responsibility and the ordinary law of negligence, the ability of the modern approaches to negligence to accommodate 'negligent misrepresentation' reveals the emptiness of those approaches. They are so wide-open, so void of content, that they are applicable to anything. It is no surprise, then, that they are incapable of solving any important issues.

The last two chapters have dealt with two of the most pressing and difficult problems facing the modern law of negligence.[162] The modern law deals with them by implementing a hoard of policies to keep liability under control. The policies are unpersuasive and are, in fact, veils for judicial intuition: 'not logic [but] . . . practical politics',[163] 'an educated reflex to the facts',[164] an 'instinctive feeling'.[165] It is ironic, though not surprising, that judges, who are experts in law, tend to utilise policy arguments, about which they on the whole have no expertise, to return more often than not to the outcomes that they would have

---

[162] The third is nervous shock and is explored in ch 11.

[163] *Palsgraf v Long Island Railroad Co* 162 NE 99 (NY CA 1928) 103 (Andrews J).

[164] *Smith v Littlewoods Organisation Ltd* [1987] 1 AC 241, 271 (HL) (Lord Goff).

[165] *Lamb v Camden London BC* [1981] 1 QB 625, 647 (CA) (Watkins LJ). This issue is also examined in A Beever, 'Particularism and Prejudice in the Law of Tort' (2003) 11 *Tort Law Review* 146.

produced had they concentrated solely on law and ignored policy altogether. Nor is it surprising that judges' instincts by and large cohere with the principled approach. But it would be preferable if we also understood the legal justifications of those instincts.

III. 'NEGLIGENT MISREPRESENTATION' AND THE PRIVATE LAW

Recall the picture of the private law discussed in Chapter 7.

Recognition of Primary Rights	Responses to Violations of Primary Rights—Secondary Rights
Property ————————	Wrongs (eg trespass, conversion, *negligence*)
Contract ————————	(Breach of) Contract
Law of Persons ————	Wrongs (eg battery, assault, defamation, false imprisonment, *negligence*)

The discussion in this chapter has revealed that this picture also is inadequate. This is because it has no place for assumptions of responsibility or for other rights and obligations that arise from consents that fall short of contracts. Some of these implicitly arise in the law of negligence. In order to accommodate these cases, the species, 'contract', needs to be replaced with the genus, 'consents'. Moreover, equity must also be added.[166]

Recognition of Primary Rights	Responses to Violations of Primary Rights—Secondary Rights
Property (equitable and legal) ————	Wrongs (eg trespass, conversion, *negligence*, some equitable wrongs)
Law of Persons ————	Wrongs (eg battery, assault defamation, false imprisonment, *negligence*)
Consents (common law and equity, including estoppel and perhaps some or all fiduciary duties)	(Breach of) Contract Breach of an Assumption of Responsibility Breach of Trust Breach of Fiduciary Duty Breach of Other Assumed Obligations (eg obligations to invitees)

---

[166] I still avoid unjust enrichment and the diagram is not intended to be complete.

Accordingly, the notion that the law of contract is a completely separate area of the law from the law of tort has done considerable harm to our understanding of the law as a whole. In fact, tort law responds to all three kinds of primary rights. Moreover, when one distinguishes between the parts of the law of tort that recognise rights (the law of persons and a subset of the law of consents) and the parts that protect rights (a subset of the law of wrongs), and also between the part of the law of contract that recognises rights (a subset of the law of consents) and the part that protects those rights (breach of contract), it becomes apparent that the distinction between tort and contract is fundamentally unstable. The formation of a contract is not a unique event in law. Rather, there are many obligations that arise from consent, contract is only the paradigm example. Hence, part of the law of tort and part of the law of contract recognise primary obligations based on consent. Moreover, other parts of the law of tort and of the law of contract respond to violations of those consent-based primary rights. Simply, breach of contract is the wrong of failing to keep one's assumed obligations in exactly the same way as 'negligent misrepresentation', breach of many trusts, or perhaps breach of a fiduciary obligation are violations of assumed obligations.[167] Tort and contract, as well as equity, are thoroughly intertwined. It is impossible fully to understand them separately.[168]

As Lord Devlin pointed out in *Hedley Byrne*, the common law requires a tort of 'negligent misrepresentation' only because the law of contract contains doctrines that limit contract formation: most importantly the doctrine of consideration.[169] Hence, before *Hedley Byrne*, consent-based obligations could not be enforced at law unless they supported an estoppel, arose in circumstances that supported the creation of a trust or fiduciary obligation or were made for consideration. This produced a gap in the law that needed to be filled. Consider again Lord Devlin's hypothetical: 'a defendant says to a plaintiff: "Let me do this for you; do not waste your money in employing a professional, I will do it for nothing and you can rely on me"'.[170] If the claimant does rely to her detriment, then it is intolerable to refuse to compensate her. Hence, this lacuna

---

[167] R Grantham and C Rickett, *Enrichment and Restitution in New Zealand* (Hart Publishing, Oxford, 2000) 49.

[168] The temptation to treat breach of contract as part of the law of consents is understandable from the perspective of the history of the common law, but it must be resisted. While contracts come into existence through consent, they are not breached by consent. Note also that the view argued for here is quite different from that promoted by PS Atiyah, *The Rise and Fall of Freedom of Contract* (Oxford University Press, Oxford, 1979) and G Gilmore, *The Death of Contract* (Ohio State University Press, Columbus, Ohio, 1974). I do not argue that contract has been absorbed into the law of tort. On the contrary, I argue that parts of the law of tort actually recognise obligations of a kind usually thought to arise only in the law of contract. Hence, I do not question the distinction between imposed and assumed obligations. I argue only that that distinction is not the distinction between tort and contract. I am no 'contorts' theorist.

[169] *Hedley Byrne & Co Ltd v Heller & Partners Ltd* [1964] AC 465, 525–6 (HL). See also B Hepple, 'Negligence: The Search for Coherence' (1997) 50 *Current Legal Problems* 69, 88; B Markesinis, 'An Expanding Tort Law—The Price of a Rigid Contract Law' (1987) 103 *LQR* 354. The issue is explored below.

[170] *Hedley Byrne & Co Ltd v Heller & Partners Ltd* [1964] AC 465, 531 (HL).

was filled by the tort of 'negligent misrepresentation'. This was well put by Lord Steyn in *Williams*:

> [T]he restricted conception of contract in English law, resulting from the combined effect of the principles of consideration and privity of contract, was the backcloth against which the *Hedley Byrne* case was decided . . . In *The Pioneer Container, KH Enterprise cargo owners v Pioneer Container (owners)*[171] . . . Lord Goff . . . said that it was open to question how long the principles of consideration and privity of contract will continue to be maintained. It may become necessary for the House of Lords to re-examine the principles of consideration and privity of contract. But while the present structure of English contract law remains intact the law of tort, as the general law, has to fulfil an essential gap-filling role. In these circumstances there was, and is, no better rationalisation for the relevant head of tort liability than assumption of responsibility.[172]

This explanation is only partial, however. Certainly, the obligation to perform responsibilities assumed without consideration could not have been recognised in contract without amending the doctrine of consideration. But this does not explain why the obligation was recognised in the law of negligence rather than in contract. *Hedley Byrne* is widely considered to be one of the most important cases of the twentieth century and to be a radical alteration to the law of negligence. Why is it acceptable to inflict upheaval on the law of negligence but not on the law of contract? Why was the doctrine of consideration not abandoned? This is a particularly pressing question, given the also widespread questioning of the doctrine of consideration and the recognition that the doctrine is an idiosyncrasy of the common law.

In part, the answer is that their Lordships in *Hedley Byrne* were still officially bound by their previous judgments.[173] But this too is insufficient to answer our question. The fact is that their Lordships and most commentators share the view that, while the established doctrines of the law of contract must be treated with considerable respect, the doctrines of the law of negligence need not be.[174] Why? The answer may in part be a belief that changes to contract law have greater and more widespread effect on the community, particularly the economy, than do changes in the law of negligence.[175] If so, that would seem to be mistaken. As many studies have shown, business people in fact make little use of contract law.[176] Moreover, given that the law of negligence is part of the general law, it has a very significant impact on the lives of all.

---

[171] *The Pioneer Container* [1994] 2 AC 324, 335 (PC).
[172] *Williams v Natural Life Health Foods Ltd* [1998] 1 WLR 830, 837 (HL).
[173] Compare *Practice Statement (Judicial Precedent)* [1966] 1 WLR 1234 (HL).
[174] This was also explored in relation to Cooke J's judgment in *Gartside v Sheffield, Young & Ellis* [1983] NZLR 37 (CA) in ch 5.
[175] See eg J Smillie, 'Is Security of Contract Worth Pursuing?—Reflections on the Function of Contract Law' (2000) 16 *Journal of Contract Law* 148 for *some* support for this view.
[176] See H Collins, *Regulating Contracts* (Oxford University Press, Oxford, 1999) which both discusses the arguments and contains an extensive bibliography of the literature.

In my view, the main reason *Hedley Byrne* was officially 'a negligence case' was that the structure of the law of negligence was and is less well understood than that of contract law. In contract law, primary rights are recognised through the explicit doctrines of formation. In the law of negligence, however, primary rights are often only implicit and unarticulated and gain recognition only indirectly by being enforced. Therefore, it was possible to recognise a new primary right 'in negligence' in *Hedley Byrne,* while fudging the nature of that right. Because the law of negligence deals with many unarticulated rights, the right in *Hedley Byrne* could simply be added to the list. The law of negligence is the common law's Swiss Army knife.

As F.S.C. Milsom has told us:

> The life of the common law has been in the abuse of its elementary ideas. If the rules of property give what seems an unjust answer, try obligation; and equity has proved that from the materials of obligation you can counterfeit the phenomena of property. If the rules of contract give what now seems an unjust answer, try tort. Your counterfeit will look odd to one brought up on categories of Roman origin; but it will work. If the rules of one tort, say deceit, give what now seems an unjust answer, try another, try negligence. And so the legal world goes around.[177]

But Milsom makes clear that this has done considerable damage to the development of the common law. The attempt to locate agreement based obligations in tort has led to considerable confusion, as has the attempt to protect testamentary rights in tort, as we saw in Chapter 7.

In this context, the attempt to see 'negligent misstatement' as belonging to the law of negligence has not boded well for the conceptual coherence of the law of negligence or of the cause of action known as 'negligent misrepresentation'. This is because the primary right recognised in 'negligent misrepresentation' cases belongs to an entirely different area of law from the other primary rights usually implicitly recognised in the law of negligence. It does not belong to the law of persons, nor to the law of property. Rather, it is a right that is derived from another's consent.[178] The resulting confusion has meant both that the law of negligence has been distorted by the attempt to incorporate 'negligent misrepresentation' within it and that the law of 'negligent misrepresentation' has been deformed by forcing it into the structure of negligence liability, creating the need for the constant application of policy. This apparent need evaporates once we have elucidated the primary right upon which the cause of action is based.

---

[177] SFC Milsom, *Historical Foundations of the Common Law* (Butterworths, London, 1981) 6.

[178] Tort law has long dealt with violations of rights to the person that are given especially strong protection only because of consent. For instance, one owes special duties to protect the bodily integrity of those one invites onto one's land. But, in these cases, the primary right remains the right to bodily integrity and hence is not created by the consent. Note that none of the above implies that the principles of the law of negligence are irrelevant to the issue of 'negligent misrepresentation' and assumption of responsibility. If the defendant assumes responsibility to perform a task carefully, then the principles of the law of negligence are likely to be relevant, though they do not directly apply. But that is because of the nature of the consent.

This discussion leads on to a crucial question: How is assumption of responsibility related to contract? In my view, the answer to this question must cause a rethink of contract formation. If 'negligent misrepresentation' exists simply to get round the doctrine of consideration in contract, then the continued existence of the doctrine must be illusory. Moreover, even if the argument of this chapter fails, the general understanding of contract is revealed to be flawed. I have argued that all successful actions for 'negligent misrepresentation' accompany an assumption of responsibility. I have not argued that all assumptions of responsibility are actionable as 'negligent misrepresentations'. That claim does not need arguing as it is already widely accepted.[179] But if that is so, then what is the point of insisting on consideration in contract any longer?

Consider the following two examples. First, A asks B to do his gardening in return for a nominal sum. B accepts but fails to perform, causing £10 loss to A. Secondly, C asks D to do his gardening in return for no consideration. D accepts but fails to perform, causing £10 loss to C. It is an article of faith that only A has a contract. Hence, only A can recover £10 for breach of a contract. But, as we have discovered, C can sue D for 'negligent misrepresentation'—that is for failure to perform a promised service.[180] Therefore, C can also recover £10 from D. Moreover, both A and C are able to recover because B and D breached an obligation they consensually undertook. Why, then, distinguish between contract and 'negligent misrepresentation'? Both enforce agreements. Only the former requires consideration, but all examples of breached contracts will also be instances of 'negligence misrepresentation' and the scope of the latter is wider than that of the former. In other words, legally binding agreements—whether we call them contracts or not—can be formed without consideration.

According to Coote's recent reappraisal of assumption of responsibility, that notion's 'significance may lie in its potential eventually to develop into what in effect, if not in theory, would be a new form of contract without consideration'.[181] But this misdescribes the situation. If the argument above is right, then it is already the case that legally binding agreements are made without consideration, both in theory and in practice. The only potential eventuality is our finally realising what has already happened.

However, as this is a book on the law of negligence, a full discussion of this question will have to be left for another time.

---

[179] See eg *A-G v Carter* [2003] 2 NZLR 160, 168 (CA).
[180] *Henderson v Merrett Syndicates Ltd* [1995] 2 AC 145 (HL).
[181] B Coote, 'Assumption of Responsibility and Pure Economic Loss in New Zealand' [2005] *New Zealand Law Review* 1, 22.

IV. THE RIGHT OF *SPRING*[182]

It remains to consider one further case: *Spring v Guardian Assurance*.[183] This must be dealt with separately and at the end of our discussion because it raises concerns that rely on the previous two chapters as well as issues relevant to the law of defamation not explored in this book.

In *Spring*, the claimant, who had worked for the defendants, applied for a position with a new company. In accordance with applicable rules,[184] the company sought a reference concerning the claimant from the defendants. The defendants were obliged by the rules to provide this reference and accordingly did so. The reference stated that the claimant lacked integrity. At trial, the claimant convinced the judge that this statement, though not made with malice, was false and was made negligently. It was alleged that the claimant was not employed by the new company, thus suffering loss, because of the statement in the reference. A majority of the House of Lords held that the defendants owed the claimant a duty of care and thus, if causation were established,[185] could recover.

Lords Lowry, Slynn and Wolf came to this conclusion based on their understanding of the ordinary law of negligence. The claimant had suffered a reasonably foreseeable factual loss as the result of the defendants' negligence. Hence, in the absence of good reasons to the contrary, it was fair, just and reasonable to find the defendants liable. Their Lordships did not believe that there were such reasons.

Lord Keith came to the opposite conclusion. According to his Lordship, reasons of public policy were sufficient in this case to negative the prima facie duty of care.[186] Lord Keith's argument was based on a comparison with the law of defamation. Clearly, the statement in the reference that the claimant lacked integrity was defamatory. Hence, on its face, the claimant could have sued the defendants for defamation. However, statements in references are protected by the defence of qualified privilege unless their publisher was guilty of malice.[187] In *Spring*, the claimant had been unable to establish malice on the part of the defendants. This was enough for Lord Keith to conclude that the defendants did not owe a duty of care in negligence to the claimant. The policy behind the existence of the qualified privilege should apply equally to the law of negligence,

---

[182]   This title contains a deliberate allusion to Lord Cooke of Thorndon, 'The Right of *Spring*' in P Cane and J Stapleton (eds), *The Law of Obligations: Essays in Celebration of John Fleming* (Clarendon Press, Oxford, 1998), which ironically contains no references to rights whatsoever, but rather considers 'the clash between apparently solidly-settled black-letter precedents and new public policy'.

[183]   [1995] 2 AC 296 (HL).

[184]   Rule 3.5(2) of the Lautro Rules 1988.

[185]   I ignore this issue in the following.

[186]   *Spring v Guardian Assurance* [1995] 2 AC 296, 307–14 (HL).

[187]   See especially *Horrocks v Lowe* [1975] AC 135 (HL).

and so the claimant should have failed. That decision was supported by the judgments of the New Zealand Court of Appeal in *Balfour v AG*[188] and the New South Wales Supreme Court in *Sattin v Nationwide News*.[189]

According to some commentators, the issue here is simply the strength of the relevant policy considerations. As Lord Cooke has said, 'most "policy" arguments on the duty of care are not capable of accurate measurement. The argument that *Spring* will discourage candid references is put in that category.'[190] But there is more to be said about the case than that. The fundamental question is: what right in the claimant, if any, did the defendants interfere with in *Spring*? There are three general kinds of answers.

The first answer is that the right is a right to reputation. If this is so, then *Spring* is an even more innovative case than most imagine. Not only does it allow one to sue for the commission of an event that would be actionable in defamation were it not thwarted by a defence, it also responds to the violation of the same right as does the law of defamation. But it is usually believed that the right to reputation is protected only by the law of defamation. Moreover, if *Spring* responded to the violation of the same right as does the law of defamation, then it is irrational for the defence of qualified privilege to exist in defamation but not in negligence. If the law responds to the same right, then the defence should either apply or not, regardless of the cause of action.

To determine whether the defence should apply or not would take us well outside the subject of this book. But it suffices to say that, if the right in question is a right to reputation, then the reasons presented by Lords Lowry, Slynn and Wolf are quite inadequate to establish their conclusion. In particular, to the extent that those judgments call for liability in negligence while leaving the defence of qualified privilege in defamation intact, they are incoherent.[191]

But perhaps their Lordships thought that the right violated in the claimant lay elsewhere. This would free them from the charge of incoherence,[192] but it is hard to see where that right might lie. The defendants did not violate the claimant's bodily integrity or property rights. Nor does it appear possible to find a more specific right, such as a right to employment, as it is trite that there is no such thing—the unemployed are not able to sue because they cannot find work, for example. Nor could we say that one has a right not to be deprived of employment by others' negligence. The potential future employees of the claimant in *Spartan Steel & Alloys Ltd v Martin & Co (Contractors) Ltd*[193] who were not hired because of the economic damage suffered could not have sued the

---

[188] [1991] 1 NZLR 519 (CA).

[189] (1996) 39 NSWLR 32 (SC).

[190] Lord Cooke of Thorndon, 'The Right of *Spring*' in P Cane and J Stapleton (eds), *The Law of Obligations: Essays in Celebration of John Fleming* (Clarendon Press, Oxford, 1998) 43.

[191] Compare P Birks, 'More Logic and Less Experience: The Difference between Scots Law and English Law' in D Carey Miller and R Zimmermann (eds), *The Civilian Tradition and Scots Law* (Duncker & Humblot, Berlin, 1997).

[192] Compare *ibid*, who neglects this point.

[193] [1973] QB 27 (CA).

defendant, for instance. Though it is not possible entirely to rule out the existence of a relevant right without a full investigation of the rights found in the private law, which cannot be undertaken here, it appears that there was no such right in *Spring* and there is nothing in the judgments of Lords Lowry, Slynn and Wolf to indicate otherwise.

But there is a third possibility that is revealed by Lord Goff's judgment. This is that the defendants' liability was based on an assumption of responsibility made to the claimant.[194] Note that if this argument succeeds, then Lord Goff was not guilty of dealing inconsistently with the laws of negligence and defamation.[195] In fact, on that point Lord Goff was in agreement with Lord Keith that, if an assumption of responsibility could not be found, then the defence of qualified privilege must also defeat the claimant's allegations in negligence.[196] On Lord Goff's view, the defendants were not liable because they damaged the reputation of the claimant, but because they promised the claimant that they would do something that they did not do. It just so happened that in not doing what they promised to do they damaged the reputation of the claimant, but that is not the basis of the cause of action. In full, the allegation was that the defendants promised the claimant to be careful in drawing up their reference but were not so, their failure to be careful resulted in damage to the claimant's reputation, and so the defendants were liable for that damage—not because they caused it per se, but because it was a reasonably foreseeable consequence of the breach of their promise. This position is entirely logical and, if the defendants did in fact assume responsibility to the claimant, then Lord Goff was assuredly right. But was the antecedent of the conditional true?

It would appear that it was not. If the reference was requested by the claimant, even if indirectly,[197] then it would have been plausible to have found that an assumption of responsibility had been made to the claimant.[198] In *Spring*, however, the reference was requested not by the claimant but by a third party. Lord Goff argued that 'where the plaintiff entrusts the defendant with the conduct of his affairs . . . the defendant may be held to have assumed responsibility to the plaintiff, and the plaintiff to have relied on the defendant to exercise due skill and care, in respect of such conduct'.[199] That is certainly true, at least as a general rule, but it does not apply to this case. The difficulty is with the word 'entrust', which tends to encourage equivocation in this context. In *Spring*, the claimant did not *en*trust the defendant with the conduct of his affairs. The request for the reference came from a third party. The claimant may have *trusted* (ie relied on) the defendant with the conduct of his affairs, but that

---

[194] *Spring v Guardian Assurance* [1995] 2 AC 296, 318 (HL).

[195] Again, compare P Birks, 'More Logic and Less Experience: The Difference Between Scots Law and English Law' in D Casey Miller and R Zimmermann (eds), *The Civilian Tradition and Scots Law* (Duncker & Humblot, Berlin, 1997).

[196] *Spring v Guardian Assurance* [1995] 2 AC 296, 316 (HL).

[197] Compare *Merrett v Babb* [2001] EWCA Civ 214, [2001] QB 1174.

[198] See *Lawton v BOC Transhield Ltd* [1987] ICR 7 (QBD).

[199] *Spring v Guardian Assurance* [1995] 2 AC 296, 318 (HL).

is another matter. The claimant's reliance was reasonably foreseeable, but there is insufficient evidence of an assumption of responsibility by the defendant to the claimant.

Moreover, the fact that the defendants were under an obligation to provide the reference indicates that they did not assume responsibility to the claimant or even to the third party. If they provided the reference only because they had to, then they were not voluntarily undertaking anything.[200]

Lord Goff attempted to meet this difficulty by locating the assumption of responsibility in the original employment relationship:

> Where the relationship between the parties is that of employer and employee, the duty of care could be expressed as arising from an implied term of the contract of employment, i.e. that, if a reference is supplied by the employer for the employee, due care and skill will be exercised by him in its preparation. Such a term . . . may be expressed to apply even after the employee has left his employment with the employer.[201]

The issue here, then, is really one of contract. According to Lord Goff, in forming an employment contract employers implicitly agree to provide with care future references for their employees. Again, whether this is so lies outside the scope of this analysis, but it appears to be highly doubtful.

This is not to say that *Spring* was wrongly decided. It may be that promises of the kind envisaged by Lord Goff are implied by employment contracts, or that the defence of qualified privilege to defamation should be altered, or that it is possible to find another right upon which to base the claimant's case. But in the absence of those proofs, we must conclude that the position taken in Australia and New Zealand is to be preferred.

---

[200] Compare the discussion of *Merrett v Babb* above, in which the defendant was under a duty to conduct the valuation, but special circumstances applied.

[201] *Spring v Guardian Assurance* [1995] 2 AC 296, 320 (HL).

9

Nonfeasance and the Liability of Public Bodies

THE GENERAL DISTINCTION between misfeasance and nonfeasance was introduced in Chapter 6. As we saw there, misfeasance is the violation of a primary right and is actionable, while nonfeasance includes actions that cause factual injury but do not violate primary rights and is therefore not actionable. In Chapter 7, we saw how this feature of the law applies in relation to economic loss. In this chapter, I explore the nature of nonfeasance in more detail.

These days, almost all the action in this area concerns the liability of public bodies. However, as we discover, the liability of public bodies raises special issues that take us outside the narrower confines of the law of negligence proper. Because of this, I begin by discussing nonfeasance in circumstances that do not involve public bodies. The relevant cases tend to be relatively old and also to come from North America where, partly because of the development of the railways, the issue has attracted more notice than it has in the Commonwealth outside North America.

I. NONFEASANCE IN GENERAL

A. The Scope of the Rule

In *Union Pacific Railway Co v Cappier*,[1] the claimant's son was struck by a train and lost an arm and a leg, while attempting to cross the tracks of a railway operated by the defendant. The defendant's employees at first did nothing to aid the claimant's son, though other employees later bound his wounds and called for an ambulance. The claimant's son subsequently died in hospital of his wounds. No negligence on the part of the defendant or his employees contributed to the initial accident, but the claimant maintained that the defendant's employees were negligent in not coming sooner to her son's aid.[2]

---

[1] *Union Pacific Railway Co v Cappier* 72 P 281 (Kansas SC 1903).
[2] Recall that in a wrongful death action of this kind, the actual claimant seeks to recover for the violation of the deceased's rights, not her own. The ability to do so is a creature of statute.

Naturally, the claimant's son had a right to bodily integrity, but the accident did not infringe that right. Hence, the cutting off of the claimant's son's arm and leg was not a violation of his bodily integrity. And, as we have seen, there is no duty to rescue. Hence, Smith J ruled that the claimant could not recover. In doing so, he distinguished *Northern Central Railway Co v The State*,[3] which counsel for the claimant had argued was analogous. In that case, the victim was struck by a train and was left in an insensible state. The defendant's employees, believing the victim to have died, failed to call for medical assistance or to inform the victim's family. Instead, they placed the victim on a plank and locked him in a nearby warehouse. The victim was found the next morning, really dead this time though his body was still warm. He had died in the night from a haemorrhage.

There were two crucial differences between this case and *Cappier*. First, as the Court in the later case noted, in *Northern Central Railway* the initial accident was caused by the negligence of the defendant's employees. The train had been travelling too fast over a crossing without sounding its whistle and there had been an insufficient number of brakemen on the train.[4] Accordingly, the initial injury to the victim was the result of the defendant's wrongdoing, and hence a duty of care was owed. Therefore, because of the initial negligence, the defendant was responsible for the condition of the victim and so was obliged to act to minimise his injury. Locking him in a warehouse did not discharge that responsibility. Secondly, in placing the victim in a warehouse, the employees of the defendant appear to have made him worse off than he would have been had he been left in the open. This is because it was impossible for anyone else to come to the aid of the victim or for him to have obtained aid for himself. Hence, this too was an interference with the victim's rights.

The distinction between these two cases is clear. Liability in *Northern Central Railway* does not imply that there should have been liability in *Cappier*. But was *Cappier* rightly decided? I suggest not, and in doing so I draw on the more recent decision of the Manitoba Court of Appeal in *Oke v Weide Transport Ltd*.[5]

While driving, the defendant non-negligently struck and knocked down a traffic sign in the gravel strip of a highway. The defendant removed the damaged sign except for a metal post imbedded in the ground that he could not shift. The defendant did not report the accident to the authorities. The following day, a driver used the gravel strip to pass another vehicle and was speared by the post, which came through the floor of his vehicle and pierced his chest. The claimant alleged that the defendant was negligent in not reporting the accident.

The majority of the Court found for the defendant on the ground that the death of the driver was not reasonably foreseeable from the perspective of the defendant's alleged negligence. That was a reasonable conclusion, given that it

---

[3] 29 Md 420 (MD CA 1868).
[4] *Union Pacific Railway Co v Cappier* 72 P 281, 282 (Kansas SC 1903).
[5] (1963) 41 DLR (2d) 53 (Man CA).

is most unusual to overtake along gravel strips and the act was prohibited. The dissent, however, held that the driver's injury was reasonably foreseeable. This meant that the dissent had to confront the problem that the alleged negligence of the defendant was that he failed to report something and that that sounds much like a duty to rescue. As Freedman JA said:

> Counsel for the defendant advanced another argument that I must now consider. Starting from the premise that the defendant's collision with the signpost was not the result of his negligence, he urged that thereafter the defendant was under no duty whatever with respect to the broken sign. Without such a duty towards other motorists, including the plaintiffs, no negligence could be ascribed to him. His position, it was argued, was no different from that of any other motorist who, driving by and observing the broken sign, did nothing about it.[6]

But Freedman JA rejected this position:.

> [E]ven if we assume that such other motorist would not be liable, it is wrong to think that the defendant's position is on all fours with his. Indeed it is decidedly different. Our other motorist did not collide with the sign; the defendant did, even if it was without negligence. . . . The former, having had no part in the destruction of the sign, was never anything more than an innocent passer-by who might not be under a legal duty to take active steps to control the situation; the defendant on the other hand participated in the creation of the hazard . . . It is entirely unrealistic, in my view, to try to assimilate his position to that of some passing motorist.[7]

Freeman JA's argument reminds us that one can create risks, even serious risks,[8] without being negligent. That will occur when it was not reasonably foreseeable that the action that created the risk would create that risk. Assuming that the injury to the driver was reasonably foreseeable as the dissent held, the defendant in *Oke* was not negligent in knocking down the sign, but his knocking down the sign nevertheless created a serious risk of injury of the kind suffered by the driver. Now, the defendant was not negligent in creating that risk. But he was negligent if, once the risk had been created, he did not act appropriately to eliminate the risk. As he could not remove the post, assuming that the driver's injury was not remote, the claimant should have been able to recover if it could have been proven that, had the defendant informed the authorities, the accident would not have occurred—probably either because the post would have been removed or because warning signs would have been put in place.

I now present these ideas more abstractly. As a moral person, one is responsible only for the consequences of one's actions. Hence, we may say, in line with

---

[6] *Ibid*, [27]–[28].

[7] *Ibid*, [28].

[8] In the following, I speak of 'serious risks' to avoid confusion with what were defined in ch 3 as 'substantial', 'small', 'real' and 'FOFF' risks, all of which require foreseeability. As I use the term here, risks are serious if they impose a high degree of risk, whether or not that would be recognised by an ordinary reasonable person at the time.

the discussion in Chapter 3, that actions and only actions are candidates for liability. The first consequence of this is the one explored in Chapter 3: that one cannot be liable for injuries that are occasioned by causes other than one's actions. In that Chapter, we also saw that in order to be liable the defendant must have created a real risk. There are two general ways in which a defendant can do so. Ordinarily, this occurs when the defendant performs an action in circumstances in which an ordinary reasonable person would recognise that the action imposed a real risk of injury to another. But this is not the only way in which such a risk can be created. Though it is much more complex and much more unusual, the defendant also creates a real risk in the following situation.

1. The defendant performs an action that imposes a serious risk of injury to another, but no reasonable person would recognise that fact;

And 2. the action has a consequence that imposes a real risk of injury to another and an ordinary reasonable person would recognise that risk;

And 3. the defendant is capable of eliminating or reducing that risk;

And 4. it is reasonable to expect the defendant to do so;

But 5. the defendant does not eliminate or reduce the risk.

This also is a situation in which the defendant is responsible for any reasonably foreseeable injury that results from the failure to eliminate or reduce the risk recognised in 2. If 1–5 hold and the claimant is injured, then the defendant created an unreasonable risk that materialised in injury to the claimant. In such circumstances, therefore, the defendant cannot rely on the nonfeasance rule to escape liability, because she is responsible for the act that created the danger, though she was not negligent in performing that act. I now illustrate this principle and its justification by applying it to some cases, hypothetical and real.

There can be no liability in the standard rescue case. I cannot be liable if I fail to rescue a drowning child, because no action of mine led to the danger that the child is in. Hence, my failure to rescue the child cannot be a violation of that child's rights. However, if it was I who knocked the child into the water, even if I did so non-negligently, I can be liable if it is apparent to the ordinary reasonable person that the child is in danger, I am capable of rescuing the child, and it is reasonable to expect me to do so. Hence, to alter the example introduced in Chapter 6, if I accidentally knock a child off a wharf into the water and can save the child merely by kicking a lifebuoy into the water, then I can be liable if I do not kick the lifebuoy into the water, even though I was not negligent in knocking the child into the water. Similarly, if I non-negligently strike a pedestrian while driving, then I cannot simply drive off safe in the knowledge that I was innocent. My driving away would be a guilty act.

Of course, I can be liable only if I was negligent. In these cases, the negligence is not the creation of the initial danger—the knocking of the child into the water, for example—but the failure to eliminate or reduce the danger that I innocently created. Accordingly, I cannot be liable if I was (or an ordinary reasonable person would have been) unaware of the danger that I created. If I could not reasonably know that I had knocked the child into the water, then I cannot be liable even if I could have rescued the child had I known. Nor can I be liable if, knowing what I have done, I refuse to rescue the child because of significant risks to myself. Remember that the point of the standard of care is to do justice between the parties. I committed no injustice in knocking the child into the water. Hence, it would be appropriate to hold that my failure to rescue the child would be negligent only if the risks to me of the rescue were not sufficiently weighty.[9]

Turning now to the actual case law, in *Oke v Weide Transport Ltd*, assuming that the death of the driver was reasonably foreseeable, the defendant should have been liable (1) because he non-negligently caused a metal post to be left in the ground, (2) because an ordinary reasonable person would have recognised that the post posed a real risk of injury to others, (3) because the defendant could have reduced the risk by informing the authorities, (4) because it would not have been difficult for the defendant to have done so, but (5) the defendant did not do so. Moreover, it appears that the defendant's omission was a factual cause of the claimant's injury, as that injury probably would not have occurred if the authorities had been informed.

Similarly, in *Cappier* the defendant should have been liable, (1) because his running the railway non-negligently caused the physical injury to the deceased, (2) because an ordinary reasonable person would have recognised that, given those injuries, there was a real risk of death, (3) because the employees could have reduced that risk by calling for aid, (4) because it would not have been difficult them to have done so, but (5) they did not do so.

Nor does this point apply only to the standard of care. It applies to duty and remoteness as well. I discuss two hypothetical examples in this context.

As we saw in Chapter 4, in *Palsgraf v Long Island Railroad Co*[10] the defendant did not owe a duty of care to the claimant, because, while the defendant's employees were negligent (ie created a real risk) to a third party, they were not negligent to the claimant. But imagine that after the packet had fallen to the ground, the defendant's employees recognised the danger to the claimant and would have been able to prevent that danger from materialising in injury to her but did not do so. Imagine, for instance, that the fireworks took a long time to explode, that it was obvious that if the fireworks exploded the claimant might be injured and there was a bucket of water nearby that could have been used to extinguish the gunpowder. In such circumstances the defendant should be found liable. In this case, the relevant negligence is not pushing the third party onto the train—this act may have been negligent, but not to the claimant—but failing to extinguish the gunpowder. Only the defendant's employees (and the defendant because of vicarious liability) could have been under a duty to extinguish the

---

[9] For a discussion of this matter see EJ Weinrib, 'The Case for a Duty to Rescue' (1980) 90 *Yale Law Journal* 247. Though Weinrib has rightly rejected the general thesis of this article, it remains valid in the limited circumstances under discussion.

[10] 162 NE 99 (NY CA 1928).

gunpowder, because only their action created the (FOFF) risk of injury to the claimant.[11]

Likewise, in *The Wagon Mound (No 1)*,[12] the defendant's employees allowed oil to spill into the bay, which unforeseeably caught fire, causing damage to the claimant's wharf. The defendant was not liable, because his employees did not create a real risk of damage by fire. However, imagine that the fire spread only slowly and that the defendant or his employees could have extinguished it before it damaged the claimant's property. In such circumstances, the defendant could have been liable, because it was the actions of those for whom he was responsible that created the (FOFF) risk of injury by fire and because those employees did not respond to the real risks that became apparent and were occasioned by the creation of that FOFF risk.

The discussion above enables us to understand the otherwise difficult decision of the Privy Council in *Goldman v Hargrave*.[13] A tree on the defendant's land was struck by lightning and caught fire. It was impossible to extinguish the fire while the tree was standing, so the defendant informed the authorities and, while waiting for the arrival of a tree feller, cleared a space around the tree and doused it with water. The tree was cut down the next day, but the defendant did not do anything more to stop the fire spreading, believing that the fire would burn itself out. A few days later, the weather changed and the fire spread, damaging the claimants' property. The Court found that the fire could have been extinguished after the tree had been cut down if water had been sprayed onto it, and that it was negligent for the defendant not to have done so.

Two features of the Privy Council's decision are crucial here. First, the defendant was found liable though he was not at fault for creating the initial risk of fire. It appears, then, that the Privy Council imposed on the defendant a duty to rescue the claimant although the reasons for doing so examined in Chapter 6 were absent. Secondly, the Privy Council ruled that:

> the existence of a duty must be based upon knowledge of the hazard, ability to foresee the consequences of not checking or removing it, and the ability to abate it. [In these cases] the standard ought to be to require of the occupier what it is reasonable to expect of him in his individual circumstances. Thus, less must be expected of the infirm than of the able-bodied: the owner of a small property where a hazard arises which threatens a neighbour with substantial interests should not have to do so much as one with larger interests of his own at stake and greater resources to protect them: if the small owner does what he can and promptly calls on his neighbour to provide additional resources, he may be held to have done his duty, he should not be liable unless it is clearly proved that he could, and reasonably in his individual circumstance should, have done more.[14]

---

[11] Remember, however, that the liability is not for the creation of the FOFF risk, but for the failure to remove the real risk caused by not preventing the explosion.

[12] *Overseas Tankship (UK) Ltd v Morts Dock & Engineering Co Ltd (The Wagon Mound, No 1)* [1961] AC 388 (PC).

[13] [1967] 1 AC 645 (PC).

[14] *Ibid*, 663.

While this approach speaks of the relationship between the parties and is thus not subjective, it is nevertheless a departure from the normal approach to the standard of care and appears to be inconsistent with the argument of Chapter 3.

With respect to the law of negligence,[15] the courts enunciated four possible positions. First, one could maintain that no duty of care was owed as the risk of fire was not created by the defendant's negligence. This was the position taken by the trial judge, Jackson SPJ, according to whom:

> the correct rule is . . . that the defendant is under no duty at common law to extinguish a fire on his property which occurs by accident, or to prevent it spreading to the property of his neighbour. This accords with the broader rule that a landowner is under no liability for anything which happens to or spreads from his land in the natural course of affairs, if the land is used naturally.[16]

However, though he rejected it, Jackson SPJ also enunciated an alternative position based on the judgment of Scrutton LJ in *Job Edwards Ltd v Birmingham Navigations Proprietors*, according to which:

> if a man finds a dangerous and artificial thing on his land, which he and those for whom he is responsible did not put there; if he knows that if left alone it will damage other persons; if by reasonable care he can render it harmless . . .; that then if he does nothing, he has 'permitted it to continue', and become responsible for it.[17]

Though this position was rejected by the trial judge, it was accepted by Taylor and Owen JJ in the High Court of Australia[18] and also by the Privy Council.[19]

Although Scrutton LJ's conjecture has undoubted intuitive appeal, it does not *argue* in favour of liability. That is, the conjecture does nothing to show *why* a defendant should be liable in such circumstances. This can be brought out by altering only one of its features: the fact that the risk arises on the defendant's land. Consider the claim that one is legally responsible for a risk that one (or those for whom one was responsible) did not create, if one knows that the risk will (or is likely to) damage other people if not eliminated, and if one can by reasonable care eliminate the risk, but one does not do so. We know that this claim is false, because it would imply a general duty to rescue. It would, for instance, apply just as much to a driver on the highway who saw a tree burning in a public park as to the defendant in *Goldman v Hargrave*.[20] Hence, if there is anything of substance to Scrutton LJ's conjecture, it lies in the idea that the risk must arise *on the defendant's land*, but the conjecture itself merely states this condition

---

[15] The claimants also maintained that the defendant was liable in nuisance and under the rule in *Rylands v Fletcher* (1868) LR 3 HL 330.

[16] *Hargrave v Goldman* [1963] WAR 102, 108 (SCWA).

[17] [1924] 1 KB 341, 357–8 (CA); quoted at *Hargrave v Goldman* [1963] WAR 102, 107 (SCWA). Scrutton LJ further clarified that liability on this basis would, in his opinion, lie in negligence and not in nuisance or be based on *Rylands v Fletcher* (1868) LR 3 HL 330.

[18] *Goldman v Hargrave* (1963) 110 CLR 40, 52 (HCA).

[19] *Goldman v Hargrave* [1967] 1 AC 645, 661–2 (PC).

[20] Compare *Goldman v Hargrave* (1963) 110 CLR 40, 66 (HCA) (Windeyer J).

without justifying its existence or showing how it, in combination with the other factors, produces liability.

This leads to the third possible basis of liability, that supported by Windeyer J in the High Court of Australia:

> The trend of judicial development of the law of negligence has been, I think, to found a duty of care either in some task undertaken, *or in the ownership, occupation, or use of land or chattels.* The occupier of land has long been liable at common law, in one form of action or another, for consequences flowing from the state of his land and of happenings there, not only to neighbouring occupiers, but also to those persons who come upon his land and those who pass by. . . . To hold that the respondent had a duty to his neighbours to take reasonable care to prevent the fire on his land spreading would be in accordance with modern concepts of a land occupier's obligations.[21]

Unfortunately, this is little better than the position taken by Taylor and Owen JJ and by the Privy Council. Windeyer J stated that the duty existed because the defendant was the owner of the land upon which the risk arose, but did not explain how that fact led to his conclusion.

In a sense, the question here concerns the law of property rather than the law of negligence per se. The question is whether it is in the nature of owning land that one owes special obligations of a kind that one would not otherwise have to one's neighbours. The positions taken by the judges in the High Court of Australia and the Privy Council imply the following picture. If a fire starts in a public park that I could easily extinguish, but I choose not to do so, though I am aware that it is likely to spread to and damage your land, I cannot be liable if that outcome occurs. However, if the circumstances are the same but for the fact that the fire started on my land, then I can be liable. This position is not implausible, but it receives no justification from the judgments of the judges in the High Court of Australia or the Privy Council.

Moreover, if it is the ownership or occupation of land that makes the difference, then it would seem that the appropriate place for that difference to be made is in the law of nuisance, not the law of negligence. This is because it is the former area of the common law that deals specifically with the relationship between neighbouring landowners, whereas the law of negligence is general. If this is right, then liability could be supported on the ground that the defendant committed a nuisance against the claimants.

Their Lordships in the Privy Council were equivocal in this regard. Lord Wilberforce said:

> Their Lordships propose to deal with these issues as stated, without attempting to answer the disputable question whether if responsibility is established it should be brought under the heading of nuisance or placed in a separate category. As this Board has recently explained in *Overseas Tankship (U.K.) Ltd. v. Miller Steamship Co. Pty. Ltd. (The Wagon Mound No. 2)* the tort of nuisance, uncertain in its boundary, may comprise a wide variety of situations, in some of which negligence plays no part, in

---

[21] Compare *Goldman v Hargrave* (1963) 110 CLR 40, 66–7 (emphasis added).

others of which it is decisive. The present case is one where liability, if it exists, rests upon negligence and nothing else; whether it falls within or overlaps the boundaries of nuisance is a question of classification which need not here be resolved.[22]

What is one to make of the claim that liability 'rests upon negligence and nothing else'? Perhaps at first glance the intention appears to have been that liability in *Goldman v Hargrave* lies in the law of negligence and not in the law of nuisance. But that interpretation renders unintelligible Lord Wilberforce's insistence that he was not deciding 'whether if responsibility is established it should be brought under the heading of nuisance or placed in a separate category'. Moreover, was Lord Wilberforce merely repeating himself when he said that nothing turns on whether the cause of action 'falls within or overlaps the boundaries of nuisance'? The liability overlaps the boundaries of nuisance if and only if it falls within those boundaries.

I suggest that the key to understanding Lord Wilberforce's claims is to notice that his Lordship uses the term 'negligence' to mean something other than *the law* of negligence. The claim that the law of nuisance deals with situations 'in some of which negligence plays no part, in others of which it is decisive' can contain no reference to the law of negligence. It would be senseless to say that a claimant can establish nuisance against a defendant only if he can first prove the defendant liable in negligence.[23] Rather, Lord Wilberforce suggested that sometimes an action in nuisance can be established only if it can be proven that the defendant was at legal fault. Hence, 'negligence' in the passage quoted above refers to the first stage of the negligence enquiry—the standard of care—rather than to the negligence enquiry as a whole. In other words, the defendant was negligent, in this sense, if he failed to take the appropriate level of care. Further, Lord Wilberforce appears to assume that in the areas of the law of nuisance in which the legal fault of the defendant is not an issue, and only in those areas, special requirements are placed on the defendant for success (perhaps this refers to the 'reasonable use of land' requirement, the relevance of the nature of the locality, etc). These requirements are irrelevant in *Goldman v Hargrave*, however, because it is a case in which liability 'rests upon negligence and nothing else'—it does not lie in that category of case where the defendant is faced with special requirements. On this reading, his Lordship's position is that liability in *Goldman v Hargrave* is based either on the law of nuisance rather than on the law of negligence (falls within the boundaries of nuisance) or on both areas of law (overlaps the boundaries of nuisance and negligence). Hence, as he asserted, Lord Wilberforce did not decide whether the *ratio* he produced properly belonged to the law of nuisance alone or to both the law of negligence and the law of nuisance.

[22] *Goldman v Hargrave* [1967] 1 AC 645, 656–7 (PC).
[23] Unless, that is, one's point was to prove that the law of nuisance in this area was redundant. For a similar argument made with respect to *Rylands v Fletcher* (1868) LR 3 HL 330, see A Beever, 'Lord Hoffmann's Mouse' (2004) 10 *New Zealand Business Law Quarterly* 161. This was clearly not Lord Wilberforce's intention.

As indicated above, if it belongs to the law of negligence, the *ratio* of the decision of the Privy Council in *Goldman v Hargrave* is inconsistent with the argument of this book. This is because it asserts that one can be liable for failing to eliminate a risk to another that one did not create. But it would be wrong to regard the case as a counterexample to the position advanced here, because the *ratio* of the case may belong, not to the law of negligence, but to the law of nuisance.

This is to not say that, if that is the case, the *ratio* is *appropriate* to the law of nuisance. That can be revealed only by a proper investigation of that area of the law. Importantly, however, even if the *ratio* of *Goldman v Hargrave* cannot be supported by a principled approach either to the law of negligence or to the law of nuisance, it would not follow that the case was wrongly decided. This is because Taylor and Owen JJ in the High Court of Australia and Lord Wilberforce in the Privy Council enunciated an alternative, fourth, basis of liability that is consistent with the principled approach to negligence. This argument relies on the notion that the defendant actually created a risk for which he was responsible.

According to Lord Wilberforce, the decision of the defendant to leave the fire to burn out:

> brought a *fresh risk* into operation, namely, the risk of a revival of the fire, under the influence of changing wind and weather, if not carefully watched, and it was from this negligence that the damage arose. That a risk of this character was foreseeable by someone in the appellant's position was not really disputed.[24]

Taking this view seriously, the following picture emerges. The risk of fire from the standing tree was not created by the defendant and so he could not be responsible for it. Nor could the defendant be liable for cutting the tree down, because it was not negligent to do so. However, in choosing to allow the fire to burn out, the defendant 'brought a fresh risk into operation' and so could be liable for the consequences of that risk.

Unfortunately, however, while this position is compatible with the principled approach, it involves an implausible interpretation of the facts. The choice to allow the fire to burn out was a choice to do nothing. This choice caused the claimants' injury, but it did not create a *new risk* of injury to the claimants. Simply, the risk that existed when the tree was cut down was the same risk that existed when the defendant allowed the tree to remain in the state that it was in when it was cut down. There is no new risk.

Moreover, if the defendant created a new risk, then his liability should have been decided in accordance with the ordinary principles of the law of negligence. In particular, the Privy Council should not have altered the normal approach to setting the standard of care. Lord Wilberforce argued that that the new approach was warranted, because:

---

[24] *Goldman v Hargrave* [1967] 1 AC 645, 656 (PC) (emphasis added).

[the defendant's] interest, and his resources, whether physical or material, may be of a very modest character either in relation to the magnitude of the hazard, or as compared with those of his threatened neighbour. A rule which required of him in such unsought circumstances in his neighbour's interest a physical effort of which he is not capable, or an excessive expenditure of money, would be unenforceable or unjust.[25]

But this is plainly inconsistent with the fact that the law does sometimes require defendants to live up to standards that they are incapable of meeting, as *Vaughan v Menlove* shows.[26] If we are to adopt the proposed standard in cases relevantly similar to *Goldman v Hargrave*, why only in those cases? Furthermore, the claim that such is unjust is, in the light of the argument in Chapter 3, false. The normal objective standard is just in the eyes of corrective justice, and hence in the eyes of the normative perspective relevant to interactions between two people.

A more plausible view was advanced by Taylor and Owen JJ in the High Court of Australia. After exploring their main argument, their Honours remarked:

This is enough to dispose of the case but it should be observed that the claim of the appellants does not rest merely upon the allegation that there was on the part of the respondent a failure to take reasonable steps to extinguish or prevent the spread of the fire in its original location in the fork of the tree. The respondent did, in fact, take some steps and these were initially taken as much for the preservation of his own property as of that of his neighbours. . . . It is, of course, a matter of general knowledge that trees in country areas are not infrequently set on fire by lightning and that, when observed, steps are taken to extinguish them or to contain them where possible as a matter of course. *But when the tree in question here was cut down a hazard of a different character was created* and it is beyond doubt that the respondent was under a duty to use reasonable care to prevent it causing damage to his neighbours in the countryside.[27]

According to this view, the defendant could not have been liable *in negligence* for the fire spreading from the standing tree. The defendant did not create the relevant risk. However, in having the tree cut down on his land, the defendant became responsible, in the sense of potentially liable, for the consequences of that action. Now, the cutting down of the tree was not negligent, so the defendant could not have been liable for that. However, if cutting down the tree (1) led to a risk of fire that (2) an ordinary reasonable person would recognise, and (3) the defendant was capable of eliminating that risk and (4) it was reasonable to expect the defendant to do so, but (5) the defendant did not do so, then the defendant should have been liable. That was the case. Hence, *Goldman v Hargrave* was rightly decided.

[25] *Ibid*, 663.
[26] (1837) 3 Hodges 51, 132 ER 490.
[27] *Goldman v Hargrave* (1963) 110 CLR 40, 52–3 (HCA) (emphasis added).

It is important to note two features of the argument above. First, the argument still requires that the defendant created a new risk or increased the original risk by his actions (though that risk creation need not have been negligent). This happened, not when the tree was left to burn as Lord Wilberforce argued, but when the tree was cut down as Taylor and Owen JJ maintained. Though this requires judgement and reasonable persons may sometimes disagree, it does appear warranted to maintain that the risk of fire spreading from a standing tree is different from that of a tree cut down and lying on the ground, particularly when one remembers that the fire is likely to be spread by dry grass close to the ground.

Secondly, the defendant could be liable only if he were capable of eliminating the risk. Hence, it is right to take into account the defendant's means in a way that is not appropriate in normal applications of the standard of care. This is because the defendant's liability is not for creating a risk, as the defendant's liability in *Vaughan v Menlove* was, but for failing to eliminate a risk that the defendant non-negligently created. Hence, the defendant can be negligent only if he were capable of eliminating the risk and it were fair as between the parties to expect the defendant to have done so. This is the best light in which to understand Lord Wilberforce's claims that:

> the law must take account of the fact that the occupier on whom the duty is cast has, *ex hypothesi*, had this hazard thrust upon him through no seeking or fault of his own. His interest, and his resources, whether physical or material, may be of a very modest character either in relation to the magnitude of the hazard, or as compared with those of his threatened neighbour. A rule which required of him in such unsought circumstances in his neighbour's interest a physical effort of which he is not capable, or an excessive expenditure of money, would be . . . unjust.[28]

The main practical difference between this position and the *ratio* actually adopted by the Privy Council is that, if the defendant had not cut the tree down but rather had done nothing, then the principled approach would lead to a finding of no liability in negligence, while the *ratio* of the Privy Council would generate negligence liability. Taylor and Owen JJ argued that this consequence of the principled approach is intolerable, because '[i]f that were the law, a man might be reluctant to try to stop a bush fire lest, if he failed in his endeavours, he should incur a liability that he would not incur if he remained passive'.[29] This argument was supported by Lord Wilberforce.[30] Put generally, the claim is that the law should not discourage people from helping (or perhaps specifically rescuing) others by refusing to impose liability on them if they refuse to help but exposing them to possible liability if they do help. This policy argument certainly possesses intuitive appeal, but it is totally inconsistent with the law of negligence which does create just this kind of incentive structure. For instance, if I witness a car accident and I refuse to help the injured victims, then I cannot

---

[28] *Goldman v Hargrave* [1967] 1 AC 645, 663 (PC).
[29] *Goldman v Hargrave* (1963) 110 CLR 40, 65 (HCA).
[30] *Goldman v Hargrave* [1967] 1 AC 645, 659 (PC).

be liable. But if I try to help but negligently make the victims worse off, then I can be liable.

This is further evidence that the *ratio* enunciated by the Privy Council does not fit into the law of negligence. Accordingly, if the *ratio* is to be restricted only to cases where the relevant risk arises on the defendant's land, then this gives more reason to think that it must properly belong to the law of nuisance, or another area of law, rather than to the law of negligence. Finally, if the law of nuisance does support the *ratio* of the Privy Council's decision, then of course the specific policy argument raised by Taylor and Owen JJ and Lord Wilberforce does not arise.

B. Assumptions of Responsibility and Nonfeasance

One can also come under a duty of care to a person where one would normally not exist because one has undertaken responsibility for that person. Recall the last map presented in Chapter 8.

Recognition of Primary Rights	Responses to Violations of Primary Rights—Secondary Rights
Property (equitable and legal)	Wrongs (eg trespass, conversion, *negligence*, some equitable wrongs)
Law of Persons	Wrongs (eg battery, assault defamation, false imprisonment, *negligence*)
Consents (common law and equity, including estoppel and perhaps some or all fiduciary duties)	(Breach of) Contract Breach of an Assumption of Responsibility Breach of Trust Breach of Fiduciary Duty Breach of Other Assumed Obligations (eg obligations to invitees)

The discussion here concerns the final category of responses to violations of primary rights: the breach of other assumed obligations. A good example of this category can be found in the decision of the Supreme Court of Canada in *Horsley v MacLaren*.[31] The defendant had invited a number of guests onto his boat. One of the guests fell into the water. Another guest attempted to rescue the first guest. Both died. It was alleged that the defendant had been negligent in manoeuvring his boat and that this had contributed to the two deaths. The

---

[31] [1972] SCR 441.

dependants of the deceased brought wrongful death actions. Here we are concerned only with the death of the first guest.

The defendant relied in part on the decision of the Ontario Supreme Court in *Vanvalkenburg v Northern Navigation Co.*[32] In that case, the Court ruled that the operators of a vessel owed no duty of care to seamen to rescue them if they fell overboard, so that the captain of a vessel was entitled simply to sail off into the horizon leaving the seaman to drown. However, a unanimous court in *Horsley* ruled that *Vanvalkenburg* should not be followed.

The majority in *Horsley* found that the defendant had not acted negligently, but all agreed that, if the defendant had been negligent, then he would have been liable. According to Laskin J, the reason for this was that:

> As owner and operator of a boat on which he was carrying invited guests, [the defendant] was under a legal duty to take reasonable care for [the] safety [of the passengers]. Having brought his guests into a relationship with him as passengers on his boat, albeit as social or gratuitous passengers, he was obliged to exercise reasonable care for their safety.[33]

In other words, in inviting the guests on board, the defendant came under an obligation to ensure their safety, an obligation that the defendant would not have possessed if he had not entered into that relationship with the guests.

Another good example of this principle is the American case of *Depue v Flateau.*[34] The claimant was a cattle buyer who visited the Minnesota property of the defendant at about 5:00 or 5:30 on the evening of 23 January 1905. He decided that it was too dark to inspect the defendant's cattle properly and asked the defendant if he could stay the night in the defendant's house and inspect the cattle in the morning. The defendant refused. The claimant then conducted some other business with the defendant and was asked to stay for a meal. The claimant accepted. After the meal, the claimant suffered a fainting spell, again asked to stay the night, but was again refused. It was clear that the claimant was very unwell and unfit to travel through a Minnesota winter's night. But he was ushered to his cutter by the defendant and left the defendant's property. He later fell from his cutter and remained on the ground for the night. He was found close to death the next morning by a farmer and revived. The claimant suffered permanent injuries because of the cold.

According to Brown J:

> In the case at bar defendants were under no contract obligation to minister to plaintiff in his distress; but humanity demanded that they do so, if they understood and appreciated his condition. And, though those acts which humanity demands are not always legal obligations, the rule to which we have adverted applied to the relation existing between these parties on this occasion and protected plaintiff from acts at their hands that would expose him to personal harm. He was not a trespasser upon their premises,

---

[32] [1913] OJ No 16 (Ont SC).
[33] *Horsley v MacLaren* [1972] SCR 441, 461.
[34] 111 NW 1 (Minn SC 1907).

but, on the contrary, was there by the express invitation of Flateau, Sr. He was taken suddenly ill while their guest, and the law, as well as humanity, required that he be not exposed in his helpless condition to the merciless elements.[35]

One does not have to take strangers into one's home. The defendant would have been entitled to turn the claimant away from the outset. But one cannot invite a person into one's home and then refuse him aid when he needs it. In inviting the claimant in to dinner, the defendant undertook responsibility for him; a responsibly that was incompatible with sending him out into the cold night given his condition.

Again, we see that the notion that the distinction between assumed and imposed obligations matches that between contract and tort is unsupportable.

II. THE LIABILITY OF PUBLIC BODIES

In light of the argument of this and the previous three chapters, the liability of public bodies must be seen in the light of a basic distinction not often made, or at least not made correctly. This is the distinction between cases in which, prima facie, the public body violated a common law primary right in the claimant and cases in which the public authority did not. Though liability may occur in either case, the cases are importantly different and must be dealt with separately. I explore them in turn before examining the case law.

A. General Theory

(i) The Liability of Public Bodies where, Prima Facie, a Common Law Primary Right has been Violated

If the claimant possessed a primary right at common law—such as the right to bodily integrity or property rights—that was violated by a public authority, then the public authority is liable in the same way, and for the same reasons, as a private defendant would be. In other words, the liability of the public body is determined in accordance with the ordinary rules of the law of negligence, and it makes no difference that the defendant is a public body.

However, it is often the case that, though prima facie the public authority violated the claimant's rights, the public body was, or purports to have been, acting with statutory authority. In fact, this situation may arise even when the defendant is a private person. There is nothing preventing the legislature from providing statutory authority to private citizens or companies, for example.[36] But the argument is usually raised in the context of the liability of public authorities.

---

[35] *Ibid*, 3.
[36] For nuisance cases of this kind see *Allen v Gulf Oil Refining Ltd* [1981] AC 1001 (HL); *Tock v St John's Metropolitan Area Board* [1989] 2 SCR 1181.

336 Nonfeasance and Public Body Liability

The general position is simple. If the behaviour of the public authority were authorised by statute, then that behaviour is not actionable. This is not determined by policy, but because the public authority cannot have committed a legal wrong in doing what the legislature authorised it to do. Hence, in these circumstances the claimant's rights were actually not violated, because the common law right was limited or extinguished by statute.

This also means that if a statute gave the public authority a discretion to act within a certain sphere and the public authority was acting within that sphere, then it cannot be liable. If the legislature gave the public authority a discretion, then the public authority cannot be acting wrongly in exercising it. Accordingly, the important question in such cases is: was the defendant acting outside the authorised sphere of discretion? This matter is appropriately settled in accordance with the rules of administrative law, according to which the actions of the defendant were covered by authority as long as they were within the sphere of activity defined by the statute unless the defendant's exercise of the discretion was 'Wednesbury unreasonable', ie irrational.[37] As Lord Brown-Wilkinson said in X (Minors) v Bedfordshire County Council:

> It is clear both in principle and from the decided cases that the local authority cannot be liable in damages for doing that which Parliament has authorised. Therefore if the decisions complained of fall within the ambit of such statutory discretion they cannot be actionable in common law. However if the decision complained of is so unreasonable that it falls outside the ambit of the discretion conferred upon the local authority, there is no *a priori* reason for excluding all common law liability.[38]

The issue under examination here has nothing to do with the law of negligence. We have already determined that, absent the purported statutory authority, the defendant would be liable in negligence. The law of negligence has no more role to play. The issue is simply whether the actions of the defendant were protected by statute, whether the defendant was authorised to act as he did.[39]

On the other hand, in Barrett v Enfield London Borough, Lord Hutton maintained that:

> where a plaintiff claims damages . . . which he alleges have been caused by decisions negligently taken in the exercise of a statutory discretion, and provided that the decisions do not involve issues of policy which the courts are ill-equipped to adjudicate upon, it is preferable for the courts to decide the validity of the plaintiff's claim by applying directly the common law concept of negligence than by applying as a

---

[37] *Associated Provincial Picture Houses Ltd v Wednesbury Corporation* [1948] 1 KB 223 (CA).

[38] [1995] 2 AC 633, 736 (HL).

[39] This is not to say that the test of *Wednesbury* unreasonableness is necessarily appropriate. I take no stand on that matter whatsoever. The position is simply that if the defendant was acting under statutory authority then he cannot be liable; while if he was not acting under statutory authority and violated a primary common law right in the claimant then the defendant must be liable. Determining the ambit of the statutory authority is the role of administrative law, not of the law of negligence.

preliminary test the public law concept of Wednesbury unreasonableness . . . to determine if the decision fell outside the ambit of the statutory discretion.[40]

This approach must be wrong. If the defendant was acting within the scope of a discretion afforded it by the legislature, then it would be inconsistent with the statute to find the defendant liable, as it would imply that, though the defendant was permitted by the statute to perform the action, the action was nevertheless illegal. Hence, for the defendant to be liable, it is necessary that the defendant's action fell outside the authority given to it by the legislature. Perhaps *Wednesbury* unreasonableness is the wrong test to determine that, but the general point that it falls to administrative law to determine this issue remains valid.[41]

(ii) The Liability of Public Bodies where, Prima Facie, a Common Law Primary Right has not been Violated

The next set of issues concern cases in which the claimant possessed no common law primary right that was violated. Generally speaking, these cases are ones in which the claimant maintains that the public authority had a duty to rescue him from danger. As we have seen, there is no common law duty to rescue others. Accordingly, if that duty exists, it must arise from outside the common law.

At least except in the most unusual cases, the right exists only if it is created by statute. That is, the claimant possesses a right if and only if a statute, expressly or impliedly, confers on the claimant that right.[42] Moreover, that right must be one held by the claimant against the defendant and actionable at common law. In other words, in these circumstances the defendant can be liable only for the so-called tort of breach of statutory duty. The appropriate analysis of that tort is itself a controversial matter, but it is passed over here because it lies outside the law of negligence. Here, it remains only to examine the case law in the light of the distinctions made above.

If there was no breach of statutory duty in such cases, then clearly there can be no liability in negligence. As Lord Hoffmann said in *Gorringe v Calderdale MBC*, '[i]n the absence of a right to sue for breach of the statutory duty itself, it would in my opinion [be] absurd to hold that the [defendant] was nevertheless under a common law duty to take reasonable care'.[43] If there was no right that the defendant held against the claimant, then the defendant cannot have committed a wrong against the claimant and there can have been no duty of care.

---

[40] [2001] 2 AC 550, 586 (HL).

[41] An alternative interpretation of Lord Hutton's argument is that decisions of public authorities that would constitute negligence at common law could not have been made in accordance with the discretion given to the authority. This is an argument about the ambit of the authority's discretion and belongs to administrative law. No stand is taken here on its validity.

[42] These statutes may include Bills of Rights, Charters, etc, that protect so-called human rights.

[43] [2004] UKHL 15, [2004] 1 WLR 1057, 1066.

B. Case Law

In the following, I explore the leading English cases in this area because they enable us to see the issues in the clearest fashion. Though the cases are widely regarded as being highly controversial, to a greater or lesser degree inconsistent with each other and, frankly, confusing, it will be seen that they are all, given certain assumptions, rightly decided, consistent with each other and *relatively* simple. The relevant assumptions are the ones made in the cases themselves that relate to areas of the law outside the law of negligence, in particular to administrative law and statutory interpretation. Because this book does not concern those issues, I simply accept the courts' analysis of them.

The leading cases are *X (Minors) v Bedfordshire County Council, Stovin v Wise*,[44] *Barrett v Enfield London Borough, Phelps v Hillingdon London Borough Council*[45] and *Gorringe v Calderdale MBC*. In all of these cases, the House of Lords ruled that the defendants did not violate any statutory duty owed to the claimants. Hence, if the claimants were to recover, it was necessary to find a primary common law right that they held against the defendants which the defendants had violated.

Bedfordshire involved three sets of appeals. In the first, the claimants had been abused by their parents and sued the defendant local councils for not intervening to protect them as they had the power to do under the Children and Young Persons Act 1969, the Child Care Act 1980 and the Children Act 1989. However, the House of Lords ruled that these acts created only public duties, and so the defendants could not be liable for breach of statutory duty. The Acts gave the defendants the power to intervene to protect the claimants from abuse, but they did not create rights in the claimants held against the defendants that the defendants so intervene. Accordingly, the claimants could have succeeded only if they could have pointed to a common law right that they held against the defendants with which the defendants interfered. The only possibility was bodily integrity, but it was the abusers, not the defendants, who interfered with that right. In other words, the claimants were insisting that the defendants had a duty to rescue them, but there was no basis for the existence of that duty, which could be founded only in statute. Accordingly, the claimants rightly failed.

In that light, the third set of appeals in *Bedfordshire* and *Barrett* were quite different cases. There, the claimants had been taken into the care of those for whom the defendant was responsible and the claimants alleged that they had suffered neglect at the hands of their caregivers causing them loss. Again, there was no statute that provided the claimants with a right held against the caregivers for care, hence the claimants also maintained that the caregivers had failed to rescue them. But in these cases the claimants did have rights to be rescued by the caregivers. That was because, in taking the children into their care, the caregivers had undertaken responsibility for the well-being of the children, similar to the situation in

---

[44] [1996] AC 823 (HL).
[45] [2001] 2 AC 619 (HL).

Horsley. Hence, on the relevant factual assumptions made, duties of care were owed and the House of Lords refused to strike out the claimants' causes of action.

The second and third appeals in *Phelps* were similar. Both cases involved claimants who alleged that they were not cared for properly by people who had the claimants under their care. In other words, the claimants' allegations were that they had not been rescued by people who had a (special) duty of care to rescue them. Those allegations were plausible and were accordingly not struck out by the House of Lords.

The first and fourth appeals in *Phelps* involved claimants who had sought advice from educational psychologists and who alleged that the advice received had been incorrect and had caused them loss. The giving of the bad advice was not a violation of a statutory duty owed to the claimants. However, in these cases the House of Lords ruled that, in giving the advice, it may have been the case that the councils had assumed responsibility to the claimants, and so their Lordships refused to strike out the claimants' actions. Here, then, the House of Lords found the possible existence of common law rights that the claimants held against the defendants and that the defendants might have violated. Whether that was so was for a trial to determine.

The second set of appeals in *Bedfordshire* resemble the cases in *Phelps* explored above, but there was one crucial difference. The infant claimant was interviewed by a psychologist and the claimants alleged that the advice given by the psychologist was bad and caused them loss. On the face of it, that would support the notion that an assumption of responsibility had been made to the claimants. That was the position taken in dissent by Lord Nolan.[46] However, the psychologist had been called in by the local authority's social services department and the psychologist had prepared her report, not for the claimants, but for the department. Accordingly, Lord Brown Wilkinson held that the psychologist was:

> retained by the local authority to advise the local authority, not the plaintiffs. The subject matter of the advice and activities of the professionals is the child. Moreover the tendering of any advice will in many cases involve interviewing and, in the case of doctors, examining the child. But the fact that the carrying out of the retainer involves contact with and relationship with the child cannot alter the extent of the duty owed by the professionals under the retainer from the local authority.[47]

In other words, any assumption of responsibility was made to the department, not to the claimants. Moreover, sections 1(1) and 2(2) of the Child Care Act 1980 placed the psychologist under a statutory (public) duty to produce her report. Hence, the report was probability not voluntarily undertaken. Accordingly, the claimants' appeal was struck out.

Stovin and *Gorringe* were cases in which claimants were injured because the highways on which they were driving were dangerous.[48] In both cases, the

---

[46] X (Minors) v Bedfordshire County Council [1995] 2 AC 633, 771–2 (HL).
[47] Ibid, 752.
[48] See also Brown v British Columbia [1994] 1 SSCR 420.

defendants had recognised the danger but, for various reasons, had not acted to eliminate it. For reasons that are not relevant here, the House of Lords in each case ruled that the defendants had breached no statutory duties that they owed to the claimants. Nevertheless, these cases are unlike those above, because it was arguable that the defendants had caused the claimants' physical injuries—ie had interfered with the claimants' bodily integrity—by putting into service dangerous highways or by allowing them to remain in service. However, in *Gorringe* Lord Hoffmann read the statutory context to imply that users of the highways were to do so at their own risk, with the exception that they had a right to expect the roadways to be in good repair.[49] The accidents in *Stovin* and *Gorringe* were not caused by the roadways being out of good repair. Hence, given the context in which the claimants were invited to use the roadways, there was no violation of the claimants' bodily integrity and also no assumption of responsibility to the claimants that was breached. Again, the claimants rightly failed.

Of course, all of the House's findings in relation to statutory interpretation are open to question. For example, one may wish to dispute Lord Hoffmann's interpretation of the legislation concerning the highways. This is, of course, an important issue, but it is not relevant to the law of negligence. The position advanced here is that *if* the interpretations of the statutory regimes given in the cases discussed above were correct, then their Lordships reached the appropriate conclusions in all of the cases examined. Moreover, the law of negligence is able to deal with these cases in a rational and consistent manner without getting entangled in the debates thought to dog this area. Again we see the superiority of the principled approach.

One might feel that this position leaves the state too free to neglect the interests of its citizens. But, even if this attitude were justified, the appropriate place to respond to the problem is not the law of tort. The problem as identified concerns the state's obligations to its citizens. Accordingly, the appropriate place to deal with this problem, if it can be dealt with in law at all, is in the area of law that controls the relationship between the state and its citizens: public law. It may be that, for instance, the state possesses special obligations to rescue its citizens from harm that private persons do not possess. If these obligations exist, their justification lies in the nature of the state, not in the structure of tort law. Moreover, if these obligations exist, it is not necessarily the case that tort law ought to protect them. Perhaps it would be better to institute or strengthen a separate public law area of accountability. Of course, these are controversial issues and no stand is taken here on how they ought to be solved. The point is only that, if the state has special obligations, those are a product of the kind (or kinds) of legal entity it is and not of the law of negligence. Again, tort law should not be used as the law's Swiss Army knife to fix potential inadequacies in public law. It has a structure of its own.

---

[49] *Gorringe v Calderdale MBC* [2004] UKHL 15, [2004] 1 WLR 1057, 1063–4

10

Defences

MOVING FROM THE previous topics discussed in this book to the defences is often seen to involve a shift in focus from the defendant to the claimant. This is superficially correct: most defences concern the claimant's rather than the defendant's behaviour. However, as we have seen, the standard of care, the duty of care and remoteness are concerned with the defendant as related to the claimant rather than with the defendant in isolation. Similarly, most of the defences focus on the claimant in relation to the defendant rather than on the claimant alone.[1] These defences function appropriately only when they are seen as relevant to the relationship between the parties, and hence in the light of corrective justice. In the following, I explore the three most important defences in the law of negligence: contributory negligence, voluntary assumption of risk and illegality.

I. CONTRIBUTORY NEGLIGENCE

At common law, contributory negligence was an absolute defence. If the claimant's negligence contributed to her injury, then she could not recover.[2] This was later qualified by the 'last opportunity' or 'last clear chance rule': if the defendant had the last clear chance to avoid the accident, then the defence was not available.[3]

Throughout the Commonwealth, the old common law rules of contributory negligence have been replaced by a statutory scheme of apportionment. In most of the Commonwealth, the relevant statutory provision is either identical or similar to the following:

> Where any person suffers damage as the result partly of his own fault and partly of the fault of any other person or persons, a claim in respect of that damage shall not be defeated by reason of the fault of the person suffering the damage, but the damages recoverable in respect thereof shall be reduced to such extent as the Court thinks just and equitable having regard to the claimant's share in the responsibility for the damage.[4]

[1] Illegality is the exception.
[2] *Butterfield v Forrester* (1809) 11 East 60, 103 ER 926.
[3] *Davies v Mann* (1842) 10 M & W 546, 152 ER 588.
[4] Section 1 Law Reform (Contributory Negligence) Act 1945 (UK).

As with any statute, issues of interpretation arise. However, I pass over these, as they do not relate to the themes explored in this book. There are two issues that we must address: Why is contributory negligence relevant and how should it be relevant?

According to the principled approach, if the defendant's negligence is relevant to the relationship between the parties, then prima facie the claimant's should be also. In negligence, the claimant brings an action against the defendant on the ground that the defendant failed to take reasonable care to prevent the claimant's injury. The claimant must, therefore, accept that her own negligence is equally relevant. The claimant cannot reasonably insist that the defendant take more care than the claimant herself.[5] This explains why contributory negligence should be taken into account even though it involves no breach of a duty of care. The claimant owes no duty of care to herself and, in committing contributory negligence, usually does not breach any duty to the defendant. Hence, when the defendant alleges that the claimant was contributorily negligent, he does not allege that the claimant committed a wrong. Rather, he alleges that the claimant's lack of reasonable care undercuts the claimant's case against him, because the claimant's lack of care is as significant as his own in evaluating the relationship between the parties.

This also reveals that apportionment is a better device for dealing with contributory negligence than the traditional approach of the common law. The original common law defence held that, if the claimant had been negligent, then the defendant's negligence was irrelevant. The last clear chance rule held that the defendant's negligence was irrelevant unless the defendant had had a last clear chance to avoid the accident, in which case the claimant's negligence was irrelevant. But, as both the negligence of the claimant and of the defendant materialised in the claimant's injury, both must always be relevant. The appropriate question, then, is not 'whose negligence was relevant?' but 'how do we take into account the relevance of the negligence of both parties?' Apportionment in terms of fault seems the most appropriate answer to this question.

Reflecting the desire of the law to do justice between the parties, the standard of care to be applied to the claimant is identical to the one applied to the defendant. This does not mean that the amount of care to be expected of the parties will necessarily be the same, but rather that the parties must be judged according to the same general standard, ie one designed to do justice as between the parties. This means that, in line with the discussion in Chapter 3, if some peculiarity of the claimant is relevant to the relationship between the parties, then that should be taken into account. For instance, if the defendant is an adult and the claimant a child and the parties are engaged in an activity together, the standard of care to be expected of the child with respect to his own safety is that

---

[5] FH Bohlen, 'Contributory Negligence' (1908) 21 *Harvard Law Review* 233, 255; EJ Weinrib, *The Idea of Private Law* (Harvard University Press, Cambridge, Mass, 1995) 169 n53.

of a child of like age, intelligence and experience. Conversely, if the claimant is an expert and that is relevant to the relationship between the parties, then the standard of care to be expected of the claimant in relation to her own safety should be raised accordingly.

Some maintain that lower standards of care are imposed on claimants than on defendants in practice.[6] Stephen Todd suggests that '[o]ne reason is that conduct putting oneself, as opposed to someone else, at risk of harm may not inspire an especially critical attitude on the part of courts'.[7] If it is true that courts impose a lower standard on claimants than on defendants and if Todd is right about the reason courts do so, then those courts are mistaken. This reasoning incorrectly assumes that the issue is whether the claimant's negligence was wrongful. In that light, one can understand why it is tempting to be harder on the defendant than on the claimant: only the former committed a wrong. But the defence does not lie in any wrong committed by the claimant but in the fact that the claimant cannot require the defendant to attain to a standard of care to which the claimant himself failed to attain. That would not be just as between the parties.

This also shows that the claimant's negligence is relevant only if the negligence is the proximate cause of the claimant's own injury. The defendant is liable only if he created an unreasonable risk of the actual injury suffered by the claimant. Hence, if the defendant created an unreasonable risk of an injury not suffered by the claimant, then the defendant's negligence is irrelevant. Fairness between the parties dictates that the same hold for the claimant's negligence. If the claimant created only a FOFF risk of the injury she suffered, then her negligence was not contributory negligence. The same holds with respect to factual causation. To undermine the claimant's case, the claimant's negligence must cause the injury for which she is suing the defendant. If her negligence causes a different injury, then the negligence is irrelevant to the relationship between the parties.

However, in one of his more remarkable judgments, *Jones v Livox Quarries Ltd*,[8] Denning LJ denied that the claimant's negligence needs to be the proximate cause of his injury. The claimant was riding on the towbar of a traxcavator when the defendant's employee drove into the back of the traxcavator, crushing the claimant. Accepting the strange decision of the trial judge that in riding on the traxcavator 'any man was running the risk, in travelling somewhere which was not a proper place to travel, of being thrown off—that is, I think, the risk which he ran, *and no other*',[9] Denning LJ concluded, *contra*

---

[6] PS Atiyah, *Accidents, Compensation and the Law*, 6th edn (Butterworths, London, 1999) 46; S Todd, 'Defences' in S Todd (ed), *The Law of Torts in New Zealand*, 3rd edn (Brookers, Wellington, 2001) 1040–1; G Williams, *Joint Torts and Contributory Negligence* (Stevens, London, 1951) 353.

[7] Todd, above n6, 1041. Todd also refers to insurance. See also J Fleming, *The Law of Torts*, 9th edn (LBC Information Services, Sydney, 1998) 126.

[8] [1952] 2 QB 608 (CA).

[9] *Ibid*, 618 (emphasis added).

Singleton and Hodson LJJ, that the claimant's injury did not fall within the ambit of the risk created by the claimant. This was because the claimant was negligent in creating a risk of injury from falling off the towbar, not from being run into.[10] Hence, Denning LJ argued that the claimant's injury was an unforeseeable consequence of his negligence and would therefore be remote. However, his Lordship also insisted that remoteness is not determinative with respect to contributory negligence:

> Once negligence is proved, then no matter whether it is actionable negligence or contributory negligence, the person who is guilty of it must bear his proper share of responsibility for the consequences. The consequences do not depend on foreseeability, but on causation. The question in every case is: What faults were there which caused the damage? Was his fault one of them? . . .
>
> [Foreseeability] is often a relevant factor, but it is not decisive. Even though the plaintiff did not foresee the possibility of being crushed, nevertheless in the ordinary plain common sense of this business the injury suffered by the plaintiff was due in part to the fact that he chose to ride on the towbar to lunch instead of walking down on his feet. If he had been thrown off in the collision, [counsel for the plaintiff] admits that his injury would be partly due to his own negligence in riding on the towbar; but he says that, because he was crushed, and not thrown off, his injury is in no way due to it. That is too fine a distinction for me. I cannot believe that that purely fortuitous circumstance can make all the difference to the case.[11]

Curiously, however, Denning LJ went on to say:

> In order to illustrate this question of causation, I may say that if the plaintiff, whilst he was riding on the towbar, had been hit in the eye by a shot from a negligent sportsman, I should have thought that the plaintiff's negligence would in no way be a cause of his injury. It would only be the circumstance in which the cause operated. It would only be part of the history.[12]

That is too fine a distinction for me.

The fact is that, in Denning LJ's hypothetical, the claimant's decision to ride on the towbar would be a factual cause of his injury. His being on the towbar would be one of the events that would lead to his being shot in the eye. Hence, if one is to say that the claimant was not contributorily negligent in such circumstances, that must reflect normative rather than factual concerns. The most natural argument is that the claimant who is shot in the eye is not contributorily negligent, because his injury is remote from his negligence. The claimant was not negligent for creating a risk that he would be shot in the eye. That was a FOFF risk.

Denning LJ's problem in *Jones v Livox Quarries Ltd* was created by his Lordship's surprising acceptance of the trial judge's extremely odd view that the claimant's injury was unforeseeable. Surely, it is perfectly foreseeable that some-

[10] [1952] 2 QB, 615.
[11] *Ibid*, 616.
[12] *Ibid*.

one riding on the towbar of a vehicle would be crushed by another vehicle. While the trial judge was right that the *main* reason one should not ride on the towbar of a vehicle is that one may fall off, that is not the only reason. As Singleton LJ said:

> It was submitted to us that the prohibition against riding upon one of these vehicles was because of the danger of a man falling off, or the danger of his becoming trapped in some part of the machine. I think there is more than that to be considered. The plaintiff, in riding on the traxcavator, was disobeying the orders of his employers. In so doing he was exposing himself to danger. It may well be that the chief danger was that he might fall off, or be thrown off, or that he might become entangled in some part of the machine on which he was riding; but those were not the only risks to which he subjected himself. He had put himself in a dangerous position which, in fact, exposed him to the particular danger which came upon him. He ought not to have been there. The fact that he was in that particular position meant that he exposed himself, or some part of his body, to another risk, the risk that some driver following might not be able to pull up in time—it may be because that driver was certainly at fault.[13]

It would have been far from odd to have said to the claimant, 'don't ride on the towbar, you may get crushed'. Accordingly, Denning LJ's claim that remoteness is irrelevant to contributory negligence should be forgotten.[14]

II. *VOLENTI NON FIT INJURIA*

A. The Two Parts of the Defence

At least outside England and Wales, the defence of *volenti non fit injuria* is today more commonly known by its English name: voluntary assumption of risk. However, the original Latin term, at least in English translation—one who wills it is not wronged—is more accurate. This is because the defence has two separate parts, only one of which is captured by the phrase 'voluntary *assumption of risk*'. Both parts of the defence rely on the basic idea that a claimant cannot be wronged if the thing about which he is complaining was suffered voluntarily by him. However, the two parts of the defence reflect the fact that the claimant could have voluntarily suffered two possible objects: the harm and the risk of

---

[13] See, eg, *ibid*, 613–14 (Singleton LJ).

[14] It is not clear whether Denning LJ really believed that remoteness was irrelevant to contributory negligence or whether he was merely trying to find a covert way to avoid the consequences of the trial judge's finding that the claimant's injury was unforeseeable. However, if the latter was the case, then Denning LJ must have believed that the trial judge's finding of fact was clearly wrong. Accordingly, instead of misrepresenting the law, it would have been preferable for Denning LJ to have deemed the finding perverse. Most importantly, in developing general understandings of the law, we must not be misled by covert strategies such as the one possibly employed by Denning LJ, and judges should not allow their desire to avoid treading on each other's toes to distort the law. Note that Singleton and Hodson LJJ interpreted the trial judge as having held that the claimant's injury was, in fact, foreseeable.

harm. That is, in raising the *volenti* defence, the defendant could intend either that the claimant suffered the harm voluntarily or that the claimant voluntarily ran the risk of harm.

There is no doubt that the second is more important in practice than the first. Few people suffer harm voluntarily and even fewer try to sue for that harm, but the distinction is important in principle because it ensures that we keep concerns relevant only to each part separate and because it enables us to understand the application of the defence to rescuers and to claims for wrongful conception.

Because the difference between the two parts of this defence is usually insignificant in practice, it is most often overlooked. For instance, it has been claimed that '[a] fair blow in a boxing match [and] an inoculation . . . are not torts, because the claimant consents to them'.[15] The conclusion that a defence based on voluntariness applies in both cases is certainly correct, but this cannot be because the claimants consent to both events in the same way. The potential damage in cases of inoculation includes the breaking of the skin, the pain of the entry of the needle, the muscle pain caused by the entry of the liquid, etc. A person who consents to an inoculation, understanding what an inoculation is, consents to all of this. Accordingly, if a person consents to an inoculation that is then given, the person consented to that inoculation. But this is not the case in a boxing match. A boxer does not consent to being punched. This is evident in the fact that the boxer tries hard not to get punched. This is not to say that the boxer has not consented to something of significance in this case that justifies the application of the *volenti* defence or its cognates. It is simply to show that these cases are different.

It may help to imagine a further case in order to see this point. Imagine a participant in a game of rugby, A, who is involved in two situations. In the first situation, A takes a crash ball into the opposition's midfield backs. The point of this move, put somewhat simplistically, is to create an effective overlap by forcing two or more opposition players to tackle A so that they will not be available to defend in the next phase. This means that A carries the ball up to the opposition back line, *intending* them to tackle him. In the second situation, later in the game, A attempts to cut through the midfield by trying to force the opposition to miss its tackles on him. However, A's strategy fails and he is successfully tackled. In the first situation, A chooses to be tackled. In the second, he does not. In the first, it is loosely right to say that he consented to the tackle,[16] but it is not correct to say this in the second. The claim is not that the tackler did anything wrong to A in the second situation. The claim is simply that it is incorrect to say that A consented to the tackle in the second situation. How could it be right to say this when A does everything that he can not to be tackled?

---

[15] WVH Rogers, *Winfield and Jolowicz on Tort*, 16th edn (Sweet & Maxwell, London, 2002) para 25.3.

[16] It is only loosely right, because consent requires communication that need not be present in these cases.

The natural reply is to say that A consented to the tackle because he consented to play rugby knowing that, in the game, players would tackle him. However, while it is perfectly true that A consented to play a game in which he knew he would be tackled, this does nothing to prove that he consented to *the* tackle in question. What A consented to was the game, not the tackle. One might say that A consented to being tackled in general during the game, but he did not consent to the individual tackle that occurred in the second situation. This means that the *volenti* defence does apply, but it does not apply in the same way as it applied to the first situation. In that case, A chose to be tackled. In the second, A did not choose to be tackled, but did choose to engage in an activity in which he knew he would be tackled. We need to refine this account later, but it suffices for the moment to express this distinction by saying that the *volenti* defence applies in the first case because A chose to be tackled but in the second case only because A consented to an activity which included the risk of being tackled during the course of the game.

This might seem to be splitting hairs, but if we are properly to understand the *volenti* defence, we must be clear about this distinction. Importantly, the two parts of the *volenti* defence function differently. This is because voluntarily suffering something possesses a distinct normative structure from voluntarily exposing oneself to the risk of something, as I now explain.

As we saw in earlier chapters, the general law provides people with a set of primary rights. One is wronged in the eyes of the law when one of these rights is violated. In corrective justice at any rate,[17] these rights are defined with reference to the right holder's will. In corrective justice, all rights are rights that certain things happen or do not happen if the rights' holder wills or does not will them to happen. Take, for instance, the right to bodily integrity. This right entails that people have control over their own bodies and no control over the bodies of others. But this right does not imply that people are forbidden to touch each other. It implies only that people are not permitted to touch each other unless the touching was willed by the person being touched. If you touch me in accordance with my will, that is consistent with me having control over my own body. Accordingly, if you do something to me to which I have consented, no violation of my rights could have taken place.

This is why *volenti non fit injuria* is part of the cause of action and its absence a precondition of liability. If the defence holds, normally the claimant was not wronged. *Volenti* is not an excuse. With respect to the defence of consent in battery, for example, people who consensually shake hands are not batterers

---

[17] The circumstances can be different in criminal law, where the state may have paternalistically imposed an obligation on people to respect others even if those others do not want to be respected. If an obligation has been imposed on A, inter alia, in order to protect B whatever B's desires and choices, then B's free choice to waive that obligation does nothing to remove it from A. In private law, however, our rights are our own. Note that this does not mean that those engaged in a fight consent to each other's batteries and therefore should not, on the view advanced here, be able to sue. Combatants realise that they may be struck, but they do not ordinarily either choose to be struck or consent to being struck. Compare *Lane v Holloway* [1968] 1 QB 379 (CA).

with an excuse; they are not batterers at all. The consent shows that they did not violate each other's rights. It does not show that, though they violated each other's rights, that was acceptable. Accordingly, if the claimant was *volens* there can be no liability, because there was no wrong.

It follows from this picture of rights that, if the claimant chose to suffer the harm, then the claimant's rights were not violated, the claimant was not wronged in suffering the harm, and so the claimant cannot recover from any person who also caused the harm. For instance, imagine *Donoghue v Stevenson*[18] with the exception that, before ingesting the ginger beer, Donoghue discovered that it contained the snail and knew that drinking the ginger beer would cause her gastroenteritis. In this case, because Donoghue chose to inflict the harm on herself, the drinking of the ginger beer was not inconsistent with her right to bodily integrity.

Note that it makes no difference to this case whether the claimant's decision to harm herself was communicated to the defendant. The point is simply that, because the harm was inflicted on the claimant in accordance with her own free will, it did not involve the violation of the claimant's rights. Hence, while it is often useful to express these points in terms of consent, to the extent that consent requires communication, as a substantive matter this part of the *volenti* defence does not require consent.[19]

But different considerations arise in cases where the claimant chooses, not to harm herself, but to expose herself to a risk of harm. If the claimant chooses to be harmed, because the harm was chosen it cannot have violated the claimant's rights. However, in choosing to undergo a risk, it does not follow that the claimant chooses to undergo a harm. Accordingly, it does not follow that, if the harm occurs, that harm is consistent with the claimant's rights. Therefore, the fact that a claimant has chosen to expose herself to a certain risk does not thereby imply that harms that result from the materialisation of that risk are consistent with the claimant's rights.

The argument can be presented in a positive fashion as follows. A person's rights protect her from certain harms being inflicted on her by others. If she chooses to undergo a risk of harm, that choice does not thereby imply that materialisations of that risk in harm are consistent with her rights.[20] I know that driving a car is a dangerous activity inter alia because others drive negligently and personal injury to me could result. Nevertheless, I choose to drive. Hence, I

---

[18]   *M'Alister (or Donoghue) (Pauper) v Stevenson* [1932] AC 562 (HL Sc).

[19]   I say 'as a substantive matter' to distinguish this point from a quite different one concerning proof. In many circumstances, it may be that the only feasible way of determining whether the claimant chose the harm is to see whether she consented to it. Even here, though, it is her choice that is normatively significant, not her consent, though we cannot tell what she chose without an investigation of her consent. Note also that choice is not identical to desire. A person can want to be touched but choose not to be. Accordingly, if a defendant touches a claimant who wants to be touched but who chooses not to be, that is a battery.

[20]   W Page Keaton *et al*, *Prosser and Keeton on the Law of Torts*, 5th edn (West Group, St Paul, Minn, 1894) 491.

choose to expose myself to the risks caused by others' negligent driving. But in doing so, neither do I choose to be harmed by negligent driving nor does it follow that those who cause me personal injury by negligently driving act consistently with my bodily integrity. If it did follow, then only the insane or ignorant could sue for road accidents. When I sue the negligent driver, I sue not for causing the risk of my personal injury—the causing of the risk could not have been a violation of my rights, because I chose to expose myself to the risk—but for the causing of the harm, ie the personal injury, in a risky (ie unreasonable) way. I sue not for the risk, but for the harm that resulted from the risk. I chose the risk, not the harm.[21]

Accordingly, the defence of *volenti non fit injuria* applies if the claimant chose to be harmed. But it does not apply merely if the claimant chose to undergo the risk of harm. In the latter case, something more is required. That is revealed by the modern name of the defence: there must be a voluntary *assumption* of risk. As we see below, this means that the claimant must expressly or impliedly waive her rights in respect of the relevant harm. This is not to say that she must have chosen to be harmed; rather only that she must either have given the defendant permission to conduct the specific activity that resulted in the harm in a risky fashion or waived her right to recover for the violation of her rights. Both of these require consent and that consent must be communicated to the defendant to be operative. If there was no consent or if the consent was not communicated to the defendant, then the defendant cannot have had permission from the claimant to engage in the relevant activity in a risky manner and there can have been no waiver of the claimant's rights.

I now examine the examples above in the light of this discussion. Recall the rugby game in which A first intends to be tackled by the opposition players and then intends to avoid their tackles. In the second case, the *volenti* defence applies because A consented to an activity, playing rugby, in which players tackle each other. In the first case, the *volenti* defence applies both because A consented to the risky activity and because A chose the particular tackle. A boxer who is punched in a match cannot sue, because he consented to the activity, boxing, which involves being punched. A person who is inoculated cannot sue, both because he consented to a 'risky' activity and because he chose the particular inoculation.

I now discuss the two parts of the defence in more detail.

B. Willing the Harm

As indicated above, the *volenti* defence applies if the claimant chose to inflict the harm on herself, even if the harm was also caused by the defendant's negligence.

---

[21] Note that the Kantian argument, that one who wills an end must will the necessary means to that end, is irrelevant here. The harm is not the end of the risk.

This is because, as the claimant chose the harm, it is impossible to regard the harm as a violation of the claimant's rights.

It is first important to remember that, for the defence to apply, the claimant must freely have chosen the harm. Hence, claimants who lack the relevant capacity, generally or temporally, are not open to the application of the defence. Courts, therefore, should be very cautious in allowing defendants to raise the defence with regard to child claimants, mentally ill claimants or any claimants whose capacity for free choice is diminished.

Moreover, in assessing the ambit of this defence, it is necessary to pay close attention to the harm that the claimant actually chose. This is a very difficult issue and it will take us some time to reach an appropriate definition of choice for this enquiry. The first point that needs to be made in this context is that choice is wider in scope than purpose. A person who decides to kill his wife with the sole purpose of claiming her life insurance does not act with the purpose of killing his wife, but he nevertheless chooses to do so. Evidently, then, the same considerations that apply to determining the scope of a person's intention also apply here.

In his helpful discussion of intention in relation to the criminal law, Andrew Ashworth concludes that the concept should be defined 'to cover not only the person who acts in order to bring about the prohibited consequence but also the person who acts "being aware that it will occur in the ordinary course of events" '.[22] As Ashworth makes clear, this means that an outcome is intended by an agent if the agent could see that the outcome would occur as the result of her action barring some unforeseen intervention.[23] In this context, of course, we are not interested in whether the claimant intended a prohibited outcome, but in whether the claimant chose a particular harm for which she is suing the defendant. This means that we must ask whether the claimant acted with the purpose of causing the harm to herself or acted knowing that her action would cause the harm barring unforeseen intervention.

A further distinction that needs to be made is between choosing *a particular* harm and choosing *to be* harmed. Though it does not make for a pleasing definition, the *volenti* defence is concerned both with whether the claimant chose the specific harm for which she is suing and whether she chose to be harmed. That is, this part of the defence can apply only if the claimant chose *both* the harm and to be harmed.

With respect to the requirement that the claimant must have chosen the particular harm, consider the following. Imagine that a claimant chooses to inject herself with heroin, knowing that heroin will harm her. However, the defendant puts not heroin but hydrochloric acid into the syringe, which causes the claimant serious internal injuries. Clearly, neither the *volenti* defence nor its

---

[22] A Ashworth, *Principles of Criminal Law*, 4th edn (Oxford University Press, Oxford, 2003) 176. Citation from Law Commission, 'Criminal Law: A Criminal Code' (Law Comm No 177, HC299, Cm 299, London, HMSO, 1989) cl 18.

[23] Ashworth, above n22.

equivalents should apply in such a case. The claimant consented to be harmed, but did not choose the harm that she actually suffered.

Consider also the following case which involves the application of the equivalent defence in battery. The claimant sets up a device to shoot herself, whereby she pulls on a string, which in turn pulls the trigger of a gun mounted on a table. At the moment the claimant pulls the string, the defendant runs into the room and pulls the trigger. The evidence suggests that either the pulling of the string or the pulling of the trigger would have been sufficient to cause the gun to fire at the time it did. The claimant is shot in the shoulder.

Here, although the claimant chose to be shot, the defendant nevertheless violated the claimant's right to bodily integrity. Recall that this right protects the ability of the claimant to control her own body. Even though the claimant chose to fire the gun at herself, she did not choose to be shot by another. That is, she chose to self-harm, not to be harmed by another.[24] Moreover, because the claimant chose to be shot in the shoulder, she cannot recover for her personal injury from the defendant—she chose to be harmed and chose that harm. But it does not follow that she cannot claim aggravated damages from the defendant for his contemptuous treatment of her as a right-less, mere thing.[25] That harm she did not choose. She did not choose to be used in this way as a means to another's end. In choosing *a* harm, one does not thereby consent to all harms.

Accordingly, this part of the *volenti* defence applies only if the claimant chose to undergo the specific harm that she suffered. But this is not sufficient; as the examples below show, it is also necessary for the claimant to have chosen to be harmed.

Consider the following cases. In each case, a defendant is driving along a narrow road. On the left side of the road is a cliff face running up and on the right is one falling into a ravine. The defendant is not keeping a proper lookout and is therefore driving negligently. The claimant is non-negligently on the road. In all cases, the defendant's car strikes the claimant throwing her off the side of the road and into the ravine. It is not possible for the claimant to avoid being injured.

In the first case, the claimant, A, does not want to be injured but is nevertheless knocked off the road. Before falling far, A grabs hold of an outcrop on the cliff's face. The outcrop is too small for A to pull herself up onto, and so she can cling there only momentarily. Hence, she is faced with a choice, she can either cling there until her fingers give out and she falls off or she can let go. After a considerable period of time, she decides to let go. She falls into the ravine and is injured. In this case, A chooses to let go knowing that, barring unforeseen intervention, she will suffer personal injury. Accordingly, she chooses to undergo that harm. But it must be clear that the *volenti* defence cannot apply to this case.

---

[24] If one doubts this, one could imagine similar cases involving, not acts of shooting, but ones of sexual contact.

[25] For this understanding of aggravated damages see A Beever, 'The Structure of Aggravated and Exemplary Damages' (2003) 23 *OJLS* 87, 88–94.

The reason is that, although A chooses the particular harm that she suffers, she does not choose to be harmed. She is faced with a choice between two options, both of which entail being harmed. Hence, though she chooses the harm that she suffers, she does not choose to be harmed, that consequence being unavoidable. The defence does not apply.

The point is even clearer in the second case, in which the claimant, B, sees the defendant coming and is faced with a choice: either to run to the left side of the road and get crushed between the defendant's car and the wall or to do something else or nothing and get thrown into the ravine. B believes that she will almost certainly die if she chooses the former, so she chooses the latter. Again, B makes a choice that she knows will cause her to be thrown into the ravine barring unforeseen intervention, and so chooses the particular harm that she suffers but she does not choose to be injured. Hence, the defence cannot apply.

More difficult is the following, slightly different, case. C sees the defendant coming and is faced with a choice. She can either do nothing, in which case the defendant's car will crash into her bicycle, or she can throw herself in front of C's car, in which case she will be thrown off the cliff but her bicycle will be saved. She chooses to do nothing and sacrifice her bicycle. Here, C not only chooses to act in a way that she knows will result in the destruction of her bicycle, she also chooses to suffer that injury. But again she does not choose to be injured. Because she chooses property damage over personal injury and there is no other option, she chooses one injury over another and therefore does not choose to be injured. Again, then, the *volenti* defence cannot apply.

A further consideration is raised in the following case, in which the claimant, D, can prevent herself from being thrown off the cliff by grabbing another person, E, and throwing him off the cliff instead. D chooses not to, however, and falls into the ravine. Again, it is clear that D chooses the injury that she suffers. But is it right to regard D as choosing to be injured? She can avoid all injury to herself by throwing E into the ravine. At this point, it is important to remember that this question arises in a legal context. Hence, the relevant question is not whether it is physically possible for D to avoid being injured. Rather, the question is whether it is possible for D to avoid being injured in the eyes of the law. Of course, the law pays close attention to facts about the world. So, if an action is physically impossible then the law should not regard it as possible. But the reverse does not necessarily follow. It does not follow from the fact that an action is physically possible that it is possible in the eyes of the law. With respect to this particular case, D could avoid injury only by throwing E into the ravine, but that is not an action that D is at liberty to perform.[26] Hence, while the law

---

[26] Note that I am assuming, as this example tends to demonstrate, either that the defence of necessity would not apply in this case and/or that the defence is in fact an excuse rather than a defence proper. That is, in raising the defence (unlike in raising the defence of consent) the defendant claims, not that he did not batter the claimant, but that he did batter the claimant but has an excuse for doing so. See EJ Weinrib, 'Deterrence and Corrective Justice' (2002) 50 *University of California of Los Angeles Law Review* 621, 632–8.

must of course recognise the physical possibility that D could violate her obligations to E, it cannot regard that as something that D is free to do. Hence, the conclusion at law must be that D is not able to avoid injury to herself and therefore did not choose to be harmed. She is, therefore, not *volens*.

The final issue is revealed in the following case, which is very similar to the first case above in which the claimant, A, is knocked into the ravine by the defendant. However, in this case, the claimant, F, sees what is happening and chooses to run into the defendant's car in the hope that it will throw her into the ravine because she wants the resulting adrenalin rush. Here, F not only chooses the harm, she also chooses to be harmed and so the *volenti* defence does apply. It is impossible to regard the defendant's negligent driving as a violation of F's right to bodily integrity, as F suffered personal injury, in part, because of her decision to collide with the defendant's car in order to be thrown off the cliff knowing that that would result in personal injury to herself.

The importance of this case is revealed in the fact that neither A's nor F's injury was avoidable. F would have been knocked into the ravine even if she had not run into the defendant's car and A would have fallen even if she had not let go. Accordingly, the question 'did the claimant choose to be harmed?' is not equivalent to the question 'was the claimant's injury unavoidable?' Though the avoidability of injury to the claimant can be a factor in determining what the claimant chose, this part of the *volenti* defence is concerned with choice and not with avoidability.

Why, then, do we say that F chose to be injured while A did not. Both injuries were unavoidable and both F and A acted knowing that injuries would result barring unforeseen intervention. The reason is that only F acted with the purpose of being injured. In cases in which injury is unavoidable, a claimant chooses to be injured only if she acted with the purpose of causing that injury.

Accordingly, for the *volenti* defence to apply, the claimant must *both* have chosen to be harmed and have chosen the harm that she suffered. We can therefore define the appropriate application of this part of the defence as follows:

The *volenti* defence applies if

(1) the claimant acted with the purpose of causing the harm to herself or acted knowing that her action would cause the harm barring unforeseen intervention,

and

(2) the claimant acted with the purpose of being harmed or acted in such a way that she knew that harm would result barring unforeseen intervention and she was able to and was at liberty to act in a way that would not result in harm.

(The defence does not apply *only if* these conditions are met, however. We are dealing with only one part of the defence at this point.)

It is also important to define what 'harm' means in particular contexts and, specifically, what it means to be able to avoid a harm. In order to see why this is an issue, it is helpful to consider the following hypothetical cases.

First, A accidentally sets fire to his own house and has no way of putting the fire out, calling the fire brigade, etc. A's act is negligent, in part, because it poses a real risk of the fire spreading to B's house. B watches the fire spread from A's property to her own. Though she has a mobile phone and could call the fire brigade, she chooses not to do so. Her house is destroyed in the fire. Had she called the fire brigade, the fire would not have spread to her property. In the second case, C negligently sets fire to D's house and has no way of putting out the fire. Noticing the blaze, D decides that she will watch the house burn down instead of calling the fire brigade on her mobile phone. D then sues C for the full cost of her house.

In neither case can the claimant recover the full cost of her house. But the reasons for this result are different. In the first case, because B chose to allow the fire to spread to her property, her property rights were not violated. She chose to be harmed and chose this harm. Hence, she has no cause of action against A. In the second case, on the other hand, D did not choose to start the fire. Hence, her property rights were violated and she does have a cause of action against C. But the amount of damages D can recover are limited by the fact that she chose to suffer some of the loss. The loss represented by the difference between the full cost of the house and the damage that she would have suffered had she called the fire brigade was chosen by her and hence, even though it was also caused, in part, by C's negligence, is D's responsibility.

It is tempting to summarise the difference between these two cases by saying that, in the first case, B consented to the injury, while in the second, D did not consent to the injury but consented to the loss. However, it is not strictly accurate, at least as a matter of law, to say that B consented to the injury because, given her choice, there was no injury in the eyes of the law. Because B chose to allow the fire to spread to her house, its doing so was not a violation of B's rights.

Though some may find this distinction to be a very fine one, it is made by the law. The first kind of case relates to the *volenti* defence: the second is said to be relevant to the claimant's so-called duty to mitigate. In practice, courts are likely to deal with the second case by saying that D failed to mitigate her loss. This is normally taken to mean that D did not act reasonably in choosing not to call the fire brigade.[27] The idea is that, if we do not approve of the fact that the claimant refused to mitigate, then we say that the claimant's failure was unreasonable and deny recovery. However, if we do not disapprove of the claimant's failure, then we say that the claimant's failure was reasonable and allow recovery.

---

[27] See, eg, J Fleming, *The Law of Torts*, 9th edn (LBC Information Services, Sydney, 1998) 286. See also *Geest plc v Lansiqout* [2002] UKPC 48, [2003] 1 WLR 3111.

Certainly, sitting down to watch the fire was an odd thing to do; it was unusual. But the issue of mitigation does not turn on the ordinariness of the claimant's behaviour or on her state of mind. Crucially, her behaviour was not unreasonable because she should have called the fire brigade per se. She was under no obligation to call the fire brigade. Though we speak of her 'duty' to mitigate, this was not a duty she owed to the defendant or to anyone else. If no risk to other people or to the property or other rights of other people was involved, then she was entitled to watch her house burn down. She was under no obligation to preserve her property. In the eyes of the law, watching her house burn down is no different from demolishing it in order to build a new one.

The general point is this. As long as she acts consistently with the rights of others, the claimant is entitled to do what she likes with her own property. While choosing not to call the fire brigade may be an odd thing to do in the circumstances, in the eyes of the law it is nevertheless a perfectly valid activity. As long as we do not injure others, judges have no business telling us that we are entitled to do only things they regard as reasonable with our property. This argument applies with even more force when the harm in question is personal injury rather than property damage. Judges clearly have no business telling us that we can do only 'reasonable' things with our bodies.

This is not to say that there is nothing unreasonable in the example above. What is unreasonable is not the claimant's refusal to call the fire brigade per se, but her attempt to sue the defendant given her refusal to call the fire brigade. She is attempting to sue the defendant for a loss to her that she could have prevented but chose not to. In this context, then, the 'duty' to mitigate is not a genuine duty at all, but is best regarded as a shorthand formulation of the principle that, if one acts in such a way as to become responsible for a loss, one cannot sue another for that loss, even though the loss would not have occurred without the prior wrongful action of another. The claimant cannot sue for the loss of her house, because in choosing to watch it burn down instead of calling the fire brigade she became responsible for that loss. She chose both to be harmed and that harm.

The claim is not that all instances of failure to mitigate are cases in which the claimant chooses to suffer a loss. It is only that *these* cases are appropriately analysed in terms of the claimant's choice to inflict harm on herself. Accordingly, the position advanced here is compatible with the notion that claimants in these cases must fail, to an extent at least, both because they consented to the harm and because they failed to mitigate. The argument is concerned with the *volenti* defence and choosing harm, not with mitigation per se.

We are now in a position to see why it is necessary to define what it means to avoid a harm. Imagine that A negligently puts B in a position where she must choose between suffering only property damage or only pure economic loss. If she chooses the former, then, in the relevant sense, she chooses both to be harmed and the specific harm that she suffers. This is because, with reference to determining liability, the only harms that count are ones that could constitute violations of the claimant's rights. As we saw in Chapter 6, an action that causes loss but does not violate a right in the claimant held against the defendant is non-feasance and is not actionable. Accordingly, it is not open to a claimant to argue that she can recover, because she was forced to choose between damage to something over which she has a right and damage to something over which she has no rights. If she chooses damage to the latter, then her rights are not violated. If she chooses the former, then she chooses that harm and to be harmed. She could have acted in a way that would not have resulted in damage to something over which she had a right. Hence, in the eyes of the law she was able to avoid being harmed in the relevant sense. This conclusion follows because, to be liable, the defendant must have harmed the claimant in the sense of having interfered with the claimant's rights.

But different considerations apply when determining, not liability, but the quantum of damages. This is because the question here is not whether the claimant's rights have been violated. That has already been decided in the affirmative. The issue is rather the extent of the claimant's loss that resulted from the violation of the claimant's rights. Accordingly, harm here is appropriately defined with respect to the claimant's loss rather than to the claimant's rights.

Imagine, for instance, that the defendant causes serious bodily injury to a claimant. Naturally, this is an injury in the eyes of the law because it violates the claimant's bodily integrity. Normally, people in the position of the claimant would take a course of painkillers such as morphine, but this claimant chooses not to because of a past drug habit. Accordingly, she suffers much more pain than an ordinary claimant would. She attempts to recover for her pain and suffering from the defendant. Despite the fact that her pain and suffering was chosen by her, and hence that she chose that harm, she should be entitled to recover for it. This is because her decision to avoid the painkillers was taken so as to avoid an even greater loss to her: drug addiction. Hence, her choice is merely to minimise the loss that results from the violation of her rights and it is not correct to regard her as choosing to be harmed. It helps to see this point if we attach numbers to these losses. Imagine that the amount of the claimant's pain and suffering would have been appropriately compensated by an award of £1,000 and the claimant's other losses by £4,000. Imagine also that, had the claimant taken painkillers, her pain and suffering would have merited an award of only £100 but that her developing drug problems would have deserved an award of £2,000.[28] On these assumptions, the claimant chose between suffering loss worth £5,000 and suffering loss worth £6,100. She chose to suffer more pain than she could have suffered, but as she could not have avoided suffering less than £5,000 loss, she did not choose to be harmed by £5,000. Hence, she is entitled to recover £5,000 from the defendant. In particular, it would be quite unfair to the claimant to deny her the £1,000 for pain and suffering on the ground that

---

[28] Of course, these figures are somewhat arbitrary, but they are not implausible. If anything, the figure given for the cost of the drug addiction is far too low compared to the others. A larger figure would strengthen my argument.

she chose it, because she chose it simply as a way of minimising the loss caused by the defendant's violation of her rights.[29] Also important are all the concerns traditionally relevant to mitigation, such as the reasonableness of the claimant's conduct.

The reason the claimant in this case is able to say that she did not choose to be harmed is the following. Given that liability is already established, for the claimant to show that she is entitled to certain damages, it is necessary to show that she was harmed, not in the sense that the defendant violated her rights, that already having been shown, but that the harm was loss suffered as a consequence of the violation of her rights. In this context, then, harm is defined with respect to loss.

C. Consenting to the Risk of the Harm

We deal now with the second part of the *volenti* defence: that relevant to willing, not the harm itself, but the risk of the harm. As indicated above, this is by far the more important part of the defence in practice and it is this part that concerns virtually all the case law.

The key to understanding the application of this part of the defence is *Nettleship v Weston*.[30] The claimant was an experienced driver who agreed to give the defendant driving lessons on the condition that the defendant carried insurance that would cover any personal injuries to the claimant that resulted from a legal wrong committed by the defendant while driving. The defendant assured the claimant that she had such insurance. In the event, the claimant did suffer personal injury as the result of the defendant's driving. While the defendant's driving was what one could have expected from a learner driver, it fell below the standard of an ordinary reasonable driver.[31] The English Court of Appeal had to decide two issues: (i) what standard of care could the claimant have reasonably expected from the defendant and (ii) was the claimant *volens*?

Lord Denning argued that the standard of care owed by the defendant to the claimant was that of the ordinary reasonable driver, not that of the ordinary reasonable learner driver. His Lordship felt that this followed from the fact that the defendant owed that level of care to other users of the highway. Prima facie, then, the defendant fell below the standard of care with respect to the claimant, and hence the claimant had a good cause of action. The remaining issue concerned the ambit of the *volenti* defence.

---

[29] For similar cases see *James Finlay & Co Ltd v NV Kwik Hoo Tong HM* [1929] KB 400 (CA); *The Griparion* [1994] 1 Lloyd's Rep 533; and *Hussey v Eels* [1990] 2 QB 227 (CA).

[30] [1971] 2 QB 691 (CA).

[31] At least, the arguments in the Court of Appeal proceeded on this basis. However, it appears to have been arguable that the defendant drove below the standard of the ordinary learner driver.

Lord Denning argued that the defence did not apply in *Nettleship*:

> Knowledge of the risk of injury is not enough. Nor is a willingness to take the risk of injury. Nothing will suffice short of an agreement to waive any claim for negligence. The claimant must agree, expressly or impliedly, to waive any claim for any injury that may befall him due to the lack of reasonable care by the defendant: or, more accurately, due to the failure of the defendant to measure up to the standard of care that the law requires of him.[32]

This point is sometimes made by distinguishing the physical risk from the legal risk.[33] On this view, it is not sufficient that the claimant consent to undergo the risk of injury; rather, the claimant must consent to being unable to recover if the risk of injury materialises. This could also be expressed by saying that, in the relevant context, the claimant must agree to waive any secondary right that would arise if her primary rights were violated. In *Nettleship*, there was no such consent. In fact, the claimant insisted on a guarantee that he was protected by the defendant's insurance, implying that he expected to be able to sue.[34]

This approach in its entirety was rejected by Salmon LJ in *Nettleship*. With respect to the *volenti* defence, Salmon LJ said that:

> if there is a duty owed to the passenger to drive safely, the passenger by accepting a lift has clearly assumed the risk of the driver failing to discharge that duty. What the passenger has done goes far beyond establishing mere 'scienter.' If it does not establish 'volens,' it is perhaps difficult to imagine what can.[35]

In other words, if the claimant knows of the (physical) risk and chooses to go along with it, then he is *volens*.

This view must be wrong. Every driver knows that others drive negligently and every driver knows of the possibility of physical injury, but that does not mean that one cannot sue if one is injured as the result of another driver's negligence. Knowing of the risk that others drive negligently and choosing to undergo that risk does not make one *volens*. Similarly, as discussed in Chapter 8, I cannot avoid liability merely by informing others that I will not take due care walking through the corridors of the faculty, even if they know about this and choose to use the corridors nevertheless. That would amount to the unilateral confiscation of their rights. In order to extinguish a right in another, I must gain that person's consent. Finally, Salmon LJ's approach to the defence is inconsistent with the law's approach to rescuers. Hence, Lord Denning's position is to be preferred to that of Salmon LJ.

However, Lord Denning's view has received short shrift from some commentators. John Fleming argues that the requirement is 'psychologically unrealistic'.[36]

---

[32] *Nettleship v Weston* [1971] 2 QB 691, 701 (CA). See also *Burnett v British Waterways Board* [1973] 1 WLR 700 (CA).

[33] G Williams, *Joint Torts and Contributory Negligence* (Stevens, London, 1951) 308; *Dube v Labar* [1986] 1 SCR 649, 657–9.

[34] *Nettleship v Weston* [1971] 2 QB 691, 702 (CA).

[35] *Ibid*, 704.

[36] J Fleming, *The Law of Torts*, 9th edn (LBC Information Services, Sydney, 1998) 334.

Why? People form agreements all the time (remembering that we are not necessarily talking of agreements that meet the formalities of contract law). Why should it be regarded as psychologically unrealistic when applied to the *volenti* defence? One possible reason is that Lord Denning's formulation of the defence may appear to imply that the defence can be raised only if the claimant explicitly stated that, if he were injured, then he would not sue: 'Nothing will suffice short of an agreement to waive any claim for negligence.'[37] At least when the claimant is not a lawyer or has not been advised by a lawyer, it is difficult to imagine claimants making agreements of this sort. However, we must not be too quick to reject Lord Denning's position. Perhaps, even though it will seldom occur, the defence should apply only in those circumstances recommended by Lord Denning. Fleming's objection seems to be that the position would not allow us to apply the defence in all those circumstances in which we would intuitively wish to apply it.[38] But we should apply the defence only when it is genuinely justified to do so. If the claimant retains a right as against the defendant, then it cannot be justified to fail to respond to the normative consequences of that right. Accordingly, more than intuition is required before we reject Lord Denning's understanding of the *volenti* defence. And, as we now see, part of the intuitive reluctance to accept Lord Denning's position may stem from a different problem that arises in *Nettleship*.

Salmon LJ's main argument in favour of the defendant was the following:

> Any driver normally owes exactly the same duty to a passenger in his car as he does to the general public, namely, to drive with reasonable care and skill in all the relevant circumstances. . . . In my judgment, however, there may be special facts creating a special relationship which displaces this standard or even negatives any duty . . . I do not agree that the mere fact that the driver has, to the knowledge of his passenger, lost a limb or an eye or is deaf can affect the duty which he owes the passenger to drive safely. It is well known that many drivers suffering from such disabilities drive with no less skill and competence than the ordinary man. The position, however, is totally different when, to the knowledge of the passenger, the driver is so drunk as to be incapable of driving safely. Quite apart from being negligent, a passenger who accepts a lift in such circumstances clearly cannot expect the driver to drive other than dangerously.
>
> The duty of care springs from relationship. The special relationship which the passenger has created by accepting a lift in the circumstances postulated surely cannot entitle him to expect the driver to discharge a duty of care or skill which ex hypothesi the passenger knows the driver is incapable of discharging. Accordingly, in such circumstances, no duty is owed by the driver to the passenger to drive safely, and therefore no question of volenti non fit injuria can arise.[39]

The argument here is not that the claimant was *volens*, but that the standard of care (though Salmon LJ spoke of duty) owed by the defendant to the claimant was not that of the ordinary reasonable driver but that of an ordinary reasonable

---

[37] *Nettleship v Weston* [1971] 2 QB 691, 701 (CA).
[38] See Fleming, above n36, 334.
[39] *Nettleship v Weston* [1971] 2 QB 691 (CA) 703–4. See also *The Insurance Commissioner v Joyce* (1948) 77 CLR 39 (HCA) 56; *Wooldridge v Sumner* [1963] 2 QB 43, 66 (CA) (Diplock LJ).

learner driver. In this, Salmon LJ was absolutely right. As discussed in Chapter 3, the standard of care is set to mediate between the interests of the parties. If the idiosyncrasies of one of the parties are relevant to the relationship between the parties, then that is to be taken into account in determining the standard of care. This is the case here. Given that the claimant knew that the defendant was a learner driver and agreed to instruct her on that basis, he cannot but expect the defendant to drive like a learner driver. To hold otherwise is to prejudice the enquiry in favour of the claimant. Similarly, if *A* knows that *B* is drunk and accepts a lift in any case, it would be unreasonable for *A* to expect *B* to live up to a standard *A* knows *B* cannot meet.[40]

The above follows from the correct approach to the standard of care and has nothing to do with a voluntary assumption of risk. The argument is that the claimant's knowledge affected the relationship between the parties in a way that meant that the claimant could not expect the ordinary standard of care from the defendant. The argument is not that the claimant's knowledge meant that the claimant consented.

Curiously, the judges in the majority in *Nettleship* seemed to recognise this, offering replies based only on policy. Lord Denning advanced three. First, Lord Denning maintained that, as the standard of care owed to other uses of the highway was that of the ordinary reasonable driver, that standard must also apply as between the claimant and the defendant. On the face of it, this argument could just as easily have gone the other way. That is, Lord Denning assumed that the defendant owed the ordinary reasonable driver standard to other uses of the highway and argued that therefore the defendant owed the ordinary reasonable driver standard to the claimant. But one could have assumed that the defendant owed the ordinary reasonable learner driver standard to the claimant and have argued that therefore the defendant owed the ordinary reasonable learner driver standard to the other uses of the highway. If we are to define the standard of care in terms of the relationship between the defendant and a group of people not including the claimant, why should that group of people be other users of the highway? Why should we not define the standard of care that the defendant owes to other users of the highway in terms of the relationship between the defendant and this claimant? This reveals that Lord Denning's approach fails to determine the standard of care in terms of the relationship between the actual parties to the case, and instead judges that relationship by examining the defendant's relationship with other people. But that is inconsistent with the point of the standard of care, which is to do justice between the actual parties.

---

[40] For policy reasons, some legislatures have decided otherwise. Road Traffic Act 1988 (UK) s149(3); Motor Accidents Act 1998 (NSW) s76. These statutes prevent 'understandings' between the parties undermining the claimant's ability to sue in tort. The reason for this is the existence of compulsory insurance in these jurisdictions. Hence, the aim of the legislation is to ensure that the claimant has access to insurance *regardless of the actual relationship between the parties*. Hence, the statutes in no way call into question the argument here.

Secondly, Lord Denning argued:

> If the driver were to be excused according to the knowledge of the passenger, it would result in endless confusion and injustice. One of the passengers may know that the learner driver is a mere novice. Another passenger may believe him to be entirely competent. One of the passengers may believe the driver to have had only two drinks. Another passenger may know that he has had a dozen. Is the one passenger to recover and the other not? Rather than embark on such inquiries, the law holds that the driver must attain the same standard of care for passengers as for pedestrians. The knowledge of the passenger may go to show that he was guilty of contributory negligence in ever accepting the lift—and thus reduce his damages—but it does not take away the duty of care, nor does it diminish the standard of care which the law requires of the driver.[41]

However, as we discovered in Chapter 3, the law routinely makes the kind of distinction Lord Denning claims would produce 'confusion and injustice'. Lord Denning admitted this by pointing out that the law considers these and similar matters when apportioning liability for contributory negligence.[42] Moreover, far from it being an impediment to justice, considering the relationship between the parties is *necessary* if justice is to be done.

Lord Denning's third response to Salmon LJ was that Salmon LJ's position erroneously equated *sciens* with *volens*. In other words, Salmon LJ held that, if the claimant knew of the risk and chose to go along with it, then the claimant voluntarily assumed the risk.[43] This is an accurate criticism of Salmon LJ's approach to the *volenti* defence, but not to his Lordship's discussion of the standard of care. Salmon LJ's claim in that regard was focused on what could reasonably have been expected as between the parties and had nothing to do with a voluntary assumption of risk.

Accordingly, those who feel that the claimant ought to have failed in *Nettleship* do not have to reject Lord Denning's understanding of the *volenti* defence. If the claimant should have failed, that would have been because the defendant was not negligent to him. However, for reasons now explored, Lord Denning's definition of voluntary assumption of risk was too narrow.

A claimant is *volens* if the harm about which she is complaining was willed by her. Imagine the following case. A wants a lift from B. B agrees, but warns A that he is not a good driver and reveals to A that he is worried about being sued by her if she is injured by his bad driving. A responds that she will not sue B if an accident occurs. An accident does occur because of B's negligent driving and A suffers personal injury. We must also assume that the standard of care owed as between B and A was violated. That is, we must assume that B's driving was

---

[41] *Nettleship v Weston* [1971] 2 QB 691, 700–1 (CA). See also ibid, 707 (Megaw LJ).

[42] See also *Cook v Cook* (1986) 162 CLR 376 (HCA); WVH Rogers, *Winfield and Jolowicz on Tort,* 16th edn (Sweet & Maxwell, London, 2002) 191. Compare S Todd, 'Negligence: Breach of Duty' in S Todd (ed), *The Law of Torts in New Zealand,* 3rd edn (Brookers, Wellington, 2001) 394–5.

[43] *Nettleship v Weston* [1971] 2 QB 691, 701 (CA). See also *Morris v Murray* [1991] 2 QB 6, 15 (CA).

even worse than his conversation with *A* indicated it was reasonable for *A* to expect. If we do not make this assumption, then no potential liability arises because *B* would not have been negligent vis-à-vis *A*.

If we agree that, at common law, *A*'s agreement means that she is not entitled to recover from *B*, then that seems to be because *A* promised *not to sue*. It does not seem to be because *B* did not violate *A*'s bodily integrity by driving negligently. Another way of putting this point is that, in agreeing not to sue, *A* cannot be taken to say that any harm she suffers as a result of negligent driving is consistent with her rights—she is not choosing to be harmed. Rather, she is saying that she will not sue *B* even if her rights are violated. Or, to put this a third, and most accurate, way, in making her agreement not to sue, *A* surrenders a potential secondary right, but she does not surrender any primary right. She merely says that, if *B* violates her primary right (to bodily integrity) she will not sue, which implies that she waives what would have been her secondary right to recover for the loss inflicted on her by *B*'s negligence.

In this example, then, *A* was *volens* because she consented to bear the loss suffered by a violation of her primary rights caused by *B*'s negligent driving. Hence, Lord Denning was right to include these cases in his definition of the defence. But people can be *volens* in a different way. A person is *volens*, not only if she waives her secondary rights, but also if she waives her primary rights. And this can be done by giving the defendant permission to conduct the activity that caused the harm in the risky manner in which it was conducted. In the light of this permission, the defendant's performance of that activity cannot have been a violation of the claimant's primary rights.[44]

It is important to see that this notion is quite distinction from, on the one hand, the concept of choosing harm relevant to the first part of the defence examined in the previous section and, on the other hand, the idea expressed by Salmon LJ in *Nettleship* that *sciens* is sufficient for the application of the defence. This can be brought out with more examples. Imagine variations on the case above in which *C* says to *B*, 'I don't mind if you drive carelessly. That should be fun.' Here, *C* does not choose to be harmed. However, she permits *B* to drive carelessly and so cannot claim that, when *B* does so and thereby causes harm to her, *B* violates her rights. Imagine also that *D* says to *B*, 'Just relax. Let's just see what happens.' Here, *D* clearly knows about the risk and chooses to go along with it. But *D* does not give *B* permission to drive negligently. Hence, in this case *D* is not *volens*.

A case of this kind is *Dann v Hamilton*.[45] The claimant passenger in the defendant's car was injured when the defendant, under the influence of alcohol,

---

[44] This also shows that T Weir, *Tort Law* (Oxford University Press, Oxford, 2002) 151 is wrong to claim that the principle in the law of nuisance, that it is no defence if the claimant comes to a nuisance, is inconsistent with the *volenti* defence. To use Weir's example, in purchasing a house next to a chip shop, one cannot be taken to have consented to the noise and the smell. The claimant may well have known about the noise and the smell, but that is another matter.

[45] [1939] 1 KB 509 (KBD).

had an accident. The claimant knew that the defendant had been drinking. Before the accident, the defendant had said to the claimant, 'You have got more pluck than I have', meaning that the claimant was very brave to be riding with him. The claimant replied, 'You should be like me. If anything is going to happen it will happen.' The Court correctly concluded that this was not a voluntary assumption of the relevant risk. The claimant clearly appreciated the possibility of physical harm, but saying that 'if anything is going to happen it will happen' does not imply that the claimant has waived her right to sue or that the claimant has waived her primary right to bodily integrity in relation to the defendant's driving. Accordingly, the defence did not apply.

In practice, the courts have exhibited a great deal of confusion in distinguishing between issues that relate to the defences of *volenti non fit injuria*, of contributory negligence and of the standard of care. A case in point is *Morris v Murray*, in which the claimant and defendant had been drinking heavily together before the claimant accepted an offer from the defendant to fly in a light aircraft. The claimant was injured when the defendant lost control of the aircraft and crashed. Though the claimant knew that the defendant was drunk and hence knew of the danger,[46] though he assisted in getting the plane ready for flight,[47] and though he actively sought the flight,[48] the Court was wrong to find that this was sufficient to show that the claimant was *volens*. For instance, the claimant may have requested the flight only in the belief that he would have had a cause of action for any injury that occurred due to the negligence of the defendant.[49] Moreover, in an attempt to justify applying the defence, Fox LJ argued that 'the wild irresponsibility of the venture is such that the law should not intervene to award damages and should leave the loss where it falls. Flying is intrinsically dangerous and flying with a drunken pilot is great folly.'[50] This is of relevance to contributory negligence, but it has nothing to do with a voluntary assumption of risk.

However, the first three concerns probably do show that it would be unfair as between the parties to find the defendant liable. If the claimant knew that the defendant had been drinking and accepted the claimant's offer in that light, then it would be unfair to allow the claimant to insist that the defendant live up to the standard to be expected of a sober person. This has nothing to do with a voluntary assumption of risk. The outcome of *Morris v Murray* is probably correct: the claimant could not reasonably expect the defendant to pilot the plane in a manner other than that of a drunk pilot. This is because the standard of care should be set with reference to both parties, rather than with reference to the defendant alone. Similarly, in *Dann v Hamilton*, as the claimant knew that the defendant was intoxicated and that affected the relationship between the parties, she could not but have expected him to drive in an intoxicated

[46] *Morris v Murray* [1991] 2 QB 6, 14 (Fox LJ), 27 (Stocker LJ), 31 (Sir George Waller).
[47] *Ibid*, 16 (Fox LJ), 31 (Sir George Waller).
[48] *Ibid*, 27 (Stocker LJ).
[49] Compare *Nettleship v Weston* [1971] 2 QB 691 (CA).
[50] *Morris v Murray* [1991] 2 QB 6, 17 (CA).

fashion. Hence, despite dealing with the *volenti* defence correctly, *Dann v Hamilton* was probably wrongly decided.

Moreover, despite what has been said above, the claimant should have been able to recover in *Nettleship v Weston*, as the majority decided for the wrong reasons. According to Lord Denning:

> Mrs. Weston . . . wanted to learn to drive. . . . She asked a friend of hers, Mr. Nettleship, if he would give her some lessons. Mr. Nettleship said he would do so, but, in case there was an accident, he wanted to check up on the insurance. Mr and Mrs. Weston assured him that they had a fully comprehensive insurance which covered him as a passenger in the event of an accident. This was correct. They showed him the policy and certificate of insurance. Mr. Weston was insured under an ordinary Lloyd's policy. By it the underwriters agreed to indemnify Mr. Weston and 'any person driving the car with his permission against liability at law for damages in respect of bodily injury to any person' including any passenger. On being so assured, Mr. Nettleship said he would give her some lessons.[51]

Why did the claimant insist on confirming this insurance? Surely, it was because the claimant wanted to be sure that if he were injured in the course of teaching the claimant to drive, he would be compensated though the defendant's husband's insurance. Hence, this indicates that, in the circumstances, the defendant had in fact *agreed* to compensate the claimant for injuries caused by her falling below the standard of an ordinary reasonable driver and that there should have been liability in that case, not for negligence, but for breach of a contract or for breach of an assumed responsibility. 'Mr and Mrs. Weston assured [the claimant] that they had a fully comprehensive insurance which covered him as a passenger in the event of an accident.' Of course, it is impossible to be sure of this conclusion, given that we know little about the actual conversation that passed between the parties, but given the evidence as it stands, the conclusion that the defendant should have been liable is justified.

To summarise: in cases where the claimant did not will the harm, the claimant is *volens* only if she waived her right to sue or waived her primary right. She will have waived her right to sue if she expressly or impliedly agreed not to sue the defendant for the materialisation of the risk which caused the harm to her. She will have waived her primary right if she expressly or impliedly gave the defendant the permission to act in the risky way that caused the harm to her. Both require communication from the claimant to the defendant. Hence, when Diplock LJ said in *Wooldridge v Sumner* that 'the maxim [*volenti non fit injuria*] in the absence of expressed contract has no application to negligence simpliciter', his Lordship was almost right.[52] The claim contains two errors. First, voluntary assumption of risk does not require a contract. The defence relies on the claimant's consent to be exposed to a certain risk. It does not require acceptance on the part of the defendant or consideration. Moreover, the

[51] *Nettleship v Weston* [1971] 2 QB 691, 697–8 (CA).
[52] [1963] 2 QB 43, 69 (CA).

claimant's consent need not be express. If the claimant conducted herself in a way that implied to the defendant that she consented, then it is reasonable as between the parties—in accordance with contract law's ordinary objective test[53]—to infer that the claimant consented. Nevertheless, we can say that the maxim in the absence of *agreement* has no application to negligence. Hence, the defence of voluntary assumption of risk is redundant except in cases where the claimant has expressly or by implication waived her legal rights.[54]

D. The *Volenti* Defence and Rescuers

It was once thought that either the *volenti* defence or the doctrine of novus actus interveniens would prevent a rescuer from recovering from a negligent party unless that rescuer had acted instinctively. For instance, in *Cutler v United Dairies (London)*, Scrutton LJ said:

> I start with this: A horse bolts along a highway, and a spectator runs out to stop it and is injured. Is the owner of the horse under any legal liability in those circumstances? On those facts it seems to me that he is not. The damage is the result of the accident. The man who was injured, in running out to stop the horse, must be presumed to know the ordinary consequences of his action, and the ordinary and natural consequence of a man trying to stop a runaway horse is that he may be knocked down and injured. A man is under no duty to run out and stop another person's horse, and, if he chooses to do an act the ordinary consequence of which is that damage may ensue, the damage must be on his own head and not on that of the owner of the horse. This is sometimes put on the legal maxim volenti non fit injuria; sometimes it is put that a new cause has intervened between the original liability, if any, of the owner of the horse which has run away. That new cause is the action of the injured person, and that new cause intervening prevents liability attaching to the owner of the horse. [55]

Similarly, in the seventh edition of his treatise on tort law, Salmond claimed that, in rescue cases, in order to recover:

> The danger must be imminent and the plaintiff must have had but a short interval in which to grasp the situation. He must not have time to think. If his action was deliberate, even though rapid, it will be a novus actus interveniens, and his error, not that of the defendant, will be held to be the cause of the accident.[56]

---

[53] Note that the question here is whether, as between the parties, it is reasonable to interpret the claimant's utterances, behaviour, etc, as a voluntary assumption of risk. The question is not whether, in assuming the risk, the claimant acted as a reasonable person.

[54] Moreover, it is possible to interpret the defence as entirely redundant. If the claimant has waived her legal rights as against the defendant, then perhaps she cannot reasonably expect the defendant to respect them. If so, then the defendant cannot have violated the standard of care if the claimant was *volens*. However, the defence is worth keeping as it reflects the correct view that 'one who wills it is not wronged'.

[55] [1933] 2 KB 297 (CA) at 303.

[56] J Salmond, *Torts*, 7th edn (Sweet & Maxwell, London, 1929) 38.

First, in light of the discussion of the doctrine in Chapter 4, it can be seen that reasonable rescues are not new intervening acts. If in creating an unreasonable risk of injury to a bystander the defendant creates a real risk that the claimant will attempt to rescue the bystander and be injured thereby, then the claimant's injury lies within the ambit of the risk created by the defendant's negligence. The only possible basis for excluding recovery, therefore, is the *volenti* defence.

For almost 100 years, however, the unanimous view has been that the *volenti* defence cannot apply in these cases.[57] However, in the following we see that the former view was not *completely* mistaken.

It is necessary to distinguish between cases in which the rescuer knowingly exposes himself to a risk of harm and ones in which the rescuer knows that she will be harmed. In the absence of an express or implied waiving of the rescuer's rights, the defence cannot apply in the first kind of case. Recall the facts in *Haynes v Harwood*:[58] the defendant's employee negligently left unattended the defendants' two-horse van. The horses became scared and bolted. The claimant saw the horses galloping along the road and saw that others were placed at risk. He ran across the road and seized one of the horses, and was injured when it fell on him. Clearly, this claimant did not choose to be harmed. Nor did he waive his right to bodily integrity or his right to recover if his bodily integrity was interfered with. In fact, no communication between the claimant and the defendant took place at all. It is patent, then, that the defence cannot apply. The vast majority of rescue cases fall into this category.

But different considerations arise when the claimant is certain to suffer harm. Imagine, for instance, that due to *A*'s negligence *B* has been caught in a machine that will kill him if he is not rescued. *C* is able to rescue *B*, but only by putting his arm into the machine. If *C* does so, then *C* will lose his arm. Seeing this and understanding the consequences, *C* rescues *B* and loses his arm. Can *C* sue *A* for the loss of his arm?

Though the conclusion is, at least at first, unintuitive and difficult to accept, it must be that *C* has no claim against *A* in negligence. This is because, in choosing to rescue *B*, *C* chose, not merely to expose himself to a risk of harm, but the harm itself. *C* chose to be harmed and chose the harm that he suffered. Moreover, he was able to avoid being harmed by doing nothing. It is, therefore, impossible to regard the loss of *C*'s arm as an invasion of *C*'s rights. *C* chose to lose his arm.

Various strategies may be employed in an attempt to avoid this result. The first is to deny that *C* chose to be harmed in the example above. It might be claimed that *C* chose merely to rescue *B*. The loss of his arm was an unfortunate and unwanted consequence of the rescue and so was not chosen by *C*. But this is to define choice too narrowly. As we saw above, choice must be defined to

---

[57] The change in England was prompted, in part, by AL Goodhart, 'Rescue and Voluntary Assumption of Risk' (1933–1935) 5 CLJ 192.

[58] [1935] 1 KB 146 (CA).

include consequences that the claimant knows are bound to result, barring unforeseen intervention. While C did not act with the purpose of being harmed, he did act knowing that the harm would result barring unforeseen intervention and he was at liberty to act otherwise. It cannot be said that C did not choose to be harmed.

Naturally, as this discussion indicates, if C was under a legal obligation to rescue B, then he would not have been *volens*. But that is to imagine a different case. In general, as we have seen in previous chapters, there is no duty to rescue. Similarly, if the alternative to the rescue would have been a violation of some right in C, then C could recover. But that is also a different case.

Secondly, one could claim that C was unable to avoid harm. Instead, C was faced with a choice between two harms: the harm of losing his arm and the psychological harm that would result by knowing that he could have rescued B but did not. This argument succeeds only if that psychological injury would have been covered by C's rights. It would work, for instance, if C would have developed a recognised psychological injury had he not rescued B, in accordance with the discussion of nervous shock in Chapter 11. But this will not often be the case. Most often, the harm that C would have suffered would have been in the order of regret and remorse. And, given that we are concerned with liability and not with the quantum of damages, that harm is irrelevant because C has no right to be free of regret and remorse.

The third strategy, and the most popular, is to deny that C *freely* chose to harm himself. For instance, Fleming claims that 'the duty, legal or moral, thrust upon the would be rescuer to intercede excludes all real choice',[59] and Jason Neyers maintains that, in these circumstances, the rescuer's decision is 'forced'.[60] As we have seen, Fleming's claim that those who conduct rescues in accordance with legal duties to do so are not open to the *volenti* defence is correct. Accordingly, these cases are put aside. But what of the general claim that rescuers do not act freely?

If this position is rightly understood to mean that, in choosing to conduct a rescue, the rescuer does not freely choose, then the position is false. The potential rescuer can always choose not to conduct the rescue. If that were not the case, then there would be no real distinction between rescues that are carried out on impulse and those that are not. Moreover, this position has the highly unintuitive consequence of implying that rescuers deserve no moral credit for what they do, because they are not free to choose otherwise. In the cases we are considering, the rescuer is free to act otherwise.

In particular, Fleming's suggestion that the ethical duty on the claimant to rescue the defendant undermines the claimant's freedom must be rejected.

[59] J Fleming, *The Law of Torts*, 9th edn (LBC Information Services, Sydney, 1998) 187. See also AL Goodhart, 'Rescue and Voluntary Assumption of Risk' (1933–1935) 5 CLJ 192, 196–200.
[60] JW Neyers, '*Donoghue* v. *Stevenson* and the Rescue Doctrine: A Public Justification of Recovery in Situations Involving the Negligent Supply of Dangerous Structures' (1999) 49 *University of Toronto Law Journal* 475, 500.

According to this view, freedom and morality (ethicality) are antagonists. But the demands of morality cannot be understood to be constraints on freedom in this way. In fact, for the Kantian at least, the demands of morality are the demands of freedom.[61] Even if one were to deny this, at the very least we must recognise that when we choose to obey the demands of morality we act freely. Decisions to place oneself in danger for others are paradigm and shining examples of acts of freedom, not of unfreedom.

A different way of interpreting Fleming's claim is to emphasise the word 'real' in 'excludes all real choice'. Similarly, Neyers maintains that the rescuer's choice is 'vitiated' by the circumstances.[62] On this view, the rescuer is faced with two options: to conduct the rescue and be harmed or to do nothing and allow the immediate victim to be harmed. This view accepts the fact that the rescuer freely chooses *between* these two options, but denies that the decision as a whole should be regarded as free because neither option is desired by the rescuer.

But it is unclear how the fact that neither option is wanted demonstrates that the choice is unfree. Many people neither want to go to their work nor to be unemployed, but it does not follow that the choice to get up and go to work each morning is unfree. Certainly, in the rescue cases, the options are forced on the rescuer by the defendant, but that does nothing to show that the choice is unfree. Moreover, there is a tendency, at least subconsciously, to slip from the idea that the choice is forced on the rescuer by the defendant to the notion that, in doing so, the defendant wronged the rescuer. That inference is invalid. In forcing the choice on the rescuer, the defendant violates no rights in the rescuer. This is evident in the fact that the rescuer remains free to avoid all injury, all violation of his rights, by refusing the rescue. If this kind of 'forcing' were wrongful, then many ordinary decisions would be likewise wrongful. For instance, if I purchase the last bottle of wine from the supermarket then you are forced to choose between two unwanted actions, viz going without or going to another supermarket. But that is no interference with your rights. The defendant in these cases constrains the number of options available to the claimant, but does so in a way that violates no right in the claimant. Therefore, it is not wrongful.

As indicated above, this must be distinguished from cases in which the defendant forces a choice on the claimant where all the options will result in a violation of the claimant's rights. That is wrongful, but it is not what occurs in the relevant cases.

In adopting this strategy, commentators sometimes appeal to the non-applicability of the *volenti* defence in the employment context.[63] In *Smith v Baker*,[64] the House of Lords held that knowledge of risk at the place of employment does not constitute consent to undergo that risk, and so ruled that the defence would

---

[61] See especially I Kant, 'Groundwork of the Metaphysics of Morals' in M Gregor (ed), *Practical Philosophy* (Cambridge University Press, Cambridge, 1996) sect 2.

[62] Neyers, above n59, 500.

[63] See eg Goodhart, above n58, 194–6; Neyers, above n59, 500 n138.

[64] [1891] AC 346 (HL).

seldom apply in these contexts. That is entirely in line with the argument presented here. But, in explaining this rule, Frances Bohlen claims that the *volenti* defence has limited applicability in employment contexts because the pressure placed on employees by employers amounts to 'duress' and undermines the freedom of the employee.[65] This has become the dominant view. But it is wrong. For a start, it is inconsistent with the law's general position on economic pressure. For instance, if I need a job and you give me one, I cannot argue that my employment contract is not binding on me because I signed it under duress. Moreover, it is obviously and recognisably the case that employees who work in risky environments are capable of refusing to undergo the risks involved. The common position is, in fact, contemptuous of these people by treating them as if they were not fully autonomous agents. This does not mean that the *volenti* defence should apply in these cases. It should not. It should not because of the reasons enunciated by the House of Lords in *Smith v Baker*: in knowing of the risk and choosing to undergo it, the employee does not thereby either choose to be harmed or waive his primary or secondary rights in relation to the materialisation of that risk. This will hold in all cases in which an employee exposes himself to *a risk* of harm in employment, but not to those, surely extremely rare, cases in which employees knowingly perform actions *certain* to cause harm to them. But in these cases either the employee is *volens* or was acting under duress. That is, the explanation for an employee choosing to perform an action that she knows will cause her harm must be because either she wants to be harmed or genuinely feels compelled to do so. But these are quite unusual cases and not the norm, as is suggested by Bohlen's position.

The fourth strategy for avoiding the conclusion argues on the basis of intuition. For instance, in *Haynes v Harwood*, Maugham LJ argued that it would be irrational for the law to adopt the position that only rescuers who act on instinct can recover:

> If you imagine a man in danger of drowning owing to the negligent management of a boat, and two persons are looking on, is it to be said that the man who jumps in immediately and tries to save the person struggling in the water has a right of action if he suffers injury, but that the man who thinks over all the circumstances and then, perhaps with even greater bravery, determines to attempt to save life, is to be regarded as not being within the protection of the law? That would be a very strange doctrine.[66]

The point here is the reverse of the one made by Fleming above. The rescuer who acts with foresight acts in a more praiseworthy fashion than one who acts instinctively.[67] This is because only the former acts freely and hence exhibits

---

[65] FH Bohlen, *Studies in the Law of Torts* (Bobbs-Merrill, Indianapolis, Ind, 1926) 499, cited in Goodhart, above n58, 195.

[66] [1935] 1 KB 146, 164 (CA). See also J Fleming, *The Law of Torts*, 9th edn (LBC Information Services, Sydney, 1998) 188.

[67] This could be doubted. Surely, the moral person is one who is at least disposed to do the right thing, not one who must calculate how to do what is right. See eg the discussion of virtue in I Kant, 'The Metaphysics of Morals' in M Gregor (ed) *Practical Philosophy* (Cambridge University Press, Cambridge, 1996) 513, [6:380].

morally praiseworthy behaviour. Therefore, it would be irrational to permit only the latter to recover.

However, this point does nothing to show that the defendant wronged the claimant in the relevant cases. Showing that the claimant was brave—which is certainly true especially in these cases in which the claimant knows that he will be harmed—does not provide any evidence to prove that he was wronged by the defendant. The fact remains that, in conducting the rescue, the claimant chooses to be harmed and his rights are therefore not violated.

A fifth strategy is to draw attention to the fact that the duty of care owed to the rescuer is independent of the duty of care owed to the person placed immediately at risk. For instance, WVH Rogers maintains that '[i]f the defendant ought to have foreseen an emergency and that someone would expose himself to danger in order to effect a rescue, then he owes a duty directly to the rescuer. To go on to hold that the rescuer was *volens* would be flatly self-contradictory.'[68] While Rogers' discussion of the duty of care is accurate, it does not show that the defence should not apply. In particular, it is hard to know what Rogers means by the claim that applying the defence would be self-contradictory. What, exactly, about itself would it contradict? In the relevant cases, the claimant chooses to be harmed. It is quite consistent, then, to say that he was owed a duty of care by the defendant but was *volens*.

A sixth strategy for avoiding the conclusion is to point out that the claimant did not consent to the defendant's negligence and therefore cannot be *volens*.[69] This argument succeeds in showing why the huge majority of rescuers are not *volens*, but does not apply in the cases under examination here. We are looking at rescuers who conduct rescues knowing that they will be injured. They are *volens* because they choose to be harmed. The fact that they did not consent to the *risk* of harm does not alter this fact.

The final strategy is to maintain that, in placing the immediate victim at risk, the defendant invited or induced the claimant to intervene.[70] We have seen a similar strategy employed in relation to negligent misrepresentation in Chapter 8. If the defendant genuinely invited the claimant to intervene in a way that implied that the defendant would be legally responsible for adverse outcomes, then of course the defendant would be liable. But the defendant would not be liable in negligence. Rather, he would be liable to compensate the claimant for his injuries because he impliedly promised to do so. The obligation, therefore, is consensual. Moreover, this kind of invitation is extremely unlikely to have occurred. On the other hand, if 'inviting' or 'inducing' the claimant to intervene means that the

---

[68] WVH Rogers, *Winfield and Jolowicz on Tort*, 16th edn (Sweet & Maxwell, London, 2002) para 25.15.

[69] *Ibid.*

[70] AL Goodhart, 'Rescue and Voluntary Assumption of Risk' (1933–1935) 5 *CLJ* 192, 198; JW Neyers, '*Donoghue* v. *Stevenson* and the Rescue Doctrine: A Public Justification of Recovery in Situations Involving the Negligent Supply of Dangerous Structures' (1999) 49 *University of Toronto Law Journal* 475, 498.

defendant made it reasonably foreseeable that the claimant would intervene, then the defendant can be liable only if the claimant did not choose to undergo the harm. But that is what happens in the cases under discussion.

We are forced, then, to the conclusion that claimants who rescue others knowing that they are going to be harmed are *volens* and therefore cannot sue in tort. There is no doubt that this conclusion is uncomfortable. But this discomfort reflects the fact that corrective justice is not all that there is to justice. There is nothing to prevent us from passing a statute to alter this situation. However, if a case of this nature were to reach the courts, they would not be entitled to find for the claimant by introducing concerns of distributive justice, ethics, etc, as these concerns cannot sensibly be contained. As we saw in Chapter 5, distributive justice cannot be relevant in some cases, such as rescue cases, but not in others without relevant reasons, which do not exist. The same holds for other areas of morality.

But perhaps the conclusion is not as unintuitive as it may at first appear. First, we must always remember that it applies only to claimants who choose to be harmed and not to those who choose to undergo a risk of harm. Given that, it is not unintuitive to insist that those who choose harm are not wronged by the suffering of that harm. In fact, the reverse is unintuitive. And, moreover, we are not forced to the conclusion that claimants in this position are unable to recover, just that they cannot recover *in tort*.

Recall the example above in which A's negligence causes B to be stuck in a machine that will kill him unless C conducts a rescue. C does so knowing that he will lose his arm as a result. In this case, not only does C benefit B, he also benefits A by preventing his negligence—for which A is of course legally responsible—from killing B. In other words, C enriches A by saving him from inevitable expenditure. And that enrichment is, of course, at C's expense. It may be possible, therefore, for C to recover this enrichment from A in what has become known as the law of unjust enrichment.[71] In fact, one can see that this area of the law is particularly suitable for dealing with this problem, because it is able to treat the claimant's intention in an especially fine grained manner. For instance, in standard cases of mistaken payment, there is a sense in which the claimant intends and does not intend the defendant to be enriched. In *Kelly v Solari*,[72] for example, the defendant insurance company paid the claimant money it believed it was obliged to pay. Later, however, it discovered that the obligation did not exist and successfully recovered the money from the claimant. When the money was paid, there can be no doubt that the claimant intended the defendant to have it. But the law of unjust

---

[71] See, for instance, *Craven-Ellis v Cannons Ltd* [1936] 2 KB 403 (CA); *Exall v Partridge* (1799) 8 Term Rep 308, 101 ER 1405; P Birks, *Unjust Enrichment* (Clarendon Press, Oxford, 2003) 48–9. R Grantham and C Rickett, *Enrichment and Restitution in New Zealand* (Hart Publishing, Oxford, 2000) 145–7 criticise the idea that an action should be available when the enrichment is for services rendered, but that is not the case here. C enriches A by preventing A becoming liable to B or to B's dependants.

[72] (1841) 9 M & W 54, 152 ER 24.

enrichment recognises that there was a defect in the claimant's intention. This defect did not mean that the claimant's enrichment of the defendant was unintended, but rather that the claimant *would not have* intended to enrich the defendant if the relevant fact was known. The intention to transfer the payment to the defendant meant that the transfer received legal effect (ie property passed), but the defect meant that the claimant could recover the enrichment. This fine grained approach to intention could also allow the rescuer to recover the defendant's enrichment in the cases explored here. While the claimant must have intended to enrich the defendant according to the definition of intention used above, there was a defect in that intention. This follows whether one adopts what Peter Birks refers to as the civilian or common law approach to unjust enrichment.[73] According to the former, the enrichment is unjust because it does not proceed on a basis recognised by law; according to the latter, because there is a defect in the claimant's intention caused, most probably, by illegitimate pressure or because of a specific overriding reason why the enrichment should be surrendered.[74]

III. ILLEGALITY

The law does not take the view that a claimant is barred from recovery merely because she was engaged in an illegal activity. However, it is felt that *some* illegal activities *sometimes* should bar recovery. In order to explore these issues, it is useful to compare the judgment of the High Court of Australia in *Gala v Preston*[75] with that of the Supreme Court of Canada in *Hall v Hebert*.[76]

A. *Gala v Preston*

After engaging in a drinking session, the claimant and the defendant stole a vehicle in contravention of section 408A of Queensland's Criminal Code. The parties took the vehicle on a joy ride and the claimant was injured by the defendant's careless driving. The High Court unanimously held for the defendant, though there was disagreement about why.

Brennan J argued that the basis for denying liability lay in the fact that 'the civil law cannot condone breaches of the criminal law'.[77] In this case:

> To admit a duty of care owed by one offender to a co-offender in the unlawful use of a vehicle would be to assure the co-offender of compensation for damage to himself occurring in the course of conduct which damages the interests of the person from whose possession the car is taken and carries the risk of damage to others. The normative influence of s. 408A would be destroyed by admitting a duty of care.[78]

---

[73] P Birks, *Unjust Enrichment* (Clarendon Press, Oxford, 2003) 88–94.
[74] *Ibid*, 92.
[75] (1991) 172 CLR 243 (HCA).
[76] [1993] 2 SCR 159.
[77] *Gala v Preston* (1991) 172 CLR 243, 270 (HCA).
[78] *Ibid*, 273.

However, Brennan J maintained that this did not imply that a claimant engaged in an illegal act would always be barred from recovering. First, the defence applies only when the claimant and the defendant were engaged in a joint illegal activity.[79] Secondly, liability will be negatived only if allowing recovery would actually amount to condoning the criminal activity.[80] Thirdly, the claimant's injury must occur in the course of carrying out the illegal activity. Imagine the following case in which the defendant and claimant agree to commit a murder.[81]

1. In order to carry out the murder, the parties drive to the intended victim's residence. The defendant drives negligently, colliding with a parked car and injuring the claimant.
2. On arrival, the parties gain access by breaking a window. The defendant negligently fails to remove broken glass from the window and the claimant is injured further.
3. Having gained access, the defendant shoots the victim. However, the bullet passes through the victim and strikes the claimant.
4. The parties hear a siren and rush from the victim's residence. (In fact, the siren belongs to a fire engine.) The parties leap into their car, the defendant accidentally places it in reverse and collides with a lamppost. The claimant suffers whiplash.

Which of these injuries occurred in the course of carrying out a joint illegal activity?

In Brennan J's view, the first injury was not sustained in the course of an illegal activity, while the second and third injuries were. It is unclear what Brennan J would say of the fourth injury. However, if the test is whether the injury occurred in the course of carrying out an illegal activity, then the claimant's best case is with respect to his fourth injury. This is because the claimant was committing no wrong at the moment he suffered an injury in that case. Conversely, in the first case, the claimant was engaged in a conspiracy to murder that involved driving to the victim's residence. If one attempts to avoid this conclusion by stipulating (implausibly) that conspiracy is not serious enough to ground the defence, then it is unclear why the claimant cannot sue for his second injury. He was not committing murder then but was merely committing a conspiracy to murder and breaking and entering. Consider also the case of the defendant who batters a claimant during a brawl. Here, the claimant's injury occurs in the course of a joint illegal activity, though the English Court of Appeal rightly tells us that the claimant may recover.[82]

---

[79] *Ibid*, 263.
[80] *Ibid*, 272.
[81] These are loosely based on Brennan J's discussion in *ibid*, 271.
[82] Compare *Lane v Holloway* [1968] 1 QB 379 (CA). The point made here operates on the assumption that the *volenti* defence does not apply. See n 17.

This demonstrates that Brennan J's approach is artificial. As it relies on the notion that liability will be negatived if the claimant's injury occurred in the course of carrying out the illegal activity, it necessitates distinguishing between injuries sufficiently connected and insufficiently connected with the illegal activity and, as there will often be more than one illegal activity, it involves arbitrarily distinguishing between these activities. This seems to reintroduce into the law the notion of 'directness' enunciated in *In re Polemis and Furness*[83] and rejected in *The Wagon Mound (No 1)*.[84] It was rejected because the notion was empty and there is no reason to think that it takes on meaningful content in this context.[85] Hence, though Brennan J insisted that the relevant principles be perspicuous,[86] his principles do not fit the bill.

I now examine the second of Brennan J's concerns: that the basis of the defence lies in the fact that 'the civil law cannot condone breaches of the criminal law'.[87] In *Gala v Preston* itself, Brennan J maintained that allowing the claimant to recover would undermine section 408A of Queensland's Criminal Code. That claim is not correct. Allowing the claimant to recover for his injuries would in no way interfere with the punitive aspect of the Code nor reduce its deterrent force. It would merely compensate the claimant for his physical injuries.[88]

Were the claimant able to recover in tort, he would be placed in the position in which he would have been had the defendant not driven negligently. This means that the Court would seek to place the claimant in the position in which he would have been had he not been *physically injured*. But this does not mean that the claimant would be compensated for the criminal sanction imposed in accordance with section 408A of Queensland's Criminal Code. In the end, the claimant's position would be that of a person uninjured *but punished*. In effect, then, denying the claimant recovery in *Gala v Preston increased* his punishment beyond that determined as appropriate by the Queensland Criminal Code, by *additionally* undermining the claimant's rights against the defendant.[89] This additional punishment is unauthorised by statute and is inconsistent with the principles of the criminal law. As Ernest Weinrib has said, 'If what lies behind the *turpis causa* tort rule is the facile assumption that plaintiff, as a wrongdoer, deserves no consideration in a court of justice, this would in itself be an abandonment, not a reinforcement, of the criminal law.'[90] In this case, Brennan J

---

[83] [1921] 3 KB 560 (CA).

[84] *Overseas Tankship (UK) Ltd v Morts Dock & Engineering Co Ltd (The Wagon Mound, No 1)* [1961] AC 388 (PC).

[85] See also EJ Weinrib, 'Illegality as a Tort Defence' (1976) 26 *University of Toronto Law Journal* 28, 33–7 and ch 4 of this book.

[86] See eg *Gala v Preston* (1991) 172 CLR 243, 260–3, 273 (HCA).

[87] *Ibid*, 270.

[88] EJ Weinrib, 'Illegality as a Tort Defence' (1976) 26 *University of Toronto Law Journal* 28, 43–7; *Hall v Hebert* [1993] 2 SCR 159, 176.

[89] Weinrib, above n87, 47.

[90] *Ibid*, 46–7.

effectively found in section 408A of Queensland's Criminal Code a justification for undermining the claimant's bodily integrity, but that is a serious violation of the rights of the claimant, who is not to be treated as a *caput lupinum*.

I turn now to the third of Brennan J's claims: that the illegality defence applies only in cases of *joint* illegality. On its face, this is not a sensible restriction. Prima facie, the innocence of the defendant ought to count in favour of the defendant, and hence in favour of the defence. But Brennan J had this the other way round. Brennan J so restricted the defence because he believed that applying it when the claimant was engaged in sole illegality would result in absurdities.[91] But, at least on its face, this restriction is itself absurd. Hence, the absurdities pointed to by Brennan J in fact reflect Brennan J's failure to elucidate the appropriate basis of the defence.

I conclude that Brennan J's view does not adequately explain the basis of the illegality defence.

Presenting an alternative account of the defence, Mason CJ and Deane, Gaudron and McHugh JJ argued that the defence applies when it would be inappropriate for a court to formulate a standard of care.[92] This occurs when setting a standard of care would require the Court to formulate a standard suitable to illegal activities:

> Thus, it would border on the grotesque for the courts to seek to define the content of a duty of care owed by one bank robber to another in blowing up a safe which they were together seeking to rob. On the other hand, to take an extreme example the other way, it would be unjust and wrong for the courts to deny the existence of the ordinary relationship of proximity which exists between the driver of a motor vehicle and a passenger merely because the driver was, with the encouragement of the only passenger, momentarily driving in a traffic lane reserved for the use of cars with three or more occupants.[93]

In the first case, the claimant must fail, as the claimant can succeed only if the court determines a standard of care expected of one bank robber to another in blowing up a safe. However, the claimant need not fail in the second case, as the standard of care owed to the claimant is not that of someone illegally driving in a lane reserved for the use of cars with three or more occupants, but that of the ordinary reasonable driver.

Note that the problem of formulating the standard of care in these cases arises because of the High Court of Australia's recognition that the relationship between the parties can affect the standard of care—a recognition that goes back to Dixon J's judgment in *The Insurance Commissioner v Joyce*.[94] Other courts are less aware of this fact and so are less sensitive to its impact on the

---

[91] *Gala v Preston* (1991) 172 CLR 243, 263, 274 (HCA).

[92] Ibid, 252–3.

[93] Ibid, 253. In the following, I ignore the references to 'proximity' in the judgment. This is because that notion has been critiqued in ch 5. See also *Gala v Preston* (1991) 172 CLR 243, 261 (HCA) (Brennan J).

[94] (1948) 77 CLR 39, 56 (HCA).

defence of illegality (as well as *volenti*). So, for instance, in *Hall v Hebert*, McLachlin J said that '[s]hifting the analysis to the issue of duty provides no new insight into the fundamental question of when the courts should be entitled to deny recovery in tort to a plaintiff on the ground of the plaintiff's immoral or illegal conduct'.[95] While this comment makes sense from the perspective in which McLachlin J was operating, it does not do justice to the fact that courts must set the standard of care with reference to the relationship between the parties. 'To conclude that [the defendant] should have observed the ordinary standard of care to be expected of a competent driver would be to disregard the actual relationship between the parties as we have described it.'[96]

The concern is that, in order to determine the standard of care in *Gala v Preston*, the Court would have had to decide how much care one car thief owes another. That does seem perverse. On this view, then, the requirement of joint illegality makes apparent sense: if the defendant was acting legally then the standard of care will not need to reflect any illegal activity.

However, no such enquiry was necessary in *Gala v Preston*. The injury to the claimant occurred after the car had been stolen and while the parties were on a joy ride. Prima facie, then, the standard of care to be expected of the defendant was that of the ordinary reasonable driver. In this case, the standard required adjusting because of the relationship between the parties, but that did not call for the Court to determine a standard of care owed by car thieves to each other. For instance, if the claimant had consented to the defendant driving negligently, then the claimant was *volens*. Moreover, if the claimant knew that the defendant would drive carelessly and chose to ride with the defendant in that knowledge, then, though the claimant was not *volens*, the standard of care that the claimant could rightly expect of the defendant was that of a careless driver.[97] These issues were explored in the previous section of this chapter. Mason CJ *et al* recognised these points:

> [E]ach of the parties to the enterprise must be taken to have appreciated that he would be encountering serious risks in travelling in the stolen vehicle when it was being driven by persons who had been drinking heavily and when it could well be the subject of a report to the police leading possibly to their pursuit and/or their arrest. In the special and exceptional circumstances that prevailed, the participants could not have had any reasonable basis for expecting that a driver of the vehicle would drive it according to ordinary standards of competence and care.[98]

---

[95] *Hall v Hebert* [1993] 2 SCR 159, 181. The context makes it clear that McLachlin J was speaking of both the standard and duty of care.

[96] *Gala v Preston* (1991) 172 CLR 243, 255 (HCA).

[97] Similarly, P Benson, 'Equality of Opportunity and Private Law' in D Friedmann and D Barak-Erez (eds), *Human Rights in Private Law* (Hart Publishing, Oxford, 2001) 227 maintains that courts can enforce contracts that involved discriminatory offers without having to endorse the discriminatory nature of the offer.

[98] *Gala v Preston* (1991) 172 CLR 243, 254 (HCA).

The concerns expressed here are related to the standard of care (and perhaps to the defence of *volenti*), but they have nothing to do with illegality.[99]

Moreover, imagine that the claimant was injured while carrying out an illegal activity. Recall the example above in which two parties are conducting a murder when one is shot by the other. In determining the standard of care here, a court need not formulate a standard of care for murderers. Instead, the court could inquire into the precautions usually imposed on those handling firearms modified only by any communication between the parties that would indicate that the claimant was *volens* or that the standard of care should be adjusted. While this will involve enquiry into the murder, it does not involve formulating a standard of care for murderers. Similarly, in *Dann v Hamilton,* explored above, a court should formulate a standard of care relevant to the parties, given that the claimant knew that the defendant was driving dangerously and under the influence of alcohol; but the Court did not need to define a standard of care for those engaged in drinking and driving.

Note that a similar enquiry will be relevant in the case of the passenger who encourages the defendant driver to drive in a lane reserved for cars with three or more occupants. This is because the claimant's encouragement of the defendant to break the law affects the relationship between the parties. Though this does not necessarily mean that the claimant will be unable to recover, it does mean that the court must enquire into such matters, contrary to the claim of Mason CJ *et al*.

I conclude that the approaches enunciated by the High Court of Australia in *Gala v Preston* do not appropriately define the scope or elucidate the basis of the illegality defence.

B. Cory J in *Hall v Hebert*

In *Hall v Hebert*, the claimant and defendant had been drinking when they decided to drive to Graveyard Road, a gravel spur. While there, they misplaced the car keys and so attempted to jump-start the car. However, this was done negligently: the car ran down a steep gravel slope and turned upside down. The claimant suffered serious head injuries.[100]

Cory J maintained that the defence of illegality should be eliminated. Instead, Cory J argued, the issues usually considered in this context should be treated as ones of public policy relevant to the second stage of the *Anns (Kamloops)* test.[101] In Cory J's opinion, in *Hall v Hebert* there was 'no reason why the appellant

---

[99] Hence, the case may well have been rightly decided, but on the ground that the defendant was not negligent to the claimant, rather than because the defence of illegality applied.

[100] The claimant was the driver. The claimant alleged that the defendant had a duty to remain sober enough to judge whether the claimant was fit to drive. This idea is not relevant to the defence of illegality and so is ignored here.

[101] *Hall v Hebert* [1993] 2 SCR 159, 209–22.

should be prevented from recovering compensation on the grounds of public policy. To permit him to recover would not offend or shock the conscience of reasonable right thinking members of the community fully apprised of the facts.'[102]

As McLachlin J pointed out in *Hall v Hebert*, dealing with this issue under the duty of care is not appropriate:

> I am not sure that much is gained by replacing the defence of *ex turpi causa non oritur actio* with a judicial discretion to negate, or to refuse to consider, the duty of care. Shifting the analysis to the issue of duty provides no new insight into the fundamental question of when the courts should be entitled to deny recovery in tort to a plaintiff on the ground of the plaintiff's immoral or illegal conduct. Moreover, it introduces a series of new problems. In the end I fear that it would prove more problematic than has the defence of *ex turpi causa non oritur actio*. . . .
>
> *Donoghue v. Stevenson* . . . the source of our modern law of negligence and of the concept of duty upon which it is founded, requires that a person exercise reasonable care toward all his neighbours. It does not say that the duty is owed only to neighbours who have acted morally and legally. Tort . . . does not require a plaintiff to have a certain moral character in order to bring an action before the court. The duty of care is owed to all persons who may reasonably be foreseen to be injured by the negligent conduct.
>
> Policy concerns unrelated to the legal rules which govern the relationship between the parties to an action have not generally been considered in determining whether a duty of care lies. This follows from the fact that the justice which tort law seeks to accomplish is justice between the parties to the particular action; the court acts at the instance of the wronged party to rectify the damage caused by a particular defendant: see Ernest J. Weinrib, 'The Special Morality of Tort Law' (1989), 34 McGill L.J. 403 at p. 408.
>
> The relationship between plaintiff and defendant which gives rise to their respective entitlement and liability arises from a duty predicated on foreseeable consequences of harm. This being the concern, the legality or morality of the plaintiff's conduct is an extrinsic consideration. In the rare cases where concerns for the administration of justice require that the extrinsic consideration of the character of the plaintiff's conduct be considered, it seems to me that this is better done by way of defence than by distorting the notion of the duty of care owed by the defendant to the plaintiff.[103]

In the following, then, I ignore Cory J's attempt to eliminate the defence.

I now explore the notion that the defence should apply only when recovery would 'offend or shock the conscience of reasonable right thinking members of the community fully apprised of the facts'.[104] This is the approach that has largely been adopted in England. Hence, in *Hardy v Motor Insurers' Bureau*, it was said that recovery would be denied when the claimant's conduct was 'sufficiently anti-social';[105] in *Thackwell v Barclays Bank plc*, when it was an 'affront

---

[102] *Hall v Hebert* [1993] 2 SCR 224.
[103] *Ibid*, 181–2.
[104] *Ibid*, 224 (Cory J).
[105] [1964] 2 QB 745, 767 (CA) (Diplock LJ).

to the public conscience';[106] and in *Kirkham v Chief Constable of Greater Manchester Police*, when it would 'shock the ordinary citizen'.[107]

These formulations point in one of two directions, each problematic. First, the suggestion could be that the claimant's ability to recover is determined by public opinion. But it is unclear why public opinion should rule here when it is usually irrelevant.[108] There are many cases in which the claimant succeeds where the public may have preferred otherwise, and many others in which the claimant fails though she enjoyed public sympathy. Tort law is not a 'law' of public opinion. Secondly, the notion may be that recovery will be denied if it *should* be opposed by the public. The problem with this view is that it is empty. In order for this view to be informative, it is necessary to elucidate what it is that should shock the community, etc. As it stands, this formulation is an empty gesture. Moreover, as McLachlin J pointed out, '[t]ort . . . does not require a plaintiff to have a certain moral character in order to bring an action before the court'.[109] It is not relevant to ask whether the claimant acted ethically.

C. Corrective Justice and Illegality: Weinrib and McLachlin J in *Hall v Hebert*

The fundamental problem with the judgments in *Gala v Preston*, with Cory J's judgment in *Hall v Hebert* and with our understanding of the defence in general is the following. The fact that the claimant acted illegally may explain our lack of sympathy with the claimant, but it does not in itself affect the relationship between the claimant and the defendant.[110] This is *especially* so in cases of joint illegality. If the claimant and the defendant were together engaged in a crime, then how can that lead to the conclusion that the claimant *rather than the defendant* should bear the loss caused by the defendant's negligence? Rather, in cases of joint illegality, the illegality seems to point both in favour of and against liability. Hence, joint illegality appears to be irrelevant.

Accordingly, if the defence has a role to play, its role can have nothing to do with the relationship between the parties.[111] Hence, though some have attempted to subsume the defence into the duty of care[112]—consistent with the

---

[106] [1986] 1 All ER 676, 687 (QBD) (Hutchison J).
[107] [1990] 2 QB 283, 284 (CA) (Lloyd LJ).
[108] *Tinsley v Milligan* [1994] 1 AC 340 (HL). T Weir, *Tort Law* (Oxford University Press, Oxford, 2002) 121 argues that this must imply that the public does not know what is fair, just or reasonable, but the better view is that the defence has nothing to do with such undefined concerns except in the specific sense in which they relate to corrective justice and the place of tort law within the legal system as a whole.
[109] *Hall v Hebert* [1993] 2 SCR 159, 182.
[110] This must be distinguished from the standard of care stage of the enquiry. In cases in which only the claimant acted illegally, it may be relevant to consider the fact that the claimant's activity was illegal in determining whether the defendant created an unreasonable risk to the claimant.
[111] *Hall v Hebert* [1993] 2 SCR 159, 181–2.
[112] See especially, *ibid*, 209–22 (Cory J); *Gala v Preston* (1991) 172 CLR 243 (HCA), (Mason CJ and Deane, Gaudron and McHugh JJ).

general trend of collapsing the whole of the law of negligence into the duty of care[113]—the defence must be treated as a separate matter.[114] As identified by Weinrib[115] and by McLachlin J in *Hall v Hebert*,[116] the defence is based on maintaining the integrity of the judicial system. Importantly, the defence must apply only when the integrity of the judicial system is at stake, otherwise the defence would be inconsistent with the principles of both tort law and criminal law. To apply the defence more widely would be inconsistent with tort law, as the claimant would be denied recovery for the violation of his rights, and it would be inconsistent with criminal law as the claimant would be punished without appropriate authority.

On this view, then, the defence of illegality comes into play only if recovery would introduce incoherence into the law.[117] This occurs in two broad situations: when allowing the claimant to recover would permit the claimant to profit from his criminal action and when allowing recovery would permit the claimant to escape the consequences of the criminal law.[118]

Weinrib discusses an example of the first situation: *Katko v Briney*.[119] In that case, the claimant was injured by a spring gun while attempting to break into the defendant's property. The claimant was awarded compensatory and exemplary damages. While the award of compensatory damages was appropriate, the award of exemplary damages could not have been, as, given that exemplary damages are a windfall to the claimant, the award allowed the claimant to profit from his wrongdoing. The claimant should be left no worse off than he would have been absent the defendant's wrongdoing, but he should not enjoy a windfall in consequence of his illegal act.[120]

Similarly, if a claimant suffers an injury that prevents him from continuing an illegal activity, the court should not permit the claimant to recover for the inability to carry on that activity. For instance, if a defendant negligently causes a 'professional' bank robber to become blind, then, while the bank robber can recover for the injury and the general loss of amenity, etc, he cannot recover for his lost future 'earnings' as a bank robber. This would permit the claimant to

---

[113] This was examined in ch 5.

[114] *Hall v Hebert* [1993] 2 SCR 159, 181–2. For additional reasons, see *ibid*, 174–5.

[115] EJ Weinrib, 'Illegality as a Tort Defence' (1976) 26 *University of Toronto Law Journal* 28.

[116] *Hall v Hebert* [1993] 2 SCR 159, 169.

[117] *Ibid*, 169, 172–7; EJ Weinrib, 'Illegality as a Tort Defence' (1976) 26 *University of Toronto Law Journal* 28, 47–51.

[118] *Hall v Hebert* [1993] 2 SCR 159, 169.

[119] 183 NW 2d 657 (Iowa SC 1971).

[120] EJ Weinrib, 'Illegality as a Tort Defence' (1976) 26 *University of Toronto Law Journal* 28, 41–2; *Hall v Hebert* [1993] 2 SCR 159, 175. I have argued that exemplary damages are inconsistent with the principled approach and with corrective justice in A Beever, 'The Structure of Aggravated and Exemplary Damages' (2003) 23 *OJLS* 87, 105–10; A Beever, 'Justice and Punishment in Tort: A Comparative Theoretical Analysis' in R Grantham and C Rickett (eds), *Justifying Remedies in Private Law* (Cambridge University Press, Cambridge, forthcoming 2007). See also EJ Weinrib, 'Punishment and Disgorgement as Contract Remedies' (2003) 78 *Chicago-Kent Law Review* 55.

benefit from illegal activities.[121] Further, if a defendant's negligence causes the destruction of a claimant's house in which the claimant had a heroin stash, the claimant can recover for the house but not for the heroin.

An example of a situation in which the defence of illegality applies to prevent the claimant escaping the consequences of the criminal law is the following. Imagine that the claimant is a 'professional' burglar who hires the defendant as a lookout man. However, due to the negligence of the defendant, the claimant is apprehended by the police, convicted and subjected to a fine or term of imprisonment. In such circumstances, the defence of illegality prevents the claimant from recovering the fine or recovering for the term of imprisonment from the defendant. This is because the alternative would allow the claimant to avoid the consequences of the criminal law and hence see tort law in conflict with the criminal law.[122]

Accordingly, the scope of the illegality defence is quite narrow. It is concerned only to preserve the law's seamless web.[123] The defence is not concerned with only joint illegality, as the examples above show.[124] Nor does the defence arise only with respect to serious offences. The sole criterion is the coherence of the legal system as a whole.

Two unanswered questions remain. First, as the defence is not concerned with the relationship between the parties, does this not imply that the defence is based on policy considerations in contradiction to the thesis of this book? Secondly, if the defence applies in order to preserve the coherence of the law as a whole, why does it do so by altering tort law rather than criminal law?

The first response to the first question is to note that the impact of criminal law on the law of negligence is an impact of *principles* of criminal law.[125] Hence, it is not appropriate to regard this as the imposition of policy. The defence is explicable with reference to legal doctrine alone.

Moreover, in answer to both questions, although the defence makes reference to the criminal law, it does not involve the trumping of tort law principles by criminal law principles. Instead, the defence reflects the interrelatedness of tort law and criminal law: the defence is witness to the fact that the common law is a seamless web.

The reason the claimant cannot recover when the defence of illegality applies is that the claimant must assert a loss of something to which she is not entitled

---

[121] EJ Weinrib, 'Illegality as a Tort Defence' (1976) 26 *University of Toronto Law Journal* 28, 42; *Hall v Hebert* [1993] 2 SCR 159, 174–5.

[122] Weinrib, above n120, 51; *Hall v Hebert* [1993] 2 SCR 159, 177–8.

[123] Weinrib, above n120, 42; *Hall v Hebert* [1993] 2 SCR 159, 176. In *Woolcock Street Investments pty Ltd v CDG pty Ltd* [2004] HCA 16, (2004) 216 CLR 515, 102, McHugh J claimed that '[l]aw is too complex for it to be a seamless web. But, so far as possible, courts should try to make its principles and policies coherent'. This can be paraphrased, consistently with the argument presented here, that it is an aspiration of the law to be a seamless web.

[124] *Hall v Hebert* [1993] 2 SCR 159, 179.

[125] In any case, the distinction between principle and policy is drawn differently in the criminal law from either here or from discussion of tort law more generally.

in law. Hence, the claimant cannot succeed, because she cannot establish in law that she suffered loss. In order to understand this point, it is necessary to distinguish it from the arguments made in Chapter 7 with respect to economic loss. Economic loss is irrecoverable because the claimant holds no primary right as against the defendant to the subject matter of that loss. Hence, economic loss is irrelevant to the relationship between the parties and defendants do not owe claimants duties of care to prevent such losses. On the other hand, when the defence of illegality applies, the claimant does possess a right held as against the defendant. Accordingly, even when the defence applies, the claimant's right is relevant to the relationship between the parties and the defendant did owe the claimant a duty of care. The reason the claimant cannot recover is not that she possessed no primary right, nor that the right was not violated by the defendant, but that *in law* the violation of the right had no *value*. In consequence, the defendant need not compensate the claimant because, in the eyes of the law and in the eyes of corrective justice, she suffered no loss.

Recall the example discussed above in which the defendant negligently caused the destruction of the claimant's heroin stash. Here, though possession of heroin is illegal, the heroin is nevertheless the claimant's property. Hence, the claimant holds a right *in rem* in the heroin and this generates obligations in others to respect that right. Accordingly, the defendant owed the claimant a duty of care in respect of the heroin. Moreover, the defendant fell below the standard of care, and was a factual cause of an injury that was proximate to his negligence. But the claimant cannot recover for the loss of the heroin, as the value of that heroin *in law* to the claimant is nothing. Because the possession of heroin is illegal, in the eyes of the law the loss of the heroin is no loss to the claimant, despite the fact that it is an interference with a property right.

None of this is to deny that the claimant suffered a loss in fact. But, as with economic loss, the question is whether the claimant suffered a loss of something over which he had a legally recognised interest. In the eyes of the law, the illegally possessed heroin had no value. The claimant cannot recover, because the criminal law shows that the claimant had no entitlement to the loss claimed. If the 'street value' of the heroin was, say, £100,000, its legal value—by which I mean the value to which the claimant was entitled as a matter of law—was £0.

This is also why a claimant personally injured and unable to continue a 'career' in bank robbing cannot recover loss of earnings as a bank robber. The claimant did possess a right as against the defendant in relation to the injury— bodily integrity—and hence the defendant owed the claimant a duty of care.[126] But, as a matter of law, the claimant is entitled to no earnings from bank robbing. Hence, in the eyes of the law, the loss of that 'career' was no loss at all.

A similar, though distinct, analysis is appropriate for defendants who demand compensation for criminal penalties. A claimant who is apprehended

---

[126] This argument does not apply—at least not immediately—to those with statutory authority to apprehend the bank robber, such as members of the police force.

because of the negligence of his accomplice cannot recover the fine or compensation for his jail term. With regard to the jail term, the claimant possessed a right as against the defendant to freedom of movement and the defendant created an unreasonable risk that the claimant would lose his freedom of movement. Hence, the defendant fell below the standard of care, owed the claimant a duty of care and factually caused an injury that was proximate to his negligence. However, the jailing of the claimant in accordance with the criminal process and statute law is no violation of the claimant's right to freedom of movement. Thus, though the defendant created an unreasonable risk of loss to the claimant, the loss actually suffered by the claimant was suffered through no violation of the claimant's rights. Similarly, with respect to the fine, while the claimant possessed a right as against the defendant to his assets, the loss to the court of some of those assets dictated by the criminal law is not a violation of the claimant's rights to those assets.

This demonstrates that no trumping of tort law by criminal law is involved. As we saw in relation to economic loss, the law of property partly determines the operation of tort law by elucidating rights to which the law responds and, by implication, non-rights to which the law cannot respond. This is not property law trumping tort law, but merely the realisation that tort law responds to rights invasions but does not directly create rights to things. It is artificial to divide the law into rigid sections: tort, property, crime, etc. The law is a seamless web. Similarly, the defence of illegality sees the criminal law denying claimants entitlements to recover for certain losses. This is not the criminal law dominating the law of tort, but the two areas of law working in tandem. And it involves no appeal to policy.

Thus, though the operation of the illegality defence is not determined in accordance with corrective justice alone, this is no exception to the general approach of the law. Corrective justice demands that the value of the damage to the claimant be given by the defendant. But corrective justice plays no role in determining that value. If I negligently destroy your £1,000,000 house, corrective justice demands that I pay you the value of your house, but it is the market that determines that your house is worth £1,000,000. Ordinarily, the value of things is determined by the relevant market or estimated in terms of social utility, but occasionally the law determines the value of things for legal purposes. For instance, in the eyes of the law the possession of heroin has no value. Hence, in such circumstances corrective justice demands that there be no compensation. Accordingly, in combination with the criminal law, corrective justice demands the defence of illegality.

11

Wrongful Birth, Wrongful Conception and Nervous Shock

THIS CHAPTER IS miscellaneous in the sense that it explores three issues that do not deserve a chapter in their own right, but must be examined at some stage. Moreover, though they appear to relate most closely to the themes of previous chapters, they must be discussed at this late stage because their resolution requires appeal to the considerations of the last five chapters. The first topic is 'wrongful birth'. In the light of what has gone before, this issue can be dealt with quickly. The second is 'wrongful conception', one of the most difficult topics in the law of negligence. The third issue is nervous shock. My treatment of this issue differs from that of the first two and from that of the other issues explored earlier in this book. This is because, for reasons elucidated below, the investigation conducted in this book cannot resolve all of the most important problems surrounding recovery for nervous shock. However, my aim is to show that corrective justice points to the resolution of these problems.

I. WRONGFUL BIRTH

In *Harriton v Stevens*,[1] the claimant was born seriously disabled because her mother caught the rubella virus while the claimant was *in utero*. The defendants were allegedly negligent in failing to diagnose the disease. The claimant's mother maintained that, had she been informed that she had rubella, she would have aborted her foetus. The claimant attempted to recover damages for past and future medical care, for pain and suffering and for loss of income. The majority of the High Court of Australia rejected the claimant's case. In doing so, they maintained that their conclusion conflicted with corrective justice but that this was appropriate in the circumstances.[2]

---

[1] [2006] HCA 15. See also *McKay v Essex Area Health Board* [1982] 1 QB 1166 (CA). In England and Wales, the common law action is no longer available. See s4 Congenital Disabilities (Civil Liability) Act 1976. The following discussion is an analysis of the common law and is not intended as an interpretation of this statute.

[2] *Harriton v Stevens* [2006] HCA 15, 271–5 (Crennan J).

In fact, however, corrective justice dictates the outcome reached by the Court. As we saw in Chapter 5, foetuses possess no rights. Only those who are born alive possess rights. Accordingly, just as there is no right not to be aborted, there can be no right to be aborted. Therefore, the birth of the claimant was no violation of its rights. Moreover, when the claimant was born, it had rights to its person and (counterfactually) the property, etc, it had when it was born. But the claimant was born with her disabilities and so those disabilities cannot be regarded as arising from the violation of the claimant's rights. The claimant's position is like that of the person who purchases a badly constructed building.

Again, this does not mean that the claimant should not be supported in other ways. It does not mean, for instance, that the state has no obligation to meet the claimant's needs. It means only that the claimant is not the victim of a tort committed by the defendant.

II. WRONGFUL CONCEPTION

For two general reasons, this is one of the most difficult areas in the law of negligence. The first reason is that the issues that arise here can be resolved only by examining many concerns relevant to the last five chapters. The second reason is that there is a strong tendency for both academics and judges to refuse to conduct this investigation because of ethical or religious beliefs, whether conservative or progressive. Moreover, these beliefs tend to cloud our perception of what the legal issues actually are. However, if we face these issues objectively, we can see how the principled approach deals with them and that it does so in a plausible and enlightening fashion.

A. Case Law

In *McFarlane v Tayside Area Health Board*,[3] the alleged facts were the following. The male claimant underwent a vasectomy after he and his wife, the female claimant, decided not to have any more children. In accordance with standard procedure, the male claimant submitted several semen samples to the defendant to test whether they contained sperm. The purpose of the tests was to determine whether the separation of the vas was permanent or whether a recanalisation had taken place. In fact, a recanalisation had occurred. The defendant incorrectly and negligently informed the male claimant that no sperm were present in the samples. As a result, the claimants ceased using birth control and the female claimant fell pregnant. The claimants decided to keep the child and attempted to recover for the cost of the pregnancy, the birth and raising the child.

---

[3] [2000] 2 AC 59 (HL Sc). Compare *Cattanach v Melchior* [2003] HCA 38, (2003) 215 CLR 1.

The House of Lords accepted the first two but rejected the last. In respect of those damages, Lord Steyn argued:

> It is possible to view the case simply from the perspective of corrective justice. It requires somebody who has harmed another without justification to indemnify the other. On this approach the parents' claim for the cost of bringing up [the child] must succeed. But one may also approach the case from the vantage point of distributive justice. It requires a focus on the just distribution of burdens and losses among members of a society. If the matter is approached in this way, it may become relevant to ask of the commuters on the Underground the following question: should the parents of an unwanted but healthy child be able to sue the doctor or hospital for compensation equivalent to the cost of bringing up the child for the years of his or her minority, ie until about 18 years? My Lords, I have not consulted my fellow travellers on the London Underground but I am firmly of the view that an overwhelming number of ordinary men and women would answer the question with an emphatic No.[4]

Elsewhere, I have argued that distributive justice cannot be introduced in this manner as it is inconsistent with the structure of tort law.[5] Though I do not pursue that argument further here, it seems to have been borne out by the decision of the House of Lords in *Rees v Darlington Memorial Hospital NHS Trust*.[6] In that case, the claimant, who suffered from visual impairment, became pregnant due to the negligence of the defendant. The Court of Appeal refused the claimant the normal costs of raising the child, but a majority allowed the claimant to recover for the additional costs of raising the child that would be incurred by the claimant because of her disability.[7] In a similar case, *Parkinson v St James and Seacroft University Hospital NHS Trust*,[8] an able-bodied mother gave birth to an unwanted child who was disabled. Again, the Court of Appeal ruled that the claimant could not recover the normal costs of raising the child, but could recover the additional costs suffered because of the child's disability. Faced with these decisions and the apparent injustice of strictly applying the decision in *McFarlane* and disallowing recovery, but not knowing what else to do in the circumstances of *McFarlane* itself, their Lordships in *Rees* adopted an extraordinary position. A majority decided that, at least in cases where the child was healthy,[9] wrongful conception will attract a conventional award of £15,000, whatever the claimant's actual loss. The dissenters preferred to send the case to trial without determining, or even providing any real guidance on, the issue upon which the appeal was brought. The House of Lords has found

---

[4] *McFarlane v Tayside Area Health Board* [2000] 2 AC 59, 82 (HL Sc). See also *Rees v Darlington Memorial Hospital NHS Trust* [2003] UKHL 52, [2004] 1 AC 309, [4]; Lord Steyn, 'Perspectives of Corrective and Distributive Justice in Tort Law' (2002) 37 *Irish Jurist* 1, 1–7.

[5] A Beever, 'Particularism and Prejudice in the Law of Tort' (2003) 11 *Tort Law Review* 146.

[6] [2003] UKHL 52, [2004] 1 AC 309.

[7] *Rees v Darlington Memorial Hospital NHS Trust* [2002] EWCA Civ 88, [2003] QB 20.

[8] [2001] EWCA Civ 530, [2002] QB 266.

[9] Their Lordships were ambivalent about the appropriate outcome should the baby be born disabled.

itself embroiled in concerns of distributive justice, concerns with which it is, entirely unsurprisingly, unable to deal.[10]

The issues of distributive justice raised by these cases are, of course, extremely politically sensitive. They strike at deeply held notions about the value of children and the autonomy of parents. Those against recovery are likely to argue that children are precious and cannot be regarded as a loss, while those in favour are inclined to maintain that adults have a right to determine their own lives and, if they choose not to have, or to have only a certain number of, children, they should not be told that that choice is unworthy of recognition because other people believe that children are priceless. Accordingly, if courts try to solve these cases by appealing to policy, they will find themselves embroiled in these highly charged emotional and political debates.[11] In *McFarlane*, the House of Lords sided with those who believe that children are priceless and cannot count as a loss, regardless of the choices of the parents; but it cannot be appropriate for judges to enforce their political preferences on society in that fashion.

The appropriate alternative is to find a genuinely legal solution to these problems. In doing so, we must recognise that the solution will not and cannot satisfy everyone's political preferences. But importantly it will not reject any of those preferences either. In making a purely legal decision, a court will produce a decision that is preferred by one political lobby or another but, if the court does not base its decision on any of the political arguments, then it cannot be accused of siding with that lobby. The court leaves the political matters to be determined by the appropriate body, which in *McFarlane* would have been the Scottish Parliament.

In the following, I explore the purely legal response to the situations raised by the cases examined above. At first, however, I ignore the issue of whether the defendant assumed responsibility to the claimants. That issue is explored only at the end of this discussion. Accordingly, at this point our examination of these issues proceeds in accordance with the principles of the law of negligence.

---

[10] See also A Pedain, 'Unconventional Justice in the House of Lords' [2004] *CLJ* 19, 21: '[i]s it not bound to make some members of the public, whose moral sensitivities their Lordships were so concerned about in *McFarlane*, uncomfortable to learn that you get £10,000 under the Fatal Accidents Act 1976 [UK] for losing a child through another's negligence, and £15,000 at common law for having one?'. B Golder, 'From *McFarlane* to *Melchior* and Beyond: Love, Sex, Money and Commodification in the Anglo-Australian Law of Torts' (2004) 12 *Torts Law Journal* 128, 128: '[t]he political context within which the recent case law is situated is the gendered construction of the family and the denial of female reproductive autonomy. It is argued that although the High Court of Australia's recent consideration of the matter in *Cattanach v Melchior* affirmed the right of plaintiffs to recover damages for this head of loss, the gendered policy reasoning which led the House of Lords in *McFarlane v Tayside Health Board* to deny the award of child-rearing damages is still evident in the reasoning of the High Court. It is argued that in the Australian context, where State legislatures such as Queensland and New South Wales have already begun to circumscribe the rights which *Melchior* gives to plaintiffs, it is more important than ever to articulate the feminist case for child-rearing damages.'

[11] See, eg, the exchanges between Gaudron J and counsel for the defendant in *Nafte v CES* (11 Sept 1996), S91/1996,.

In conducting this argument, it is necessary on occasion to draw analogies between the claimant's case in *McFarlane* and cases involving damage to chattels. Naturally, some will balk at these analogies. However, the point in making them is not to suggest that children are morally analogous to chattels but to reveal the normative structure of the claimant's or defendant's contentions. It is certainly not presumed that children are in any way morally equivalent to chattels.

B. The Law of Negligence

For the claimants to have succeeded in *McFarlane*, it was first necessary for them to have demonstrated that the defendant had violated their rights. In informing the male claimant that he was sterile, the defendant exposed the female claimant to an unreasonable risk of injury through pregnancy. Though some deny that having a child constitutes injury,[12] this mischaracterises the issue that needs to be decided.[13] An injury in the eyes of the law includes the invasion of the claimant's right to bodily integrity. Hence, whether or not pregnancies are usually desired, whether or not we are inclined to describe pregnancy as an injury in non-legal contexts, if the claimant did not desire to become pregnant but became so because of the negligence of the defendant, then her right to bodily integrity was violated. As Lord Millet said:

> The contention that the birth of a normal, healthy baby 'is not a harm' is not an accurate formulation of the issue. In order to establish a cause of action in delict, the pursuers must allege and prove that they have suffered an invasion of their legal rights (*injuria*) and that they have sustained loss (*damnum*) as a result. In the present case the *injuria* occurred when (and if) the defenders failed to take reasonable care to ensure that the information they gave was correct. The *damnum* occurred when Mrs. McFarlane conceived. This was an invasion of her bodily integrity and threatened further damage both physical and financial.[14]

Here we see, most unusually, the appropriate concern being given to the claimant's rights. No doubt, this was in large part because the case was heard on appeal from Scotland.[15]

---

[12] This formed the basis of the argument in the courts below the House of Lords. See also C Witting, 'Physical Damage in Negligence' (2002) 61 *CLJ* 189. In any case, surely pregnancy does cause physical injury as any mother will attest.

[13] *McFarlane v Tayside Area Health Board* [2000] 2 AC 59, 81 (Lord Steyn), 87 (Lord Hope), 107–8 (Lord Millett).

[14] *Ibid*, 107. Note that Lord Millett's analysis assumes that the defendant is liable because of an assumption of responsibility and that assumption of responsibility is best analysed in terms of the negligence model. Only on this approach does the *injuria* occur when the statement was made. On the approach under examination at the moment, the *injuria* occurred when the claimant conceived.

[15] In fact, it is interesting to observe that a substantial number of the leading cases in the law of negligence are appeals from Scotland. Could it be that they become leading cases because the civilian background forces judges to think more deeply about legal structure? In any case, the focus on rights was short-lived. Lord Millet directly went on to say that '[t]he admission of a novel head of damages is not solely a question of principle. Limitations on the scope of legal liability arise from

The cost of raising the child is loss that flows from the violation of the mother's bodily integrity. In more familiar but less helpful language, it is consequential economic loss. Accordingly, prima facie, the mother can recover those costs. However, the father has no claim. This is because, unless the defendant assumed responsibility to the father (an issue that we return to below), no right in the father has been violated. There is no violation of the male claimant's bodily integrity and he has no common law right not to have children.[16] Accordingly, I ignore the male claimant for the most part in the following.

The second requirement for success is that the claimant must have suffered loss in respect of that for which she was claiming. This issue is highly contentious. But this is in part because it is often misunderstood. As discussed in more detail in the following, in determining whether the child is a loss, it is necessary also to take into account the benefits that the child brings. Accordingly, Lord Millett claimed that 'if the court assesses the monetary value of the child at a sum less than the costs of maintaining him, it will have accepted the unedifying proposition that the child is not worth the cost of looking after him'.[17] To say that the child is a loss is to say that he is not worth the cost of raising him.

But this is wrong. In insisting that she suffered a loss, the claimant is not required to make any assertion about the value of the child. I take it that all agree that children are priceless in the sense that they possess, in Kantian terms, dignity rather than price.[18] Children are moral persons and they are sources of value rather than merely objects of value. The claimant's position is not that her child lacks value in that sense, but that he causes a loss *to her*. This is entirely compatible with the notion that the child is priceless in himself.

Also mistaken is Frances Trindale and Peter Cane's assertion, referred to by Lord Steyn in *McFarlane*,[19] that it is:

> inconsistent to allow a claim by the parents [in cases such as *McFarlane*] while that of the child, whether healthy or disabled, is rejected [in accordance with the discussion of wrongful birth above]. Surely the parents' claim is equally repugnant to ideas of the sanctity and value of human life and rests, like that of the child, on a comparison between a situation where a human being exists and one where it does not.[20]

---

legal policy, which is to say "our more or less inadequately expressed ideas of what justice demands" . . . The court is engaged in a search for justice, and this demands that the dispute be resolved in a way which is fair and reasonable and accords with ordinary notions of what is fit and proper': *ibid*, 108, citing W Page Keaton *et al* (eds), Prosser *and Keeton on the Law of Torts*, 5th edn (West Group, St Paul, Minn, 1894) §41.

[16] If there were such a right, then men could sue women who have children against the will of the men where the children could have been aborted.

[17] *McFarlane v Tayside Area Health Board* [2000] 2 AC 59, 111 (HL Sc).

[18] I Kant, 'Groundwork of the Metaphysics of Morals' in M Gregor (ed), *Practical Philosophy* (Cambridge University Press, Cambridge, 1996) 84, [4:434–435]

[19] *McFarlane v Tayside Area Health Board* [2000] 2 AC 59, 83 (HL Sc).

[20] FA Trindale and P Cane, *The Law of Torts in Australia*, 3rd edn (Oxford University Press, Melbourne, 1999) 434.

It does not. The claimant's position in *McFarlane* says nothing about the value of human life whatsoever. It says something only about the value of one human life (the child) to another person (the claimant).

In fact, pointing to the value of children could defeat the claimant only if children were tradable. If you acquire a priceless chattel as a result of my negligence, then of course it does not lie in your mouth to say that I caused you a loss. But this is because, if you do not want the chattel, you can sell it for gain. But this course of action is, naturally, not open to the claimant in *McFarlane*. There, she may have 'acquired' a priceless 'object' but, as she cannot sell it, it is not unreasonable for her to regard it as a loss.

A different kind of reply to the claimant would be to insist that children are never a loss to their parents in that they always bring more than they take. But the amount that children give and take depends importantly on the attitude of the parents. There is no natural law that insists that all people must want children and many parents choose to give their children up for adoption, indicating that, at least in many of these cases, they do not regard them as an overall gain. It is contemptuous of these people to insist that their judgements are simply wrong, because one happens to regard children otherwise. Nor is Lord Millett's suggestion helpful that '[i]n ordinary life . . . the birth of a healthy and normal baby is a harm only because his parents, for whatever reason, choose to regard it as such'.[21] This makes it sound as if the only reason having a child would be a loss to a person is if that person, on a whim, decides to regard it as such and suggests that this could be altered if that person simply changed his mind. Whether children are a gain or a loss to us is, at least in part, determined by deep seated understandings of who we are, our life goals and the place of children within them. For some people, asking them to regard having children as a benefit to them is like asking them to change the people they are.

In deciding not to have any more children in the first place, the claimant in *McFarlane* made a decision that having four children (or less!) would be better than having five. That, after all, was why she and her husband chose for him to have a vasectomy. Those who argue that a child cannot be a loss to its parents insist that this decision must have been a mistake as children are always, on balance, valuable to their parents. If this argument were right, then it would follow that family planning would be irrational. Barring health problems and similar issues, we should all seek to have as many children as possible because in doing so we would be maximising our utility functions. But this is not plausible.

For that reason, Lord Millett's claim that '[i]t is morally offensive to regard a normal, healthy baby as more trouble and expense than it is worth'[22] is either irrelevant or wrong. The claim could be given three different interpretations. First, it is morally offensive for a claimant to regard the birth of a child as a loss to her. I see no reason whatsoever to accept this claim. Moreover, unless one believes that we should all have as many children as possible, it is false to

[21] *McFarlane v Tayside Area Health Board* [2000] 2 AC 59, 112 (HL Sc).
[22] *Ibid*, 114.

suggest that the birth of a child is always a gain to its parents. That means that, on this interpretation, Lord Millett suggested that it is immoral for the claimant to recognise the truth. But that could not be the case.

A second interpretation of Lord Millett's argument is that, though it may be morally permissible for a claimant to regard the birth of a child as a loss to her, society, including the courts, are not morally permitted to recognise that the birth of the child is a loss to the claimant. But this implausibly implies that it is immoral for the courts to recognise the truth. This would be a strange, 'ostrich' morality. It would also oddly imply that it would be immoral of society to recognise that family planning can be rational. A different slant on this argument would be to insist that courts must not make the relevant claim because it would signal to the child that he was unwanted by his parents. But again that is the truth. The child's parents chose not to have any more children. It does not require the court to say that the parents would have preferred to give the child away. They did not. Perhaps the problem is that we do not want children *discovering* that they were unwanted. But, if this concern is compelling, there are more rational ways of dealing with it. One could, for instance, allow name suppression of the claimants or conduct the trials in a closed court.

The third interpretation of Lord Millett's position, and the one I believe was intended, is that society must not regard the birth of the child as bringing into the world, on balance, disvalue. Society must regard the birth of every person as a valuable event. This claim is surely right. But it is irrelevant to the issue that needed to be decided in *McFarlane*. As we have seen, the issue there was not whether the child was valuable in himself, but whether his birth was a loss to the claimant. It is neither immoral nor implausible to regard it as such.

Accordingly, the rights of the female claimant in *McFarlane* were violated, and it is not inappropriate for her to maintain that she suffered loss as a result. The discussion below proceeds on that basis.

However, a difficulty arises for the claimant at this point. If it is true that having the child was a loss to the claimant, then, on the face of it, she ought to have avoided that loss by giving the child up for adoption. (A crucial reply to this is examined below.) To put this another way, in choosing to keep the child, the claimant became responsible for the relevant costs.[23]

This conclusion is usually and unfortunately expressed by saying that the claimant had a 'duty' to mitigate her loss by offering her child for adoption and, if she chose not to do so, that loss was her responsibility. Representing the issue in this way is disastrous because of the way in which the duty to mitigate is usually understood. In regard to mitigation, John Fleming maintains that 'the defendant [must] prove that the plaintiff's refusal to mitigate was unreasonable'.[24] This is an appeal to policy. The idea is that, if we do not approve of the fact that the claimant refused to mitigate, then we say that the claimant's failure was unrea-

---

[23] *CES v Superclinics (Aus) Pty Ltd* (1995) 38 NSWLR 47, 84–5, 87 (NSWCA).

[24] J Fleming, *The Law of Torts*, 9th edn (LBC Information Services, Sydney, 1998) 286. See also *Geest plc v Lansiqout* [2002] UKPC 48, [2003] 1 WLR 3111.

sonable and deny recovery. However, if we do not disapprove of the claimant's failure, then we say that the claimant's failure was reasonable and allow recovery. On this view, then, the claimant in *McFarlane* failed to mitigate her loss only if she acted unreasonably in keeping the child. But that is arrant nonsense.

Thus, in *Nafte v CES*, Gaudron J said, '[t]hat would be about the cruellest and most inhumane submission I have heard put in this Court since I have been here. I must say, it took my breath away when I read the judgments below suggesting that that was a proper form of mitigation'.[25] Similarly, in *McFarlane*, Lord Steyn said:

> I cannot conceive of any circumstances in which the autonomous decision of the parents not to resort to even a lawful abortion could be questioned. For similar reasons the parents' decision not to have the child adopted was plainly natural and commendable. It is difficult to envisage any circumstances in which it would be right to challenge such a decision of the parents.[26]

And Lord Slynn rejected the argument because '[t]here was no legal or moral duty to arrange . . . an adoption of an unplanned child'.[27]

But, correctly understood, nothing of the sort is involved. Of course, if the question were whether the claimant's decision to keep the child was reasonable, then no issue could arise. But that is not the right question. The reaction witnessed above is prompted by a common misunderstanding of the nature of the relevant issue, a misunderstanding that, once again, can be traced to the predominant role of policy in the modern law.

Recall the following case, which was discussed in Chapter 10. *D* negligently sets fire to *C*'s house and has no way of putting out the fire. Noticing the blaze, *C* decides that she will watch the house burn down instead of calling the fire brigade on her mobile phone. *C* then sues *D* for the full cost of her house. As we saw, in the eyes of the law *C* is entitled to watch her house burn down. At law, there is nothing unreasonable about this behaviour, despite its oddity and unusualness. What is unreasonable is not *C*'s refusal to call the fire brigade but *C*'s attempt to sue *D* given her refusal to call the fire brigade. She attempted to sue *D* for a loss to herself that she could have prevented. Hence, *C* chose to suffer that loss and thereby became responsible for it and could not recover it from *D*.

The claimant in *McFarlane* was, as a matter of law, at liberty to have her child adopted (but not aborted[28]). Of course, she was entitled to keep her child. But

[25] (11 Sept 1996), S91/1996.
[26] *McFarlane v Tayside Area Health Board* [2000] 2 AC 59, 81 (HL Sc). See also at 98 (Lord Hope), 105 (Lord Clyde), 113–14 (Lord Millett). Lord Millett implausibly claimed that the claimants were not *free* to have their child adopted in the sense that they were *incapable* of doing so.
[27] *Ibid*, 74.
[28] Most claimants are not at liberty to have their foetuses aborted. This is because, as a matter of law, foetuses can be aborted only on medical grounds. As Lord Millett pointed out in *McFarlane*, above n26, at 112, the abortion of the claimant's child would have been illegal. The fact that this does not represent actual practice is irrelevant. See Abortion Act 1967 (UK) s1(1); Crimes Act 1961 (NZ) s187A(1). Hence, failure to abort a foetus cannot be relevant: *Emeh v Kensington and Chelsea Area Health Authority* [1985] QB 1012 (CA).

if she chose to keep the child and thereby exposed herself to the cost of raising the child, then prima facie she was legally responsible for those costs. Note that the claim is emphatically not that it was unreasonable for the claimant to have kept her child. Nor is the assertion that the claimant should have placed her child for adoption. *No stand whatsoever is taken on the ethics of adoption.* The claim is merely that, on its face, there is no legal basis for the claimant to recover the costs of raising the child when she acquired those costs because of her choice not to do something that she was at liberty to do when she knew that that choice would impose those costs on her.

In order to see this point, it may help to distinguish this case from an apparently similar one. Imagine that a claimant is physically injured due to the carelessness of another. Though he was at liberty to suffer with the injury without medical treatment, he chose to obtain and pay for normal treatment. It may appear that, according to my argument, the claimant could not recover his medical expenses as he was at liberty to avoid them, but that is clearly not the law. However, this problem arises only if one analyses the ability of claimants to recover medical expenses differently from the way suggested in Chapter 7. On the account presented there, claimants are able to recover medical expenses because they represent an aspect of the cost to the claimant of the violation of the claimant's bodily integrity. Hence, those losses are suffered whether or not the claimant chooses to have medical treatment. Allowing the claimant to recover the costs of the medical treatment is simply one way of calculating the cost to the claimant of the violation of his bodily integrity.

This point is more obvious when the injury is property damage. A claimant's ability to claim for damage to, say, his vehicle is unaffected by whether he chooses to have the vehicle repaired. The injury is the violation of the claimant's property right in the vehicle and the cost of repair is merely one way of calculating the cost of that violation to the claimant, which would exist even if the claimant chose not to repair the vehicle. Hence, it is not possible to argue that a claimant who unnecessarily chooses to have his vehicle repaired should not be able to recover for damage to his vehicle, as those costs are awarded because they represent part of the cost to the claimant of the violation of the claimant's rights in the vehicle. Put simply, the choice to repair the car did not impose the cost on the claimant. That loss existed the moment the damage occurred. Similarly, in the hypothetical case under discussion, the claimant was in a certain position, let us call it x, before the claimant was injured, and fell to position y the moment he was injured. In measuring the difference between x and y it is usually sufficient to consider the cost of getting the claimant from y back to x.

These cases are quite distinct from *McFarlane*, where it appears that the claimant's loss occurs only because she chooses to keep the child when she is under no legal obligation to do so. When the claimant fell pregnant, on the assumptions we are making her position fell from x to y, but that fall did not include the costs of raising the child. Her position did not fall in that regard until she actually decided to raise the child. That is a cost that she imposed upon herself. Accordingly, though that decision was perfectly understandable and even laudable, there appears to be no strict legal justification for making the defendant pay for the costs of it.

At law, on the assumptions we are currently making, the claimant's position in *McFarlane* is identical to the following. Imagine that D damages C's car. The car can be repaired in one of two ways. First, it could be repaired all at once for £x. Secondly, it could be partially repaired now for £x, would deteriorate over a year to need another partial repair for £y, the year after for £z and so on and on. C chooses the latter and attempts to sue D for £x + y + z + . . . n. In such a case, however, a court should hold D liable only for £x. In *McFarlane*, this means finding the defendant liable only for the costs of the pregnancy and the birth.

As a result of the above, we seem forced to the position that the claimant's decision not to have her child adopted meant that she chose to impose the costs of raising the child on herself and therefore cannot recover those costs from the defendant. And note that it is no reply to argue that the costs were unwanted. In accordance with the definition of choice given in Chapter 10, the claimant acted in such a way that she knew would result in the harm barring unforeseen intervention and she was at liberty to avoid that harm.

However, there is another, and very important, reply that the claimant could give. This is that choosing to have had her child adopted would have caused her an even greater harm than the harm imposed by the cost of raising the child. In other words, the claimant maintains that there were three possible scenarios. First, no child is born. Secondly, a child is born and raised by the claimant. Thirdly, a child is born and is given up for adoption. It is perfectly plausible for the claimant to insist that, for her, the second is worse than the first and the third is the worst of all. This would be because, in giving up the child for adoption, the claimant would suffer loss that can generally be described as bereavement at giving up the child, in both the short and long term. It is not implausible to suggest that this would exceed the value of the costs of raising the child.

Note that this reply is open to the claimant because the issue concerns, not whether the defendant violated the claimant's rights, but whether the claimant chose to suffer a loss as a result of the defendant's violation of her rights. In Chapter 10, we discovered that in these contexts a claimant chooses a harm if and only if she freely acts with the purpose of being harmed or acts in such a way that she knows that the harm will result barring unforeseen intervention and she is at liberty to act in a way that would have resulted in lesser harm to her, whether that harm was something covered by her legal rights or not. Suffering bereavement does not necessarily result from a violation of one's rights, but that matter is irrelevant as we have already established that the claimant's rights were violated. Her assertion is that, in choosing to keep the child, she chooses the lesser harm to herself, and that means that we cannot regard her as having chosen to harm herself.

Note that the reverse argument also applies. If the claimant chooses to give up her child for adoption, then she is entitled to recover for her bereavement from the defendant, as long as that loss to her was less than the loss she would have suffered had she kept the child.

In principle, then, the claimant in *McFarlane* was entitled to recover the loss caused to her by having the child. But at this point it is crucial to note that this is not what she claimed. She claimed the costs of raising the child. This is importantly different and caused the majority of their Lordships to misunderstand the crucial issue of the claimant's loss.

Their Lordships considered the argument (accepted above) that, in assessing the loss to the claimant, it was necessary to take into account the benefit to the claimant that the child will bring. However, the argument was accepted only by Lord Hope.[29] It was explicitly rejected by Lords Steyn,[30] Clyde[31] and Millett.[32] According to Lord Clyde, 'in attempting to offset the benefit of parenthood against the costs of parenthood one is attempting to set off factors of quite a different character against each other and that does not seem to me to accord with principle'.[33]

In fact, however, the issue is not one of set off. The defendant's argument at this point was understood by the majority of their Lordships as follows: the claimant's loss in having the child is correctly calculated by reference to the costs of raising the child. However, the claimant also makes gains by having the child. Hence, as a matter of justice, those gains need to be set off against the claimant's losses. That position was rejected. But the defendant's argument is better represented as follows: the claimant maintains that having a child will cause her loss. She also maintains that it is appropriate to calculate that loss with reference to the cost of raising the child. But to concentrate solely on that matter is to overestimate the claimant's loss, because it does not take into account the benefits that the claimant will accrue from having the child.

This difference is crucial. On the first interpretation, the claimant suffered loss x but the defendant should have to pay $x-y$ because the defendant caused the claimant to gain y. On the second interpretation, however, the claimant lost, not x, but $x-y$. The second is the better interpretation because it is only by looking at the claimant's *overall* position with respect to her child that one can see how much she lost or gained. The claimant's loss is not correctly calculated with reference to the cost of raising the child alone. It is calculated by comparing the position that the claimant would have been in had she no child with the position that she is in. Therefore, it must take into account the benefit to the claimant of having the child. That is necessary to determine the position that the claimant is in. Hence, Lord Clyde was wrong to maintain that considering this issue is contrary to principle. It is the ordinary approach of the law.

---

[29] *McFarlane v Tayside Area Health Board* [2000] 2 AC 59, 97 (HL Sc). At 87 Lord Hope rejected its application to the claimant's claim for pain and suffering.

[30] *Ibid*, 81–2.

[31] *Ibid*, 103.

[32] *Ibid*, 111.

[33] *Ibid*, 103.

Therefore, assuming that adoption would have been worse for the claimant than keeping the child, we have discovered that the claimant in *McFarlane* was entitled to recover the loss caused to her by having a child, though not the costs of raising the child. Objections to this position come in two kinds, both of which were raised in *McFarlane*.

The first is that it would be too difficult to calculate the award of damages. For instance, Lord Slynn claimed:

> Of course judges have to evaluate claims which are difficult to evaluate, including assessments as to the value of the loss of a life, loss of society or consortium, loss of a limb or a function. But to do so and to get it even approximately right if little is known of the baby or its future at the time the valuation has to be made is very difficult. It may not be impossible to make a rough assessment of the possible costs of feeding, clothing and even housing a child during the likely period of the child's life up to the age of 17 or 18 or 25 or for whatever period a parent is responsible by statute for the support of a child. But even that can only be rough. To reduce the costs by anything resembling a realistic or reliable figure for the benefit to the parents is well nigh impossible unless it is assumed that the benefit of a child must always outweigh the cost which . . . I am not prepared to assume. Of course there should be joy at the birth of a healthy child, at the baby's smile and the teenager's enthusiasms but how can these be put in money terms and trimmed to allow for sleepless nights and teenage disobedience? If the valuation is made early how can it be known whether the baby will grow up strong or weak, clever or stupid, successful or a failure both personally and careerwise, honest or a crook? It is not impossible to make a stab at finding a figure for the benefits to reduce the costs of rearing a child but the difficulties of finding a reliable figure are sufficient to discourage the acceptance of this approach.[34]

There are two separate arguments embedded in this passage: the cost imposed on the claimant by the child is too difficult to calculate because it involves an assessment of future contingencies and because there is an incommensurability between the kind of gains and losses involved and monetary sums. It is important to notice, however, that the assessment of many injuries faces exactly these problems. Imagine, for instance, a child born disabled because of the negligence of the defendant, such as occurred in *Renslow v Mennonite Hospital* discussed in Chapter 4.[35] In such cases, the court has to assess very similar future contingencies as it would in wrongful conception cases. The court must estimate both the likely course of the claimant's life, including disadvantage in career opportunities, social circumstances, extra financial costs, etc, and compare this with an assessment of what the claimant's life would have been like had she not been born disabled. There is no reason to think that the future contingencies are any more difficult to calculate in *McFarlane* than they are here. Nor is the purported incommensurability between the loss and gain on the one hand and monetary awards on the other any greater in *McFarlane* than here. It is no more or less difficult to assess the monetary value of a disabled life, loss of life expectancy,

---

[34] *Ibid*, 74–5.
[35] 351 NE 2d 870 (Ill CA 1976).

personal injury, etc, than it is with respect to the claimant's loss in *McFarlane*. If Lord Slynn's argument were acceptable, there would never be recovery for any kind of non-pecuniary loss.

In fact, their Lordships use this argument in two different and rather conflicting ways. First, they argue that the benefits of having the child cannot be set off against the cost of raising the child, because it is too difficult to estimate the benefits. Secondly, they argue, or at least suggest, that the claimant should not receive the costs of raising the child, in part, because it is too difficult to calculate the benefits of raising the child.[36] The first argument contends that it is right to ignore the benefits to the claimant of having the child. But the second argument has plausibility only if that contention is false. That is, if it is right to ignore the benefits, then the fact that it is difficult to calculate the benefits cannot possibly argue against recovery.

Moreover, according to the first argument, we are sure that the claimant suffered a loss, though we are not certain how much that loss is. However, prima facie, the claimant should be awarded compensation that we are certain is much in excess of that loss, because it is difficult to calculate the extent of the claimant's loss. This argument cannot succeed. The difficulty of awarding an amount that is appropriate cannot justify awarding an amount that we can be sure is inappropriate (here, because it is too much).

The second argument faces similar difficulties. If we are sure that the claimant has suffered a loss, then it cannot be right to award the claimant nothing in the way of damages because it is difficult to calculate the exact amount of the claimant's loss. The difficulty of awarding an amount that is appropriate cannot justify awarding an amount that we can be sure is inappropriate (here because it is too little). In general, the difficulty of assessing a damages award can never justify failing to award damages. If we are sure that the claimant has wrongfully suffered loss because of the defendant, then courts must do their best to determine an appropriate level of compensation. In a personal injury case, for instance, where the defendant has negligently caused the claimant to become a quadriplegic, while we cannot justify in an open manner an award of, say, £200,000 rather than an award of £400,000 or some other figure,[37] the difficulty of settling on a particular sum could not possibly justify the refusal to give the claimant any compensation at all.

The reasoning seems more plausible in *McFarlane*, however, because we are uncertain whether the claimant will suffer loss. Accordingly, it is more plausible to argue that damages should not be awarded because they are too difficult to calculate, when the background assumption is that there is a very real chance that no damages are deserved. But the problem is that this is to deny the claimant's perfectly reasonable assertion that she would have been better off

[36] See eg *McFarlane v Tayside Area Health Board* [2000] 2 AC 59, 102–3 (Lord Clyde), 111 (Lord Millett).
[37] WVH Rogers, *Winfield and Jolowicz on Tort*, 16th edn (Sweet & Maxwell, London, 2002) para 22.22.

without this child—in the specific circumstances of *McFarlane*, that she would have been better off having four children rather than having five. For the reasons discussed above, this denial is not acceptable.

The modern law has adopted a strategy for dealing with the problem of assessing damages for non-pecuniary loss.[38] First, courts attempt to achieve consistency in their awarding of such damages by having quoted to the trial judge previous awards in similar cases. These awards are always open to criticism, and courts adjust the levels of the awards in the light of that criticism. The idea is to achieve a rough consensus on appropriate levels of compensation. A very similar approach is adopted in determining remoteness and other issues, as we saw in Chapter 4. Because of the existence of these guidelines, or tariffs as they are known, the assessment of non-pecuniary loss is more than 'a stab at finding a figure'.[39] Though the tariffs are flexible and allow the court to make judgments on whether the claimant's loss in the instant case is greater or less than the tariff, they are nevertheless invaluable tools in the setting of damages for non-pecuniary loss. But before the tariffs existed, the courts had to start with very rough estimates of the appropriate amounts. If courts in those cases had accepted the argument under examination, then we would not have recovery for non-pecuniary loss and the tariffs would not exist. The courts must start somewhere, even if that somewhere is not a particularly good place, and build the tariffs up over time. That is what they have done with respect to non-pecuniary loss and what they ought to do in cases like *McFarlane*.

However, there is nevertheless something special about the loss in cases such as *McFarlane*. This is that there is a natural focal point for the damages award in a sense that I now explain. The more that the claimant asserts that she lost as a result of having the child, the more she implies that she will get little benefit from the child. This means that, the more loss the claimant asserts, the harder it is to believe that she would have lost less had she given her child for adoption. Put shortly, if the child is such a loss, then it is hard to believe that avoiding bereavement was worth it. This is not only because the higher the loss the closer it must come to the potential bereavement, but also because, in indicating that the child is a large loss, the claimant indicates that she does not have the degree of attachment to children that would ordinarily lead to a large amount of bereavement. Conversely, in cases in which the claimant has given her child for adoption and is claiming for her bereavement, the greater the amount she claims, the harder it is to believe that she would have suffered a greater loss had she kept the child. This is not only because of the sums involved, but also because in asserting that she is suffering great bereavement, the claimant indicates that she is the kind of person who was likely to have gained much from having the child.

---

[38] For discussion of this in the context of English law, see *ibid*.
[39] *McFarlane v Tayside Area Health Board* [2000] 2 AC 59, 75 (HL Sc) (Lord Slynn).

These points are important because, if the claimant would have suffered less had she done the converse of what she did, then she chose part of the loss that she suffered and was responsible for that loss. Recall the definition of the relevant part of the *volenti* defence from Chapter 10.

The *volenti* defence applies if:

(1) the claimant acted with the purpose of causing the harm to herself or acted knowing that her action would cause the harm barring unforeseen intervention,

and

(2) the claimant acted with the purpose of being harmed or acted in such a way that she knew that harm would result barring unforeseen intervention and she was able to and was at liberty to act in a way that would not result in harm.

In these cases, because the claimant's rights have been violated, harm is defined as loss. This means that the loss that the claimant in either case can recover has a certain narrow plausible range.

In the light of this, the proper approach of the courts is to set a tariff for the losses involved. And, for the reasons discussed above, the tariff ought to be the same whether the claimant chooses to keep her child and sue for the loss involved or to give up her child for adoption and claim bereavement.[40] Finally, the tariff should be relatively small. The £15,000 set as a 'conventional award' by the House of Lords in *Rees* would be as good a start as any for a tariff.

A second objection to the idea that the claimant's loss should be calculated with reference to the benefits of having a child is that such would force courts to engage in immoral enquiries. Lord Steyn, for example, raised the issue of wealthy parents recovering more than poor parents because, for instance, they choose to send their child to public (ie private) school.[41] Putting the issue this way reveals the fallacy in the argument. Children do not need to be sent to private schools. It is perfectly acceptable, and quite in accordance with the parent's legal obligations, to send the children to state schools. This is not to question parents' decisions to send their children to private schools, but it is to treat those decisions as such, ie as choices. The costs that arise are costs that parents place on themselves that they are at liberty to avoid. Therefore, they are responsible for them, not potential defendants. The defendant has to compensate the claimant for the claimant's losses, but cannot be required to pay for the benefits that the claimant may wish

---

[40] This reflects the notion that, if the former is bigger than the latter, then the child ought rationally to have been adopted, while if the latter is bigger than the former, the child ought rationally to have been kept. The oughts here are not legal or moral oughts. They reflect merely the losses and gains to the claimant and therefore the impact of the claimant's choices on her ability to recover damages.

[41] *McFarlane v Tayside Area Health Board* [2000] 2 AC 59, 79 (HL Sc).

to extend to the child.[42] Nor is it relevant that the claimant's other children may have gone to private schools. The desire not to make the youngest child feel left out or 'under'-privileged may explain the claimant's choice to send him to a private school, but that choice remains a choice. This argument applies to all 'elective' expenditure. The tariff should be set with reference to the costs of raising a child in an acceptable fashion, not in a privileged one.

A different kind of argument was advanced by Lord Clyde, who maintained that the approach advanced here would mean that parents of difficult children would be able to recover more than parents of children who are easier to raise.[43] But what is wrong with that conclusion? As any parents or expectant parents know, difficult children are more of a problem to raise—and therefore more of a loss or less of a gain *to their parents*—than children who are a delight to raise. That, after all, is why they are called difficult. Why, then, should this fact not be reflected in the claimant's damages? If the reason is to spare the child humiliation, then his can be dealt with by granting name suppression, etc.

In fact, the ability of the courts to depart from the normal tariff to reflect special losses caused by either the claimant's or the child's peculiarities is necessary in order to do justice in the circumstances thrown up by cases like *Parkinson* and *Rees*, introduced above. If the claimant has a disability that imposes special costs, then the court ought to increase the amount recoverable by the claimant above that of the tariff. The same result follows if the peculiarities of the child impose special costs.[44] Moreover, if the peculiarities of the claimant or child lead to special savings, then this should be reflected in a lowering of the award below that suggested by the tariff.

The position argued for is, then, remarkably similar to that adopted by the House of Lords in *Rees*. But, apart from the argument used to reach the conclusion, there are two important differences. The first difference is that the majority of the House of Lords in *Rees* ruled that £15,000 was a 'conventional award', meaning that it would be given in all relevant cases and there would be no flexibility to adjust this award in the light of special circumstances. However, their Lordships left open the possibility that, if the child was disabled, then that award could be increased. This approach is too inflexible. The £15,000 figure should be regarded as a tariff and not as a 'conventional award'. Trial courts should be free to adjust the award in the light of special circumstances, not merely when the child is disabled.

[42] One possible reply is to argue that some parents would be worse off themselves if they did not send their children to private school. But this reply relies on an implausible psychological egoism—the idea that people only ever act in their self-interest. The reason people send their children to private schools is to benefit them, the children, not to benefit themselves; still less to prevent loss to themselves, which the argument requires.

[43] *McFarlane v Tayside Area Health Board* [2000] 2 AC 59, 103 (HL Sc).

[44] These conclusions are subject to the claimant's injuries being foreseeable. Note that consideration of the claimant's peculiarities here is not inconsistent with the argument of ch 3. There, the question was whether the defendant wronged the claimant. Here, the question is, given that the defendant wronged the claimant, how much worse off was the claimant as a result?

The second difference is that the majority of the House of Lords set the figure of £15,000 as if it were legislating. But this figure ought to be seen as the beginning, rather than the end, of a debate about the appropriate level of compensation. In other words, the £15,000 should be seen as the first step in setting a lasting tariff, and not as a quasi-legislative determination of the award in all future cases.

One way of expressing both of these points is to say that the decision in *Rees* ought to be brought back into the mainstream of the common law. The decision in *Rees* is remarkable in that the majority of their Lordships accepted that the claimant suffered a loss in having an unwanted child but refused to compensate for that loss, but then gave a conventional sum that seemed to be plucked out of nowhere. Treating the £15,000 as a tariff, however, would be entirely in accordance with *ordinary* common law principles, and also demanded by corrective justice. That is the path that the Court should take in future.

Accordingly, I disagree with Lord Steyn's claim in *Rees* that these cases involved a conflict between two (or more) equally plausible views.[45] Naturally, I accept that, in terms of ethics, distributive justice, etc, there are competing reasonable views. But Lord Steyn overlooked the law's perspective on the issue. Not only are there reasonable competing political views on this matter, there is a legal view that involves no appeal to such concerns.

I am not claiming that the solution proposed here is ethical or distributively just. But nor have I denied that claim. Whether the solution accords with ethics and distributive justice is to be determined by another debate. But the result is correctively just. It is just, then, from the perspective appropriate to the law of negligence. Hence, the solution is not merely an 'escape mechanism' for avoiding the political pitfalls of the modern approaches—though it does allow that escape—it really does do justice between the parties. Justice between the parties is not all that there is to justice, but it is all that a court can legitimately do in such cases.

C. Recovery under an Assumption of Responsibility

In *McFarlane*, Lord Steyn said:

> I have taken into account that the claim in the present case is based on an assumption of responsibility by the doctor who gave negligent advice. But in regard to the sustainability of a claim for the cost of bringing up the child it ought not to make any difference whether the claim is based on negligence simpliciter or on the extended *Hedley Byrne* principle.[46]

Nothing could be further from the truth.

---

[45] *Rees v Darlington Memorial Hospital NHS Trust* [2003] UKHL 52, [2004] 1 AC 309, 324.
[46] *McFarlane v Tayside Area Health Board* [2000] 2 AC 59, 83–4 (HL Sc).

First, for the reasons discussed above, in the absence of an assumption of responsibility, there could be no liability to the male claimant. But in the presence of an assumption of responsibility by the defendant to the male claimant, then naturally the defendant can be liable to the male claimant. That is, if the defendant assumed responsibility to the male claimant that he would have no further children, then the defendant is responsible for the losses of the male claimant if he breaches that responsibility.

Even more importantly, it is evident that an assumption of responsibility can make crucial differences to the loss recoverable by the claimants, especially given Lord Steyn's conclusion in *McFarlane* that the claimants could not recover the costs of raising their child. Imagine, for instance, that the defendant had said something of the following sort to the claimants: 'Oh, don't worry. There is absolutely no chance that you will have another child. In fact, I am so confident about this that I pledge to pay for the costs of raising the child myself if you have one.'[47] It cannot be maintained that this would make no difference to the case.

In short, if the defendant assumed responsibility to the claimant or claimants for their not having another child, then there ought to be no difficulty coming to the conclusion that the defendant should be liable for the claimants' losses.

It is impossible to decide whether this occurred in *McFarlane*, however. This is because the contents of the representations made by the defendant to the claimants are not revealed in the law reports. Accordingly, though, for instance, Lord Slynn's claim that the defendant had assumed responsibility only for the costs associated with the pregnancy and birth, and not for the future costs of raising the child, was not implausible, we do not have sufficient information to make any judgement on this matter.

However, this line of thought must also cast doubt on the availability of any recovery in all of these cases. Although none of the judgments discussed above mentions any communication between the claimants and the defendants prior to the communication to the claimants that they were sterile, it is not unlikely that at least some of the defendants had informed the claimants of the risk of pregnancy. In *McFarlane*, for instance, it is possible that the claimant was warned about the chance of recanalisation of the vas. This would almost certainly undermine the idea that the defendant had assumed responsibility to the claimants that the female claimant would not fall pregnant. Moreover, in warning the female claimant of the potential risks of pregnancy—or, strictly, in not leading her to believe that there were no such risks—the defendant could no longer be regarded as having violated the claimant's bodily integrity when she fell pregnant. The defendants may even have disclaimed any responsibility for future pregnancies. That would completely defeat any possible assumption of responsibility. And if the claimants chose to have unprotected sex in the light of

---

[47] Of course, we must assume that the defendant is, or at least appears to be, sincere in making this offer. And note that if the issue is that we do not want the NHS to pay for the costs in these cases, the appropriate solution is not to remove the doctor's responsibility, but to break the chain between the doctor and the NHS.

the disclaimer, a pregnancy that resulted could not be regarded as the violation of their bodily integrity. As it were, the defendants would have said to the female claimants, 'you may still get pregnant and if you do I'm not responsible'. However, given that we do not know of any such communication, that must remain speculation.

III. NERVOUS SHOCK

No one doubts that the law surrounding recovery for nervous shock is a mess. Jane Stapleton has argued that this area of law is 'where the silliest rules now exist and where criticism is almost universal'.[48] Nevertheless, it is important to show how corrective justice and the principled approach would deal with nervous shock; not least because some claim that no approach based on corrective justice can resolve the issue.[49]

First, what is nervous shock? At least in English law,[50] a claimant suffers nervous shock if she develops a physical injury or a recognised psychiatric illness as the direct result of a traumatic event of some kind in which she is not physically injured.[51] Importantly, nervous shock does not include grief or other ordinary vicissitudes of life and cannot result merely from reading or hearing about an accident. Hence, grief caused by witnessing an accident is not *nervous* shock, while a recognised psychiatric injury caused by reading about an accident is not nervous *shock*.

A. Primary Victims

In *King v Phillips*,[52] Denning LJ maintained that a claimant could recover for nervous shock only if the defendant, as a reasonable person, could foresee that the claimant was placed at risk of nervous shock. Moreover, in *Bourhill v Young*,[53] the House of Lords ruled that the claimant could recover only if her injury was of a kind that could reasonably foreseeably have been suffered by a

---

[48] J Stapleton, 'In Restraint of Tort' in P Birks (ed), *The Frontiers of Liability* (Oxford University Press, Oxford, 1994) 95.

[49] P Cane, 'Distributive Justice and Tort Law' [2001] *New Zealand Law Review* 401, 403, 410–12.

[50] Compare *Tame v New South Wales* [2002] HCA 35, (2002) 211 CLR 317. The differences between this case and the English cases, while important, do not relate to the issues explored here. This is because, for reasons discussed below, the examination of nervous shock cannot be completed here.

[51] In the following, I ignore physical injury that results from nervous shock. In recent times, courts have preferred the label 'psychiatric injury' to 'nervous shock'. However, the former term is misleading. This is because courts continue to insist that the claimant must have suffered psychiatric injury consequent to shock. K Wheat, 'Proximity and Nervous Shock' (2003) 32 *Common Law World Review* 313, 316.

[52] [1953] 1 QB 429, 441 (CA).

[53] [1943] AC 92 (HL).

person of 'customary phlegm'.[54] Accordingly, a claimant could not rely on any unusual susceptibility to mental injury.

However, these conclusions were qualified by a majority of the House of Lords in *Page v Smith*.[55] In that case, their Lordships ruled that the restrictions on recovery outlined in *King v Phillips* and *Bourhill v Young* apply to 'secondary victims' but not to 'primary victims'. Lord Lloyd defined primary victims as those who participated in the accident or were 'directly involved in the accident, and well within the range of foreseeable physical injury'. Conversely, secondary victims are those 'in the position of a spectator or bystander'.[56]

Lord Lloyd seems to have believed that the restrictions on liability enunciated in *King v Phillips* and *Bourhill v Young* were a policy-based departure from the ordinary principles of the law of negligence, designed to prevent an overly extensive liability. Moreover, Lord Lloyd believed that the application of this policy was unjustified when the claimant was a primary victim. After all, primary victims are (at least usually) a well-defined class and hence no problem of indeterminate liability arises in respect of these victims. Accordingly, Lord Lloyd ruled that primary victims could recover if they were placed at a reasonably foreseeable risk of psychological *or* physical injury, while secondary victims had to show that they were placed at a reasonably foreseeable risk of psychological injury.

The distinction between primary and secondary victims is opaque. In English law, this difficulty has centred on how to categorise the position of rescuers. Recall that Lord Lloyd defined a primary victim as one who participated in the accident or was placed at physical danger. These tests are not identical. One may participate without being placed in physical danger, and vice versa. The view that participation is sufficient was supported by the House of Lords in *Alcock v Chief Constable of the South Yorkshire Police*[57] and in *W v Essex County Council*.[58] However, the alternative position, that the claimant must have been placed in physical danger, was preferred by the House in *White (or Frost) v Chief Constable of South Yorkshire Police*.[59] In *W v Essex County Council*, Lord Slynn said that the definition of rescuers in English law was 'developing' and had to be approached incrementally.[60]

I doubt that anyone thinks that this is satisfactory, even supporters of the incremental approach. The fact is that we have no clear basis upon which to distinguish primary from secondary victims. This is no surprise, because there is no account of the normative basis of the distinction. If the distinction reflected genuine normative differences between victims, then the enquiry into how the

---

[54] *Ibid*, 117.
[55] [1996] 1 AC 155 (HL).
[56] *Ibid*, 184.
[57] [1992] 1 AC 310, 407–8 (HL) (Lord Oliver).
[58] [2001] 2 AC 592, 599–601 (HL) (Lord Slynn).
[59] [1999] 2 AC 455 (HL).
[60] [2001] 2 AC 592, 600 (HL).

distinction should be drawn would make sense and have a direction. But the distinction reflects nothing but a rough sense of policy. Accordingly, as the conceptual and normative distinction between primary and secondary victims is itself arbitrary, the precise line between the two in practice will remain arbitrary as well.

The fundamental problem here is that the distinction between primary and secondary victims is of no relevance to the justice of the claimant's case against the defendant. The claimant is suing for *nervous shock*, for *mental* injury. Hence, it cannot matter whether she was placed at risk of *physical* injury or whether she participated in the accident. The issue is whether the claimant can demonstrate the relevant normative connection between her *mental* injury and the defendant's negligence, not whether she can show that the defendant's negligence may have, though it did not, caused a different injury for which she is not suing. Focusing on the distinction between primary and secondary victims completely loses sight of the relationship the law is meant to analyse.

As indicated above, in *Page v Smith* Lord Lloyd seems to have thought that the restrictions on liability enunciated in *King v Phillips* and *Bourhill v Young* were motivated by policy. That was wrong. Those restrictions were an ordinary application of the principled approach. The defendant is liable only if he creates an unreasonable risk that materialises in the claimant's injury. If the injury suffered by the claimant is of an unforeseeable kind, the injury is too remote.[61] This is because the defendant was not negligent in creating the risk of the claimant's actual injury, that risk being only FOFF. Accordingly, *Page v Smith* does not remove a limitation on liability over and above the principled approach that has been imposed for reasons of policy; rather, it extends liability beyond the principled approach for no good reason. This error of the majority is the more remarkable, given that it was clearly pointed out by the dissenting judges.[62]

The errors in *Page v Smith* are more deleterious consequences of the distorted prominence given to the duty of care in the modern law; a prominence created by the *Anns* test and preserved by the incremental approach. For the majority in *Page v Smith*, the predominant issue was whether the defendant owed the claimant a duty of care. Hence, the rules enunciated in *King v Phillips* and *Bourhill v Young* were seen as restrictions on the duty of care. In this false light, the rules do appear to be departures from the principled approach, as, on that approach, the claimant was owed a duty of care because he was placed at unreasonable risk of some injury. But the duty of care is only one stage in the negligence enquiry. A duty of care may be owed by the defendant to the claimant, though the claimant's injury was too remote from the defendant's negligence to justify recovery.

---

[61] There is some attempt to justify liability in terms of the thin skull rule. However, the claimant's initial injury in *Page v Smith* was property damage, not personal injury, and the thin skull rule is in any case inconsistent with corrective justice and with the principled approach, as outlined in ch 4.

[62] *Page v Smith* [1996] 1 AC 155, 168–9 (Lord Keith) 1712 (Lord Jauncey).

The distinction between primary and secondary victims is entirely unprincipled and must go, along with the confusions promoted by the policy-based approach to negligence that supports it.

B. Secondary Victims

In *Alcock*, the House of Lords set out its approach to determining the duty of care owed to secondary victims. The claimants were friends and relatives of people who had died in the Hillsborough football stadium disaster. As a result of those deaths, the claimants suffered mental injury.

In *Alcock*, their Lordships enunciated a set of restrictions on liability. However, Lords Ackner and Oliver also acknowledged that these restrictions should not be arbitrary and could not rest entirely on policy. For instance, Lord Ackner argued against the notion that the duty of care should be owed only to the immediate family of the immediate victims, asking:

> how do you explain why the duty is confined to the case of parent or guardian and child and does not extend to other relations of life also involving intimate associations; and why does it not eventually extend to bystanders? As regards the latter category . . . I see no reason in principle why he should not [recover], if in the circumstances, a reasonably strong-nerved person would have been so shocked. In the course of argument your Lordships were given, by way of an example, that of a petrol tanker careering out of control into a school in session and bursting into flames. I would not be prepared to rule out a potential claim by a passer-by so shocked by the scene as to suffer psychiatric illness.[63]

Hence, Lord Ackner rejected the idea that the answer to the question 'why does liability end here?' could be that 'it is all a question of expediency'.[64] How could it be expedient given the facts in *Alcock*? Similarly, Lord Oliver maintained that the terminus of the duty of care 'cannot, I think, be attributable to some arbitrary but unenunciated rule of "policy" which draws a line as the outer boundary of the area of duty'.[65]

However, their Lordships also insisted that the duty of care is ordinarily owed only to those with a sufficient degree of love and affection for the immediate victims.[66] Why? Lord Ackner insisted that this could have nothing to do with reasonable foreseeability,[67] but went on to say:

> As regards claims by those in the close family relationships . . . the justification for admitting such claims is the presumption, which I would accept as being rebuttable, that the love and affection normally associated with persons in those relationships is

[63] *Alcock v Chief Constable of the South Yorkshire Police* [1992] 1 AC 310, 403 (HL).
[64] *Palsgraf v Long Island Railroad Co* 162 NE 99, 104 (NY CA 1928) (Andrews J).
[65] *Alcock v Chief Constable of the South Yorkshire Police* [1992] 1 AC 310, 410 (HL).
[66] *Ibid*, 403–4.
[67] *Ibid*, 403. See text accompanying above n63. See also *Alcock v Chief Constable of the South Yorkshire Police* [1992] 1 AC 310, 398 (HL) (Lord Keith).

such *that a defendant ought reasonably to contemplate* that they may be so closely and directly affected by his conduct as to suffer shock resulting in psychiatric illness. While as a generalisation more remote relatives and, a fortiori, friends, can *reasonably be expected* not to suffer illness from the shock, there can well be relatives and friends whose relationship is so close and intimate that their love and affection for the victim is comparable to that of the normal parent, spouse or child of the victim and should for the purpose of this cause of action be so treated.[68]

The emphasised passages indicate that reasonable foreseeability is relevant after all.

Moreover, Lord Ackner maintained that:

Whether the degree of love and affection in any given relationship, be it that of relative or friend, is such that the defendant, in the light of the plaintiff's proximity to the scene of the accident in time and space and its nature, should *reasonably have foreseen* the shock-induced psychiatric illness, has to be decided on a case by case basis.[69]

Finally, Lord Ackner denied that a duty of care was owed to one of the claimants, Robert Alcock, because, as Alcock had lost 'only' his brother-in-law, 'h[e] was not, in my judgment, *reasonably foreseeable* as a potential sufferer from shock-induced psychiatric illness'.[70]

Lord Ackner was right the first time. The rule that there must be a sufficient relationship of love and affection between the claimant and an immediate victim has nothing to do with reasonable foreseeability. This is clearly demonstrated in *Alcock*. Ninety-six people were crushed to death in the Hillsborough disaster and more than 400 people were injured. This posed a plainly foreseeable risk of nervous shock to a wide range of people. Why, then, did their Lordships attempt to justify the restrictions imposed in terms of reasonable foreseeability?

In my view, the answer is that the only alternative was to base the restriction on the raw intuition that allowing the claimants to recover would extend liability too far. This would be unlikely to convince the claimants or anyone who did not already agree with this conclusion. And, especially given the seriousness of the circumstances of this case and the plight of the claimants, if raw intuition is all the judges can give us, then the appropriate response is contempt for the law.[71]

In that light, it is interesting to note that their Lordships did not even attempt to justify their two other limitations: that the claimant must have been proxi-

---

[68] *Alcock v Chief Constable of the South Yorkshire Police* [1992] 1 AC 310, 403 (HL) (emphasis added). See also at 397 (Lord Keith).

[69] *Ibid*, 404 (emphasis added).

[70] *Ibid*, 406 (emphasis added). See also *Gifford v Strang Patrick Stevedoring Pty Ltd* [2003] HCA 33, (2003) 198 ALR 100, 112–14 which purports to reject the 'control mechanisms', but reintroduces them in the name of foreseeability.

[71] Note, however, that while this line of argument is clearly abhorrent in this case given the horrendous nature of the Hillsborough Stadium disaster, frequently claimants will be facing situations that are *to them*, though not to onlookers such as judges and commentators, equally harrowing.

mate in time and space to the accident,[72] and that the claimant must either see or hear the accident or be present at its immediate aftermath.[73] The first rule is a return to the days before *Donoghue v Stevenson*[74] and is obviously arbitrary.[75] The second rule appears to be nothing more than an ad hoc and arbitrary restriction on recovery.[76]

The basic problem with all three 'control mechanisms' is that none of them has anything to do with the normative connection between the defendant's negligence and the claimant's injury.[77] Hence, they are irrelevant to the relationship between the parties. The rule that the claimant must see or hear the accident or be present at its immediate aftermath is entirely arbitrary. The notion that the claimant must be close to the accident in time and space defines the relationship between the parties in terms of morally irrelevant concerns. The rule that the claimant must have suffered nervous shock as the result of physical injury to someone for whom he has love and affection defines the relationship between the claimant and the defendant in terms of a third party.

C. Nervous Shock and the Rights of the Claimant

In an important article, Michael Jones argues that the rules relating to the recovery of nervous shock should be brought back into line with the mainstream of the law of negligence.[78] In particular, Jones argues that the thin skull rule should not apply to nervous shock cases, the distinction between primary and secondary victims should be abolished, the categories restricting recovery for secondary victims should be eliminated, and the ordinary remoteness rule should always apply. Jones also argues that the law should not rely, as it has tended to do in recent times, on definitions of psychiatric injury taken from psychiatrists' manuals such as the American Psychiatric Association's *Diagnostic and Statistical Manual of Mental Disorders* and the World Health Organisation's *International Classification of Mental and Behavioural Disorders*. This is because these works contain accounts of psychiatric conditions that would not normally be regarded as injuries and are often highly controversial within the psychiatric community.

[72] *Alcock v Chief Constable of the South Yorkshire Police* [1992] 1 AC 310, 397 (Lord Keith), 404–5 (Lord Ackner).
[73] *Ibid*, 398 (Lord Keith), 400–1, 405 (Lord Ackner).
[74] *M'Alister (or Donoghue) (Pauper) v Stevenson* [1932] AC 562 (HL Sc). See discussion in ch 4.
[75] For additional criticism, see K Wheat, 'Proximity and Nervous Shock' (2003) 32 *Common Law World Review* 313, 318–21.
[76] The fact that the rule can be traced to cases such as *McLoughlin v O'Brian* [1983] 1 AC 410 (HL) makes no difference to this conclusion. The issue is not the rule's pedigree but its justification.
[77] K Wheat, 'Proximity and Nervous Shock' (2003) 32 *Common Law World Review* 313, 322.
[78] M Jones, 'Liability for Psychiatric Damage: Searching for a Path between Pragmatism and Principle' in JW Neyers, E Chamberlain and SGA Pitel (eds), *Emerging Issues in Tort Law* (Hart Publishing, Oxford, forthcoming 2007). See also N Mullany and P Handford, *Tort Liability for Psychiatric Damage: The Law of 'Nervous Shock* (Sweet & Maxwell, London, 1993).

410 Wrongful Life and Nervous Shock

In drawing attention to this last issue, Jones puts his finger on the most fundamental problem with the law surrounding nervous shock—a common problem, as we saw earlier—the common law's focus on remedies at the expense of rights. The basis of the cause of action, the primary right that the cause of action protects, receives almost no attention. In *Alcock*, Lord Keith described the claimants' injuries as 'a secondary sort of injury brought about by the infliction of physical injury, or the risk of physical injury, upon another person'.[79] The potential right in the claimants, then, is seen as parasitic on the third party's right to bodily integrity. But this will not do. It is necessary to identify the right *in the claimant* that grounds the cause of action.

WVH Rogers argues that the distinction between physical damage and nervous shock must lie in policy, as nervous shock is sometimes caused by chemical changes in the brain and so must be physical injury in fact.[80] But this too can be seen to be an error caused by focusing on remedies rather than rights. From a purely physical perspective, all known injuries involve alterations in brain states. But then again, purely physically, the distinction between objects is entirely arbitrary.[81] Hence, there is no purely physical story that one can tell to distinguish my property from yours. But this should not lead us to conclude that, if someone damages your property, the fact that you can recover and I cannot is a matter of policy. Moreover, there is no purely physical story that can be told to distinguish your body from mine, in the sense that one is yours while the other is mine. They are, after all, simply collections of atoms. The reason my body is mine while your body is yours, my property is mine while your property is yours, is that I have a *right* to my body and my property while you have a *right* to yours.[82] This conception of rights is utterly foundational to the law and to our ordinary moral understanding of ourselves. It is remarkable that the common law tries so hard to do without it.

Similarly, there is no need to appeal to policy to explain why one cannot (generally) recover for psychiatric injury not caused by personal injury, while it is routine to recover for such injury if consequent on personal injury. As one has a right to bodily integrity, one can recover for the extent to which violations of that right make one worse off, including psychiatric injury. However, as there is no clear right to psychological integrity, there cannot be recovery for psychological injury unless it flows from the violation of some right.

[79] *Alcock v Chief Constable of the South Yorkshire Police* [1992] 1 AC 310, 396 (HL).

[80] WVH Rogers, *Winfield and Jolowicz on Tort*, 16th edn (Sweet & Maxwell, London, 2002) 177.

[81] For instance, while Jupiter is distinct from Saturn, this distinction is no more or less arbitrary from the perspective of nature than the distinction between the main bodies of Jupiter and Saturn on the one hand and the rings of those planets on the other. To human beings, the former distinction appears to be the more fundamental, but this is because of our *practical* concern with the world. Attention to rights is an important part of our practical concern in general.

[82] What counts as my body is, in other contexts, not defined by my rights. But those are not the relevant contexts. My friend does not commit battery (or conversion) when he vacuums up the particles of skin and hair that I left (abandoned) on his couch. Sometimes we say that the skin and the hair are mine, but usually not when we are thinking morally or legally.

Returning to the issue of recovery for nervous shock, one possibility, the easiest one, is to deny that there is any right to psychological integrity. For instance, it is arguable that Kantian right would disallow a primary right to psychological integrity on the ground that psychological integrity is not sufficiently public to be relevant to the relationship between the parties.[83] Alternatively, one could argue on grounds of Kantian right that one has a right to one's psychological integrity only to the extent to which that integrity is public. On this view, then, the need to show a recognised psychiatric illness would not be a policy-based restriction on recovery, but would reflect the nature of the right itself.

I do not argue here that either view necessarily captures the correct understanding of Kantian right nor that Kantian right necessarily provides the best understanding of interpersonal morality. My claim is that we need to decide whether people have a right to their psychological integrity or not. And if we decide that they do, we need to elucidate that right. When we have done so, the rest should fall into place. 'Name the right, define it, and the rest is mere application in light of the circumstances. More juris, less prudence.'[84]

It is not unlikely that when this task has been achieved, the right will entail that liability has a greater or smaller scope than at present. But that should not bother us. At present, we are told that expanding liability (much) beyond its current boundaries would be to extend it too much; however, as we do not understand the right involved, this is empty assertion. Similarly, those who would object to a further restriction on recovery have no juridical basis on which to do so. The appropriate scope of liability is determined entirely by the right that it is the job of the cause of action to protect.

It is, perhaps, disappointing that a definition of the right is not explored here. However, as indicated in Chapter 2, that task cannot be undertaken here. In previous chapters, I have taken common law rights as I have found them whilst acknowledging that there are arguments for and against their reform. Here, I have found no rights at all. Nevertheless, discussion of the nature and scope of the rights protected by the law of negligence is beyond the scope of this book. This is because it is likely that such an investigation will need to explore the potential right under discussion in the context of the rights found in private law as a whole. This is not the place for such a wide ranging discussion.[85]

Despite the fact that the argument is incomplete, I have shown that it is premature to conclude that corrective justice cannot deal with nervous shock. In fact, as corrective justice demands the identification of primary rights, corrective justice holds out the best hope we have for treating the cancer that is the modern law of nervous shock.

---

[83] See eg Kant's discussion of wishes in I Kant, 'The Metaphysics of Morals' in M Gregor (ed), *Practical Philosophy* (Cambridge University Press, Cambridge, 1996) 374–5, [6:213].

[84] D Stevens and JW Neyers, 'What's Wrong with Restitution?' (1999) 37 *Alberta Law Review* 221, 227.

[85] Incidentally, the attention that the issue of nervous shock has received from other commentators is likely to be relevant and important to determining the nature of the relevant right.

12

Causation

THIS CHAPTER EXAMINES the role of factual causation in the law of negligence. It begins by explaining why factual causation belongs to the negligence enquiry. The reason is that, though factual causation is not in itself normative, it is an essential element of corrective justice.

The second part of the chapter explores the nature of factual causation per se. It is crucial to identify at the outset that factual causation is not a normative issue. It is a question about the mechanism by which things produce consequences. On the face of it, then, to say that causation is, even in part, a normative or a policy matter is to imply that our judgements or preferences for deciding liability determine the fundamental nature of the universe; as if, were human beings not to exist, or were even just law to be abolished, the fundamental nature of the universe would change. This is, of course, nonsense.

In that light, the claim that causation is, in part, a normative or policy matter is likely to mean, not that causation is determined by policy, but that *what the law regards as causation* is in part a normative or policy matter. This position implies that the law should sometimes treat an event *as if* it caused an effect though it did not, or that the law should sometimes treat an event *as if* it did not cause an effect though it did. Perhaps this is justifiable, but it can only confuse matters to describe these debates as ones concerning factual causation.

Accordingly, this section of the chapter examines approaches to determining *factual* causation found in the case law and academic commentary: the but for, substantial factor, material contribution, targeted but for and NESS tests. Though all these tests are rejected, it insists that there can be no *legal*, as opposed to scientific or philosophical, conception of causation.

The third part of the chapter deals with the undoubted normative considerations that do arise in this context. These are issues that flow from causal over-determination as they relate to liability and damages. It argues that these issues must not be seen as part of causation per se, but are rather to be solved by focusing on the role of causation in determining and realising corrective justice.

I. WHY CAUSATION?

Why does the law insist on causation? As we have seen in previous chapters, the standard of care, the duty of care, remoteness and the defences fit together in a unified normative enquiry. Causation is different. It is not normative. Why, then, is it an element in the enquiry at all?

Corrective justice has a simple answer. The law of negligence seeks to remedy wrongs committed by one person against another. I have expressed this earlier by saying that the defendant will be liable if and only if he created an unreasonable risk of the actual injury that the claimant suffered. But if the defendant did not cause the claimant's injury, then the claimant did not suffer an injury as the result of the defendant's wrongdoing. Hence, the law of negligence is uninterested in activities that do not result in injury. Accordingly, though the focus of this chapter is somewhat different from that of those above, causation is as essential to the negligence enquiry as any other stage.

To understand this point fully, it is necessary to comprehend the failure of an important argument against the causation requirement. This is the notion that causation is morally arbitrary.[1] The argument is that a person is good or bad depending on her intentions. If she intends well, then she is a good person. If she intends ill, then she is a bad person. But causation is unrelated to intention, and hence is morally arbitrary. For instance, one badly intentioned person may cause injury while another equally badly intentioned person may not. While only the first person can be liable in negligence, the two are equally blameworthy and so negligence law is morally arbitrary.

This argument fails for two related reasons. First, as we discovered in Chapter 3, the law often imposes liability on ethically innocent defendants. But this does not mean that the law is immoral or amoral. Rather, the focus of the law, and the focus of corrective justice that motivates the law, is on the claimant and the defendant taken as a unit rather than on the defendant alone. Accordingly, the law is not interested in the ethical qualities of the defendant per se. Moreover, the law is interested in the defendant only if the defendant violated a right in the claimant. Hence, causation is not morally arbitrary but is internal to corrective justice. We are not looking for a defendant who should pay money to someone and a claimant who should receive compensation from someone. Rather, we are looking for a defendant who should pay because he violated the claimant's rights and a claimant who should receive because his rights were violated by the defendant. The law may be *ethically* arbitrary, but it is not *morally* arbitrary. It is motivated by corrective justice and corrective justice is the appropriate understanding of morality in this context.

---

[1] This argument is expounded by CH Schroeder, 'Corrective Justice, Liability for Risks, and Tort Law' (1990) 38 *University of California of Los Angeles Law Review* 143 and is examined in A Ripstein and BC Zipursky, 'Corrective Justice in an Age of Mass Torts' in GJ Postema (ed), *Philosophy and the Law of Torts* (Cambridge University Press, Cambridge, 2001) 221–5. See also EJ Weinrib, *The Idea of Private Law* (Harvard University Press, Cambridge, Mass, 1995) 155–6.

II. THE NATURE OF FACTUAL CAUSATION

A. Case Law: The But For Test and its Alternatives

The positive law has an inadequate test for factual causation: the 'but for' test. According to this test, *C* is the cause of *E* if and only if *E* would not have occurred but for the occurrence of *C*. Famously, this test produces inappropriate results when applied to cases of over-determination. If 100 mg of a substance is enough to kill someone, and you and I each separately inject 100 mg of the substance into our enemy, then, according to the but for test, neither you nor I are the cause of our enemy's death. This is because you can rightly say that our enemy would have died without your action and I can correctly say that he would have died without mine. This means that our enemy's death was uncaused: it was a miracle.

Similarly, in *Lambton v Mellish*,[2] the claimant was driven to distraction by barrel organs operated by two defendants. The claimant sought an injunction in nuisance to stop the noise.[3] The defendants argued that 'two rights cannot make a wrong'.[4] In other words, as each defendant produced insufficient noise to constitute a nuisance, each defendant's action alone was rightful. Hence, the combination of the defendants' activities could not amount to a wrong. However, Chitty J held that the amount of noise produced by each defendant alone was sufficient for a nuisance, but went on to say that, even if that were not so, the defendants would remain liable.[5]

In fact, however, that is the easy case. If the noise produced by each defendant on its own was insufficient for a nuisance, but the noise combined was sufficient, then each defendant was a but for cause of the nuisance. But Chitty J found that the noise produced by each defendant was alone sufficient for the nuisance. Hence, neither defendant was the but for cause of the nuisance, though that did not prevent him being found liable.

Likewise, in *Corey v Havener*,[6] the claimant was riding in a carriage along the highway. The defendants, riding motor tricycles that emitted smoke and loud noise, rode up on either side of the claimant at high speed. This frightened the claimant's horse, causing the claimant to lose control of the horse and resulting in personal injury to the claimant. The Court found that both defendants were negligent and that either defendant's act alone was sufficient to cause all of the claimant's injury. This means that neither defendant was a but for cause of the claimant's injury. Nevertheless, the defendants were found liable.

[2] [1894] 3 Ch 163.
[3] The differences between negligence and nuisance are not relevant here.
[4] *Lambton v Mellish* [1894] 3 Ch 163, 165.
[5] *Ibid*, 165–6.
[6] 65 NE 69 (Mass SJC 1902).

Note that in each of the above cases the but for test tells us that the injury was uncaused, that it was a miracle. This is, of course, absurd. But it is important to be clear about the nature of this absurdity. Commentators tend to describe the absurdity in terms of recovery. For instance, John Fleming maintains that 'it would be idiotic for the victim to be denied redress while each defendant was endlessly shifting the blame to the other'.[7] Similarly, Stephen Todd argues that the results in *Lambton v Mellish* and *Corey v Havener* are determined by policy, 'for it would seem clearly unjust that a strict causal test be applied in such circumstances'.[8]

Again, we see the deleterious impact of the law's remedial mentality and the inappropriateness of its reliance on policy. To apply the but for test in *Corey v Havener* is not to apply an accurate test of causation in inappropriate circumstances, but to apply an inaccurate test of causation. The but for test indicates that the claimant's injuries were uncaused. That is palpably false. The problem with the but for test is not that it conflicts with policy, but that it is an inaccurate test for factual causation. The test is clearly not 'theoretically satisfactory'.[9] Nor can it be appropriate to avoid the undesirable consequences of the but for test by supplementing it with policy. If the test is the wrong test, then it is incumbent on academics to search for a better understanding of causation. Adding policy to the but for test may enable us to generate the right results, but it cannot remove the errors with the but for test. Accordingly, as always, the utilisation of policy to improve the law leaves the original problem intact and clouds our ability both to understand that problem and to formulate theoretically appropriate methods of surmounting it. Moreover, while the addition of policy to the but for test may allow us to achieve the right results, we cannot know if that is so without a theoretically appropriate understanding of causation, the development of which is hampered by the reliance on policy.

Our task must be to understand factual causation as it actually is. We should not be looking for a heuristic model of factual causation that generates liability in accordance with our instinctive feelings, unconcerned whether the model is accurate or not. Simply, lawyers cannot say that C was the cause of E when it was not, or that C was not the cause of E when it was. To do so is, literally, to part company with reality.[10] It is sometimes said that a philosopher is someone for whom a tragedy is a good theory destroyed by the facts. If so, then a lawyer is someone for whom a tragedy is a favoured legal outcome prevented by the truth.

[7] J Fleming, *The Law of Torts,* 9th edn (LBC Information Services, Sydney, 1998) 219. See also J Stapleton, 'Perspectives on Causation' in J Horder (ed), *Oxford Essays in Jurisprudence* (Oxford University Press, Oxford, 2000) 966 n 61, 968.
[8] S Todd, 'Causation and Remoteness of Damage' in S Todd (ed), *The Law of Torts in New Zealand,* 3rd edn (Brookers, Wellington, 2001) 991.
[9] Against:J Fleming, *The Law of Torts,* 9th edn (LBC Information Services, Sydney, 1998) 219.
[10] This is an example that reveals the absurdity of the claim that theory loses touch with reality while focussing on the practice of the law is the best way of keeping one's feet on the ground.

The but for test is so clearly wrong that one might have expected the law to jettison it. But it has not. In fact, the Privy Council has recently recommitted itself to the test.[11] The reason for this is twofold. First, the but for test often generates the correct conclusions. Secondly, alternatives to the test do not seem forthcoming. Accordingly, although it is widely recognised that the test is flawed, it is retained because there appears to be no better option. I argue that this view is mistaken. It is open to the law to adopt a more rational approach to factual causation.

One alternative to the but for test, favoured in some case law, is to ask whether the defendant's negligence was a 'substantial factor' in,[12] or 'materially contributed' to,[13] the claimant's injury. These tests are extremely vague. As a result, the approaches are utilised only when the but for test generates inappropriate results. In practice, then, the law adopts for the most part an inappropriate test for factual causation, but, when that test generates absurd results, relies on an alternative that is effectively meaningless. This is not good.

The second and more important problem with the substantial factor and material contribution tests is that they introduce irrelevant concerns. In determining factual causation, we are interested in whether the defendant's negligence was a causal factor in, or causally contributed to, the claimant's injury. It makes no difference whether the factor was substantial or whether the contribution was material. To take the clichéd example, if the wings of a butterfly in Brazil caused a hurricane in Texas, then the butterfly was a cause of the hurricane of course. But it would not seem right to say that it was a *substantial* factor in, or *materially* contributed to, the hurricane.[14] Frankly, the law is floundering here.

The basic problem with the but for test is that it is a test for necessity. It examines whether C was a necessary condition for E. But the cases involving over-determination show that being a cause of E is not the same as being a necessary condition for E. Moreover, causation is centrally concerned with sufficiency rather than with necessity. Accordingly, I now explore two leading attempts to define causation by incorporating the notion of sufficiency. These are Jane Stapleton's targeted but for test[15] and Richard Wright's NESS test.[16]

[11] *Channel Islands Knitwear Co Ltd v Hotchkiss* [2003] PC 68, [36]–[37].

[12] Eg *March v Stramare* (1991) 171 CLR 506 (HCA).

[13] Eg *McGhee v National Coal Board* [1972] 1 WLR 1 (HL Sc).

[14] See also RW Wright, 'Once more into the Bramble Bush: Duty, Causal Contribution, and the Extent of Legal Responsibility' (2001) 54 *Vanderbilt Law Review* 1071, 1081–4.

[15] J Stapleton, 'Perspectives on Causation' in J Horder (ed), *Oxford Essays in Jurisprudence* (Oxford University Press, Oxford, 2000); J Stapleton, 'Legal Cause: Cause-in-Fact and the Scope of Liability for Consequences' (2001) 54 *Vanderbilt Law Review* 941.

[16] RW Wright, 'Causation in Tort Law' (1985) 73 *California Law Review* 1735; RW Wright, 'Causation, Responsibility, Risk, Probability, Naked Statistics and Proof: Pruning the Bramble Bush by Clarifying the Concepts' (1988) 73 *Iowa Law Review* 1001; RW Wright, 'Once more into the Bramble Bush: Duty, Causal Contribution, and the Extent of Legal Responsibility' (2001) 54 *Vanderbilt Law Review* 1071. The NESS test has its origins in HLA Hart and T Honoré, *Causation in the Law,* 2nd edn (Clarendon Press, Oxford, 1985).

B. The Ness Test and the Targeted But For Test

(i) Introducing the Tests

The NESS test holds that 'a condition contributed to some consequence if and only if it was necessary for the sufficiency of a set of existing antecedent conditions that was sufficient for the occurrence of the consequence'.[17] On the other hand, the targeted but for test calls for the following enquiry:

> [T]ake all factors existing at the time of the actual transition, including the factor that we are investigating . . . If there is a notional sequence of removing factors from that set such that
>
> —a stage is reached where, given the remaining factors the actual transition to the outcome might still have occurred, but that
> —the further removal of the targeted factor leaves a set that would not (in the course of things that we now know happened) have produced the transition,
> —then the targeted factor played a role in the history of the original transition.[18]

The targeted but for test cannot be accepted as it stands. This is because it cannot explain the simple cases of causation. Imagine that *D* drives negligently causing injury to *C*, and if *D* had not driven negligently *C* would not have suffered any injury. Here, there is no 'notional sequence of *removing* factors' that would generate the result that *D* caused *C*'s injury. This problem can be avoided by altering the *insistence* that factors be removed to *permission* to remove such factors, and that amendment appears consistent with the spirit of the test.

I now use examples to elucidate these approaches.[19] First, recall *Corey v Havener*. On the NESS test, each defendant was the factual cause of the claimant's injury as each was necessary for the sufficiency of a set of existing antecedent conditions sufficient for the claimant's injury. This is because the conditions created by each defendant were 'necessary for the sufficiency of a set of existing antecedent conditions that contained it but not the' conditions caused by the other defendant.[20]

Similarly, imagine a case in which seven defendants each negligently release one unit of toxic effluent into a stream that injures a downstream claimant. The claimant would have suffered identical injury if only five units had been released but would not have been injured at all if only four units had been released. Again, all defendants were NESS causes of the claimant's injury. This is because each release was necessary for the sufficiency of a set of existing antecedent con-

[17] R W Wright, 'Once more into the Bramble Bush: Duty, Causal Contribution, and the Extent of Legal Responsibility' (2001) 54 *Vanderbilt Law Review* 1071, 1102–3.

[18] J Stapleton, 'Legal Cause: Cause-in-Fact and the Scope of Liability for Consequences' (2001) 54 *Vanderbilt Law Review* 941, 959–60.

[19] These are based on R W Wright, 'Once more into the Bramble Bush: Duty, Causal Contribution, and the Extent of Legal Responsibility' (2001) 54 *Vanderbilt Law Review* 1071, 1104, 1106–7.

[20] *Ibid*, 1104.

ditions sufficient for the claimant's injury. If we label the defendants D_1 to D_7, then we can see that D_1's release was a NESS cause of the claimant's injury as it was necessary for the sufficiency of, say, the releases by D_2, D_3, D_4 and D_5. The same can be said for each of the defendants, showing that they were all NESS causes of the claimant's injury.

I now apply the targeted but for test to these cases. In *Corey v Havener*, each defendant—let us call them D_1 and D_2 —was the targeted but for cause of the claimant's injury. We begin with D_1. If we take the events in *Corey v Havener* but subtract D_2 from the picture, then the claimant's injury still would have occurred. However, if we additionally remove D_1's negligence, then the claimant would not have been injured. Hence, D_1's negligence was a targeted but for cause of the claimant's injury. An identical analysis is appropriate for D_2.

In the effluent case, D_1 was a targeted but for cause of the claimant's injury, as we can remove, say, D_2 and D_3—leaving D_1, D_4, D_5, D_6 and D_7—and the claimant's injury would still have occurred, but the additional removal of D_1 would mean that the claimant would not have been injured. The same analysis can be applied to all the other defendants.

(ii) Problems with the Targeted But For Test

These are similar approaches, but there is one important difference between them. The NESS test asks simply whether there is a set of conditions such that the one under examination is necessary for the sufficiency of that set. Conversely, the targeted but for test asks one imaginatively to subtract some conditions and ask whether the outcome would have occurred. This difference has led Stapleton to describe her approach as the more scientific and as the easier to use.[21] It is easier to use because it involves subtraction rather than asking the rather complex question: 'Was the defendant's act necessary for the sufficiency of a set of existing antecedent conditions that was sufficient for the occurrence of the claimant's injury?' I take it that Stapleton believes that the targeted but for test is the more scientific because subtraction mirrors experimentation in the sciences. But this is not correct. Experimentation is insufficient to establish causation if applied to a single case, even if applied repeatedly. This reflects the fact that the targeted but for test, like its ancestor, generates inappropriate results in at least one type of case.[22]

[21] J Stapleton, 'Legal Cause: Cause-in-Fact and the Scope of Liability for Consequences' (2001) 54 *Vanderbilt Law Review* 941, 958–61.

[22] The following criticism is based on RW Wright, 'Once more into the Bramble Bush: Duty, Causal Contribution, and the Extent of Legal Responsibility' (2001) 54 *Vanderbilt Law Review* 1071, 1112–19. Wright also argues that the targeted but for test cannot handle cases in which two defendants cause the claimant's injury where one defendant's actions were independently sufficient for the claimant's injury but one defendant's actions were not. However, I believe that the targeted but for test and the NESS test generate identical results in these cases: both defendants are causes of the claimant's injury.

Imagine that two defendants—D_1 and D_2—seek to kill a desert traveller. D_2 does so by poisoning the traveller's water supply. However, before the traveller drinks any of the poison, D_1 empties the water supply. The traveller dies of dehydration.[23] On the targeted but for test, both D_1 and D_2 are causes of the traveller's death. D_2 is a cause of the traveller's death as, if D_1's action is subtracted from the collection of events, then the traveller still would have died: if the water had not been emptied, then the traveller would have been poisoned. However, on the additional assumption that D_2 had not poisoned the water, the traveller would not have died. D_2, then, is a targeted but for cause of the traveller's death. But D_2 was not a cause of the traveller's death. The fact that the traveller would have been killed by D_2 had D_1 not acted does nothing to show that D_2 was a cause of the traveller's death. The targeted but for test generates the unacceptable conclusion that D_2 was a cause of the traveller's death, though we are certain that no causal chain ran from the poisoning to the traveller's death, as the traveller did not ingest the poison. Hence, the targeted but for test generates a result that is wrong. Therefore, it cannot be an appropriate test for factual causation.

In this light, it can be seen that the targeted but for test can be applied to generate most unintuitive conclusions. Imagine, for instance, that D_1 and D_2 are driving negligently. C, crossing the road, is hit by D_1. D_2 drives past without injuring C. However, C can prove that if she had not been hit by D_1 she would have been hit by D_2 and hence that her injury would have occurred even if she had not been hit by D_1. According to the targeted but for test, D_2 is a cause of C's injury because removing D_1 from the picture would still have resulted in injury to C but the additional removal of D_2 would not. But this conclusion is plainly wrong. There is no causal chain that runs from D_2's negligent driving to C's injury. The test is unsatisfactory.

At this point, it may be noted that the targeted but for test is being rejected partly on the basis that it conflicts with intuition. This is not inappropriate. As explored in the context of interpretive legal theory in Chapter 1, reflective equilibrium calls for both intuition and theory to have a role in determining what we ought to say about these cases. The targeted but for test produces consequences that are so unintuitive that we may accept the theory only if no more intuitive theory can be found. But, despite its problems, the NESS test reveals that such a theory is available.

Against this, however, it has been suggested to me that colleagues who poll students as to their response to these cases generally discover that the students are unsure what to say and give widely divergent answers when pushed. When asked whether the poisoner was a cause of the traveller's death, for instance, I am told that roughly as many students say that he was as say that he was not. However, law students are probably the last people who should be polled on

[23] This example is discussed in J Stapleton, 'Perspectives on Causation' in J Horder (ed), *Oxford Essays in Jurisprudence* (Oxford University Press, Oxford, 2000) 82–4.

this question as, unless they are well prepared, they are almost certain to confuse the question 'did the poisoner cause the traveller's death?' with the question 'should the poisoner be liable for the traveller's death?' or perhaps, more specifically, 'should the causation stage of the enquiry prevent the poisoner being liable for the traveller's death?' This is not necessarily problematic, but if the students have also been taught the law of negligence along the lines of the modern approaches, then they are likely to think that the poisoner should be liable for roughly the same reasons as he should be criminally liable for attempted murder. That is, the student's understanding is likely to be that the poisoner should be liable if he was negligent—which is understood as doing something socially undesirable, like trying to kill someone—unless there are good reasons of policy to the contrary, and there appear to be no such reasons. Moreover, the students are also likely to confuse the question 'did the poisoner cause the traveller's death?' with the question 'should the poisoner be liable, not for causing the traveller's death, but for making it inevitable?' That is, the real question in the mind of the student may be 'should making inevitable rather than causing be the test that satisfies the factual causation stage of the negligence enquiry?'. That is highly likely given that the but for test confuses precisely those questions, and hence in studying the judicial use of that test students have been trained to use 'causation' to refer to the concept of making inevitable instead of the concept of causation. In any case, in my experience these tests of student opinion often reflect the teacher as much as the students. Conversely, imagine that the desert traveller is taken to a mortuary and a doctor is required to fill out a death certificate identifying the cause of death. It cannot seriously be contended that the doctor will write that the traveller died of dehydration and poisoning. There is no poison in his system. The fact that lawyers are tempted to reach that conclusion demonstrates the extent to which they confuse causation with other issues (a confusion reflected in their students when they are polled).

On the other hand, the NESS test produces the correct result in the desert traveller case: only D_1 caused the traveller's death. Dehydration was a necessary condition for the sufficiency of the set of existing antecedent conditions sufficient for the traveller's death. Conversely, as the traveller did not ingest the poison, there was no set of *existing antecedent conditions* for which the poisoning was necessary for its sufficiency. Hence, D_2 was not a cause of the traveller's death.

Again, the targeted but for test fails because it gives too prominent a role to necessity. At heart, the targeted but for test is a test of necessity, but it allows sufficiency to play a role by permitting the enquirer to subtract certain facts. It is, as it were, a necessity test limited by sufficiency. But the concept of causation is most fundamentally related to sufficiency rather than to necessity. The NESS test does better because at heart it is concerned with sufficiency, though it is limited by necessity. However, this does not prevent the NESS test from facing insurmountable problems.

(iii) Problems with the Ness Test

There are two general problems with the NESS test. The first is philosophical and concerns the test's reliance on controversial or question begging notions of sufficiency. This has been explored by Richard Fumerton and Ken Kress and is not examined further here.[24] The second is more practical, though, as we will see, it has philosophical consequences. That problem is explored here.

It has been suggested by David Fischer that the NESS test cannot handle cases of multiple omissions.[25] Take the following example. D_1, a mechanic, negligently fails to repair the brakes of D_2's car. Later, driving the car, D_2 collides with and injures C. D_2 negligently did not apply the brakes. Had the brakes been in good repair and had D_2 applied them appropriately, then C would not have been injured. However, given that D_2 did not apply the brakes, C would have been injured even if D_1 had repaired the brakes, and given that D_1 did not repair the brakes, C would have been injured even if D_2 had applied the brakes. How does the NESS test deal with this case?

Wright initially argued that:

> Under the NESS test, it is clear that [D_2's] negligence was a preemptive cause of [C's] injury, and that [D_1's] negligence did not contribute to the injury. [D_2's] failure to try to use the brakes was necessary for the sufficiency of a set of actual antecedent conditions that did not include [D_1's] failure to repair the brakes, and the sufficiency of this set was not affected by [D_1's] failure to repair the brakes. A failure to try to use brakes will have a negative causal effect whether or not the brakes are defective. On the other hand, [D_1's] failure to repair the brakes was not a necessary element of any set of antecedent actual conditions that was sufficient for the occurrence of the injury. Defective brakes will have an actual causal effect only if someone tries to use them, but that was not an actual condition here. The potential negative causal effect of [D_1's] failure to repair the brakes was preempted by [D_2's] failure to try to use them.[26]

However, Fischer responds that:

> [Wright] assumes that [D_1's] failure to repair the brakes did not occur because he excludes this omission from the pertinent set of actual antecedent conditions [when asking whether D_2 was a NESS cause of C's injury]. Subtracting this negative fact (failure to repair the brakes) has the same effect as adding an imaginary positive fact (that the car was equipped with good brakes). Failure to apply these good brakes then becomes the cause of the accident. Thus, Wright's analysis is based on an assumption that does not square with reality. The argument can be manipulated by assuming that the driver attempted to apply the brakes, that is, excluding the driver's failure to apply the brakes from the set of actual conditions to which the failure to repair the brakes belongs. The result is that [D_1], rather than [D_2], caused the accident.

[24] R Fumerton and K Kress, 'Causation and the Law: Preemption, Lawful Sufficiency, and Causal Sufficiency' (2001) 64(4) *Law and Contemporary Problems* 83.
[25] DA Fischer, 'Causation in Fact in Omission Cases' [1992] *Utah Law Review* 1335, 1358–9.
[26] RW Wright, 'Causation in Tort Law' (1985) 73 *California Law Review* 1735, 1801.

Thus, in multiple-omission cases, the NESS test can be manipulated to produce differing results.[27]

Fischer's conclusion is that the NESS test 'does not appear to provide a definitive solution to multiple-sufficient-cause cases involving twin omissions'.[28]

On the face of it, this conclusion does not follow from Fischer's argument. Rather, Fischer's conclusion ought to have been that, according to the NESS test, both D_1 and D_2 were causes of C's injury. It is not that the NESS test 'can be manipulated to produce differing results' and therefore 'does not . . . provide a definitive solution'; rather, it does provide a definitive solution, viz that D_1 and D_2 were the causes of C's injury. This is problematic only if we assume that that result is incorrect. That is indeed Wright's view, but one might doubt that it is right. Nor is Fischer correct to maintain that the failure of the NESS test leads to the conclusion that the causation enquiry is rightly determined, in part, by policy concerns.[29] This is yet another example of the unfortunate tendency of common lawyers to fall back on policy instead of solving the real problem. If the NESS test is wrong, then we need a new approach to factual causation. We do not need to depart from factual causation and argue instead about normative concerns such as policy. That would be to turn our backs on the problem we ought to be addressing.

However, Fischer's point concerning the need for Wright to import falsehoods into his test is crucial. Wright can generate the conclusion that D_2 was a cause of C's injury only by assuming for the purposes of the application of the NESS test that the brakes were in good condition. That is 'an assumption that does not square with reality'. Hence, Wright does not merely ignore some fact— as we ignored one of the defendant's actions in assessing *Corey v Havener* above—but asserts a falsehood. While it would be legitimate to ignore the fact that D_1 had not repaired the brakes, it is quite something else to imagine that the brakes were in good working order. D_2's failure to apply the brakes was a NESS cause of C's injury only on the assumption that the brakes were in good working order, but the brakes being in good working order was not an *actual* antecedent condition of C's injury.

This demonstrates that Fischer actually mislocates the source of his objection to the NESS test. In fact, it has nothing to do with omissions per se. Consider the following case. D_3 negligently cuts the brake cable in D_4's car. D_4 negligently drives at excess speed and has an accident, colliding with and injuring C. If D_3 had not cut the cable and D_4 not driven too fast, then C would not have been injured. However, given that D_3 had cut the cable, C would have been injured even if D_4 had not been driving too fast, and given that D_4 was driving too fast, C would have been injured even if D_3 had not cut the cable. Consider first the position of D_4. D_4's driving too fast was a NESS cause of C's injury only if there

[27] DA Fischer, 'Causation in Fact in Omission Cases' [1992] *Utah Law Review* 1335, 1359.
[28] *Ibid*, 1358.
[29] *Ibid*, 1359–60.

was a set of actual antecedent conditions such that driving too fast was neces-sary for the sufficiency of that set. There was no such set. That set would have existed only if the cable had not been cut. Again, then, we have not merely to subtract D_3's action, we have to imagine a falsehood, something that was not an actual antecedent condition. A similar argument applies with respect to D_3.

Perhaps, however, one could reply that the assumptions of such falsehoods can be appropriate. But this response would lead to the NESS test giving the wrong response in the desert traveller case explored above. Recall that in that case one person poisons the desert traveller's water supply while another subse-quently empties the water and the traveller dies of dehydration. We saw that the poisoner is not a NESS cause of the traveller's death, because there was no actual antecedent set of conditions such that the poisoning was necessary for the sufficiency of that set. In other words, the poisoning of the water was a NESS cause only on the assumption that the traveller drank the water, but he did not. That fact allows the NESS test to generate the right result in this case, but if the reply under examination were adopted—if we were allowed to add falsehoods to our set of conditions—then there appears nothing to prevent us from adding the falsehood that the traveller drank the water and thus the poisoner would become a NESS cause of the traveller's death. Moreover, we appear to be adding this falsehood in this case for exactly the same reason Wright adds his falsehood to the case involving the traffic accident. That is, for the purposes of the test Wright assumes that the brakes were in good condition in order to eliminate the effects of D_1's actions/omissions from the operation of the NESS test and in our current treatment of the desert traveller example we assume that the traveller drank the water in order to eliminate the effects of the actions of the person who emptied the water.

More recently, Wright has argued for a notion of causal priority.[30] Generalising from the failure to brake example, Wright notes that in relevantly similar cases safeguards work only if they are used. In those cases, then, Wright maintains that the use of the safeguard is causally prior, even though temporally subsequent, to the provision of the safeguard. Accordingly, 'the activation of the safeguard depends on someone's first attempting to use it, so that if no such attempt is made, "the (temporally) first omission (the failure to provide a work-ing safeguard) is not causal because it never came into play"'.[31] The basic point is this: the use of a safeguard is causally prior to its existence, because, if it was not used, its non-existence cannot have been an existing antecedent condition that was sufficient for the occurrence of the consequence, because the non-

[30] RW Wright, 'Once more into the Bramble Bush: Duty, Causal Contribution, and the Extent of Legal Responsibility' (2001) 54 *Vanderbilt Law Review* 1071, 1128–31. See also RW Wright, 'Acts and Omissions as Positive and Negative Causes' in J Neyers (ed), *Emerging Issues in Tort Law* (Hart Publihing, Oxford, forthcoming 2007).

[31] RW Wright, 'Once more into the Bramble Bush: Duty, Causal Contribution, and the Extent of Legal Responsibility' (2001) 54 *Vanderbilt Law Review* 1071, 1128. The quotation is from DA Fischer, 'Causation in Fact in Omission Cases' [1992] *Utah Law Review* 1335, 1361.

existence of the safeguard did not play any role in the events that led to the effect.[32]

The conclusion is right, but it does nothing to save the NESS test. Because of D_2's failure to apply the brakes, D_1's failure to repair the brakes never came into play, but it remains true that there was no set of actual antecedent conditions such that D_2's failure to apply the brakes was necessary for the sufficiency of that set in causing C's injury. Moreover, the reply does not apply to our other case in which D_3 cuts the brake cable and D_4 drives too fast. Here there is no causal priority at all. Hence, the problem with NESS cannot be solved by reference to causal priority.

The problem with the NESS test is the same as the problem with the but for and targeted but for tests: the reliance on necessity. D_2's failure to apply the brakes was part of the set of conditions sufficient for C's injury, but it was not necessary for the sufficiency of that set. But that does not stop it being a cause of C's injury. With this point in mind, we now explore the nature of causation in very general terms.

C. The Nature of Factual Causation in Outline

We must first distinguish between the notion that something is *the* cause of something else and the idea that something is *a* cause of something else. To say that C is *the* cause of E is to say that if C happens then E must happen; it is not to say that E could not happen without C. It is, therefore, focussed on sufficiency and not at all on necessity. *The* cause of an effect includes all those conditions that were part of the set that was sufficient for the effect. So, for instance, oxygen, heat, a fuel source, the absence of an extinguishing agent and so on are *the* cause of fire. In this sense of causation, it would be inaccurate to say that heat was the cause of the fire—there are many elements that go together to make up causation.

Of course, this concept of causation is of little use in law. The search for *the* cause of an event is a search for all those factors that contributed to the event, but in law we are not interested in *the* cause of the claimant's injury, but only in whether the defendant's alleged wrongdoing was *a* cause of that injury. The question now is what it means for something to be *a* cause of an effect.

At an abstract level, the answer is easy. Something is *a* cause of an effect if that something was an element of the set that was *the* cause of the event. To spell this out in more detail, we might say that C is *a* cause of E if and only if C was a member of the set of conditions that were sufficient for E and led to E. Any test inconsistent with this definition must be mistaken. The but for, targeted but for and NESS tests are examples. This is because they adopt, in different ways, the

[32] RW Wright, 'Acts and Omissions as Positive and Negative Causes' in J Neyers (ed), *Emerging Issues in Tort Law* (Hart Publishing, Oxford, forthcoming 2007).

strategy of using a test of necessity to determine whether an alleged event was a member of the set of events that led to an effect. But there is no reason to think that necessity is an appropriate test. In fact, in the light of the problems that flow from over-determination, there is every reason to think that it is not. Accordingly, we must conclude not only that the but for, targeted but for and NESS tests are flawed but that any test incorporating necessity must also be.

Of course, however, there is a crucial problem with the definition of being a cause given above. It is circular. The notion of 'leading to' is just the notion of causation in disguise. In order to avoid this circularity, the NESS test appeals to necessity—it holds that C was a member of the set of conditions that led to E if and only if C was necessary for the sufficiency of that, or of some restricted, set. But the concept of 'leading to' cannot be cashed out in terms of necessity. 'Leading to' is consistent with over-determination, while necessity is not.

Ideally, one would provide an analysis of 'leading to', but one is not currently available. It is, as Fumerton and Kress remark, 'a concept that has resisted philosophical analysis for millennia'.[33] They also warn that 'if the law is waiting for philosophers to offer something better than a prephilosophical grasp of what is involved in one thing causing another, the law had better be very patient indeed'.[34]

But perhaps things are not quite as bad as they may appear. Theories that fail are not useless. In particular, the NESS test has taught us much about causation, even though it ultimately fails. In the language of reflective equilibrium, we have yet to produce a theory that satisfies our deeply held intuitions concerning causation, intuitions that are so important that we are unable to surrender them. But in the process of theorising about causation, we have refined our other intuitions and improved on them. Not all is lost.

But we must accept the fact that we have no test for causation. There is no formula that can be applied to settle difficult cases. This does not mean that we must rely on policy arguments. Though we cannot define factual causation satisfactorily, it remains factual and not normative. The failure to provide a definition in no way calls for policy. Nor does it mean that, because philosophy is yet to provide a definition of causation, it is acceptable for lawyers to ignore philosophical accounts and adopt their own legal conception. That would be like saying that lawyers are free to invent a legal account of morality or truth because philosophers disagree over those subjects. Neither does it mean that we must rely on our uneducated intuitions when judging causal claims. We should educate our intuitions as much as we are able, and while we have no definitive standard against which to prove our intuitions right against those whose views differ, we are still able to argue intelligently and profitably about such matters.

[33] R Fumerton and K Kress, 'Causation and the Law: Preemption, Lawful Sufficiency, and Causal Sufficiency' (2001) 64(4) *Law and Contemporary Problems* 83, 93.
[34] *Ibid*, 105.

It remains the job of academics to analyse and criticise the findings of courts regarding causation, for instance, and those academics should be informed about the latest philosophical and scientific theories of causation. In courtrooms, this means that more emphasis needs to be placed on expert testimony and less on the guesswork of judges. But that would be entirely appropriate. With respect to factual causation, judges have no special expertise.[35]

D. Exploring Factual Causation

Because we have no formula for determining factual causation, the best that we can do is to examine the difficult cases that arise in the light of our educated intuitions. In this section, I examine some of the examples that have been suggested by case law and commentary. Naturally, this discussion does not provide a general theory of causation, but it is intended as a contribution to our understanding of causation in general. It is an attempt to educate our intuitions. I begin with a case that will also be explored in the next section of this chapter: the decision of the Supreme Court of Canada in *Sunrise Co Ltd v Ship 'Lake Winnipeg'*.[36]

The claimant's boat, the *Kalliopi L*, suffered physical damage when it went aground due to the defendant's negligence. Later, the *Kalliopi L* again went aground and suffered further physical damage due to the claimant's own carelessness. To repair the damage caused by both groundings, the *Kalliopi L* needed to be removed from the water for 27 days. The claimant wished to recover the loss of profits suffered because of the need to remove the *Kalliopi L* from service for that length of time. However, if the first accident had not occurred, the *Kalliopi L* could have been repaired in 14 days, while, if the second accident had not occurred, the *Kalliopi L* could have been repaired in 27 days. That is, the second accident did not add to the length of time required to repair the *Kalliopi L*, as the repairs could be conducted concurrently. Consequently, the second accident did not add to the quantum of the relevant loss. Therefore, the claimant argued, the second accident was irrelevant to the claimant's cause of action.

Writing for the majority, L'Heureux-Dubé accepted the claimant's position. Her Honour insisted that 'there is no causal link between the second incident

---

[35] In practice, this is made difficult by the adversarial nature of legal procedure and the fact that most experts are hired by the parties rather than appointed by the court. This means that judges or juries must assess often conflicting expert testimony. In my view, this is irrational and the common law would do well to look to the Continent for an alternative. See R Taylor, 'A Comparative Study of Expert Testimony in France and The United States' (1996) 31 *Texas International Law Journal* 181. See also R Goldberg, *Causation and Risk in the Law of Torts: Scientific Evidence and Medicinal Product Liability* (Hart Publishing, Oxford, 1999) 124–31; S Haack, 'Truth and Justice, Inquiry and Advocacy, Science and Law' (2004) 17 *Ratio Juris* 15.

[36] [1991] 1 SCR 3.

and the loss of profit suffered by the owners of the Kalliopi L'.[37] But that is wrong. The *Kalliopi L* had to be removed from the water for 14 of the 27 days both because of the defendant and because of the claimant.

However, Stephen Waddams supports L'Heureux-Dubé's reasoning, arguing that:

> the damage for which the defendant is responsible causes an immediate diminution in the capital value of the ship, to be measured, in the relevant respect, by its diminished future earning capacity: as a saleable asset the ship is worth less for this reason in consequence of the defendant's wrong. Even if this approach puts the plaintiff in some cases in a better position than she would have occupied if the wrong had not been done, the result can be supported on grounds of simplicity and convenience.[38]

We explore this argument in detail below, but at this point we must note that it cannot support L'Heureux-Dubé's actual claim in *Sunrise*: that 'there is no causal link' between the second accident and the claimant's loss. There was a causal link. Waddams argues that we should proceed *as if* there were no causal link, but not that there was no such link.

It will be useful to explore several variations on *Sunrise* discussed by Waddams in order to clarify the causal issue. Case 1: imagine *Sunrise* with the following two exceptions: (i) both groundings were the result of defendants acting negligently and (ii) the first grounding completely destroyed the ship. Here, Waddams argues that the second defendant is not liable for any damage, since she merely 'shot a corpse'. Case 2: imagine *Sunrise* with the exception that the second grounding (innocently caused) completely destroyed the ship. Waddams argues that in this case the first event is analogous to shooting a corpse. 'It then seems impossible to say that event one has caused any loss of earning capacity; the ship . . . had no future as a profit earning machine.'[39]

However, focusing on factual causation for its own sake, rather than with an eye on the wanted remedy, enables us to see that these cases are not analogous to each other and that it confuses the causal issue to treat them as such. First, Waddams is right that the second defendant did not cause any loss to the claimant in Case 1. However, this is because she did not cause any damage. It is not because she caused damage incorporated by that of the first defendant. This is why it is impossible to imagine an instance of Case 1. If the ship was completely destroyed in the first grounding, how could it later be damaged by the second defendant?

In Case 2, on the other hand, the first defendant did cause damage. Hence, the cases are not analogous. We need to look further at what it means to shoot a corpse.

[37] *Ibid*, 20 (L'Heureux-Dubé J).
[38] SM Waddams, 'Causation in Canada and Australia' (1993) 1 *Tort Law Review* 75, 81 (citation omitted).
[39] *Ibid*, 79.

Case 3: D_1 and D_2 consecutively shot at a person, P. D_2's shot hit P's body, but only after he had been killed by D_1. D_2 shot a corpse. Accordingly, D_2 did not cause P any damage, as P was already dead when hit by D_2's shot. So, D_2 can rightly claim that he did not cause P any loss. But this is not the situation in *Sunrise* or in Case 2. In *Sunrise*, the first event caused 27 days' damage, the second 14 days. In Case 2, the first event caused 27 days' damage, while the second destroyed the ship.

Take this further example. Case 4: two ships sail excessively close to the bank of a river. This causes the port side of the ships' hulls to collide with a sub-merged rock, resulting in dents in the hulls of the ships that will take 10 days in dry dock to repair. Later, the first ship hits its starboard side on the rock. This damage can be repaired in the same 10 days for no extra cost. On the other hand, the second ship is again too close to the bank on its port side. Had the dent in the ship's hull not already been created, the second ship would have struck the rock. As it happened, however, because of the presence of the dent, the ship did not strike the rock.

The second incident with the second ship is akin to the shooting of a corpse; the second incident with the first ship is not. Both events are causes of the 10 days' loss for the first ship, but only the first event causes the loss for the second ship. *Sunrise* and Case 2 are related to the circumstances relevant to the first ship but not the second. Hence, despite the fact that the damage caused by one of the events is completely incorporated by that caused by the other, both events are causes of the loss. These are not examples of shooting corpses. The first event in Case 2 does not add to the aggregate of damage that the ship suffers. But casting this as analogous to the shooting of a corpse obscures the issue.

The confusion over these cases may be a product of the belief that the total damage must be an aggregate of each individual instance of damage caused by each event. Hence, if I claim that the first event in *Sunrise* caused 27 days' damage and the second event caused 14 days' damage, then this means that the total damage must be 41 days. But that is wrong, as it neglects the possibility of over-determination. Thirteen days' damage was caused by the first event alone, 14 days' by both events. It is impossible to apportion causal responsibility for the loss of revenue for those over-determined 14 days. Both events are causally responsible for all of the 14 days' damage.

To clarify further, it is necessary to distinguish *Sunrise* from a hypothetical case explored by Tony Honoré.[40] Honoré asks us to imagine a wrestler, C, who is unable to continue wrestling because of a permanent injury caused by A. Moreover, six months after that injury, C is also injured by B. C's second injury is such that C would have been unable to continue his career as a wrestler even if he had never been injured by A. The issue Honoré asks us to consider is A's and B's potential liability to C if C sues after the second injury.

---

[40] T Honoré, 'Necessary and Sufficient Conditions in Tort Law' in D Owen (ed), *Philosophical Foundations of Tort Law* (Oxford University Press, Oxford, 1995) 379–80.

On its face, this looks the same as *Sunrise*, but it is crucially different. In order to see this clearly, it is necessary to identify the injury for which the claimants (real or potential) are suing. While we say that the claimant in *Sunrise* is suing for loss of profit and C in the wrestler case is suing for lost earnings, as discussed in Chapter 7 this is not the correct legal analysis. The claimant in *Sunrise* had no right held against the defendant to the profits and C in the wrester case had no right held against either A or B to his future earnings. In *Sunrise*, the claimant's potential causes of action lay in the defendant's interference with the claimant's property right in the *Kalliopi L.* In the wrestler case, C's potential causes of action lie in A's and B's violation of C's bodily integrity. However, in *Sunrise*, the claimant is able to recover 'loss of profit' because that loss represents the value to the claimant of the interference with the property right. Similarly, in the wrestler case, 'loss of earnings' is a measure for quantifying the value of A's and B's violation of C's bodily integrity.

The failure to see this leads to the erroneous conclusion that the second incident in *Sunrise* was causally irrelevant: because the 27 days' profit was already effectively gone by the time the second incident occurred, that incident was not a cause of the claimant's injury. But that is the wrong analysis. The injury was the physical damage to the *Kalliopi L.* The issue that we are struggling with in *Sunrise* and the wrestler case is not causation of injury—there is indubitably over-determining causation in both cases. Rather, the issue is one of valuation of damage.

In Honoré's wrestler case, it seems clear that B should not have to compensate C for the loss of C's career. This is because C did not have and could not have had a career as a wrestler when injured by B. The value of the personal injury caused by A includes loss of amenity, pain and suffering, etc, and loss of career earnings as a wrestler. However, that final element is not part of the value of the injury caused by B. Put simply, C's body was worth less after the injury caused by A,[41] and that should be reflected in the damages payable by B.

However, now imagine that the injury caused by A could have been healed. Let us say that the injury caused by A would have taken two years to heal, whereupon C could have immediately resumed his career as a wrestler. However, one year after C suffered his injury caused by A, B permanently injured C so that C could never return to wrestling. Moreover, C's 'life expectancy' as a wrestler was a further five years from the point at which he was injured by B and that C's career was worth £100,000 per annum. In this case, it does seem right to find B liable for C's 'loss of earnings' as a wrestler. This is because the value of the injury is calculated, in part, by reference to what the injury prevents the claimant from doing. Here, the injury caused by B does prevent C from continuing his career as a wrestler. In this case, then, A is potentially liable for £200,000 and B for £600,000. The £100,000 for which both A and B are responsible should be apportioned between the defendants in accordance

[41] At least, so Honoré's example assumes.

with the contribution rules. (Hence, C should receive a total of £700,000 in relation to his loss of earning capacity.)

Imagine further that the injury caused by B could also be healed, so that C could return to wrestling two years after being injured by B. In this case, then, A is potentially liable for £300,000 and B for £200,000, with the £100,000 for which both A and B are responsible apportioned between the defendants. (This solution is also applied to *Sunrise* and variations in the next section of this chapter.)

Quite different from these cases are those that involve, in Wright's terminology, prior or pre-empting causation. In the case explored above involving the failure to repair breaks, only the driver was the cause of the claimant's injury as the mechanic's failure to repair the brakes was causally pre-empted by the driver's failure to use them. (Recall that no objection was stated to this aspect of Wright's argument.)

The lesson of the discussion above is the importance of distinguishing between the causation of injury and the evaluation of loss. This distinction plays a crucial role in the following.

These particular observations are all that I have to say about factual causation per se. In the following, I explore a different issue. Even assuming that we can agree on the existence of factual causation, disagreements over the implications of over-determination for liability may still arise. These disagreements are normative. They are not about causation, but about the consequences of causation for liability. Accordingly, I argue that they should be determined in accordance with corrective justice.

III. LIABILITY IN CASES OF OVER-DETERMINATION

In the previous section of this chapter, I explored the nature of factual causation primarily in connection with the issue of factual over-determination. I concluded that we must regard over-determining causes as causes. However, as I explore in this section, this creates problems for our understanding of the law, because, in cases that involve over-determination, defendants are sometimes not liable for apparently wrongfully causing claimants' injuries. As always, the answer to this problem is to return to corrective justice.

A. The Problem

I now explore two fact patterns that involve over-determination. In order to facilitate this investigation, it is helpful to distinguish between defendants who would be liable but for the causation enquiry and those who would not be liable. In order to do so, I say that a defendant is prima facie liable if affirmative answers are given to the first three of the following questions and a negative answer to the fourth:

(i)   Did the defendant's behaviour fall below the standard of care?
(ii) Did the defendant owe the claimant a duty of care?
(iii) Was the claimant's injury within the ambit of the risk created by the defendant?
(iv) Are any defences available to the defendant?

In the following, persons who are prima facie liable are referred to as defendants or by the symbol '*D*'. Conversely, those who played some causal role in the claimant's injury but who are not prima facie liable are referred to as blameless or innocent parties and labelled '*B*'. Sometimes, '*B*' refers not to a person but to a natural event such as an earthquake or storm.

We begin with the following two fact patterns in which two events are independently sufficient for the claimant's injury:

1. D_1 and D_2 injured the claimant. Had either D_1 or D_2 not acted, the claimant would have been injured nevertheless.
2. D and B injured the claimant. Had either D or B not acted, the claimant would have been injured nevertheless.[42]

An example of pattern 1 is *Corey v Havener* explored above. An example of pattern 2 is a variation on *Corey v Havener* in which the place of one of the defendants is taken by lightning. In pattern 2, then, the claimant's horse was scared both by the negligence of a defendant and by lightning.

In pattern 1, D_1 and D_2 are factual causes of the claimant's injury. Hence, both defendants are liable. In pattern 2, D and B are also factual causes of the claimant's injury. Of course, B cannot be liable. But the difficulty is with the position of D in pattern 2. As D was prima facie liable and was a factual cause of the claimant's injury, the necessary conclusion seems to be that D must be liable. But this is not the position taken by the common law, where it is said that, as the claimant's injury would have occurred without D's negligence, D cannot be liable. In court, the claimant is likely to fail in her cause of action against D on the ground that she cannot establish factual causation on the but for test. However, whatever the common law's pretended solution, there is no escaping the fact that D caused (ie was *a* cause of) the claimant's injury.

It is tempting, then, to argue that, if it is right to excuse D because of the claimant's failure to establish 'factual causation', then factual causation cannot exhaust the 'factual causation' stage of the negligence enquiry. Instead, there must be some normative considerations that establish why D_1 and D_2 are said to be the 'factual causes' of the claimant's injury in pattern 1 but why D is said not to be the 'factual cause' of the claimant's injury in pattern 2. Moreover, this explanation must be consistent with the fact that all defendants are prima facie

---

[42] For reasons of clarification, I express each fact pattern in more technical language in footnotes. D_1 and D_2 in pattern 1 and D and B in pattern 2 are independently sufficient and jointly necessary for the claimant's injury.

liable and all were factual causes of the claimant's injury. It is hard to see how this could be done.[43]

But there is an alternative—a more principled response. In order to elucidate it, it is first necessary to deal with two preliminaries. The first concerns the nature of common law rights in relation to negligence and the nature of damages. The second involves distinguishing an apparently similar view from the one proposed here.

B. Negligence and Nominal Damages

Nominal damages are awarded when a defendant has violated the claimant's rights but left the claimant factually no worse off as a result. For instance, if *A* breaches a contract with *B* but *B* suffers no factual loss thereby, then though compensation cannot be appropriate, the law awards nominal damages in order to recognise that *A* violated *B*'s rights by breaching the contract.

It is often believed that nominal damages cannot be awarded for negligence. The argument for that conclusion can be represented as follows:

1. Nominal damages are awarded only when the defendant violated a right in the claimant but left the claimant factually no worse off.
2. In negligence, the claimant can sue only if she suffered actual damage.
3. But, if the defendant caused actual damage to the claimant, then the defendant must have left the claimant factually worse off.
4. Hence, nominal damages cannot be available in negligence.

That argument is unsound. In fact, 3 is false. It is possible for a defendant to cause a claimant an actual loss that leaves the claimant no worse off than the claimant would have been had the defendant not acted. This occurs in cases involving over-determination—the very cases under discussion. In such circumstances, as the defendant violated a right in the claimant by causing the claimant actual loss, and as the defendant left the claimant no worse off than the claimant would have been had the defendant not acted negligently, the defendant should in principle be liable for nominal damages. I show shortly that this insight enables us to solve the problems encountered above.

In the following, it is important to recall that nominal damages are a symbolic award designed to recognise that the defendant violated the rights of the claimant though the defendant made the claimant factually no worse off. There is no argument here to suggest that this recognition must be in the form of nominal *damages*. I argue merely that in the relevant cases the court should recognise that the defendant violated the claimant's rights, even though the claimant is left no worse off as a result.

---

[43] I attempted such an explanation in A Beever, 'Cause-In-Fact: Two Steps Out of the Mire' (2001) 51 *University of Toronto Law Journal* 327. However, for reasons I discuss in the following, I now believe that position to be mistaken.

C. Wright on Damages

My argument below is similar to one made by Wright. In this section, I briefly explore Wright's view in order clearly to distinguish it from mine.

Recall our two fact patterns. In pattern 1, the actions of two defendants are independently sufficient for the claimant's injury. Our example is *Corey v Havener*. In pattern 2, the actions of one defendant and one innocent party are independently sufficient for the claimant's injury. Our example is *Corey v Havener* with the exception that the place of the second defendant is taken by lightning.

Under the heading 'Distinguishing the Damages Issue', Wright notes that courts faced with cases falling into pattern 2 are inclined to fall back on the but for test and deny liability on the ground that the defendant did not cause the claimant's injury.[44] Of course, this reasoning is fallacious. Instead, Wright insists, the defendant should be able to avoid liability because of 'policy limitations, rather than the false denial of causation'.[45] On the other hand, when dealing with pattern 1, 'given the usual policy limitations, the defendant should not escape liability when the duplicative or preempted condition was also of tortious origin'.[46] Instead, in pattern 1, both defendants 'are tortious duplicative causes of the injury, and liability should be imposed jointly on both tortfeasors with a right of contribution'.[47] Wright also claims that the relevant policies are connected to proximate causation.[48]

In my view, while Wright draws the correct conclusions, his reasoning is inadequate. First, if it is true that the defendant in pattern 2 should not be liable, that conclusion can have nothing to do with proximate causation. In our hypothetical example, the defendant placed the claimant at an unreasonable risk of just the sort of injuries that occurred. The claimant's injuries were not remote. Moreover, the defendant in our hypothetical example appears to be in exactly the same position as the defendant in *Corey v Havener*. Hence, the distinction between the cases cannot lie in remoteness. Secondly, the appeal to policy is unfortunate, even recognising that the term has, for Wright, a more constrained sense that it does for Commonwealth lawyers. On its face, given that we have a negligent defendant and an innocent claimant, policy would seem to argue in favour of, rather than against, liability. Moreover, the conclusion that the defendant in pattern 2 should not have to compensate the claimant for his injury seems to result, not from a policy-based addition to the law, but from the structure of the law itself. That is, it seems inconsistent with the nature of the law of negligence for the claimant to be compensated in pattern 2—at least so it seems to me—a fact that may explain

---

[44] RW Wright, 'Causation in Tort Law' (1985) 73 *California Law Review* 1735, 1799–800.
[45] *Ibid*, 1800.
[46] *Ibid*.
[47] *Ibid*, 1801.
[48] *Ibid*, 1798.

why courts are inclined to say that there was no factual causation in these cases, despite the fact that that claim is obviously false.

Finally, Wright is not clear about the impact of the relevant policies. He argues that policy demonstrates that 'the defendant should be able to *avoid liability* in such circumstances'.[49] This indicates that policy negatives liability. But he also suggests that these matters are related to damages,[50] indicating that the defendant should remain liable but should not have to pay compensation. To the extent that policy argues for either conclusion, it seems to favour only the second. That is, if the claimant's injury would have occurred in any case, this may (perhaps) show why the defendant should not have to pay damages to the claimant. But it is hard to see how the fact that the claimant would have been injured without the defendant's negligence shows that the defendant should not be liable, when Wright accepts that the defendant's negligence caused the claimant's injury. The basic problem here is that B in pattern 2—the lightning in our example—is not relevant to the relationship between the claimant and the defendant. Hence, it is unclear why the presence of B should make any difference to the defendant's potential liability. If Wright holds that the defendant in these cases should be liable but not have to pay damages, then his conclusion is the same as mine, though he attempts to justify his view by reliance on policy while I base mine in corrective justice.

D. The Claimant's Rights and Factual Causation

As indicated above, the position of the common law is that the defendant in pattern 2 is not liable, even though both defendants in pattern 1 remain so, despite it being the case that all defendants are prima facie liable and all defendants are factual causes of their claimants' injuries.

I begin with the position of the defendant in pattern 2. We must answer two questions: Should the defendant be liable and, if so, what is the quantum of damages that the defendant must pay?

In answer to the first question, the defendant should be liable if he was prima facie liable and a cause of the claimant's loss or damage. In our example, the defendant was prima facie liable and a factual cause of the claimant's personal injury. Hence, the defendant must be liable.

We turn now to the second question: what is the quantum of damages that the defendant must pay? This is answered by considering the difference between the position that the claimant is in and the position that the claimant would have been in had the defendant not acted negligently. In pattern 2, the claimant would have suffered exactly the same injury had the defendant not acted negligently. Hence, the quantum of damages is zero. In other words, the claimant is entitled only to nominal damages.

[49] *Ibid*, 1800 (emphasis added).
[50] *Ibid*, 1798.

Let us represent the position of the claimant before injury with the variable PoC and say that the claimant's personal injury was correctly valued at £100. In pattern 2, the defendant's negligence was a factual cause of the claimant's personal injury. Hence, the defendant is liable for the claimant's personal injury. Now, in order to compensate the claimant, the defendant must pay a sum of money that places the claimant in the position that the claimant would have been in had the defendant not acted negligently. Ignoring any potential secondary rights in the claimant in relation to the defendant's negligence, the position of the claimant after the accident is PoC–£100. The position the claimant would have been in had the defendant not acted negligently is also PoC–£100 (because of the lightning). Hence, although the defendant was a cause of the personal injury worth £100 to the claimant, the defendant owes the claimant nothing in the way of compensation. That is, no secondary rights to compensation need to be created in order to place the claimant in the position that he would have been in had the defendant not violated the claimant's primary right to bodily integrity. Accordingly, although the defendant violated the claimant's rights causing factual injury, in doing so the defendant left the claimant no worse off than the claimant would have been had the defendant not acted negligently. Hence, the correct award is nominal damages. Of course, this is unusual. Nominal damages will be available only in cases involving over-determination. But, as a matter of principle, they should be available.

The main difficultly with the argument above is reconciling it with the fact that both defendants must compensate the claimant in pattern 1, in which, it seems, each defendant can rightly allege that the claimant would have been no better off absent their negligence. In fact, this allegation is wrong. Though the claimant's injury would have occurred without either D_1's or D_2's negligence, neither D_1 nor D_2 can claim that his failure to compensate the claimant would leave the claimant no worse off than the claimant would have been had that defendant not wronged the claimant.

Let us begin with D_1. Without D_1's negligence, the claimant would have suffered the same injury, but would also have had a cause of action against D_2. However, if in pattern 1 the claimant cannot recover compensation from D_1, because D_1 can maintain that the claimant's injury would have occurred without D_1's negligence, then the claimant also cannot recover compensation from D_2. This is because D_1 and D_2 are in the same legal position: both defendants created unreasonable risks that materialised in the claimant's injury. Therefore, there is no principled basis for distinguishing D_1 from D_2. This means that, if the claimant cannot recover from D_1, then D_1's act *alone* would leave the claimant worse off than the claimant would have been had D_1 not acted.

Honoré expresses this conclusion by saying that D_1 would deprive the claimant of a remedy against D_2.[51] However, it is crucial to see that the point is

[51] T Honoré, 'Necessary and Sufficient Conditions in Tort Law' in D Owen (ed), *Philosophical Foundations of Tort Law* (Oxford University Press, Oxford, 1995) 380.

not that such deprivation is a wrong. Rather, the deprivation relates to the quantum of damages, as it demonstrates the extent to which the defendant leaves the claimant worse off.[52] Using the figures discussed in connection with pattern 2, ignoring the claimant's secondary rights in relation to the incident under discussion, the claimant's position immediately after the accident is PoC–£100. However, had D_1 not acted, then the claimant would have had a cause of action against D_2. Hence, taking into consideration the claimant's secondary rights, the position of the claimant would have been PoC–£100+£100 (owed by D_2): ie PoC. However, if D_1 is permitted not to compensate the claimant, then it must follow that the claimant cannot recover from D_2 and hence the claimant would be left in the position PoC–£100, ie £100 worse off than the claimant would have been had D_1 not acted. Accordingly, in order to avoid leaving the claimant worse off, D_1 must be liable for £100. The same argument applies to D_2.[53]

But, it may be argued, this reasoning fails if D_2 is, for example, impecunious or impossible to locate. In such circumstances, even taking into account the claimant's potential cause of action against D_2, if D_1 had not acted then the claimant's position would have been PoC–£100. Hence, D_1's failure to compensate the claimant leaves the claimant in exactly the position that the claimant would have been in had D_1 not acted.

The error is, again, to ignore the claimant's legal position and focus instead on the facts alone. Whether or not D_2 is impecunious or impossible to locate, the fact remains that had D_1 not acted, the claimant would have had a good cause of action against D_2. Hence, the claimant's legal position would have been PoC–£100+£100 (owed by D_2), or PoC. The fact that the claimant will be unable actually to get the £100 from D_2 in no way affects the claimant's legal position.

I now apply this approach to two decisions of the House of Lords: *Baker v Willoughby*[54] and *Jobling v Associated Dairies Ltd*.[55] In *Baker*, the defendant injured the claimant in a car accident. As a result, the claimant suffered from a stiff leg, causing inter alia loss of amenity and loss of earning capacity. I refer to this loss as L_1. Later, but before trial, the claimant was shot in the same leg by a burglar. The leg had to be amputated. This caused further loss of amenity, earning capacity, etc. I refer to this additional loss as L_2. The claimant attempted to recover L_1 from the defendant. The defendant replied that 'the second injury submerged or obliterated the effect of the first'.[56]

---

[52] Note also that the claim is not that D_1 has caused evidential damage to the claimant. Compare A Porat and A Stein, *Tort Liability Under Uncertainty* (Oxford University Press, Oxford, 2001) ch 6.

[53] The damages will be divided between the defendants in accordance with the contribution rules.

[54] [1970] AC 467 (HL).

[55] [1982] AC 794 (HL).

[56] *Baker v Willoughby* [1970] AC 467, 491 (HL) (Lord Reid). This argument was accepted by the Court of Appeal.

Lord Reid argued that this could not be accepted as:

A man is not compensated for the physical injury: he is compensated for the loss which he suffers as a result of that injury. His loss is not in having a stiff leg: it is in his inability to lead a full life, his inability to enjoy those amenities which depend on freedom of movement and his inability to earn as much as he used to earn or could have earned if there had been no accident. In this case the second injury did not diminish any of these. So why should it be regarded as having obliterated or superseded them?[57]

Lord Reid went on to say:

These cases exemplify the general rule that a wrongdoer must take the plaintiff (or his property) as he finds him: that may be to his advantage or disadvantage. In the present case the robber is not responsible or liable for the damage caused by the respondent: he would only have to pay for additional loss to the appellant by reason of his now having an artificial limb instead of a stiff leg.[58]

This line of reasoning caused problems in *Jobling*. In that case, the claimant had suffered a slipped disc due to the defendant's negligence. This meant that the claimant could perform only light work, reducing his earning capacity: L_1. However, the claimant later developed symptoms of a cervical myelopathy that resulted in total incapacity: L_2. If Lord Reid's judgment were followed, we would be forced to say that the cervical myelopathy was irrelevant and the defendant should have had to compensate the claimant for L_1.

However, the House of Lords in *Jobling* refused to reach that conclusion. Lord Keith argued that Lord Reid had failed to take into account the 'vicissitudes principle',[59] the idea that:

[I]f no accident had happened, nevertheless many circumstances might have happened to prevent the plaintiff from earning his previous income; he may be disabled by illness, he is subject to the ordinary accidents and vicissitudes of life; and if all these circumstances of which no evidence can be given are looked at, it will be impossible to exactly estimate them; yet if the jury wholly pass them over they will go wrong, because these accidents and vicissitudes ought to be taken into account. It is true that the chances of life cannot be accurately calculated, but the judge must tell the jury to consider them in order that they may give a fair and reasonable compensation.[60]

However, this reasoning creates problems in turn. Why was the burglar's shooting in *Baker* not a vicissitude? Lord Keith's response was that:

Additional considerations come into play when dealing with the problems arising where the plaintiff has suffered injuries from two or more successive and independent tortious acts. In that situation it is necessary to secure that the plaintiff is fully compensated for the aggregate effects of all his injuries. As Lord Pearson noted in *Baker* v. *Willoughby* it would clearly be unjust to reduce the damages awarded for the first tort

---

[57] *Ibid*, 492.
[58] *Ibid*, 493.
[59] *Jobling v Associated Dairies Ltd* [1982] AC 794, 813–14 (HL).
[60] *Phillips v London & South Western Railway Co* (1879) 5 CPD 280, 291–2 (Brett LJ).

because of the occurrence of the second tort, damages for which are to be assessed on the basis that the plaintiff is already partially incapacitated. I do not consider it necessary to formulate any precise juristic basis for dealing with this situation differently from the case of supervening illness. It might be said that a supervening tort is not one of the ordinary vicissitudes of life, or that it is too remote a possibility to be taken into account, or that it can properly be disregarded because it carries its own remedy. None of these formulations, however, is entirely satisfactory. The fact remains that the principle of full compensation requires that a just and practical solution should be found.[61]

In other words, '[i]t is all a question of expediency'.[62]

But that approach is not needed to solve these problems, nor is it very helpful.[63] In *Baker*, the defendant is liable for causing the claimant's leg injury and for causing the claimant's leg to become stiff (L_1). In *Jobling*, the defendant is also liable for causing the claimant to suffer a slipped disc (L_1). However, in *Jobling* the defendant must pay only nominal damages as he can say that compensating the claimant for either the first or second loss would make the claimant better off than the claimant would have been had the defendant not wronged the claimant. This is not something that the defendant in *Baker* can rightly allege, as this would entail that the claimant could not recover from the burglar—both wrongfully caused the over-determined loss.

Again, we see that the principled approach is able to deal with seemingly intractable issues without appeal to policy.

E. Applying the Theory to More Complex Fact Patterns

In the following, I apply the theory elucidated above to more complex fact patterns. This is important in order to discover whether the theory functions outside the two simple patterns examined above.

3. *D* and *B* injured the claimant. *D*'s act alone would have caused all of the claimant's injury. *B*'s act alone would have caused some but not all of the claimant's injury.[64]

An example of this pattern faced the Supreme Court of Canada in *Sunrise*. Recall that the claimant's boat ran aground due to the defendant's negligence causing 27 days' worth of damage, and then ran aground again due to the claimant's own carelessness causing 14 days' damage. The damage could be repaired concurrently.

---

[61] *Jobling v Associated Dairies Ltd* [1982] AC 794, 815 (HL).

[62] *Palsgraf v Long Island Railroad Co* 162 NE 99, 104 (NY CA 1928) (Andrews J).

[63] See WVH Rogers, *Winfield and Jolowicz on Tort*, 16th edn (Sweet & Maxwell, London, 2002) 217–18 for discussion of the uncertainty created by *Jobling v Associated Dairies Ltd* [1982] AC 794 (HL).

[64] *D* is necessary and sufficient for the whole of the claimant's injury. *B* is sufficient but not necessary for some of the claimant's injury.

As indicated above, a majority of the Supreme Court of Canada accepted the claimant's view that the second accident was irrelevant. L'Heureux-Dubé claimed that the second incident was causally inert.[65] As we also saw, although this claim is mistaken, Waddams supports the outcome reached by the Court by arguing that 'the result can be supported on grounds of simplicity and convenience'.[66]

The claimant's entitlement is to have the injury inflicted on him by the defendant removed as far as the law is able to do so. In practice, this means that the court must award the claimant a sum of damages that, as far as possible, places the claimant in the position in which he would have been had the defendant not wronged the claimant. To do less is an injustice in corrective justice to the claimant, as the claimant is left with less than he deserves. To do more is also an injustice in corrective justice, this time to the defendant, as it takes more from the defendant than is required to place the claimant in the position he would have been in had he not been wronged. Neither form of injustice can be justified on the ground that it is simple and convenient for the court. The defendant's obligation is to make up for his wrong. His property is not to be confiscated in the name of judicial simplicity and convenience.

Moreover, the decision of the majority of the Court in *Sunrise*—finding the defendant liable for the full 27 days' damage—does not seem consistent with the fact that there is no liability in pattern 2. In such cases, courts say that the claimant cannot recover, as she would have been injured in any case. In *Sunrise*, all but 13 days' worth of damage would have occurred in any case.

In dissent in *Sunrise*, McLachlin J contended that the defendant should be liable for only 20 days: the 13 days for which he was solely to blame and half of the remaining 14 for which there was dual responsibility.[67] Her Honour maintained that this outcome 'conforms with the fundamental principle that the claimants are entitled to be placed in the same position as they would have been in had the tort never occurred'.[68] But this also is wrong. If the claimant in *Sunrise* had not been wronged, he would have suffered 14 days' loss, not seven days' loss.

Significantly, in *Athey v Leonati*, a case involving personal injury, the Supreme Court of Canada implicitly accepted these conclusions. Major J said that:

> the essential purpose and most basic principle of tort law is that the plaintiff must be placed in the position he or she would have been in absent the defendant's negligence (the 'original position'). However, the plaintiff is not to be placed in a position better than his or her original one. It is therefore necessary not only to determine the plaintiff's position after the tort but also to assess what the 'original position' would have been.[69]

---

[65] *Sunrise Co Ltd v Ship 'Lake Winnipeg'* [1991] 1 SCR 3, 20.
[66] SM Waddams, 'Causation in Canada and Australia' (1993) 1 *Tort Law Review* 75, 81.
[67] *Sunrise Co Ltd v Ship 'Lake Winnipeg'* [1991] 1 SCR 3, 34–40.
[68] *Ibid*, 39.
[69] *Athey v Leonati* [1996] 3 SCR 458, 472.

While this is entirely correct, it does not explain why it is correct to treat personal injury differently from property damage.

Mitchell McInnes attempts the rationale for this distinction between the treatment of personal injury and of property damage:

> [T]he plaintiff . . . is entitled to compensation from the defendant if the loss in question arises from property damage, rather than personal injury. That distinction may be defensible on the basis that the losses attendant on property damage occur immediately, whereas those attendant upon personal injury are of a continuing nature. Consequently, it has been argued that in the latter situation, but not the former, the subsequent non-tortious cause remains causally relevant.[70]

The argument here is that the loss due to personal injury does not happen all at once but accumulates over time, while the loss that accompanies damage to property is instantaneous. Accordingly, it is reasonable to make the defendant pay for a loss that occurs immediately, regardless of what happens afterwards; while it is not reasonable to exact payment for a loss that takes time to materialise, when subsequent events would bring about the loss without the defendant's negligence.

However, losses consequent on damage to property can be continuing, and those connected with personal injury can be immediate. An example of the former is *Sunrise* itself. The value of the relevant injury in *Sunrise* was the loss of profit due to the need to have the *Kalliopi L* out of the water for 27 days. Before the claimant had suffered any of this loss, the claimant damaged his own boat, causing 14 days' worth of damage. On the other hand, personal injuries can be immediate. If my leg is instantaneously amputated as the result of someone's negligence, no time is required for some of my loss to materialise. The distinction between the treatment of personal injury and the treatment of property damage is not sustainable.

The correct approach is to require the defendant to compensate the claimant only for 13 days' damage. This is because the defendant can correctly argue that to require him to pay for more than 13 days would force him to place the claimant in a better position than the claimant would have been in had the defendant not wronged the claimant.

I now discuss two patterns together.

4. D_1 and D_2 injured the claimant. D_1's act alone would have caused all of the claimant's injury. D_2's act alone would have caused some but not all of the claimant's injury.[71]

For this case, imagine *Sunrise* with the exception that the second event was caused by a separate defendant's negligence. Hence, the claimant's ship went

---

[70] M McInnes, 'Causation in Tort Law: Back to Basics at the Supreme Court of Canada' (1997) 35 *Alberta Law Review* 1013, 1023.

[71] D_1 is necessary and sufficient for the whole of the claimant's injury. D_2 is sufficient but not necessary for some of the claimant's injury.

aground because of D_1's negligence causing 27 days' damage and later went aground because of D_2's negligence causing 14 days' worth of damage. The damage could be repaired concurrently.

5. *D* and *B* injured the claimant. *B*'s act alone would have caused all of the claimant's injury. *D*'s act alone would have caused some but not all of the claimant's injury.[72]

Imagine here *Sunrise* with the accidents reversed: that is, the claimant first inflicted 27 days' worth of damage on his own boat and the defendant later caused the boat to run aground, causing 14 days' worth of damage that can be repaired concurrently.

Given that L'Heureux-Dubé said that the claimant's carelessness was causally irrelevant in *Sunrise*, her position must be that D_2's negligence would also be inert in pattern 4. This would mean that D_1 would be liable for the full 27 days while D_2 would not be liable at all. This conclusion seems quite wrong. In pattern 4, both defendants are causally responsible for some of the claimant's injury and both are prima facie liable. Accordingly, in this case, McLachlin J seems to have the preferable view. Applying McLachlin J's judgment in *Sunrise* to pattern 4, D_1 would be liable for 20 days and D_2 would be liable for seven days.

Compare this with pattern 5. Applying L'Heureux-Dubé's reasoning in *Sunrise*, the defendant would entirely escape liability as his negligence is said to be causally inert. Conversely, McLachlin J would hold the defendant liable for seven days' loss of profit, this being half of the damage for which there was dual responsibility. But in this case, McLachlin J's position puts the claimant in a better position than he would have been in had he not been wronged.

On the view advanced here, both defendants are liable for the injuries they caused in pattern 4. This means that D_1 owes the claimant compensation for 27 days and D_2 for 14 days. Of course, the damages will be divided between the defendants in accordance with the contribution rules.

At one level, this resembles McLachlin J's apportionment of liability in *Sunrise*. But it is quite distinct. McLachlin apportions *liability*, this approach apportions *damages*. Apportionment of liability is not consistent with the general approach of tort law.[73] This is because a defendant is liable for an injury if he wrongfully caused that injury. In pattern 4, both defendants wrongfully caused the over-determined 14 days' loss to the claimant. Hence, both defendants should be liable for that loss. Moreover, it is by no means clear that apportionment of liability will secure the claimant's secondary rights, since it is not unlikely that one of the defendants will be, for example, impecunious or impossible to locate. Given that both defendants wrongfully caused the over-

---

[72] *B* is necessary and sufficient for the whole of the claimant's injury. *D* is sufficient but not necessary for some of the claimant's injury.

[73] This matter is also explored with respect to factual uncertainty in ch 13.

determined 14 days' loss, the risk that one of the defendants should be impecunious must be borne by the other defendant, not by the claimant. The contribution rules create rights in defendants as against one another; they do not remove rights in the claimant. This is not policy but is dictated by corrective justice. Liability is determined in accordance with the relationship between the parties. That D_2 is or is not impecunious is of no relevance to the relationship between D_1 and the claimant. Hence, D_2's impecuniosity cannot negative any right that the claimant holds against D_1. Accordingly, as D_1 wrongfully deprived the claimant of the over-determined 14 days, if D_2 is impecunious, the claimant can recover the whole of that loss from D_1.[74]

Finally, a strict application of the principled approach shows that both defendants are jointly and severally liable for all the damage they inflicted. Naturally, each defendant is liable only for what he caused—D_1 27 days' damage and D_2 14 days'—but each should be fully liable for that.

In pattern 5, the defendant should have to pay only nominal damages, as compensating the claimant would place the claimant in a better position than the claimant would have been in had the defendant not acted.

Before we leave the discussion of the nature of factual causation, it is useful to examine three more fact patterns. When we have done so, we will have covered all the fact patterns that could arise in dual causation cases. It should be easy to apply the conclusions reached here to cases with three or more causal elements.

6. *D* and *B* injured the claimant. Had *D* not acted, the claimant would not have suffered any injury. Had *B* not acted, the claimant would have suffered exactly the same injury she did in fact suffer.[75]

Imagine that *D* negligently lit a fire with an intensity of 100 units. That fire combined with an innocently lit fire of 50 units. The fire then spread, igniting and destroying the claimant's house. Imagine also that a fire with an intensity of fewer than 100 units would not have spread so far and would not have made contact with the claimant's house. On the other hand, any fire with an intensity of 100 units or more would have spread to and destroyed the claimant's house.

In pattern 6, despite its similarity to pattern 3, the defendant must compensate the claimant for the whole of the claimant's loss. This is because, unlike pattern 3, the claimant would not have lost anything absent the defendant's wrongdoing. Hence, the defendant cannot say that compensating the claimant would place the claimant in a better position than the claimant would have been in had the defendant not wronged the claimant.

[74] This point has unfortunately been overlooked in the recent tort reform in Australia. See eg ss30–31 Civil Liability Act 2003 (Qld).
[75] *D* is necessary and sufficient for the claimant's injury. *B* nevertheless contributes.

7. *D* and *B* injured the claimant. Had *B* not acted, the claimant would not have suffered any injury. Had *D* not acted, the claimant would have suffered exactly the same injury she did in fact suffer.[76]

This case is simply the reverse of the above. Imagine that a fire with an intensity of 100 units was innocently lit. That fire combined with a negligently lit fire of 50 units. The fire then spread, igniting and destroying the claimant's house. A fire with an intensity of fewer than 100 units would not have made contact with the claimant's house, but any fire with an intensity of 100 units or more would have spread to and destroyed the claimant's house.

The reasoning here is the same as that in pattern 2. That is, *D* must pay only nominal damages. This is because requiring *D* to pay compensation would place the claimant in a better position than the claimant would have been in had *D* not wronged the claimant.

8. D_1 and D_2 injured the claimant. Had D_1 not acted, the claimant would not have suffered any injury. Had D_2 not acted, the claimant would have suffered exactly the same injury she did in fact suffer.[77]

For this case, imagine fact patterns 6 and 7 with the difference only that both fires were negligently lit.

In pattern 8, both defendants are liable for the loss they caused. In this case, both defendants are liable for the destruction of the claimant's house. This is because, if D_2 can claim that he must pay only nominal damages for the over-determined damage, then D_1 could claim this also, leaving the claimant worse off than he would have been had D_2 not acted. Damages are to be apportioned in accordance with the contribution rules.

---

[76] *B* is necessary and sufficient for the claimant's injury. *D* nevertheless contributes.

[77] D_1 is necessary and sufficient for the claimant's injury. D_2 nevertheless contributes.

13

Proof and Uncertainty

I SSUES OF PROOF and uncertainty pose problems for the law of negligence in three main areas: in proving whether the defendant was negligent, in establishing whether the defendant caused the claimant's loss and in the so-called 'loss of a chance' cases. On its face, it may seem odd to discuss these issues in a book focusing on substantive legal principle. Issues of uncertainty appear to have more to do with the ins and outs of legal practice and with the law of evidence. However, as corrective justice has important things to say about these matters, it is worth exploring them here.

In relation to the burden of proof, the argument is that corrective justice dictates that the claimant should bear the burden of having to establish the elements of the cause of action (excluding the defences). Hence, no exception to this principle is to be permitted. In particular, to the extent that it still exists, the doctrine known as *res ipsa loquitur* must be abolished. I then explore cases that involve factual uncertainty. I argue that cases such as *Cook v Lewis*,[1] in which a claimant is unable to determine which of two negligent people caused the injury for which he is suing, is best resolved by examining the rights of the claimant. I argue that the claimant can recover from either or both potential defendants, because, in reasonably foreseeably preventing the claimant from recovering from another for the violation of a right, each defendant violates that very right. Conversely, I examine three problematic decisions of the House of Lords—*McGhee v National Coal Board*,[2] *Wilsher v Essex Area Health Authority*,[3] and *Fairchild v Glenhaven Funeral Services Ltd*[4]— and argue that the outcomes of these cases required no appeal beyond the ordinary principles of the law. I maintain that these cases are difficult because they have difficult fact patterns, but when the facts are correctly understood they are easily settled by the law's ordinary principles. Finally, I explore the issue of loss of a chance. I maintain that the concept of loss of a chance is incoherent and is merely a confused form of factual uncertainty.

---

[1] [1951] SCR 830.
[2] [1972] 1 WLR 1 (HL Sc).
[3] [1988] AC 1074 (HL).
[4] [2002] UKHL 22, [2003] 1 AC 32.

THE BURDEN OF PROOF

The default position is that the claimant must prove on the balance of probabilities that the defendant was negligent, that the defendant owed the claimant a duty of care, that the claimant's injury was not remote and that the defendant caused the claimant's injury. (For convenience, I refer to this as 'breach, duty, and proximate and factual causation'.)

Corrective justice demands that the standard of proof be the balance of probabilities. Because the parties are to be treated as equals and because the parties stand to gain and lose the same thing, the standard of proof ought to be balanced fairly between them. The burden of proof is also demanded by corrective justice and by the principle that one is innocent until proven guilty. The defendant does not come to court faced with the assumption that he committed a tort against the claimant. Rather, the claimant must prove that she was wronged by the defendant. Accordingly, the claimant must prove breach, duty, and proximate and factual causation.

However, on the face of it, this biases the enquiry in favour of the defendant. For instance, if a claimant has established duty and proximate and factual causation on the balance of probabilities, why does the claimant also have to show on the balance of probabilities that the defendant was negligent?

The reason is that breach, duty, and proximate and factual causation are parts of a conceptual whole. In arguing these elements of the cause of action, the claimant attempts to establish that the defendant's creation of an unreasonable risk materialised in her injury. This is required in order to show that she was wronged by the defendant. Hence, from the perspective of the law of negligence, as well as from the perspective of corrective justice, the defendant is *entirely innocent* (with respect to the claimant) unless the claimant establishes *all* elements against the defendant. For instance, although the defendant's employee in *Doughty v Turner Manufacturing Co Ltd*[5] was negligent in the sense that he created an unreasonable risk of injury, although that risk was created to the claimant, and although the defendant's employee caused the claimant's injury, as the injury was remote from the defendant's employee's negligence the defendant's employee committed no wrong *whatsoever* to the claimant in the law of negligence or in the eyes of corrective justice.

This also shows that the need for the claimant to establish breach, duty, and proximate and factual causation on the balance of probabilities—ie 50 per cent *plus 1*—is not merely a matter of convenience or a way of breaking ties.[6] Rather,

---

[5] [1964] 1 QB 518 (CA).

[6] Compare A Ripstein and BC Zipursky, 'Corrective Justice in an Age of Mass Torts' in GJ Postema (ed), *Philosophy and the Law of Torts* (Cambridge University Press, Cambridge, 2001) 241–3. Note that, strictly, probabilities are not correctly expressed as percentages. Nevertheless, it remains common in law to express them as such, and I follow that convention here.

a party who shows that a proposition is as likely to be true as it is to be false cannot be said to have *proven* the proposition according to any standard. Hence, a claimant who has established only that it was as likely as not that the defendant was negligent has not shown that she was wronged by the defendant.

While it is the claimant's task to prove breach, duty, and proximate and factual causation, the defendant must show any relevant defences. The default position is that people are expected to have acted reasonably unless there is evidence to the contrary. This is another way of saying that guilt must be proven. This explains why the claimant must show that the defendant was negligent in order to establish a cause of action, but it also demonstrates why the defendant must prove that the claimant was negligent in order to enjoy the defence of contributory negligence. That is demanded by the formal equality of the law. Similarly, the *volenti* defence applies only if the claimant surrendered a right to the defendant. The law must not presume that people surrender their rights but must look for adequate evidence of such. Accordingly, the defendant has the burden of proof. With respect to illegality, the claimant's primary right has been violated, but the claimant cannot recover because, in the eyes of the law, her claim has no value. This is despite the fact that the claimant has suffered a factual loss. Hence, given that the claimant suffers a loss in fact and prima facie has a good cause of action against the defendant, it is up to the defendant to show that this should be negatived because of illegality.

II. UNCERTAINTY OVER WHETHER THE DEFENDANT WAS NEGLIGENT

Uncertainty over whether the defendant was negligent is covered by the thorny doctrine known as *res ipsa loquitur*. In *Byrne v Boadle*,[7] a barrel of flour fell from the defendant's warehouse injuring the claimant. Apparently, the defendant's employees had been hoisting barrels into the warehouse using a set of pulleys. However, the claimant knew very little about the specific activities of the defendant's employees. Accordingly, as the claimant could not point to any particular act of negligence, the defendant argued that the claimant should have been nonsuited. However, Pollock CB rejected this reasoning, claiming:

> It is the duty of persons who keep barrels in a warehouse to take care that they do not roll out, and I think that such a case would, beyond all doubt, afford prima facie evidence of negligence. A barrel could not roll out of a warehouse without some negligence, and to say that a plaintiff who is injured by it must call witnesses from the warehouse to prove negligence seems to me preposterous. . . . Or if an article calculated to cause damage is cut in a wrong place and does mischief, I think that those whose duty it was to cut it in the right place are prima facie responsible, and if there is any state of facts to rebut the presumption of negligence, they must prove them. The

---

[7] (1863) 156 ER 299.

present case upon the evidence comes to this, a man is passing in front of the premises of a dealer in flour, and there falls down upon him a barrel of flour. I think it apparent that the barrel was in the custody of the defendant who occupied the premises, and who is responsible for the acts of his servants who had the control of it; and in my opinion the fact of its falling is prima facie evidence of negligence, and the plaintiff who was injured by it is not bound to shew that it could not fall without negligence, but if there are any facts inconsistent with negligence it is for the defendant to prove them.[8]

Some of the language used by Pollock CB gives the impression that the burden of proof was reversed in *Byrne v Boadle*, so that the defendant had to show that neither he nor his servants were negligent. Hence, in *Voice v Union Steam Ship Co of New Zealand Ltd*, Gresson J said:

In my opinion, the principles to be extracted from these authorities as to the application of the doctrine [of *res ipsa loquitur*] are as follows:

(i)   In every case there arises the question which is one of law—namely, whether there is any evidence on which the jury could properly find in favour of the party on whom the onus of proof lies—that is, find for the plaintiff on the basis that the defendant was negligent.

(ii)   If the plaintiff proves a happening of such a nature that *res ipsa loquitur*, the onus is on the defendant—that is to say, he is presumed to have been negligent.

(iii)   The onus of displacing this impression of negligence will be discharged by showing either:

> (a)   That the happening was due to something which was not negligence on the part of the defendant or those for whom he is responsible; or
>
> (b)   That the defendant, though unable to explain the happening, exercised all reasonable care.

(iv)   The onus of disproving negligence which lies on the defendant by reason of his presumptive negligence remains throughout the proceedings, so that, if the evidence is too meagre or too evenly balanced for that issue as a question of fact to be capable of determination, then, by force of the presumption, plaintiff is entitled to succeed.[9]

If this is the correct approach, then the crucial question is: 'what is "a happening of such a nature that *res ipsa loquitur*" '? In *Britannia Hygienic Laundry Co v Thornycroft*,[10] Bankes LJ's answer was that the *res ipsa loquitur* rule would apply when the claimant had no knowledge or no reasonable way of knowing what the defendant actually did. Similarly, in *Ybarra v Spangard*,[11] the claimant's shoulder was injured during an operation while he was under general anaesthetic. As any one of five potential defendants could have caused the injury, the claimant could not establish proof of negligence on the balance of

---

[8]   *Ibid*, 301.
[9]   [1953] NZLR 176, 189–90 (SC); affirmed in *Voice" v Union Steam Ship Co of New Zealand Ltd* [1953] NZLR 176 (CA).
[10]   (1925) 95 LJKB 237 (CA).
[11]   154 P 2d 687 (Calif SC 1944).

probabilities against any one person. However, the California Supreme Court insisted that *res ipsa loquitur* applied and the defendant, one of the five people in the operating theatre, had to show on the balance of probabilities that he was not negligent.

The problem with this approach is that it irrationally favours the claimant who knows very little about what happened over the claimant who actually knows something. In this sense, then, the less one knows about the defendant's activities the better—the less evidence one has the better. As a general strategy, it will often make sense for claimants to plead ignorance in order to shift the burden to the defendant. Moreover, reversing the burden of proof entails that the law may impose liability on a defendant when there is insufficient evidence reasonably to conclude that the defendant wronged the claimant. But that cannot be justified.

To understand what actually happened in *Byrne v Boadle*, it is necessary to examine legal procedure imagining that jury trials were still the norm. The relevant rules are that the claimant must establish a prima facie case against the defendant or the claimant will be nonsuited. This means that the claimant must convince the judge that a reasonable juror *could* reach the conclusion that the defendant was negligent. If the claimant cannot do this, then the claimant will be nonsuited: the case will not be sent to the jury and the claimant will fail. This does not mean that, in order to establish a prima facie case, the claimant must convince the judge *on the balance of probabilities* that the defendant was negligent. Rather, the judge must be satisfied only that the jury *would not be acting unreasonably* in finding for the claimant, even if the judge herself believes that the evidence tends to show that the defendant was innocent.

In *Byrne v Boadle*, the claimant had been nonsuited because the assessor took the view that the claimant had failed to make out a prima facie case. It was this view that Pollock CB rejected. Hence, the claim that the accident provided 'prima facie evidence of negligence'[12] does not mean that the mere fact that the accident occurred implied that the defendant had to exonerate himself. Rather, Pollock CB meant that the fact that *this* accident occurred in the way that it did was sufficient to show that a reasonable jury *could* have come to the conclusion that the defendant was negligent. Hence, the claimant should not have been nonsuited. Barrels do not fall out of windows every day. In *Byrne v Boadle*, then, it was not *unreasonable* to conclude, on the balance of probabilities, that the defendant's employees had been negligent (even if, in fact, the defendant's employees had not been negligent). Accordingly, the case could not rightly have been withdrawn from the jury.

Res ipsa loquitur is often confused with what John Fleming calls the burden of persuasion.[13] If the claimant establishes on the balance of probabilities that the defendant was negligent, then, *as a matter of strategy*, the defendant must

---

[12] *Byrne v Boadle* (1863) 156 ER 299, 301.
[13] J Fleming, *The Law of Torts*, 9th edn (LBC Information Services, Sydney, 1998) 361.

attempt to undermine the claimant's evidence or introduce new evidence tending to exonerate herself if she does not wish to be found to have been negligent.[14] As it were, if the claimant has shown that it is 60 per cent likely that the defendant was negligent, then the defendant will need to lead evidence to bring this down to 50 per cent or below, or the defendant will be found to have been negligent. In cases where *res ipsa loquitur*, the fact that the accident happened may itself be sufficient to show that it was more likely than not that the defendant was negligent. This seems to have been the case in *Byrne v Boadle*. Given what we know, it was more likely than not that the defendant's employees had acted negligently. Hence, to escape a finding of negligence, the defendant had to lead evidence to show that he and his employees were not negligent. There is no reversal of the burden of proof here. The burden remains on the claimant, but the defendant must lead evidence to avoid a finding of negligence because the claimant has met this burden.

In *Hawke's Bay Motor Co Ltd v Russell*,[15] the claimant's coach was damaged when the defendant driver of another vehicle failed to negotiate a corner and collided with the coach. The coach had been entirely on the claimant's side of the road. On its face, this was enough to conclude that the crash occurred because of the defendant's negligence. However, the defendant alleged that he had suffered a turn or a blackout due to a calcified aneurysm on one side of his brain, and hence was not acting when the accident occurred. There was some evidence to support this contention. It will help our understanding if we arbitrarily attach some numbers to the probabilities here.

Let us say that, if we knew only that the accident had occurred entirely on the claimant's side of the road, then it would have been 75 per cent likely that the defendant was negligent. Moreover, we also know that the chance that the defendant suffered a blackout was 33.33 per cent. This means, then, that the chance that the defendant was negligent was actually 50 per cent (50 being 66.67 per cent of 75).

In *Russell*, the claimant appealed to the doctrine of *res ipsa loquitur* and insisted that the defendant prove on the balance of probabilities that he had suffered a blackout. This argument rested on the notion that *res ipsa loquitur* causes the burden of proof to be reversed and, as the claimant had established the circumstances in which *res ipsa loquitur* should apply, the burden of proving lack of negligence fell on the defendant. Given that, as the defendant had established only that it was 33.33 per cent likely that he suffered a blackout, the defendant had failed to establish on the balance of probabilities that he was not negligent. Therefore, the defendant should lose.

Beattie J rejected this argument and insisted that the burden of proof remains on the claimant. Hence, as the evidence was evenly balanced—it was 50 per cent

[14] She may be happy to be found negligent. For instance, she may feel that the claimant will fail to establish a duty of care or suffered a remote injury.
[15] [1972] NZLR 542 (SC).

likely that the defendant was negligent and 50 per cent likely that he was not—the claimant failed. No more analysis is required than an assessment of the probabilities revealed in the evidence presented before the court.

In this light, it is best not to regard *res ipsa loquitur* as a doctrine. It is nothing more than the *observation* that sometimes the fact that the accident occurred is sufficient to establish on the balance of probabilities that the defendant was negligent. Accordingly, *res ipsa loquitur* adds nothing to the law. It is merely the observation that, as it were, things sometimes speak for themselves. 'There is therefore no need to subsume the maxim into the general body of tort law: it is already fully consonant with it.'[16] Hence, it is misleading to say that *res ipsa loquitur* 'allows the court to draw an inference of negligence from the mere fact that an event as happened' or that the maxim 'can ease the burden of proving that the person responsible for it was at fault'.[17] *Res ipsa loquitur* does not allow the court to do anything, nor does it ease the burden of proof on the claimant. There is nothing that courts can do with *res ipsa loquitur* that they could not do according to the ordinary principles of the law. As Fleming correctly puts it:

> Res ipsa loquitur is no more than a convenient label to describe situations where, notwithstanding the plaintiff's inability to establish the exact cause of the accident, the fact of the accident by itself is sufficient in the absence of an explanation to justify the conclusion that most probably the defendant was negligent and that his negligence caused the injury. The maxim contains nothing exceptional; it is based on common sense, since it is matter of ordinary observation and experience in life that sometimes a thing tells its own story.[18]

Ideally, as *res ipsa loquitur* adds nothing to the law, references to the maxim should disappear. Major J intended to support this view in *Fontaine v British Columbia (Official Administrator)*:

> It would appear that the law would be better served if the maxim was treated as expired and no longer used as a separate component in negligence actions. After all, it was nothing more than an attempt to deal with circumstantial evidence. That evidence is more sensibly dealt with by the trier of fact, who should weigh the circumstantial evidence with the direct evidence, if any, to determine whether the plaintiff has established on a balance of probabilities a *prima facie* case of negligence against the defendant. Once the plaintiff has done so, the defendant must present evidence negating that of the plaintiff or necessarily the plaintiff will succeed.[19]

Unfortunately, however, this suggests the old view of *res ipsa loquitur* found in cases such as *Voice, Britannia Hygienic* and *Ybarra,* examined above. A claimant who has established a prima facie case has shown only that a reasonable person

---

[16] *Schellenberg v Tunnel Holdings* (2000) 200 CLR 121, 141 (HCA) (Gleeson CJ and McHugh J).
[17] S Todd, 'Negligence: Breach of Duty' in S Todd (ed), *The Law of Torts in New Zealand*, 3rd edn (Brookers, Wellington, 2001) 410. Compare ibid, 414, where *res ipsa loquitur* is correctly described.
[18] J Fleming, *The Law of Torts*, 9th edn (LBC Information Services, Sydney, 1998) 353.
[19] [1998] 1 SCR 424, 435. See also *Roe v Minister of Health* [1954] 2 QB 66, 87 (CA) (Morris LJ).

could come to the conclusion that the defendant was negligent, not necessarily that a reasonable person *should* or *must* come to the conclusion that the defendant was negligent. However, if we delete 'a *prima facie* case of' from the paragraph above, we have a correct statement of the law.

On the other hand, a recent attempt has been made to resuscitate the doctrine. Arial Porat and Alex Stein argue that one must distinguish:

> between the two ways—one statistical and the other individualised—in which negligence can be established. Normally, a plaintiff is required to establish the defendant's negligence by case-specific evidence, that is, by evidence that points to a concrete act or omission committed by the defendant. If such an act or omission amounts to negligence and if it is causally responsible for the plaintiff's damage, then the defendant should be held liable. This normal proof requirement is individualised in nature. But there are cases in which there is no evidence that could point to a specific act or omission by which the defendant negligently damaged the plaintiff; at the same time, general experience instructs the judges that in the given type of cases, the defendant's negligence is predominantly responsible for the plaintiff's respective damage. Statistical inference of negligence consequently becomes available. Normally, no such inference may be drawn against the defendant even when it is sound from a probabilistic point of view. A person should be held responsible only for what he or she did individually rather than for being affiliated by the judge to some statistically significant group of people, in which the wrongdoers form the majority. As the famous saying goes, 'For statistics there are no individuals, and for individuals no statistics.'[20]

Accordingly, Porat and Stein insist that, although *Fontaine* officially abandoned *res ipsa loquitur* in Canada, the doctrine remains in force in fact, as statistical evidence is permissible in the relevant cases.[21] In Porat and Stein's view, *res ipsa loquitur* 'allows judges to infer negligence under uncertainty even when that inference is unwarranted from an epistemological point of view. The presumption thus allows judges to assume risk of error in their final verdict and to shift that risk to the defendant.'[22]

However, it cannot be appropriate for 'judges to infer negligence . . . when that inference is unwarranted from an epistemological point of view'. If a claim is not warranted from an epistemological point of view then it is not warranted. Porat and Stein insist that the court should say that the defendant was negligent though the evidence suggests that she was not. This means that judges should say that something happened when the evidence suggests that it did not.

Moreover, the distinction between individual and statistical evidence is unimportant in law.[23] Despite Porat and Stein's assertions, statistical evidence is probative. In fact, even if it is not explicitly adduced in evidence, statistical evidence

---

[20] A Porat and A Stein, *Tort Liability Under Uncertainty* (Oxford University Press, Oxford, 2001) 87.

[21] *Ibid*, 92.

[22] *Ibid*, 85.

[23] Much of the confusion in this area is caused by the decision of the House of Lords in *Hotson v East Berkshire Area Health Authority* [1987] AC 750 (HL). That case is examined below. As we will see, the decision did not involve a rejection of statistical evidence.

must always be relied on because our understanding of the world is dependant on (rough) statistical generalisations. Without them, the world would appear chaotic. Furthermore, if statistical evidence establishes on the balance of probabilities that the defendant was negligent, then finding the defendant negligent is epistemologically warranted; in fact it is epistemologically demanded. Finally, the claim that '[a] person should be held responsible only for what he or she did individually rather than for being affiliated by the judge to some statistically significant group of people, in which the wrongdoers form the majority'[24] mistakes the issue. The relevance of statistics is not to show merely that *people in the defendant's position* are usually negligent. Rather, it is to show that, given that people in the defendant's position are usually negligent, it is more likely than not that *the defendant* was negligent. Hence, a defendant found liable on the basis of statistical evidence is 'held responsible only for what he or she did individually'. We come to a conclusion about what he or she did partly on the basis of evidence about what other people do in relevantly similar circumstances, but we hold him or her responsible for what we believe, and have good reason to believe, he or she did.

Accordingly, *res ipsa loquitur* has no role to play in the modern law of negligence. The phrase should be expunged from our vocabulary.

III. UNCERTAINTY OVER FACTUAL CAUSATION

A. The Principled Approach to Factual Uncertainty

The issue of factual uncertainty arises when it is unclear whether the defendant's negligent action caused the claimant's injury. I begin by exploring two intriguing cases: *Cook v Lewis* and *Sindell v Abbott Laboratories*.[25]

In the former case, two potential defendants, Cook and Akenhead, negligently shot in the direction of the claimant, Lewis, while hunting. The claimant was injured, but was hit by only one of the potential defendants.[26] Hence, the claimant could show only that it was 50 per cent likely that Cook (or Akenhead) had shot him. Accordingly, Locke J held that the claimant had failed to establish factual causation. However, a majority of the Supreme Court of Canada held otherwise.

In *Sindell*, the defendants were drug manufacturers who produced and marketed diethylstilbestrol (DES). The claimants' mothers took DES during pregnancy and the claimants developed ovarian cancer as a result. However,

---

[24] A Porat and A Stein, *Tort Liability Under Uncertainty* (Oxford University Press, Oxford, 2001) 87.

[25] 607 P 2d 924 (Calif SC 1980). In the following, I treat the case as one of negligence and ignore the special rules concerning 'products liability' that exist in the US.

[26] In fact, it is not clear in either *Cook v Lewis* or *Summers v Tice* whether the claimants were hit by only one defendant or by both. In each, however, the Courts dealt with the issues on the basis that the claimants had been shot by only one defendant.

many potential defendants produced DES, and no individual claimant could show specifically which manufacturer produced the DES taken by her mother. Hence, each claimant failed to show on the balance of probabilities that any particular defendant had caused her injuries. Nevertheless, in a 4–3 decision, the Supreme Court of California found the defendants liable.

In *Cook v Lewis*, although the claimant could not show on the balance of probabilities that he was injured by the defendant, Cartwright J ruled that the burden of proof should be reversed, in accordance with the decision of the Supreme Court of California in *Summers v Tice*:

> When we consider the relative position of the parties and the results that would flow if plaintiff was required to pin the injury on one of the defendants only, a requirement that the burden of proof on that subject be shifted to defendants becomes manifest. They are both wrongdoers—both negligent toward plaintiff. They brought about a situation where the negligence of one of them injured the plaintiff, hence, it should rest with them each to absolve himself if he can. The injured party has been placed by defendants in the unfair position of pointing to which defendant caused the harm. If one can escape the other may also and plaintiff is remediless. Ordinarily defendants are in a far better position to offer evidence to determine which one caused the injury.[27]

In an important article on corrective justice and causation, Arthur Ripstein and Benjamin Zipursky support this reasoning.[28] They argue that, while the burden of proof usually lies on the claimant to establish causation, this is by no means essential to the structure of the law.[29] Instead, Ripstein and Zipursky insist that, as a matter of principle, the law may decide for either party when the evidence is evenly balanced. Usually, the claimant must meet the burden, because the claimant is asking the state to interfere with the defendant. Hence, usually when the evidence is evenly balanced the claimant will lose. However, this should be reversed when the normal rule 'is guaranteed to lead to a misfortune being left with the wrong person'.[30] According to Ripstein and Zipursky:

> On the cusp, a court normally has no choice but to take a 50 percent chance of making a mistake. In *Summers* [*v Tice* and *Cook v Lewis*], though, the ordinary rule would have guaranteed a mistake; the changed rule still enables the plaintiff to proceed against the defendant who did not in fact cause his injury, but the chance of this error is only 50 percent, which is ordinarily deemed acceptable. Although ordinary procedures ordinarily approximate justice, employing them in this case would ensure injustice.[31]

---

[27] *Cook v Lewis* [1951] SCR 830, 842; citation from *Summers v Tice* 199 P 2d 1 (Calif SC 1948) 4.

[28] A Ripstein and BC Zipursky, 'Corrective Justice in an Age of Mass Torts' in GJ Postema (ed), *Philosophy and the Law of Torts* (Cambridge University Press, Cambridge, 2001). Note that Ripstein and Zipursky refer to *Summers v Tice* rather than to *Cook v Lewis*. However, their analysis is equally applicable to the latter case.

[29] Ripstein and Zipursky, above n28, 241.

[30] *Ibid*, 242.

[31] *Ibid*. See also *Fairchild v Glenhaven Funeral Services Ltd* [2002] UKHL 22, [2003] 1 AC 32, 69 (Lord Nicholls).

The claim, then, is that finding for the defendant in these cases would guarantee injustice, because it would mean that a claimant who definitely deserves to be compensated fails to recover. On the other hand, finding for the claimant may impose an injustice on a particular defendant, but the chance of that being so is only 50 per cent. Hence, imposing liability on a defendant is the most likely way to avoid injustice.

Ripstein and Zipursky insist that this argument would not apply if there were more than two hunters who shot in the direction of the claimant. This is because the probability of any one defendant having injured the claimant would be only 33.33 per cent and hence, even reversing the burden, each defendant could show that it was 66.67 per cent likely that he did not shoot the claimant, and so the claimant must fail. Consequently, Ripstein and Zipursky conclude that the solution adopted by the majority in *Summers v Tice*, and by implication the majority in *Cook v Lewis*, has nothing to offer in *Sindell* where there were more than two potential defendants.[32]

However, Ripstein and Zipursky support recovery in *Sindell*. They do so by arguing that 'the plaintiffs had no real difficulty in proving that each of the defendants had breached a duty of non-injury to the claimants'.[33] Accordingly, 'the problem in *Sindell* is not exactly about causation'.[34] Instead, Ripstein and Zipursky insist that the issue is one of the burden and standard of proof.[35] Ultimately, Ripstein and Zipursky maintain that the burden must lie with the defendants. This is because, if the burden was with each claimant, no claimant would be able to show on the balance of probabilities that she was injured by any defendant. But this would mean that each defendant:

> implicitly concedes responsibility for injuries to some other plaintiff. To allow [the argument] would be to allow each defendant to assert serially both that it was not responsible for [one plaintiff's] injuries (when confronted by her) and that it was responsible for them (when confronted by others). Such a merry go round of defences would have allowed each defendant to show, as to each plaintiff, that its negligence had not caused her any injury, even while conceding that it had caused a significant number of injuries of precisely that type to some, unidentifiable members of the pool of plaintiffs.[36]

This analysis is ingenious. However, there are important problems with it. With respect to *Sindell*, the major problem is that the argument appears to work only because *Sindell* was a class action. Recall Ripstein and Zipursky's claim that 'the plaintiffs had no real difficulty in proving that each of the defendants had breached a duty of non-injury to the plaintiffs'.[37] This is true if both the defendants and the claimants are taken as a group. But if they are taken individually,

---

[32] Ripstein and Zipursky, above n28, 243.
[33] *Ibid*, 232.
[34] *Ibid*.
[35] *Ibid*, 233.
[36] *Ibid*, 234.
[37] *Ibid*, 232.

then it is clearly not true. Ripstein and Zipursky are able to conclude that the main issue is not one of causation only because we know, or at least it is likely, that each defendant injured some of the claimants. Therefore, Ripstein and Zipursky's argument is that the defendants must be liable because, taken together, their actions materialised in injury to the claimants, also taken as a group. Here, the focus is not on the relationship between one claimant and one defendant, but between groups of persons.

This is almost conceded when Ripstein and Zipursky argue that the difficulties of proof for the claimants arose because the defendants engaged in generic marketing that meant that it was impossible to trace the drugs to particular defendants.[38] This argument suggests that, because their drugs were marketed together, the defendants should be liable because they were, in some sense, a single entity. But that was not in fact the case.

Ripstein and Zipursky also treat the claimants as a unit. The crux of Ripstein and Zipursky's argument can be represented as follows:

1. D_1 states that on the balance of probabilities he did not injure C_1.
2. This implies that D_1 injured some other claimant (C_n).
3. But D_1 could use the argument made in 1 on $C_2, C_3 \ldots C_n$.
4. Hence, D_1 would not be liable to any claimant.
5. But 2 and 4 are inconsistent.

This relies on the notion that the claimants can make their case together, as a unit. But this is a departure from corrective justice. The fact that D_1 cannot be liable to C_n has no bearing on the relationship between D_1 and C_1. The fact remains that it is more likely than not that D_1 did not injure C_1 and so it appears that the claimant must lose, even if the burden is reversed.

This failure of Ripstein and Zipursky's position can also be seen in the following comment: '[g]iven the evidence that each of the defendants had completed a tort, the only remaining question concerns the identity of the plaintiff against whom they have committed it'.[39] On this view, we have guilty defendants and innocent claimants, and the task of the court is to put them together. But, according to corrective justice, the defendant commits no wrong against the claimant unless she creates an unreasonable risk that *materialises* in the claimant's injury. Though the defendants may have acted unethically, Ripstein and Zipursky do not show that any defendant committed a wrong against any particular claimant. Hence, no claimant can establish that any defendant caused her an injustice in corrective justice. According to corrective justice, there is no inconsistency between 2 and 4 above, as we are interested in a defendant's relationship with a claimant, not in the defendant's relationship with someone else or to some other set of persons. Hence, Ripstein and

---

[38] Ripstein and Zipursky, above n28, 234–5.
[39] *Ibid*, 234.

Zipursky's analysis is in tension with one of the main functions of the causation enquiry: to link particular acts of wrongdoing to particular injuries, to link particular defendants to particular claimants.[40]

Ripstein and Zipursky's discussion of *Summers v Tice*, and by implication *Cook v Lewis*, is also flawed along the same lines as is their exploration of *Sindell*. First, Ripstein and Zipursky are wrong to conclude that their argument applies only to cases in which there are two potential defendants. Recall that the argument was that a defendant should be liable in *Summers v Tice* and *Cook v Lewis* because finding for the defendant would guarantee—ie would make it 100 per cent likely—that a deserving claimant would go without recovery, while finding for the claimant would make it only 50 per cent likely that an innocent defendant would be found liable. Imagine now that there were three hunters who negligently shot in the direction of the claimant. In this case, a finding of no liability would also make it 100 per cent likely that a deserving claimant would go without recovery. Conversely, finding for the claimant would make it only 66.67 per cent likely that an innocent defendant would be found liable. According to Ripstein and Zipursky's argument, here too justice seems to lie with the claimant. The most likely way to avoid injustice on this view is, *contra* Ripstein and Zipursky, to impose liability on a defendant. In fact, this conclusion will follow no matter how many hunters are involved.

This is not necessarily a problem for Ripstein and Zipursky because, as we see below, the conclusion that three or more defendants should be liable is attractive. However, while three or more hunters should be liable in such cases, Ripstein and Zipursky's argument cannot show why that is. This is because Ripstein and Zipursky ignore the relationship between the parties. They are right to say that, if liability is imposed in *Summers v Tice* and in *Cook v Lewis*, then the chance of an innocent potential defendant being found liable is 50 per cent. But they are wrong to insist that, if liability is not imposed, the chance of a deserving claimant going without recovery is 100 per cent *as between the parties*. This is because, as between the claimant and any one defendant, the chance that the claimant should recover from this particular defendant is 50 per cent. Hence, the justice is evenly balanced between the parties. In the eyes of corrective justice, it is no more or less unjust for the claimant to recover from the defendant if it was not the defendant who shot the claimant than it is unjust for the claimant to fail to recover from the defendant if it was the defendant who shot the claimant. Moreover, as discussed above, corrective justice calls for the burden of proof to be on the claimant.

We cannot say that the claimant is deserving of recovery and leave it at that. It is irrelevant to corrective justice that the claimant deserves recovery from *someone*—viz either the actual defendant or the potential defendant. In corrective justice, it is necessary to say that the claimant is deserving of recovery *from*

---

[40]   This was analysed in the first section of ch 12. See also EJ Weinrib, 'A Step Forward in Factual Causation' (1975) 38 *MLR* 518, 518–19.

some particular person. Hence, as against one defendant, the chance that the claimant deserves recovery is only 50 per cent.

Despite the promise offered by Ripstein and Zipursky's arguments, then, they fail to justify the results in *Cook v Lewis*, *Summers v Tice* or *Sindell*. Accordingly, I now present an alternative position.

Recall the claim made in *Summers v Tice*, endorsed by Cartwright J in *Cook v Lewis*, that both potential defendants were wrongdoers.[41] What does this mean? It could mean simply that they were prima facie wrongdoers in the sense defined in Chapter 12: ie they violated the standard of care, owed the claimant a duty of care and the injury that the claimant suffered was not remote. But this does not appear to capture the full sense in which the defendants were wrong-doers. Both defendants would have been wrongdoers in this sense even if the claimant had remained uninjured. Rather, it is the fact of the claimant's injury coupled with the circumstances that mean that the claimant cannot prove who caused that injury that makes these two defendants wrongdoers in a stronger sense than merely prima facie wrongdoers. But how are we to make sense of this claim? If one of the potential defendants did not hit the claimant, then how could he be a wrongdoer in more than the prima facie sense? In his extra-ordinary judgment in *Cook v Lewis*, Rand J attempted to answer this question:

> [I]n this case, the essential obstacle to proof is the fact of multiple discharges so related as to confuse their individual effects: it is that fact that bars final proof. But if the victim, having brought guilt down to one or both of two persons before the court, can bring home to either of them a further wrong done him in relation to his remedial right of making that proof, then I should say that on accepted principles, the barrier to it can and should be removed. . . . What, then, the culpable actor has done by his initial negligent act is, first, to have set in motion a dangerous force which embraces the injured person within the scope of its probable mischief; and next, in conjunction with circumstances which he must be held to contemplate, to have made more difficult if not impossible the means of proving the possible damaging results of his own act or the similar results of the act of another. He has violated not only the victim's substantive right to security, but he has also culpably impaired the latter's remedial right of establishing liability. By confusing his act with environmental conditions, he has, in effect, destroyed the victim's power of proof.[42]

One way of reading this is to take Rand J as arguing that the claimant had a right to the *evidence* he needed to establish a cause of action. On this view, as both defendants in *Cook v Lewis* interfered with that evidence, both defendants interfered with the claimant's rights.[43]

However, this view is highly problematic. Rights to evidence are rights to things (not necessarily corporeal things). Moreover, in order to bind both defen-

---

[41] *Cook v Lewis* [1951] SCR 830, 842; citation from *Summers v Tice* 199 P 2d 1 (Calif SC 1948) 4.
[42] *Cook v Lewis* [1951] SCR 830, 831–2.
[43] A Porat and A Stein, *Tort Liability Under Uncertainty* (Oxford University Press, Oxford, 2001) ch 6. See also A Porat and A Stein, 'Indeterminate Causation and Apportionment of Damages: An Essay on Holtby, Allen, and Fairchild' (2003) 23 *OJLS* 667.

dants in *Cook v Lewis*, including the defendant who did not shoot the claimant (whoever that was), the right to the evidence must have generated obligations in all comers. In other words, if there was a right to evidence, that right must have been a property right *in rem*. But the law of property governs whether such rights exist. They cannot be manufactured 'in tort' in order to generate desired results in tricky cases. Sometimes there will be such property rights, but usually there will not. Tellingly, there were no such rights in *Cook v Lewis*.

In any case, I doubt that the above accurately captures Rand J's intention. Nor was his claim that the burden of proof should be reversed or that some risk should be transferred to the defendant.[44] Rather, Rand J's suggestion was that the remedial right is a right that belongs to the law of persons as the term was defined in Chapter 6. Hence, in *Cook v Lewis*, *both defendants harmed the claimant*: one shot the claimant, while the other or both injured the claimant's personal remedial right to prove liability. Hence, there is no issue of causation, as we know for certain that both defendants violated the claimant's rights.

Though Rand J's position points to a major breakthrough, the difficulty with his proposal is the unargued assertion that a claimant has a right to establish a case against a defendant. There is no such right. If there were then, at the very least, the burden of proof would always be on the defendant. This is not the position of the common law. However, what we need is not a replacement for Rand J's view but merely a way of limiting its application to the appropriate cases. I provide that in the following.

The solution to the problem presented by *Cook v Lewis* is again to be found by focusing on the normative rather than the factual. I argue that both defendants injured the claimant in *Cook v Lewis*, though only one caused material injury. This is because both defendants interfered with the claimant's rights.

In line with the argument of the previous chapters, a claimant has a good cause of action against a defendant only if the defendant violated a right that the claimant held against the defendant. In *Cook v Lewis*, the relevant right was the right to bodily integrity. Hence, the claimant ought to have been able to recover from either Cook or Akenhead only if he could prove on the balance of probabilities that one or both of those parties had violated his right to bodily integrity. Note, then, that the subject matter of our enquiry is the *right* to bodily integrity. It is not the claimant's body. We are not asking whether the defendant violated the claimant's body, but whether he violated the claimant's right to bodily integrity. The first question, then, is whether it is possible to violate a person's right to bodily integrity without touching his body.

The converse is certainly the case. It is possible to touch, even to damage, someone's body without violating her right to bodily integrity. If I unintentionally and non-negligently cut someone's arm off, then I have clearly damaged that person's body, but I have not violated that person's right to bodily integrity.

---

[44] Compare HLA Hart and T Honoré, *Causation in the Law*, 2nd edn (Clarendon Press, Oxford, 1985) 424–5.

Hence, the body and the right to bodily integrity are distinct. But is it possible to do the reverse: to violate someone's bodily integrity without touching their body?

Apparently, the common law answers this question in the affirmative. At least that is so if we assume that the tort of assault protects the right to bodily integrity. This assumption seems reasonable, because the torts of assault and battery are usually thought of as close relations and the criminal law actions are now typically treated synonymously, indicating that they are likely to respond to violations of the same interest. Although this is not the appropriate place to analyse the tort of assault in detail, it appears that the law regards one's right to bodily integrity as extending beyond one's body to protect one from the *apprehension* of unwanted physical contact. One can violate another's bodily integrity without touching him by assaulting him.

The question now is whether noting the distinction between bodily integrity and the body helps us to solve the riddle presented by *Cook v Lewis*. The argument will be that, in acting as he did, the defendant who did not hit the claimant nevertheless violated the claimant's right to bodily integrity.

An impediment to understanding this argument is that we find it difficult to see monetary awards as genuine compensation for personal injury. Accordingly, the argument will be clearer if we change the example for a moment and imagine a case in which genuine compensation can obviously be given. Imagine a case in which D_1 and D_2 independently set out to steal C's car. D_2 was successful, but, while C can prove that either D_1 or D_2 stole the car, he cannot prove which of the two it was. Moreover, the reason C cannot prove which defendant stole the car was that they were both attempting to steal the car at the same time. C wants the car to be returned or, failing that, damages for its loss. Imagine also that this is a case in which a court will be prepared to order the return of the car if C is able to prove who possesses it.

In the eyes of the private law, D_2 is a wrongdoer to C because he violated C's right to the car, inter alia, by depriving C of the physical possession of the vehicle. Consequently, if D_1 had not tried to steal C's car, then C would have been able to sue D_2 and regain possession of the vehicle. But D_1 did act, and this prevents C from proving that it was D_2 who stole the car. Hence, if D_1 cannot be liable, then D_1's attempt to steal the car would have the consequence of depriving C of physical possession of the car.

Now, that is not enough to make D_1 liable. The mere fact that D_1 did something that had the consequence of depriving C of the car is insufficient for liability. The defendant's employees in *Palsgraf v Long Island Railroad Co*[45] deprived Ms Palsgraf of her health, but that did not make them liable. However, in our example, the consequence to the claimant connects with D_1's prima facie wrongdoing. That is, D_1 tried to steal C's car and stealing is wrong, inter alia, because it deprives the owner (or legal possessor) of physical possession of the

---

[45]   162 NE 99 (NY CA 1928).

asset, and, on the assumption that D_1 cannot be liable, D_1's attempt to steal the car deprives C of physical possession of the car. In other words, D_1's act was prima facie wrongful, inter alia, because it would have the consequence of depriving C of physical possession of the car and, on the assumption that D_1 cannot be liable, D_1's action would deprive C of physical possession of the car. Accordingly, the assumption must be false and D_1 must be liable. This is not necessarily to say that D_1 *converted* C's car, but it is to say that in trying to steal C's car in a way that prevented C from recovering the car from D_2, ie in a way that deprived C of physical possession of the car, D_1 wronged C.

We must now apply this argument to *Cook v Lewis*. Crucial to the argument is the notion that an adequately compensated for injury is no longer an injury in the eyes of the law. Hence, if A steals B's car and then adequately compensates B, the law regards B as no longer suffering an injury. This is despite the fact that B does not get his car back. The factual injury remains, but it is no longer legally significant. Similarly, if C shoots D in the arm causing a physical injury and if C compensates D, then in the eyes of the law D is no longer suffering an injury even though he will still have a wounded arm. Again, the physical injury remains, but it is no longer legally relevant. We see once more that injuries at law are normative, not purely physical, entities.

Imagine that it was Akenhead who shot the claimant. According to this scenario, Akenhead wronged the claimant by causing the physical injury. If Cook had not fired, then, Lewis would have been able to recover for his injury from Akenhead and, in the eyes of the law, Lewis would no longer be injured. Now, on the assumption that Cook cannot be liable, the fact that he fired in the direction of the claimant means that Lewis cannot recover from Akenhead. That means that Cook injured Lewis in the eyes of the law, because Cook's action created an unreasonable risk of the very injury that Lewis suffered and Lewis is suffering that injury (ie Lewis cannot get compensation from Akenhead) because of Cook's action. Hence, the assumption must be false, Cook must be liable.

Note that the claim is not that in firing at the same time as Akenhead Cook caused a right to come into existence. The argument is that Cook violated Lewis' primary right to bodily integrity, though he did not (or on the assumption that he did not) harm Lewis' body. The argument does not rely on any new right, but on the one that always existed: the right to bodily integrity. Cook is liable for violating Lewis' primary right to bodily integrity, an action that he did by creating a real risk of the injury that Lewis suffered and causing that injury by preventing Lewis from recovering from Akenhead. Hence, even on the assumption that it was Akenhead who shot the claimant, Cook violated the claimant's bodily integrity.

At this point is it important to recall that it is not sufficient for liability that a defendant merely act in such a way that the claimant cannot vindicate his rights against another defendant. Imagine that D_1 shot C in circumstances that meant that C could not prove that that occurred, except that the incident was captured on closed circuit television. However, D_2 negligently destroyed the videotape showing the incident. Here, C cannot sue D_2 for violating his right to bodily integrity. This is because D_2 was not negligent in creating a risk of physical injury to C. The result in *Cook v Lewis* should be imitated only if the defendant who did not physically injure the claimant—or who we assume *arguendo* did not physically injure the claimant—created an unreasonable risk of that injury, ie the physical injury that the claimant suffered. An alternative result would mean that the claimant would be recovering for a violation of a different right, and a right that would have to be manufactured to justify recovery.

Before I discuss further consequences of this view, I should admit that, at least initially, the argument is not particularly intuitive. But I have two responses. First, no such arguments are intuitive at first. We are dealing with an area of great intuitive conflict and it is unreasonable in such circumstances to expect intuitive explanations.[46] Moreover, given the difficulty of reaching an intuitive judgement about *Cook v Lewis* itself, it is not surprising that the theory presented here to justify it is also intuitively uncomfortable. Secondly, if we are looking for an explanation of why both defendants were wrongdoers, and not merely prima facie wrongdoers, then some explanation of the kind is required. This is not an attempt to insulate the theory from criticism, however. If in time the unintuitive features of the theory do not fade—or indeed if they cannot be revised—then of course the theory must be rejected. In any case, I go on now to explore the consequences of the theory.

The conclusion reached above is invariant to the number of potential defendants. If there were three hunters who negligently fired in the direction of the claimant, then all three would have violated the claimant's right to bodily integrity, and so all should be liable. Using labels again, in the following we are interested in D_1's liability. Assuming that D_3 hit the claimant, D_1 and D_2 must also be liable because they were both prima facie negligent in creating an unreasonable risk of the injury that the claimant suffered and caused that injury by preventing the claimant recovering from D_3. Hence, even on the assumption that it was D_3 who shot the claimant, D_1 and D_2 must also be liable. The same argument applies if there were four or more potential defendants.

Moreover, the liability of the party who did not shoot the claimant in *Cook v Lewis* is in no way parasitic on the liability of the party who did shoot the claimant. Assuming again that Akenhead shot Lewis, given *the fact* that Akenhead shot Lewis, Cook's shooting interfered with the claimant's bodily integrity. But the argument is not that, because Akenhead *should be liable* to Lewis, Cook should also be liable. Cook's liability to Lewis is direct: it arises because Cook violated one of Lewis' rights. In this sense, then, *Cook v Lewis* is no different from the novus actus interveniens cases explored in Chapter 4. The position, then, is not that Cook was in any way responsible for what Akenhead did.

---

[46] Compare the account of the clash between intuitions such as 'what you don't know can't hurt you' and 'it is bad when people are unfaithful' explored in T Nagel, 'Death' (1970) 4 *Nous* 73.

   Finally, if the defendant did not shoot the claimant and has evidence to that effect, the defendant can escape liability by presenting that evidence. For instance, if Cook could have presented evidence suggesting that it was Akenhead who shot Lewis, then Cook's firing would not have interfered with Lewis' right to bodily integrity as it would not have prevented Lewis from recovering from Akenhead. By showing that the chance that Akenhead shot the claimant was greater than 50 per cent, Cook would have removed the claimant's inability to vindicate his right to bodily integrity and thus would no longer be interfering with that right.

   This also follows in the three hunters case, but only if the defendant can show that one of the other hunters was more than 50 per cent likely to have shot the claimant. For instance, if D_1 can show on the balance of probabilities that D_3 shot the claimant, then the claimant can recover from D_3 and hence D_1 is not interfering with the claimant's right to bodily integrity. But this does not succeed unless D_1 can establish on the balance of probabilities that D_3 (or D_2) shot the claimant. Imagine that D_1 shows that the chance that she shot the claimant was 25 per cent, the chance that D_2 shot the claimant was 30 per cent and the chance that D_3 shot the claimant was 45 per cent. Here, D_1 cannot escape liability. This is because this would leave the claimant unable to vindicate her right to bodily integrity as against either D_2 or D_3. Hence, D_1 would still be interfering with the claimant's right. (We could not say that, given that D_1 is out of the picture as it were, the chance that D_2 shot the claimant was 40 per cent while the chance that D_3 shot the claimant was 60 per cent. It is true that the chance that D_3 *as opposed to* D_2 injured the claimant is 60 per cent, but that is not the relevant question. That question is: what is the chance that D_3 shot the claimant? The answer to that question remains 45 per cent.)

   The reasoning supported here is directly applicable to *Sindell*. As it were, in that case many defendants shot in the direction of the claimants and no defendant could show on the balance of probabilities that any one defendant was the cause of the physical injuries of any one of the claimants. Hence, all defendants interfered with all of the claimants' rights. This similarity between *Sindell* and *Cook v Lewis* is somewhat obscured by the fact that it is difficult to see a defendant who is not the factual cause of the claimant's physical injury as the proximate cause of that injury.[47] This is due to the infelicity of the term 'proximate *cause*'. It must be remembered that x counts as the proximate cause of y if y is a reasonably foreseeable outcome of x. In *Sindell*, the injury to each claimant was a reasonably foreseeable consequence of each defendant's manufacture of DES, whether or not that consequence materialised.[48] Hence, although we can be sure that no defendant

---

[47] Recall that we are ignoring the 'products liability' context of this litigation.

[48] However, both *Sindell* and the similar case, *Hymowitz v Eli Lilly* 539 NE 2d 1069 (NY CA 1989), employ methods not countenanced here. In *Sindell*, liability was apportioned. I argued against apportionment of liability, as opposed to apportionment of damages, in the previous chapter. In *Hymowitz*, it was declared that a defendant could be held liable even if he could prove that he was not the factual cause of the claimant's injury. Naturally, these findings are inconsistent with my position. It is uncontroversial, however, that these features of the cases are highly anomalous. In

was the factual cause of every claimant's physical injury, we can also be sure that each defendant was a proximate cause of every claimant's physical injury.

Mirroring the treatment of causation in the previous chapter, we end this discussion by distinguishing between a number of fact patterns in order to determine whether the solution presented here works outside the relatively simple cases we have been discussing. Again, people who are potentially liable are referred to as defendants or represented by the symbol 'D'. Those who played some causal role in the claimant's injury but who are not potentially liable are referred to as blameless parties and labelled 'B'. Sometimes claimants are labelled C. In each pattern, we must assume that it is not possible to trace a particular injury to a specific action. The uncertainty, then, surrounds causal responsibility for instances of damage (though at times we know that both actions caused some injury).

When there is one claimant:

1. D_1 and D_2 injured the claimant.[49]
2. Either D_1 or D_2 injured the claimant.
3. Either D or B injured the claimant.

When there is more than one claimant:

4. Either D_1 or D_2 acted negligently towards C_1 while the other defendant acted negligently towards C_2. C_1 and C_2 were injured.
5. Either D_1 or D_2 acted negligently towards C_1 while the other defendant acted negligently towards C_2. C_1 only was injured.

We have seen that D_1 and D_2 are liable in pattern 2. This must imply that both defendants are also liable in pattern 1. However, the defendant cannot be liable in pattern 3. This is because, if the claimant was injured by B, then his rights have not been violated. Hence, as the claimant cannot prove that his rights were violated at all, D's failure to reveal the cause of the claimant's injury cannot amount to a violation of the claimant's rights.

Nor should there be any recovery in pattern 4 or 5. This may seem counterintuitive, particularly in pattern 4. There we know that both defendants have negligently caused injury to a claimant, yet they escape liability. However, this is a product of the character of tort law and of corrective justice. Unless the claimants can make their case together—that is, as a unit—then neither can

---

my view, in *Sindell* each manufacturer should have been liable for all the claimants' injuries, though the damages should have been apportioned in accordance with the relevant contribution rules. See also A Ripstein and BC Zipursky, 'Corrective Justice in an Age of Mass Torts' in GJ Postema (ed), *Philosophy and the Law of Torts* (Cambridge University Press, Cambridge, 2001).

[49] It may appear that there is no causal issue here, as we are certain that each defendant harmed the claimant. However, the issue concerns liability for instances of damage. Say, for example, that one defendant, though we do not know which one, injured one of the claimant's arms while the other, we do not know who, injured the claimant's legs. Here, the claimant cannot prove factual causation on the balance of probabilities against either defendant in relation to any instance of damage.

prove on the balance of probabilities that either defendant wronged her. This is because neither claimant can establish factual causation against any defendant.

B. Applying the Principled Approach to Cases of Factual Uncertainty

In the light of the above, I now examine three perplexing decisions of the House of Lords: *McGhee, Wilshire* and *Fairchild*. Merely applying the criteria outlined above and in Chapter 12 cannot solve these cases, because the uncertainty extends to the issue of which fact patterns the cases instantiate. Nevertheless, the preceding analysis can be used to clarify the background structure against which these cases should be decided and, hence, clear the way for their solution. This discussion is very important because it again shows the strength of the principled approach and the ability of that approach, when taken seriously, to solve problems that appear to require the addition of policy.

(i) McGhee[50]

The claimant's employment necessitated that his skin be covered in abrasive brick dust until the end of his shift. Moreover, because appropriate washing facilities were not provided at the place of employment, the claimant could not remove the dust until after his return home. As a consequence of his exposure to the dust, the claimant developed dermatitis. It was agreed that the defendant was negligent in failing to provide washing facilities, but not for exposing the claimant to dust at work. The defendant maintained that the claimant could not prove that the dermatitis was a result of the failure to provide washing facilities. In fact, the defendant contended, it was highly likely that McGhee would have developed dermatitis even if a shower had been provided.

According to Lord Reid, the expert testimony called in *McGhee* led to four important deductions. First, dermatitis is caused by repeated abrasions of the skin. Secondly, brick dust on skin causes abrasions. Thirdly, if the claimant did not wash after work, then the abrasions would have continued until the claimant washed at home. Fourthly, abrasions have a cumulative effect in the sense that the longer one is exposed to abrasion the more likely one is to develop dermatitis. As Lord Reid noted, there were two possible conclusions. The first was that the claimant's dermatitis resulted when he had received sufficient exposure to the dust. That is, the claimant developed his injury at the moment when the aggregate of his exposure to abrasive dust reached a certain threshold level. This would mean that, at this moment, each exposure to abrasive dust would have been necessary for the injury. According to this possibility, it is certain that

---

[50] Throughout this discussion, I accept the facts as presented in the House of Lords. However, see A Beever, 'Cause-In-Fact: Two Steps Out of the Mire' (2001) 51 *University of Toronto Law Journal* 327, 360–1.

the defendant's negligence was a cause of the claimant's injury. However, the second possibility was that each abrasion merely *increased the chance* of the claimant developing dermatitis in a sense examined below.[51] On this reading, we cannot be sure that the failure to provide showers was a cause of the claimant's injury.

In finding for the claimant, Lord Reid argued:

> I am inclined to think that the evidence points to the former view. But in a field were so little appears to be known with certainty I could not say that that is proved. . . . But I think that in cases like this we must take a broader view of causation. The medical evidence is to the effect that the fact that the man had to cycle home caked with grime and sweat added materially to the risk that this disease might develop. It does not and could not explain just why that is so. But experience shews that it is so. *Plainly that must be because what happens while the man remains unwashed can have a causative effect, although just how the cause operates is uncertain. I cannot accept the view . . . that once the man left the brick kiln he left behind the causes which made him liable to develop dermatitis. That seems to me quite inconsistent with a proper interpretation of the medical evidence.* Nor can I accept the distinction drawn by the Lord Ordinary between materially increasing the risk that the disease will occur and making a material contribution to its occurrence.[52]

Despite recent reinterpretations of this passage, explored below, the most natural reading is that Lord Reid said that, on the balance of probabilities, the defendant's negligence caused the claimant's injury. That view was also supported by Lords Simon, Kilbrandon and Salmon.[53] All of their Lordships, rightly or wrongly, insisted that the claimant in *McGhee* could establish causation on the balance of probabilities.[54] Hence, in *Wilsher*, Lord Bridge correctly insisted that *McGhee* 'laid down no new principle of law whatever. On the contrary, it affirmed the principle that the onus of proving causation lies on the pursuer or plaintiff.'[55]

Conversely, in *Fairchild*, four out of five of their Lordships rejected Lord Bridge's interpretation of the judgments in *McGhee* and insisted that *McGhee* varied the default approach to factual causation.[56] Lord Bingham enunciated five reasons for reaching this conclusion.

First, Lord Bingham argued that 'the House was deciding a question of law. Lord Reid expressly said so . . . The other opinions, save perhaps that of Lord Kilbrandon, cannot be read as decisions of fact or as orthodox applications of settled law'.[57] The passage in question from Lord Reid's judgment follows his

---

[51] *McGhee v National Coal Board* [1972] 1 WLR 1, 3–5 (HL Sc).

[52] *Ibid*, 4–5 (emphasis added).

[53] *Ibid*, 8 (Lord Simon), 10 (Lord Kilbrandon), 12–13 (Lord Salmon).

[54] The exception is Lord Wilberforce who argued that the burden of proof should be reversed: *ibid*, 6.

[55] *Wilsher v Essex Area Health Authority* [1988] AC 1074, 1090 (HL).

[56] See also Lord Hope, 'James McGhee—A Second Mrs. Donoghue?' (2003) 62 *CLJ* 587, 597.

[57] *Fairchild v Glenhaven Funeral Services Ltd* [2002] UKHL 22, [2003] 1 AC 32, 55. See also Lord Hope, above n56, 598.

Lordship's brief summary of the facts (216 words), and introduces his Lordship's discussion of the issues with the claim that the case 'raises a difficult question of law'.[58] It is specious to take this as proof that Lord Reid's decision turned on the introduction of a novel approach to causation. Moreover, as we have seen, it cannot be correct to claim that it is *impossible* to interpret the other judgments in *McGhee* as turning on an interpretation of the facts.

Lord Bingham's second argument was that the relevant question in *McGhee* was whether the claimant should succeed even though he could not show on the balance of probabilities that his injuries were caused by the defendant's negligence. But this question cannot be settled by reference to the facts. Hence, the question in *McGhee* must have been one of law.[59] This argument is circular. If we assume that the claimant could not establish his case on the balance of probabilities, then the issue in *McGhee* was not one of fact but must have been one of law. But this assumes the truth of the issue at hand.

Thirdly, Lord Bingham maintained that, on the ordinary approach, there would have been no liability in *McGhee*. However, Lord Bingham insisted, their Lordships in *McGhee* regarded that as a plainly unjust result. Hence, their Lordships had to replace the ordinary approach with an alternative view.[60] Again, this argument is circular as it relies on the assumption that the claimant could not establish his case on the balance of probabilities. Most importantly, Lord Bingham misinterpreted the expert testimony in *McGhee*, claiming that 'it was not open to the House to draw a factual inference that the breach probably had caused the damage: such an inference was expressly contradicted by the medical experts on both sides'.[61] That is not true. The medical experts said that it was not possible to prove—in a sense of proof to be examined below—that the defendant's negligence caused the claimant's injury, but, as the medical experts were not applying the balance of probabilities, that does not imply that it was proved that the defendant did not cause the plaintiff's injury. If, for instance, I say that it was not shown to be 90 per cent likely that the defendant caused the claimant's injury, that does not mean that it was 90 per cent likely that the defendant did not cause the claimant's injury. In *McGhee*, the medical experts refused to be drawn on whether the defendant did *or did not* cause the claimant's injury.

Lord Bingham's fourth and fifth arguments are more impressive and more important. They must also be examined together. The fourth is that their Lordships in *McGhee* could not have concluded that the claimant's injury was caused by the defendant's negligence on the balance of probabilities, because that was inconsistent with the medical evidence.[62] The fifth argument is that

---

[58] *McGhee v National Coal Board* [1972] 1 WLR 1, 3 (HL Sc).
[59] *Fairchild v Glenhaven Funeral Services Ltd* [2002] UKHL 22, [2003] 1 AC 32, 55.
[60] *Ibid*, 55, 66.
[61] *Ibid*, 55.
[62] *Ibid*. See also *ibid*, 70–1 (Lord Nicholls), 75–6 (Lord Hoffmann). Compare *ibid*, 86–90 (Lord Hutton).

their Lordships in *McGhee* concluded that the claimant's injury was caused by the defendant's negligence, not because the defendant's negligence caused that injury, but because the defendant's negligence *increased the risk* of that injury. Hence, causation was inferred because of risk creation. But increasing the risk of something does not equal causing it. Therefore, *McGhee* did indeed introduce a new approach to causation.[63]

Although it will be important to examine the fourth argument in detail below, it is already apparent that it invalid. Even if it were true that the medical evidence in *McGhee* demonstrated that one could not reasonably come to the conclusion that the claimant's injury was caused by the defendant's negligence, that could not show that their Lordships in *McGhee* did not reach that conclusion. Unless we suppose that their Lordships in *McGhee* were infallible as to the impact of the medical evidence, it is possible that they made a *mistake* in interpreting that evidence. Hence, even on the assumptions made by Lord Bingham, there is no evidence of any novel approach to deciding issues of factual causation in *McGhee*.

More interestingly, as I now argue, their Lordships in *McGhee* did not incorrectly interpret the medical evidence.

First, it is important to be clear about the nature of the uncertainty in *McGhee*. Crucially, the experts did not say that there was no proof of a causal link between dust and dermatitis. If the position had been that there was no proof that dust did or did not cause dermatitis, then the claimant should have failed. This is because it is a sound principle of explanation, in the natural sciences and elsewhere, that propositions should be accepted only if there is adequate evidence to support them. Accordingly, if it were impossible to prove that dust did or did not cause dermatitis, then the correct conclusion would be that it could not be proven that dust causes dermatitis. But that is not this case. In *McGhee*, the experts were clear that dust causes dermatitis. The issue was only that it was impossible to prove specifically whether the dust that was on the claimant's skin *after work* caused the claimant's dermatitis.

It is certainly true that increasing the risk of an event is not the same as causing the event.[64] Recall the desert traveller example explored in the previous chapter. The victim was a desert traveller who died because D_1 emptied his water supply. Moreover, D_2 had poisoned the water supply, so that the traveller would have died even if D_1 had not emptied the water supply. When D_2 acted, he increased the likelihood that the traveller would die, but, as the traveller did not drink the poisoned water, D_2 did not cause the traveller's death.

Imagine the following variation on the desert traveller case. The traveller is aware that there is a threat to his life and so places a padlock on his wagon to protect his water. In order to poison the water, D_2 removes the padlock. Later,

---

[63] *Ibid*. See also *Fairchild v Glenhaven Funeral Services Ltd* [2002] UKHL 22, [2003] 1 AC 32, 98 (Lord Rodger).

[64] For discussion of the importance of this point and of some surrounding issues, see JCP Goldberg and BC Zipursky, 'Unrealized Torts' (2002) 88 *Virginia Law Review* 1625.

but before the traveller drinks any of the water, D_1 empties the water supply. Had D_2 not removed the padlock, D_1 would have done so. Nevertheless, D_2's removal of the padlock made D_1's emptying of the water supply easier.

In this example, both of D_2's actions—removing the padlock and poisoning the water—made the traveller's death more likely (in a sense to be examined below). But only the former was a cause of the traveller's death.[65] With respect to that action, the fact that D_2's action made the traveller's death more likely does lead to the conclusion that D_2 caused the traveller's death. Increasing the risk of an event is not sufficient for causation, but that does not mean that it is necessarily irrelevant.

D_2's poisoning of the water is not causally relevant, because, although it makes the traveller's death more likely, it plays no role in the actual events that lead to the traveller's death. The traveller was not poisoned. Conversely, the removal of the padlock did play a role in the actual events that led to the traveller's death. The padlock needed to be removed so that D_1 could gain access to the traveller's water keg in order to empty it so that the traveller would die of dehydration.

D_2's poisoning of the water made the traveller's death more likely ex ante but not ex post facto. That is, the chance that the traveller would die was higher after D_2 had poisoned the water but before D_1 had emptied the water than it was before D_2 had poisoned the water. However, ex post, the poisoning of the water did not increase the actual chance of the traveller's death, because, after D_1 had emptied the water, the chance that the traveller would die was unaffected by the poison. Conversely, D_2's removal of the padlock made the traveller's death more likely both ex ante and ex post. This is because the removal of the padlock was a necessary condition for D_1 to empty the water.

Recall that the two possibilities enunciated by Lord Reid in *McGhee* were (i) that the claimant's dermatitis resulted when he had received sufficient exposure to the dust—in which case each exposure to the abrasive dust was necessary for the injury, and hence the defendant's negligence would have been a factual cause of the claimant's injury—or (ii) that each abrasion merely increased the chance of the claimant developing dermatitis. In fact, there were three possibilities; the second outlined above could relate to two different ideas. The full list is the following:[66]

1. Each exposure to the brick dust was a necessary condition for the development of dermatitis.
2. Each exposure to the brick dust increased the risk (ex post) that the claimant would develop dermatitis.

---

[65] Note, however, that it was not a but for cause of the traveller's death. Again, this shows the deficiencies of that test.

[66] For a similar analysis see M Stauch, 'Causation, Risk, and Loss of Chance in Medical Negligence' (1997) 17 *OJLS* 205, 212–31.

3. Some exposures to the brick dust were necessary conditions for the development of dermatitis or increased the risk (ex post) that the claimant would develop dermatitis, but some exposures to dust were causally inert.

According to 3, each exposure increased the risk of developing dermatitis ex ante but not ex post. On this view, exposure is like Russian roulette. One is more likely to be shot if one plays 10 times than if one plays once, even though the chance of being shot on any one occasion remains 16.67 per cent no matter how many times one plays.[67]

Crucially, 2 is different from 3 in that each exposure to the dust made the chance of contracting dermatitis more likely ex post. One might compare this to a game of Russian roulette in which the chamber is spun before the first time the trigger is pulled but not thereafter. The chance of being killed by the first shot is 16.67 per cent, by the second 20 per cent, by the third 25 per cent and so on.

If *McGhee* fits with 1 or 2, then the defendant must have been a cause of the claimant's injury. On either of these possibilities, *McGhee* resembles the removal of the padlock rather than the poisoning of the water in the variation on the desert traveller case discussed above. On 2, *McGhee* is analogous to the second game of Russian roulette rather than the first. On 3, however, it remains *possible* that the exposure to dust after work played no role in the claimant's injury.

But this possibility must now seem very unlikely indeed. For the exposure after work not to have contributed to the claimant's injury, 1 and 2 must have been false and 3 must have been true. Moreover, even assuming the truth of 3, the defendant caused the claimant's injury unless we *additionally* assume that all of the exposures after work were causally inert. This is not impossible, but the claimant could establish his case *on the balance of probabilities*. I assume that this is why Lord Reid expressed himself with such confidence while, at the same time, acknowledging the uncertainty:

> The medical evidence is to the effect that the fact that the man had to cycle home caked with grime and sweat added materially to the risk that this disease might develop. It does not and could not explain just why that is so. But experience shews that it is so. Plainly that must be because what happens while the man remains unwashed can have a causative effect, although just how the cause operates is uncertain. I cannot accept the view . . . that once the man left the brick kiln he left behind the causes which made him liable to develop dermatitis. That seems quite inconsistent with a proper interpretation of the medical evidence.[68]

This is sufficient to demonstrate that the claimant established on the balance of probabilities that the exposure to dust after work caused his injury. In fact, then,

---

[67] This is like the poisoning of the water in the desert traveller example. D_1 and D_2 each put a bullet in a chamber, but it was D_1's bullet that was fired, not D_2's.

[68] *McGhee v National Coal Board* [1972] 1 WLR 1, 4–5 (HL Sc). See also *Hotson v East Berkshire Area Health Authority* [1987] AC 750, 786 (HL) (Lord Mackay).

the issue of causation in *McGhee* is relatively simple. Much more difficult, however, is that of the evaluation of damages. However, at least keeping these issues separate allows us to deal with them appropriately.

As we discovered in the previous chapter, if despite being causally involved in the claimant's injury the defendant's negligence made the claimant no worse off, then the claimant is entitled only to nominal damages. That was a real possibility in *McGhee*. On all three possibilities above, it may have been the case that, even if the defendant's negligence was a cause of the claimant's injury, that injury would have occurred without the defendant's negligence. In other words, the claimant's injury may have been over-determined. Again, there are three relevant possibilities (I continue to use consecutive numbering to avoid confusion, although the following list involves possibilities of a different kind from the above):

4. The claimant's injury would not have developed had the claimant been exposed to any less dust. Hence, no injury would have developed had the defendant not been exposed to dust after work.
5. Although the claimant's injury could have occurred with less total exposure to dust, in fact the extent of the injury suffered by the claimant would not have occurred without exposure to dust after work. Hence, the occurrence of dermatitis was over-determined, but its extent was not.
6. The claimant would have developed dermatitis, and developed dermatitis to the same extent, even if only exposed to dust during work. Hence, both the occurrence of dermatitis and its extent were over-determined.

On 6, the claimant should have been able to recover only nominal damages. On 5, the damages should have been reduced so that the claimant could recover only for the extent of his injury that would not have occurred without the defendant's negligence. On 4, the claimant was entitled to recover for the entirety of his injury.

The medical evidence could not determine which of these possibilities occurred. But this is not to say, as was implied in *Fairchild*, that the medical evidence was that 6 was just as likely as 4 and 5 combined. The expert witnesses in *McGhee* refused to take any stand on this matter. They declined to attach any probabilities to 4, 5 or 6. Therefore, it must be wrong to conclude automatically, as did the majority in *Fairchild*, that the claimant failed to establish on the balance of probabilities that the defendant's negligence made him worse off.[69]

Crucially, the Court cannot simply side with the defendant when expert witnesses cannot or will not express their views on the probabilities. That would bias the enquiry in favour of the defendant. It would mean that the claimant alone bears the risk of scientific uncertainty. But that is a breach of corrective justice and does not treat the parties as equals. If the expert witnesses refuse to take a stand on the probabilities, the Court must substitute its own judgment as

---

[69] In *McGhee*, this would have been a matter for the trial judge if the case had gone to trial.

to where the balance of probabilities lies. In *McGhee*, as the experts would not be drawn on the matter, their Lordships were forced to make such a judgment, and they did so quite plausibly.

(ii) Wilsher

Very similar issues were traversed in *Wilsher* and *Fairchild*. In the former case, the claimant was born prematurely and developed retrolental fibroplasia (RLF), which caused total blindness in one of his eyes and impaired his vision in the other. It was known that this condition can be caused by fluctuations in the partial pressure of oxygen (ppO_2). Accordingly, the defendant's employees inserted a catheter into the claimant to measure the ppO_2 in order, inter alia, to prevent the development of RLF. However, the catheter was negligently misplaced. As a result, the claimant was administered oxygen in order to raise his ppO_2 level when it was likely that his ppO_2 level was adequate. Hence, it was likely that the defendant's employees' negligence in misplacing the catheter caused a dangerous fluctuation in the claimant's ppO_2 level.[70]

However, fluctuation in ppO_2 was only one of a number of possible conditions known to cause RLF. It was likely, although not certain, that the claimant suffered from one or more of those conditions.[71] Accordingly, Lord Bridge decided that, on the facts as presented to the House of Lords, the claimant had not met the burden of proof. Moreover, his Lordship maintained that, as the trial judge was operating under a false understanding of causation that confused the issue to be decided, it was impossible to make accurate judgements about where the balance of probabilities lay. Hence, his Lordship ordered a retrial.

(iii) Fairchild

There were three claimants in *Fairchild*. The third was a man who had developed mesothelioma. It was highly likely that this disease was a consequence of exposure to asbestos dust. The first two claimants were widows of men who had died of mesothelioma. Those deaths were also likely to have been caused by exposure to asbestos dust. In the following, for simplicity, I explore only the position of the third claimant.

The problem for the claimant in *Fairchild* was that, although his injury was very likely to have been caused by exposure to asbestos, and although he had been exposed to asbestos by a number of parties all of whom were negligent and had breached a duty of care to the claimant,[72] it appeared that the claimant

---

[70] In A Beever, 'Cause-In-Fact: Two Steps Out of the Mire' (2001) 51 *University of Toronto Law Journal* 327, 363, I neglected this important point.

[71] *Wilsher v Essex Area Health Authority* [1988] AC 1074, 1081 (HL).

[72] The relevant duty was also a breach of s63 of the Factories Act 1961 (UK). However, as the result in *Fairchild* is meant to apply also in negligence, I explore the issues from that perspective below.

could not prove on the balance of probabilities *which* party caused his injury. The reason for this was neatly summarised by Lord Bingham:

> [T]he condition may be caused by a single fibre, or a few fibres, or many fibres: medical opinion holds none of these possibilities to be more probable than any other, and the condition once caused is not aggravated by further exposure. So if C is employed successively by A and B and is exposed to asbestos dust and fibres during each employment and develops a mesothelioma, the very strong probability is that this will have been caused by inhalation of asbestos dust containing fibres. But C could have inhaled a single fibre giving rise to his condition during employment by A, in which case his exposure by B will have had no effect on his condition; or he could have inhaled a single fibre giving rise to his condition during his employment by B, in which case his exposure by A will have had no effect on his condition; or he could have inhaled fibres during his employment by A and B which together gave rise to his condition; but medical science cannot support the suggestion that any of these possibilities is to be regarded as more probable than any other.[73]

Importantly, even those of their Lordships who in *Fairchild* rejected the interpretation of *McGhee* that Lord Bridge propounded in *Wilsher*, accepted that *Wilsher* was rightly decided. Hence, the task facing their Lordships in *Fairchild* was to elucidate an approach to causation that would generate the desired result in *Fairchild*, that would explain the outcome in *McGhee* on the assumption that the claimant could not prove causation on the balance of probabilities, and would also be consistent with the outcome in *Wilsher* and other relevant cases. This was no small task. The most obvious suggestion would have been to follow Lord Wilberforce's notion in *McGhee* that, in relevant circumstances, the burden of proof should be reversed,[74] while finding some way of distinguishing *Wilsher*. Curiously, however, in *Fairchild* all of their Lordships rejected that solution. Instead, their Lordships opted for a far more dramatic and far-reaching resolution.

Lord Hoffmann argued that claimants should be held to have satisfied the causation stage of the negligence enquiry when:[75]

1. The defendant owed the claimant a duty to protect the claimant from a particular kind of injury.
2. The duty is intended to create a right to compensation.[76]
3. The defendant's breach of duty increased the likelihood that the claimant would suffer that particular kind of injury.
4. Medical science cannot prove or disprove that the defendant caused the particular kind of injury.
5. The claimant suffered that particular kind of injury.

---

[73] *Fairchild v Glenhaven Funeral Services Ltd* [2002] UKHL 22, [2003] 1 AC 32, 43.
[74] *McGhee v National Coal Board* [1972] 1 WLR 1, 6 (HL Sc).
[75] *Fairchild v Glenhaven Funeral Services Ltd* [2002] UKHL 22, [2003] 1 AC 32, 74.
[76] This is of particular relevance to the impact of the Factories Act 1961 (UK) on the case.

However, this reasoning directly applies to *Wilsher*,[77] as well as to a number of similar cases in which there is scientific uncertainty. Lord Hoffmann's position is too wide.[78] Consequently, sitting on the Privy Council in *Channel Islands Knitwear Co Ltd v Hotchkiss*, another case involving factual uncertainty, Lord Hoffmann declined to apply his own view.[79]

Returning to *Fairchild*, Lord Bingham maintained that (i) when two or more potential defendants[80] fail to live up to a duty of care that they owe to the claimant (ii) to protect the claimant from a certain kind of injury, (iii) that injury materialises and (iv) it is not plausible that the claimant's injury had a cause other than that for which the potential defendants were responsible, but (v) the state of science is such that the claimant cannot prove which defendant, on the balance of probabilities, caused her injury, then this is sufficient to satisfy the requirements of factual causation against those defendants.[81] This is narrower than Lord Hoffmann's view, because it implies that a defendant can be liable only if the other potential causes of the claimant's injury were also tortious. But this is ad hoc. On Lord Bingham's view, it is unclear why the ability of a claimant to recover from a defendant should be affected by whether the other potential causes were tortious or not. This view was also rejected in the later decision of the House of Lords in *Barker v Corus (UK) plc*.[82]

Although Lord Nicholls insisted that protecting the defendant from injustice implies that '[t]here must be good reason for departing from the normal threshold . . . test', ie the but for test, his Lordship maintained that '[p]olicy questions will loom large when a court has to decide whether the difficulties of proof confronting the claimant justify taking this exceptional course. It is impossible to be more specific.'[83] But it is the task of judges in the House of Lords to be more specific if they are to introduce wide-open concepts of causation. This is particularly so if their Lordships later refuse to apply those concepts to what appear to be relevantly similar cases.[84]

In *Barker*, the House of Lords tightened the meaning of *Fairchild* so that it applies only to cases in which the potential causes of the claimant's injury were

---

[77] Against:*Fairchild v Glenhaven Funeral Services Ltd* [2002] UKHL 22, [2003] 1 AC 32, 76–7. A possible reply to this is that the defendant's negligence in *Wilsher* increased the risk of the claimant's injury if and only if it caused that injury. This reply is correct, but, for reasons examined below, destroys the position taken by their Lordships, with the exception of Lord Hutton, in *Fairchild*.

[78] See also J Morgan, 'Lost Causes in the House of Lords: *Fairchild* v *Glenhaven Funeral Services*' (2003) 66 *MLR* 277, 279–80.

[79] [2003] PC 68, [36]–[37].

[80] Note that some of the parties were no longer in existence and hence could not be sued. But they remain potential defendants in the sense that, but for the enquiry into factual causation, they would in principle have been liable had they existed.

[81] *Fairchild v Glenhaven Funeral Services Ltd* [2002] UKHL 22, [2003] 1 AC 32, 44. Here I have run the second and third stages of Lord Bingham's presentation together. I have also assumed that this rule does not apply solely to cases involving mesothelioma.

[82] [2006] UKHL 20, [2006] 2 WLR 1027.

[83] *Fairchild v Glenhaven Funeral Services Ltd* [2002] UKHL 22, [2003] 1 AC 32, 70.

[84] *Channel Islands Knitwear Co Ltd v Hotchkiss* [2003] PC 68, [36]–[37].

all of the same kind.[85] Apparently, this distinguishes *Fairchild* from both *Wilsher* and *Hotchkiss* where the potential causes of the claimants' injuries were various. But what is the justification for this rule? Lord Hoffmann gave none. In fact, his Lordship himself noted that, in *Fairchild*, he thought that the rule had no basis.[86] In *Barker*, he maintains that he was mistaken in *Fairchild*, but he does nothing to explain why.[87] In *Barker*, his Lordship correctly points out that without adopting the rule he cannot justify the distinction between *Wilsher* and *Fairchild*,[88] but that does not justify the rule. In fact, the rule seems to be nothing more than an arbitrary restriction on the application of *Fairchild* and, moreover, appears to be intended as such.[89]

A further problem with *Barker* is that a majority of their Lordships held that that a defendant would be liable in cases like *Fairchild* even if one of the potential causes of the claimant's injury was innocent.[90] This is not always inappropriate, but would mean that, for example, a person who was exposed to asbestos for 99 days due to his own fault and then for one day due to the fault of the defendant could recover from the defendant, despite it being the case that the defendant was very likely not to have caused the claimant's injury.[91] Their Lordships mitigate the consequences of this rule by maintaining that the defendant should be liable only for the risk he created—here 1 per cent of the claimant's loss.[92] Their Lordships feel that these alterations to the normal approach are necessary in these particular types of case to ensure justice,[93] but they are nevertheless very definite departures from the law's traditional approach. Moreover, they raise the question why apportionment of loss is not the approach of the general law and why, as a matter of principle, the *Fairchild* approach is not applied across the board, or at least to all cases involving any kind of uncertainty (which is at least almost across the board). If it really is necessary to go down this road, then perhaps it can be justified, but, as we see now, it is not necessary.

How should *Fairchild* have been decided? First, if the probabilities were as their Lordships described them, then *Fairchild* would have presented the same situation that faced the Supreme Court of California in *Sindell*. Hence, *Fairchild* should have been decided in accordance with the discussion of *Sindell* above.

[85] *Barker v Corus (UK) plc* [2006] UKHL 20, [2006] 2 WLR 1027, paras [18]–[24] (Lord Hoffmann).
[86] *Ibid*, [22]; *Fairchild v Glenhaven Funeral Services Ltd* [2002] UKHL 22, [2003] 1 AC 32, 77.
[87] He claims that '[t]he question which I raised about different kinds of dust is not so much about the principle that the causative agent should be the same but about what counts as being the same agent'. But that is plainly wrong.
[88] *Barker v Corus (UK) plc* [2006] UKHL 20, [2006] 2 WLR 1027, [24].
[89] *Ibid*.
[90] *Ibid*, [17] (Lord Hoffmann).
[91] An alternative reading, explored in the next section of this ch, is that the defendant's liability is for creating a risk of injury and not for creating the injury itself.
[92] But why that figure? That issue is explored below.
[93] See especially *Barker v Corus (UK) plc* [2006] UKHL 20, [2006] 2 WLR 1027, [43] (Lord Hoffmann), [101] (Lord Roger), [108] (Lord Walker), [122]–[127] (Baroness Hale).

On this interpretation of the probabilities, then, the outcome of *Fairchild* was correct, although the reasoning was inappropriate.

More importantly, however, their Lordships' interpretation of the probabilities was faulty. In order to see this, it is helpful to return to *Cook v Lewis*. Imagine that there were not two, but three equally likely possibilities in that case: that Cook had shot Lewis, that Akenhead had shot Lewis, or that both Cook and Akenhead had shot Lewis.[94] In this scenario, Lewis would face no difficulty proving on the balance of probabilities that either Cook or Akenhead shot him. The chance that Cook alone shot Lewis was 33.33 per cent. The chance that Akenhead alone shot Lewis was also 33.33 per cent. And the chance that both Cook and Akenhead shot Lewis was, of course, also 33.33 per cent. This means that the chance that Cook shot Lewis was 66.67 per cent. The same conclusion applies to Akenhead.

The difficulty in *Fairchild* was caused, not by any inadequacy in the law's traditional approach to causation, but by misunderstanding the medical evidence and failing to understand this feature of probability. The latter failure arises because a very important distinction is overlooked. In the version of *Cook v Lewis* described above, the chance that Cook shot Lewis was 66.67 per cent and the chance that Akenhead shot Lewis was 66.67 per cent. That result is clear from the description of the case. But it is crucial to recognise that this does not imply that the chance that Cook and Akenhead shot Lewis was 66.67 per cent. The chance that Cook and Akenhead shot Lewis is stated in the above; it is 33.33 per cent. Probability does not aggregate in this manner. The chance that Cook shot Lewis is 66.67 per cent, the chance that Akenhead shot Lewis is 66.67 per cent, the chance that both shot Lewis is 33.33 per cent, not 66.67 per cent. The chance that *either* shot Lewis must not be conflated with the chance that *both* did.

The problem here is to think in the following way. If the chance that A caused E is x and the chance that B caused E is also x, then the chance that A and B caused E must be $2x$. This is because adding A and B together appears to suggest that the chances associated with A and B should also be added together. But this can be seen to be wrong as soon as one remembers that, if A and B caused E, then *both* A and B must have caused E, and that means that the chance that A and B caused E can never be greater, and will almost always be lower, than x.

One must also be careful not to be caught by what is really the same fallacy in reverse, as revealed in the following argument. Only Cook and Akenhead could have caused Lewis' injury. Hence the chance that Cook or Akenhead or both were responsible was 100 per cent. Accordingly, as it was no more likely that Cook shot Lewis than that Akenhead shot Lewis, the chance that either shot Lewis must have been 50 per cent. This is because two possible people caused Lewis' injury, both people were equally likely, and 100 divided by two is 50. But the fact that it was no more likely that Cook shot Lewis than that

---

[94] In fact, this was not far from the truth. See above n26.

Akenhead shot Lewis shows only that the chance of either must be equal. It does not show that it must be 50 per cent. Probability does not divide in this manner. It is specifically this version of the fallacy that lay behind the difficulties in *Fairchild*.

With these issues in mind, we need to return to that case. Recall Lord Bingham's presentation of the legal issue. The claimant's condition may be caused:

> by a single fibre, or a few fibres, or many fibres: medical opinion holds *none of these possibilities to be more probable* than any other . . . C could have inhaled a single fibre giving rise to his condition during employment by A, in which case his exposure by B will have had no effect on his condition; or he could have inhaled a single fibre giving rise to his condition during his employment by B, in which case his exposure by A will have had no effect on his condition; or he could have inhaled fibres during his employment by A and B which together gave rise to his condition; but medical science cannot support the suggestion that *any of these possibilities is to be regarded as more probable* than any other.[95]

On this version of the facts, it is clear that A (and B) caused C's injury on the balance of probabilities.

This can be revealed by considering the possible scenarios. I label the fibres after their 'owners' in lower case. Imagine first that C's injury was caused by one fibre. Here the possibilities were that C's injury was caused by *a* or by *b* and neither 'of these possibilities is to be regarded as more probable' than the other. The chance that A caused C's injury would therefore be 50 per cent. Imagine now that two fibres caused C's injury. The possibilities would be *aa, ab, bb*, each equally likely. Hence, the chance that A caused C's injury would be 66.67 per cent.[96] Moreover, if the first and second situations are equally likely, then the chance that A caused C's injury, assuming at it was caused by one or two fibres, would be 58.33 per cent. Imagine now that C's injury was caused by three fibres. The possibilities would be *aaa, aab, abb, bbb*, where these possibilities are equally likely. Accordingly, the chance that A caused C's injury would be 75 per cent. And if the first, second and third situations were equally likely, then the chance that A caused C's injury, assuming that it was caused by one, two or three fibres, would be 63.88 per cent.

Though we have far from exhausted the possibilities, it must now be apparent that, on the balance of probabilities, A caused C's injury. On the assumption that one fibre caused C's injury, then the chance that A caused C's injury is 50 per cent. On any other assumption, it is higher than 50 per cent. And it is no

---

[95] *Fairchild v Glenhaven Funeral Services Ltd* [2002] UKHL 22, [2003] 1 AC 32, 43 (emphasis added).

[96] Note that I am assuming that it does not matter which order the fibres come in. This is most likely to be the case as it cannot matter to the causation of mesothelioma which defendant was responsible. However, if somehow this did matter, then the possibilities would be *aa, ab, ba, bb*. In this case, the chance that A caused B's injury would be 75 % on the assumption that these possibilities were equally likely.

more likely that *C*'s injury was caused by one fibre than by any other number. On the balance of probabilities, therefore, *A* caused *C*'s injury. And note that, even if we were sure that only one fibre caused *C*'s injury, then the position discussed above in relation to *Cook v Lewis* and *Summers v Tice* should have applied.

The conclusion is only slightly less clear when three or more potential causes are involved. Imagine that *A*, *B* and *C* are the potential causes of *D*'s mesothelioma. On the assumption that one fibre caused *D*'s injury, then the chance that *A* caused *D*'s injury is only 33.33 per cent.[97] However, on the assumption that two fibres caused *D*'s injury, then the chance that *A* caused *C*'s injury would be 50 per cent; on the assumption that three fibres caused *D*'s injury, the chance would be 60 per cent; on the assumption that four fibres caused *C*'s injury, the chance would be 66.67 per cent; and so on. Hence, on the assumption that one, two, three or four fibres caused *C*'s injury and that each was equally likely, the chance that *A* caused *C*'s injury was 52.5 per cent.

Imagining now that there were four potential causes, that *A*, *B*, *C* and *D* are the potential causes of *E*'s injury, the chance that *A* caused *E*'s injury is 25 per cent on the assumption that one fibre was involved, 40 per cent on the assumption that two fibres were involved, 50 per cent on the assumption that three fibres were involved, 57.14 per cent on the assumption that four fibres were involved, 62.5 per cent on the assumption that five fibres were involved, 70 per cent on the assumption that six fibres were involved and so on. Hence, on the assumption that one, two, three, four, five or six fibres caused *C*'s injury and that each was equally likely, the chance that *A* caused *C*'s injury was 50.77 per cent.

The importance of these figures is that the median number of fibres likely to cause the claimant's injury in *Fairchild* was well above these figures. The medical evidence was not, for instance, that it was likely that six or fewer fibres caused the claimant's injury. Rather, it was that an unknown number of fibres caused the injury, no number being any more likely than any other. Hence, the medical evidence was to the effect that the defendant's negligence caused the claimant's injury on the balance of probabilities. Though, for reasons discussed in the following section, the medical experts did not testify in this manner and would not have thought it appropriate for them to have done so, that is the appropriate conclusion to reach from what they did say.

It is also important to note that the above has shown not only that *A* was the cause of the claimant's injury on the balance of probabilities in the cases examined, but that the other potential defendants were also. So, for instance, on the assumptions that there were four potential defendants and six fibres were required in order to cause the claimant's injury, the chance that *A* or *B* or *C* or *D* caused the claimant's injury was 70 per cent. Hence, the claimant would be able to recover from any or all of them. But note again that this does not imply

---

[97] Although the *Cook v Lewis* [1951] SCR 830 approach should apply.

that on the balance of probabilities all defendants caused the claimant's injury. It implies only that on the balance of probabilities A caused the claimant's injury, and on the balance of probabilities B caused the claimant's injury, and on the balance of probabilities C caused the claimant's injury, and on the balance of probabilities D caused the claimant's injury. These claims are quite distinct. To say that it was likely that A caused the injury and that it was likely that B caused the injury does not imply that it was likely that A and B caused the injury.

In *Barker*, Lord Hoffmann described the rule in *Fairchild* as follows:

> The purpose of the *Fairchild* exception is to provide a cause of action against a defendant who has materially increased the risk that the claimant will suffer damage and may have caused that damage, but cannot be proved to have done so because it is impossible to show, on a balance of probability, *that some other exposure to the same risk may not have caused it instead.*[98]

This passage contains a clear example of the fallacy above. Lord Hoffmann assumed that if it were more probable than not that something other than the defendant's negligence caused the claimant's injury, then it must follow that it was not probable that the defendant caused the claimant's injury. But that does not follow. Probability does not divide in this fashion. It is possible, and in the relevant cases it is true, that it was more probable than not that both the defendant caused the claimant's injury and that something else did.[99]

Similarly, the Court of Appeal held that:

> It was . . . common ground on these appeals that it could not be said whether a single fibre of asbestos was more or less likely to have caused the disease, alternatively whether more than one fibre was more or less likely to have caused the disease. In the latter event, it could not be shown that it was more likely than not that those fibres came from more than one source. In other words, none of these scenarios could be proved on the balance of probabilities.[100]

But the conclusions drawn in this passage do not follow from what comes before. All that was established was that no possibility was any more likely than any other. That does not mean that the chance of each possibility was 50 per cent or less.

Against this argument, Lord Bingham maintained that '[t]here is no way of identifying, even on a balance of probabilities, the source of the fibre or fibres which initiated the genetic process which culminated in the malignant tumour'.[101] This is either correct but irrelevant or false. If Lord Bingham meant that it was not possible for the claimant to prove on the balance of probabilities

---

[98] *Barker v Corus (UK) plc* [2006] UKHL 20, [2006] 2 WLR 1027, [17] (emphasis added).

[99] This does not mean that the defendant and something else probably cause the claimant's injury.

[100] *Fairchild v Glenhaven Funeral Services Ltd* [2001] EWCA Civ 1881, [2002] 1 WLR 1052, 1064.

[101] *Fairchild v Glenhaven Funeral Services Ltd* [2002] UKHL 22, [2003] 1 AC 32, 43. See also Lord Hope, 'James McGhee—A Second Mrs. Donoghue?' (2003) 62 *CLJ* 587, 598.

that the defendant caused his injury, then the claim is false, as we have seen. If, however, Lord Bingham meant that it was impossible for the claimant to trace his disease to a specific fibre or fibres and then back to a particular defendant, then the claim is true, but would be relevant only if the claimant was trying to sue a fibre. The claimant was under no obligation to locate on the balance of probabilities the specific fibre or fibres that caused his injury. He needed to show only on the balance of probabilities that at least one of those fibres, whichever they were, came from the defendant. Similarly, if the wife of a claimant is shot by 100 bullets from the defendant's machine gun, the claimant does not fail in a wrongful death action because he cannot locate the actual bullet that killed his wife. We know that the defendant killed her, and that is enough. Likewise, we know that the probabilities were that the defendant was responsible for at least some of the asbestos that injured the claimant in *Fairchild*.

Another possible reply to the above is to maintain that the chances were not all equal in *Fairchild* itself. This is to say that Lord Bingham's presentation of the legal issue to be decided in *Fairchild* does not latch on to the facts in that case. To return to that presentation, one might say that, to fit *Fairchild*, that presentation must be rephrased such that the potential causes of C's injury are either A or B (but not both) and, though medical science cannot show which was more likely, there are other means of determining that one was more likely. But if this were so then, at least in the case described by Lord Bingham, the problem would not have arisen in the first place. That is, on this description of the facts, it is clear who should be liable. If it was more probable that A caused the injury, then A should be liable; if it was more probable that B caused the injury, then B should be liable.

However, one might further claim that this misdescribes the facts in *Fairchild* where, with respect to the third claimant, there were four possible causes. Hence, one might imagine that case in the following light. The chance that the claimant's injury was caused by A was 40 per cent, and the chance that it was caused by B, C or D, was 20 per cent each. Here it is not possible to say on the balance of probabilities who caused the claimant's injury.

There are three problems with this reply. First, the facts it describes bear no resemblance to those in *Fairchild*. In that case, it was possible, in fact highly likely all things considered, that the claimant's injury was caused by two or more of the potential defendants. This means that the percentage numbers, as listed above, must have added up to more than 100 to reflect the fact that the claimant's injury was likely to have been caused by more than one of the potential defendants.[102]

Secondly, if the case was as described above, then the appropriate way to deal with it is in line with the discussion of *Cook v Lewis* and *Summers v Tice* above. Thirdly, and most importantly, the whole basis of the discussion in *Fairchild*

---

[102] The idea that the sum total of *these* percentages must be 100 is an example of the fallacy discussed above.

assumes that the chances cannot be calculated in this fashion. It was not for no reason that Lord Bingham described the issue as he did. His Lordship described it in that way because he thought that that was the consequence of the medical evidence. The rule in *Fairchild* is meant to deal with situations in which the chances cannot be ascribed as above, because of scientific uncertainty. Hence, the reply is not really a reply to this criticism of *Fairchild* at all.

In any case, in determining the likelihood that a particular defendant caused the claimant's injury, the inequality of chances will only sometimes matter, depending on the extent of the inequality. But then it should sometimes matter. If A exposes the claimant for 10 years and B for 10 minutes, then that ought to make a difference to our assessment of the chance that A or B caused the injury. The exact probabilities can be extremely difficult or impossible to calculate, and probability is a notoriously unintuitive subject, but that does not mean that we should invent special legal approaches to causation to avoid having to grapple with it. Though the exact probability that the defendant caused the claimant's injury in *Fairchild* is not apparent, it is clear that it was more than 50 per cent.

A final objection, suggested by Porat and Stein's discussion of *res ipsa loquitur* above, is that 'statistical evidence' of this kind is not normally admissible. But this cannot be right. The point of examining the probabilities above is to determine the likelihood that the defendant's negligence caused the claimant's injury. Though it may be unusual for courts to engage in probability analysis in the way I have, this shows only that courts normally conduct themselves in this area in an intuitive rather than mathematical fashion. Courts must always assess the probabilities in one way or another. Hence, though the specific method of analysis employed here may be unfamiliar, it cannot be right to say that evidence of this kind is inadmissible. In any case, it would not be sensible to bar evidence of this kind only to create special rules such as *res ipsa loquitur* and the *Fairchild* approach to let it all back in again.

It is ironic that the result in *Fairchild*—one of the longest and most confusing judgments in this area—could have been reached without any legal (as opposed to mathematical) difficulty. And note that even on the assumption that the claimants' injuries were caused by only one fibre or that the probabilities were quite other than that described by Lord Bingham, the result in *Fairchild* would follow from the discussion of *Cook v Lewis* above. There is an important lesson here. The principled approach to the law of negligence has more going for it than many assume. It is quite capable of dealing with difficult cases such as *Fairchild* if we take it seriously. We should do so.

The confusion in *Fairchild* has now been reflected in *Barker* which, in many ways, exacerbates the problems with the former case. The husband of one of the claimants, who had died of mesothelioma, had been exposed to asbestos during three periods: once when working for the defendant, once when working for a company now insolvent, and once when he was self-employed. Rightly, the House of Lords ruled that the defendant could be liable to the claimant. This conclusion follows from the argument above: On the balance of probabilities, the defendant caused the claimant's injury. However, the House of Lords found for the claimant in accordance with the discussion in *Fairchild*. Moreover, the majority of their Lordships rejected the position advanced by Lord Bingham in *Fairchild*, according to which the claimant could recover under *Fairchild* only if all potential causes of the claimant's injury were tortious. According to Lord Hoffmann in *Barker*, for instance, 'it should be irrelevant whether the other exposure was tortious or non-tortious by natural causes or human agency or by the claimant himself'.[103]

In *Barker*, it did not make any difference to the enquiry into liability that one of the possible causes was non-tortious.[104] This is because the defendant's negligence caused the claimant's injury on the balance of probabilities. It was therefore irrelevant that there were other non-tortious causes. But Lord Hoffmann was certainly wrong to state that it can never make a difference. Imagine, for instance, that the claimant's husband had been non-tortiously exposed to asbestos for 40 years and then had been exposed for 30 seconds to asbestos because of the defendant's negligence. Are we really to conclude what Lord Hoffmann suggests: that it is impossible to estimate whether the defendant's negligence caused the claimant's injury on the balance of probabilities and that, in the circumstances, the defendant must be liable?

Apparently, the Court of Appeal thought that the answers to these questions must be in the affirmative. Kay LJ argued:

> Mr Feeny [for the defendant] pointed to a situation where 99% of the exposure was during periods of self-employment . . . In such circumstances, if the period of self-employment was not a bar to the claimant succeeding, he would recover in full from the defendant who was only responsible for 1% of the exposure since there would be no contributory negligence. This, he submitted, could not be right.
>
> Unsurprisingly Mr Allan [for the claimant] countered with the reverse situation where the employer was responsible for 99% of the exposure and the self-employment counted for only 1% . . . For such a claimant to recover nothing . . . would be manifestly unjust.
>
> Such arguments to my mind only serve to highlight the policy element inherent in developing the law to provide the most equitable solution to the problems inherent in a situation such as this. . . . The policy decision has to be made on the basis of the generality looking for the fairest solution when the matter is considered in the round.[105]

The claimant must prove on the balance of probabilities that the victim was injured as a result of the defendant's negligence. There is no difficulty accepting the position of both Feeney and Allan. It is strange, though somewhat understandable in the light of *Fairchild*, that the Court of Appeal had difficulty with this, as it is routine for claimants who fit the first situation to fail as it is routine for those who fit the second to succeed. To consign this to the realm of policy is

---

[103] *Barker v Corus (UK) plc* [2006] UKHL 20, [2006] 2 WLR 1027, [17].

[104] It may make a difference regarding damages. That issue is broached below.

[105] *Barker v Saint Gobain Pipelines plc* [2004] EWCA Civ 545, [2005] 3 All ER 661, [39]–[41].

to lose sight of a crucial element of the fundamental structure of the law of negligence.

In *Barker*, Lord Hoffmann softened the unintuitive consequences of his judgment by ruling that liability in such cases would be several only, rather than joint and several. This means that, although the defendant would be liable in the case above in which he was responsible for exposing the victim to asbestos for only 30 seconds, his liability would be very small.

But this reintroduces injustice in different areas. Imagine *Fairchild* with two potential defendants, A and B, where B is impecunious. According to *Barker*, the claimant could recover for only part of her injury. But this is not appropriate. She should be able to recover for the whole of her injury, as the whole of her injury was caused by A (and B) on the balance of probabilities. Thankfully, the rule in *Barker* has been abolished by legislation, though only in respect of injuries caused through mesothelioma.[106]

At least according to the House of Lords in *Barker*, *Fairchild* instituted a new regime in relation to causation under conditions of scientific uncertainty.[107] As Lord Hoffmann expressed the idea, 'the basis of liability is the wrongful creation of a risk or chance of causing the disease, the damage which the defendant should be regarded as having caused is the creation of such a risk or chance'.[108] Hence, the defendant is liable for creating the risk of the mesothelioma, not for causing the mesothelioma, and the actionable damage that the victim suffered is the risk of the mesothelioma, not the mesothelioma itself. For convenience and for reasons discussed below, I describe the general position as holding that the defendant's liability is for creating *the risk of harm* to the claimant rather than causing *harm* itself, identifying the mesothelioma in *Fairchild* and *Barker* with 'harm'. Another way to represent the issue is to maintain that the risk of the mesothelioma in *Fairchild* and *Barker* is the harm and find another general term to refer to the normally physical injury that the claimant suffers, such as the disease in *Fairchild* and *Barker*. However, nothing here turns on the difference between these formulations. No stress is placed on the word 'harm'. In summary, then, according to the House of Lords in *Barker*, under appropriate conditions, the defendant is liable, not for causing the harm that the victim suffered, but for creating the risk of that harm, and the damage that the victim is said to have suffered is not the harm itself, but the risk thereof.

In fact, however, this is an illusion. Despite their Lordships' aversions, *Fairchild* and *Barker* present no new position but represent no more than a misunderstanding of the law's traditional approach. This is because, against their explicit assertions, their Lordships defined the damage to the victim in such a way that it cannot be identified with the risk of harm to the victim but must be seen as identical to the harm itself. In the following, I first explore their

---

[106] Section 3 Compensation Act 2006. This legislation, however, is problematic in its own way and may entrench the mistakes made in *Fairchild* and *Barker*.

[107] See also Lord Hope, 'James McGhee—A Second Mrs. Donoghue?' (2003) 62 *CLJ* 587.

[108] *Barker v Corus (UK) plc* [2006] UKHL 20, [2006] 2 WLR 1027, [35].

Lordships' explicit position in terms of a rights analysis. This reveals that the explicit position advanced by their Lordships is untenable. This is both because it is immoral and because it would be impossible to realise in practice. Consequently, whatever their Lordships' explicit claims, *Fairchild* and *Barker* should not and cannot be understood to institute a regime of liability for risk creation. I then reveal how this point plays out in *Barker*, showing that the case does not, in fact, attempt the impossible; that it does not even attempt to impose liability for risk creation.

The position taken in *Barker* implies the following picture. Under normal circumstances people possess rights not to be harmed in certain ways. However, in some extraordinary circumstances people also possess rights not to be placed at risk of harm. But that right cannot exist. If people had rights not to be placed at risk of harm, then almost all actions would be wrongful. My walking down the street places others at risk. According to the view that people have rights not to be placed at risk of physical harm, that means not only that I am wronging those others by walking down the street but that I am causing actionable damage to them even if I cause no harm to them. On a normative level, this is not supportable, because it is palpably false to suggest that an ordinary walk down the road is a legal wrong and because the position violates the principle that people cannot be guilty merely through acting.[109] According to this position, the exercise of agency is itself a legal wrong, but this cannot be right.

It is no reply to point out that the *Fairchild* approach is meant to apply only in conditions of scientific uncertainty. First, that only narrows the range of cases in which the approach produces an immoral result. It does not remove the immorality. Secondly, from this perspective the conditions placed on the approach must appear arbitrary. Why should it be the case that people have rights not to be placed a risk of harm only under conditions of scientific uncertainty? How could the state of science affect our rights in this manner? On this view, scientific discovery robs us of our rights by removing rights not to be placed at risk of harm in favour only of rights not to be harmed. This is not plausible. Even less plausible is the notion, advanced in *Barker*, that people possess rights not to be placed at risk of harm only when the risk arises because of a single causative agent. That position is normatively bizarre.

The position is also unworkable as a legal rule. We cannot have a situation in which everyone I pass on the street can sue me even if they have suffered no harm. Even if we allow the arbitrary restrictions on the rule as proposed in *Fairchild* and *Barker*, we cannot have people suing just because they were exposed to risks of harm. And indeed, as we see, the House of Lords in *Barker* did not open up this possibility. And that shows that the House of Lords did not really institute a regime of liability for risk creation.

---

[109] I Kant, 'The Metaphysics of Morals' in M Gregor (ed) *Practical Philosophy* (Cambridge University Press, Cambridge, 1996) 394, [6:238] refers to this as the principle of being 'beyond reproach'.

On the face of it, the explicit claims made in *Barker* are inconsistent with the decision of the House of Lords in *Gregg v Scott*.[110] That case, examined in detail below, dealt with the issue of loss of a chance. A paradigmatic example of such a case is the following: *A* has cancer. If *A* is treated properly, then there is a 40 per cent chance that *A* will be cured. However, *B*, *A*'s doctor, treats *A* negligently, meaning that *A* is now in the position that he has only a 10 per cent chance of a cure. Medical science is unable to say whether *A* would have been cured had he been treated properly. Can *A* recover from *B* the loss that the fall in his chances of a cure is said to represent?

While these cases are presented as involving loss of a chance, they can also be described as ones involving risk creation. In the example above, the allegation is that *B* increased the risk that *A* would not be cured. On this description, the question is whether *A* can recover for the risk created by *B*.

In *Gregg v Scott*, a majority of the House of Lords, including Lord Hoffmann, ruled that the law does not recognise the loss of a chance as actionable damage.[111] But, given that loss of a chance can be described as the creation of a risk, this must also imply that the law does not recognise the creation of a risk as actionable damage. Hence, *Gregg v Scott* is inconsistent with *Barker*. In *Barker*, Lord Hoffmann attempted to deal with this difficulty by saying that allowing recovery in *Gregg v Scott* 'would in effect have extended the *Fairchild* exception to all cases of medical negligence, if not beyond, and would have been inconsistent with *Wilsher*, in which the negligent doctor had increased the chances of the baby suffering RLF (or reduced his chances of escaping it)'.[112] This is just to say that the rule should not be applied in *Gregg v Scott* because that would be inconsistent with another decision of the House of Lords that this bench does not want to upset, without justifying that desire. Why not overturn *Wilsher*? In fact, the explicit position adopted by their Lordships in *Barker* indicates that both *Wilsher* and *Gregg v Scott* must have been wrongly decided. If the wrongful damage was the defendant's negligent creation of the risk of harm, then the claimants in *Wilsher* and *Gregg v Scott* suffered wrongful damage and should have been able to recover. Accordingly, the fact that their Lordships in *Barker* did not draw this conclusion indicates that they did not adopt their explicit position.

Moreover, if the actionable damage is the risk of the mesothelioma, then how are the damages payable to be calculated? What is the worth of a risk? In answering this question, it is helpful to consider the following example. Imagine that a raffle is being held with 100 tickets, each costing £2, and a single prize of £1,000.[113] You buy one ticket and the others are sold to other people. For the

---

[110] [2005] UKHL 2, [2005] 2 AC 176.

[111] *Ibid*, [79].

[112] *Barker v Corus (UK) plc* [2006] UKHL 20, [2006] 2 WLR 1027, [39]. This reveals that Lord Hoffmann recognised that no distinction can be made between the loss of a chance and the creation of a risk.

[113] One has to imagine that the prize was donated for this raffle to make sense. That is often the case in reality, particularly where the prize is not monetary.

sake of simplicity, let us stipulate that the ticket is worthless apart from its providing a chance to win the £1,000. How much is your ticket worth? In accordance with the discussion of loss of a chance below, the courts would ordinarily hold that your ticket is worth £10, that being one onehundredth of £1,000. But imagine now that the raffle is held and you do not win. How much is your ticket worth now? It is worthless.

The problem for *Fairchild* and *Barker* is that the position of the claimants in those cases resembles the situation that exists after the raffle has taken place and not before it has taken place. In those cases, though we are unsure about just who caused what, we are sure that the mesothelioma has occurred. In a nutshell, the problem is this: If the defendant's negligence caused the mesothelioma, then the risk created by the defendant had negative value to the claimant, but if the defendant's negligence did not cause the mesothelioma, then that risk had no negative value to the claimant. At least in circumstances where the mesothelioma has occurred, it is possible to say that the risk created by the defendant's negligence made the claimant worse off only if we assume that it caused the mesothelioma. As we have seen, that assumption is justified on the balance of probabilities, but the House of Lords in *Fairchild* and *Barker* denied that that assumption could be made. However, in holding that damages for the mesothelioma should be awarded against the defendant, the House of Lords implicitly ruled that the defendant did, at least on the balance of probabilities, cause the mesothelioma, there being no other basis for making the defendant pay anything by way of compensation to the claimant. In short, if the risk that the defendant created caused the mesothelioma, then the risk had a negative value to the claimant and the claimant was rightly compensated, but if the risk created by the defendant did not cause the mesothelioma, then the risk had no negative value to the claimant and there was nothing for which to compensate. The defendant did have to compensate the claimant. Therefore the House of Lords implied that the defendant caused the claimant's injury.

A related problem is that it is meaningful to speak of the risk of mesothelioma after the mesothelioma has occurred only if it is assumed that the risk in question caused the mesothelioma.[114] Recall that in *Barker* the claimant's husband had been exposed to asbestos first when working for a company now insolvent (A), secondly when working for the defendant (B) and thirdly when self-employed (C). And recall that the House of Lords insisted that it could not be determined whether A or B or C caused the mesothelioma on the balance of probabilities and that A, B and C had increased the risk of the mesothelioma. But, given the assumptions made by the House of Lords, that conclusion cannot be justified. For instance, on the assumption that A caused the mesothelioma, nothing B or C did increased the risk of the mesothelioma. The chance of the mesothelioma occurring was already 100 per cent. If it were true that it were impossible to determine causation on the balance of probabilities, then the

---

[114] I owe this very important observation to John Murphy.

difficulties that would arise could not be avoided by shifting focus to the risk of injury. This is because this approach still requires us to make assessments about the causal link between the risk and the harm. And that is what their Lordships did. When their Lordships spoke of B increasing the risk of mesothelioma, they were referring to the chance that B caused the mesothelioma and awarded damages appropriately, though they denied that that was what they were doing.

This point can also be seen later in Lord Hoffmann's judgment, where his Lordship claimed that '[a]lthough the *Fairchild* exception treats the risk of contracting mesothelioma as the damage, *it applies only when the disease has actually been contracted'*.[115] But why does it apply only then? If the actionable damage is *the risk* of contracting mesothelioma, then why does the victim need to contract mesothelioma in order for the defendant to be liable? In fact, the refusal to compensate the defendant's former employees unless they suffer mesothelioma reveals that the actionable damage is the mesothelioma and the consequences thereof, and not the risk of mesothelioma.

The general point here is that, if it were the risk of mesothelioma that were actionable, then there would be no need for the claimant's husband to have developed mesothelioma for him to have had a cause of action.[116] It would be sufficient for the claimant's husband to have been negligently exposed to the risk of mesothelioma. It would also mean that anyone who had been exposed to asbestos would be able to sue, whether they had developed mesothelioma or not. But that is not the position actually adopted by the House of Lords. The idea that these cases involve liability for risk creation is an illusion.

Furthermore, recall that the House of Lords in *Barker* ruled that the defendant's liability would be several only, though this has been overturned by legislation. Nevertheless, on what basis did the House of Lords argue that the scope of the defendant's liability should be decided?

Consider the following, perplexing passage from Lord Hoffmann's judgment:

> Treating the creation of the risk as the damage caused by the defendant would involve having to quantify the likelihood that the damage (which is known to have materialised) was caused by that particular defendant. It will then be possible to determine the share of the damage which should be attributable to him.[117]

The issue with this passage concerns the use of the term 'damage'. Is it being used univocally or equivocally? If it is being used univocally, then the passage should be paraphrased as follows:

> Treating the creation of the risk as the damage caused by the defendant would involve having to quantify the likelihood that *the risk* (which is known to have materialised) was caused by that particular defendant. It will then be possible to determine the share of the risk which should be attributable to him.

---

[115] *Barker v Corus (UK) plc* [2006] UKHL 20, [2006] 2 WLR 1027, [48] (emphasis added).

[116] Of course, the claimant can sue only if her husband has died. That is determined by the Fatal Injuries Act 1976.

[117] *Barker v Corus (UK) plc* [2006] UKHL 20, [2006] 2 WLR 1027, [36].

The problem is that this does not make sense. If the damage to the claimant is the risk of developing mesothelioma, then there would be no need to quantify *the likelihood* that the risk was caused by the defendant. On this view, we are certain that the risk was caused by the defendant as that was the basis upon which he was found liable.[118] The question here concerns merely *the scope* of the defendant's liability. Nor does the last sentence in the passage make sense on the reading given to it here. The defendant created the whole of the relevant risk. It does not make sense to speak of attributing any share of that risk to him. Moreover, deciding the share of the risk attributable to the defendant does nothing to determine the extent of the defendant's responsibility for the mesothelioma. The general problem here is that the defendant was required to compensate the claimant for some of the consequences of the mesothelioma, not of the risk of the mesothelioma. Because the mesothelioma had occurred, the risk of the mesothelioma could not be relevant unless it materialised in the mesothelioma. Accordingly, if the passage above is to help us decide the extent of the defendant's liability for the consequences of the mesothelioma, it must be interpreted in a way that links the risk created by the defendant to the mesothelioma and its consequences. Hence, the passage must be given the following interpretation, which is, in any case, the most natural reading of it:

> Treating the creation of the risk as the damage caused by the defendant would involve having to quantify the likelihood that *the mesothelioma* (which is known to have materialised) was caused by that particular defendant. It will then be possible to determine the share of *the mesothelioma and its consequences* which should be attributable to him.

This view solves the problem above, but it renders the whole approach in *Fairchild* and *Barker* redundant. According to this view, the scope of the defendant's liability is determined in accordance with the likelihood that he caused the mesothelioma in comparison with the chance that the other potential causes did. But if we knew how to calculate that, then the issue that produced the problems in *Fairchild* and *Barker* would not arise. The issue in those cases occurs only on the assumption that it is not possible to prove on the balance of probabilities whether or not the defendant caused the mesothelioma. But when the House of Lords in *Barker* demanded the apportionment of liability, it required something much more precise than that. It required courts to put a specific figure on the extent of the defendant's responsibility for the mesothelioma vis-à-vis the other potential causes. If this can be done, then it cannot be impossible to say that the defendant caused the mesothelioma on the balance of probabilities. I agree that it can be done in a rough fashion, but that means that the problem said to face the Court in *Fairchild* is not even on the horizon.

Consider also the suggestion made by Lord Walker that the scope of the defendant's liability in *Barker* could be determined in accordance with 'the

---

[118] In the above, I argued that this view was mistaken. Nevertheless, it is accepted here as it is the view taken by the Court.

duration and intensity of the claimant's [husband's] exposure to asbestos during' the claimant's husband's employment with the defendant.[119] Why are these
features thought to be significant? Surely, it is because it is thought—and
thought plausibly—that the longer and more intense the claimant's husband's
exposure to asbestos in the defendant's employ, the higher the chances that he
developed the conditions that would produce mesothelioma there. But that is
just to say that the longer and more intense the claimant's husband's exposure
to asbestos in the defendant's employ, the more likely that the defendant caused
the mesothelioma. That intuition is perfectly valid, but it is not consistent with
the notion that it cannot be said on the balance of probabilities whether the
defendant caused the mesothelioma. Here, then, Lord Walker is quite rightly
assessing the likelihood of causation, though his Lordship explicitly denied that
he was able to do so.

Accordingly, though *Fairchild* and *Barker* officially institute a regime of
liability for risk creation, that is not the reality. In *Barker*, despite the formal
position that causation cannot be assessed, the House of Lords considered that
very issue in exploring the ambit of the defendant's liability. That exploration
was highly plausible, but it was, in part, an exploration of the chance that the
defendant caused the mesothelioma. This is the law's traditional approach in
confusing disguise.

Finally, it is also important to remember that, in assessing the damages
payable by the defendant, it is necessary to take into account the loss that the
claimant would have suffered even if the defendant had not acted negligently.
Hence, if the claimant's husband's self-employment in *Barker* was likely to have
exacerbated his condition, then that is to be taken into account in reducing, not
the defendant's liability, but the damages payable by the defendant.[120] And, of
course, the damages payable amongst the defendants should be divided in
accordance with the contribution rules. The result, then, is not unlike that
reached in *Barker* itself, though the difference is important when more than one
tortious agent is involved and one or more of those agents cannot be sued or are
impecunious, etc. Again, we see the modern law adopting a host of confused
policies to reach almost the very conclusion that it would have reached if it had
simply adopted the principled approach. In fact, in conjunction with the
Compensation Act 2006, in relation to mesothelioma the law has now through
contorting itself ended up in exactly the position it would have been in had it not
contorted itself in the first place. It is hoped that the law can now unwind.

(iv) Scientific Uncertainty and Uncertainty in General

As we have seen above, the fundamental problem in *Fairchild* was to take the
expert testimony that none of the potential causes of the claimants' injuries was

[119] *Barker v Corus (UK) plc* [2006] UKHL 20, [2006] 2 WLR 1027, [106].
[120] That appears not to have been the case however. *Fairchild v Glenhaven Funeral Services Ltd*
[2002] UKHL 22, [2003] 1 AC 32, 43: 'the condition once caused is not aggravated by further exposure'.

more likely than the others to have caused the mesothelioma to imply that it could not be proven on the balance of probabilities that the defendants caused the mesothelioma. It is not unlikely, then, that the problem was that the experts were asked the wrong questions. To use Lord Bingham's presentation of the issue, the experts should not have been asked whether it was more likely that *A* or *B* had caused *C*'s injury. They should have been asked simply whether *A* caused *C*'s injury on the balance of probabilities. But even if they were asked this question, their reply may have been misleading to lawyers, as I now explain.

Much of the confusion in the cases arises because of a tendency to treat scientific uncertainty differently from uncertainty in other contexts.[121] For instance, in *Byrne v Boadle*, we are happy to say that on the balance of probabilities the negligence of the defendant or his servants caused the claimant's injury, though we know very little about the connection between that behaviour and the claimant's injury. No scientists were involved in *Byrne v Boadle*, but the defendant could have called expert witnesses, physicists perhaps, who might have suggested that it was impossible to prove scientifically that any negligence on the part of the defendant or his employees caused the claimant's injury. Similarly, if a child has influenza, the child's parents encounter no one else with the disease and the parents contract influenza, we are inclined to infer by induction that the parents caught the disease from the child. But at least under normal conditions, science is not capable of establishing whether the parents did or did not contract the disease from the child. It is possible that the parents contracted the virus from the environment, though medical science is normally incapable of tracing the disease to a particular virus cell or of determining whether the cell or cells came from the child. But, if the parents chose to sue the child for giving them influenza, a court should not apply a special, *Fairchild*-like, approach to factual causation.

These examples are not on all fours with *McGhee*, *Fairchild* and *Barker* because, while it is known how negligence in loading barrels into a warehouse may cause injury and how viruses cause diseases, it is or was not known how dust causes dermatitis or how asbestos fibres cause mesothelioma. But this is not a difference of any legal significance. This uncertainty makes it more difficult for judges to ascertain where the balance of probabilities lies, but it does not alter the essential question: did the defendant cause the claimant's injuries on the balance of probabilities? Hence, this difference does not call for a special approach to determining factual causation.

The fundamental problem is that lawyers misunderstand the testimony of the scientists in these and in similar cases. Scientists are used to dealing with a much higher standard of proof than are private lawyers. Hence, when they are asked whether the defendant caused the claimant's injuries, they tend to reply in the affirmative only if they think that that was *very likely*. The standard of proof

---

[121] See eg *ibid*, 74; J Stapleton, 'Lords A'Leaping Evidentiary Gaps' (2002) 10 *Torts Law Journal* 276.

adopted by scientists, then, is more like the criminal law standard of beyond reasonable doubt, and may in some cases be even higher. Hence, to conclude from the fact that the claimant could not satisfy the scientific standard of proof that the claimant failed to satisfy the appropriate legal standard would bias the enquiry in favour of the defendant and would violate the equality of the parties.

Moreover, we must bear in mind that when scientific experts say things such as 'I could not say whether it was more likely than not that the defendant caused the claimant's injury' they may mean something quite different from what a lawyer would mean in making this utterance. In general, scientific experts will be happy making predictions with regard to a phenomenon only when they believe that they understand the underlying causal nature of that phenomenon. But when they do not have that understanding, they generally refuse to make any prediction at all. Hence, because medical experts understand the action of viruses on the human body, they will generally be happy to say that the parents in our hypothetical example above most likely contracted influenza from their child. But medical experts in cases such as *Fairchild* will be likely to refuse to express any opinion at all, because they do not have sufficient understanding of the causal process that connects the breathing of asbestos fibres to the development of mesothelioma. This is not, or need not be, because they simply have no idea where the likelihoods lie, but is rather because they feel that their instincts about such issues are not scientifically justified, because they have insufficient understanding of the relevant phenomena, and so they should not, *as scientists* or *as expert witnesses*, express that opinion. This is especially so when they are being asked to speak as scientists in as formal a place as a court of law. In fact, however, individual scientists are not unlikely to have very strong opinions about the likelihoods and those opinions are likely to guide their future research by forming the basis of hypotheses that they will test in future. Were scientists not to have such opinions, then science would be a wild goose chase. But, as mentioned, the scientist is very reluctant to express these opinions in public, particularly in fora where she is asked to speak as a scientist. Asking a scientist to state her opinion, or *hunch* as she would probably put it, in such fora is like asking a lawyer to state a proposition, no matter how obvious, without judicial authority.

In cases such as *McGhee, Fairchild* and *Barker*, because of the scientific uncertainty, courts are unwilling to assess the probabilities for themselves. Hence, because determining factual causation in terms of the scientific testimony on its own would inappropriately favour the defendant, it appears that an exception to the ordinary principles should be made in order to do justice between the parties.

This is not necessary, because the ordinary principles of the law demonstrate that factual causation should not be determined entirely in accordance with this kind of scientific testimony. In light of that testimony, the court must determine whether *on the balance of probabilities* the defendant caused the claimant's injury. If the expert witnesses refuse to be drawn on that question, the court must substitute its own judgment. As Sopinka J said in *Snell v Farrell*, a case of medical misadventure, '[i]t is not . . . essential that the medical experts provide a firm opinion supporting the plaintiff's theory of causation. Medical experts ordinarily determine causation in terms of certainties whereas a lesser standard is demanded by the law'.[122] Science wants certainty, or something like it; the law wants 50 per cent plus one. Once this is remembered, there is no need for *Fairchild*-like approaches to factual causation.

Consider again the comments of Lord Reid in *McGhee*:

> In the present case the evidence does not shew—perhaps no one knows—just how der-matitis of this type begins. It suggests to me that there are two possible ways. It may be that an accumulation of minor abrasions of the horny layer of skin is a necessary precondition for the onset of the disease. Or it may be that the disease starts at one particular abrasion and then spreads, so that multiplication of abrasions merely increases the number of places where the disease can start and in that way increases the risk of its occurrence.
>
>   I am inclined to think that the evidence points to the former view. But in a field were so little appears to be known with certainty I could not say that that is proved.[123]

What could Lord Reid have meant by 'proved' here? If the evidence points to the former view, then the former view is proved *on the balance of probabilities*. Of course, that is not nearly sufficient proof to satisfy the medical expert. But that matter is irrelevant in law. In fact, Lord Reid should have said, and actually con-cluded, that the former view was proven on the balance of probabilities, and hence Lord Reid held the defendant liable.

Note that the position is not that the law should adopt a special understand-ing of causation. Causation was dealt with in the last chapter, where it was maintained that the scientific and philosophical understanding of causation must be accepted in the law. The issue here is not causation but proof of causa-tion. While we must adopt the scientific understanding of causation, that does not imply that we must adopt the scientific understanding of proof of causation. In the private law, we must not adopt that standard, because it would be unfair as between the parties. In private law, we ask whether the claimant can prove on the balance of probabilities scientific causation. That is demanded by the principled approach.

IV. LOSS OF A CHANCE

A. The Problem: *Gregg v Scott*

In *Gregg v Scott*, the House of Lords confronted the issue of recovery for the loss of a chance in cases of medical negligence. Their Lordships, by a majority of

[122] [1990] 2 SCR 311, 330.
[123] *McGhee v National Coal Board* [1972] 1 WLR 1, 4 (HL Sc).

3–2, refused to recognise loss of a chance as a recoverable head of damages. In the following, I explore this case because it very usefully portrays the problem presented by loss of chance cases. Moreover, the first two judgments in the case, those of Lords Nicholls and Hoffmann, present not only the most compelling cases for, respectively, the dissent and the majority, but they also each contain a crucial ambivalence that lies at the heart of this issue and that causes judges and commentators to struggle with the concept of loss of a chance. I explore this ambivalence by distinguishing between their Lordships' 'main' and 'secondary arguments'. I end by suggesting that this ambivalence should be resolved in favour of the position taken by the majority of the Court, though not quite for the reasons given by Lord Hoffmann.

The facts as accepted by the majority of the House of Lords were as follows.[124] The defendant negligently misdiagnosed the claimant's malignant cancer as benign. As a result, the claimant's treatment was delayed for nine months. This delay reduced the claimant's chances of being 'cured' of the cancer from roughly 42 per cent to 25 per cent.[125]

The problem facing the claimant was that, before the defendant's negligence, his chance of being cured was only 42 per cent. This meant that, on the balance of probabilities, the defendant did not deprive the claimant of a cure. According to the normal understanding of the general principles of the law of negligence, and in line with cases such as *Barnett v Chelsea and Kensington Hospital Management Committee*[126] and, most importantly, *Hotson v East Berkshire Area Health Authority*,[127] the claimant could not establish that the defendant was the factual cause of any loss suffered, and so the claimant had to fail. This was the conclusion reached both at first instance and by the Court of Appeal.

Therefore, the claimant argued, inter alia, that although he could not recover for the failure to be cured per se, he ought to be entitled to recover for the loss of the chance of a cure that he suffered because of the defendant's negligence. Consequently, he argued that he should have been able to recover for 17 *per cent* of the value of a cure.

(i) Lord Nicholls' Main Argument

Lord Nicholls' main argument is in fact very simple and compelling: loss of a chance is a genuine loss and therefore, if it is reasonably foreseeable, etc, it should be recoverable in negligence. Lord Nicholls accepted that the law has traditionally focused on outcomes rather than chances, and so recovery has usually been denied in such cases because the courts have insisted that the claimant

---

[124] Lord Hope interpreted the facts in an importantly different way. However, I propose to ignore this in order to focus on the issue of loss of a chance.
[125] Here, 'cure' is used in its medical sense to imply survival for 10 years. This technical definition of 'cure' is not important for our purposes.
[126] [1969] 1 QB 428 (QBD).
[127] [1987] AC 750 (HL). See also *Lawson v Laferriere* [1991] 1 SCR 541.

prove on the balance of probabilities that the defendant's negligence deprived him of a certain valuable outcome. But, Lord Nicholls argued, there is no justification for that focus. As Lord Nicholls pointed out, in simple cases the distinction between outcome and opportunity may not be important—if I saw your leg off with a chainsaw, the chance that I deprived you of your leg and the chance that I deprived you of the opportunity to retain your leg come to much the same thing—but when dealing with cases in which the outcome is uncertain, such as *Gregg v Scott*, the distinction between outcome and opportunity comes to the fore. Moreover:

> the greater the uncertainty surrounding the desired future outcome, the less attractive it becomes to define the claimant's loss by whether or not, on balance of probability, he would have achieved the desired outcome but for the defendant's negligence. This definition of the claimant's loss becomes increasingly unattractive because, as the uncertainty of outcome increases, this way of defining the claimant's loss accords ever less closely *with what in practice the claimant had and what in practice he lost by the defendant's negligence.*[128]

That is, focusing solely on outcomes blinds courts to the real loss suffered by the claimant, ie the loss of the chance of a cure, and, without good reason, courts should not so blind themselves. As Lord Nicholls concluded this argument:

> In order to achieve a just result in such cases the law defines the claimant's actionable damage . . . by reference to the *opportunity* the claimant lost, rather than by reference to the loss of the desired *outcome* . . . In adopting this approach the law does not depart from the principle that the claimant must prove actionable damage on the balance of probability. The law adheres to this principle but defines actionable damage in different, more appropriate terms.[129]

One might also add, in support of this argument, that the distinction between outcome and opportunity is theoretically unstable. This is because an opportunity can always be described as an outcome. In *Gregg v Scott*, for instance, there appears to be nothing preventing the claimant from claiming that the defendant's negligence did deprive him of a desirable outcome, namely of being in the position of having a 42 per cent chance of being cured. Simply, if loss of a chance is a real loss, then it should be compensatable.

(ii) Lord Nicholls' Secondary Argument

However, despite the powerful argument examined above, Lord Nicholls then appeared to accept that, at least in this kind of case, the loss of a chance was no loss at all. For Lord Nicholls, this was because of the need for the claimant to rely on statistical evidence.

---

[128] *Gregg v Scott* [2005] UKHL 2, [2005] 2 AC 176, [16] (emphasis added).
[129] *Ibid*, [17].

The trial judge had come to the conclusion that the defendant's negligence had reduced the claimant's chances of a cure largely because of statistical evidence relating to people with similar conditions to the claimant's. Hence, with respect to the claimant's chances of survival given prompt treatment, Lord Nicholls said:

> Take as an example the statistical evidence that 42% of the patients suffering from the same disease as Mr Gregg achieved ten year survival if treated at the stage when, but for the negligence, Mr Gregg would have been treated, this figure dropping to 25% when the treatment was not given until the disease had reached the more advanced stage at which Mr Gregg was actually treated. Who can know whether Mr Gregg was in the 58% non-survivor category or the 42% survivor category? There was no evidence, peculiar to him or his circumstances, enabling anyone to say whether on balance of probability he was in the former group or the latter group. The response Mr Gregg would have made if treated promptly is not known and never can be known.
>
> This difficulty was the foundation of a submission based on the proposition that a 'statistical chance' has no value, so its 'loss' cannot attract an award of compensation.[130]

Crucially, Lord Nicholls accepted the first conclusion of this argument: that the claimant had only a statistical chance and that the loss of that chance had no value. Hence his Lordship rejected the second conclusion, not by arguing that the statistical chance had value, but by maintaining that '[i]n suitable cases courts are prepared to adapt their process so as to leap an evidentiary gap when overall fairness plainly so requires'.[131]

This argument is curious because it is inconsistent with Lord Nicholls' main argument. Recall that Lord Nicholls maintained that the claimant ought to be able to recover his lost chance because that was a real loss. If that is so, then what prompts the conclusion that the claimant possessed only a statistical chance of a cure and that that chance had no value?

In the passage quoted above, Lord Nicholls maintained that it was impossible to know whether the claimant belonged to the non-survivor group (which contained 58 per cent of the people sampled) or the survivor group (which contained 42 per cent of the people sampled). But this assumes that the claimant did in fact belong to one of those groups and, if that were so, then *the claimant had no chance at all*. He either would have or would not have survived.[132]

On this view, then, there are two relevant possibilities. First, the claimant belonged to the non-survivor group and would not have been cured even if he had been treated promptly. In that case, the defendant's negligence would not have deprived the claimant of anything. Secondly, the claimant belonged to the survivor group and would have been cured had he been treated promptly, in

---

[130] *Ibid*, [29]–[30].

[131] *Ibid*, [31]. His Lordship cited *Fairchild v Glenhaven Funeral Services Ltd* [2002] UKHL 22, [2003] 1 AC 32 as evidence of this claim.

[132] Strictly, the claimant's chance was 100% or 0%. In law, however, we tend to speak of the claimant having a chance only if the chance was greater than 0% and less than 100%.

which case the defendant's negligence would have deprived the claimant of the cure. But it is more likely, ie 58 per cent, that the claimant belonged to the former group. Hence, on the balance of probabilities the defendant's negligence did not cause any loss to the claimant.

Moreover, when an evidentiary gap of this kind exists, how can it be justified to conclude that it is proper to leap it in the name of justice? In this case, if it was not clear that the claimant suffered a loss as a result of the defendant's negligence, why is it plain that fairness demands recovery? Fairness demands recovery only if the defendant did cause the claimant loss, but that is just the evidentiary gap that exists—ie we do not know whether the defendant caused the claimant loss. To argue for leaping this gap on the ground that justice so requires is entirely circular, as it *assumes* precisely what is at issue, namely that the defendant did cause the claimant loss. Of course, Lord Nicholls was prepared to make this assumption because he believed that the claimant did indeed suffer a loss, namely the loss of a chance. But if that is a real loss, as his Lordship claimed in his primary argument, then there is no need to leap any evidentiary gaps in order to recognise and compensate for it. We are back with the question: Is loss of a chance a real loss or not? If it is, then the claimant deserves to be compensated; if it is not, then the claimant does not deserve to be compensated. Lord Nicholls said that the loss of a chance both was and was not a genuine loss.

This inconsistency is not unique to Lord Nicholls' judgment; it is also contained, to a greater or lesser extent, in the judgments of their other Lordships, including that of Lord Hoffmann.

(iii) Lord Hoffmann's Main Argument

Lord Hoffmann's main argument is also very simple: the claimant was not entitled to damages for the loss of his chance of a cure because, at least in the eyes of the law, loss of a chance is not a genuine loss. This is because:

> the law regards the world as in principle bound by laws of causality. Everything has a determinate cause, even if we do not know what it is. . . . The fact that proof is rendered difficult or impossible . . . makes no difference. There is no inherent uncertainty about what caused something to happen in the past or about whether something which happened in the past will cause something to happen in the future. Everything is determined by causality. What we lack is knowledge and the law deals with lack of knowledge by the concept of the burden of proof.[133]

In other words, Lord Hoffmann accepted the premise of Lord Nicholls' secondary argument: that the claimant belonged either to the survivor or non-survivor class, that he either would have or would not have been cured had he been treated promptly. On this understanding, the claimant never had a 42 per cent chance of recovery. He either had a 100 per cent chance or a 0 per cent chance, though we do not know which. We say that there was a 42 per cent

---

[133] *Gregg v Scott* [2005] UKHL 2, [2005] 2 AC 176, [79].

chance of recovery, not because there was one, but because we *do not know* whether the claimant would have recovered or not. That is, the figure of 42 per cent relates, not to the claimant's condition, but to our knowledge or lack thereof: we *say* that there was a 42 per cent chance of a cure because we *do not know* whether the claimant would have been cured or not but, in general, 42 per cent of peole in a similar position to the claimant are cured. Hence, the defendant either did deprive the claimant of a cure or he did not, and, given the state of our knowledge, the chance of the former was 42 per cent and of the latter 58 per cent. It was more likely than not, then, that the defendant did not cause any injury (of the relevant kind) to the claimant. Moreover, on this view, the claimant's case in *Gregg v Scott* was no different from an ordinary case involving factual uncertainty and, the odds being as they were, the claimant had to fail.

(iv) Lord Hoffmann's Secondary Argument

Interestingly, however, later in his judgment Lord Hoffmann also accepted the first of Lord Nicholls' claims: that the claimant's 'loss of a chance' was a real loss. He said:

> Academic writers have suggested that in cases of clinical negligence, the need to prove causation is too restrictive of liability. . . . In the present case it is urged that Mr Gregg has suffered a wrong and ought to have a remedy. Living for more than 10 years is something of great value to him and he should be compensated for the possibility that the delay in diagnosis may have reduced his chances of doing so.[134]

Crucially, his Lordship's response to this point was not, as the above would suggest, to reassert that there was no loss. Instead his Lordship argued that allowing recovery would be inconsistent with authority and would result in too much litigation that would be impossible to constrain through the adoption of sensible 'control mechanisms'.[135] Neither of those replies would be necessary if, as Lord Hoffmann had earlier suggested, the claimant had suffered no loss as the result of the defendant's negligence. In fact, such replies would be extremely odd. If the defendant did not cause the claimant loss, then what is the point of appealing to such authority and floodgates arguments when a result in favour of the defendant would be axiomatic? Accordingly, replying in this fashion implicitly admits that the claimant did suffer such a loss.[136]

---

[134] *Ibid,* [84].

[135] *Ibid,* [85]–[90].

[136] In *Hotson v East Berkshire Area Health Authority* [1987] AC 750 (CA), the Court of Appeal accepted the premise of Lord Nicholls' main argument and in *Hotson v East Berkshire Area Health Authority* [1987] AC 750 (HL) the House of Lords adopted that of Lord Hoffmann.

B. What Does it Mean to Say that There Was a Chance?

Obviously, the crucial question here is: is loss of a chance a real loss or not? If it is, then it seems to follow that recovery for such loss ought to be permitted. If loss of a chance is not a real loss, however, then clearly it should not be compensatable.

The question turns on the distinction between objective and epistemological probability. Objective probability is a feature of the world. An event has an objective probability (of greater than 0 per cent and less than 100 per cent) if there really is a chance that it will or will not happen. Perhaps the paradigm example of such is the decay of a Uranium atom. According to quantum theory, Uranium atoms decay in an indeterminate fashion, in the sense that the moment of decay is to a degree random. Even given complete knowledge of the world and its laws, it would be impossible to say with certainty when an atom will decay. Accordingly, there is an objective chance that a Uranium atom will decay at any point in time. Epistemological probability, on the other hand, is not a feature of the world but reflects only our understanding of the world. On this level, probability is concerned with practical predictability. Imagine that we are playing a game with a die. I roll the die and it falls off the table and out of sight. We are inclined to say that the chance it landed on a 6, say, is 16 per cent. But we say this knowing that the die either has or has not landed on a 6. In that sense, we do not believe that there is any *chance* that it has landed on a 6: it either has or it has not. But we say that there is a 16 per cent chance that it has landed on 6, because we would predict that (over time) the die would land on 6 16 per cent of the time.

According to Lord Nicholls' main and Lord Hoffmann's secondary arguments, the claimant in *Gregg v Scott* possessed an objective chance of a cure, and that chance was reduced by the defendant's negligence.[137] However, according to Lord Hoffmann's primary and Lord Nicholls' secondary arguments, the claimant possessed only an epistemological chance of a cure. The reason for this difference is that their Lordships assumed that the contracting and development of cancer are both a deterministic and indeterministic process. It is necessary briefly to examine these notions.

Causation is deterministic if effects are uniquely determined by causes. Determinists hold that for every event there exists a preexisting state of affairs—the cause—that is related to the event in such a way that it would violate a law of nature for that state to exist but the event not to happen. Indeterminists deny this claim. It is important to realise that only indeterminism allows for the existence of objective probabilities. According to determinism, there are no objective chances, as the world is completely and deterministically governed by natural laws.

---

[137] Of course, according to this view the claimant also possessed an epistemological chance of a cure, but that is not significant for our purposes.

It is this scientific and philosophical question that lies at the heart of *Gregg v Scott* and similar cases, and these cases cannot adequately be settled without confronting it. It is clear that the law has traditionally adopted the view that the world is deterministic.[138] In the following, I explore two important arguments that suggest that this position should be abandoned.

(i) The Argument from Quantum Physics

It is sometimes said that quantum physics has put an end to the notion of universal determinism, and that it follows from this that courts should also adopt an indeterministic understanding of causation and recognise, at least in some cases, the existence of objective chances.[139] But this argument almost certainly commits a fallacy of composition. Though it does follow from the truth of quantum physics, if indeed the theory is true,[140] that the world is to an extent indeterministic, it does not follow that 'real' chances—in a sense of 'real' to be explained in the following—exist with respect to the kinds of situations that face courts.

In particular, it is important to remember that quantum physics is a theory about the behaviour of sub-atomic particles. It would involve an enormous leap to apply the conclusions of quantum physics directly to events such as motor vehicle accidents, house fires and the development of cancer. The reason for this is succinctly summarised by Roy Weatherford:

> [T]he randomness and uncertainty taken as implied by quantum mechanics operates primarily at the micro-particle level. As more and more particles enter the calculations, a statistical smoothing occurs. Thus, while the theory implies that there is some chance that all the particles in a table will simultaneously and randomly happen to move upwards, so that the table will levitate, the odds against such an occurrence are so astronomical that it is not reasonable to expect an event of this sort even once in the entire history of the universe.[141]

This is why quantum physics is a theory of physics, and not of chemistry, biology, engineering, etc. The point is not that quantum theory *excludes* the existence of quantum effects above the sub-atomic level, but rather that the theory says nothing about such effects and one cannot assume that because some quantum activity takes place at the sub-atomic level it takes place

---

[138] H Reece, 'Losses of Chances in the Law' (1996) 59 *MLR* 188, 205 suggests that this may be because the legal rules were largely developed in the 19th century, when universal determinism was at its most fashionable in the sciences and/or because a belief in determinism is encouraged by retrospective investigation of events.

[139] See, in particular, *ibid*, 193f.

[140] It is important to remember that quantum theory is inconsistent with relativity theory, according to which the universe is entirely deterministic. Perhaps these views will one day be reconciled, but there is no reason to assume that the reconciliation will preserve quantum theory's commitment to indeterminism.

[141] RC Weatherford, 'Determinism' in T Honderich (ed), *The Oxford Companion to Philosophy* (Oxford University Press, Oxford, 1995).

elsewhere. Accordingly, even if indeterminism were true, the chances that exist with regard to phenomena relevant for courts are so low as to be negligible. Indeed, it would be irrational for courts to take them into account. It is right, then, for courts to ignore such chances. With respect to *Gregg v Scott*, for instance, while there may have been an objective chance that the claimant either would or would not have been cured, this chance is so low, so astronomically low, that courts can and must ignore it. The claimant belonged to the survivor group or to the non-survivor group *simpliciter*, or he belonged prima facie to the survivor or non-survivor group but had an objective chance of not being or of being cured, respectively, so low that 'the odds against such an occurrence [ie not being or being cured] are so astronomical that it is not reasonable to expect an event of this sort even once in the entire history of the universe'. For all practical purposes, then, the claimant belonged to either the survivor or non-survivor group and had no real chance of a cure.

Note that this point has nothing to do with the *de minimis* rule. It is not only courts that should ignore such small possibilities, but scientists working on the relevant phenomenon as well. If we assumed that the development of cancer, for instance, is indeterministic in the way lawyers sometimes suggest, then this would imply that there was no point in scientists looking for the causes of cancer. What is the point of looking for the causes of a random process?

It is important to stress the implications of this point. Consider the following passage from Baroness Hale's judgment which explores *Hotson v East Berkshire Area Health Authority*.[142] In that case, the claimant suffered a fall which injured his hip. He was then taken to the defendant's hospital where, due to the defendant's employees' negligence, his knee but not his hip was X-rayed. He was then told to go home and return in 10 days if necessary. The claimant developed pain and returned to the hospital. His hip was then X-rayed and a risk of avascular necrosis was discovered. This risk existed because of inadequate blood supply to the region. The claimant was operated on, but the operation did not prevent the development of avascular necrosis. The trial judge found that it was 75 per cent likely that the claimant's blood vessels were so damaged when the claimant first presented in hospital that avascular necrosis would have occurred even had prompt treatment been given. In *Gregg v Scott*, Baroness Hale remarked:

> The House of Lords [in *Hotson*] treated this as a case in which the die was already cast by the time the claimant got to the hospital (or at least the claimant could not prove otherwise). The defendant had not even caused the loss of the chance of saving the situation, because by the time the claimant got to them there was no chance. The coin had already been tossed, and had come down heads or tails. But there must be many cases in which that is not so. The coin is in the air. The claimant does have a chance of a favourable outcome which chance is wiped out or significantly reduced by the negligence. The coin is whipped out of the air before it has been able to land.[143]

[142] [1987] AC 750 (HL).
[143] *Gregg v Scott* [2005] UKHL 2, [2005] 2 AC 176, [211].

The talk of the coin is, of course, metaphorical; but it is perhaps the central metaphor in this context, most often relied on by courts and commentators. And the metaphor is revealing. It is assumed by Baroness Hale that after a coin has landed there is a fact of the matter about whether it landed on heads or tails, but after it has been tossed but before it has landed there is no fact as to where it will land. But that is wrong. When the coin is in the air there is a fact of the matter as to which side it will land on, and it would be possible for people with sufficiently sensitive equipment to determine which side that is. There is, then, no objective chance here.[144] Nor does it matter whether interference occurs. If the coin is 'whipped out of the air' before it lands, it remains true that it would have landed on heads or on tails, and again sufficiently sensitive equipment would enable us to determine which result would have occurred.

Nevertheless, we *say* that there is a 50 per cent chance that a tossed coin will land either on heads or on tails. We mean that when we toss a coin, under usual circumstances, it is *impossible to predict* which side it will land on, and that all we are able to say is that *we can be no more certain* that it will land on heads than on tails. The 'chance', then, refers not to the coin but to our knowledge. It is an epistemological but not objective chance.

Similarly, when we say that smoking raises the chance of cancer, we do not mean that smoking sets off a random process within the body that may result in cancer. If we did, then there would not be any point in looking for the causal connection between smoking and cancer. We mean that smoking produces many causally determined processes to begin in the body that may or may not produce cancer. Because we do not know enough about these processes, and because the processes are largely impossible to observe, we say that smoking increases the chance of cancer. Again, the 'chance' has nothing to do with what goes on inside the smoker's body, but with our knowledge.[145]

With respect to *Gregg v Scott*, then, the 42 per cent chance of a cure that the claimant was said to have had had he been treated promptly refers, not to the claimant's condition, but to our lack of knowledge. What this figure meant was that, though we are sure that the claimant belonged either to the survivor or non-survivor group, we do not know which group. And we know that 42 per cent of people in the position that the claimant was in, as we understand that position, are cured. Therefore, we say that there was a 42 per cent chance of a cure. But that '42 per cent chance' was never something that the claimant actually had. It was an epistemological and not an objective chance. The claimant

---

[144] Or, rather, no objective chance that makes any practical difference.

[145] Incidentally, the philosophical debate that occurs in this context is largely over the following kind of question: If smokers do not always develop cancer, can it be right to say that smoking causes cancer? Many wish to answer this question in the affirmative, and so develop accounts of causation that are in some sense probabilistic. But none of this is to suggest that the underlying processes in producing cancer are in any way random or indeterminate. The debate is over the appropriate use and meaning of the term 'causation', not over the fundamental structure of the universe. It is quite mistaken to take these debates over probabilistic causation as having anything to do with the debate between determinism and indeterminism of the kind we are discussing here.

either would have been cured or he would not have been. Therefore, he did not lose any chance when the defendant failed to treat him promptly. There should be no recovery for loss of a chance, because it is not a real loss. It is simply a form of factual uncertainty.

(ii) Free Will

In *Gregg v Scott*, Lord Hoffmann claimed that:

> One striking exception to the assumption that everything is determined by impersonal laws of causality is the actions of human beings. The law treats human beings as having free will and the ability to choose between different courses of action, however strong may be the reasons for them to choose one course rather than another.[146]

This claim is strongly to be resisted. On its face, it is obviously wrong. Imagine that a court is faced with the odd claim that the defendant flew merely by flapping his arms. Of course, courts would reject such testimony, but why? The answer is that flying by flapping one's arms is physically impossible—ie inconsistent with the laws of nature. It would be ridiculous for courts (or anyone else) to even entertain the possibility. But that argument applies to all actions. Courts (and others) should never accept that peole violate the laws of nature. And that means that the behaviour of people *is* determined by natural laws. The alternative is to believe that, in effect, human action is literally miraculous. Whatever freedom of the will entails, it does not imply independence of the laws of nature.

Moreover, it would be wrong to think that the distinction between causal determinism and causal indeterminism is directly related to the issue of freedom of the will. First, in line with the argument above, quantum physics tells us nothing significant about the predictability of human behaviour; it is a theory about sub-atomic particles, not about brains, for instance.

> In terms of the number of particles involved, the brain, and even an individual neuron, is an enormous object for which no such deviation from 'expected' behaviour is likely to occur. Thus even if quantum mechanics as interpreted is true, the bodies of human beings are so near to deterministic as makes no difference.[147]

Secondly, as indeterminism posits randomness, it has nothing to do with freedom.[148] If human behaviour is to an extent random, that does not imply that human beings are free, only that they are to some extent random.

Freedom of the will is, of course, far too complex to be examined here. Suffice it to say, however, that the consensus of opinion amongst the philosophers who research in this area is that some form of compatiblism is the preferred account of free will. Compatiblists hold that freedom is consistent with causal deter-

---

[146] *Gregg v Scott* [2005] UKHL 2, [2005] 2 AC 176, [82].

[147] RC Weatherford, 'Determinism' in T Honderich (ed), *The Oxford Companion to Philosophy* (Oxford University Press, Oxford, 1995).

[148] H Reece, 'Losses of Chances in the Law' (1996) 59 *MLR* 188, 197f, *Gregg v Scott* [2005] UKHL 2, [2005] 2 AC 176 appears to equate indeterminism with freedom.

mination.[149] At the very least, courts should not adopt the bizarre position that human beings are somehow independent of natural laws.

(iii) Loss of Chance and Factual Uncertainty

As we have seen, then, so called 'loss of a chance' is in fact a form of factual uncertainty. Ignoring the infinitesimally small chances that arise according to quantum physics, to say that A lost a chance of x because of y is to say nothing more than that we do not know whether A would have achieved x were it not for y. We misunderstand the phenomenon when we conceptualise it as the loss of a chance.

As we have seen, *Barker v Corus (UK) plc* concerned a victim of mesothelioma who was exposed to asbestos on three discrete occasions, two of which were the responsibility of potential defendants, the third of which was the victim's own responsibility. The House of Lords held that potential defendants in these situations, and in cases such as *Fairchild*, should be liable because of they *created the risk* of the victim's injury. As we also saw, the creation of a risk of injury that has occurred is just another way of conceptualising the causing of a loss of a chance of avoiding that injury. Imagine a *Fairchild*-type situation with the following differences: there are four potential defendants—A, B, C and D— only one of whom caused the claimant's injury, each is 25 per cent likely to have caused the claimant's injury, and we do not know who actually caused the injury. We can regard these defendants as creating a 25 per cent risk of the claimant's injury or as causing the claimant to lose a 25 per cent chance of avoiding the injury. This means that the notion of risk creation is subject to the same difficulties as the idea of loss of a chance. There is no such thing as loss of a chance, nor is there, *in the relevant sense*, any such thing as the creation of a risk.

First, however, it is important to specify what 'creation of a risk' means in this context. In particular, it is important to distinguish this idea from the notion of risk explored primarily in Chapters 3 and 4 above. There, we discovered that a defendant is found liable if he created a real risk of the claimant's injury. It is crucial to note that the idea of risk relevant to that enquiry is entirely different from the notion of risk pertinent here. In relation to the earlier enquiry, the operative notion of risk is foresight. That is, the defendant is found to have been negligent only if, as a reasonable person, he could have predicted that his actions posed a real risk of causing the claimant's injury. This notion of risk is perfectly compatible with that of factual uncertainty. The defendant creates a risk if he puts into play causal factors that either will or will not injure the claimant. It is his inability to predict the consequences of his actions that gives rise to the

---

[149] I do not mean to imply that this view is universally held, however I mean to use the term 'compatiblism' widely to include all views that hold that human beings do not violate the laws of nature. In this sense, then, 'compatiblism' is consistent with views such as the one Henry Allison attributes to Kant in HE Allison, *Kant's Theory of Freedom* (Cambridge University Press, Cambridge, 1990), which Allison takes to be anti-compatiblist.

notion of risk. In this sense, then, risk refers to epistemic not objective probability. Think, for instance, of *Doughty v Turner Manufacturing Co Ltd.*[150] Recall that, in that case, an asbestos and cement cover was negligently knocked into a cauldron containing a sodium cyanide solution at 800 degrees Celsius by one of the defendant's employees. For reasons that, at the time, no one was aware of, an explosion occurred expelling the solution from the cauldron, burning the claimant. The English Court of Appeal held that the defendant could not be liable, because he did not create a real risk of the explosion. This means that the defendant's employee, as a reasonable person, could not have predicted this outcome. It does not mean that the defendant's employee did not actually create a risk of the explosion. Of course he did create such a risk; in fact, coupled with other factors, a certainty. Risk, as it operates in terms of the standard of care, duty of care, remoteness, etc, is an epistemic notion.

However, correctly understood, risk in the context of causation cannot be epistemic but must be objective. Causation, after all, is concerned with the world. To say that the defendants in *Barker* created a risk of the victim's disease in terms of causation is to say that the defendant created an objective probability of that injury. But there are no such things, or at least no such things of which it would be rational for judges to take cognizance. Take again the example in which the claimant is injured by one of four defendants, though we do not know who. According to the House of Lords in *Barker*, we can find all liable because each caused the risk of the claimant's injury. But that is wrong. If *A* caused the claimant's injury, then *B* did not create any objective risk of that injury at all. The same holds for *C* and *D*. Dealing with cases of factual uncertainty in terms of risk creation involves muddying an already difficult issue in order to appear to solve it.

C. Another Kind of Loss of a Chance

It is important to distinguish two kinds of cases. In the first type of case, of which *Gregg v Scott* is an instance, the uncertainty surrounds whether the defendant violated a right in the claimant. In these cases, the issue is simply one of causation and should be dealt with according to the discussion in the section above and in Chapter 12.[151] There, 'loss of a chance' is simply a synonym for factual uncertainty. Conversely, there are cases in which it is certain that the defendant violated the claimant's rights, but uncertainty surrounds the extent of the claimant's consequent injury. The contract case, *Chaplin v Hicks*, is a case

---

[150] [1964] 1 QB 518 (CA).

[151] Hence, most of the cases referred to in J Fleming, 'Probabilistic Causation in Tort Law' (1989) 68 *Canadian Bar Review* 661 and J Fleming, 'Probabilistic Causation in Tort Law: A Postscript' (1991) 70 *Canadian Bar Review* 136 are irrelevant in this context, including *Melec v J C Hutton pty Ltd* (1990) 169 CLR 638 (HCA) which is a case involving over-determination, not loss of a chance.

in point.[152] The defendant breached his contract with the claimant by refusing to allow her to enter a beauty contest. The court assessed the damages by dividing the total prize money by the number of entrants and awarded the claimant that amount. There was no question that the defendant had violated the claimant's rights. In fact, the defendant's argument was not that he should escape liability but that nominal damages should have been awarded. Hence, given that the claimant's right was violated, she was entitled to the value of her expectation. This was appropriately calculated by estimating the claimant's likely winnings. This is in no way analogous to *Gregg v Scott*.

A similar case, this time in negligence, is *Mulvaine v Joseph*.[153] The defendant negligently injured the claimant's hand. The claimant, a professional golfer, was unable to compete in tournaments, and recovered in accordance with the court's assessment of his likely winnings. Again, there is no question that the defendant interfered with the claimant's rights, in this case his bodily integrity. The issue was solely how much that interference was worth to the claimant, how much worse off the claimant was as a result. In order to determine this, it was necessary to take into account the claimant's likely earnings as a golfer. That required the court to estimate the claimant's potential winnings. Again, this is nothing like *Gregg v Scott*.[154]

Once more we see that focus on the parties' rights and taking seriously the principled approach solves apparently problematic issues with the modern law of negligence.

---

[152] [1911] 2 KB 786 (CA).

[153] (1968) 112 Sol J 927 (QBD). See also *Kitchen v Royal Air Force Association* [1958] 1 WLR 563 (CA); *Sellars v Adelaide Petroleum NL* (1994) 197 CLR 332 (HCA).

[154] J Fleming, 'Probabilistic Causation in Tort Law' (1989) 68 *Canadian Bar Review* 661, 673–4 argues that to distinguish *Hotson* from *Chaplin* and *Mulvaine v Joseph* 'on the ground that [the latter] deal with quantification of damages, not with causation, does not make the loss any less speculative than the other'. This point is quite correct, but it is irrelevant. Moreover, M Stauch, 'Causation, Risk, and Loss of Chance in Medical Negligence' (1997) 17 *OJLS* 205, 219, following suggestions in *Hotson* itself, mistakenly maintains that the distinction between these two types of cases lies in a perceived distinction between past and future damage.

14

Conclusion

I. CORRECTIVE JUSTICE AND LEGAL CHANGE

BEFORE I CONCLUDE, it is important to consider a reply to the entire argument of this book. I have contended that the law of negligence has a structure based on corrective justice. I have also criticised departures from this structure as, inter alia, unprincipled and chaotic. Perhaps, however, the modern law's departure from corrective justice heralds not chaos but a new law of negligence with a different structure. At present, the law appears chaotic, but this is because it has yet fully to shake off corrective justice. But when it does so it will reveal itself as no less principled than the view I support here. Surely, I cannot be arguing that the law should forever be captured by its past.

First, however, although I have argued that the law of negligence possesses an enduring structure, this does not entail that change in the positive law is unacceptable. As indicated in Chapter 2, our ideas of the implications of corrective justice are bound to alter over time as we reject unfounded prejudices. It was once widely accepted that it was no injustice for a man to beat his wife or for a man to own another human being. This was because classes of human beings were once viewed as being less than fully moral persons. Conversely, Grotius believed that it was equally unjust to kill a man as to seduce his wife.[1] Our view of these matters has changed and the positive law has followed suit. Hence, that the law of negligence is always about corrective justice does not mean that it cannot develop.[2]

An example of the modern development of the common law was seen in Chapter 3 in our discussion of *McHale v Watson*.[3] We discovered that, although a majority of the High Court of Australia enunciated the correct principles, they applied those principles incorrectly because of the judges' sexist views. No doubt, there are many similar mistakes that haunt the contemporary positive law and it is the task of academic commentators and others to point them out

---

[1] H Grotius, *The Law of War and Peace* (trans FW Kelsey, Clarendon Press, Oxford, 1925) 60, [I II 7].

[2] This is also why it is impossible to imagine this argument being raised with respect to distributive justice. No one would argue that Parliament should not enforce distributive justice because public policy should change over time.

[3] (1966) 115 CLR 199 (HCA).

and eliminate them.[4] Hence, far from being an impediment to the law's development, corrective justice demands development.[5]

Secondly, in light of the previous chapters, it cannot be said that the departures from the principled approach suggest an alternative *structure*. Instead, they appear to be almost random. It is also telling that those who oppose the notion that the law of negligence is based on corrective justice are unable to suggest a credible alternative structure. Distributive justice will not do. This is because, as is obvious to anyone living in modern democratic societies, there is widespread disagreement on the nature and content of distributive justice. Hence, distributive justice is not able to direct judicial decision making in a meaningful way.[6] Moreover, although the fact that judges belong to the same socio-economic elite tends to restrict the amount of disagreement between them as to distributive justice, this is not a good argument in favour of basing law on distributive justice. Accordingly, opponents of the principled approach sometimes suggest that the law serves a multiplicity of often competing functions.[7] But that is to give up on the notion that the law possesses a coherent structure. We really are faced with a stark choice: the law of negligence is either based on corrective justice or it has no perspicuous structure whatsoever.

Thirdly, corrective justice is a fundamental aspect of morality.[8] Though it is no more important than ethics or distributive justice, it is also no less important. The notion that one must make good one's wrongdoing is central to our understanding of ourselves and of our relationships with other people. Moreover, although it has become fashionable for legal academics to think of private law as if it were a kind of public law—a law that imposes rules for the public interest rather than a law that achieves justice between individuals, as if our only meaningful connection to one another were through the medium of the state, a surely absurd view that has rendered the legal academy blind to at least half of human existence—the fact remains that our interactions with other individuals *as individuals* remain pervasive and we will always require the law to police it. Accordingly, there will always be a demand for the law to reflect corrective justice. Therefore, I do not argue that the law of negligence should be trapped by the notions of the past. It should be captured by notions that have been at the forefront of Western legal analysis since ancient Greece because they are funda-

---

[4] A good example of this is M Moran, *Rethinking the Reasonable Person: An Egalitarian Reconstruction of the Objective Standard* (Oxford University Press, Oxford, 2003).

[5] See also LE Weinrib and EJ Weinrib, 'Constitutional Values and Private Law in Canada' in D Friedmann and D Barak-Erez (eds), *Human Rights in Private Law* (Hart Publishing, Oxford, 2001) especially 48–51, 59–67.

[6] The same is not true of corrective justice. See EJ Weinrib, *The Idea of Private Law* (Harvard University Press, Cambridge, Mass, 1995) 210–14; A Beever, 'Aristotle on Justice, Equity, and Law' (2004) 10 *Legal Theory* 33, 44–7.

[7] See eg P Cane, *Responsibility in Law and Morality* (Hart Publishing, Oxford, 2002) 57.

[8] Private law 'is the repository of our must deeply embedded intuitions about justice and personal responsibility': EJ Weinrib, *The Idea of Private Law* (Harvard University Press, Cambridge, Mass, 1995) 1.

mental to our moral world view.[9] This is no entrapment, no straitjacket,[10] unless reason itself is a prison.

Moreover, though I have argued that the modern approaches to the duty of care and other issues are inadequate, we have also seen that the modern law frequently recommends the same outcomes as the principled approach. The differences concern not so much what we do but how we understand what we do. In the end, then, no matter what approach is adopted, no matter how large the apparent influence of policy, I predict that the law of negligence will always tend back to corrective justice. In that light, this book does not recommend the principled approach out of a desire to preserve corrective justice. Corrective justice can look after itself.[11] Rather, this book is an attempt to reveal what the law is and will always be predominantly about. The question is not whether the law of negligence should reflect corrective justice, but whether, given that it always will reflect corrective justice to a large extent, whether we are able to understand the law and deal rationally with it.

At this point, it may be useful to consider further how corrective justice can produce legal change. I do so by examining in detail Lord Diplock's seminal discussion in *Home Office v Dorset Yacht Co Ltd* of the way in which judges appropriately alter the positive law with respect to the duty of care.[12] In general, according to Lord Diplock, in approaching an individual case:

> the judicial development of the law of negligence rightly proceeds by seeking first to identify the relevant characteristics that are common to the kinds of conduct and relationship between the parties which are involved in the case for decision and the kinds of conduct and relationships which have been held in previous decisions of the courts to give rise to a duty of care.
>
> The method adopted at this stage of the process is analytical and inductive. It starts with an analysis of the characteristics of the conduct and relationship involved in each of the decided cases. But the analyst must know what he is looking for, and this involves his approaching his analysis with some general conception of conduct and relationships which ought to give rise to a duty of care.[13]

---

[9] Aristotle, *Nicomachean Ethics* (trans T Irwin, Hackett, Indianapolis, Ind, 1999) 72–6, [1131b25–1134a16]; EJ Weinrib, *The Idea of Private Law* (Harvard University Press, Cambridge, Mass, 1995) 6.

[10] Compare *Sutherland Shire Council v Heyman* (1985) 157 CLR 424, 497 (HCA) (Deane J); J Stapleton, 'Comparative Economic Loss: Lessons from Case-Law-Focused "Middle Theory"' (2002) 50 *University of California of Los Angeles Law Review* 531, 532.

[11] At least this is so unless departures from corrective justice are imbedded in statute. Two examples of this are New Zealand's Injury Prevention, Rehabilitation, and Compensation Act 2001 and the recent negligence reforms in Australia such as the Civil Liability Act 2002 (NSW) and Civil Liability Act 2003 (Qld). As New Zealand's Injury Prevention, Rehabilitation, and Compensation Act is justified (correctly or not) on the basis that the distributive justice concerns it promotes are more important than the corrective justice concerns it replaces, it is unobjectionable from the perspective of the argument presented here. However, the Australian Acts, in as far as they pretend to capture and clarify the law of negligence while in fact altering it significantly, are insidious.

[12] *Home Office v Dorset Yacht Co Ltd* [1970] AC 1004, 1058–9 (HL)

[13] *Ibid.*

In other words, the first stage of the enquiry is to discover whether the facts in the instant case fall under a principle developed in other cases. The relevant facts of the instant case are discovered by looking at the conduct of the parties and the relationship between them, ie in accordance with corrective justice. Moreover, the principles are themselves designed to reflect normatively salient features of interactions between parties, also in accordance with corrective justice. As Lord Diplock rightly noted, this process is inductive in the sense that it involves judgement.

Lord Diplock then described in more detail the process of elucidating these principles from the cases.

> This analysis leads to a proposition which can be stated in the form:
>   'In all the decisions that have been analysed a duty of care has been held to exist wherever the conduct and the relationship possessed each of the characteristics A, B, C, D, etc., and has not so far been found to exist when any of these characteristics were absent.'[14]

Hence, these principles are the product of abstraction from the individual decided cases. If all (or, more realistically, a sufficient majority of) past cases in which factors A, B, C and D were present led to the existence of a duty of care, then a principle exists according to which a duty of care exists in cases in which A, B, C and D are present. '[T]hat proposition is converted to: "In all cases where the conduct and relationship possess each of the characteristics A, B, C, D, etc., a duty of care arises."'[15]

Lord Diplock then explored how these principles help the judge to decide whether a duty of care exists in the instant case:

> The conduct and relationship involved in the case for decision is then analysed to ascertain whether they possess each of these characteristics. If they do the conclusion follows that a duty of care does arise in the case for decision.[16]

If the instant case falls under the relevant principles, then a duty of care arises. If it does not, then no duty of care exists.

But that is not the end of the matter. Because it is open to the judge we are imagining to alter the positive law, she must consider whether the extant principles should be revised. Lord Diplock described this process as follows:

> But since ex hypothesi the kind of case which we are now considering offers a choice whether or not to extend the kinds of conduct or relationships which give rise to a duty of care, the conduct or relationship which is involved in it will lack at least one of the characteristics A, B, C or D, etc. and the choice is exercised by making a policy decision as to whether or not a duty of care ought to exist if the characteristic which is

---

[14] *Ibid*, 1059.

[15] Lord Diplock claims that this process is deductive, but this is a mistake. All steps in this process involve judgement.

[16] *Home Office v Dorset Yacht Co Ltd* [1970] AC 1004, 1059 (HL).

lacking were absent or redefined in terms broad enough to include the case under consideration.[17]

It is open to the judge to revise the principles and the decision to undertake this revision is guided by policy.

On the face of it, this is an appeal to the policy driven approach, and that is surely how it would be taken by the majority of modern academics. That conclusion is also suggested by Lord Diplock's association of his own view with Lord Denning's.[18] But Lord Diplock's understanding of policy is not the modern one. Nor does it share much with Lord Denning's. According to Lord Diplock:

> The policy decision will be influenced by the same general conception of what ought to give rise to a duty of care as was used in approaching the analysis. The choice to extend is given effect to by redefining the characteristics in more general terms so as to exclude the necessity to conform to limitations imposed by the former definition which are considered to be inessential.[19]

The 'general conception of what ought to give rise to a duty of care as was used in approaching the analysis' is, as we saw above and as we have seen throughout this book, corrective justice—'characteristics that are common to the kinds of conduct and relationship between the parties'.[20] For Lord Diplock, then, the appeal to policy does not involve a reference to distributive justice or other concerns. Rather, it is the acknowledgement that corrective justice should be used to shape the law. If the analysis reveals that the extant positive legal principles do not achieve corrective justice, then those principles must be revised so that they do. That is what used to be called the law working itself pure.

Here we see the appropriate and important difference between proper judicial and academic reasoning in relation to the law of negligence. The academic is permitted to begin with the relevant moral principles—corrective justice and the principles of the principled approach—and deduce appropriate outcomes. Largely, that has been my task here. But common law judges are not permitted to reason in that fashion. Rather, they are constrained by precedent as academics are not. Hence, they must begin with the case law as it is and deduce principles from it. But, while these principles may be binding for lower court judges, they hold only prima facie for appellate judges, particularly those in final appellate courts. Not only must those judges have a good understanding of the principles that arise from the case law, they must also have or develop a sophisticated account of the 'general conception of what ought to give rise to a duty of care' or liability in general. In other words, they must have an understanding of a 'general conception of relations giving rise to a duty of care [and other aspects of liability], of which the particular cases found in the books are but

---

[17] *Ibid.*
[18] *Ibid*, 1058.
[19] *Ibid*, 1059.
[20] *Ibid*, 1058.

instances'.[21] That has been missing from modern legal analysis and this book is an attempt to fill some of that gap.

II. POLICY AND PRINCIPLE: REDISCOVERING THE LAW OF NEGLIGENCE

According to the principled approach, a defendant is liable to a claimant if and only if the defendant created an unreasonable risk of the actual injury suffered by the claimant. A risk is unreasonable if it was substantial or if it was small and there was no good reason for failing to eliminate the risk. That question is determined by examining the relationship between the parties. An injury is the violation of a primary legal right. Also, the claimant has a secondary right to recover only for the extent to which the defendant's wrongdoing made him worse off. Finally, the value of the claimant's loss is sometimes determined by the law. This occurs when the law states that the claimant is not entitled to enjoy the subject matter of the loss. In summary, that is the whole of the law of negligence as examined in this book.

Though it can be difficult to apply this approach in certain circumstances, the approach itself is a simple and elegant account of a kind of moral responsibility: viz corrective justice. Partly because of its simplicity and elegance, and partly because it captures corrective justice in this area, it encounters none of the problems that haunt the modern law of negligence. Conversely, as I summarise now, those problems arise because of the tendency of modern lawyers to ignore various parts of the principled approach.

First, it is said that, according to the ordinary principles of the law, a defendant owes a duty of care to a claimant if the defendant placed the claimant at a reasonably foreseeable risk of injury. Moreover, the modern law understands 'reasonably foreseeable' to mean conceivable. But there are a great many injuries that are reasonably foreseeable in that sense, and it would be inappropriate to impose duties of care with regard to all of those injuries. Hence, there is a need to restrict the ambit of the duty of care. This is done arbitrarily by restricting the duty of care in terms of a vacuous notion of proximity, by appealing to an equally vacuous notion of incrementalism, by articulating politically controversial and usually inadequately enunciated and argued for policies said to call for restrictions on liability, or by treating remoteness as a policy-based constraint on liability.

This problem arises because the unity of the law of negligence has been forgotten. According to the principled approach, the defendant owed a duty of care to the claimant only if the defendant created an unreasonable risk of the claimant's injury, and unreasonable risk is defined as discussed above. This approach is able to determine liability within a well-defined and justifiable sphere. It has no need to appeal to policy.

---

[21] *M'Alister (or Donoghue) (Pauper) v Stevenson* [1932] AC 562, 580 (HL Sc).

Secondly, it is believed that the standard of care is set in accordance with the interests of the public. The most obvious standard is the one adopted in the criminal law, essentially a subjective standard. After all, if both criminal law and tort law are aimed at protecting the public interest, it appears that they should set the same standard. As we saw in Chapter 3, in *Mansfield v Weetabix Ltd*,[22] the English Court of Appeal applied a subjective test. It did so in the belief that it would be unreasonable for the public to expect a defendant to live up to a standard that he was incapable of meeting. On this approach, the ordinary objective standard is seen as an exception to general principle that must be justified in terms of policy.[23] Moreover, given that the law sometimes adjusts the ordinary objective standard, it is necessary to invent yet more policies to explain and justify those adjustments. Furthermore, this approach must understand the defence of contributory negligence in terms of policy. For instance, one may argue that contributory negligence is designed to preserve the incentive on claimants to look out for their own interests.[24]

These problems are caused because it has been forgotten that the standard of care should be set to achieve justice between the parties. On this view, the ordinary objective standard, the adjustments to that standard and the defence of contributory negligence are designed to do justice between the parties and require no justification from policy. As Cardozo CJ worried, the modern approaches ignore 'the fundamental difference between tort and crime'.[25] The account of wrongdoing that those models presuppose is the criminal one: falling below a standard determined in accordance with the interests of the public as a whole. And the limitations—the duty of care and remoteness—are seen as limitations enforced for the public interest. This is a very considerable distance indeed from the model propounded in our foundational cases in the law of negligence.

Thirdly, it is believed that the principles of the law of negligence would generate recovery limited only by reasonable foreseeability. This would allow recovery for, inter alia, all foreseeable economic loss, including but not restricted to loss suffered in reliance on statements. That result would produce indeterminate liability. Consequently, there is a need to devise policies in order to restrict recovery for economic loss.

This problem arises because it has been forgotten that an injury at law is the violation of a legal right. Because relational and pure economic losses do not flow from the violation of a right in the claimant, they are irrecoverable according to the ordinary principles of the law. Moreover, because rights to rely on statements are created only if the defendant assumed responsibility for that

---

[22] [1998] 1 WLR 1263 (CA).

[23] Alternatively, T Honoré, *Responsibility and Fault* (Hart Publishing, Oxford, 1999) ch 2 argues for an account of ethical responsibility that accommodates the law of negligence. For reasons explored in J Evans, 'Choice and Responsibility' (2002) 27 *Australian Journal of Legal Philosophy* 97, I do not believe that this attempt is successful.

[24] Compare RA Posner, *Economic Analysis of Law*, 2nd edn (Little, Brown and Co, Boston, Mass, 1977) 123–4.

[25] *Palsgraf v Long Island Railroad Co* 162 NE 99, 101 (NY CA 1928).

reliance, recovery in this area is well defined and is in no need of limitations based on policy.

Finally, it is believed that policies must be invented to demonstrate why a claimant who consents to the defendant's behaviour cannot recover, why sometimes a claimant who has engaged in illegal activities is not entitled to compensation, why sometimes a claimant can recover though she cannot show on the balance of probabilities that the defendant caused her loss and why a claimant cannot recover compensation for over-determined loss where one of the over-determining causes was innocent (thus instituting a peculiarly legal understanding of factual causation).

All of those problems arise because the common law neglects the rights of the parties. The defence of voluntary assumption of risk applies because the defendant does not violate the claimant's right if the claimant wills the defendant's action. The defence of illegality applies because some factual losses are, in the eyes of the law, losses of no value. A claimant can recover when a defendant creates an unreasonable risk that prevents the claimant from vindicating her secondary rights because, in creating that risk, the defendant violates the claimant's primary rights. And claimants cannot recover for over-determined losses when one of the causes of those losses was innocent, because the claimant has a secondary right to recover only for the extent to which the claimant was made worse off by another's wrongdoing. Again, none of this requires appeal to policy.

The modern law of negligence is a mess because we have forgotten what its principles actually are. The modern approaches create the mess by distorting the principles of the law. They then seek to tidy the mess by inventing policies to determine the scope of liability. But those policies increase the mess by moving us further from the principles of the law. In consequence, there is a new mess that attracts new policies that create more mess and so on and on. None of this is necessary. Without the modern approaches, there would be no mess in the first place. Recall from Chapter 1 Jane Stapleton's view that it is '[s]imply not feasible' to ignore policy concerns in describing the law of negligence.[26] This is a self-fulfilling prophesy. We should not be captured by it. When we rediscover the principles of the law of negligence, we see that the law is able to determine liability without any appeal to policy whatsoever.

It is no small historical irony that at the same moment when, in many countries, governmental advisors (especially economists) lost confidence in their and in their governments' ability to utilise specific policies to produce desirable outcomes, advisors for courts (especially economist academics) began in earnest to argue that courts should utilise specific policies in order to produce desirable outcomes. Whatever the situation in government, there seems little doubt that judicial recourse to policy has been damaging.

It is time we returned to a more humble approach to law. Despite its rejection of the modern methodology, this book recommends just such an approach. In

---

[26] J Stapleton, 'The Golden Thread at the Heart of Tort Law: Protection of the Vulnerable' (2003) 24 *Australian Bar Review* 135, 136.

particular, instead of seeing ourselves as creating the law *ex nihilo* in accordance with our political aspirations, the corrective justice model sees the law as lying in norms inherent in human interaction. On this view, the task of lawyers is not to create but to discover: to look at the ways in which human beings interact and extract norms of conduct from that interaction. We should not set out to create a desirable world using the law as a tool, but should create a desirable world by focusing on what we already understand about how human beings interact. This calls for more attention to be paid to the past, particularly to legal history. Not history of the 'realist' kind, where past cases are treated as an occasion to invent policy-based explanations (much in the way post-modern philosophers 'read' texts); a kind of freewheeling and undisciplined neo-Marxism motivated by a plethora of political perspectives. Rather, the appropriate historical approach is to attempt to understand how the court understood the justice of the case. Attention must be paid to what the court actually said. It also involves study of the history of ideas (of which history of law is a part). Justice is something that has been discussed in the West since the days of ancient Greece. It does the subject a considerable disservice when, in the name of justice, courts abandon the principled approach, which was itself carefully designed to reflect justice, without reference to any of the vast history of this discussion, as *frequently* happens in our courts. Only the modern law thinks that justice was invented yesterday. Though our views of justice have changed, justice itself has not changed over the years; nor is it one thing among the English and another among Australians, Canadians or New Zealanders. It is our task to elucidate it and, for lawyers, that means to express justice in principles of law.

There are, I do not doubt, errors in the argument of this book. On occasions I will not have understood corrective justice properly or will have misapplied it to the law of negligence. There will be other areas that I have explained incorrectly. Moreover, there are many issues that I have not traversed. But I hope above all to have shown that the kind of analysis I have pursued here is both possible and rewarding. The law of negligence is not a disaster that needs constant rescuing from policy, or it need not be. It is capable of being understood legally. Seen through the lens of corrective justice, the law is perfectly principled and indeed an extraordinary creation. It is an area of law that deserves our respect rather than the contempt that has been poured on it since 1977, intentionally or not. Academics, at least, should attempt to understand it for itself, rather than use it as a vehicle for expressing and pursing our personal political preferences.

Of course, it may turn out that, even correctly understood, the law of negligence is undesirable. The Eiffel tower may be an impressive structure, but I would not like to live in it. If the law of negligence is indeed undesirable, then we can of course replace it through statute. But we should not ignore it. Those charged with the upkeep of the Eiffel tower should not pretend that it is l'Hôtel de Ville because they would rather live there. The law of negligence has a structure, and it is our primary role as academics to discover what that structure is. That is the first, though by no means the only, task of legal analysis.

Bibliography

ALLISON, HE, *Kant's Theory of Freedom* (Cambridge University Press, Cambridge, 1990).

American Law Institute, *Restatement of the Law of Torts* (American Law Institute Publishers, St Paul, Minn, 1934).

AQUINAS, T, *Summa theologica* (trans English Dominicans, Benziger Bros, New York, 1947).

ARISTOTLE, *Nicomachean Ethics* (trans T Irwin, Hackett, Indianapolis, Ind, 1999).

ASHWORTH, A, *Principles of Criminal Law*, 4th edn (Oxford University Press, Oxford, 2003).

ATIYAH, PS, *The Rise and Fall of Freedom of Contract* (Oxford University Press, Oxford, 1979).

—— 'Personal Injuries in the Twenty-First Century: Thinking the Unthinkable' in P Birks (ed), *Wrongs and Remedies in the Twenty-First Century* (Clarendon Press, Oxford, 1996).

—— *Accidents, Compensation and the Law*, 6th edn (Butterworths, London, 1999).

ATKIN, Lord, 'Law as an Educational Subject' [1932] *Journal of the Society of Public Teachers of Law* 27.

BARKER, K, 'Unreliable Assumptions in the Modern Law of Negligence' (1993) 109 *LQR* 461.

BEEVER, A, 'Cause-In-Fact: Two Steps Out of the Mire' (2001) 51 *University of Toronto Law Journal* 327.

—— 'The Structure of Aggravated and Exemplary Damages' (2003) 23 *OJLS* 87.

—— 'The Law's Function and the Judicial Function' (2003) 20 *New Zealand Universities Law Review* 299.

—— 'All at Sea in the Law of Negligent Misrepresentation' (2003) 9 *New Zealand Business Law Quarterly* 101.

—— 'Particularism and Prejudice in the Law of Tort' (2003) 11 *Tort Law Review* 146.

—— 'Perspectives of Responsibility in Law and Morality' (2003) 27 *Melbourne University Law Review* 905.

—— 'Aristotle on Justice, Equity, and Law' (2004) 10 *Legal Theory* 33.

—— 'A Rights-Based Approach to the Recovery of Economic Loss in Negligence' (2004) 4 *OUCLJ* 25.

—— 'Lord Hoffmann's Mouse' (2004) 10 *New Zealand Business Law Quarterly* 161.

—— 'Justice and Punishment in Tort: A Comparative Theoretical Analysis' in R Grantham and C Rickett (eds), *Justifying Remedies in Private Law* (Cambridge University Press, Cambridge, forthcoming 2007).

—— and Rickett, C, 'Interpretive Legal Theory and the Academic Lawyer' (2005) 68 *MLR* 320.

BENDER, L, 'A Lawyer's Primer on Feminist Theory and Tort' (1988) 38 *Journal of Legal Education* 3.

BENSON, P, 'The Basis for Excluding Liability for Economic Loss in Tort Law' in D Owen (ed), *Philosophical Foundations of Tort Law* (Oxford University Press, Oxford, 1995).

BENSON, P, 'The Idea of a Public Basis of Justification for Contract' (1995) 33 *Osgoode Hall Law Journal* 273.
—— 'The Unity of Contract Law' in P Benson (ed), *The Theory of Contract Law: New Essays* (Cambridge University Press, Cambridge, 2001).
—— 'Equality of Opportunity and Private Law' in D Friedmann and D Barak-Erez (eds), *Human Rights in Private Law* (Hart Publishing, Oxford, 2001).
—— 'Philosophy of Property Law' in J Coleman and S Shapiro (eds), *The Oxford Handbook of Jurisprudence and Philosophy of Law* (Oxford University Press, Oxford, 2002).
—— 'Should *White* v. *Jones* Represent Canadian Law: A Return to First Principles' in JW Neyers, E Chamberlain and SGA Pitel (eds), *Emerging Issues in Tort Law* (Hart Publishing, Oxford, forthcoming 2007).
BENTHAM, J, *The Principles of Morals and Legislation* (Prometheus Books, Amherst, NY, 1988).
BIRKS, P, *Introduction to the Law of Restitution*, 2nd edn (Clarendon Press, Oxford, 1989).
—— 'The Concept of a Civil Wrong' in D Owen (ed), *Philosophical Foundations of Tort Law* (Oxford University Press, Oxford, 1995).
—— *Harassment and Hubris: The Right to an Equality of Respect* (University College Dublin Faculty of Law, Dublin, 1996).
—— 'Definition and Division: A Meditation on *Institutes 3.13*' in P Birks (ed), *The Classification of Obligations* (Clarendon Press, Oxford, 1997).
—— 'More Logic and Less Experience: The Difference between Scots Law and English Law' in D Carey Miller and R Zimmermann (eds), *The Civilian Tradition and Scots Law* (Duncker & Humblot, Berlin, 1997).
—— *Unjust Enrichment* (Clarendon Press, Oxford, 2003).
BISHOP, W, 'Negligent Misrepresentation Through Economists' Eyes' (1980) 96 *LQR* 360.
BLOM, J, 'The Evolving Relationship Between Tort and Contract' (1985) 10 *Canadian Business Law Journal* 257.
BOHLEN, FH, 'The Moral Duty to Aid Others as a Basis of Tort Liability' (1908) 56 *University of Pennsylvania Law Review* 217.
—— 'Contributory Negligence' (1908) 21 *Harvard Law Review* 233.
—— *Studies in the Law of Torts* (Bobbs-Merrill, Indianapolis, Ind, 1926).
BRIDGE, MG, 'Mitigation of Damages in Contract and the Meaning of Avoidable Loss' (1989) 105 *LQR* 398.
BROWN, R, 'Still Crazy After All These Years: *Anns, Cooper v. Hobart* and Pure Economic Loss' (2003) 36 *University of British Columbia Law Review* 159.
—— 'Justifying the Impossibility of Recoverable Relational Economic Loss' (2004) 5 *OUCLJ* 155.
BYRD, SB, and HRUSCHKA, J, 'Duty to Recognize Private Property Ownership: Kant's Theory of Property in his *Doctrine of Right*' (2006) 56 *University of Toronto Law Journal* 217.
—— and —— 'Kant on "Why Must I Keep my Promise?"' (2006) 81 *Chicago-Kent Law Review* 47.
CANE, P, *Tort Law and Economic Interests*, 2nd edn (Clarendon Press, Oxford, 1996).
—— 'Corrective Justice and Correlativity in Private Law', (1996) 16 *OJLS* 471.
—— 'Retribution, Proportionality, and Moral Luck in Tort Law' in P Cane and J Stapleton (eds), *The Law of Obligations: Essays in Celebration of John Fleming* (Oxford University Press, Oxford, 1998).

—— 'Distributive Justice and Tort Law' [2001] *New Zealand Law Review* 401.

—— *Responsibility in Law and Morality* (Hart Publishing, Oxford, 2002).

—— 'Tort Law as Regulation' (2002) 31 *Common Law World Review* 305.

—— 'Reforming Tort Law in Australia: A Personal Perspective' (2003) 27 *Melbourne University Law Review* 649.

CARRIGAN, F, 'A Blast from the Past: The Resurgence of Legal Formalism' (2003) 27 *Melbourne University Law Review* 163.

CHRISTIE, GC, 'The Uneasy Place of Principle in Tort Law' in D Owen (ed), *Philosophical Foundations of Tort Law* (Oxford University Press, Oxford, 1995).

COASE, R, 'The Problem of Social Cost' (1960) 1 *Journal of Law and Economics* 1.

COLEMAN, J, *The Practice of Principle* (Oxford University Press, Oxford, 2001).

COLLINS, H, *Regulating Contracts* (Oxford University Press, Oxford, 1999).

COOKE, R, *Turning Points of the Common Law* (Sweet & Maxwell, London, 1997).

COOKE, LORD, OF THORNDON, 'The Right of *Spring*' in P Cane and J Stapleton (eds), *The Law of Obligations: Essays in Celebration of John Fleming* (Clarendon Press, Oxford, 1998).

COOTE, B, 'The Effect of Hedley Byrne' (1966–1967) 2 *New Zealand Universities Law Review* 263.

—— 'Assumption of Responsibility and Pure Economic Loss in New Zealand' [2005] *New Zealand Law Review* 1.

DWORKIN, R, *Taking Rights Seriously* (Harvard University Press, Cambridge, Mass, 1977).

ENGLARD, I, *The Philosophy of Tort Law* (Dartmouth, Aldershot, 1993).

EPSTEIN, RA, 'A Theory of Strict Liability' (1973) 2 *The Journal of Legal Studies* 151.

EVANS, J, 'Choice and Responsibility' (2002) 27 *Australian Journal of Legal Philosophy* 97.

FELDTHUSEN, B, *Economic Negligence,* 4th edn (Carswell, Scarborough, 2000).

FINNIS, J, *Natural Law and Natural Rights* (Clarendon Press, Oxford, 1980).

FISCHER, DA, 'Causation in Fact in Omission Cases' [1992] *Utah Law Review* 1335.

FLANNIGAN, R, 'Privity—The End of an Era (Error)' (1987) 103 *LQR* 564.

FLEISCHACKER, S, *A Short History of Distributive Justice* (Harvard University Press, Cambridge, Mass, 2004).

FLEMING, J, 'Remoteness and Duty: The Control Devices in Liability for Negligence' (1953) *Canadian Bar Review* 471.

—— 'Probabilistic Causation in Tort Law' (1989) 68 *Canadian Bar Review* 661.

—— 'Probabilistic Causation in Tort Law: A Postscript' (1991) 70 *Canadian Bar Review* 136.

—— *The Law of Torts,* 9th edn (LBC Information Services, Sydney, 1998).

FLETCHER, G, 'The Fault of not Knowing' (2002) 3 *Theoretical Inquiries in Law* 265.

FRIEDMANN, D, and BARAK-EREZ, D (eds), *Human Rights in Private Law* (Hart Publishing, Oxford, 2001)

FUMERTON, R, and KRESS, K, 'Causation and the Law: Preemption, Lawful Sufficiency, and Causal Sufficiency' (2001) 64(4) *Law and Contemporary Problems* 83.

GARDNER, J, 'The Purity and Priority of Private Law' (1996) 46 *University of Toronto Law Journal* 459.

GARNER, BA, *A Dictionary of Modern Legal Usage* (Oxford University Press, Oxford, 1995).

—— *Black's Law Dictionary,* 7th edn (West Group, St Paul, Minn, 1999).

GILMORE, G, *The Death of Contract* (Ohio State University Press, Columbus, Ohio, 1974).

GOLDBERG, JCP, and ZIPURSKY, BC, 'Unrealized Torts' (2002) 88 *Virginia Law Review* 1625.

GOLDBERG, R, *Causation and Risk in the Law of Torts: Scientific Evidence and Medicinal Product Liability* (Hart Publishing, Oxford, 1999).

GOLDER, B, 'From *McFarlane* to *Melchior* and Beyond: Love, Sex, Money and Commodification in the Anglo-Australian Law of Torts' (2004) 12 *Torts Law Journal* 128.

GOODHART, AL, 'Rescue and Voluntary Assumption of Risk' (1933–1935) 5 *CLJ*192.

GRANTHAM, R, and RICKETT, C, 'Directors' "Tortious" Liability: Contract, Tort or Company Law?' (1999) 62 *MLR* 133.

—— and —— *Enrichment and Restitution in New Zealand* (Hart Publishing, Oxford, 2000).

—— and —— 'Property Rights as a Legally Significant Event' (2003) 62 *CLJ* 717.

GRASSIAN, V, *Moral Reasoning: Ethical Theory and some Contemporary Moral Problems* (Prentice-Hall, Englewood Cliffs, NJ, 1981).

GROTIUS, H, *The Law of War and Peace* (trans FW Kelsey, Clarendon Press, Oxford, 1925).

HAACK, S, 'Truth and Justice, Inquiry and Advocacy, Science and Law' (2004) 17 *Ratio Juris* 15.

HART, HLA, and HONORÉ, T, *Causation in the Law,* 2nd edn (Clarendon Press, Oxford, 1985).

HEDLEY, S, 'The Empire Strikes Back? A Restatement of the Law of Unjust Enrichment' (2004) 28 *Melbourne University Law Review* 759.

HEPPLE, B, 'Negligence: The Search for Coherence' (1997) 50 *CLP* 69.

HEUSTON, RFV, '*Donoghue* v. *Stevenson* in Retrospect' (1957) 20 *MLR* 1.

HEYDON, JD, 'Judicial Activism and the Death of the Rule of Law' (2003) 23 *Australian Bar Review* 110.

HOBBES, T, *Leviathan* (Oxford University Press, Oxford, 1996).

HOLMES, OW, *The Common Law* (Dover Publications, New York, 1881).

HONORÉ, T, 'Are Omissions Less Culpable?' in P Cane and J Stapleton (eds), *Essays for Patrick Atiyah* (Clarendon Press, Oxford, 1991).

—— 'Necessary and Sufficient Conditions in Tort Law' in D Owen (ed), *Philosophical Foundations of Tort Law* (Oxford University Press, Oxford, 1995).

—— *Responsibility and Fault* (Hart Publishing, Oxford, 1999).

HOPE, LORD, 'James McGhee—A Second Mrs. Donoghue?' (2003) 62 *CLJ* 587.

HURD, HM, and MOORE, MS, 'Negligence in the Air' (2002) 3 *Theoretical Inquiries in Law* 333.

IBBETSON, DJ, *A Historical Introduction to the Law of Obligations* (Oxford University Press, Oxford, 1999).

—— 'How the Romans did for Us: Ancient Roots of the Tort of Negligence' (2003) 26 *University of New South Wales Law Journal* 475.

JAFFEY, AJE, *The Duty of Care* (Dartmouth, Aldershot, 1992).

JANSEN, N, 'Duties and Rights in Negligence: A Comparative and Historical Perspective on the European Law of Extracontractual Liability' (2004) 24 *OJLS* 443.

JENSEN, D, 'Punitive Damages for Breach of Fiduciary Obligation' (1996) 19 *University of Queensland Law Journal* 125.

JONES, M, 'Liability for Psychiatric Damage: Searching for a Path between Pragmatism and Principle' in JW Neyers, E Chamberlain and SGA Pitel (eds), *Emerging Issues in Tort Law* (Hart Publishing, Oxford, forthcoming 2007).

KANT, I, *Critique of Pure Reason* (trans NK Smith, St Martin's Press, New York, 1965).

—— 'The Metaphysics of Morals' in M Gregor (ed), *Practical Philosophy* (Cambridge University Press, Cambridge, 1996).

—— 'Groundwork of the Metaphysics of Morals' in M Gregor (ed), *Practical Philosophy* (Cambridge University Press, Cambridge, 1996).

—— 'Critique of Practical Reason' in M Gregor (ed), *Practical Philosophy* (Cambridge University Press, Cambridge, 1996).

—— *Critique of Pure Reason* (trans P Guyer and A Wood, Cambridge University Press, Cambridge, 1998).

—— *Critique of the Power of Judgment* (trans P Guyer and E Matthews, Cambridge University Press, Cambridge, 2000).

KAPLOW, L, and SHAVELL, S, 'Fairness Verses Welfare' (2001) 114 *Harvard Law Review* 961.

KEATING, GC, 'The Idea of Fairness in the Law of Enterprise Liability' (1997) 95 *Michigan Law Review* 1266.

KELLY, JM, 'The Inner Nature of the Tort Action' (1967) 2 *Irish Jurist (NS)* 279.

KRIPKE, SA, *Wittgenstein on Rules and Private Language: An Elementary Exposition* (Blackwell, Oxford, 1982).

Law Commission for England and Wales, 'Contracts for the Benefit of Third Parties', 1996 242

LEVIN, A, 'Quantum Physics in Private Law' (2001) 14 *Canadian Journal of Law and Jurisprudence* 249.

LINDEN, AM, *Canadian Tort Law* (7th edn, Butterworths, Markham, 2001).

LLOYD, D, 'Note' (1951) 14 *MLR* 499.

LOKE, AF, 'Damages to Protect Performance Interest and the Reasonableness Requirement' [2001] *Singapore Journal of Legal Studies* 259.

LUNTZ, H, and HAMBLY, D, *Torts: Cases and Commentary* (4th edn, Butterworths, Sydney, 1995).

MACCORMICK, N, *Legal Reasoning and Legal Theory* (Clarendon Press, Oxford, 1978).

MARKESINIS, B, 'An Expanding Tort Law—The Price of a Rigid Contract Law' (1987) 103 *LQR* 354.

MARKESINIS, BS, and UNBERATH, H, *The German Law of Torts: A Comparative Treatise*, 4th edn (Hart Publishing, Oxford, 2002).

McBRIDE, NJ, 'Duties of Care—Do they Really Exist?' (2004) 24 *OJLS* 417.

—— and Bagshaw, R, *Tort Law*, 2nd edn (Pearson Education Ltd, Harlow, 2005).

McINNES, M, 'Causation in Tort Law: Back to Basics at the Supreme Court of Canada' (1997) 35 *Alberta Law Review* 1013.

MEGARRY, RE, *Miscellany-at-Law: A Diversion for Lawyers and Others* (Stevens & Sons Ltd, London, 1955).

MILL, JS, 'On Liberty' in JS Mill, *Three Essays* (Oxford University Press, Oxford, 1975).

—— *Utilitarianism* (Hackett, Indianapolis, Ind, 1979).

MILSOM, SFC, *Historical Foundations of the Common Law* (Butterworths, London, 1981).

MORAN, M, *Rethinking the Reasonable Person: An Egalitarian Reconstruction of the Objective Standard* (Oxford University Press, Oxford, 2003).

MORGAN, J, 'Tort, Insurance and Incoherence' (2004) 67 *MLR* 384.
—— 'Lost Causes in the House of Lords: *Fairchild* v *Glenhaven Funeral Services'* [2003] 66 *MLR* 277.
MULGAN, T, 'The Place of the Dead in Liberal Political Philosophy' (1999) 7 *Journal of Political Philosophy* 52.
MULLANY, N, and HANDFORD, P, *Tort Liability for Psychiatric Damage: The Law of 'Nervous Shock'* (Sweet & Maxwell, London, 1993).
MULLENDER, R, 'Corrective Justice, Distributive Justice, and the Law of Negligence' (2001) 17 *Professional Negligence* 35.
NAGEL, T, 'Death' (1970) 4 *Nous* 73.
NEYERS, JW, '*Donoghue* v. *Stevenson* and the Rescue Doctrine: A Public Justification of Recovery in Situations Involving the Negligent Supply of Dangerous Structures' (1999) 49 *University of Toronto Law Journal* 475.
—— 'Distilling Duty: The Supreme Court of Canada Amends *Anns'* (2002) 118 *LQR* 221.
NOZICK, R, *Anarchy, State, and Utopia* (Blackwell, Oxford, 1975).
OAKESHOTT, M, 'The Concept of a Philosophical Jurisprudence: Part I' [1938] *Politica* 203.
—— 'The Concept of a Philosophical Jurisprudence: Part II' [1938] *Politica* 345.
PEDAIN, A, 'Unconventional Justice in the House of Lords' [2004] *CLJ* 19.
PENNER, JE, *The Idea of Property in Law* (Clarendon Press, Oxford, 1997).
PERRY, SR, 'The Moral Foundations of Tort Law' (1992) 77 *Iowa Law Review* 499.
—— 'Tort Law' in D Patterson (ed), *A Companion to Philosophy of Law and Legal Theory* (Blackwell, Cambridge Mass, 1996).
—— 'On the Relationship Between Corrective and Distributive Justice: Fourth Series' in J Horder (ed), *Oxford Essays in Jurisprudence* (Oxford University Press, Oxford, 2000).
—— 'Responsibility for Outcomes, Risk, and the Law of Torts' in GJ Postema (ed), *Philosophy and the Law of Torts* (Cambridge University Press, Cambridge, 2001).
POLLOCK, F, *The Law of Torts,* 13th edn (Stevens, London, 1929).
PORAT, A, and STEIN, A, *Tort Liability Under Uncertainty* (Oxford University Press, Oxford, 2001).
—— 'Indeterminate Causation and Apportionment of Damages: An Essay on Holtby, Allen, and Fairchild' (2003) 23 *OJLS* 667.
POSNER, RA, *Economic Analysis of Law,* 2nd edn (Little, Brown and Co, Boston, Mass, 1977).
—— *Cardozo: a Study in Reputation* (Chicago University Press, Chicago, Ill, 1990).
PROSSER, WL, 'Palsgraf Revisited' (1953) 52 *Michigan Law Review* 1.
—— *et al, Prosser and Keeton on the Law of Torts,* 5th edn (West Group, St Paul, Minn, 1894).
PUFENDORF, S, *Of the Law of Nature and Nations* (trans HC and WA Oldfather, Clarendon Press, Oxford, 1934).
RACHELS, J, *The Elements of Moral Philosophy,* 3rd edn (McGraw-Hill, New York, 1999).
RAWLS, J, *The Law of Peoples* (Harvard University Press, Cambridge, Mass, 1999).
—— *A Theory of Justice: Revised Edition* (Belknap, Cambridge, Mass, 1999).
—— 'Outline of a Decision Procedure for Ethics' in S Freeman (ed), *John Rawls: Collected Papers* (Harvard University Press, Cambridge, Mass, 1999).

—— 'The Independence of Moral Theory' in S Freeman (ed), *John Rawls: Collected Papers* (Harvard University Press, Cambridge, Mass, 1999).

RAZ, J, *Practical Reason and Norms,* 2nd edn (Oxford University Press, Oxford, 1999).

REECE, H, 'Losses of Chances in the Law' (1996) 59 *MLR* 188.

RICKETT, C, 'Extending Equity's Reach through the Mutual Wills Doctrine?' (1991) 54 *MLR* 581.

RIPSTEIN, A, *Equality, Responsibility, and the Law* (Cambridge University Press, Cambridge, 1999).

—— 'Three Duties to Rescue: Moral, Civil, and Criminal' (2000) 19 *Law and Philosophy* 751.

—— 'Authority and Coercion' (2004) 32 *Philosophy and Public Affairs* 2.

—— and Zipursky, BC, 'Corrective Justice in an Age of Mass Torts' in GJ Postema (ed), *Philosophy and the Law of Torts* (Cambridge University Press, Cambridge, 2001).

ROBERTSON, B, 'The Court System Through the Eyes of the Citizenry' [2002] *New Zealand Law Journal* 267.

ROBINSON, OF, FERGUS, TD, and GORDON, WM, *European Legal History,* 2nd edn (Butterworths, London, 1994).

ROGERS, WVH, *Winfield and Jolowicz on Tort,* 16th edn (Sweet & Maxwell, London, 2002).

SALMOND, J, *Torts,* 7th edn (Sweet & Maxwell, London, 1929).

SCHROEDER, CH, 'Corrective Justice, Liability for Risks, and Tort Law' (1990) 38 *University of California of Los Angeles Law Review* 143.

SEAVEY, WS, 'Mr. Justice Cardozo and the Law of Torts' (1939) 39 *Columbia Law Review* 20.

SIMESTER, AP, and Chan, W, 'Inducing Breach of Contract: One Tort or Two?' [2004] *CLJ* 132.

SMART, JJC, 'An Outline of a System of Utilitarian Ethics' in JJC Smart and B Williams (eds), *Utilitarianism: For and Against* (Cambridge University Press, Cambridge, 1973).

SMILLIE, J, 'Let's Abolish Negligence: Commentary on a Paper by J G Fogarty QC', *1996 New Zealand Law Conference Papers* (New Zealand Law Society,Dunedin 1996).

—— 'Formalism, Fairness and Efficiency: Civil Adjudication in New Zealand' [1996] *New Zealand Law Review* 254.

—— 'Certainty and Civil Obligation' (2000) 9 *Otago Law Review* 633.

—— 'Is Security of Contract Worth Pursuing?—Reflections on the Function of Contract Law' (2000) 16 *Journal of Contract Law* 148.

SMITH, JC, and BURNS, P, '*Donoghue* v. *Stevenson*—The Not So Golden Anniversary' (1983) 46 *MLR* 147.

SMITH, L, 'Restitution: The Heart of Corrective Justice' (2001) 79 *Texas Law Review* 2115.

SMITH, SA, *Contract Theory* (Clarendon Press, Oxford, 2004).

SMITS, JM, *The Good Samaritan in European Private Law: On the Perils of Principles without a Programme and a Programme for the Future* (Kluwer, Deventer, 2000).

STAPLETON, J, 'In Restraint of Tort' in P Birks (ed), *The Frontiers of Liability* (Oxford University Press, Oxford, 1994).

—— 'Torts, Insurance, and Ideology' (1995) 58 *MLR* 820.

—— 'Duty of Care Factors: A Selection from the Judicial Menus' in P Cane and J Stapleton (eds), *The Law of Obligations: Essays in Celebration of John Fleming* (Clarendon Press, Oxford, 1998).

STAPLETON, J, 'Perspectives on Causation' in J Horder (ed), *Oxford Essays in Jurisprudence* (Oxford University Press, Oxford, 2000).
—— 'Legal Cause: Cause-in-Fact and the Scope of Liability for Consequences' (2001) 54 *Vanderbilt Law Review* 941.
—— 'Lords A'Leaping Evidentiary Gaps' (2002) 10 *Torts Law Journal* 276.
—— 'Comparative Economic Loss: Lessons from Case-Law-Focused "Middle Theory"' (2002) 50 *University of California of Los Angeles Law Review* 531.
—— 'The Golden Thread at the Heart of Tort Law: Protection of the Vulnerable' (2003) 24 *Australian Bar Review* 135.
STAUCH, M, 'Causation, Risk, and Loss of Chance in Medical Negligence' (1997) 17 *OJLS* 205.
—— 'Risk and Remoteness of Damage in Negligence' (2001) 64 *MLR* 191.
STEVENS, D, and NEYERS, JW, 'What's Wrong with Restitution?' (1999) 37 *Alberta Law Review* 221.
STEYN, LORD, 'Perspectives of Corrective and Distributive Justice in Tort Law' (2002) 37 *Irish Jurist* 1.
STONE, M, 'The Significance of Doing and Suffering' in GJ Postema (ed), *Philosophy and the Law of Torts* (Cambridge University Press, Cambridge, 2001).
TAYLOR, J, 'The Conceptual Basis of the Tort of Negligent Misstatement' (2003) 9 *New Zealand Business Law Quarterly* 177.
TAYLOR, R, 'A Comparative Study of Expert Testimony in France and The United States' (1996) 31 *Texas International Law Journal* 181.
TETTENBORN, A, 'Property Damage and Economic Loss: Should Claims by Property Owners Themselves be Limited?' (2005) 34 *Common Law World Review* 128.
TODD, S, 'Negligence: Particular Categories of Duty' in S Todd (ed), *The Law of Torts in New Zealand,* 3rd edn (Brookers, Wellington, 2001).
—— 'Negligence: Breach of Duty' in S Todd (ed), *The Law of Torts in New Zealand,* 3rd edn (Brookers, Wellington, 2001).
—— 'Defences' in S Todd (ed), *The Law of Torts in New Zealand,* 3rd edn (Brookers, Wellington, 2001).
—— 'Negligence: The Duty of Care' in S Todd (ed), *The Law of Torts in New Zealand,* 3rd edn (Brookers, Wellington, 2001).
—— 'Causation and Remoteness of Damage' in S Todd (ed), *The Law of Torts in New Zealand,* 3rd edn (Brookers, Wellington, 2001).
—— 'Policy Issues in Defective Property Cases' in JW Neyers, E Chamberlain and SGA Pitel (eds), *Emerging Issues in Tort Law* (Hart Publishing, Oxford, forthcoming 2007).
TREITEL, GH, *The Law of Contract,* 11th edn (Sweet & Maxwell, London, 2003).
TRINDALE, FA, and Cane, P, *The Law of Torts in Australia,* 3rd edn (Oxford University Press, Melbourne, 1999).
UNDERWOOD, P, 'Is Ms Donoghue's Snail in Mortal Peril?' (2004) 12 *Torts Law Journal* 39.
UNGER, R, 'The Critical Legal Studies Movement' (1983) 96 *Harvard Law Review* 561.
—— *What Should Legal Analysis Become?* (Verso, New York, 1996).
VORSTER, JP, 'A Comment on the Meaning of Objectivity in Contract' (1987) 103 *LQR* 274.
WADDAMS, SM, 'Causation in Canada and Australia' (1993) 1 *Tort Law Review* 75.
—— *Dimensions of Private Law: Categories and Concepts in Anglo-American Legal Reasoning* (Cambridge University Press, Cambridge, 2003).

—— 'Breach of Contract and Claims by Third Parties' in J W Neyers, E Chamberlain and SGA Pitel (eds), *Emerging Issues in Tort Law* (Hart Publishing, Oxford, forthcoming 2007).

WALKER, DM, *The Oxford Companion to Law* (Clarendon Press, Oxford, 1980).

WATSON, A, *Legal History and a Common Law for Europe* (Institutet för Rättshistorisk Forskning, Stockholm, 2001).

WEATHERFORD, RC, 'Determinism' in T Honderich (ed), *The Oxford Companion to Philosophy* (Oxford University Press, Oxford, 1995).

WEINRIB, EJ, 'A Step Forward in Factual Causation' (1975) 38 *MLR* 518.

—— 'Illegality as a Tort Defence' (1976) 26 *University of Toronto Law Journal* 28.

—— 'The Case for a Duty to Rescue' (1980) 90 *Yale Law Journal* 247.

—— 'Towards a Moral Theory of Negligence Law' (1983) 2 *Law and Philosophy* 37.

—— 'Legal Formalism: On the Immanent Rationality of Law' (1988) 97 *Yale Law Journal* 949.

—— *The Idea of Private Law* (Harvard University Press, Cambridge, Mass, 1995).

—— *Tort Law: Cases and Materials* (Emond Montgomery Publications Ltd, Toronto, 1997).

—— 'Does Tort Law Have a Future?' (2000) 34 *Valparaiso University Law Review* 561.

—— 'Restitutionary Damages as Corrective Justice' (2000) 1 *Theoretical Inquiries in Law* 1.

—— 'Correlativity, Personality, and the Emerging Consensus on Corrective Justice' (2001) 2 *Theoretical Inquiries in Law* 107.

—— 'Corrective Justice in a Nutshell' (2002) 52 *University of Toronto Law Journal* 349.

—— 'Deterrence and Corrective Justice' (2002) 50 *University of California of Los Angeles Law Review* 621.

—— 'Punishment and Disgorgement as Contract Remedies' (2003) 78 *Chicago-Kent Law Review* 55.

WEINRIB, LE, and WEINRIB, EJ, 'Constitutional Values and Private Law in Canada' in D Friedmann and D Barak-Erez (eds), *Human Rights in Private Law* (Hart Publishing, Oxford, 2001).

WEIR, T, *Economic Torts* (Clarendon Press, Oxford, 1997).

—— 'The Staggering March of Negligence' in P Cane and J Stapleton (eds), *The Law of Obligations: Essays in Celebration of John Fleming* (Clarendon Press, Oxford, 1998).

—— *Tort Law* (Oxford University Press, Oxford, 2002).

WHEAT, K, 'Proximity and Nervous Shock' (2003) 32 *Common Law World Review* 313.

WHITTAKER, S, 'Privity of Contract and the Tort of Negligence: Future Directions' (1996) 16 *OJLS* 191.

WILLIAMS, G, *Joint Torts and Contributory Negligence* (Stevens, London, 1951).

—— 'The Risk Principle' (1961) 77 *LQR* 179.

WINFIELD, PH, 'The History of Negligence' (1926) 42 *LQR* 184.

WITTING, C, 'Justifying Liability to Third Parties for Negligent Misstatements' (2000) 20 *OJLS* 615.

—— 'Distinguishing Between Property Damage and Pure Economic Loss in Negligence: A Personality Thesis' (2001) 21 *LS* 481.

—— 'The Three-Stage Test Abandoned in Australia—or Not?' (2002) 118 *LQR* 214.

—— 'Physical Damage in Negligence' (2002) 61 *CLJ* 189.

WOOD, A, *Kant's Ethical Thought* (Cambridge University Press, Cambridge, 1999).

WRIGHT, RW, 'Causation in Tort Law' (1985) 73 *California Law Review* 1735.

Wright, RW, 'Causation, Responsibility, Risk, Probability, Naked Statistics and Proof: Pruning the Bramble Bush by Clarifying the Concepts' (1988) 73 *Iowa Law Review* 1001.

—— 'Once more into the Bramble Bush: Duty, Causal Contribution, and the Extent of Legal Responsibility' (2001) 54 *Vanderbilt Law Review* 1071.

—— 'Negligence in the Courts: Introduction and Commentary' (2002) 77 *Chicago-Kent Law Review* 425.

—— 'Justice and Reasonable Care in Negligence Law' (2002) 47 *American Journal of Jurisprudence* 143.

—— 'Hand, Posner, and the Myth of the "Hand Formula"' (2003) 4 *Theoretical Inquiries in Law* 145.

—— 'Acts and Omissions as Positive and Negative Causes' in JW Neyers, E Chamberlain and SGA Pitel (eds), *Emerging Issues in Tort Law* (Hart Publishing, Oxford, forthcoming 2007).

Zimmermann, R, *The Law of Obligations: Roman Foundations of the Civilian Tradition* (Oxford University Press, Oxford, 1996).

—— *Roman Law, Contemporary Law, European Law: The Civilian Tradition Today* (Oxford University Press, Oxford, 2001).

Zipursky, BC, 'Civil Recourse, Not Corrective Justice' (2003) 91 *Georgetown Law Journal* 695.

Index

risk as actionable damage, 475, 483–9
  loss of a chance, 485
  quantum of damages, 485–9
Rogers, WVH, 50, 99n, 179, 190n, 370, 410
rule of law, 7, 12–14

Salmond, John, 2, 365
scientific uncertainty, 465–92
  corrective justice, 471–2
  testimony of expert witnesses, 489–92
secondary rights, *see* rights, definition of
    primary and secondary
Simester, Andrew, 271n
Smith, JC, 177n
Smith, Stephen, 21–5, 27–8
standard of care:
  action, 74–8
  adjustment for circumstances/persons,
    87–96, 659–60
  assumption of responsibility/negligent
    misrepresentation, 301–2
  contributory negligence, 342–3
  corrective justice, 103–6, 103–6
  emergencies, 108–11
  illegality, 375–7
  reasonable care, 96–103
  volenti non fit injuria, 359–64
  where risk creating act was innocent, 326–7,
    330–2
  see also ordinary reasonable person
Stapleton, Jane, 3–18, 32, 171–2, 194–5, 210,
    404, 418–21, 514
Stauch, Marc, 505n
Stein, Alex, 452–3, 481
Stevens, David, 232–3

thin skull rule, 162–6
Todd, Stephen, 4, 99n, 107n, 171, 176, 178,
    190n, 254, 290, 343, 416
tort law, relationship with negligence, 195–7,
    269–71, 306–9

Trindale, Frances, 390–1

Underwood, Peter J, 7–8
Unger, Roberto, 53n
unreasonable risk, 105–6

vicarious liability, 35–36
volenti non fit injuria, 257, 287–8, 345–72
  consent to harm, 347–57, 366–72
  consent to the risk of harm, 347–9, 357–66
  contributory negligence, 363–4
  mitigation, 354–5
  rescuers, 365–72
  standard of care, 359–64
  two parts of, 345–9
voluntary assumption of risk, *see volenti non
    fit injuria*
vulnerability, 194–5, 210

Waddams, Stephen, 266n, 428–9, 440
Weinrib, Ernest, 34n, 45n, 61n, 63n, 48, 63–66,
    98n,112n, 117, 174, 176–7, 202, 210n, 374,
    378–83, 508n
Weir, Tony, 84, 101n, 216–7, 232n, 271n, 300n,
    362n, 379n
Williams, Glanville, 165–6
Winfield, PH, 1
Wright, Richard, 96n, 100, 418–25, 431, 434–5
wrongful birth, 385–6
wrongful conception, 386–404
  assumption of responsibility, 402–4
  bereavement, 395–6
  mitigation, 392–5
  quantification of damages, 397–402
  regarding children as losses, 390–2
  rights of the parties, 389–90
  set off, 396
wrongful death, 36

Zimmermann, Reinhard, 58
Zipursky, Benjamin, 454–8